CONDO & VILLA VACATIONS RATED

United States and Canada

Clinton Burr & Ellen Burr

PRENTICE HALL TRAVEL

NEW YORK · LONDON · TORONTO · SYDNEY · TOKYO · SINGAPORE

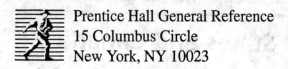
Prentice Hall General Reference
15 Columbus Circle
New York, NY 10023

PRENTICE HALL and colophon are
registered trademarks of Simon & Schuster, Inc.

Library of Congress Catalog Card Number: 93-083871
ISBN 0-671-86987-6

Edited by Catherine Fay
Typeset by Bruce Burdick and Charles H. Seymour
Maps by Ortelius Design

Manufactured in the United States of America

10   9   8   7   6   5   4   3   2   1

First Edition

CONTENTS

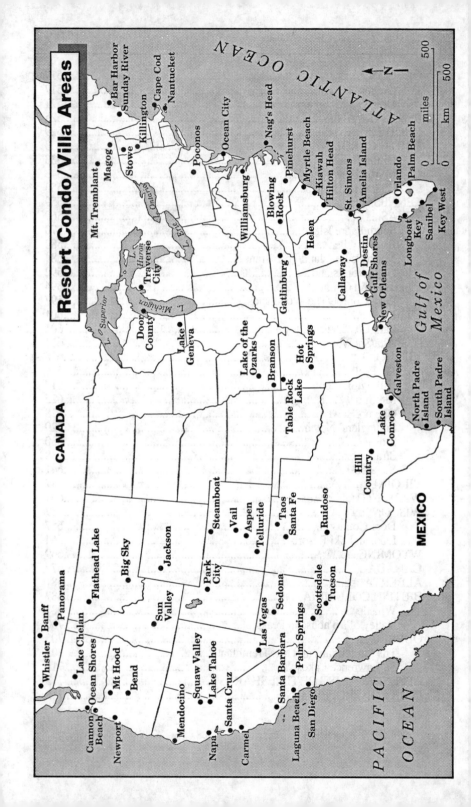

Resort Condo/Villa Areas

INTRODUCTION

The focus of this book is resort properties—condos, villas, and cottage colonies—which you can rent for your vacation in the United States and Canada. These are privately owned second homes, that offer luxurious accommodations in a resort setting; where you will enjoy the privacy of at least two or three separate rooms and the convenience of a kitchen for morning coffee or light meals. Not commercial properties like Holiday Inn or Hilton Hotels, these resorts have character. Many of these individual condos and villas have personalized interior decor, created by a designer where the furnishings alone cost over $50,000. Character here, also means a sense of quiet confidence about each resort where many of the people around the pool are owners and knowledgeable annual visitors. These unspoiled resorts are the sort which you've dreamed of, but before this book, were unable to find. What we find interesting is that Hyatt Hotels surveyed its frequent travellers to find out what sort of vacations they wanted the most. Guess what the answer was? "A private condo or villa on a tropical beach where the vacation could be shared with a spouse or significant loved one." What we find so impressive is that this is a hotel company admitting that consumers dream of taking vacations at non-commercial condos or villas.

The first criteria for inclusion in this guide begins with private ownership. Almost all of the properties we review and recommend are privately owned. The average price to purchase one of these resort properties would probably run $200,000. By using this book, however, you can locate condos and villas where the rental rate, for six people, averages $900 per week. That's $22 per night per person. To top it off, it has been estimated that four people staying in a condo will save approximately $100 per day on vacation food expenditures because there is a kitchen. Unlike hotels where a family or a group of four will spend $25 for breakfast, $50 for lunch, and $25 on snacks, in a resort property you'll have the luxury of your own kitchen. You can prepare exactly what you want when you want it.

Resort properties are comprised primarily of condominiums where the individual units are privately owned. All of the units generally share ownership of a central recreation facility, including a pool, beach cabana, tennis court, watersports center, or some other amenity.

What is a resort condo? A resort condo is a second home (not a primary residence) where at least one wall of each unit is shared with a neighboring unit. This includes apartments, townhouses, and duplexes. What is a villa? A villa is a separate structure, often within a community of similar villas which, like condos, share a central recreation facility. There are also villas that are separate homes on individual lots. Our description of each property gives you a layout of the community as well as a report on the individual condos and villas that we have personally inspected. Geared to those who appreciate the fantasy and luxury of a private vacation home—and not a hotel room—this book introduces you to a new dimension in travel. You'll find many exciting alternatives to just staying in a hotel or taking a regimented cruise.

Why Choose
A Resort Property For Vacation?

Some may wonder why they should choose a resort property over a hotel when they go on vacation. The answer is that no other lodging provides both the enchantment and the convenience of a home away from home. Consider the following:

- Save money because resort properties generally cost less to rent than a hotel room.

- Break away from the monotony of another hotel room by experiencing the fantasy of a vacation home, many of which have been decorated by interior designers in fulfillment of the owner's personal vacation dreams.

- Avoid the commercialism of a resort hotel, often so overrun with conventioneers that the individual is a second-class guest.

- Live the lifestyle of the rich and famous as many of the owners congregating by the pool are millionaires and these condos and villas are their play toys.

- Savor the space and privacy of a living room, den, separate bedrooms, and private patio.

- Enjoy the convenience of a kitchen for meals or snacks.

- Save money by only going out to restaurants in the evening, instead of for all meals.

- Relish the beauty of your own residence, often with the luxury of a private pool.

Resort properties won't appeal to all travelers. In most cases, the level of service at a condo or villa resort will be less than at a hotel. The major benefits are the freedom and the convenience of doing what you want to do, when you want to do it. You don't have to be tied to the regimen of someone else's schedule. Additionally, you can avoid those travelers who want group activities or the swinging singles lifestyle. Condos and villas tend to be more sedate. In some cases, however, condos have become part of a larger hotel property. Proving so popular that guests return year after year, many hotels now have sections where individuals can buy their own piece of paradise, yet still continue to enjoy all the social activities and services offered by the hotel.

Each one of the listed properties has its own distinct identity. Generally unknown to most vacationers, these are enclaves where sophisticated travelers eventually go because these resort properties offer all the comforts of home in exotic destinations.

More and more travelers prefer resort properties when they go on vacation. Not only do condos and villas offer more space and convenience, but also they offer a true sense of adventure. Resort condos are the play toys of millionaires and they are often fancifully decorated. You can expect many to have a video tape player (VTP) in the living room, a sunken jacuzzi bath, or even a Boogie board in the closet for body surfing in the waves. The owner may have a few more toys than you'd expect, such as the complimentary use of a power boat. Resort properties are great vacation homes that combine all the comforts you desire in an exciting new resort locale.

To give you an idea of the amazing range of exciting and personalized accommodations, here are some quick sketches of the more intriguing properties.

Toyland — Condos decorated completely with toys and games. Shelves lined with toys you've never seen before, Mickey Mouse telephones and comfortable adult-sized furniture where your favorite cartoon character holds the reading light.

At the Track — Condos in the Poconos where each has a private champagne glass jacuzzi bath and poolside activity includes parimutuel betting on three-year olds in floating sea horses, splashing against each other as they make Ben Hur circuits of the pool. Odds are given and bets placed before the race begins.

Murder She Wrote — Condos where each week the guests are invited to participate in solving a murder mystery. You can expect one clue to be spelled out during the bingo game.

PGA Pro Golf Training — Condos often are along golf courses and the local pro plays on the circuit. But one condo resort is at the former PGA training course where the pros were given instruction on how to be pros.

Jungleland — Condos which include a boardwalk where animals and exhibits have been set up to resemble the Jungle Cruise at neighboring Disney World. Canopied beds with mosquito netting drawn back combine with interior decor to bring the fantasy alive.

Get-in-Shape — Condos built around a spa/health club where you'll be put on a regimen so, hopefully, a new you will emerge after a week.

Shangri-La — Condos located on a mountaintop twelve miles from town. Enjoy the massive stone fireplace, in the lobby or the comfort of your own Kiva-style fireplace as you look out over mountain peaks and fields of snow.

Oregon Trail — Vacation homes and condos surrounding a golf course on the dry side of the mountains where rain is a rarity. Decorated with San Francisco sophistication on the inside, just step outdoors, unhitch your horse, and ride off into the hills.

Ocean Fantasy — Vacation homes on Martha's Vineyard which blend in with Cape Cod's "saltbox" architecture. But step inside and you'll find period furniture that belongs in a major metropolitan museum.

Midwest Escape — Within hours of midwestern cities, you can be on the rocky shoreline of Lake Michigan where, with the lighthouses and the rocky coastline, you'll feel like you are in Maine.

These are just a few examples of resort properties that can be rented for vacation instead of staying in a hotel room. Expect the unexpected as you search for the resort condo that's just right for you.

Terms Defined

Resort properties are usually full-size villas, bungalows, cottages, townhouses, or apartments and not just hotel bedrooms. We have categorized these properties according to the number of bedrooms each has since that usually is indicative of the size of the living room and kitchen. Of course each unit has bathrooms, generally one for each bedroom. The size of the unit will fall into one of these classifications:

Studio: Features one large room with sleeping accommodations for two to four people, a kitchenette, and one bath. When we say two to four we mean designed for a couple, or a couple with two small children.

One-Bedroom: One separate bedroom, full kitchen, living room and one bath. The unit accommodates up to four people with convertible couch or pull-out bed in the living room. The kitchen will be complete with china, table linens, and cookware. A one-bedroom condominium is comfortable for a family of four.

Two-Bedroom: Two full bedrooms, full kitchen, living room, one or two full baths. It accommodates four to six people with the use of a convertible couch or pull-out beds in the living room. Two-bedroom condominiums or villas are good for families or two couples.

Three-Bedroom: Three full bedrooms, full kitchen, living room, two or three full baths. It accommodates six to eight people with the use of a convertible couch or pull-out bed in the living room.

Loft: Upstairs sleeping area which is out of sight of the living room, but without a separate wall for privacy. One advantage of a loft unit is a living room that usually has a spacious cathedral ceiling.

In our descriptions of the condos you will find that we have used the following terms:

Full Kitchen: Everything including a dishwasher and a garbage disposal. A few deluxe condos also have a washer/dryer unit in the kitchen or in a small utility room just off the kitchen.

Kitchenette: Cooking area not necessarily walled off from the living room. Studios have kitchenettes instead of kitchens. Expect a small refrigerator, two burners, a sink, coffee-maker and maybe a microwave oven. A few kitchenettes have dishwashers.

Cooking Facility: A small refrigerator, a microwave, and a coffee maker. Adequate for light breakfasts or lunch, but inadequate to prepare a family meal.

Each unit is individually owned and decorated. Some condominiums are operated as a **condo-hotel** where, by agreement, all the units must have similar decor. Otherwise, each unit has its own distinct decor and personality. Therefore, when we speak of how the condos are furnished and decorated, we are painting with a broad brush. We are describing those units we have seen plus pictures and reports based upon correspondence from 22,000 other vacationers. **You will find discrepancies between our descriptions and your visit.** We are providing generalized guidelines. Some resorts will have units better than what we have described. We doubt you will find worse. During inspections, we were incognito and sometimes we saw the resorts through the eyes of the housekeeping staff—people who really know how the units are maintained.

The RPOA Ratings

The ratings are the most important part of this guide—and we use the word deliberately. This is not a directory that just lists names, addresses, and resort amenities. This guide gives you information on the FLAVOR of each resort so you will know how to plan a vacation that fits your personal expectations.

Hotels and motels have all been inspected and rated by AAA, Mobil, or the Michelin guide. RPOA (Resort Property Owners Association) has developed a ratings system for resort condos and villas that, because they are privately owned and individually decorated, have previously defied a systematic ratings program. RPOA's ratings system does have standards and parameters, but all of our ratings also include the intangible FLAVOR of a resort.

Everyone knows that a Hyatt Hotel is luxurious or that if a building is on the beach (not a block away), it has a great location. But how are you going to know if a resort is oriented toward families or seniors, or that hospitality on check-in is limited only to handing out keys and a bill?

With RPOA ratings, you'll know a lot about a resort (or a great deal about a resort) before you go. At RPOA, we inspected over 4,500 condo and villa resorts in the U.S.A., Canada, Mexico, and the Caribbean. We then rated each on a scale of one to ten, with one the lowest quality and ten the highest. Privately owned condo or villa units generally have a wide range of tasteful interior decor. Some condo-hotel properties, where all units are committed by contract to be in the rental program, (and the rental manager has control over interior decor), are more standard.

How did we research and inspect these resorts? Not by any traditional means. First by acting like another vacationer, we go straight to the pool and talk to the guests about their vacations and whether they would recommend this resort in preference to another in the area. Then we go see the maids. They are the best source of information and they'll tell you the "dirt" (if there is any) about the resort or management. In our opinion, it is the people outside the marketing office—who actually provide the services for visitors—who are the best source of information about a resort. If sloppiness is tolerated, you'll know right away. If the staff is overworked and feeling underpaid, then how can you expect great service? Finally, we'll go to the manager or the local realtor and ask to see several units, all the while continuing to pose as just another vacationer to the area.

When you read that a resort has its own golf course, elegant interiors, three pools, a children's program, and we have rated it as a "9," you'll know what to expect. When you read about indifferent service, and that the resort lacks a resort ambience, you'll understand what we mean by a "3" rating. Vacation villas that are on individual lots and not part of a development or enclave are marked by a 🏠 symbol.

There will be no rating next to the description of a single private home. In some cases, because of temporary remodeling or closure, we do not rate the condo/villa resort. We simply have an **"NR"** symbol for Not Rated.

We briefly tell you what we have observed about the interior decor during our undercover inspection. Generally all interior decor should be in the style or range which we have described for each resort. In order to facilitate descriptions we have used certain terms as aids. For example, "skierized" is a term we coined to describe the furniture found at many ski resorts. These sofas, tables and chairs have a boxy modular look, and are very functional. Dark oak or pine with dirt concealing synthetic fabrics are standard. It can withstand the normal abuse of boots, snow, slush, and fireplace soot and smoke common to ski condos. "Early attic" is another term we use to describe mismatched furniture that has seen better days. "Early Pier 1" or

Pier 1 furniture is reminiscent of the 60s and early '70s rattan furniture, hanging lamps, and often the Philippine capiz shell used in everything from lampshades and wastebaskets to placemats and mobiles. "Island style" is a medium grade of rattan furniture with medium-grade fabrics, oftentimes designer knock-offs. Island style decor offers simplicity and a light, airy atmosphere with glass-top tables and beach or nautical prints on the walls.

The RPOA ratings system is a "desirability" index that includes comparisons among resorts in a given area. Our ratings focus on two items: (1) resort facilities, which account for 40% of the score (including location of the property, building maintenance, facilities for resort living, and appearance of the interiors), and (2) personal inspection of the resort's services, which account for 60% (including cleanliness, hospitality, check-in, activities, services, and congeniality). In addition to our personal inspections, we rely upon letters and reports from 22,000 consumers about their vacations in resort condominiums. The ratings scale is not scientific, but we give you our best judgment after visiting and comparing these resort properties. The final test comes when we debate the merits of staying at one resort over another in the same locality.

The ratings give a clear indication of what you'll find upon visiting the property. Combined with the descriptions, the ratings will help you choose vacation destinations to suit your personal expectations—whether its whimsy, romance, or plain good value.

We believe that our ratings will tell you:

Scale	Meaning
10	Everything is in perfect order. A top-quality, world-class resort. To be a "10" this must be a self-contained "destination resort" where you will not need to leave the property confines for recreation, such as golf or tennis.
9	A great resort with beautiful units, fabulous decor, many owner services, and usually a social director. Many are homes of millionaires, but these resorts do not have their own golf courses, tennis center, etc.
8	A better than average resort with superior location, design, and decor. Highly recommended. You will find spacious units, probably with professionally decorated interior decor, some on-site recreation facilities, and perhaps a social director.
7	An above-average resort that will provide you with good accommodations and some on-site recreation area, such as a pool. Expect the resort to be landscaped or have a beautiful reception area. The resort environment evokes good character, and management offers quiet, efficient services.
6	A comfortable, quiet resort setting. The resort manager may view herself/himself as almost an "innkeeper." These resorts offer privacy

and are good for extended stays. Don't expect to see interior designer decor.

5   Spacious condos, townhouses, or apartments, but probably without on-site management. Should the need arise, assistance may be available a half-block away or two miles away. Expect the interior decor to be adequate, but the style will probably be a bit dated.

4   A mature resort. A great spot 15 years ago, but the facilities and services just haven't kept up with today's expectations. Interior decor, to be polite, has seen better days.

3   Spacious condos, but often aged and in need of refurbishment— "Early attic" furniture. Generally the property reveals a casual attitude toward maintenance. Don't expect much service, as the property managers often view their responsibility as limited to handing out keys or issuing checks to the lawn or pool care services.

2   These are in need of improvement. Sometimes, these are converted motel units which are being called "condos" in an effort to post a higher room rate.

1   Economy lodgings or appropriate for groups of college students at spring break. "If the kids don't finish it off, maybe a hurricane will." Rebuilding or remodeling is needed.

Sometimes you will see that we have a "+" sign next to the rating. That means there is something special about this resort. These "+" resorts offer something different, perhaps even unique, which makes a more memorable vacation.

With our ratings system, we have tried to tell you which resorts are in top-notch shape, and those which have experienced lackluster management. We have given you our best advice—consumer to consumer.

How To Rent A Resort Property— Rental Resources

The consumer has a real advantage in booking a resort condo, rather than reserving a hotel room. With hotels, there is one source that controls the rates for all the rooms. There are multiple sources for renting a unit in resort condos. Each has its own pricing structure. You can shop these Rental Resources and negotiate the best rate for yourself.

Several resources you may wish to consider when shopping for a condo rental are:

1. **Real Estate Brokers** — offer a selection of rentals at a wide range of properties in each locale.

2. **Reservations Services** — specialized knowledge of condo rentals and work with travel agents.

3. **Travel Agents** — have search to find accommodations that suit your needs.

4. **Resorts** — have agents handling the "in-house" rental pool.

5. **Property Owners** — are always eager to rent directly and avoid paying a commission.

A **Rental Resources** list is included at the end of each resort section. Those lists are by no means definitive but should give you a good starting point. Some rental resources are also found in the "Where to Stay" section and are identified with the ℭ symbol. The telephone numbers which appear with the resort descriptions are for the on-site rental company. There are some properties where there is no on-site management. Nor is there a mail receptacle for the resort which we've named. That doesn't mean there is something wrong or that we left something out. The truth is that many resorts were built to be true "second homes" and the planners didn't anticipate the emergence of the condo rental boom. Others are intentionally, and intensely private. The owners just don't want a lot of vacationers discovering the serenity of their pool area, which may have been unutilized and hence very private during the past few years. With these resorts, you *must* use the services of one of the off-site rental agents listed below, or else call upon someone who might own a unit there. You'll find this particularly to be the case with celebrity resorts where film stars or Supreme Court justices spend their vacations. They don't want anything that smacks of a commercial atmosphere, and when one is on an uninhibited tropical vacation, privacy is sometimes a jealously guarded asset.

We urge you to call the off-site rental agents not only because they are price competitive, but also because they will have a couple of units at sixty or perhaps a hundred different resorts. You'll hear about some exceptional opportunities and in the wide open world of condo-villa rentals we encourage you to explore all avenues before choosing your vacation accommodations.

How To Use This Book

This book focuses upon condo and villa properties available for rent in the continental United States and Canada. Hawaii, with over 700 condo and villa resorts, is covered separately in the companion book, **CONDO & VILLA VACATIONS RATED — HAWAII, MEXICO, AND THE CARIBBEAN.** We have endeavored to show you what we have seen so that you will know what is available and approximately what it will cost. We have also told you about negotiating for competitive rental rates by contacting the agencies listed under Rental Resources. Accordingly, we have divided this book into chapters by state. Some states such as Alabama or Maryland have all the vacation condos clustered into one area such as Gulf Shores or Ocean City. Then there are other states like Colorado and Florida which we have subdivided into eleven separate, identifiable vacation areas. We have provided information on each of these resort areas so that you'll clearly understand the distinctions and be able to choose one over the other.

Each chapter begins with an overview. Here, we tell you about the resort area, how it developed, and who goes there. **"Where to Stay"** is the heart of the book. Here, you are let in on the kind of inside information about resort condominiums that you would receive from a friend. We tell you about the neighborhoods and give you exact information about the resort and the standards you can expect to find. Sometimes our descriptions touch upon the local real estate market so you can appreciate the value of the properties described.

The rates which appear in the resort descriptions are the ranges from low to high season quoted by the on-site rental company. They should serve as a point of reference and are by no means an absolute. Condo rental rates are as elastic, volatile, and as varied as airline ticket prices. The season, the length of your stay, and which days you stay all impact the rates. This is in addition to the variations among the different rental sources. The rates are also negotiable. More than one agent has made reference to the adage "a half a loaf is better than none." Another wrinkle is package rates. Many rental companies now offer car, golf, ski, dive, and even air packages which may be better than the best rates you may find quoted separately. Packages may also be your best choice in some areas during the high season when car rentals or tee times can be difficult to arrange.

Whatever the source, condo and villa vacations are the best resort travel value available today. With this guide you can find the one best for you.

ALABAMA

"Jubilee" is the cry up and down the beach when it happens. The ones who come first to the Jubilee have no trouble filling buckets with shrimp, crab and flounder. Mobile Bay is so nutrient-rich that there are periods of mass exodus of marine life to the surface in search of oxygen. This phenomenon is called "Jubilee" and shellfish literally propel themselves ashore to the delight of Alabamians. Similarly Alabamians stream to Gulf Shores when they are in search of good times, great beaches, fishing, or golf.

Gulf Shores is just 45 minutes southeast of Mobile. The "center" is the intersection of Highway 59 (from Mobile) with Highway 182 (Gulf Shores Blvd.). Most distances are usually measured from this point, which is the oldest part of the area.

Gulf Shores offers 18 miles of crystalline white sand beaches running both east and west from the Highway 59 intersection. At the western tip is Ft. Morgan founded in 1702 by the Sieur de Bienville. It was made famous by Admiral Faragut during the Civil War when he proclaimed, "Damn the torpedoes (from Ft. Morgan) full speed ahead." The western part of this sandbar island was developed first. Then the area east of town became home to dozens of high-rise condominiums during the 1980s. Now the new development, and most luxurious condos, are out on Romar Beach, next to the Florida state line and Perdido Key. Less than two hours from New Orleans and minutes from Florida, the area has a cultural identity all its own. You'll find Gulf Shores at the western end of Florida's Panhandle map on page 178.

Condo rentals in Alabama must be booked through a licensed real estate broker. In the case of the condos listed below, rentals are available in most of these buildings through the realtors listed in our Rental Resources section. Almost none of the resorts have on-site management or telephone numbers.

Gulf Shores was devastated by Hurricane Frederic in 1979 and most buildings have been rebuilt since then. Expect to find some older two-story wooden structures on stilts where a lazy tropical island ambiance has been created. You can sit on your porch, listen to the Gulf surf, sip a cool drink, and peel a few shrimp for an appetizer after a hard day of fishing, sailing, biking, or walking the beach. The newer condos are in mid-rise to high-rise towers built of concrete and capable allegedly, of withstanding the gale-force winds. We hear the new condos are a great improvement but somehow those two-story "beach-house style" condos were the ones that said "BEACH VACATION" to us.

WHERE TO STAY

7 **BOARDWALK**
409 E. Gulf Shores Blvd., Gulf Shores, AL 36542
Amenities: Beach, pool.

Boardwalk is a ten-story high-rise in the main part of Gulf Shores just before you get to the new Romar Beach area. These pleasant condos each have a view of the Gulf. Helpful management is quietly efficient. The Boardwalk condominium has a wooden boardwalk along the beach and its own pier for boats, fishing, and swimming.

7   THE BREAKERS
25466 Perdido Beach Blvd., Gulf Shores, AL 36542
Amenities: Beach, pool

The Breakers offers two-bedroom condos overlooking the Gulf at Romar Beach, six miles east of the Highway 59 intersection. This new eight-story concrete building contains 32 stylish units. Interior decor is superior to many other condos in the area.

4   CASA VERANA
1143 West Beach Blvd., Gulf Shores, AL 36542
Amenities: Beach

This is a quiet motel-style building located about a mile west of the center of Gulf Shores. Facing the beach, each unit is adequately furnished for a comfortable stay.

7   EDGEWATER (East and West)
1001–1007 West Beach Blvd., Gulf Shores, AL 36542
Amenities: Beach, pool

These twin eight-story buildings are located on a popular section of beach about a mile west of the Highway 59 intersection. Cheerfully furnished with rattan furniture, deck chairs, and poster art, these units are designed for casual beachfront living.

6   FOUR SEASONS OF ROMAR BEACH
East Highway 182, P.O. Box 1648, Gulf Shores, AL 36542
205-981-6759
Amenities: Pool, exercise room w/ universal gym.

This complex consists of two, nine-story high-rise towers out at Romar Beach, commanding one of the area's best strips of sand. Beautifully land-scaped, the pool area is a compliment to the beach. Four Seasons has its own pier for boats, fishing, and swimming. The condos are designed so each unit has a view of the Gulf. Furnishings are modern and comfortable with light woods covered with solid pastels. This is a good bet for all age groups.

7 GULF HOUSE CONDOMINIUMS
511 E. Gulf Shores Blvd., Gulf Shores, AL 36542
Amenities: Beach, pool

This is one of the newer and more impressive buildings near the old center of Gulf Shores. These units are superior in space and decor to many of their neighbors. Frankly, the interior decor is more typical of those found in the new Romar Beach area.

7 GULF SHORES PLANTATION
P.O. Box 1299, Gulf Shores, AL 36542, 800-554-0344
Amenities: Beach, indoor and outdoor pools, health club

One of the largest resorts in the Gulf Shores area, this resort sees lots of activity. Built in several stages, there's a variety of styles among these offerings. You'll be able to choose between three-story buildings, five-story buildings, and an eight-story tower. The best feature of these is all the mirrors that make them seem even larger. The furnishings carry out the theme of relaxed beach-front living without sacrificing comfort. You'll find light colored woods in the living room and steelcase furniture in the dining area. There's lots of activity in the summer when children are on vacation; lots of activity in the spring and fall with golf and tennis players.

6 GULF VILLAGE
1027 West Beach Blvd., Gulf Shores, AL 36542
Amenities: Beach, pool

This condo complex is on both sides of the highway. On the beach side, there are three, three- and four-story condo buildings. Across the street with a view to the lagoon, there's a cluster of individual beach bungalows surrounding the pool. Although the bungalows don't have the ocean view, they are superior because you can run in and out of your beach house all day without using the elevator.

4 ISLAND SUNRISE
427 E. Gulf Shores Blvd., Gulf Shores, AL 36542
Amenities: Beach, pool

This is located right in the center of Gulf Shores. The building has two arms creating a small courtyard effect around the sheltered pool area. Interior decor is aged and maintenance appears to be haphazard. Think twice before selecting Island Sunrise.

4-5 ISLAND WINDS (East and West)
407 West Beach Blvd., Gulf Shores, AL 36542, 205-968-7363
Amenities: Beach, pool

Located right in the heart of Gulf Shores, these twin towers are a pleasant place for an active vacation. Friendly, helpful management will get your vacation off to a good start. These units are older than many in the Gulf Shores area and as such, there's a wide difference in the quality of decor. Some are downright dingy; others are new and sparkle. This is a popular place. We recommend it, but check before you go to ensure you'll receive the quality you want.

8   PHOENIX
Highway 182 East, Gulf Shores, AL 36542, 205-968-7363
Amenities: Pools, tennis, racquetball, game room.

The Phoenix offers rejuvenation for young executives. A week of beach, tennis, and racquetball should restore your well being. The Phoenix offers superior modern condo accommodations in twin twelve-story towers in the Romar beach section of Gulf Shores. Expect casual contemporary or island-style rattan furniture. After all, this is a place at the beach. The three-bedroom penthouse condos are luxurious, however, with private whirlpools.

8   SEASIDE BEACH AND RACQUET CLUB
24522 Perdido Beach Blvd., Gulf Shores, AL 36542
205-981-6921
Amenities: Beach, indoor and outdoor pool, hot tub, tennis

This is one of the nicest developments in the area because of the grounds taht are landscaped with palms and palmettos. These two-bedroom condos have an efficient floor plan, and interior decor is superior to most in the area. The traditional rattan furniture has been made stylish through the use of designer and colorful fabrics. Lots of glass-top tables and sea shell arrangements have been used as accents. It is a very attractive development.

4-5 SHORELINE TOWERS
1155 West Beach Blvd., Gulf Shores, AL 36542, 205-948-5373
Amenities: Beach, pool

On the beach, it's in a great location. But the building shows age and the condos could be spruced up. The resort is refurbishing the condos and you'll find some of the newly decorated units to be quite attractive with floral prints, lots of pillows, and bric-a-brac. Each condo has a Gulf view and the beach-side pool is popular at noon and at the cocktail hour.

8+ SUMMERCHASE
25800 Perdido Beach Blvd., Gulf Shores, AL 36542
205-981-9731
Amenities: Pool, hot tub, beach, gazebo

Located in the newly developing Romar Beach section of Gulf Shores, this modern high-rise is one of the best choices. The sand beach is wide and white. Each condo has a private balcony directly overlooking the Gulf. You can lie in bed at night and hear the surf. The interior decor is attractive with casual wicker furniture and sharp designer fabrics emphasizing lemon yellow and cotton-candy pink. The master bathroom has a vanity area including a mirror surrounded by lights. Lots of golfers and tennis players choose this resort as well as those looking for a family vacation at the beach.

And for a lagniappe, we found one special condo resort hidden among the rolling hills of central Alabama.

8+ STILL WATERS
1000 Still Waters Drive, Dadeville AL 36853, 800-633-4554
Amenities: Lake, golf, tennis, clubhouse, restaurant, horseback riding, hunting, fishing, pool

The Old South lives! This resort is a corporate retreat or "camp." It's not a beach-side condo. When we say "camp" we don't mean campground for RVs. Nor do we mean a camp with kiddies. This is an old-time, private resort built by Dadeville Lumber for executives and special friends. Now it has been opened to the public as a condo resort. Located and and one-half hours northeast of Mobile or an hour south of Montgomery, this resort is in an unlikely location—Backwoods Alabama. Forget the "Dukes of Hazard" image—this is a first class resort with private cottages in a compound. You're likely to hear classical music coming from a cottage. There are 16 villas and a full staff at your service. There is a private 18-hole golf course waiting for you. One hole was featured in "Golf Digest." Nearby, the forests offer limitless fishing and hunting opportunities. Still Waters is located on Lake Martin, so you can fish and water ski right at the resort. The restaurant is your private club for a week.

RENTAL RESOURCES
Associated Property, 205-968-5676
Bender Realty, 205-948-5256
Boardwalk Rentals, 205-861-3992
Brett/Robinson Gulf, 205-968-7363
Century 21 Gulf Bay, 205-943-7653
Charter Realty, 205-948-6716
Coldwell Banker, 205-968-8888
Commander Realty, 205-948-5000
ERA Commander Realty, 205-948-6836
Ft. Morgan Rentals, 205-540-7325
Gulf Towers Rentals, 205-948-2556
Jennings Real Estate, 205-968-2386

Kaiser Realty, 205-968-6868
Meyer Real Estate, 205-968-7516
Ocean Village Condos, 205-948-7318
Perdido Dunes, 205-948-4358
Sand Dollar Realty, 205-968-7634
Sandpiper Rentals, 205-948-5256
Sugar Sands Realty, 205-981-6981
Sunswept, 205-981-4949
Ward Real Estate, 205-968-8423
Wind Drift, 205-981-8907
Young's Realty, 205-968-4400

ARIZONA

Once viewed as a destination for just winter vacations, Arizona has become a year-round playground. The reasons? The cool temperatures of the mountains, water sports on Lake Havasu, and the dry climate of Phoenix/Scottsdale keep vacationers from noticing those high temperatures, especially when condo rental rates drop as much as 80 percent in the summer.

Arizona has five distinct tourist areas, each with a climate and set of attractions all its own.

1. Phoenix/Scottsdale
2. Sedona/Flagstaff
3. Lake Havasu/Lake Powell
4. Pinetop/White Mountains
5. Tucson

For more detail, consult the map of Arizona/New Mexico on page 462.

1. PHOENIX / SCOTTSDALE

With warm winter sun and a dry climate, Phoenix/Scottsdale has attracted residents as well as vacationers. It now is the tenth largest city in the U.S. by population. Surprisingly, with all this growth, the resorts have maintained an escapist environment.

The Superstition Mountains break the geographic sprawl of Phoenix and have created natural pocket areas where you'll find the golf courses of Paradise Valley and Scottsdale. You can play tennis from 8 A.M. until 10 P.M., and with the dry climate you won't feel as weary. The pools of Scottsdale are famous for developing a deep tan that won't fade until weeks later. Old Town Scottsdale is a recreation of a western village where cars give way to horse-drawn carriages. There are lots of shops and fountains to attract your attention here. Or if you want the wild west, drive out to Rawhide. Children love this area of stagecoach rides, mine explorations, and shootouts. For $2 you can have someone arrested and jailed until you bail them out.

The European influence has been brought to Scottsdale. The Borgatta is a recreation of an Italian village and is one of the most unusual shopping areas in the country. North of town, the Italian designer Paolo Soleri has created an architectural fantasy, a city of the future called Arcosanti.

Several of the condo choices are part of larger resort communities that include hotels, extensive tennis facilities, and each has a private golf course. A third choice is north of Scottsdale in the unique community of Carefree. Here, all construction must be approved by the zoning commission to blend in to the natural desert environment. Then there are two other choices in the metropolitan area. They cater to families and are without the attendant hotel/golf course facilities. These have attractive rental rates, so you can enjoy this exclusive environment at half price.

WHERE TO STAY

9 ALAMOS CONDOS AT COTTONWOODS RESORT
6160 N. Scottsdale Rd., Scottsdale, AZ 85253, 602-483-6848
1BR $110–175, 2BR $150–285
Amenities: Pool, tennis, golf

This couldn't have a more central location, right at the intersection of Scottsdale Road and Lincoln. Four of the best golf courses in the metropolitan area are within a stone's throw. The Borgatta and Scottsdale shopping centers are within walking distance. At night around the pool, you can look up and see the lights on Camelback or Mummy Mountains. The two-bedroom condos here are Southwestern in style with beamed ceilings, a mini-bar and a beehive fireplace. Each condo has a private whirlpool spa on a private patio bordered by flowers. This is a great place for a romantic weekend or perhaps spring vacation as a family. It just doesn't get better than this! One drawback: no full kitchens. But never fear, room service is just a call away. Or you can go over to the main part of the hotel for dining, swimming, tennis, or just socializing. The Alamos is a great choice.

10 THE BOULDERS
34631 N. Tom Darlington Dr., Carefree, AZ 85377, 602-488-9009
1BR $150–495, 2BR $275–620, 3BR $325–670
Amenities: Golf, tennis, pools, fitness center

You have to know Carefree to appreciate this resort. Unlike any other resort destination except maybe Tucson's La Paloma, this community has fought to preserve the natural desert environment. You won't find yards with grass or beds of flowers in Carefree. Instead, you'll be impressed by the rugged rocks and boulders. The main vegetation is the statuesque saguaro cactus. All buildings in this community are strictly controlled by the zoning commission and most feature a Frank Lloyd Wright style of architecture. Offsetting the stark desert, is the rolling 27-hole golf course and the activity on the six tennis courts.

The Boulders was conceived and designed under the direction of David Rockefeller as an elite refuge. Millions of dollars have been invested in the pottery, rugs, and Indian art adorning the accommodations at this resort. Away from the main hotel structure, there are 45 casita patio homes available for rent along the golf course. The design of the condos has the "boxy" pueblo look, but many have elaborate and lavish interiors. The fireplaces are a nice addition and enhance the glow of the evening. But in some of the condos, you'll feel as though you are living in a museum. Although children are welcome, this is more a choice for a honeymoonette or that "unforgettable" vacation.

6 CORNERSTONE INN
4301 N. 24th St., Phoenix, AZ 85016, 602-954-9220; 1BR $85
Amenities: Pool

This is a casual budget choice for those who want to enjoy the Phoenix/ Scottsdale area without paying for glamorous extras. There are studios and one-bedroom casitas equipped with full kitchens that have been decorated with hotel furniture. Conveniently located in mid-town Phoenix, you are halfway between downtown and the golf resorts of Paradise Valley/ Scottsdale. It is practical and attractively priced.

8+ ORANGE TREE GOLF RESORT
10601 N. 56th St., Scottsdale, AZ 85254; Suite $80–240
Amenities: Golf, tennis, pool, restaurant

This country club resort is just what so many are looking for in Arizona— but is often so hard to find. This resort is built around golf, not just next to it. Set on 128 acres, the 160 suites overlook the fairways of the PGA-rated championship golf course, one of the most popular golf courses in all of Arizona. New management has spruced up the accommodations and added a host of services, intended to please a wide range of vacationers. These time-share suites are a little on the small side, and they don't have private kitchens. But there's a frige and a wet bar that will accommodate groceries for breakfast or those late night-snacks. Each suite has a big screen television, a VCR, and a private terrace where you can watch activity on the golf course. Every whim is catered to here.

9+ THE POINTE AT SQUAW PEAK
7677 N. 16th St., Phoenix, AZ 85020, 602-997-7777
1BR $115–250, 2BR $250–325
Amenities: Golf course

Located at the base of one of Phoenix's most beautiful mountain pre-serves, The Pointe is a full-service resort. Some units are part of the Hilton Hotel complex and there are 94 condo villas. The design is Spanish/ Mediterranean with courtyards, fountains, and exotic flowers. The units are well decorated and somewhat standardized, so they lack individual personality. There are two main reasons to choose The Pointe: the golf and the high quality restaurants/social programs available to guests. You'll find a social director who will help you plan excursions for jeeping in the desert, ballooning over the Superstition Mountains, or perhaps even a private tour to the Grand Canyon. Periodically, The Pointe runs specials and discounts for condo rentals. It's the personal touch that makes this resort outstanding. Popular as a corporate retreat or for small medical meetings, this resort has the flavor of a retreat for the privileged.

8   RESORT SUITES OF SCOTTSDALE
7677 E. Princess Blvd., Scottsdale, AZ 85255, 602-585-1234
2BR $110–160, 4BR $165–200
Amenities: Pool, tennis. Golf nearby.

Phoenix/Scottsdale has an abundance of retirement homes and lively deluxe hotels, but there are only a few collections of resort condos that are available for short-term rentals. Resort Suites is one of those few alternatives. Originally designed and built to be vacation-home condos overlooking the Princess golf course, economic hard times caused a change of plans. Instead, all of the condos are owned by one person who operates the property as an all-suite hotel. Here you have commercial service, residential accommodations, and an attentive management who is highly motivated to make sure you enjoy your stay.

Resort Suites is located on the north side of Scottsdale within 20 minutes of 18 different golf courses. Focusing on the golf, the Resort Suites staff have made special arrangements with Stonecreek, The Phoenician, Tatum Ranch, and Red Mountain Ranch for golfing guests to get special rates and starting times at those courses. They even have a special staff devoted to tournament planning for the occasional small conference centered at Resort Suites.

The units are available in one-, two-, and four-bedroom models. Interior decor is light and casual in keeping with the surrounding desert. Expect to find neutral colors in the furniture and fabrics, but colors of the sky and sunset have been added with pillows and art. Each has a kitchen and breakfast bar that opens out onto the living room to create a sense of spaciousness. The pool is a pleasant place to make friends—not one of those affairs where guests are reserving lounge chairs at 7 A.M.

In Scottsdale, this will provide quality and convenience at an efficient price.

7+   SCOTTSDALE CAMELBACK RESORT
6302 E. Camelback Rd., Scottsdale, AZ 85251, 602-947-3300
1BR $100–110
Amenities: Pool, health club, tennis, golf

This is set right in the heart of Scottsdale's glamour and a short distance away from the top-rated golf courses of Paradise Valley. Some of the most elegant shopping areas in the nation are nearby. The resort is designed to provide a family with a full, well-rounded vacation. The condos are elaborately decorated in Southwestern style with lots of pastel colors. Each condo has a private patio or balcony for sunbathing. This is a great choice for anyone going to Arizona for a winter vacation. Summer is a time for rock-bottom bargain rentals and you'll be surprised to find that the climate is more enjoyable than Dallas or Los Angeles in the summer.

7   **SCOTTSDALE MANOR**
      4807 Woodmere Fairway Dr., Scottsdale, AZ 85251, 602-994-5282
      2BR $100–200
      Amenities: Pools, tennis, hot tub

Located right in the heart of Scottsdale, this is an exceptional find because it is one of the very few local condo/suite resorts that caters to the short-term vacationer. Guests are given the same "welcome to our home" reception whether one stays for a single night or for three months. Of course the daily rate fluctuates with the length of your stay. Secluded and quiet, the 72 units in this garden setting offer a truly residential atmosphere, free from the commercialism of a hotel. This is Arizona at your pace. Management is friendly and highly personalized. The two-bedroom suites each have a full kitchen, and furnishing tends to be traditional with a couple of country French accents. Each cluster of twelve units has its own private pool and a garden that faces majestic Camelback Mountain. Close to the Arizona Canal, there is a jogging trail as well as two tennis courts. This is what many hope to find in Arizona, but often are unable to book for short-term stays.

10   **THE WIGWAM**
       300 E. Indian School Rd., Litchfield Park, AZ 85340
       602-935-3811, 1BR $175, 2BR $220
       Amenities: Pools, tennis, golf, horseback riding

One of the grande dames of the resort world, the Wigwam is indeed a special place. To begin with, it's 15 miles from Phoenix and 20 miles from Scottsdale, separated from the city by acres of cotton fields. Originally built as a corporate retreat by Goodyear Tire & Rubber Company, the Wigwam soon became popular with film celebrities as well as corporate executives. Like Sun Valley, Idaho, this was a place where guests were welcomed into the family and many stayed to build million dollar homes along the golf course. Among the vacation homes and villas available for rent are some unusual bubble structures dating from the 1950s. These were an experiment by Goodyear to use rubber casings as a construction technique to reduce building costs. The experiment was abandoned, but the domed half-bubble, white stucco buildings remain. The condos are the latest addition, featuring southwestern architecture, tile floors, Indian rugs, and lodge-pole furniture.

These villas and condos are available for daily, weekly, or monthly rentals. With three championship golf courses, sunset horseback trail rides, tennis, and two dozen pools, you'll find plenty to do. The main lodge with its restaurants is one of a handful of establishments to receive a five star rating from Mobil.

RENTAL RESOURCES
ReMax Excaliber Real Estate, 800-678-0083
Russ Lyon Realty, 602-488-2400
West USA Realty, 602-488-2400

2. SEDONA / FLAGSTAFF

Just 120 miles north of Phoenix, Sedona and Flagstaff are two communities at opposite ends of Oak Creek Canyon that enjoy an entirely different climate. Still within the dry Sonora desert, Sedona/Flagstaff doesn't have the winter sun and warmth so popular to the south. Winter is dry, and although better then Duluth, you won't be able to lie by the pool during the winter months. However, summer here is magnificent with cool mountain breezes and afternoon thunderstorms during July and August that moderate the temperature.

Sedona is a picturesque artists' hideaway that has become a chic resort destination. It sits at the southern end of Oak Creek Canyon in an area surrounded by "painted" or red rocks. It's a 30-minute drive through the canyon north to Flagstaff. To reach Sedona from Phoenix, drive north for 125 miles along Interstate 17. Sedona is a center for relaxation, nature lovers, and sports enthusiasts, with a wide variety of activities available: white-water rafting, jeeping in the mountains, horseback trail rides, stream fishing parties, and hiking. Oak Creek Canyon, 16 miles long, is not as overwhelming as the Grand Canyon. First-timers to Arizona explore the Grand Canyon, but the experienced devote time to the Oak Creek area.

Flagstaff is a cowboy town that is becoming an urban center. Surrounded by pine-forested mountains, the air in Flagstaff is cool and fresh. Just north of the city, you'll find the state's largest ski resort, Fairfield Snowbowl. Flagstaff makes a good base of operations for those planning to explore scenic Arizona. A trip to the Grand Canyon, 80 miles away, is an easy day trip as is an excursion to the set for *"The Young Riders"* and other western shows. The Painted Desert is 100 miles away and Arizona's famous Meteor Crater is only 45 miles away.

For those who enjoy exploring the Old West, nearby is the town of Jerome, once a copper mining town, then a ghost town, and now a tourist center. Built on a geologic fault, the buildings in town move several inches each year. Just south of Jerome is Montezuma's Castle, so called because the first explorers who saw the cliff dwellings believed that this was where the Aztec King had hidden his fabled gold. It is the best preserved of the Indian cliff dwellings. The U.S. Park Service has a good display on the natural history of the Verde Valley.

WHERE TO STAY

8 **ARROYO ROBLE RESORT**
100 Arroyo Roble Rd., Sedona, AZ 86336, 602-282-7777
Suite $95–105, Cottage $130
Amenities: Health club, tennis, pool, spa

Located amid Sedona's beautiful mountain scenery and historic sites, the Arroyo Roble is a memorable five-story, Spanish style complex with townhouse condos spread over six acres. The townhouses are removed from the main hotel operation as they are down a steep hill along the banks of Oak Creek. The creekside setting, directly opposite a mountain, creates that self-contained exclusive resort feeling. The vistas of the canyon and the red rocks will fill you with awe. The units are decorated with heavy southwestern furniture, blue carpets, and durable brown/tan fabrics dating from the early 1970s. Accents include Southwestern Indian wall hangings, tile floors, and lot's of wood. There's a large whirlpool tub in each unit and you can lounge outside by the pool. This resort is exceptional in that it provides the Old Southwest vacation atmosphere in a gracious way. The nearby Tlaquepaque shopping area is a reconstruction of a quiet Mexican village. The artists' shops in Tlaquepaque are quite exclusive.

10 **ENCHANTMENT**
525 Boynton Canyon Rd., Sedona, AZ 86336
602-282-2900, 800-826-4180
1BR $155–210, 2BR $220–330, Hopi House $410–560
Amenities: Tennis, pools, health club, spa, pitch n'putt golf

This is one of the most remarkable resorts in North America, and it fulfills the fantasy many Easterners have about vacationing in the Arizona desert. Within the mystic setting of Boynton Canyon, ten miles from the village of Sedona, this enclave resort is surrounded by the dramatic red rock mountains for which this area is so famous. The main lodge is built in the adobe style with glass walls reaching three stories high and classical music piped in the background. The condos and villas are in keeping with this style. Called casitas, each unit has wood beamed ceilings, fireplaces, original southwestern art, and custom-made furniture. Huge sliding glass doors assure that you'll never lose sight of your breathtaking surroundings.

You'll never be bored at Enchantment with a dozen tennis courts, a full health club, spa, pools, and a pitch n'putt golf course.

7 **FAIRFIELD FLAGSTAFF**
2580 North Oakmont Dr., Flagstaff, AZ 86001, 602-526-3232
1BR $55–90, 2BR $75–110
Amenities: Golf, tennis, pools, riding stables

Although a surprise to many, both 1991 and 1992 have been record years for skiers in Arizona. The Fairfield Snowbowl resort is just 25 miles north of Flagstaff and the ski conditions have recently rivaled those of several Colorado resorts. The condos for skiers and golfers are in a different location, ten miles east of town in an area called Fairfield Flagstaff.

This golf resort community is truly exceptional. High and dry, you'll be surrounded by dramatic mountains and stands of pine trees. Although the mountains are snowcapped, the golf course is playable ten months out of the year (and all year long for the hard core). There are three distinct areas of condos here: **Walnut Canyon Hills, Ridgewood,** and **Tanglewood.** Many of the Walnut Canyon Hills condos and those at Ridgewood are occupied by their owners for half of the year.

Well built and attractive you won't find many short-term vacationers here. But over at Tanglewood it's a different story. Weekly or weekend rentals are the norm. These two-story units feature walls of glass, cedar woodwork, and moss rock fireplaces. These building materials are a natural compliment to the surrounding high desert. Inside furnishings are a mixture of traditional, with wing chairs, and Southwestern Indian weavings and fabrics. Truly spacious, these units make an excellent base for exploring the Arizona desert, Sedona, or the Grand Canyon. Children will enjoy the recreation center while adults tend to socialize across the street over at the Country Club.

8   JUNIPINE
8351 N. Highway 89A, Sedona, AZ 86336, 602-282-3375
1BR $160–200, 2BR $210–230
Amenities: Restaurant, creek waterslide nearby, hiking trails

Uniquely situated in the narrow chasm of Oak Creek Canyon, Junipine is a world unto itself. Surrounded by the pines and the red rock canyon walls, you'll feel totally removed from the pressures of the 20th Century. This is a village of 50 "creekhouses" surrounding a lodge that blends western rusticity with the sophistication of oriental rugs and brass lamps. There's a dining room out back on an outdoor deck overlooking the creek. As for the creekhouse units, each has two bedrooms, a full kitchen, dining area, and a spacious living room where the fireplace is the centerpiece. Some units have lofts, which children find especially intriguing. A large part of the charm of this resort comes from the creekside setting—like none other on earth.

8   L'AUBERGE DE SEDONA
301 L'Auberge Ln., P.O. Box B, Sedona, AZ 86336
800-272-6777, 1BR $95–175
Amenities: Restaurant

Nestled along the banks of Oak Creek, beneath the majestic Red Rocks, L'Auberge is a special little retreat. Most of the units here are suites and some are little cottages. Each has the rustic log cabin exterior and each has a fanciful "country French" interior. You'll find brass beds, globe lamps, lots of ruffles, and yards and yards of fabrics. Most of the units do not have kitchens and you'll be encouraged to dine at the inn's excellent restaurant. The larger units have separate living rooms and kitchens. Each has a fireplace. This is a property with a unique blend of two different cultures—resulting in a resort of character.

8 LOS ABRIGADOS
160 Portal Ln., Sedona, AZ 86336, 602-282-1777
Suite $150, 2BR $195
Amenities: Spa, golf, tennis, horseback riding

This is what you would hope to find in Arizona. On arrival, you are greeted next to the enormous Spanish colonial fountain just over the red tile bridge. At Los Abrigados no expense has been spared to create the finest, most romantic environment in Arizona. Added to the man-made splendor is the dramatic scenery of Sedona's Red Rocks and the entrance to Oak Creek Canyon. The resort is built around 22 giant sycamore, cypress, and cottonwood trees. Care has been taken to preserve the best of the Old Southwest. The condos are in a maze of two-story buildings, decorated with understated good taste using native woods, adobe walls, navajo rugs, and Indian art work. The casitas are all very private. The individual fireplaces are especially welcome on those cool mountain evenings. Although they do not have fully equipped kitchens, each casita has a refrigerator. Los Abrigados was once a location for filming western movies and you'll be hard pressed to find a resort that more fully captures that Arizona feeling.

7 POCO DIABLO RESORT
1752 Highway 179, Sedona, AZ 86336, 602-282-7333
Amenities: Golf, tennis, racquetball, pools

Located in the foothills of Northern Arizona, where Oak Creek cuts a colorful canyon through the massive bright red and gold mountains, this resort overlooks a nine hole golf course and is nestled within the calm beauty of Red Rock country, two miles south of the center of Sedona. There are 32 villas in addition to the main hotel section. Each has a private fireplace and is furnished in southwestern style with soft desert hues. The comfort of the guests comes first with the friendly, well-trained staff. Each condo has a small refrigerator and wet bar but no full-service kitchen.

RENTAL RESOURCES
Blue Chip Realty, 602-282-2000
Red Rock Realty, 602-282-7254
Canyon Mesa Country Club, 602-284-2176
Coldwell Banker, 602-284-1740

Foothills Real Estate, 800-369-RENT
Northern Shadows Realty, 602-282-1791
Sedona Rentals, 602-282-7109

3. LAKE HAVASU / LAKE POWELL

Where the stark Arizona desert meets the jagged red rocks and the Colorado River, two man made lakes designed to enhance Western agriculture have become the setting for resort communities. Lacking the heat of the desert cities like Phoenix, these two recreational areas are favorites among retirees. Good golf and tennis weather all year, excellent watersports in the summer, with waterskiing and houseboating as two favorites.

Lake Powell and Lake Havasu have been formed by the Colorado River in the northern corners of Arizona. Lake Powell is popular with vacationers from all over the intermountain West in the summer. Lake Havasu triumphs as a year-round resort with a retirement community as a base. The condos in Lake Havasu are around London Bridge Village and golf course. There's a beach along the river, but that's not the draw. In summertime, the area comes alive with water sports enthusiasts, sailing and waterskiing under the constant clear blue sky.

The Lake Powell houseboating adventure can be a lot of fun especially when two families or a group of friends embark on a cruise to nowhere for a week.

WHERE TO STAY

6   INN AT TAMARISK
3101 London Bridge Rd., Lake Havasu City, AZ 86403
602-764-3033
Amenities: Pool, barbecue area Beach nearby.

This quiet condo development is a great choice for golfers, seniors, or families with well-behaved children. The condos are comfortable and modestly furnished.

6   LAKE HAVASU DUNES
Lake Havasu City, AZ 86403, 602-855-6626
Amenities: Clubhouse, pool

Located across the street from the Lake Havasu Marina, these 24 condos have been constructed in a contemporary California/Spanish style. Palm trees line the entrance to the resort. The one- and two-bedroom condos are spacious and attractively furnished to provide a comfortable environment.

7+ LAKE POWELL HOUSEBOATING
c/o Del Webb Recreational Properties
2916 N. 35th Ave., Suite 8, Phoenix, AZ 85017, 602-278-8888
Amenities: None

Can a houseboat be a condo? Absolutely! These flat bottom houseboats are privately owned by groups of 12 families. Under the purchase arrangement the houseboats are managed by the Del Webb corporation, which makes reservations and handles hospitality for guests just as at any other condo project. You'll spend your days on deck fishing, sunning, or dining on the water. Down below, quarters are efficient with three bedrooms and a dining table that converts (with cushions) to a double bed. Don't expect luxury or comfort, but do expect fun.

This can be an exciting and memorable vacation. These houseboats are called the "Winnebagos of the Waves." There are three sizes to choose from, depending upon how large your group is: 36, 44, or 50 feet. After a short one-hour lesson on operations and navigation, these beauties can be yours. Explore the narrow side canyons, where sheer walls rise straight from the water, or pull up on a private sandy beach for a Robinson Crusoe picnic.

7 NAUTICAL INN RESORT
1000 McCulloch Blvd., Lake Havasu City, AZ 86403
602-855-2141
Amenities: Golf, tennis, recreation center

The Nautical Inn has its own nine-hole golf course. There are a few condos for rent along the golf course and these are choice because of their size. The resort offers full hotel services and you can arrange for room service to come to your condo.

5 SANDS VACATION RESORT
240 Mesquite Ave., Lake Havasu, AZ 86403, 602-855-1388
Amenities: Pool, hot tub, tennis

The Sands Vacation Resort offers spacious suites complete with living room, kitchen, and separate bedrooms.

4. PINETOP / WHITE MOUNTAINS

A surprise awaits you in Arizona's White Mountains in the north central part of the state. This is one of the most beautiful and yet little known recreational areas in all of Arizona. The forest consists of approximately 170,000 acres of some of the most diverse and beautiful scenery in all the Southwest. The topography is dominated by the Mogollon Rim, a rim which Zane Grey referred to as the "Tonto Rim" in his writings. The Rim also defines the climate of the White Mountain National Forest and the resort town of

Pinetop. Semi-desert temperature and moisture conditions are found below the rim while typical mountain conditions are found above the rim. Summer temperatures may top 100 degrees in the canyons, while temperatures above the rim are in the '70s and '80s. The cool moist plateau above the rim is covered with spruce and fir trees.

The high country now lures thousand of retirees each year as well as sports enthusiasts attracted to the wide open spaces. At Pinetop, the snow glistens and drops from the winter pine trees like soft cotton, while the cross-country skiers pass underneath. Summer hikers enjoy beautiful woodland trails and trout fishermen catch their limit on the lakes lining the lush forest.

WHERE TO STAY

6 **NORTHWOODS**
Highway 260, P.O. Box 397, Pinetop, AZ 85935, 602-367-2966
Amenities: Pool

A quiet condo resort that is ideal for young families or the nearly retired. Not too expensive, it offers large, well-furnished condos and a pleasant resort atmosphere. The pool area is quiet, but at this small resort you're bound to make new friends quickly. You'll find your fireplace to be a welcome comfort on those chilly mountain evenings.

7 **ROUNDHOUSE RESORT**
Buck Springs Resort, Pinetop, AZ 85935, 602-369-4848
Amenities: Skiing, health club, racquetball, pool

Nestled in the mountains about two hours east of Phoenix, this quiet resort area caters to Phoenix residents looking to escape the heat and city congestion. The resort has preserved the Western cowboy flavor. There is skiing nearby in winter and a wide range of outdoor activities during the other nine months of the year. It is best for peace and quiet, as there is a limited number of restaurants and night spots in this area.

6 **WHISPERING PINES RESORT**
Highway 260, P.O. Box 307-A, Pinetop, AZ 85935, 602-367-4366
Amenities: Golf

Tucked away in the Ponderosa pines, just around the corner from the golf course, you'll find Whispering Pines. The condos have several grades of quality here from rustic cabins for fishing parties to comfortable villas for the golfers. The units have some cooking facilities, but at this "compound" guests gather at the Fireside Inn restaurant. It is a quiet and rustic resort.

5. TUCSON

Tucson enjoys the warm winter sun every bit as much as Phoenix. While most of the nation shivers in January, vacationers can lie by the pool in Tucson. Even better though, is the climate for golf and tennis. Because of the dry air, you won't feel the heat and you'll find your game has just a little more pep than it did back home. Summer can be hot and we can't apologize for August. You can play golf when it's 110 degrees and not feel the heat, but touch metal and you'll know its hot.

Tucson is one of those rare places that has it all: winter sunshine; nearby mountain forests; southwestern history and architecture blended with the convenience of a modern city.

The more obvious evidence is found in the world of downtown, where glass and concrete skyscrapers cast shadows on buildings with hand-crafted adobe walls. Northeast of the city just beneath the foothills of the Santa Catalina mountains with their jagged peaks, newly built modern homes surround lush golf courses. This is where the master planned golf, resort and retirement communities are located. Surprisingly many of what appear to be resort condos within the confines of these golf communities are not for rent. These condos are true second homes occupied by the owners in season.

In Tucson, we have selected condos surrounding two golf resorts. These provide an opportunity for you to enjoy the privacy and convenience of a condo, yet also let you take advantage of the golf, tennis, and social activities that are part of the resort environment. We have selected one urban condo complex for families or Tucson visitors who don't want the golf or the related built-in expense. And finally we've selected a group of condos in a retirement community offering a tranquil environment. These four selections are a sampling of the variety that Tucson has to offer.

WHERE TO STAY

6   **SUN CITY VISTOSO**
14023 Green Tree Dr., Tucson, AZ 85737, 800-433-9611
Amenities: Pool, golf, racquetball

Rancho Vistoso is a master-planned community located about eight miles north of metropolitan Tucson. It sits alone, surrounded by desert, awaiting its destiny as a major resort community ten years from now. The first development at Rancho Vistoso is the 1,000-acre Sun City development created by Del Webb corporation. The attraction is an 18-hole golf course as well as complete peace and privacy in the desert. The 27 townhouse condos available for rent are luxurious and reasonably priced for rental or purchase. Only weekly rentals are allowed. As this community was designed for seniors, no guests under age 16 are allowed. These condos are new and offer high quality accommodations at a very reasonable price.

8+ TUCSON NATIONAL RESORT & SPA
2727 W. Club Dr., Tucson, AZ 85741, 602-297-2271, 1BR $135
Amenities: Golf, spas

These villa suites are located in low-rise contemporary buildings along the golf fairways or overlooking the desert. Tucson National is a golf-oriented community on the northern edge of town. Just beyond the resort, there's open desert for as far as you can see. Maybe this is why Tucson National has preserved the charm of Arizona's heritage. The 27-hole golf course has been the home of NBC's Tucson Open for years as well as *Golf Digest's* golf training program. The center of the resort is the hotel, which has 24 one-bedroom suites, but for families or long-term stays you can arrange to rent one of the condos along the fairways. The southwestern heritage has been preserved in the interior decor of most units.

8 VENTANA CANYON GOLF & RACQUET CLUB
6200 N. Clubhouse Ln., Tucson, AZ 85715, 602-577-1400
Suite $95–235
Amenities: Golf, tennis

Set at the foot of the Santa Catalina mountains, Ventana Canyon enjoys a spectacular location. Do not confuse this with the Loew's Ventana Canyon Resort that is next door. Although both offer outstanding recreational and dining facilities, Ventana Canyon is a condo-hotel where the spacious one- and two-bedroom suites have a congenial, comfortable atmosphere. Whereas the Loew's Resort has more glitz, Ventana Canyon is the sort of place you would enjoy as much after two weeks as on the first day. The condo interiors are decorated in dusty rose and cheerful pink colors. The wall separating the living room from the master bedroom is actually an entertainment center arranged so you can reverse the VTP/television for viewing in either room; yet you can seal it off to make two totally private rooms. This resort caters to golf and tennis players. There are special golf package rates that can mean even greater savings. This is clearly one of the best choices in Tucson for families with small children.

5 VILLA SERENAS
8111 E. Broadway, Tucson, AZ 85710, 602-886-5537
Studio $55–90, 1BR $79–119, 2BR $99–128
Amenities: Pools, health clubs

This is a surprising choice for the budget traveler seeking a week in the sun. Villas Serenas is partially a residential condo property/partially a resort vacation rental property. The project is huge and encompasses nine, five-story buildings surrounding five pools and four fountains. The furniture in the condos is, as you would expect, functional and comfortable. Management is very friendly and helpful but don't expect many hotel-style services other than housekeeping and grounds keeping.

ARKANSAS

Arkansas will surprise you. You might not expect to find the rugged mountain hills, unspoiled green forests, and variety of sophisticated attractions "up in the hollows." There are some great golf resorts in the state. Bella Vista, Fairfield Bay, Los Indios, and Los Lagos are more affordable and less crowded than similar resorts in Florida and California. Moreover, the golf season lasts nine to ten months. The fishing in the Ozarks is also great and water sports are unlimited on the man-made lakes created during the past 50 years. Unlike the ocean, the waters are always calm and therefore ideal for waterskiing and wind surfing. At night, you'll hear country music jamborees in the hills—a part of the enduring frontier culture. We have divided the Arkansas chapter into two sections:

1. Ozark Mountains
2. Hot Springs

Most of the vacation homes in Arkansas are privately-owned cabins, generally along the shore of one of the lakes. Because Arkansas law requires condo/vacation home rentals to be handled by a real estate broker, you'll need to consult our Rental Resources section to arrange a vacation rental.

1. OZARK MOUNTAINS

The frontier culture is very much alive in this unspoiled region of the country. Settled by Scottish and Irish immigrants who had come from hill country cultures, these people have maintained their old ways through the generations. Listening to the mountain men talk, you can almost hear a little Scottish accent in the conversation. The commercial center of this area is Eureka Springs, but the condo resorts are in their own self-contained communities along the lakes. Eureka Springs extends along a twisted mountain road that drops more than 500 feet from one end of town to the other. As a result, nothing is level. The Victorian homes were built into the side of the hills, and some of them seem to lean. Because Main Street is twisted and narrow, the town runs an old-fashioned trolley car to help you get around. Every night, there are country music shows and special performances in Basin Spring Park. Eureka Springs is also home to the nation's most important Passion Play, similar to performances at Oberammergau, Austria.

South of Harrison you will find Dogpatch USA, one of the most interesting of the Ozarks' tourist centers. Dogpatch is a family entertainment area peopled by characters from Li'l Abner. Heading south toward Hot Springs you'll find the Ozark National Forest. It is densely wooded, but there are marked hiking trails. From a hilltop, you can see nothing but a green forest canopy. If you exit the forest at Mountain View, you can visit Blanchard Springs Caverns and hike the underground Dripstone and Discovery Trails. These provide good exercise in unique underground passageways. Or you

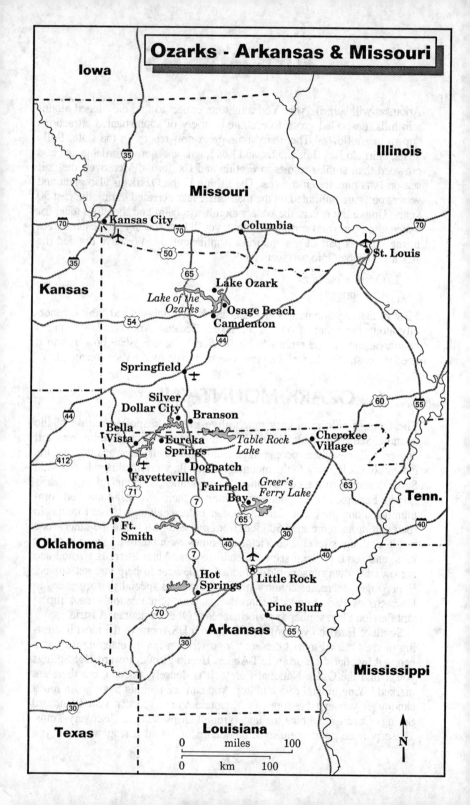

can visit the Ozark Folk Center, another family entertainment area. This one is devoted to traditional skills, crafts, and music.

Heading north to the Missouri state line, you will find Bull Shoals Lake, a lake created by the U.S. Army Corps of Engineers in the 1950s. Stocked with freshwater fish, the lake's size and depth allow the fish to grow extra large. You can rent a boat or join a fishing expedition on one of the pontoon boats and see for yourself. The Ozarks present opportunities for do-it-your-self adventure. If you see an interesting sight when puttering around the mountains, stop, relax, and enjoy yourself.

WHERE TO STAY

BELLA VISTA
430 Town Center, Route 3, Box 175, Bella Vista, AR 72714,
501-525-1321, 800-225-9030; 2BR $60–100
Amenities: Golf, tennis, horseback riding, pools, hot tub, boating,
racquetball, game room

Bella Vista is a major retirement/vacation community developed across 1,200 acres of rolling Arkansas hills. The focal points are the golf course and the country club. Unlike some of the more popular states like Florida or California, Bella Vista gives guests the best opportunities to play golf and tennis on uncrowded facilities. You can play all day long if you have the stamina, and you won't have to leave because of someone else's court or tee time. Bella Vista offers several groups of vacation condos for rent, all of which are about the same quality. The major difference between the various complexes is the location.

The Greens (8) The Greens is a good choice because of the unusual design of the condos. Built of redwood, they feature the best of the Ozarks, but each unit's design around an atrium is more in the contemporary California style. What's exceptional about this property is, it has a neatness more reminiscent of New England than of the mountain country. This is a first-class resort for visitors from all over because of its location and golf facilities.

FAIRFIELD BAY
P.O. Box 3008, Fairfield Bay, AR 72088, 501-884-3347,
800-643-9790; 2BR $500–780/wk
Amenities: Golf, tennis, pools, horseback riding, marina

Fairfield Bay is on the southern edge of the Ozarks. It is only 85 miles north of Little Rock and is conveniently located for touring the Ozark National Forest and the Ozark Folk Center. This 14,000-acre destination resort is unquestionably the finest in the area. It features two 18-hole golf courses, the Indian Rock tennis complex (providing one of the finest training programs in the U.S.), and a full marina for boating, fishing, and sailing. In addition, it is possible to scuba dive in Greer's Ferry Lake. The wide variety of accommodations to choose from here includes chalets, three-story condo buildings and townhouses. Every unit has a full kitchen and professional interior decorator furnishings. Naturally, some are newer and more stylish than others.

Cliffside Lodge Villas (7) These condos are located on the mountain near the Racquet Club. They are our favorite because of the view and the close location to the pool and the restaurant. Cathedral ceilings, fireplaces and stylish, contemporary decor are special characteristics of these condos.

The Terraces (6) These condos are in a convenient location. They are not as stylish as Cliffside condos, however they are just as popular as vacation rentals. The social director and the staff have planned week-long activity programs for adults and children. The "Murder She Wrote" style mysteries are especially interesting. Guests discover "clues" during the week and compete to solve the crime and win a prize. The restaurant at the country club features sandwiches as well as gourmet specials at reasonable prices. The resort is so complete that you can return year after year and never want to leave. The resort condos are part of a large community that also has condos that are owned and occupied part of the year by the semiretired. There are also lots for retirement or vacation homes.

5   THE LODGE ON WHITNEY MOUNTAIN
Route 1, 1657 Lodge Dr., Lost Bridge, Garfield, AR 72732,
501-359-3201; Suites $50–80
Amenities: Restaurant, pool, tennis

This resort lodge/restaurant offers suites and condos behind it that face the lake.

6   TABLE ROCK RESORT
95 Woodside Dr., Holiday Island, One Landing Dr.,
Holiday Island, AR 72632, 501-253-7733, 800-255-9381
1BR $45–75, 2BR $55–95, 3BR $65–110
Amenities: Marina, golf, tennis, pool

Table Rock Resort is on Holiday Island, separated from the mainland by arms of the lake. Holiday Island is connected to the mainland by a narrow mountain road and a rope suspension bridge. The flavor of a Tom Sawyer lifestyle is here. There's an 18-hole golf course, tennis courts and a marina/general store. One cluster of condos is on the golf course, the rest are within walking distance of the marina overlooking the lake. Table Rock Lake has bluffs, coves, and surrounding forests. It's a primitive backwoods area with a certain appeal. The condos are spacious townhouses with country casual furniture.

Good for groups of golfers or fishermen, it is also popular with active families who like the sporting life in summer. Complimentary greens fees are included with the price of a rental. There are no on-site facilities at any of the individual condominium developments, but the clubhouse up the hill with its Olympic size pool and its diner-style restaurant are available. It is comfortable with a country-friendly atmosphere.

2. HOT SPRINGS

Founded as a mineral springs spa, this community has evolved into a full-fledged vacation center that will keep you busy all week, year after year. The city is older, with many buildings dating from before World War II. Five miles from the city center is Lake Hamilton, which is the focal point for new development. There are marinas where you can rent boats for waterskiing, fishing, sailing, windsurfing, or just floating on the lake. Pontoon boats are popular here, with daily rentals for outings. The town is interesting. Bathhouse Row is now listed on the National Register of Historic Places. You will see the bubbling springs behind glass near the Maurice Bathhouse or next to the Arlington. No one knows why the thermal springs are warm or why they bubble, but theories abound. Mountain Valley Waters, the Mid-South's answer to Perrier, is bottled here. The water is naturally sterile and pure. A tour of the bottling plant provides an excellent education on Hot Springs as a community. The most exciting attraction is the horse racing during the spring season that culminates in the Arkansas Derby. Hot Springs is Little Rock's playground. More sophisticated than the Ozarks, Hot Springs attracts the gentry from Little Rock on weekends. Why not? The climate is mild in the winter and cooler than the city in summer. Hot Springs is also popular as a golfer's resort. There are 20 golf courses in the area, and starting times are never a problem.

WHERE TO STAY

7   **EMERALD ISLE CONDOMINIUMS**
7005 Central Ave., Hot Springs, AR 71913, 501-525-4685
Studio $600/wk, 1BR $650, 2BR $750
Amenities: Beach, marina, pool, tennis

Emerald Isle consists of 40 units on Lake Hamilton. Quality and fun are emphasized at this resort. Well managed and maintained, this complex has a marina for guests to bring their boats, as well as a full-service health spa with indoor and outdoor pools. The condominiums are in three-story buildings overlooking an arm of Lake Hamilton. The condos are new, modern, and stylishly decorated. They have the interior decor you might expect in California: light woods, solid-colored fabrics, fireplaces, and VTPs. Some condos even have a private whirlpool in the master bath. What's outstanding here? The activities program. It is one of the best in Arkansas. You'll find a bubbly staff dedicated to making sure that you and your children have a happy vacation.

6 **LAKE SHORE RESORT & YACHT CLUB**
Highway 270 West, Box 2540, Hot Springs, AR 71914,
501-767-8408; 2BR $100
Amenities: Beach, indoor and outdoor pools, tennis

These townhouse condo units are located on the Sheraton Resort & Conference Center property, a short walk away from the main hotel lodge. Strung along the lake shore, each has a great view and a private patio. The decor is modern and spiffy, but the furniture is hotel style. The condos are spacious, private, and convenient to all of the hotel activities. The resort offers quiet ambiance and bustling activity. Sheraton also manages a separate group of townhouse condos on the opposite shore of the lake. They are more spacious than these condos, but not as convenient to the hotel's recreational facilities.

9 **LOS LAGOS**
1 Los Lagos Blvd., Hot Springs, AR 71909, 800-222-4892
2BR $60–140
Amenities: Golf, golf club, tennis, health spa, lake, pools

Los Lagos is the choice resort at Hot Springs. It is spread over 1,100 acres and managed by the same people who created Bella Vista and Cherokee Village. It is another integrated community where vacation condos are only part of a larger development. This property attracts golfers and a smart crowd from Little Rock. These townhouse condos along the fairway with private enclosed patios on one side, offer a full expansive view of the golf course on the other. Designed with lots of wood trim and half-timber beams, you'll find sunken living rooms and cathedral ceilings that make the units seem even more spacious. A stone-hearth fireplace and a private whirlpool are in the master bath. Is this what you were expecting? The best part is the wealth of activities available from 18 holes of golf, eight tennis courts, two pools, and a golf club with a 19th hole for sharing stories. The majority of owners are from northern climates and have an interest in building a vacation home or retiring to this community some day. Do they plan to sell their vacation condos when the house is built? No. This is a vacation villa for children or guests to visit.

4 **NORTH SHORE RESORT**
200 Pretti Point Rd., Hot Springs, AR 71901, 501-525-4691
Amenities: Lake, beach, racquetball, restaurant, pool, tennis

This is a small development where 12 units are part of a timeshare plan. The two-bedroom units are will furnished and there are indoor and outdoor pools as well as tennis facilities for guests. This resort is quiet by comparison with the others and there is no activities program.

7   SOUTH SHORE LAKE RESORT
201 Hamilton Oak Dr., Hot Springs, AR 71913, 501-525-8200
Amenities: Lake, restaurant, pool, and tennis

This 268-unit resort occupies an entire peninsula overlooking Lake Hamilton. The three-story buildings were designed and furnished to be a top quality resort. It occupies 40 acres and is a world unto itself, with clubhouses, pools, tennis courts and a health spa.

7   SUN BAY BEACH CLUB/LODGE
6110 Center Ave., Hot Springs, AR 71913, 501-525-4691,
800-847-0090; 1BR $60–159, 2BR $90–219
Amenities: Marina, racquetball, tennis, pools

The three-story condominiums at Sun Bay Beach Club are older than the suites next door in the Sun Bay Lodge, but the Beach Club condos have a sense of "vacation home." This is one of the most popular resorts in the state of Arkansas because of all the social activities, children's programs, restaurants, and the bar. Every unit has a view of Lake Hamilton, and downtown Hot Springs is only a mile away. Staying at Sun Bay Beach Lodge is more like staying in a hotel because the condos are along a hallway. The Lodge condos are suites with kitchens. They are only four years old, and have newer, lighter furniture. The entrance is off a central corridor. At Sun Bay Beach Club, the apartments are larger and more "Ozarks" or country because of the heavy woods and ruffles. The Beach Club condos have their own individual entrances.

6   THE WHARF
240 Central Ave., Hot Springs, AR 71913, 501-525-4604
$500–650/wk
Amenities: Pool, tennis

This was built by the same developer as Sun Bay Lodge/Sun Bay Beach Club. These three-story condo units are on Long Island, a short two-mile drive from the main part of Hot Springs. The resort overlooks Lake Hamilton and has a dock and swimming pool. Guests have full membership privileges at Sun Bay's facilities.

RENTAL RESOURCES
Albright Realty, 501-624-4451, Hot Springs
Coldwell Banker Spa Realty, 501-525-4457, Hot Springs

Greer Real Estate, 501-253-9000, Eureka Springs
Holiday Isle Vacation Rentals, 800-848-4688
Lakeland Realty, 501-253-8750, Eureka Springs
Little Switzerland Realty, 501-253-9182, Eureka Springs
Mountain Country Properties, 501-253-9660, Eureka Springs
Rainbow Realty, 501-321-1277, Hot Springs
Slezak Realty, 501-623-9064, Hot Springs
South Shore Rentals, 501-984-7700, Hot Springs
Village Villas, 501-922-0303, 800-643-1000, Hot Springs
VR Rentals, 800-222-4892, Bella Vista

CALIFORNIA

California offers a wide range of climates and activities for vacationers. Southern California has its beaches, golf courses, and attractions such as Disneyland. Palm Springs offers a desert environment perfect for golf or tennis players. Just above the desert floor, the San Bernardino mountains offer skiing in the winter and an alpine lakes region in the summer when the snow melts. The north central Pacific Coast area has dramatic scenery and a number of unique attractions such as the artist's colony of Carmel and America's favorite city, San Francisco. Lake Tahoe is a year-round resort with the largest concentration of ski areas in the U.S., as well as watersports in summer and casino nightlife all year long. Finally the Mammoth area appeals to skiers in winter and nature lovers wishing to explore Yosemite in the summer.

You'll find a range of condo accommodations in each of these areas. We have divided this chapter into five sections, so you can concentrate on the selections in the areas of your choice:

1. Southern California Coast (San Diego & Orange Counties)
2. Inland Empire (Palm Springs & San Bernardino Mountains)
3. Pacific Coast (Carmel to Mendocino)
4. Lake Tahoe and Squaw Valley
5. Mammoth

1. SOUTHERN CALIFORNIA COAST

The Southern California coastal area has two distinct resort regions: Orange County and San Diego County. Camp Pendleton, the Marine Corps base, provides a twenty-mile gap between the beach resorts of Orange County and San Diego County.

SAN DIEGO COUNTY

The northern part of San Diego County is a land of small towns, farms, horse ranches, acres of flowers, and tourist attractions. There are several distinct neighborhoods in San Diego County and the following will help you select your destination.

Beginning with Oceanside, 30 miles north of downtown San Diego, this beach community is being reborn, and prices are rising swiftly with the change. Carlsbad is the next community south of Oceanside along the coast. The town was named after Carlsbad in Bavaria when it was discovered that the water has the same chemical properties as the mineral spas in Germany. Perhaps the most famous spa of all, La Costa, is located here. This is where today's Hollywood stars go to rejuvenate and get in shape. With an 18-hole

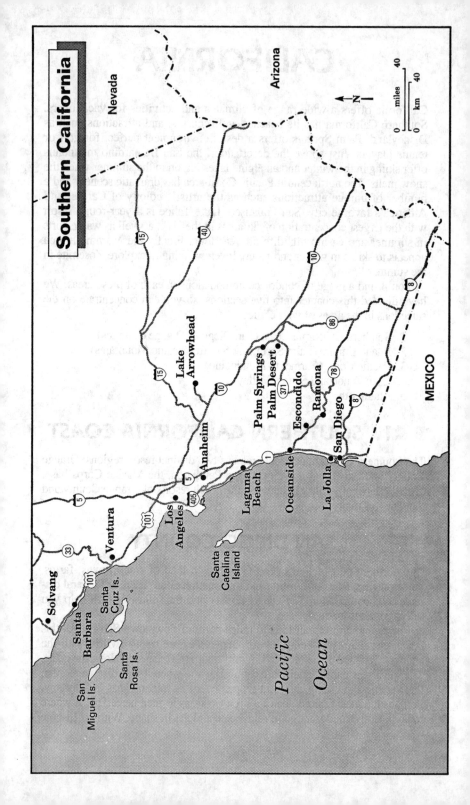

Southern California

golf course and a dozen tennis courts, this is one of Southern California's most outstanding resorts.

Del Mar, where "turf meets the surf," is located on the coast just north of La Jolla. Its famed racetrack is home to thoroughbred racing from late July through mid-September. The resorts of Del Mar are small and smart.

La Jolla is technically part of San Diego, but both residents and visitors agree that it's a world apart. Many condos along La Jolla Shores Beach used to be vacation rentals, but are now permanent residences. The good news is that La Jolla still enjoys that fabulous year-round climate where temperatures in this coastal town generally range between 65° and 80° all year long. With rugged sea cliffs and forests of torrey pines and eucalyptus, it is home to spectacular golf courses and legendary beaches. Downtown La Jolla remains La Jolla, an exclusive enclave where many of the cute storefronts house very expensive art galleries.

In San Diego there are two areas of resort condominiums: Mission Bay Beach and Coronado Island in the middle of the bay, connected to the mainland by a bridge. Mission Bay Beach is just north of Sea World and convenient to the sailboat marina and port for fishing charters. For families planning a week in the San Diego area, Mission Bay Beach makes an ideal base of operations because of its convenient access to the sights of San Diego and the beachfront location for those moments of "downtime" recreation.

Coronado Island, dominated by the famous resort Hotel del Coronado, is an ideal vacation spot because of the broad sandy beach. Just ten minutes away from downtown San Diego, the island operates on "island time." The condos for rent on Coronado Island, with one exception, have a minimum rental period of one month because of a local zoning ordinance designed to maintain the island's quiet residential nature and to prevent commercial development of the beachfront by hotels and vacation condos. However, we hear that weekly rentals frequently occur on Coronado, so if a one-month stay is not your style, call around and you might find what you want.

Heading inland, the mountains are home to numerous golf resort communities. Eucalyptus groves were planted in the area soon after the turn of the century as an experimental source of railroad ties. The wood proved unsuitable, so today the air is fragrant with the smell from the remaining groves of eucalyptus trees. The area now sprouts green fairways and condo developments where golfers and mature travelers can take advantage of 330 days of sunshine each year.

The Lawrence Welk Resort, a huge complex which has two 18-hole golf courses, can be divided into three sections: the Champagne Village retirement area, the hotel, and the golf course Fairway Villas. Pala Mesa nearby in Fallbrook is home to the University of Golf, a 7 or 14-day training program. Rancho Santa Fe, with its RSF course and an additional 18 holes at Whispering Palms, is one of the nation's most exclusive communities where the average home has a price tag in excess of $1,000,000. Surrounded by groves of eucalyptus and citrus, this is where Old Southern California meets the new millionaires from the East.

Further inland there's the mountain resort town of Julian, famous for its apple festival. To escape the constant good weather, San Diegans take to the hills for a change of pace. Destinations include Warner Springs Ranch and the desert community of Borrego Springs. With a Palm Springs-like climate, Borrego offers the same desert experience at half the price.

WHERE TO STAY

5 **BEACHCOMBER VILLAGE**
620 S. The Strand, Oceanside, CA 92054, 619-755-8686
1BR $450–695/wk, 2BR $795–1095/wk
Amenities: Beach, pool, hot tub

Right across the street from one of the best beaches in Southern California, this cluster of condos looks like an overgrown motel. These one and two-story structures have seen their better days. But serendipity is in store because these units have been beautifully and tastefully decorated on the inside. Expect to find pale pastels, a touch of lavender and splashes of burgundy. Mirrors bring the oceanview inside and silk flowers make a dashing touch. Sometimes you can't judge a book by its cover.

6 **BLUE SEA LODGE (Best Western)**
707 Pacific Beach Dr., San Diego, CA 92109, 619-483-4700
1BR $115, 2BR $175–225, 3BR $235
Amenities: Pool, beach, fishing. Sailboat rentals nearby

Blue Sea Lodge is a good choice for people who want to vacation in San Diego's Mission Bay area (San Diego's playground). Mission Bay offers something for everyone including sailing, beaches, and deep-sea fishing charters. Blue Sea Lodge's location, across the street from the beach, is especially good for young, active vacationers. The units in this three-story building are relatively new and decorated in a contemporary style with lots of peach and blue furnishings. Since our first review this has switched from being a condominium, where units are owned by individuals, to an all-suite hotel managed by Best Western. There has been no change in the units, but management is now more formal and institutionalized.

6 **CAPRI BY THE SEA**
4767 Ocean Blvd., San Diego, CA 92109, 619-435-4137
Studio $97, 1BR $99–175, 2BR $115–275
Amenities: Beach, pool

Capri by the Sea is located on Coronado Island in a partially residential high-rise tower. Monthly rentals are encouraged, although daily rentals are available. This is a unique feature on Coronado Island where all *other* properties supposedly are only available on a monthly basis. In the summertime, the swimming pool is a fun place to be. The condos are spacious and furnished with contemporary furniture. Some of the units haven't been maintained as well as others. Ask about what you will be getting before you rent.

7   CARLSBAD INN BEACH RESORT
3075 Carlsbad Blvd., Carlsbad, CA 92008, 619-434-7020,
800-235-3939; Studio $95–105, 1BR $160
Amenities: Beach, restaurant, pool, spa, health club

The Carlsbad Inn is a lovely English Tudor style resort located just off the beach at Carlsbad. English accessories, wing chairs, and floral designer fabrics grace the interior of the main building. This resort offers a tasteful blend of picturesque resort architecture with all of the modern comforts of home. Stylishly decorated, each has "country club" charm. The 132 luxury condos surround a green and are in a three-story structure with its own private entrance. The children generally converge around the pool while the adults take advantage of the facilities in the spa and health club. A full exercise room with a variety of weight training equipment is provided. Scheduled parties and spontaneous get-togethers are common at this resort. In addition, a list of organized activities (different for each day of the week) is offered. One noteworthy observation: housekeeping and maintenance are immaculate with nothing out of place. For those seeking a superior vacation, close to the beach and with all the comforts of home, this is highly recommended for San Diego's North County.

8   CORONADO SHORES
Silver Strand Blvd., P.O. Box 220, Coronado, CA 92118,
619-435-6238; 1BR $1500/mo, 2BR $2000/mo, 3BR $2500/mo
Amenities: Beach, pools, tennis, gym, saunas, hot tub

Coronado Shores is a village of ten, 18-story high-rise condo buildings located next to the Hotel del Coronado. It's a complete community with a unique location on Coronado Island. The condos were designed as residences as well as vacation homes. Three hundred of the 1,500 condos are available for rent. They are spacious and tastefully furnished for comfort with a neutral decor. Although the interiors are somewhat standardized, the styles vary according to the owner's tastes. Purchase prices begin at $200,000 and rapidly escalate to a million dollars. After all, this strip of Coronado Island is unique real estate.

The city of San Diego passed a zoning ordinance prohibiting rentals for less than 30 days. The city fathers didn't want residential real estate completely converted to a resort hotel atmosphere. The reasoning was that the increased prices would edge out the beachfront citizens from their homes. Therefore, rentals are quoted for a 30 day minimum. But in practice, we hear that some of these condos are rented by the week. If this is what you want, investigate. This condo village has its own private beach, four pools, eight tennis courts, a gym with exercise equipment, saunas, and hot tubs. There's also a teen center and a children's recreation room.

8   IMPERIAL BEACH CLUB
712 Seacoast Dr., Imperial Beach, CA 92032
Amenities: Beach, pool, hot tub, exercise room

Imperial Beach Club is a brand new, three-story beachfront condo complex with gabled roofs and painted steel tube railings around the balconies. Every one of these two and three-bedroom condos has a view of the ocean. Each condo also has a fireplace and a spacious deluxe kitchen, quite a change from the galley quarters most cooks are used to. There's a landscaped courtyard, pool, hot tub, and exercise facility that is popular with visitors and residents alike at the end of the day.

7+   LA CASA DEL ZORRO
3845 Yaqui Pass Rd., Borrego Springs, CA 92004, 619-767-5323
1BR $150
Amenities: Pools, hot tubs, putting green, restaurant, tennis

Borrego's most famous resort is a complex of Spanish-style tile and stucco buildings surrounded by palms and luxuriant landscaping. In the empty desert, it appears as an oasis. Most units are hotel rooms, although there are two, three, and four-bedroom casitas. These are the best accommodations you'll find at Zorro's house because they have a fireplace, private patio, and a whirlpool. The clear skies and absence of lights make the stars seem brighter. The evening landscape is enhanced by night-lit pools. The tennis program is excellent with nine courts and a teaching pro. Try it for a change of pace, or if you plan activities in neighboring Anza-Borrego Desert State Park.

10   LA COSTA
Costa del Mar Rd., Carlsbad, CA 92008, 619-438-9111
800-854-6564; 1BR $195–400, 2BR $255–825
Amenities: Golf, tennis, pools, spa, hot tubs

"If I'm good, when I die I'll go to La Costa" is the remark sometimes heard in Beverly Hills. La Costa is the southern California resort by which other golf and spa resorts are judged. Twenty-five years ago, La Costa was designed as a spa where Hollywood celebrities and national business leaders could rejuvenate. It began a trend, and today there are a host of imitations, but La Costa will always be the real thing.

La Costa is set in the foothills of North San Diego County about three miles from the ocean and beach in an area of eucalyptus and pine forests.

The contour of the hills has been used to create La Costa's championship 27-hole golf course. There are 28 tennis courts, a stadium court, and a team of top notch instructors for clinics or private lessons. La Costa hosts a number of golf and tennis tournaments including the Carl Reiner Celebrity Pro Am.

La Costa is most famous for its spa, and the spa restaurant is known throughout Southern California for gourmet lean cuisine. This really is one of the spots where the stars go to get in shape and workouts can be a unique social experience. The layout of the resort begins at the reception center, a pink stucco building with a great hall lobby, crystal chandeliers and massive paintings in gilded frames. The view from the terrace is enchanting, especially when the sun sets around 5 P.M. and the air is fragrant with eucalyptus trees. The condos are hidden in two-story buildings and private bungalows. There is plenty of landscaping to preserve privacy. Inside you'll find elegant decor with large living rooms, dining rooms and full-size kitchens. Some have a private whirlpool in the master bath. The style of the decor may vary with the owner's individual tastes, but the resort maintains the highest standards and evaluates each condo before placing it in the rental program.

Sounds like an exclusive resort where children wouldn't be welcome? Absolutely not true. Camp La Costa is one of the leaders in activity programs for young children and sports instruction programs for juniors. In addition, there are horseback riding stables and over 21 miles of riding trails within the resort.

After a week of workouts, sports and exceptional dining, you'll be able to test the hypothesis that La Costa is next to heaven.

9   LA JOLLA BEACH AND TENNIS CLUB

2000 Spindrift Dr., La Jolla, CA 92037, 619-454-7126
1BR $105–210, 2BR $140–290
Amenities: Beach, pool, 9 hole pitch-n-putt, restaurant

This is an exclusive but friendly retreat on the beach just north of San Diego. Located on the best part of the beach in La Jolla, this is a private club where members and those with introductions can rent condos. The condos on this ten-acre property are in a series of Spanish-style stucco buildings with red tile roofs. Most face the water. Interior decor is beach casual but done to perfection. Each unit has a small kitchenette. Before passing judgment on this one, remember that these condos were developed nearly 30 years before superlative features such as whirlpool bathtubs became commonplace. Members and guests have been returning here year after year as families grow up and long-time friendships are formed. This is more than just a place to stay.

8   LA JOLLA COVE SUITES
155 Coast Blvd., La Jolla, CA 92037, 619-459-2621
Amenities: Beach, pool, racquetball, exercise room

This is a great spot. La Jolla Cove is one of the prime reasons to visit La Jolla for divers and swimmers. La Jolla Cove Suites is directly across the street. There are two buildings here—one four stories, the other seven stories. Each has a private balcony overlooking picturesque Scripps Park, the palms and the Pacific. Interior decor ranges from classic French to Danish modern, depending upon the personal tastes of the condo owner. More personalized than most condo rental properties, this is like being a guest in someone's home. There are sports facilities but you'll really appreciate being next to the cove with its pretty beach and clear water. This location is a block away from the heart of La Jolla's restaurant and shopping district.

7   LA JOLLA RACQUET CLUB
2600 Torrey Pines Rd., La Jolla, CA 92037
Amenities: Pool, hot tub, tennis

More residential than vacation oriented, these condos are an example of what has happened to the second home market in La Jolla/Del Mar. Originally built to be "playtoys," these were vacation homes for Angelenos or visitors from the Bay who came for the San Diego sunshine. Originally priced at under $100,000, today the prices are $200,000 to $238,000 for a two-bedroom condo. Therefore, most of the part-time owners have sold out to La Jolla residents who live here full time. There are still some vacation rentals at this attractive complex only two miles from the beach at La Jolla Shores, but it has lost the carefree vacation atmosphere.

9   LA JOLLA SHORES CLUBDOMINIUMS
Camino del Oro at Vallecitos, La Jolla, CA 92037
Amenities: Beach, pool, hot tub, tennis

Located across the street from the beach at La Jolla Shores and next door to the Beach and Tennis Club, you couldn't have a better location in La Jolla. The spacious condos in these modern four-story buildings are some of the most sought after in the La Jolla area. With price tags of $300,000 or more for a two-bedroom unit, you know this property has got to be good. Beautifully decorated, we saw one that combined tiled floors, Persian carpets, glass-top tables, and art from Santa Fe. This unit is eclectic and a visual feast. This is a private clubby community. Count yourself among the fortunate few if you're able to arrange a summertime rental— no matter the price.

9 **LAWRENCE WELK RESORT VILLAS**
8858 Lawrence Welk Dr., Escondido, CA 92026, 619-749-3000
2BR $220
Amenities: Lake, pools, tennis, restaurant, golf, health club, spa, theater

Don't let the name mislead you. This part of the resort is not to be confused with the neighboring Welk Retirement Community. This beautiful resort is for the young and active, and everything has been developed to a level of near perfection. There are 12 tennis courts and two golf courses: one a championship 18-hole course and the other an executive par 3. It is the only condo resort that offers real Broadway plays on site with a stage for touring theater productions. This resort is fabulous in every respect. Nearly 300 condominium units cluster in little groupings around the golf course and park, spread over 150 acres. Each unit was designed to capture the best views of the fairway and the mountains beyond. The whole resort, including the retirement village, Champagne Estates, encompasses more than 1,000 acres. The spacious condominiums are beautifully decorated. An added advantage here is that the resort is only 15 minutes from the beach if you decide to visit for a day. This resort delivers unforgettable vacations. Rentals may be expensive because the owners really do use this resort as much as they can.

7 **NORTH COAST VILLAGE**
999 N. Pacific St., Oceanside, CA 92054
Amenities: Beach, pools, tennis, hot tub, sauna

North Coast Village is located in Oceanside on one of the widest and safest beaches in California. The slope is gentle, the water is shallow and the waves are mild. Many of the condos have a view of the Oceanside Yacht Marina. The resort is a huge village of 26 separate three and four-story buildings. Some of them are part-time residential, while others are for vacation rentals. Recently furnished in a casual contemporary style, each condo is comfortable and has its own fireplace. There are three recreation centers in this village and two full size pools (one's an Olympic size). In addition, a huge hot tub in a secluded fern grotto is available. For those who don't get enough activity with Boogie boarding, surfing, fishing, golf and tennis, there's a health club with an exercise room and saunas. Rentals are by the week.

8 **OCEAN FRONT WALK VILLAS**
3325-3725 Ocean Front Walk, San Diego, CA 92108
Amenities: Beach and marina nearby

Located on the southern tip of the western shore of Mission Bay, this is a special community of three-story townhouses. Ultra-modern in architecture, they are right on the beach. This location is an almost unheard of luxury in the San Diego area where oceanfront development has been limited. We saw one that had a rooftop sun deck with a private hot tub large enough for four. Designer decorated, you can expect colorful fabrics with peach, lavender, and aqua colors tastefully used throughout. Pass-through kitchens have an open table for cooking so the cook can look into the living room and view the evening sunset beyond. Absolutely beautiful, there's a fireplace for the occasional foggy morning or a cool evening. If you have been dreaming of the California beach or boating experience, this exceptional place is for you.

8+ PALA MESA RESORT
2001 Old Highway 395, Fallbrook, CA 92028, 619-728-5881, 800-822-4600; 1BR $125, 2BR $160
Amenities: Golf, pool, clubhouse, tennis, hot tub

A real sleeper, Pala Mesa provides all of the advantages offered by more celebrated resorts, yet it is quite undiscovered. It is located ten miles inland from the coast, twenty miles north of San Diego, and enjoys a temperate climate. The winter weather is dryer than San Diego and the Coast, but it's not desert like Palm Springs. The area is surrounded by fragrant eucalyptus trees. This is a golfer's resort and home to the University of Golf, an intensive training program with clinics, practice and video critiques. Along the rolling fairways you'll find townhouse-style condominiums. Each two-bedroom townhouse can be locked off to create a one-bedroom apartment and a hotel room. The two-bedroom units have a spiral staircase leading to the second floor. The basic decor is comfortable and casual. The pool and hot tub are in an attractive landscaped garden setting. This is one of the best choices for golfers in the San Diego area.

PENNY REALTY
3803 Mission Blvd., San Diego, CA 92109, 619-488-4129
800-748-6704

This is the largest vacation rental company in the La Jolla/Mission Bay area. One telephone call will put you in touch with over 350 vacation properties ranging from cute Ocean Walk townhouses at the tip of the Bay, to ultra-modern beachside cottages in Del Mar. The latter are favored by film celebrities and corporate executives from the East seeking to find the "true California" experience. Prices range from $300 per week to $19,500 for a month. As you can see, there is a wide, wide range of rental alternatives. Check the list of Rental Resources for the competition.

6 RAMS HILL
1881 Rams Hill Rd., Borrego Springs, CA 92004, 619-767-5000
1BR $170, 2BR $215, Casita $160
Amenities: Golf, tennis, pools, restaurant

Hoping to compete with the desert golf community of Palm Springs, Rams Hill was developed in the 1980s as "the next place to go." Theoretically when the Coachella Valley is built out, we'll all troop down to Borrego. This golf-oriented resort community looks a little wan as though its waiting for the guests to arrive. After reviewing all of the facilities and the amenities, this is clearly the best resort in the Borrego area. But where are all the people? Each condo is tastefully furnished but lacks the drama created by Palm Springs decorators. There's a fireplace for those cool mountain nights and a patio where you'll enjoy beautiful views of the mountains. Rams Hill is for pioneers.

 ## SAN DIEGO VACATION RENTALS
2613 Mission Dr., Suite 8, San Diego, CA 92108, 619-755-8686

Rarely do we mention a property management service since this is a directory of properties, not rental agents. But in San Diego there is an inventory of beachfront bungalows and condos for rent through this company. Increasingly San Diego, with its charming Mission Bay Park District or quaint La Jolla, is becoming urbanized. Now with over 1,000,000 citizens, it's California's second largest city. Yet the combination of climate, wide white beaches, mountains, and clear diving waters make this the ultimate California vacation destination. San Diego Vacation Rentals has carefully selected an array of homes and condos which can be rented by the day, the week, the month or the season. Other companies rent out condos or villas on behalf of the owners; this company makes it easy for you, the consumer, to find and rent these accommodations. Examples of some of the properties are:

Carmel Cloisters — Small two-bedroom condos on the boardwalk next to the Mission Bay Beach. Sit on your balcony and watch the surfers. Casual, contemporary decor. So much better than a hotel.

Entertainer's Delight — A two-story living room with glass walls to capture the ocean view. Stereo and VCR equipment in a tiled-floor living room. Upstairs the master bath has a whirlpool.

Mission Point Views — On the channel at South Mission Bay you can watch both the ocean and the boats on their way into the bay. Just 100 yards from the ocean, there's an exercise room and sauna for this cluster of townhouses.

Beach House on the Bay — A three-bedroom modern wood beach house overlooking the bay. Casual, tranquil, and a sailor's delight. The ocean is five minutes away.

6+   **SAN VICENTE RESORT**
24157 San Vicente Rd., Ramona, CA 92065
Amenities: Golf, tennis, pool

This peaceful golf course-oriented master community development is isolated in the hills about 30 miles northeast of San Diego. It's a world unto itself with fragrant air from the eucalyptus forest and rows and rows of condominiums lining the golf course. The condos are either retirement homes, vacation homes (used by San Diegans on the weekends) or rentals (daily, weekly, or monthly). The condos are located in one and two-story buildings. They are adequately furnished, but they're nothing special. This is a good place to stay to play golf and tennis, or to just meet friends. Socializing takes place around the country club, especially in the afternoons at the 19th hole. Each cluster of condos has its own pool.

6   **SEA BLUFF**
1750 N. Hwy. 101, Leucadia, CA 92024
Amenities: Pools, tennis

Sea Bluff is located 20 miles north of downtown San Diego. The location is convenient for people interested in driving to the beaches at Del Mar and Oceanside. A stairwell leads to the beach in front of Sea Bluff. The townhouse condos are located on a bluff overlooking the beach in North County. They are spacious and have a private walled patio or sun deck. The two-bedroom condos have interesting loft units upstairs. For pleasure, two heated swimming pools and five lighted tennis courts are available.

7   **SEASHORE ON THE BLUFF**
708 Fourth St., Encinitas, CA 92024, 619-458-6746
1BR $495–695/wk, 2BR $695–995/wk
Amenities: Pool

These three-story condos are perched on a bluff, 200 feet above the ocean. You'll hear the crashing surf and enjoy unparalleled ocean vistas. Beach access is just a short walk away. These casual condos have beautiful interior decor, yet the rental rates would be a winner on "The Price is Right." Expect to find muted pastel fabrics, mirrors to enhance the view and lovely silk flower arrangements. This is superior to the furnishings of most beach houses. Many guests take advantage of the discounts on monthly rentals. Sea Bluff is warm and friendly, and is a very good value.

7   **SEASHORE ON THE SAND**
2805 Ocean St., Carlsbad, CA 92008, 619-755-8686
Studio $450–750/wk, 1BR $695–1250/wk, 2BR $950–1750/wk
Amenities: Beach, pool

These studio, one, and two-bedroom condos are a surprising find right on the beach in Carlsbad. Unpretentious on the outside, they are beautifully decorated on the inside with painted wood furniture and pink and grey fabrics. Pictures and flowers help create a romantic setting. They have weekly rates as low as $1750 for a two-bedroom beachfront condo. Compare this to neighboring (and very exclusive) La Costa where the stars stay for $750 a night. Considering the facilities and location, this is one of the best values in Southern California.

7   SHADOW MOUNTAIN RANCH

2771 Frisius Rd., Julian, CA 92036, 619-765-0323
Tree House $60
Amenities: Indoor pool, hot tub, library, billiards room

Nestled at 4,200 feet above sea level in the mountains of San Diego County, an hour and a half northeast of the San Diego Airport, Julian attracts those who march to a different drummer. It is one of the most unusual collections of "cabins in the woods" that we've found anywhere. One of the cabins, the "Tree House," is actually built into the arms of a giant live oak next to the main house of a genuine working ranch. Several other cabins have been scattered in the woods and the attraction here is an escape from civilization into rustic seclusion. Interior decor is traditional country with checkered fabrics and lots of ruffles. Never mind the schmaltz, these cabins have views of the valley and the mountains beyond, and provide a bit of New England fantasy in sunny Southern California.

7   SOUTHERN CALIFORNIA BEACH CLUB

121 S. Pacific, Oceanside, CA 92054, 619-755-6666
1BR $135, 2BR $150
Amenities: Hot tub, beach, clubhouse

Southern California Beach Club, located across from one of the best beaches in California, is the perfect choice for beach lovers. The resort is surrounded by the ocean surf, the smell of the sea and sometimes, just a little ocean mist. The structure looks Moroccan from the outside, probably because of the orange color and the Marrakesh architecture. The units are terraced along the hillside toward the water. Step inside and you'll find beautifully decorated units that aren't formal enough to detract from the beach-house feeling. The resort is great for a traditional family vacation. The Oceanside community is undergoing a rapid transition. During the past two years, the downtown area has been torn down and completely replaced with a dazzling new mall that caters to a more sophisticated clientele. Leading the way, this resort has retained the charm of coastal California and has infused new style with a touch of elegance. With an exceptional activities program designed to keep both young and old occupied, this resort offers memorable vacations. Don't miss this one.

6   **TAMARACK BEACH RESORT**
3200 Carlsbad Blvd.,Carlsbad, CA 92008, 619-729-3500
1BR $120–170, 2BR $150–200
Amenities: Hot tub, pool, tennis, restaurant

Tamarack Beach Resort, located across the street from the broad sandy beach at Carlsbad, commands a superb location. Lying in your room, you can almost hear the surf at night. Tamarack places a strong emphasis on services for guests by offering a full-scale activities program, as well as extensive recreational facilities. In the summer, special programs for children are offered. The condos are in a large three-story hotel-style building.

7   **VENTANAS AL MAR**
3631 Ocean Front Walk, San Diego, CA 92109, 619-459-7125
1BR $105 & up
Amenities: Beach

This cozy three-story condo building is located on Mission Beach. You'll smell the ocean and hear the surf. These cute little condos are nicely decorated with grasscloth wallpaper and sturdy "skierized" furniture. A fireplace and a Roman-style tiled whirlpool bath for two is located in every condo. The kitchen is separated from the living room by a breakfast bar. This resort is a good choice for a family planning a week in San Diego because the location is convenient to many attractions.

9   **VILLA L'AUBERGE**
1570 Camino del Mar, Del Mar, CA 92014
1BR $525/day
Amenities: Pool, hot tub, health spa with supervision and massage, beach. Racetrack nearby

Clearly the most stylish choice in Del Mar, a sleepy community of half timbered, English Tudor cottages. L'Auberge was opened in 1989 with a lot of flash. The lobby is intimate and elegant with oak woodwork, crystal chandeliers, and lots of fresh flowers. This five-story complex is on a bluff overlooking the beach, only a short ride away. Del Mar racetrack is nearby and this was developed as a special place for horse owners to stay during the racing season. Most of L'Auberge is a hotel, but there are some elegant timeshare bungalows. These are not what you think of when you hear the word timeshare. These are sophisticated and exclusive with rental price tags at $525 per night. Elegantly decorated, each villa has a small kitchen, a gas log fireplace, and some have whirlpools. Service is superb and was meant to rival the much more famous La Costa. There's a small health spa with exercise equipment, steam rooms and therapeutic massages. This is a good choice for a special intimate weekend, a honeymoonette, or the day your horse wins at nearby Del Mar.

5   VILLA MARINA
      2008 Harbor Dr. North, Oceanside, CA 92054
      Amenities: Pool, hot tub, sauna. Next marina

This is an apartment hotel at Oceanside Harbor popular with fishermen or those who have just come back from a yacht charter. These one-bedroom suites have kitchens, fireplaces and great views of the new marina area.

8   WAVE CREST
      400 Ocean Ave., Del Mar, CA 92014, 619-755-0100
      Studio $650–975/wk, 1BR $800–1200/wk, 2BR $1000–1500/wk
      Amenities: Amenities: Hot tub, beach, boating, pool, golf

Wave Crest is a charming traditional California beachside inn. There are two seasons to stay here; surf and turf. Turf is the high season when the races are on at Del Mar and the weather is perfect for the beaches. Surf is the remaining ten months of the year. This small resort with only 31 condos is just steps away from the main area of Del Mar village. Its picturesque, California-style wooden villas line a ridge crest just above the ocean. The condos are small and stylishly decorated. For a congenial, sophisticated resort with style, Wave Crest is an exceptional value.

9   WHISPERING PALMS
      4000 Concha de Golf, Box 3209, Rancho Santa Fe, CA 92067,
      619-756-2471; 1BR $140
      Amenities: Golf, tennis, pools

Next to one of America's most exclusive communities, Whispering Palms is an 18-hole golf course lined with condos. Some are residential, some are weekend retreats, but most are for seasonal rentals of two months or more during the winter or during the summertime race season. Only four miles from the Del Mar racetrack, this is an ideal location for those active vacationers to enjoy equestrian camaraderie and who want golf at their doorstep. There is a main lodge with hotel rooms. However, the condo rentals are not connected with the hotel. These two-story townhouses have been constructed in either a California ranch style with lots of wood, or in a Spanish Mediterranean style, with white stucco and red tile roofs. Stylishly decorated, the one we saw was in keeping with the spirit of Old California: tile floors, whitewashed walls, and heavy Conquistador wood furniture. This is a prestigious community, eight miles inland from the beach, where rentals can be expensive.

6   WINNERS CIRCLE BEACH AND TENNIS RESORT
      550 Via De La Valle, Solana Beach, CA 92075, 619-755-6666
      Studio $75, 1BR $110, 2BR $250
      Amenities: Pool, hot tub, tennis, restaurants

Winners Circle Resort is located across the street from the Del Mar Racetrack on the Solana Beach side of the road. This beach and the racetrack are the most popular spots in San Diego County during summertime. The beach is just over a small hill, a two-minute drive from the resort. Del Mar is a small resort town that maintains its "beach community" atmosphere distinct from nearby San Diego. It has one of the best beaches in southern California. The sandy shore slopes at just the right angle for surfing and body-surfing. On either side of the resort are two of the most popular restaurants in the community, the Fish Market and Tracton's. Its 94 units are in four, two-story structures. Recently redecorated, the units have a stylish contemporary decor using a palette of pastel colors, although the units are on the small side. The resort's pool and four tennis courts make it a good choice for families. This is a lively spot for a week's vacation, and the value is exceptional for this part of San Diego County. This resort lives up to its name.

RENTAL RESOURCES
T. Akins Condo Vacations, 619-268-0287
Bay View Properties, 619-455-5903
Beach & Bayside Vacations, 619-488-3691
Beach Connection, 619-456-9411
Benardo Hills, 619-451-6500
Cairncross Management, 619-488-8312
Capri Beach Accommodations, 619-483-5011
Capri By The Sea Rentals, 619-483-6110
Coldwell Banker, 619-459-3851
Crown Point, 619-270-6588
Lincoln Properties, 619-793-1001
McMillin Realty, 619-459-8291
Ocean Vacation Rentals, 619-488-4654
San Diego Beach Resort, 619-485-7319
San Diego Beach Vacations, 619-583-5387
San Diego Vacation Rentals, 619-755-8686
Sandcastle Beach Rentals, 619-488-1395
Seascape Suites, 619-438-8900
Seashore Resorts, 800-438-6746
Trade-Inn, 619-492-8656
Willis Allen, 619-459-4033

ORANGE COUNTY

Orange County has become an expensive suburb of Los Angeles, but it still provides some exceptional resorts in communities such as Laguna Beach and San Clemente. The nucleus of the tourist industry in Orange County began 35 years ago with the advent of Disneyland. Knott's Berry

Farm added attractions and soon Orange County became a destination for family vacations.

Laguna Beach with its seaside bluffs first attracted beach lovers, and then was discovered by the artists. Although a real city now with many shops, galleries and boutiques, it still retains its original beach/artist colony flavor. San Clemente rocketed to fame when it became the Western White House during the Nixon administration. One of the area's condo resorts hosted members of the Nixon entourage and the charms of this seaside town were discovered. Today, there are several options to choose from depending upon whether you want a peaceful vacation environment or one where the children will be entertained.

WHERE TO STAY

8+   ALISO CREEK INN
31106 Coast Hwy., South Laguna, CA 92677, 714-499-2271
1BR $130
Amenities: Golf, tennis, pool, hot tub, restaurant, bar

This apartment hotel has studio and one-bedroom suites in a spectacular setting. Located half a mile from the ocean in a coastal canyon, this resort has truly captured the Southern California ranch feeling. Overlooking its own nine-hole golf course, the style here is "understated good taste." There's a rustic chic style favored by those who otherwise would live in the lap of luxury. Aliso Creek is a place of escape for the doctor or lawyer who wants to return to a simpler age. With this in mind, everything has been done to preserve the timeless charm of Southern California. Each unit has a kitchen, and either a private patio or balcony where you can soak up the view.

7   CAPISTRANO SURFSIDE INN
34680 Pacific Coast Hwy., Capistrano Beach, CA 92624,
714-240-7681; 1BR $120–145, 2BR $140–165
Amenities: Beach, pool, sauna, exercise room

This is the way California was meant to be. The Capistrano Surfside Inn is one of the few remaining inns along the California coast that combines old charm with informal beach life. The Inn is a three-story wooden structure at the base of a bluff across the street from the beach. It sits by itself, so you will not be fighting urban congestion or crowds. Everything has been carefully planned to create a good vacation environment for romantic couples, as well as families with children. The condos are beautiful and decorated in a casually elegant beach style. Blond wood furniture, fabrics with Southwestern colors, art objects, and pieces of coral are characteristic. A mellow attitude will enable you to enjoy this resort.

7 LAGUNA RIVIERA BEACH RESORT
825 S. Coast Hwy, Laguna Beach, CA 92651
Amenities: Pool, hot tub

Located on a hillside above the beach, this property was designed architecturally to create a flow down to the sea. Some units are one-bedroom suites, others are studios. The one-bedroom units are handsomely furnished and with all the glass and mirrors, the view seems to come inside. There's a whirlpool in the master bath.

7 LAGUNA SHORES
419 N. Coast Hwy., Laguna Beach, CA 92651, 714-494-0748
Studio $575–885/wk, 1BR $855–975/wk
Amenities: Beach, pool, hot tub

Laguna Shores is nestled on a bluff and overlooks the ocean. It is recommended for second honeymooners, but you'll sometimes find families with well-behaved older children. The condos in the modern brick building are just a little on the small side, but they're very well designed and are appropriate to the lifestyle of Laguna Beach. Small kitchens for light meals are provided. The interior decor is stylish. You'll find floral prints and blonde wood furniture (California contemporary). This is the kind of place where you'll relish sitting on your balcony, just listening to the surf and watching the sea gulls play over the beach.

5 LAGUNA SURF
611 South Coast Hwy., Laguna Beach, CA 92651, 714-497-6299
Amenities: Beach, pool, hot tub

Laguna Surf is located next door to Laguna Shores, but the tone and atmosphere of the two resorts are quite different. These 25 units are located in a two-story complex just above the beach. Every unit has a simply breathtaking view of the ocean. The condos are decorated in a fanciful California style with muted pinks and blues. VTPs and microwaves are an extra touch. Laguna Surf is more social and family oriented and not as romantic as Laguna Shores.

7 RESIDENCE INN — ANAHEIM
1700 S. Clementine St., Anaheim, CA 92802
Amenities: Pool, hot tubs, racquetball

It's sad to report, but there are no condo rentals available in Anaheim, site of Disneyland and close to Knott's Berry Farm. So many people want to find a condo close to these theme parks that we have elected to include an all-suite resort. The Residence Inn suites all have a sitting room, kitchen, bedroom and bath. The second floor units with gabled ceilings are most desirable. There is a complimentary breakfast in the mornings and afternoon cocktails/buffet. It's a good location for a few days with the kids.

7+ SAN CLEMENTE COVE
104 South Alameda Ln., San Clemente, CA 92672, 714-492-6666
Studio $85-105, 1BR $90–125
Amenities: Beach, pool, hot tub

This is a great place for a special hideaway for the weekend or home base for a week in Southern California. The architecture at San Clemente Cove invokes the Arabian Nights, but at the same time it looks like Spanish California. The resort is located across the street from the fishing pier and the beach. The condos are new and have sharp designer interiors. You'll find lots of extra touches such as VTPs. Management makes sure that everything is operating at peak efficiency. Since the kitchen facilities are limited, this resort will appeal to vacationers who want to explore restaurants in the area. A popular seafood restaurant is located right on the pier; it's great for Sunday brunch. San Clemente is only 30 minutes from Disneyland and Knott's Berry Farm.

6 SAN CLEMENTE INN
2600 Avenida Del Presidente, San Clemente, CA 92672,
714-492-6103; Studio $85–100, 1BR $100–125
Amenities: Restaurant, pool, tennis, Golf and beach nearby

The atmosphere at San Clemente Inn is presidential. President Nixon's staff used the inn for six summers (this resort has a history). A few of the guests who return year after year were on the former President's staff. This is a friendly resort. You'll get to know your neighbors by the pool or at the festive barbecues offered weekly. A restaurant/cocktail lounge with live music makes for a pleasant evening. The inn has 96 units in a lodge-type setting. The units are actually small suites with a casual decor. The resort is a block from the beach and less than a mile from a golf course.

5 VILLA DEL MAR
612 Avenida Victoria, San Clemente, CA 92672
Amenities: None. Beach across the street

This cozy condo complex is across the street from a park and the beach. Beautifully furnished, the decor pales by comparison with the view from the balcony. It's spiffy, new, and well done. The only drawback is the unavoidable noise from occasional trains running along the coast next to Villa del Mar.

RENTAL RESOURCES
All Resort Condos, 714-447-8873, Timeshare all over California

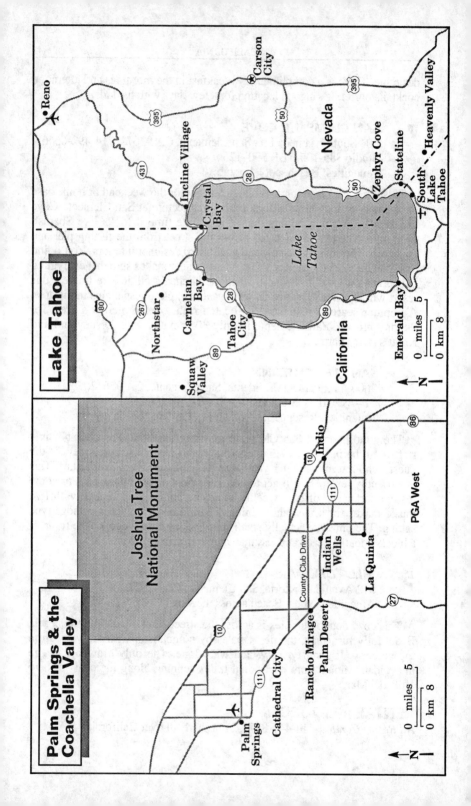

Vacation Resorts International, 800-874-8770, Timeshares all
    over California
Trading Places, 800-624-1618, Timeshares all over California

2. INLAND EMPIRE

This is the area east of metropolitan Los Angeles which encompasses the
dry expanse of Palm Springs (including the Coachella Valley communities
of Rancho Mirage, Palm Desert, Indian Wells, and La Quinta) and the
alpine mountain resorts of Big Bear and Lake Arrowhead in the San
Bernardino Mountains.

PALM SPRINGS and the COACHELLA VALLEY

Palm Springs, at the western end of the Coachella Valley, is located 120
miles due east of Los Angeles. It is usually protected from the Los Angeles
smog by the barrier peaks of the Santa Rosa mountains. It may also have
the most dependable warm winter climate in the Continental U.S. with winter average temperatures somewhere in the 70s. It rarely rains in the
Coachella Valley—there are over 320 days of sunshine each year—but
January can be windy.

The arid Coachella Valley is home to the resort communities of Palm
Springs, Cathedral City, Palm Desert, Rancho Mirage, Indian Wells, La
Quinta, and Indio (see map on page 48). Although long popular with the
Native Americans, the area was first discovered as a winter retreat for
Hollywood celebrities seventy years ago. Today, it is one of the nation's
major golf areas and claims over forty 18-hole courses. Originally, the "season" in Palm Springs was February and March, but now it runs from
November to May. As Los Angeles County grows in population, many people are discovering that the dry summer heat of the desert is tolerable, and
the golf and tennis facilities are less crowded making the Coachella Valley
popular in summer, too.

Although Palm Springs is the most well-known of the desert resort communities, all of the cities in the Coachella Valley offer something special for
the visitor. Cathedral City is an "in between" area of commercial strips and
resort developments. Rancho Mirage is known for its exclusive golf and tennis resorts—including one developed by former President Gerald Ford—and
for its "restaurant row." Palm Desert and Country Club Drive have turned
green with golf courses and palm trees. You've never seen such a line-up of
spectacular golf resorts.

Indian Wells is home to the very exclusive El Dorado Country Club and
the area's most expensive resorts. La Quinta has four new golf courses,

including the PGA tournament course built with grassy terraces for tournament spectators. Indio, once an agricultural community, is being engulfed by new country club and condominium developments.

WHERE TO STAY

8 **CATHEDRAL CANYON RESORT**
34567 Cathedral Canyon Dr., Palm Springs, CA 92264,
619-321-9000; 1BR $150–190
Amenities: Golf, tennis, pool

Three groups of condos are available for rent at the Cathedral Canyon Resort. Cathedral Canyon encompasses 200 secluded acres, yet it's only minutes from the famous restaurants and shops of Palm Springs. The architecture is California/Mediterranean-style and the environment is serene. It is perfect for retirees who plan to spend a lot of time in the desert. In addition to the golf course there are 10 tennis courts and a private swimming pool for every condo cluster. Some of the interior decor is stunning. Plenty of pink, lavender, and pastel green colors are used. The decor is contemporary with some high-tech touches. If you don't feel like cooking, the hotel is only two minutes away.

7 **DESERT ISLE**
2555 East Palm Canyon Dr., Palm Springs, CA 92262,
619-327-8469; 1BR $150–220
Amenities: Pools, tennis, health club, racquetball, restaurant

Desert Isle is located on bustling Palm Canyon Drive. Once past the resort's entry gates, you will discover a peaceful and gracious world. The design is unusual because there are single-story villas spread over 17 acres surrounding decorative ponds, pools, and fountains. Since Desert Isle caters to adult vacationers, the loudest sounds come from the bubbling waters. But don't get the wrong idea; this resort also welcomes families with children. The condo interiors are a modern desert style with earth-tone colors of dusky orange and muted greens. There are plenty of decorator accessories, such as ceramic vases with whitewashed dried branches.

9 **DESERT PRINCESS**
Vista Chino at Landell, Palm Springs, CA 92234, 619-322-7000
800-637-0577; 1BR $110–225, 2BR $160–325
Amenities: Pool, golf, tennis, spa, racquetball, restaurant

These condominiums are on the grounds of the 360 acre Desert Princess golf resort. Doubletree Hotels now manages the condos, as well as the hotel property. The units are new and glamorous. Mirrors have been used to enhance the golf course views. Every condo is a decorator's model with some of the finest interiors in the desert. There are dramatic touches, such as indirect track lighting and neo-Art Deco accessories. Overly large beds and sofas that you sink into are typical features. Guests can choose between the privacy of a quiet pool surrounded by a cluster of condos, or the main pool at the hotel where you'll find lots of activity. This resort promises luxury, tranquility, and many social activities. The tennis center and health club make this an outstanding choice. Desert Princess is great for families as well as seniors who value all of the services available through the hotel.

6 INDIAN PALMS COUNTRY CLUB
48630 Monroe Ave., Indio, CA 92201, 619-347-0688
2BR $75–125
Amenities: Hot tub, golf, restaurant, pool, tennis

Surrounded by groves of date palms, this resort was developed in the Spanish style, the single-story villas having white washed walls and red tile roofs. Olive and eucalyptus trees provide shade and flowering bougainvillaea add beauty. Indian Palms features a 27-hole golf course and was home to President Eisenhower for seven years during the time he was writing his memoirs. The centerpiece of the resort is the clubhouse overlooking the 18th fairway. The restaurant is casual, but at night it takes on a different character; guests dance to music from the big band era. This is one of the oldest golf course community resorts in the desert. Some of the interiors could be freshened up to appeal to today's consumer. The location is only two miles from the exclusive courses of La Quinta, but you won't be paying those top prices. Indian Palms is a friendly, casual resort where visitors return year after year.

10 LA QUINTA GOLF & TENNIS RESORT
49-499 Eisenhower Dr., Box 69, La Quinta, CA 92253,
619-564-4111, 800-854-1271; 1BR $225–450
Amenities: Pool, tennis, golf, restaurant, shops

Dating from 1926, La Quinta has always been one of Southern California's most spectacular resorts. The main building has thick adobe walls, tile floors, and cool alcoves. Everyone from Clark Gable and Ginger Rogers to Mickey Rooney came here to play. The 45 casitas spread over the resort's 200 acres have flowering gardens, private patios, fireplaces, and many have private pools. The casitas are uniformly furnished in a low-key, Southwestern style. Twenty-three pools are available for the 45 casitas. Across the street the condos are privately owned and prices average $400,000. These condos are top-of-the-line and you would recognize some of the owners' names. Remember, this is where many of the Betty Ford Clinic's celebrities find seclusion while they recover. The condos are one-story affairs with individual, professionally decorated interiors. Even the "standard" condos are decorated better then most homes. You must be a guest or a club member to use the golf course. The tennis club with its 20 courts and two stadium courts is one of the glitziest in the desert, and you'll find a lively crowd that often includes some excellent players.

8   THE LAKES COUNTRY CLUB
      76-300 Country Club Drive, Palm Desert, CA 92260, 619-345-5695
      2BR $185–215, 3BR $250–410
      Amenities: Golf, tennis, pool, hot tub

Located along Country Club Drive across the street from Palm Valley Country Club, the Lakes is another desert golf community punctuated by lakes and waterfalls. Low-rise condos with a "California ranch" architecture line the fairways. The interiors are spacious and all have private patios. These are more for part-time residents than many of the other condo resorts in this area. If you are planning a stay for a month or two, this is one of your best bets.

9   MARRIOTT'S DESERT SPRINGS VILLAS
      74855 Country Club Dr., Palm Desert, CA 92260, 619-779-1208,
      800-526-3597; 2BR $110–330
      Amenities: Pools, clubhouse, tennis, spa, golf

Marriott's Desert Springs Resort is a true pleasure dome in the desert. The centerpiece hotel has a spectacular lobby with boats and swans passing by on the lower level. A waterway behind the hotel allows people to travel by boat to the villas on the golf course (or you can drive directly to the villas). No matter how you arrive, you are sure to enjoy staying in these luxurious two-bedroom condos. You'll discover some of the most elegant interior decor in the area. Persons who stay in the villas will be able to enjoy a private pool and clubhouse and the hotel pool and tennis courts. One of the outstanding features at this resort is the full-service spa offering invigorating herbal wraps and beauty treatments such as seaweed-mud facials. Indulgence is the key word here with every desire anticipated by the resort.

8   MARRIOTT'S RANCHO LAS PALMAS
      41000 Bob Hope Dr., Rancho Mirage, CA 92270, 619-345-5695
      1BR $140–250, 2BR $155–350, 3BR $185–390
      Amenities: Golf, tennis, pool, hot tub

Rancho Las Palmas Country Club Resort occupies an ideal location. It is just half a mile from the intersection of Bob Hope and Palm Canyon Drive. The location is great for golfers and first time visitors to the desert. It is also great for extended stays because of its proximity to Eisenhower Medical Center and the Betty Ford Clinic. The area is absolutely beautiful. The 27 holes of golf are separated by lakes and the tennis complex features 25 courts. The Marriott hotel complex is host to small, exclusive executive conferences and conventions. The condos along the golf course are great for families or those who want an unforgettable week of golf, tennis, or sunning in the desert. Once you enter this 450 acre resort complex, you are immediately aware of the exquisite beauty of the landscape architecture, the flowers and date palms, and the snow-capped mountains beyond the desert.

The single-story condos at Rancho Las Palmas have a Spanish California style with red tile roofs and exposed wooden beams. Today these are called "patio homes" because, although there is a common wall on two sides of the condos, you have the sense of your own home with a private patio and garden or lagoon view. All have a "contemporary formal" ambiance with desert decor or high-tech styles. Expect desert colors such as dusky rose, orange, tan, and sagebrush green. Each cluster of condos has a private swimming pool and hot tub. It is important to note that some pools are restricted to adult use so make sure you rent a condo in the cluster that's right for you.

9   MONTEREY COUNTRY CLUB
41-500 Monterey Ave., Palm Desert, CA 92260, 619-568-5985
2BR $155–285, 3BR $185–350
Amenities: Pools, golf, country club, tennis

Monterey Country Club enjoys a great location in Palm Desert. It is near the intersection of Monterey and Country Club drives, directly accessible from all directions. The resort is 15 miles east of Palm Springs (which has plenty of shops and tennis clubs), about three miles north of the heart of Palm Desert and the shopping center on Highway 111, and about five miles west of the La Quinta/PGA West complex. The resort is beautiful and luxurious with one and two-story condos lining the fairways. Most condos have interiors designed by professional decorators that emphasize a desert style (i.e. light colors, contemporary furniture, track lighting, cactus plants, and southwestern art). Many have fireplaces and wet-bars, and a couple even have private whirlpool spas. Each cluster of condos has its own private pool. Weekends are popular but the resort is at its best during the week. There are 27 holes of golf to play.

8   PALM VALLEY COUNTRY CLUB
76-200 Country Club Dr., Palm Desert, CA 92260, 619-345-2737
1BR $140–285, 2BR $185–335, 3BR $215–410
Amenities: Golf, tennis, spa, racquetball, aerobics studio

Palm Valley Country Club is one of the liveliest communities in Palm Desert. It is located about 5 miles north of the center of Palm Desert. Country Club Drive is, as you would expect, a row of spectacular golf course communities. his one stands out because of all the activity. The condos line the golf course and the styles vary to include townhouses as well as flats in two-story buildings. All have a private patio for sunbathing and a few have fireplaces for those chilly desert evenings. We like Palm Valley because it is possible to enjoy the privacy of your golf course condo and all of the activities at the clubhouse.

10   PGA WEST
55-955 PGA Blvd., La Quinta, CA 92253, 619-564-PGAW,
800-PGAWEST; 2BR $155–285, 3BR $185–350
Amenities: Golf, pools, tennis

PGA West is an incredible golf community. There's nothing else like it, except maybe Pebble Beach. Thirty-six holes of golf designed by Arnold Palmer, Jack Nicklaus, and Pete Dye are offered. It is home to the Skins Game and the PGA Cup Matches. You'll find unexpected bunkers and greens surrounded by water, accessible only by footbridge. There are two major condo groupings along the fairways of PGA West: Legends and Champions. All are luxurious, but the Legends condos can easily cost $500,000 and their owners have invested accordingly in interior decor. Most condos have been professionally decorated to create an elegant home and a pleasant place to entertain. Some are townhouses, some are patio homes, and a few are upper/lower condos with private balconies/patios. Each cluster of condos has a private heated swimming pool, in addition to the pool at the tennis club. Just because PGA West is known for the golf, don't underestimate the tennis. Currently there are 19 courts and the master plan calls for 60! It's hard to beat PGA West.

5   SANDS OF INDIAN WELLS
75188 Highway 111, Indian Wells, CA 92210, 619-364-8113
Studio $65, 1BR $95
Amenities: Pool, hot tub, restaurant. Golf nearby.

This resort is full of surprises. From the street it looks like an average motel, but inside there is a Spanish-style courtyard and swimming pool (what you would hope for in Palm Springs). There's a pool and sun deck on one side, and an eye-pleasing lawn and garden area on the other. The condos are adequate and furnished with a contemporary style that suggests Mexico. The helpful management is friendly and you'll be called by your first name during your stay. This is a cozy resort. Pot luck suppers sometimes happen around the pool in the evenings. One of the favored restaurants in the desert, The Nest, is located here, and "Restaurant Row" is nearby.

8   SHADOW MOUNTAIN RACQUET CLUB
45750 San Luis Rey, Palm Desert, CA 92260,
619-346-6123, 800-472-3713;
Studio $85–140, 1BR $125–195, 2BR $175–280, 3BR $225–350
Amenities: Tennis, pool

Shadow Mountain is ideal for tennis players. Each morning you'll hear the quiet plop of a perfectly placed shot or the occasional cry of victory. This is a quiet, lush tennis oasis where the condos are arranged in two-story wings overlooking the figure-eight swimming pool, the 16 tennis courts, or the mountains in the distance. There are teaching pros on site to give you tennis lessons and help in the group clinics. Some of the accommodations are only hotel rooms, but the real attractions here are the one, two, and three-bedroom condos. They are tastefully decorated in desert pastels with lots of glass and chrome. The particular charm of this resort is the social atmosphere.

5   SMOKE TREE INN
1800 Smoke Tree Lane, Palm Springs, CA 92262, 619-327-8355
Studios $52–84
Amenities: Pool

This intimate resort enjoys a great location just two blocks from the main "strip" in Palm Desert. What a difference two blocks can make! Smoke Tree offers an attractive "Old California Ranch" atmosphere that is laid back and unpretentious. The whole complex is one story and the tiny studios are spread over four acres. It's quiet and casual. Well-attended gardens and good management provide a backdrop for conversations around the pool. A good choice for families with well-behaved children and young couples, Smoke Tree Inn exudes understated good character.

6   SUNDANCE
2901 Avenida Caballeros, Palm Springs, CA 92262, 619-325-3888
2BR $310, 3BR $350–420
Amenities: Private and clubhouse pools, hot tubs, tennis, racquetball

Nestled at the foot of the San Jacinto Mountains, you'll find Sundance, fourteen individual bungalows set within a compound. Each condo is totally private with its own swimming pool and hot tub surrounded by a five foot high brick wall. It's a skinny-dippers delight. Each condo also has its own private patio and garden. The units are stylishly decorated in contemporary decor with the modern "desert" look. Each unit has its own private fireplace in the living room and a two-car garage. However, in spite of the best laid plans of the original development, management has allowed this one to slip.

7   THE TENNIS CLUB & HOTEL
701 West Baristo Rd., Palm Springs, CA 92262, 619-325-1441
Studio $95–125, 1BR $115–145, 2BR $200–240
Amenities: Hot tubs, restaurants, pools, tennis, pro shop

The Tennis Club, built in 1937, occupies a unique and sheltered location at the foot of the San Jacinto Mountains and Tahquitz Canyon. In this tranquil atmosphere you'll find cubist architecture with lattice roofs providing shade from the sun. The condos are clustered into private groups of four, with the lattice roof covering the passageway. The decor is neutral with accessories from the desert. The whole resort is meticulously cared for— even the flower beds look manicured. Nothing can disturb the calm environment here. All the activity is reserved for the tennis courts on the far side of the resort near the pro shop. There are three quiet pools, five whirlpools, an isolation tank, and 11 tennis courts. This resort is operated as a functioning hotel and provides a disco, room service, and restaurants.

6 WOODHAVEN COUNTRY CLUB
41429 Woodhaven Drive, Palm Desert, CA 92260
1BR $550–880/wk, 2BR $650–950/wk, 3BR $850–1150/wk
Amenities: Golf, country club, exercise club, racquetball, tennis

This resort caters to those who spend several weeks in the desert each year. Not exactly a resort complex with lots of services, Woodhaven instead offers a quiet community for golfers and people who just enjoy the warm desert environment. The condos are fairly plain, so don't expect the glitz and glamour you would find at other desert resorts.

RENTAL RESOURCES
California Desert Rentals, 619-345-2637
Continental Vacation Rentals, 619-773-9951, 800-869-1129, Palm Desert
Country Club Condos, 619-776-2200, Rancho Mirage
Cove Condo Rentals, 619-360-6565, 800-777-2615, Palm Desert
Desert Condo Rentals, 619-320-6007, 800-248-2529, Palm Springs
Desert Sunshine Rentals, 619-568-9629, 800-654-8754, Palm Desert,
    Whole Valley
Frontier Vacation Rentals, 800-284-5527, Palm Springs
La Quinta Leasing, 619-564-6098, La Quinta
Lobland Waring Properties, 619-568-0777, 800-753-3325, Whole Valley
McLean Company Rentals, 619-322-2500, Whole Valley
Mission Properties, 619-346-9690
Palm Desert Tennis Club, 619-346-5683, Palm Desert
Palm Springs Resort Villas, 619-327-3744
PGA West, 619-771-5000
Rental Connection, 619-320-7336, 800-468-3776, Whole Valley
San Tropez Villas, 619-341-4443, Apartments, Palm Desert
SAP Locator, 619-773-4495, Apartments
Sunrise Company, 619-345-5695, Largest rental agency in the area.
    Covers country club developments in Palm Desert, Rancho Mirage, and
    La Quinta.

SAN BERNARDINO MOUNTAINS

Located 100 miles east of Los Angeles, the San Bernardino mountain resorts offer competition with Lake Tahoe, but on a less grand scale. Big Bear Lake and Lake Arrowhead are the two core resort communities. Mostly popular in summer, they also are popular in winter when there's snow on the 5500 foot mountains at Idyllwild, Big Bear, and Snow Valley. Lower in elevation than the Sierras, the past five years of drought conditions have not been kind to these ski areas. All of that changed in 1993 with the record snowfall.

This is primarily a weekend getaway area for Angelenos, but the fresh air and natural beauty, and the ease of transportation through nearby Ontario airport have caused these resorts to emerge as popular centers for corporate conferences. We have reviewed several area condominium complexes as well as a cute village of individual log homes.

WHERE TO STAY

5   CAPE COD MOUNTAIN COTTAGES
652 Jeffries Rd., Box 3329, Big Bear Lake, CA 92315,
619-866-8296
Amenities: None

This is a cute romantic spot for a weekend getaway or accommodation for skiers. Each Cape Cod-style cottage has a living room with fireplace, bedroom, and kitchen. Tucked away in the pines, the air is fragrant.

5   COZY HOLLOW LODGE
40409 Big Bear Blvd., Box 1288, Big Bear Lake, CA 92315,
619-866-9694
Amenities: Hot tub, volleyball

These are log cabins, where each with a kitchenette and a fireplace. Some have private whirlpools.

7   FOREST SHORES ESTATES
40670 Lakeview Dr., Big Bear Lake, CA 92315
Amenities: Beach, dock, hot tub, sauna, game room

These two-story condominiums are on the beach at Big Bear Lake. In summer there's a boat dock. Superior to other accommodations, they are individually decorated with upbeat contemporary furniture. Ski posters adorn the walls. Each has a gas log fireplace, but the centerpiece is the picture-window view of the lake.

5   LAGONITA LODGE
183 Lagonita Lane, Big Bear Lake, CA 92315, 909-866-6531
1BR $65–110, 2BR $110–190
Amenities: Marina, clubhouse, lake, sauna, skiing in winter, golf,
horseback riding, hiking, hunting, and indoor pool

These attractive two-story units are on the shore of Big Bear Lake in the
San Bernardino National Forest. Simple in design, they give a sense of openness and tranquility.

5   LAKE ARROWHEAD CHALETS
199 Rock Ledge Lane, Box 2293, Lake Arrowhead, CA 92352,
909-337-0457; 2BR $140, 3BR $160
Amenities: Pool, sauna, clubhouse, hiking trails, gym, four boat docks
for boat rentals, restaurants, beach, and horseback riding nearby

Located on Lake Arrowhead in the San Bernardino National Forest, this
resort offers skiing in the winter and watersports in the summer. The two
and three-bedroom chalets feature a large window box that brings sunshine
into the unit.

5   QUIET CREEK INN
26345 Delano Dr., Idyllwild, CA 92349
Amenities: None

Hidden in the pines above Strawberry Creek, this small community of
duplexes offers spacious accommodations at modest prices. Each studio,
one, and two-bedroom unit has a stone fireplace and kitchenette. These are
simple accommodations.

7   SNOW SUMMIT TOWNHOUSES
861 Thrush Dr. #40, Big Bear Lake, CA 92315
Amenities: Pool, saunas, game room

Right next to the Snow Summit ski lifts, these units are the best choice for
skiers in the area. These spacious two and three-bedroom townhouses each
have a living room and a full kitchen. Some have private hot tubs on the
deck or in the master bedroom.

RENTAL RESOURCES
All Seasons Resort Rentals, 909-866-5851, Big Bear
Arrowhead Estates Realty, 909-337-2531, Lake Arrowhead
Realty World/Mountain Resorts, 909-337-4413, Lake Arrowhead

3. PACIFIC COAST

The Pacific Coast of California offers spectacular scenery and opportunities for a variety of outdoor activities. Spring is a great time to visit because the valleys are green, the flowers are in bloom, and the air is a brisk 65°. Summer invites hiking (and biking) the coastal nature trails, or just poking around the shops of the seaside towns. Fall is sometimes the warmest time of the year when you can play golf or tennis under dependably sunny skies and temperatures that just touch 80°. Winter can be rainy; that's when you'll appreciate having a fireplace and a bottle of wine.

The resort areas along the Coast that are covered in this section are:

Carmel/Monterey/Pebble Beach
Santa Cruz
San Francisco
Sonoma/Marin/Napa/Mendocino Counties.

Accordingly, we have divided this section into these four geographic groupings.

CARMEL / MONTEREY / PEBBLE BEACH

Unique is the word to describe the Monterey Peninsula. Pebble Beach's lone cypress has become an emblem signifying the struggle of life against the forces of rock and sea. The peninsula sticks out like a thumb into the Pacific Ocean, separating Monterey Bay from Carmel Bay. Three of the famous Pebble Beach golf courses wander along this rocky shoreline. As a result of ocean currents, the weather here is different. Often foggy in the mornings, the afternoons are predictably warm and sunny. The ocean winds provide clean air and some of the brightest light to be found anywhere. This combination of light and scenery made the area a natural magnet for artists from all over the world. Carmel was once a community of artists who built cozy, Hansel & Gretel or English garden cottages. Today's popularity and rising prices have driven the artists out and replaced them with legions of tourists. There are nearly 100 art galleries in this small community so Carmel has retained its importance as a center of the California art world.

Next door to Carmel is Pebble Beach, home to the towering pines and picturesque cypress of the Del Monte Forest. The Seventeen Mile Drive loops the circumference of the forest. Admission to this area of private homes and condos is $6 unless you are a resident or staying in one of the condos. Weekly rentals here are popular with both golfers and returning visitors to the area.

The next community is Pacific Grove. Like Carmel, it is a residential area of cute Victorian bungalows surrounded by pines, eucalyptus, and flowers. Many artists who would otherwise live in Carmel have moved to less congested, less expensive Pacific Grove.

Monterey is adjacent to the huge Ft. Ord military installation, yet it has also been a popular tourist and retirement community for over 50 years. With one foot in each world, Monterey has always had a mixed reputation, although with the base closing, tourism is clearly becoming the mainstay of its economy. It has several neighborhoods where resort properties are located. The first is the Del Monte beach area, right along the 11-mile sweep of Monterey Bay. Another is Skyline Forest, just over the line from Pebble Beach's Del Monte Forest. To the visitor, the line of demarcation is not clear and guests in condos in the Skyline Forest area are only ten minutes away from the golf courses of Pebble Beach. Some condos at the top of this ridge, dividing the Monterey peninsula into two sides (Monterey and Carmel/ Pebble Beach), command views of both coastlines.

The undying popularity of this area has made resort managers somewhat jaded. The quality of service can sometimes be poor because there's a confidence born of 98% occupancy figures that, when you leave, there will always be another paying guest. Although citizens of Carmel have initiated efforts to "keep the tourists out," much of this area is unincorporated so short term daily or weekly rentals are indeed possible. Accommodations in these cute cottages are readily available through several of the area's rental agencies. One caveat; this past summer both Carmel and Monterey enacted ordinances prohibiting vacation rentals for less than 30 days. You may stay at one of these vacation homes for only two weeks but you'll need to technically arrange the rental for a full 30 days.

South of town, and beyond this Carmel city ordinance, is Carmel Valley Ranch. A recent real estate development, it has clusters of townhouse condos around the tennis club. This is one of the area's most popular destinations among conference attendees who rent condos for only five days or a week at a time.

WHERE TO STAY

9+ CARMEL VALLEY RANCH (Club Place Townhouses)
Old Ranch Rd., Carmel, CA 93923, 408-625-9500,
800-4-CARMEL; 1BR $235–385, 2BR $650–700
Amenities: Golf, tennis, conference center, restaurant, pools

Located six miles south of Carmel, Carmel Valley Ranch is far enough into the valley to escape the cold and fog, yet only ten minutes from the art galleries and restaurants of Carmel. Built along the side of the Santa Lucia Mountains, Carmel Valley Ranch is renowned for the championship 18-hole golf course designed by Pete Dye. This resort complex dates from 1976 and in the eyes of many Carmel locals, it still is a place for newcomers to the area. And what a place it is! Aside from the golf club, there is a tennis club and an inn that revolve around the conference center. There are few individual guests; instead, the meeting facilities are filled with corporate executives attending a national strategic planning meeting or some seminar. Most visitors opt to stay in the deluxe townhouses of Club Place. These 46 units are surrounded by the 8th, 9th, and 18th fairways and have spectacular golf-course views. The tennis club is there for your convenience and you can walk to the conference center or take one of the golf carts which are frequently shuttling along the path. The living rooms have 9-foot cathedral ceilings designed to capture the view and create a sense of spaciousness. The kitchens have greenhouse windows and there's a redwood deck for cocktails outside. Each master bedroom has a fireplace and there's a Roman whirlpool tub in the bath. Interior decor involves a subtle blend of muted colors and styles including English furniture punctuated by high-back carved Spanish chairs. Remember, this is not Carmel and the six miles make a big difference in the climate. Carmel Valley Ranch may be warm and sunny on days when Carmel is experiencing heavy fog or drizzle.

7   CYPRESS VILLA
   1170 Jewell, Pacific Grove, CA 93950
   Amenities: Pool, hot tub. Golf nearby

Located just across from the Pacific Grove Municipal Golf Course, near the northwestern tip of the Monterey Peninsula, these two-story, wood townhouse-style units are in a cute neighborhood of artist's cottages and turn-of-the-century bungalows that are being restored as half million-dollar weekend retreats. With a garage downstairs, each one-bedroom unit has a large living room with a fireplace. These are timeshare units where weekly rental rates are quoted at $1000. Ironically, you can also buy these time-shares for prices beginning at $1000 per week and you'll own the use of it every year for the rest of your life.

7   DEL MISSION COURT
   1 N. Mission St., Carmel, CA 93923
   Amenities: None

Right in the heart of downtown Carmel, a few steps from the shops, galleries, and restaurants of Ocean Avenue, you'll find Del Mission Court. These cute, one-bedroom condos are efficient with space and there's a sofa bed in the living room for families with children. Very attractively decorated, and with an eye to the artistic, expect to find mirrored walls and shutters to adjust the light, white wicker furniture, and a tropical ceiling fan in the sunken living room. These are very tastefully done, and you can't beat this location.

7   DEL MONTE BEACH CONDOMINIUMS
   63 La Playa, Monterey, CA 93940
   Amenities: Beach, heated pool

Located just five minutes from Fisherman's Wharf and Monterey along the beach, these townhouse condos are in a charming neighborhood of restored gingerbread cottages. The complex is beautifully landscaped and overlooks weathered Monterey cypress trees as well as the ocean. The pool is surrounded by an attractive deck area that is a great place to experience the rhythms of Monterey Bay. Each townhouse has a split-level living/dining room with two bedrooms upstairs. Your attention will be divided between the beachfront views out the sliding glass doors and the cozy wood-burning fireplace. The Monterey Peninsula bike path passes right behind this complex. With your own beach, this is what many hope for but never find when planning vacations to this area.

8   HACIENDA DEL SOL
       70 Forest Ridge, Monterey, CA 93940
       Amenities: None

Up in the hills, in the prestigious Skyline Forest area, these condos have very picturesque views of the sweeping arc of Monterey Bay. These three-story townhouses are built into the side of the hill with the garage on the ground level, living rooms on the second, and the bedrooms on the third level. This way you have a glimpse of the bay from the living room. Furnished in a solid, traditional style, this is a perfect residence for someone who wants to spend a month in the area playing the championship golf courses. Pebble Beach, the seventeen Mile Drive, and the Del Monte Forest are just over the ridge down the backside of the hill. Hacienda del Sol is excellent for mature travelers.

7   LA PLAYA TOWNHOUSES
       63 La Playa, Monterey, CA 93940, 415-364-7118
       Amenities: Beach, pool

Some of the Del Monte Beach Townhouses are promoted as "La Playa Townhouses." There is no difference other than the name. For a full description, see Del Monte Beach Condominiums.

8   MOUNTAIN SHADOWS
       249 Forest Ridge, Monterey, CA 93940
       Amenities: None

Located up in the hills in the Skyline Forest area, these one-story bungalows have views of Monterey Bay. The Del Monte Forest is just a stone's throw away over the ridge and the championship Poppy Hills golf course of Pebble Beach is just ten minutes away. These bungalows are enhanced by extensive landscaping. Often touched with fog, this area is a sensual delight with fireplace smoke, juniper, and eucalyptus trees. Interior furnishings are solid and comfortable as befitting a $350,000 two-bedroom bungalow. There are no amenities, but this is a convenient location for those who plan a month of golf and browsing through the streets of Monterey or Carmel.

9   OCEAN PINES
17 Mile Drive, Box 171, Carmel, CA 93921, 408-625-1400
1BR $125
Amenities: None

One of only three condominium developments inside the Pebble Beach covenant, these units are located at the top of Huckleberry Hill on the Seventeen Mile Drive. Surrounded by pines and deep in the forest, there is no ocean view. The championship Poppy Hills golf course is only two minutes away and the links at Spyglass Hill are just a ten-minute roll down the hill from Ocean Pines. Many of these condos are residences; others are second homes available for vacation rentals. There are five, three-story buildings designed with a touch of the Frank Lloyd Wright style; timbered archways and slabs at angles. At first glance it appears that these buildings are suspended in the forest. Beautifully decorated, many are highly customized with oriental art and treasures from European journeys. Some reflect a lifetime of accomplishments. Ocean Pines condos are handsome and ideal for Pebble Beach golfers.

6   PACIFIC GROVE PLAZA
620 Lighthouse Ave., Pacific Grove, CA 93950, 408-373-0562
1BR $100–145, 2BR $135–195
Amenities: None

Located in the heart of Pacific Grove, this is at once a downtown arcade of shops and restaurants and two stories of suites upstairs. This is a good base for exploring the Monterey Peninsula. Cannery Row is only five minutes away and the entrance to Pebble Beach and the Del Monte Forest is five minutes further west. Interior decor is spiffy and all units are decorated similarly in shades of tan and beige. This timeshare lacks the cuteness of Pacific Grove but it has a central location.

6   PINE ACRES LODGE
1150 Jewel Ave., Pacific Grove, CA 93950, 408-372-6651
Studio $70, 1BR $105, 2BR $165
Amenities: None

This is part of the same development as Cypress Villa at the eastern edge of Pacific Grove. The ocean is just a few blocks away and there's nothing else to the west until you hit Japan.

☎   PINE CONE RENTALS
P.O Box 221236, Carmel, CA 93922, 408-626-8163

This is one of the two major agencies offering vacation homes for rent in the Carmel/Monterey Peninsula area. Some Pebble Beach estates will go for prices as high as $24,000 a month (that's rent, not purchase). Most cottages and the few condo offerings are available at much more reasonable prices. Just to give you an idea:

Prospect House — This five-bedroom house commands a panoramic view from Monastery Beach all the way up to Carmel River Beach. Modernistic in design, there's a simplicity that whispers of Frank Lloyd Wright. Wood and stone frame the dozens of full-length glass windows that capture the view. Luxuriously furnished, there are three fireplaces and a dining room capable of seating ten.

English Country Castle — This private estate in Pebble Beach has four bedrooms and has been aesthetically decorated for those with the most discriminating taste.

Carmel Charm — Located just a few blocks from Ocean Avenue and the heart of Carmel, this two-bedroom bungalow has been furnished by an interior designer to create the English country house effect. Built of pine and stucco, this is a quiet retreat.

California Ranch — Located on the fairway in Pebble Beach, this spacious ranch-style home has lots of glass windows to make the most of the forest and ocean views.

 SAN CARLOS AGENCY
P.O. Box 22123, Carmel, CA 93922, 408-624-3846

One of two major vacation rental operations in Carmel, the San Carlos Agency offers over 120 properties to Carmel/Monterey Peninsula visitors. Many rentals are for 30 days but some are shorter. Of course, longer term rentals may be easily arranged. Here you can rent one of those cute one-bedroom bungalows in Carmel or make arrangements for a five-bedroom estate in Pebble Beach. The selection ranges from modern condominiums in the Skyline Forest section of Monterey to the quaint neighborhoods of Carmel. Examples of their inventory are:

Seagate — Overlooking the ocean and the cypress trees, this cute two-bedroom cottage is in a residential neighborhood of Carmel. You can walk to Ocean Avenue. The living and dining areas are on split levels and there's a den with French doors that open onto a carefully tended garden.

Mexican Cottage — This adobe home has beamed ceilings, hardwood floors, Mexican tile in the kitchen and touches of art. It's in a residential Carmel neighborhood where you can walk to town.

Hansel & Gretel — Right from the pages of a story book, this cute two-bedroom cottage has a crooked little roof, shutters, and flower boxes.

Inside there is a fireplace in the living room and a private garden with hundreds of flowers.

SAN SOUCI
Dolores at Third, Carmel, CA 93923
Mail to Watson, 1143 Boynton St., San Jose, CA 95117

This is an example of the bungalows that are available for a 30-day rental in Carmel. Just to the north of Ocean Avenue, in a wooded area of winding hillside lanes, Sans Souci is a cute two-bedroom house. It's only a few blocks to town and down to the beach. Built of wood and covered with stucco, there's a brick fireplace for those cold, foggy mornings. This cute and compact bungalow has oak-beamed ceilings in the living room and two small bedrooms.

9 SHEPHERD'S KNOLL CONDOMINIUMS
17 Mile Drive, Pebble Beach, CA 93953
Amenities: None

With only three condominium developments in all of Pebble Beach, there's not much of a choice. Fortunately, these luxury three-bedroom condos were built in a large oval so none view a neighbor. Each has an unobstructed view of the forest—and what a view that is! Perched atop Shepherd's Knoll, there's a spectacular vista of Monterey Bay and the San Gabriel Mountains. You'll enjoy the privacy and serenity of your tiled garden patio. Inside, the rooms have extra large dimensions. The fireplace is a joy on foggy evenings. The master bedroom, in a wing completely removed from the main part with the other two bedrooms, has a tiled roman whirlpool tub. With price tags of $500,000, interior decor is highly individual and each has an ambiance of confident, quiet luxury.

9 SKYLINE CREST
12 Skyline Crest Dr., Monterey, CA 93940
Amenities: None

Only a couple of these half million-dollar condos are available for rent, but they are so spectacular that they must be mentioned. These two-story condos sit high atop the ridge dividing the Monterey Peninsula into the communities of Pebble Beach and Monterey. Views are of Pebble Beach with its rocky coastline and, on the other side, of the sweeping arc of Monterey Bay. Other locations may be more famous but none can match the beauty of this location. Inside, interior decor favors chandeliers, an attractive large fireplace hearth, and furnishings that look like a showroom. There are no gimmicks here, just a strikingly handsome habitat. If you have the time for a month in the Monterey Peninsula, this is worth the expense.

10 **SPANISH BAY**
Spanish Bay Cr., Box 130, Pebble Beach, CA 93953, 408-647-8700
3BR $650–1175
Amenities: Golf, tennis, pool, restaurant, spa

Some of the most expensive condominiums in the world, these three-bedroom units are priced for sale between $1,450,000 and $2,395,000. The reason is the location, one of the last remaining sites for development within the Pebble Beach covenant. These are elegantly furnished by decorators flown in from Los Angeles, New York, and San Francisco. Some are single-story models arranged around a courtyard; others are two-story townhouses. Inside, the floor-to-ceiling windows capture views of the sand, surf, and rocks for which Pebble Beach is so famous. In addition to the three bedrooms, there's also a den facing the private courtyard. Some have the extra feature of a curving staircase, under a skylight, leading to the second floor. Upstairs, the master bedroom has a dressing room and a fireplace. The master bath will either have a private whirlpool tub, steam shower, or private sauna.

The Spanish Bay Country Club conference center is only steps away and throughout most of the year this is popular with executive conferences and corporate strategy retreats. After all, at these rates, how many people can afford to rent these condos? One extra touch—piped bagpipe music plays ever so softly over speakers in the parking lot.

7 **TANGLEWOOD**
18 Tanglewood Pl., Monterey, CA 93940
Amenities: Pool

Modest and unpretentious, these two-story wood condos are in the Skyline Forest area. Mainly a residential and retirement condominium area, some units are available for vacation rentals. There are great views of Monterey Bay. The location is very convenient, being only minutes away from Pacific Grove and the entrance to Pebble Beach. Monterey and its waterfront are also close at hand. The interior decor is comfortable with tweed fabrics and lots of beige and earth-tone colors.

RENTAL RESOURCES
Bay Lodging, 408-655-1426
Garden Court Realty, 408-625-3500, Carmel
Don Lauria Realty, 408-375-2537, Monterey
Monterey Bay Vacation Rentals, 408-649-8216
Monterey Dunes, 408-633-4883
Resort II, 408-649-9250

SANTA CRUZ

The 33-mile-long arc of Santa Cruz Bay with its beaches and ocean cliffs is just 35 miles from the San Jose airport. With wide open areas of sand dunes and unspoiled forests, this is the California that many beach-loving vacationers hope to find. The water is cold (witness the many surfers in wet suits), but the temperature on the beach and the fairway is usually warm and sunny. Winter is chilly and foggy, but for nine months of the year this is a great place to enjoy the fruits of California. Spring is incredibly beautiful with clear skies, bright green grass, and flowers everywhere. The local strawberry, asparagus, and artichoke festivals are fun and popular. Summer days are a great time to sample local wines, and the fall is colorful with all the pumpkinfests.

Only a few resort communities have been established here, but generations of San Franciscans have owned vacation homes in the Santa Cruz area.

WHERE TO STAY

8   **PAJARO DUNES**
2661 Beach Rd., Watsonville, CA 95076,
408-722-4671, 800-564-1771
1BR $75–150, 2BR $100–175, 3BR $125–225, 4BR $145–280
Amenities: Beach, conference center. Tennis Club next door

For beach lovers, this is one of California's best kept secrets. It's truly unique. Located on a mile and a half of a wide, sandy beach, you are as close to nature as one can be. One of the very last resorts to be developed along the California Coast, this was built in an era when environmentalism was rising. Pajaro Dunes is an expanse of sand dunes covered by natural vegetation, bordered on one side by the ocean and on the other by weathered wood condominiums that seem to blend into the landscape. Not at all what you would normally find in California, yet this is what you had hoped for. The architecture is boxy and angular, yet at the same time, fun. Some buildings are almost treehouses. Two units have entryways on the lower level but rooms and balconies upstairs are cantilevered so they seem suspended in space, like branches of a tree. Another is a narrow three-story tower with three rooms arranged vertically and topped by a windmill. Vaulted ceilings, picture windows and sliding glass doors make the most of the beachfront setting and the waving sea oats atop the dunes. Interior decor is generally contemporary and upbeat, yet very casual as befitting a beach house. Most units have microwaves in the kitchens and VTPs in the living room. Fireplaces make the condos cozy on those foggy mornings. Unpretentious, this place offers everything you need for a California beach vacation.

6 **SEACLIFF INN**
7500 Old Dominion Ct., Aptos, CA 95003
Amenities: Conference center, restaurant, pool, hot tub

This lovely resort is on the Pacific Coast Highway across from Seacliff Beach. Midway between Santa Cruz and Monterey, the beach runs for thirty miles along the arc of Santa Cruz Bay. Primarily a hotel, there are a dozen suites, luxuriously decorated in softly muted colors and plush carpets. Each suite has an extra-large whirlpool tub in the master bath. For cooking, there's a mini-fridge, coffee maker, and microwave. Seacliff Inn is or those who want all the services of a hotel yet extra space.

SAN FRANCISCO

This cosmopolitan city ranks with New Orleans, Paris, and Venice as a place to visit time and again. The vistas can never be seen too often and the sights of Ghiradelli Square, Sausalito, and Golden Gate Park never became old and are always changing. For those who want the comforts of home in this exciting city and who plan to stay for more than two days, we have listed the apartments and ownership properties which can be rented, or even purchased. Most have strategic locations so you can walk or take a cable car to most of the city's attractions, shops, and fine restaurants.

WHERE TO STAY

 AMERICAN PROPERTY EXCHANGE
170 Page St., San Francisco, CA 94102, 415-863-8484, 800-747-7784
Studios from $85. Discounts on weekly and monthly stays

This is not really a resort, but a collection of apartments and condos in San Francisco and the Bay Area that have been designed and decorated to be vacation rentals. Many of these apartments and condos are perfect for families or groups desiring a week in sophisticated, urban San Francisco. Much more convenient than a hotel, these properties all have living rooms (some with fireplaces), kitchens, and decorator accessorized interiors.

7 **CLUB DONATELLO**
501 Post St., San Francisco, CA 94102, 415-441-7100
1BR $200, 2BR $400
Amenities: Health club with pool, restaurant

These are luxury suites on two floors atop the deluxe Hotel Donatello. Once the best, management is now indifferent. Appeal is fading fast.

2 **JACKSON COURT**
2198 Jackson St., San Francisco, CA 94115, 415-929-7670
Studio $98
Amenities: None

Weekly or monthly rentals are preferred. This is a tired and inexpensive timeshare in a residential area. You can buy one for $500.

6 **NOB HILL INN**
1000 Pine St., San Francisco, CA 94109, 415-673-6080
1BR $165–195, 2BR $225
Amenities: Nob Hill location

Nob Hill Inn is an urban retreat that offers Victorian Belle Epoque condominiums instead of a standard hotel room. The condo interiors are appropriately decorated with brass beds and Victorian globe light fixtures. This property gives special value to those who want the space of a complete condominium apartment in the heart of the city. Compare prices with the hotel rooms down the street and you'll see what a great value this is.

7 **POWELL PLACE**
730 Powell St., San Francisco, CA 94108, 415-362-7022
Studio $90, 1BR $135–165
Amenities: Nob Hill location, cable car stop

Powell Place is located on Nob Hill, across from all of the activity at the Fairmont. This resort offers an excellent location because you can walk to Chinatown and take the cable cars to Fisherman's Wharf and the financial center. The "San Francisco of 1910" theme runs throughout the building and the suites. Some suites have small, private bricked courtyards covered with ivy. This is a surprising find considering that it's located in the heart of the city. New management has planned this resort and we hope to see improvements soon.

8 **SAN FRANCISCO SUITES**
710 Powell St., San Francisco, CA 94108, 415-433-9700
Studio $175, 1BR $275
Amenities: Nob Hill location

San Francisco Suites offers refined elegance. If you had a rich uncle, he probably would have lived in an atmosphere like this. This resort exudes good taste and refined elegance from the moment you step in the lobby. The style can best be described as "English country home." There are lots of fresh flowers, pictures of fox hunting scenes, brass lamps, and a concierge seated at an Empire style desk. Instead of standing in line to check in, the concierge welcomes you and offers an overview of all that is available. Do the suites upstairs live up to this introduction? Absolutely. Every suite is decorated individually with more framed English hunt scene pictures, fine fabrics, brass beds, and comforts that you probably don't have at home. What's the cost? Rentals are expensive, but a great value when compared to nearby hotel rooms. It's worth every penny!

8 **TRINITY SUITES**
845 Pine St., San Francisco, CA 94109; Suites $235
Amenities: Nob Hill location

On Nob Hill, this elegant little inn offers each studio suite with a living room area as well as two double beds. There's a microwave, coffeemaker, and small refrigerator. The suites are just large enough that friends can visit without feeling like they're in your hotel room. Each suite is decorated with "country French" furniture and beige and cream colors. Nothing dramatic, this is just a pleasant environment in a convenient location on Nob Hill, well-suited for a week's stay.

SONOMA / MARIN / MENDOCINO / NAPA COUNTIES

North of the San Francisco Bay Area, the beaches, cliffs and forests of this fog-shrouded coast have generally evaded the tide of development that has swept most of California. The local residents for years have been fighting a pro-environment, anti-development battle to save the pristine quality of this area. They've been right so far because the attraction of this area is that it's about the only place left along the Coast where mythical California still survives.The result is a scarcity of lodgings in an area that is mushrooming in popularity for vacations. Over on the other side of the mountains in the Napa Valley, the temperatures are 10 to 15 degrees warmer with long sunny days from June until the last of the grapes are brought in during October. The Wine Country of the Napa and Sonoma Valleys has become a place to just waste a week on self-indulgence.

Starting at the Golden Gate Bridge and heading northwest, you enter an area of dramatic ocean beaches, migrating shore birds, and meadows of spring wildflowers that attract hikers, artists, and those who want to escape from 21st-Century California. The Pacific Coast Highway offers an ever-changing spectacle of ocean, bay, forest, and valley. The first stop is the broad expanse of Stinson Beach National Monument, Bolinas Bay, and the nearby Seadrift Lagoon. Preserved as a refuge for migrating waterfowl, the vacation homes here are a far cry from what you would expect from bird watchers. Although laid back, the sophistication of San Francisco can be found in the local shops and coffeehouses. Point Reyes is also a National

Park with over 500 acres. Unlike Stinson, it draws hundreds of visitors on any given day to the beaches and marshes where wildlife may be observed.

Tomales Bay will remind you of the lochs of Scotland. Formed by a fault, the bay is long and narrow and the fogs bless it with the romance of Bonnie Prince Charlie. Dillon Beach is at the western tip of the peninsula while Bodega Bay is across on the mainland side. Bodega Bay is the vacation home center of the Sonoma Coast. You'll find only one condo development at Bodega Bay Country Club, otherwise all of the vacation rentals are homes. Larger than condos, you'll find the prices to be relatively reasonable. Further up the coast you'll come to Jenner and hundreds of architecturally unique vacation homes along the Russian River.

The Sea Ranch is a special development which spiritually belongs down on the Big Sur, but it was developed 100 miles north of the Bay Area and a million miles from anywhere. It's hard to believe that this escape from time is so close to a major metropolitan area. From Gualala on up the Mendocino Coast, the homes are singular and you won't find communities of vacation homes sharing a central recreation facility.

Crossing over the mountains and heading down through the wine country of Sonoma and Napa, you'll find an exciting area to visit. Yet surprisingly, condo and vacation homes have not really taken hold here. Napa is an area of small country inns and bed and breakfast lodgings. There are two golf resort communities offering condos, a famous restaurant with suites in the back, and a winery that built condos in the woods to encourage longer duration stays.

The climate along the Coast is foggy and chilly in Summer and usually inundated with rain in the Winter. Napa is temperate like the Mediterranean. Transportation to this area is by automobile from San Francisco airport. Napa is an hour north of the city. Sonoma's Stinson Beach and Bodega Bay are one and one half hours north, and Mendocino is a good two hours north.

WHERE TO STAY

7+ **AUBERGE DU SOLEIL**
180 Rutherford Hill Rd., Napa, CA 94558
Amenities: Restaurant, heated pool, tennis

This is a restaurant which grew a colony of vacation apartments to satisfy its clientele. The warm French country inn atmosphere has been extended to the 36 suites which command a stunning view of the mountains surrounding the Napa Valley. Nine separate two-story buildings house these units with kitchenettes, fireplaces, and redwood decks. Combine two of these suites and—voilà—you have a one-bedroom apartment.

BODEGA HARBOR COUNTRY CLUB
Pacific Coast Hwy., Bodega Bay, CA 94923 (No mail. Contact
local agents for rentals generally priced from $250 a night to $400).
Amenities: Pool, hot tub, restaurant, tennis

This country club development includes over 50 vacation homes available
for short-term rentals along the fairway flowing down the hill from the
Bodega Bay Inn. Just outside of town you'll be charmed by the ocean views,
the opportunity for walks along the shore, and tennis and golf opportunities.
Each of these homes has three, four, or five bedrooms so they are most suitable for families who want a place for a month or so where they can entertain houseguests or relatives. All vacationers at properties within the master
resort development of Bodega Harbor Country Club have guest privileges
for the golf course, tennis courts, and club dining room. The best feature is
the view of the ocean with the surf crashing upon the rocks.

7 **EMBASSY SUITES**
1075 California Blvd., Napa, CA 94558
Amenities: Pool, hot tub, sauna, restaurant, tennis

So many vacationers want to find a condo in the Napa Valley area so they
can stay for a couple of days and sample the area's delights. However, many
condo or vacation home rentals in this area require a seven-day stay. Others
are part of a golf club and the rental rates subsidize the golf course. So, this
all-suite hotel is the best choice we could find for those vacationers who
want the space and convenience of a condo in Napa, but don't want to stay
for a week or pay for the golf.

 GRAY'S RETREAT
Box 56, Point Reyes Station, CA 94956, 415-663-1166; $150

Originally the Point Reyes Schoolhouse, this rustic cedar home is in an
open pasture surrounded by a cypress windbreak. Decor is eclectic featuring
yards and yards of English country home fabric, antiques, and a Franklin
stove for a fireplace. This is good for families who want to experience mythical California. It is right on the edge of the National Seashore Park, at the
head of hiking trails, and a short walk from a children's playground.

 MAUI ON DILLON BEACH
29 Renz Road, Mill Valley, CA 94941, 415-383-5928; $125

Located 50 miles north of San Francisco, this is typical of many of the
vacation homes available for rent along the Mendocino and Sonoma Coast
through the local rental agents. We have given you the mailing address but
the home is on Dillon Beach just south of Bodega Bay. This three-bedroom plus loft home is what you would hope to find in California. It's built

of natural woods with an abundance of glass and a redwood deck over-looking the ocean. Inside you'll find this comfortably furnished as befitting a beach house. There's a VCR and a fireplace for the nippy nights along this shore. So what's Hawaiian about this? Absolutely nothing except that the streets in the subdivision are named after Polynesian destinations such as Tahiti or Kona.

8+ MEADOWWOOD RESORT
900 Meadowwood Ln., St. Helena, CA 94574
Amenities: Wine school, golf, tennis

This all-suite resort capitalizes on the lack of condos in the area and the high demand for accommodations where vacationers who stay for a week also have the comforts of home. There are 56 very private suites spread over 256 wooded acres. Some have views of the golf course. The central attraction here is the wine school, so many who stay for a week or two want their own kitchenette for trying out new skills.

POET'S LOFT
Box 1184, Ross, CA 94057, 415-453-8080; $150

Built on pilings on the shores of Tomales Bay, this vacation home is for dreamers. More fitting in Nantucket than California, this ramshackle home will transport your worried mind to another world. The fireplace and red-wood hot tub are nice extra touches but they aren't necessary to make this a distinctive vacation retreat.

THE SEA RANCH
Highway 1, Sea Ranch, CA 95497
(No mail. Contact any of the seven rentals agents in the Sea Ranch area listed in Rental Resources).
Amenities: Golf, tennis, beach

The Sea Ranch is a unique area, being one of the most environmentally conscious developments in North America. Up here along the Sonoma-Mendocino Coast, local residents have long fought a bitter battle to prevent the coastline from becoming developed. Only a few vacation homes have been allowed and over 300 vacation homes within the Sea Ranch are available for vacation rentals. The Sea Ranch is a master resort community spread over 5,000 acres on the Sonoma County Coast less than two hours north of San Francisco. It occupies a breathtaking site with bluffs covered with redwoods and fir forests overlooking the ocean. Many homes have romantic California redwood architecture. Some have an almost New England-style architecture. With their gabled roofs, shutters and dormer windows, the houses blend well with the turbulent skies and strong ocean breezes. For a moment, you'll forget you are in California, but step inside and you'll be impressed by the California redwood hot tubs and walls of glass. Some of the houses are rustic cabins in the woods, but inside you'll find modern appliances and interior decor that exudes a sparse, Pacific Northwest feeling. Some have been decorated with a southwest Native American motif. Each is different so shop around to find one that fulfills your fantasy. This resort community attracts returning visitors year after year so there is a certain amount of clubbiness. The Sea Ranch is romantic and great for those who prefer their landscape natural.

8 THE SEA RANCH CONDOMINIUMS
Sea Ranch, CA 95497
Amenities: Golf, tennis, beach, pool, clubhouse, hiking trails

Built in 1964 on the desolate, rocky coast some 100 miles north of San Francisco, this is the only group of condominiums at The Sea Ranch. Unlike traditional resort areas, the environment of Sea Ranch does not lend itself to lounging in the sun or other programmed recreation. The dramatic site where sheep once grazed is characterized by grassy slopes and rugged cliffs that collide with the sea. Rows of cypress which stripe the landscape deflect the bracing winds. The challenge for architects was to create multi-unit housing without destroying the landscape. The condos are grouped tightly together to leave as much of the site open as possible and still create a strong sense of community. The modified pitch of the shed roofs deflects the wind and mirrors show off the jagged silhouette of the cliffs. The architectural simplicity of the condominiums and the use of untreated redwood reflects the environment. If you are looking for something really different for your next vacation, this is an unforgettable place.

7 SEACLIFF
Box 697, Gualala, CA 95445, 707-884-1213
Amenities: None

Located on the Mendocino Coast two hours north of San Francisco, this is a special place for a romantic interlude. Families that also relish nature and hiking along the rocky coastline or in the hills will also enjoy this area, but we would advise them to look for accommodations elsewhere. Seacliff is a community of flats in two-story townhouses where "privacy" in this fog-shrouded area is the key word. Operated as an all-suite inn, each unit has a wood burning fireplace, whirlpool spas with ocean views, and a coffee maker/refrigerator area. The best feature is the balcony where you'll be alone with the ocean and the gulls. This is a unique spot—one that you would hope to find.

SEADRIFT LAGOON
2 Dipsea Rd., Stinson Beach, CA 94970, 415-459-1976
2BR $1200/wk, 3BR $1500/wk
Amenities: Beach, clubhouse

For those who saw the movie *Basic Instinct,* you already know that Seadrift Lagoon is a unique community of very expensive second homes wedged into an unspoiled area of the Sonoma Coast just 25 miles north of San Francisco. There is nothing else like it. This private, gated community sports ultra-modern redwood beach houses with unexpected walls of glass, traditional Hilton Head-style plantation homes, homes that seem to be huge greenhouses with beds and living areas tucked away discretely, and much more. Some have simple but exquisite beach house interiors. Others are formally decorated. This is a perfect place for an unforgettable week at the beach in California, and surprisingly, prices generally run between $1200 and $1500 per week. That's around $200 a night for lodgings that will accommodate 6 to 8 people—and we assure you that each of these homes are unforgettable. You could probably negotiate a rate better than these asking prices.

8   SILVERADO
1600 Atlas Peak Rd., Napa Valley, CA 94558, 707-257-0200
800-532-0500; 1BR $175–195, 2BR $310–330, 3BR $380–465
Amenities: Golf, tennis, pools, restaurant

Silverado, a 1,200 acre resort, lies in the very heart of California's famous wine country just 45 minutes north of San Francisco. For those who want to spend a few days or a week in the wine country and also have the option to play golf and tennis under Napa's sunny skies, this is for you. The centerpiece of the resort is the historic French/Italian mansion built in 1870. The brick colonial style sets the tone for the two-story condo buildings and bungalows. Each cluster of condos has hidden courtyards and its own swimming pool, so you're never more than a few steps away from a pool. There's also an Olympic-size pool at the main lodge.

Each condo has a fireplace, dining area, and wet bar for entertaining. There's also an umbrella table and chairs on the private patio for the villas. The decor emphasizes neutral colors and sturdy furniture. Wicker sofas with tan cushions, pine tables and chairs, and nubby tweed fabrics are characteristic of most interiors.

An 18-hole golf course, 20 tennis courts, and a tennis pro are available. The concierge can arrange vineyard tours, restaurant reservations, or hot-air balloon rides. Silverado is the best choice for those who want an active vacation in the wine country. Children will have a good vacation too.

VACATION RENTALS INTERNATIONAL
Box 38,1580 East Shore Rd., P.O. Box 38, Bodega Bay, CA 94923,
800-548-7631, prices begin at $125 a night for 1BR or 2BR
homes to a maximum asking price of $470.

With over 80 vacation homes and cottages available for rent, this is one of
your best bets for lodging in the Bodega Bay area. Minimum rentals are for
two nights and there are discounts for stays of a week or more. Locations
vary and you can take your pick from the wind-swept hills overlooking
Bodega Harbor, the delicate marshlands and dunes at Salmon Creek, the Bay
View homes nestled in and around Bodega Bay, the ragged cliff lines of
Gleason and Wright's Beach, and the coastal river town of Jenner where the
Russian River flows into the sea. All of these vacation homes are well-maintained and set up for short term rentals. Even your firewood is included. The
following is a brief description of representative accommodations offered:

Bodega Harbor — These two, three, and four-bedroom luxury homes are
along the fairways of the golf course. Most have excellent views of the
ocean and harbor. Beautifully furnished, you can expect the sophistication of
San Francisco in a rural, fog-shrouded setting. Guests here have a private
access beach that stretches out to Doran Park. Tennis players and golfers
will favor this area.

Bay View — These comfortable, two and three-bedroom homes all have
lofts and extra large living rooms with cathedral ceilings and lots of glass to
capture the spectacular harbor view. You can see Point Reyes and the ocean
hills in the distance. Or watch the village activities as the fishing boats return
at sunset with their catch. You can easily walk to the state park beach and
the windswept sand dunes.

Salmon Creek — These cozy cabins have a great view of the creek as it
runs into the ocean, and also of the rocky coastline to the north. It's a short
walk over the sand dunes to the two-mile long Salmon Creek Beach.

Ocean View — These homes offer the best value in the area. They have
ocean views and are only a short walk from Schoolhouse Beach.

RENTAL RESOURCES
Beach Rentals, 707-884-4235, Sea Ranch area
Bodega Bay & Beyond, 800-888-3565, Wide selection
California West Properties, 707-878-2731
Coastal Lodging of West Marin, 415-663-1351
Dancing Coyote, 415-669-7200, Tomales Bay cottages
Don Berard Sea Ranch Rentals, 707-884-3211, Large inventory
Guala Getaways, 800-726-9997
Irish Beach Rentals, 707-882-2467
Kennedy's Sea Ranch Rentals, 707-884-9600

Kerr's Sea Ranch Rentals, 707-758-2570
Mendocino Coast Reservations, 707-937-5033
Ocean View Properties, 707-884-3539
Oceanic Realty, 415-868-0717, Stinson Beach
Orca Vacation Homes, 800-229-2156, Mendocino
Point Arena Lighthouse Rentals, 707-882-2777, Lightkeepers' cottages
Ram's Head Realty, 707-785-2427
Sea Ranch Escape, 707-785-2426
Sea Ranch Rentals, 707-785-2579
Sea Coast Hideaways, 707-847-3278, Russian River
Seadrift Realtors, 415-868-1791, Stinson Beach
Shoreline Properties, 707-964-1444, Mendocino
Sirensea, 707-884-3836
West Marin Network, 415-663-9543

4. LAKE TAHOE and SQUAW VALLEY

Lake Tahoe on the California-Nevada state line is the most spectacular alpine lake in North America. A sportsman's paradise in summer with boating, fishing, golf, hiking, and tennis opportunities galore, Lake Tahoe is equally famous as a wintertime ski area. The climate varies with the altitude. The most dramatic example is from the top of Heavenly Valley. While knee-deep in California snow, you can look out over the parched Nevada desert. In winter, the higher mountains at Lake Tahoe enjoy excellent snow conditions for their ski resorts. In summer, it's beach weather along the lake shore, while 2,000 feet farther up the mountain it's cool enough for a jacket.

Two-thirds of the lake shore is in California, one-third in Nevada. The western shore (the California side), has sheer cliffs that drop straight into the lake. The roads here twist among ponderosa pine and spruce. The Truckee River, which flows into the lake, is one of the most picturesque in California with clear bubbling waters. The best views of the California mountains and shoreline are ironically from the Nevada side. Emerald Bay on the south end of the lake is one of the most photographed areas in California. Squaw Valley is actually ten miles inland from the lake.

Many of the condos in this section are at the south end of the lake in the community appropriately named South Lake Tahoe. Some are on the lakeshore, others are in the forest clustered around the base of Heavenly Valley. With one exception, Tahoe Seasons, none of the condos have ski-in, ski-out access to Heavenly Valley. Most skiers take the shuttle bus up to the parking lot and chair lifts.

Tahoe City is where the babbling Truckee River empties into the lake. This was the first area of development and many older and exclusive private homes line the shore here. Granlibakken is a granddaddy conference center in the area. Nordic in design, there's a small ski lift on the property. Most of the newer condos are around Dollar Point just north of town. This is where you'll find Star Harbor, St. Francis Lakeside, Lake Forest Cove, and Dollar Hill.

Continuing north you come to the areas of Carnelian Bay and Kings Beach where the highway is lined by firs, colonies of cabins and motels. Carnelian Bay offers a unique community of vacation houses, all within a 100-acre forested compound.

Heading inland five miles, there are so many condos around Squaw Valley, that it almost deserves its own section. All properties with a Squaw Valley address are skier-oriented, although the spectacular new Squaw Creek Conference Center and the new golf course are attracting summertime visitors who otherwise might have stayed along the lake. Alpine Meadows, almost next door, offers equally good skiing; however, very few of these condos are set up for vacation rentals. River Run is the one exception.

Also to the north and twelve miles from the lake is Northstar, a master-planned ski and golf resort community. With a conference center and a spectacular country club, Northstar hosts many small business conferences and retreats. Northstar has its own private ski mountain and the cost of a lift ticket is often included in the price of a winter rental.

Although the Lake Tahoe area is home to a dozen ski areas, most of the visitors are from California or the West. Tahoe doesn't have the local transportation system that you'd find in other communities like Aspen or Breckenridge. If you come for the skiing and are not staying close to the lifts, you'll need a car.

Transportation to Lake Tahoe is easy with interstate highways and nonstop flights from Reno to most major U.S. cities. One of the secrets to the success of Lake Tahoe is the abundance of inexpensive airfares to Reno from just about everywhere.

WHERE TO STAY (See also Nevada—Lake Tahoe)

8 **THE ASPENS**
100 Winding Creek Rd., Squaw Valley, CA 96146
Amenities: Hot tub, tennis

Located right at the intersection of Highway 89, connecting Tahoe City with Interstate 80 and Squaw Valley Road, these condos are a healthy three miles from the ski lifts at Squaw Valley and the fun of the village. This is a secluded, peaceful setting along Squaw Creek where the only sound is the occasional tooting from a truck horn on the highway in the distance. These two and three-bedroom condos are superior to most of what you'll find in Squaw Valley. It is a great place for families or groups that have brought their own agenda for fun at Squaw.

7 BROCKWAY SPRINGS RESORT
101 Chipmunk, Kings Beach, CA 96413, 916-546-4201
1BR $115–125, 2BR $125–140, 3BR $140–160
Amenities: Tennis, pool, saunas, clubhouse, lake dock

Occupying a nice strip of rocky shoreline, this has an atmosphere similar to what you might find in Maine. Surrounded by looming firs, these condos are in a parklike setting. There is also a high-rise, seven-story tower. The condo interiors are decorated with contemporary furniture with lots of wood and soft pink colors. Comfortable and well maintained, nothing is out of order. This resort has a conference facility and specializes in small gatherings of doctors and other professionals. In addition, an impressive sports center with pools, saunas, and a hot tub, provides a great place to relax after a day of skiing or conferencing.

6-7 CARNELIAN WOODS
5101 N. Lake Blvd., Carnelian Bay, CA 96140, 916-546-5547
1BR $165, 2BR $225, 3BR $225, 4BR $275
Amenities: Pool, saunas, hot tub, tennis, game room

This is a community of private townhouses and detached A-frame villas scattered over a 281-acre site. This is like renting your own home at Lake Tahoe because the condos are spread out through the forest and are very private. Yet it is within a community where all of the condos have access to the recreation center. The interiors of the condo units vary in quality. Some of them are amply furnished and others need to be spruced up. Every unit has a fireplace and private patio. They are also very spacious, and are therefore great for young active families or groups of friends. The recreation center is the heart of the resort—it has an outdoor pool, an indoor hot tub spa, saunas, and a game room. This is where families come after skiing to relax, play, and socialize. Incline Village and the Nevada state line are only about 15 minutes away and Northstar, Alpine Meadows, and Squaw Valley are 30 minutes away. This resort is different from other developments because of the amount of land and well-spaced distribution of the houses.

10 CHINQUAPIN
Box RR, Tahoe City, CA 96415, 916-583-6991
1BR $140–160, 2BR $180–240
Amenities: Pool, hot tubs, boat dock, tennis

Welcome to the world of "Old Money." This small, exclusive resort caters to people who want solid comfort and privacy. Chinquapin is hard to find and isn't locally advertised. This is a resort for families from San Mateo and Piedmont who remember what Tahoe used to be like. The condos are all cedar villas scattered in a pine forest that overlook the lake. Only about half of the condos are offered for vacation rentals; the remainder are used as vacation toys by their owners. Some have striking, colorful interior decor. Others have that traditional "north woods cabin" look. Each one is immaculate. Nearby is Tahoe's Emerald Bay, one of the most spectacular, and often photographed. When you've had enough privacy, drive about 15 minutes and you're at the casinos of Incline Village.

8   **CHRISTY HILL**
         1610 Christy Lane, Box 2449, Squaw Valley, CA 96146
         916-583-3451; 2BR $120–225
         Amenities: None

Among the most luxurious large condos you'll find in Squaw Valley, these are located a quarter mile from the lifts and the village. Down below is the post office and a small shopping center. The brand new golf course is across the street and becomes a Nordic ski area in winter. You can walk to the tram, but it's a hike. Beautifully decorated, some have European, ski-chalet themed interiors; others are just plain comfortable. There's a stone fireplace that is the centerpiece of the living room. Christy Hill has a sunny location, easy access, and beautiful views.

7   **DOLLAR HILL**
         3170 N. Lake Blvd., Tahoe City, CA 96415
         Amenities: None

Overlooking the lake from its hillside location, the shore is a half mile away downhill. These condos were built townhouse-style and many have the kitchen/living/dining room upstairs with the bedroom down below. This gives you the best view from the living room. Individually furnished by the owners, each is comfortable and many are accented by treasures from the attic. An attractive development, interior decors vary a lot in quality, but all have fireplaces.

6   **DONNER LAKE VILLAGE**
         15695 Donner Pass Rd., P.O. Box 11109, Truckee, CA 96160,
         916-587-6081; 1BR $62–92, 2BR $135–155
         Amenities: Sauna, restaurant, bar

This resort has a quiet location on the southwest end of Lake Tahoe on the California side. It's close to Emerald Bay and the almost-hidden Bliss State Park. This is for nature lovers. If you want to be near the woods for hiking, but you don't want to sleep in a tent, try Donner Lake. The crowd here enjoys Sierra Club magazine and appreciates the wilderness. The condos are amply furnished with sturdy furniture, neutral colors, and lots of tweedy fabrics. Some enjoy great views of the lake. There is a fireside lodge, which is a good place to socialize in winter, or you can just relax in the peace of a sauna. Alpine Meadows and Squaw Valley are just 15 minutes away. The resort is about ten minutes from nightlife in either Tahoe City or Stateline. Enjoy a quiet and pleasant environment.

6-7+ GRANLIBAKKEN
Granlibakken Rd., Tahoe City, CA 96415, 916-583-4242
Studio $105, 1BR $156, 2BR $177, 3BR $225
Amenities: Tennis, pool, saunas, hot tub, skiing, conference center

Granlibakken is located a mile inland from Tahoe City. Nestled in a private valley, it provides a quiet retreat for special vacation escapes. The lodge is famous because in 1932 it was the site of the Olympic ski trials. Granlibakken is a four-season resort featuring one, two and three-bedroom condos. The condos combine European charm with the practicality of Lake Tahoe's sporting lifestyle. Kitchens, fireplaces, dining areas, cozy lofts, and decks or patios are included in most of the condos. Rental rates include a full buffet breakfast offered daily at the main lodge. Nature trails wind beneath towering pines throughout the grounds. During the winter you can schuss down Granlibakken's small ski hill or enjoy a saucer run on the nearby sledding hill. Two cross-country ski trails also traverse the resort's wooded acreage. Granlibakken is very popular with small conventions and group meetings. It's a lively place to stay.

6 KINGSWOOD VILLAGE
1001 Commonwealth Dr., Kings Beach, CA 96413, 916-546-2501
1BR $190, 2BR $225, 3BR $260
Amenities: Pool, gym w/exercise room, sauna, hot tub

Kingswood Village is located on Highway 267 between Northstar and Incline Village. The location is convenient for skiing or visiting the lake. Both areas are only 15 minutes away. Northstar is five miles away and Incline is eight miles away. The condos are in a three-story building that is surrounded by a forest. The loft units are architecturally appealing because of the cathedral ceilings in the living room. The furniture is durable and the color scheme consists of brown and burnt orange. Every unit has a private washer/dryer and a fireplace. This is a spacious and pleasant condo project. Although it is a bit isolated, it is good for families and groups of skiers who intend to bring their own fun.

7-8 LAKE FOREST GLEN
3101 Lake Forest Rd., Tahoe City, CA 96415
Amenities: Pool, tennis, hot tub

Down in the meadowlands below the main highway, yet not quite lake front property, this village of townhouse-style condos is popular with weekenders. Some have been beautifully, and expensively, decorated. We saw one with oriental touches including a huge Japanese fan over the moss rock fireplace. Other treasures from travel in the Orient adorn this superior unit. These are among the largest condos you'll find in the Lake Tahoe area. They have two, three, and four bedrooms. The activity center gives Lake Forest Glen a friendly social atmosphere.

8+ LAKELAND VILLAGE BEACH & SKI RESORT
3535 Hwy 50, South Lake Tahoe, CA 96150, 916-541-7711
Studio $65–85, 1BR $80–150, 2BR $90–185, 3BR $145–285
Amenities: Beach, dock, tennis, pool, hot tub, saunas

Tucked away on Lake Tahoe's south shore, yet only a four-minute drive to the casinos on the state line, is Lakeland Village Beach & Ski Resort. It's a gem because it is a self-contained resort which enjoys a private beach and dock for boating. It's only a mile or so from Heavenly Valley ski area. Spread over 19 forested acres, the condos are in three-story townhouse buildings with flats downstairs and two-story units upstairs. All are spacious, well designed, and decorated with lots of wood, forest green carpets, and pastel fabrics for the furniture. You'll be pleased with the immaculate maintenance. The grounds surrounding the buildings are forested, but landscaped and lined with flower beds in summer. Although there's a beach, you'll find most social life over at the main building where the pool and hot tubs are located.

9+ NORTHSTAR AT TAHOE
Hwy 267, Truckee, CA 96160, 916-562-1113, 800-533-6787
Condos: 1BR $112, 2BR $159, 3BR $199,
Villas: 3BR $227, 4BR $268
Amenities: Pool, private ski mountain, tennis, golf, horseback riding, restaurants, health club, children's programs

Northstar is a completely self-contained ski community tucked away in the High Sierras only 20 minutes from the shores of Lake Tahoe. The BIG advantage here is that Northstar has its own ski mountain primarily for Northstar guests. Ticket sales are limited and Northstar guest have first option. This is a BIG plus on a crowded day at Tahoe and by staying at Northstar you can avoid those long lift lines. Northstar has over 300 condos strategically placed around its 2,700 acres. Some condos have ski-in, ski-out access and the rental rates are at a premium. Others line the golf fairways, and still others are sheltered by the forest. Expect to find California redwood construction with lots of glass and angles that create additional space and bring in the sunlight and mountain views. The interior decor may differ in style, but expect high quality furnishings. Some are designer decorated with pink and blue fabrics, oversized ceramic vases with sprays of dried branches, and lots of accessories like hand-stitched quilts. Others have a rustic north woods style with a stone fireplace and hearth, Early American tables and chairs, and accessories such as duck decoys or hunting scenes. Ski Trail

Condos are the best choice for skiers because they are actually on a ski trail above the resort plaza. For children, there's the Minor's Camp as well as programs for ski, golf, and tennis instruction. There are three pools, but the Olympic-sized pool at the clubhouse is clearly the most popular. There are also three restaurants, a health club featuring massages, a weight room, and a game room for children. For outdoor activities, there are stables, hiking trails, and bike rentals for exploring the miles of trails.

8+ OLYMPIC VILLAGE INN
1900 Squaw Valley Rd., Olympic Valley, CA 96146
1BR $95–195
Amenities: Pool, hot tubs, tennis, beach, golf, restaurants

Located at the base of the lifts, this resort features a million dollar "water-garden" laced with 30,000 flowering bulbs, an imposing grand lodge with two major restaurants, and a mountain-view bar. The lobby has a huge copper fireplace with a crackling fire every day in winter. Throughout each of the 90 one-bedroom suites, a Swiss provincial motif is evident. Silk flowers, designer wallpapers, colorful old world stenciling, even a down comforter are the rule here. Bedroom furnishings include a cedar-lined hope chest and an old world armoire in bleached pine. The living rooms include camel beige sofas that easily convert into queen-sized beds. Each unit has a mini-kitchen. Most of the units have stereos and VTPs.

10 RESORT AT SQUAW CREEK
400 Squaw Creek Rd., Box 3333, Olympic Valley, CA 96146,
916-583-6300; 1BR $475, 2BR $575
Amenities: Golf, tennis, horseback riding, conference center, restaurants, shops, pools, spa

This is what Squaw Valley has needed ever since the 1960 Winter Olympics were held here. Set on 626 hillside acres, the main lodge is about a mile away from the main skiers' village of Squaw Valley. That's just fine. This is a whole new way of looking at Squaw Valley—a sophisticated resort conference center cum condos and cabins. The old part of Squaw Valley for years has had all the charm of a college dorm. The Resort at Squaw Creek is just what the area needed to reinstall itself as a spectacular mountain hide-away. It is removed from the pressures of urban life.

The lodge is the core. Piped-in classical music gently wafts in the background throughout the day. You can survey the scene from a spare, almost Frank Lloyd Wright, lobby area bathed in sunlight streaming through windows three stories high. The townhouses radiate from the lodge and although not as impressive as the lodge, they nevertheless have a sophisticated charm. Natural woods, clean angles, and skylights create the living space. Area rugs, Indian weavings, and occasional ceramic pieces punctuate the interior. An all-natural environment surrounds you with nothing out of order. Many of these condos are rented by CEOs attending conferences at the lodge. Some are rented by urbanites seeking a honeymoonette. Not a family resort, this is perfect for two or three couples who want a week at Squaw Creek to be an unforgettable interlude in their lives.

6   RIVER RUN CONDOS
Alpine Meadows at Hwy. 89, Tahoe City, CA 96415,
916-583-0137; 1BR $100–155, 2BR $130–190, 3BR $155–235
Amenities: Pool, tennis

River Run condos, located close to the Alpine Meadows ski area, are only a five-minute drive from either Lake Tahoe or Squaw Valley. Alpine Meadows is an excellent ski area and a favorite of those who know Tahoe well. The drawback is that River Run is remote. You have to drive if you want to go out in the evening. It is 30 minutes over to Incline Village on the north side of Lake Tahoe if you want glamour or gambling. Consequently, River Run is an option for athletic families or those seeking peace and quiet away from Tahoe's frenzied summertime activity. The interiors are adequately furnished with durable, "skierized" furniture. The condos are comfortable and provide a great setting for après-ski by the fireplace. A unique feature here is the river rafting parties in the summertime. If possible, try to stay in the condo decorated as "Toyland." Toys are everywhere. You'll never forget it.

8   ST. FRANCIS LAKESIDE
Lake Forest Rd., Tahoe City, CA 96415
Amenities: Pool, tennis, hot tub

Enjoying a lakeside setting, these luxurious townhouse condos were designed so each has a partial view of the lake. The upstairs loft bedroom is a favorite with children. Interior decor varies but we saw one with gorgeous lake views, comfortable skierized furniture, and a VTP in the living room. Beautifully managed, everything is well tended on the outside. This is a good spot for families and the activities center is a popular destination.

9   SQUAW VALLEY LODGE
201 Squaw Peak Rd., Olympic Valley, CA 96146, 916-583-5500
Studio $75–180, 1BR $100–170
Amenities: Health club, horseback riding, golf, pool, restaurants

Squaw Valley Lodge is just 84 steps from the Squaw Valley tram, you can't get any closer. There are five, three-story buildings surrounding a pool and health club. The studio and one-bedroom condos are on either side of a central hallway and the buildings are connected by glass enclosed passageways. Architectural flourishes create angular ceilings and little nooks and crannies. These are designed for families or groups of friends; there isn't

enough privacy for two couples to share a condo. The condos have professional designer decor that emphasizes oak chairs and tables with solid color
fabrics. Southwestern accents are provided by pictures, pillows, and throw
rugs. Decor is very imaginative with simple, bold strokes. Sorry, there are
no fireplaces. The lobby always sees lots of activity. It is at the core of
Squaw Valley Ski Resort. It's especially lively after skiing when the aerobics classes come into full swing. A large fieldstone fireplace is the attraction for those who prefer more sedentary activities such as wine tasting. A
health club with an exercise room, hot tubs and saunas is available.

7   SQUAW VALLEY MEADOWS
Squaw Valley Rd., Olympic Valley, CA 96146
Amenities: Golf

One of the newer properties at Squaw Valley, this overlooks the fairways
of the new golf course. In winter, it becomes a Nordic Center and the tram is
within walking distance. Inside, the units have stone fireplaces and are
trimmed with redwood. Aesthetically appealing to all, the environmentally
conscious will enjoy these units most.

8   STAR HARBOR
2350 N. Lake Blvd., Tahoe Vista, CA 96418
Amenities: Beach, pool, tennis, boat docks, pier

Located on one of Tahoe's best sandy beaches, this is a favorite among
boaters. Bring your own boat or rent one for your stay. These condos have
their own docks and there is a boater's spirit among the owners here.
Beautifully furnished, this is a good choice all year-round. It's exceptional
in summer.

3   TAHOE EDGELAKE BEACH CLUB
7860 N. Lake Blvd., Tahoe Vista, CA 96418, 916-546-5974
Studio $50, 1BR $75, 2BR $120
Amenities: Hot tub, pool

Tahoe Edgelake is a quiet, relaxed spot with redwood townhouses and
motel-style condos located right on the edge of the lake in the Kings Beach
area. A variety of accommodations are available, and some units are larger
than others. We like the new townhouses best. They are spacious with high
ceilings, neutral beige colors, lots of woodwork, private fireplaces, and
views of the lake. The units in the main building are smaller and dark by
comparison. This is a family resort that is popular with children. It is a great
place to make new friends. The casinos on the Nevada side are a short drive
away. The swimming pool is closed in the winter, but the hot tub that overlooks the lake operates year-round.

THE TAHOE ESCAPE
245 N. Lake Blvd., Box UU, Tahoe City, CA 96415,
916-583-0223

Specializing in personalized service, The Tahoe Escape rents vacation homes and villas on the California side of Lake Tahoe. They take the time to match the individual to the property. This rental agency surveys vacationers and then sends a collection of pictures to help you select the vacation retreat that's right for you. You just can't beat this personalized service. The following describes a few of the 164 properties they handle.

Ridgewood Highlands — This modern three-bedroom home has views of the mountains and lake. Sparsely furnished and decorated in Japanese style, it even has futons should you desire to sleep on the floor. It makes an impact on the eye that you'll long remember after your vacation is over.

Two Attorneys — This Alpine three-bedroom home with wraparound deck is right on the lake. Sit in your private hot tub and enjoy nature at its finest. Owned by two lawyers, their wives spared no expense in decorating this dream house with the finest from Laura Ashley. Four poster beds and lots of ruffles contrast with the polished blond woodwork. There's a VTP and stereo for those cold winter evenings when you want to stay home.

Serendipity — A getaway cabin in the woods above Tahoe Vista, this has been decorated in a southwestern country style. Lots of blue and white colors, gingham fabrics, and wood carvings from the Old West over the mantel. One bedroom has bunk beds and a toy chest — now that's planning for a family vacation.

Drummer House — A light, bright A-frame in the woods angled to capture the winter sun. Rustic decor and a wood-burning stove make this a cozy place for an escape from civilization.

The Ranch — This sprawling four-bedroom ranch-style home is one of the older properties in Lake Tahoe. Comfortable and handsomely furnished, there's a range of features from a private hot tub to a VTP and Nintendo system.

7+ **TAHOE SEASONS**
3901 Saddle Rd., South Lake Tahoe, CA 96150, 916-541-6010
1BR $79–120, 2BR $150–270
Amenities: Pool, tennis, restaurant, game room, hot tub

Tahoe Seasons is great for skiers because it's located right next to the lifts at Heavenly Valley. The best way to explain the location of this resort is that it shares Heavenly Valley's parking lot. You couldn't be closer to the gondola. There is a small outdoor pool, a good restaurant, and a large après-ski cocktail lounge/game room. At this resort, they want you to have fun. All of the 160 condos are attractively decorated with wood paneling and deep forest green colors. Each condo has a private Japanese bath, not a whirlpool, but a real spa separated by sliding Japanese screens. These hot tubs can easily accommodate four. The kitchen area includes a refrigerator, sink, microwave, and dishes. While adequate for small meals, you should plan to go out for dinner. Tahoe Seasons has a classic, contemporary ambiance and is as good a choice for families as it is for couples on a honeymoon. In fact, this may be one of Tahoe's best choices for those seeking a romantic interlude.

9 TAHOE TAVERN
300 W. Lake Blvd., Tahoe City, CA 96415
Amenities: Pool, tennis, pier

Located south of Tahoe City, these are among the most expensive condos in the area that enjoy a prime lakeside location. Dark on the outside, interior design has captured the best of the lake view by creating sunken living rooms. Each has a rear deck and private side patio.

7 TAHOE TYROL
3351 Pine Hill Rd., South Lake Tahoe, CA 96150, 916-544-6017
1BR $110–130, 2BR $130–150, 3BR $160–180
Amenities: Pool, hot tub, sauna, meeting room

This is a community of two to four-bedroom private alpine chalets just four blocks below the community recreational center. It is located on a slope above Lake Tahoe. The individual two-story chalets have fancifully carved wood trim and elaborate motifs similar to what you would find in Austria. The chalets are spacious, although the interior decor leaves a lot to be desired. Sturdy "skierized" furniture is featured where you can be comfortable with or without your boots. The centerpiece is the large fireplace and hearth in the living room. This is a great choice for groups of skiers because they will have plenty of space and will enjoy the use of the recreation center. This resort is different and offers good value.

5 TAVERN INN
227 Squaw Valley Rd., Squaw Valley, CA 96146, 916-583-1504
1BR $100–275, 2BR $145–330, 3BR $175–385
Amenities: Pool, hot tub, sauna. Golf next door

Tavern Inn is the budget choice in Squaw Valley. These half-timbered English Tudor-style units are close to Highway 89 and with over 150 units, it is its own little community, complete with convenience store. You'll need to drive or take a shuttle bus to the lifts at Squaw Valley or for fun in the evening. There's a wet bar in the living room. These units are designed for gregarious skiers or golfers who want to have fun. This resort has its own full-amenity complex—a rarity among Squaw Valley lodgings.

RENTAL RESOURCES

Accommodations Station, 916-541-2355
Alpine Meadows Realty, 916-583-1545
Alpine Place, 916-583-1890
Bavarian Village Rentals, 916-541-8191
Beach Comber, 916-544-2426
Better Homes Realty, 916-544-7010
Carnelian Bay Rentals, 916-546-5547
Coldwell Banker Fraser & Fraser, 916-587-3316, 800-345-0102
Donner Lake Realty, 916-587-6055
ERA Alpine Realty, 916-544-6978
First Resort Realty, 916-583-1000
Hauserman Rental Group, 916-583-3793
Lake of the Sky Properties, 916-542-0557
Lake Tahoe Realty & Rentals, 916-541-1444
M & M Vacation Rentals, 800-542-2100
Northstar Properties, 916-562-1140
Prudential Golden West, 916-587-7772
Sierra Vacation Rentals, 916-546-8222
Ski West Vacation Rentals, 916-587-9218, 800-339-5535
Squaw Valley Realty, 916-583-3451
Tahoe Park Realty, 916-583-6942
Tahoe Riverfront Realty, 916-583-3483
Tahoe Timberline Properties, 916-581-0183
Tahoe Vacation Properties, 916-583-6985
Vacation Property Management, 916-587-1236
Wells & Bennet, 916-583-4292

5. MAMMOTH

Mammoth Mountain, on the eastern slope of the Sierra Nevadas, is a complete destination resort with perhaps, the best powder skiing in California. It is one of the largest ski areas in the United States. It has 29 lifts and 150 trails. Winter is the main season, although travelers are starting to discover that Mammoth is a sleeping giant of a summer resort. Close to June Lake for boating, waterskiing, and fishing, Mammoth is also a good place from which to discover the Yosemite Valley. Because of the altitude, summer is sunny yet cool. Hiking into the John Muir Wilderness, backpacking through the high country, fishing, and mountain climbing also draws visitors. Two miles away, the resort town of Mammoth Lakes is a good base for short excursions into the surrounding area.

Most condo owners and visitors to the Mammoth Lakes area come from the cities of Southern California, a six-hour drive through the desert on the east side of the Sierras. Mammoth has challenging skiing and the potential to be a national destination, but so far that hasn't happened. The town has friendly cafes, western bars, and some excellent restaurants. Shopping is limited mainly to items for local consumption, although boutiques are springing up along Old Mammoth Road.

There are several distinct areas. Main Street is just a highway lined with motels and restaurants. South of town, the Old Mammoth area borders a meadowlands where you'll find golf and horseback riding in the summer. Chair lift 15 provides mountain access to this area in winter. Most of the condos are in the Canyon Blvd. residential area between town and the base of the ski mountain. This is a veritable sea of two and three-story wood condo buildings separated from each other by pine and fir landscaping. These condos are along either Canyon Blvd. or Lakeview. Here you'll find the Warming Hut II Ski Center with four separate ski lifts. The condos in this area are, therefore, ideally located for skiers.

Three miles out of town, along Minaret Road, is the main base and gondola for the ski area. Here your choices are the condos of the Mammoth Mountain Inn and the Mammoth Mountain Chalets. The Chalets are intriguing A-frames where the driveways are snowed-in in winter. You can either use your skis or the resort provides transportation on its snow cat.

New development is starting to take place higher up at Lake Mary. But in winter the Lake Mary Road is sometimes closed for a few hours due to heavy snow conditions.

Transportation to Mammoth is poor. Almost everyone drives from Southern California. Although it has a Northern California location, the passes from the San Francisco Bay area are closed in the winter, so auto traffic is routed through Lake Tahoe. There is a commuter airline to L.A. and San Francisco. Our secret route is to fly to Reno and drive two hours south through the desert. The drive past Mono Lake is fascinating. The former undersea rock and "stalactite" formations are now visible from the road along the lakeshore.

WHERE TO STAY

8+ **THE BRIDGES**
Lake Mary Rd., Box 1452, Mammoth Lakes, CA 93546,
619-934-8919, 800-654-1143; 2BR $95–180
Amenities: Ski-in/ski-out access

Unique on Mammoth Mountain, this is one of the rare finds where you can ski home in the evening. Specifically, it is a half mile above Chairs 15 and 24, so good skiers can ski down to the lifts in the morning. As you would expect with this mountainside location, the views are spectacular over Crowley Lake to the Sierra peaks beyond. These luxury condominiums and townhouses are only five years old. Each has a microwave for convenience in the kitchen, and the living rooms have vaulted ceilings and stone fireplaces. Most have VTPs and we saw one with an elaborate stereo system. Some units have a private whirlpool. These two and four-bedroom condos are among the best in the Mammoth area.

8   CANYON SKI AND RACQUET CLUB
Lakeview Blvd., Box 7296, P.O. Mammoth Lakes, CA 93546,
619-934-4747; 2BR $105, 3BR $119
Amenities: Hot tub, sauna, racquetball, tennis

The resort is located just a short walk from the skiers' shuttle bus stop at the intersection of Main Highway and Minaret Road. In an area thick with condominiums, this is a handsome community of cedar-sided townhouses. These two and three-bedroom loft units have vaulted ceilings, wood burning fireplaces and contemporary decor with accents to create that "ski chalet" feeling. The kitchens are fully equipped and even have microwaves. There's a wonderful activities center here with a racquetball court, tennis court, sauna, and hot tub. Good value can be found here.

6   CHAMONIX
803 Canyon Blvd., Mammoth Lakes, CA 93546, 619-934-6792,
800-421-9799; 1BR $110–145, 2BR $145–175
Amenities: Hot tubs, game room

Among the forest of condominiums along Canyon Blvd., Chamonix is closest to the Warming Hut II ski lift. At this location you don't have to take the shuttle bus in the morning. These two-story wooden buildings are arranged in a village, clustered around the recreation area that has three large hot tubs and a game room with video games and a billiards table. Inexpensively decorated, you'll find some furniture a little faded or replaced with "treasures from the attic." Never mind the style, these one and two-bedroom units (half with lofts) are reasonably priced and offer a great location for skiers.

5   DISCOVERY 4
Lake Mary Rd., Box 789, Mammoth Lakes, CA 93546,
800-538-4751; 1BR $95–165, 2BR $130–210
Amenities: Pool, hot tub, sauna, game room with billiards

For cross country skiers, these condos are a great choice. Away from the main part of town and surrounded by pines, these two-story wood condos are on the way up to Lake Mary. The cross country ski center is just up the hill. Looking a little like a college dorm, these basic units have a stone fireplace as the centerpiece in the living room. The second-story units have vaulted ceilings and great views of the mountains and valley. For the hearty, several chair lifts are within walking distance.

8 **1849 CONDOMINIUMS**
Lakeview Blvd., Box 835, Mammoth Lake, CA 93546,
619-934-7525; 1BR $125–185, 2BR $160–200, 3BR $230–255
Amenities: Pool, hot tubs, sauna, exercise room

One of the most popular condo complexes in Mammoth, partially because of its location in the Canyon Blvd. section of Mammoth and partially because it is across the street from the ski center, close to the Warming Hut II chair lift. In the evening, you can ski right to your terrace. These two and four-story buildings are practical, without architectural flourish. The units are 15 years old; some have been well maintained, others have been dressed up by new owners who have introduced attractive new furniture packages. All units have fireplaces and VTPs for your enjoyment. The location is very convenient.

4 **KRYSTAL VILLA EAST**
Mammoth Tavern Rd., Box 1132, Mammoth Lake, CA 93546,
619-934-2669; 1BR $70–100
Amenities: Pool, hot tub, sauna

These one-bedroom and one-bedroom loft condos are located in the Canyon Blvd. section of Mammoth, close to the intersection of Minaret and Main Street where the shuttle bus stops. Reasonably priced, these offer comfortable accommodations in the area. Some of the units could be spruced up. This is choice for younger visitors who plan to be outside all day—and for a good part of the evening too.

6 **MAMMOTH ESTATES**
221 Canyon Blvd., Box 1117, Mammoth Lakes, CA 93546,
619-934-2884; Studio $55–115, 2BR $80–140, 3BR $95–180
Amenities: Pool, hot tub, sauna

Located in the Canyon Blvd. section of town, it's a long, long walk to the Warming Hut II lifts. You'd be better advised to take a shuttle bus. These two-story condos are densely packed together, which limits the view and makes you aware of your neighbors. Built ten years ago, they have a boxy appearance on the outside, but are light and airy on the inside. Skylights bring even more sunshine into the upstairs loft units. Surrounded by trees, there's a friendly pool and hot tub.

7 **MAMMOTH MOUNTAIN CHALETS**
Minaret Rd., Box 513, Mammoth Lakes, CA 93546, 619-934-8518
Chalets $120
Amenities: Ski-in/ski-out access

These A-frame chalets have one of the best locations in the area across from the gondola at the main ski area. Mammoth town is three miles away, but there's a lot of activity next door at the inn in the evenings. The chalets make an interesting choice because they are free-standing houses with a large living room, kitchen, and two or three bedrooms. Children will especially enjoy the loft upstairs with its steeply slanted roof lines. This is an excellent choice for families with small children as it's right across from the Children's Ski School. During winter you can't drive to your individual chalet; transportation is provided on the resort's snow cat, but you can ski in and ski out.

8   MAMMOTH MOUNTAIN INN
     Minaret Rd., Mammoth Lakes, CA 93546, 619-934-2581
     1BR $79–160, 2BR $90–215
     Amenities: Hot tubs, restaurant

Mammoth Mountain Inn, located across from the gondola, is the central lodge for the ski area. It is part hotel and part condo resort and sees lots of activity. You can enjoy the kitchen in your suite or wander downstairs to the popular bar and restaurant. The condos are beautifully decorated with Bavarian blond wood furniture, fine floral prints, wing chairs, and little touches that create the romance of Europe. There are three indoor hot tubs in the main lodge. Real advantages here are the supervised activities program for children and the opportunities for teenagers to have fun.

6   MAMMOTH SKI AND RACQUET CLUB
     Canyon Blvd., Mammoth Lakes, CA 93546, 619-934-6891
     1BR $60–130, 2BR $70–155
     Amenities: Pool, hot tubs, saunas, tennis

Located in the Canyon Blvd. section of Mammoth, it's an easy walk to the Ski Center and the Warming Hut II ski lifts. The special feature here is that each two-story building with only four units has its own private sauna. In this sea of buildings, there are 13 saunas plus two hot tubs and an indoor swimming pool. Creeping up on 20 years of age, these condos have seen better days. Most are decorated in earth-tone colors, with burnt orange the most popular. Most have VTPs. The upstairs loft units with the extra windows are bright and far superior to the ground floor condos.

7   MEADOW RIDGE
     3005 Meridian, Box 8290, Mammoth Lakes, CA 93546,
     619-934-3808; 1BR $115, 2BR $150–185, 3BR $195
     Amenities: Whirlpool, pool, tennis

Meadow Ridge consists of townhouse condos located near Chair 15. Away from town and down in the valley, you are surrounded by views of the mountains. Each condo has a full kitchen, fireplace, and a stereo. The loft units have vaulted ceilings and extra space, something that's needed as the dimensions of the rooms are on the small side. This fact is a surprise considering that these are some of the more expensive condos in Mammoth.

8 MOUNTAINBACK AT MAMMOTH
Mammoth Lakes, CA 93546, 619-934-4549
2BR $110–220
Amenities: Pool, hot tubs

Located in the Canyon Blvd. section of Mammoth, this complex is on a long plot of ground with some units close to the Warming Hut II ski lifts. Other units, back by Lake Mary Road, require the use of the shuttle bus. This is one of Mammoth's newer and larger developments. Mountainback at Mammoth is distinguished by its offering of luxury condos. All units have stone fireplaces, natural wood walls, and full kitchens. Vaulted ceilings and lofts create a sense of openness in the living room and oak paneling enhances the forest setting. You'll feel very much in the woods here. Mountainback offers a heated pool and there's a private hot tub for each building of six condos. These are good for groups of skiers or families with older children. Mountainback is a prestigious place.

7 SEASONS 4
Lakeview Blvd., Box 2249, Mammoth Lakes, CA 93546,
619-934-2030; 1BR $60–135, 2BR $72–1190
Amenities: Heated pool, hot tub, game room

This small group of condos is a popular choice. It is located in the Canyon Blvd. section of Mammoth. These condos are distinguished by their log cabin exteriors and the vaulted, beamed ceilings on the inside. Extra spacious with a breakfast bar that opens into the living room, you'll probably want friends to come over for parties in the evening. The large stone fireplace is especially attractive. There's also a large indoor hot tub that is the size of a small pool, and an outdoor heated pool. Teenagers enjoy the game room.

6 SHERWIN VILLAS
Box 2249, Mammoth Lakes, CA 93546, 619-934-4773
1BR $75–95, 2BR $90–150, 3BR $105–170
Amenities: Pool, hot tub, tennis

Located in the area known as Old Mammoth, this is next to the shops. This is a good choice for families or groups if one member doesn't ski. In summer, it's even better because it is close to the Equestrian Center, the starting point for many trail rides. These practical two-story buildings offer cheerful, comfortable units. Generally there is nothing spectacular about the decor, but it is solid and well maintained.

9   SNOW COUNTRY
Old Mammoth Rd., Box 8228, Mammoth Lakes, CA 93546,
619-934-8634; 2BR $85–120, 3BR $95–145
Amenities: Access to Snowcreek Athletic Club

These two-story condos are located in the Old Mammoth area near the
shops, cross country skiing at Sierra Meadows, and right across the street
from the golf driving range. The upstairs loft units are spectacular with
mostly glass walls. The end units are best with three rows of glass windows
on just one wall—17 framed picture windows. The brick fireplace sits in the
middle of the living room and effectively divides the space into two sections.
Equipped with all the modern appliances, there are Jenn-air grills in the
kitchen and a whirlpool in the master bath. For amenities, there are guest
passes for the Snow Creek Athletic Club next door. Other condos may be
more expensive, but these are some of the best units in town.

9+ SNOWCREEK
Old Mammoth Rd., Mammoth Lakes, CA 93546, 619-934-3333
Amenities: Athletic club, pool

Snowcreek is its own world. Located in a meadowlands area between
Pyramid Peak and Mammoth Mountain, it is two miles from the village.
This is one of our favorites in the area because of the quality. The condos are
grouped in clusters and leave open spaces of land so that each condo enjoys
an open view of the mountains. The spacious condos have an elegant simplicity about them. They have a somewhat Japanese feeling because of the
use of wood, stone, glass, and the open space. No floral or designer fabrics
here! The special advantage is the Snowcreek Athletic Club with exercise
room, swimming pool, sauna, and hot tub. There is a courtesy shuttle bus to
the resort, but frankly, you'll make friends and probably prefer to stay in the
convenience of this enclave.

6   SUNRISE VILLAGE
Box 9139, Meadow Lane, Mammoth Lakes, CA 93546,
619-934-7260; 1BR $85–105
Amenities: Pool

A development of two-story redwood buildings surrounding the pool area,
located not far from the village in a wooded area. In summer, horseback riding is available nearby so this attracts the equestrian set.

6   SUNSHINE VILLAGE
Box 1085, Mammoth Lakes, CA 93546, 619-934-3340
1BR $65–105, 2BR $85–170
Amenities: Pool, hot tub, sauna, game room, tennis

This village of one and two-bedroom condos offers reasonably priced condos down near the shops of Old Mammoth. Chair lift 15 is a five-minute walk away. Good for families and especially popular with groups of young skiers, this resort is well cared for and pleasant.

5 WILDFLOWER
Box 1576, Arrowhead Dr., Mammoth Lakes, CA 93546, 619-934-4600; 1BR $65–105, 2BR $100–165
Amenities: Pool, hot tub

This cluster of 18 three-story buildings is located in the Old Mammoth area. A resort village, this has a recreation center with a pool and hot tub is popular in the evenings after skiing. Contemporary and casual, the loft units upstairs are the best. It is popular in summer as well as winter because golf and horseback riding are close at hand.

7 THE WOODLANDS
Box 7338, Mammoth Lakes, CA 93546, 800-321-3261
2BR $110–150
Amenities: Pool, hot tub, sauna

Located in the Old Mammoth area, just above Mammoth Creek, these are secluded, wooded townhouses. Surrounded by pines, the air is fragrant and in summer you can hear the creek. It is a wonderfully peaceful and private spot. If you want to make friends, walk over to the pool/hot tub area. Although remote for skiers, these are superior units.

RENTAL RESOURCES
800 Mammoth, 800-MAMMOTH
Mammoth Reservation Bureau, 800,462-5571
Mammoth Sierra, 800-325-8415

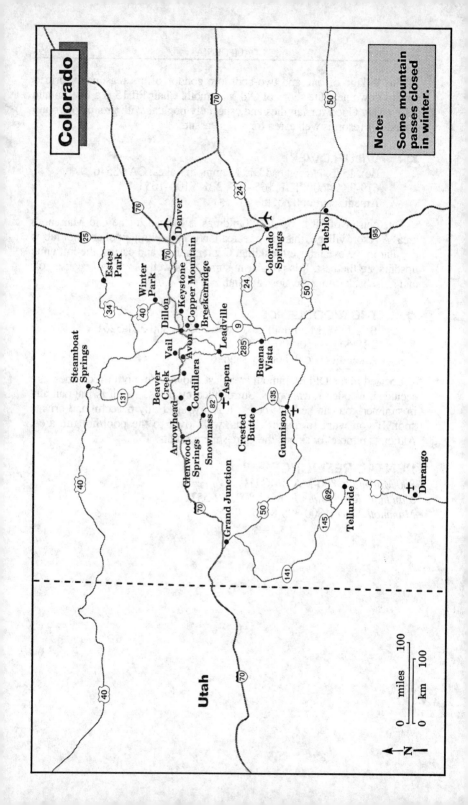

COLORADO

With over 25 million tourists annually you would think the concept of a private condo in the mountains would be impossible, but the Rockies include a lot of territory.

Colorado's ski resorts have been among the most popular areas for condominium development in North America and with nearly 500 in number ranks second only to Florida. For purposes of organization we have focused on 12 resort areas that attract visitors from around the U.S., Latin America, and Europe. Those resort areas are:

1. Aspen/Snowmass
2. Beaver Creek/Avon
3. Breckenridge
4. Copper Mountain
5. Crested Butte
6. Dillon/Frisco
7. Durango/Purgatory
8. Keystone
9. Steamboat Springs
10. Telluride
11. Vail
12. Winter Park

1. ASPEN / SNOWMASS

This is a tale of two towns that, because one grew from the other, are usually considered to be one resort area. Yes, you can enjoy both communities. They are only nine miles apart. But we think you'll find your vacation experience influenced by the initial decision of where to stay. Even though this is one resort destination, we have divided this section into two groupings of lodgings.

There are several reasons why Aspen continues to attract so much attention. One is the mystique of the mountain. Another is the well-known people who visit from stars like Barbra Streisand (who has called for a boycott until the anti-Gay law is changed) to Mr. Mellow himself, John Denver. Count yourself lucky if you're NOT in town for the John Denver Ski Week when Hollywood's finest compete with the wealthiest from New York and Europe for restaurant reservations. Although it is exciting to shop for groceries with the stars, do not underestimate the local merchants and their interpretation of the pecking order.

The most important reason why vacationers choose Aspen is the town itself. Despite all the speciality shops, the cuisine, and the much talked about night life, Aspen is still the queen of ski resorts because it has character. It's quaint, cozy, and like most other ski resort areas, a little on the quirky side with pieces of the past popping up when you can least expect them. Grand old Queen Anne and Victorian homes and cute miners' cottages where the gardens are brimming with flowers in Summer are available here. Funky antiques, horse drawn sleigh-rides; the list could go on and on. Aspen is a quaint town where traffic almost became a real problem. Now, streets have been "ended" to prevent through traffic, and pedestrian malls have replaced streets. You'll find most of the condos clustered by the base of the mountain, a couple of blocks from the main restaurant and shopping district. Aspen is a town where most everything is a short walk from your condo and, like New York, part of the fun is just being out in the streets. One piece of advice about condo lodgings in Aspen—don't expect too much. The condos in Aspen are older than in most resort communities and many are showing their age. Interior decor of some condos are "aged" and others are dreadful, but the owners and the rental companies can get away with this because it's ASPEN where there is always high demand. Although the prices are some of the highest that you'll pay for condo vacations anywhere, this is a community where the condo owners seem to like things the way they were. Nowhere will you find sprays of artificial flowers or the decorator traps prevalent in many second homes. Don't get us wrong, there's nothing wrong with these accommodations and they are luxury homes owned by multi-millionaires, but renovation just doesn't seem to be a high priority.

Most assume that Snowmass is the same as Aspen because they are so close together. Wrong. Only nine miles away, Snowmass is a world apart. Purposely built as a ski resort twenty years ago with convenience in mind (and an aversion to automobile traffic), you'll find that every shop, restaurant, and condominium development is a stone's throw from the slopes. Snowmass is a place where families can be together—and parents can be left alone if the mood strikes them. Drop the kids off to be Big Burn Bears. Sip hot cappuccino in the Paradise Bakery. Try a few Steeps On The Wall. Or just cruise, at your own pace down Sheer Bliss, or Coney Glade, or any one of the numerous intermediate runs. Snowmass is entirely different as 95% of the condos are designed to be ski-in, ski-out. The most popular part of Snowmass Mountain for skiers is the Big Burn. During the 19th century when the local Arapaho Indians were being driven from this area, the mountainside forest was torched after defeat in battle. They truly followed a "scorched earth" policy. Hence the name the "Big Burn." Snowmass resort was designed to be a unique pedestrian village with 16 levels cascading down the hillside. Most of the restaurants and shops are located in the central mall, from which the lodges and condominiums stretch both up and down the slope. Skiers walk a level path to the sides of the slope where everyone puts on skis and slides down to the nearest chair lift. At night, if you want to explore Aspen's glamorous off-beat restaurants, there's a frequent shuttle bus, so if you stay at Snowmass, you'll never need nor even want a car.

Skiers in the Aspen area have the choice of four different ski areas: Aspen Mountain, Buttermilk, Snowmass, and Aspen Highlands. The first three are all owned by the Aspen Ski Corporation, and the three-day and six-out-of-seven-day lift ticket packages offer the possibility of skiing at all the mountains. Because Aspen Highlands is a ski area under different ownership, management has developed competitively priced offers. The ski terrain varies among Aspen's four mountains. Buttermilk, located a mile west of town, offers primarily beginner and intermediate terrain. Snowmass, with acres of open terrain and forested trails, is the ultimate intermediate paradise. Aspen Mountain, overshadowing the town of Aspen, has terrain for better intermediates and experts. Aspen Highlands, partway between Aspen and Snowmass, has a blend of terrain for all skill levels. The free Aspen Ski Corporation buses shuttle skiers between the town and its three resorts. Aspen Highlands has its own free "jelly bean" bus.

Transportation to Aspen can be easy or it can be a problem. Not close to a major airport, you must either take an expensive commuter flight or, as so many Aspenites prefer, you can bring your own private plane. The Aspen airport has an acre of tarmac parking for all the private planes. United Express has frequent flights to Denver and seasonal nonstop service to Chicago, Dallas and L.A. Driving to Aspen is quite another story. It takes six long hours from Denver. In summer, driving time shortens to four hours for those willing to endure the tortuous curves of Independence Pass.

WHERE TO STAY... Aspen

9   ASPEN ALPS
700 Ute Ave., Aspen, CO 81611, 303-925-7820
2BR $155–440, 3BR $200–480
Amenities: Pool, hot tub, sauna

Some of the oldest most established condos in Aspen, these are located at the base of Aspen mountain. These luxurious condos are owned and used by some of Denver's leading families. Although not ostentatious, this is one of Aspen's most prestigious addresses. The resort is convenient for skiers and is two blocks from the main shops and restaurants of Aspen. The condos are individually furnished. You should expect to find a handsome environment furnished with lots of wood and quality fabrics. Each has a fireplace, and the views will make you believe you are alone with the mountain, even though you're in one of Aspen's most convenient locations.

6   ASPEN COUNTRY INN
38996 Highway 83, Aspen, CO 81611, 303-925-2700, Suite $155
Amenities: Pool, hot tub, fishing, restaurant

The Aspen Country Inn is located about one and one-half miles from town and a half mile from the airport. It's self-contained and great for families with teenage children because after skiing there's lots of activity. Each unit is romantically furnished with brass beds and wing back chairs, but there are no kitchens. There's a shuttle bus that travels frequently from the Inn to town and the ski lifts. In summer, the Inn is ideally situated for hiking or for fishing in the streams on the back of the property. In winter, this is a good choice for families with small children or new skiers because it's close to Buttermilk Mountain, which features Aspen's gentle beginner slopes.

7   ASPEN MOUNTAIN CONDOMINIUMS
623 S. Monarch, Aspen, CO 81611, 303-925-2260
1BR $200, 2BR $300
Amenities: Ski lift location

This has a great location nestled between the gondola and Lift A at the base of Aspen Mountain. It's two blocks to the center of town. The townhouse units are modern and well furnished with dramatic touches like track lighting and black-against-white furniture. The focal point is each unit's private fireplace. No on-site management, instead management is from a central office about a block away. This is for couples seeking a great location for skiing and who want to be close to the nightlife of Aspen. There is no pool on site.

8   ASPEN SQUARE
617 E. Cooper Ave., Aspen, CO 81611, 800-862-7736
Studio $85, 1BR $110, 2BR $185
Amenities: Pool, hot tub

This is simply the best location in Aspen. Located right in the heart of town, this three-story brick-condo complex offers pleasant condos and great value. Although it's not a budget choice, this resort offers high quality for a reasonable price. Arranged around an atrium, the studio, one and two-bedroom condos are well built so you won't hear your neighbors. Interiors are nice with neutral woods and some colorful woven fabrics. Aspen Square is equally popular with singles and families.

7   CHATEAU EAU CLAIR/CHATEAU ROARING FORK
1034–1039 E. Cooper St., Aspen, CO 81611, 800-222-7736
1BR $120–180, 2BR $170–520, 3BR $225–495
Amenities: Pool, hot tubs

These twin complexes are located on the banks of the Roaring Fork River, just three blocks from downtown Aspen. Chateau Eau Claire has balconies; Chateau Roaring Fork doesn't. Don't be discouraged by outside appearances; once inside you'll be favorably impressed. Both three-story buildings share Aspen's largest condo pool complex, which also has two hot tubs. These two and three-bedroom units have superior furniture and the decor follows the themes of "ski chalet," "western cowboy," or "Santa Fe eclectic." In a quiet location, this is a private community within walking distance of Aspen's nightlife.

8   THE DURANT
      7185 Galena, Aspen, CO 81611, 303-925-2260
      1BR $110–125, 2BR $135–340
      Amenities: Pool, hot tub, ski-in/ski-out access

What better place to enjoy all that Aspen has to offer. The Durant is located in a cul-de-sac two blocks from the center of town and one block from the Aspen Mountain gondola. Ski-in/ski-out access is a big plus as so many in-town condos don't have this. At The Durant, you have a panoramic view of the mountains and town. These modern stylish condos are well furnished in neutral colors and feature spacious living rooms with a fireplace. It's a good choice for adults.

8   FASCHING HAUS
      747 S. Galena St., Aspen, CO 81611, 303-925-2260
      Studio $135, 1BR $200, 2BR $335.
      Amenities: Pool, hot tub

An attractive dark wooden building at the base of the Aspen Mountain gondola, Fasching Haus offers a convenient location just two blocks from the center of town or a block from the Ajax ski lift. The exterior has cute Austrian shutters and flower boxes, but inside most of the condos have an upbeat, contemporary decor. In general, the condos are decorated with lots of wood accented by beige and brown fabrics. It's a memorable spot.

8   FIFTH AVENUE CONDOMINIUMS
      800 S. Mill St., Aspen, CO 81611, 303-925-2260
      1BR $185, 2BR $290.
      Amenities: Pool, hot tub, ski-in/ski-out access

Modernistic wooden structures with interesting angles, windows, and stairwells, Fifth Avenue is distinguished from the other condos at the base of Aspen Mountain because of its ultra-modern architecture. However, many of the interiors are a disappointment, with standard arrangements of "skierized" furniture in tweed fabrics and with lots of pillows. Some of the units have cathedral ceilings and windows that bring in streaming sunlight. Ski-in/ski-out access makes this especially attractive for an in-town Aspen condo.

6+   THE GANT
      610 W. End St., Aspen, CO 81612, 800-642-4210
      1BR $110–225, 2BR $135–340
      Amenities: Pools, hot tubs, tennis

Good for hospitality and service, The Gant, a condo-hotel and conference center, is a self-contained retreat near the base of Aspen Mountain. Located four blocks from the center of Aspen and two blocks from the ski lifts, these condos have great views up Aspen Mountain. Although the lobby and pool are inviting, the size of the condos is a little disappointing. You'll find narrow boxy floor plans with fireplaces and balconies. The most unusual and helpful part of The Gant is its outstanding service. "The Gantman" will meet you at the airport, pick you up after a concert, secure a preferred tee time, or pick up groceries. This is one concierge who takes his job seriously.

9   POMEGRANITE
22094 Highway 83, Aspen, CO 81611, 303-925-1400
1BR $160, 2BR $235
Amenities: Golf

Located on the new Grand Champions golf course, these one-, two-, and three-bedroom units in a three-story building have wraparound views of the mountains surrounding Aspen. All four ski mountains are only ten miles away. Alone on the golf course, these are among Aspen's most private condos and rental values are good, considering all the space and, after all, this is Aspen.

4   SHADOW MOUNTAIN QUARTERS
809 S. Aspen, Aspen, CO 81611, 800-222-7736
1BR $155, 2BR $250
Amenities: Pool

Located next to Lift 1A on the side of Aspen Mountain, this is a cute cluster of Austrian chalet-style condos. Beautifully decorated by interior designers, some have European style and others reflect the art galleries of Santa Fe. The indifferent management, however, leaves us cold. Although rental rates are some of the lowest and the accommodations are all dressed up, there's something missing.

5   SNOWFLAKE INN
221 E. Hyman Ave., Aspen, CO 81611, 303-925-3221
1BR $100, 1 Deluxe $124, 2BR $205
Amenities: Pool, hot tub

Welcome to the heart of Aspen. It's only a short two blocks to the ski lifts, but in the evenings you are in the center of the action. These cozy condos have some of the most cheerful interiors that you'll find. Blond wood with lots of red and green tartan fabrics—light, friendly, comfortable. All condos have full kitchens or kitchenettes. For families, this is a relatively inexpensive choice in Aspen. Consider the "one-bedroom deluxe" units where you get just about as much room as in the two-bedroom units. Snowflake provides good value for your money.

6 **TIPPLE INN**
747 S. Galena St., Aspen, CO 81611, 303-925-2260
Studio $165, 2BR $235
Amenities: Ski lift location. Nearby pool and hot tub

Right next to the Little Nell ski lift at the base of Aspen Mountain, the
Tipple Inn has a good location and an unassuming appearance. The condos
are studios, designed for a twosome. These units are an "add-on" to one of
Aspen's long-standing watering holes, the Tipple Inn.

WHERE TO STAY... Snowmass

6 **ASPENWOODS**
Snowmass, CO 81615, 303-923-2711
Studio $75, 1BR $115, 2BR $165
Amenities: ski-in/ski-out location

Located two levels above the Village Mall, this has convenient access to
the slopes. The attractive condos, which are a little on the small side, feature
good furniture and some have richly patterned wallpaper and royal blue carpet. Interior decor seems to vary according to the time the owner bought the
unit—some when thick carpeting on the walls was in vogue. Some of the
newer acquisitions have been updated with a more contemporary look. More
than elsewhere, you'll find a wide range of styles reflected in the interior
decor here. Some condos are very dark. Others are on the small side and
bunk beds preserve precious space. Each condo has a brick fireplace to
brighten the evening after skiing. The advantage to this resort is its central
location just above the Village Mall and ski-in/ski-out accessibility.

9 **CHAMONIX**
Wood Rd., Snowmass, CO 81615, 303-923-3232
Amenities: Pool, hot tub, game room, tennis courts

Located a quarter mile below Snowmass village with ski-in/ski-out convenience, these new condos are built in a French architectural style
featuring Mansard roofs. Chamonix offers some of the highest quality, most
attractive condos in Snowmass and they are luxuriously decorated with lots
of peach colors, off-white fabrics, and glass-top tables. You'll find the staff
at this resort provides some of the most helpful service in town. In short,
you'll be treated like royalty. Although this is one of Aspen's most exclusive resorts, you'll be pleased with the friendly social atmosphere around the
pool in the evenings. Or if you prefer, each condo has a private whirlpool for
relaxing after a hard day of skiing.

8 CRESTWOOD
400 Wood Rd., Snowmass, CO 81615, 800-356-5949
1BR $100, 2BR $220, 3BR $320
Amenities: Pool, hot tub, sauna, exercise room

Located at the base of Fanny Hill, a long walk below the main Village Mall, Crestwood is one of the largest condo complexes in Snowmass. Crestwood is a classic new condo building, with high quality and good service. For skiers there is ski-in/ski-out access. There's also a shuttle bus to Aspen town or Aspen Highlands and management will even pick up groceries for you. These condos have great views and some are fancifully decorated with carved Bavarian blond wood furniture and Austrian quilts with ruffles. The loft units are spectacular with two stories of glass and cathedral ceilings. Also, some of the condos have private saunas—a real plus. Crestwood is a good choice for that honeymoon getaway or for two couples looking for a first-class mountain home.

9 DEERBROOK
381 Ridge Rd., Snowmass, CO 81615, 800-543-0839
4BR $800–900
Amenities: Ski-in/ski-out access

Located on the slopes of Assay Hill at the base of Snowmass Village, these are some of the largest and most luxurious units in all of Aspen/Snowmass. With over 3000 square feet of living space, these four-bedroom townhouses feature two master suites. With sales prices of $1,000,000 or more, you can well imagine that no expense has been spared on the interior decor. Some have private hot tubs. Ski-in/ski-out accessibility and sweeping mountain views complete the picture.

9 ENCLAVE
Wood Rd., Snowmass, CO 81615, 303-923-3232
Amenities: Pool, hot tub

Fresh flowers in your condo! Located between Lift-6 and Lift-11 (the triple chair) at Snowmass' Elk Camp area, the Enclave combines ski-in/ski-out access with handsomely appointed furnishings. These condos have a sense of privacy because of the view from the living room. The top-floor units have vaulted ceilings and an extra sense of spaciousness. Designer decorated, some of these units have extraordinary views.

6 POKOLODI LODGE
25 Daly Ln., Snowmass, CO 81615, 800-666-4556, Suite $85–130
Amenities: Lap pool, hot tub, Mall location

With one-bedroom condos selling at $53,000, these are the most inexpensive units in Snowmass. Small on the inside, they have a big advantage—the location is next to the Snowmass Mall and the central pool. Not just a splash tub, this Olympic-length lap pool is a real asset. Recently redecorated, they are the perfect choice for those attending a conference at Snowmass. This one gets better and better each year. It, too, has ski-in/ski-out accessibility.

9   THE RIDGE
229 Faraway Rd., Snowmass, CO 81615, 800-222-7989
2BR $330–420, 3BR $410–560
Amenities: Outdoor heated pool, hot tubs

These luxurious condos are within walking distance of the slopes at Snowmass (one of the few selections without ski-in/ski-out access). Some of the newest units in the Snowmass area, they are superior in design, comfort, and decor. Best of all, there's a private sauna, steam room, and whirlpool tub area in each individual condo. The disadvantage of the location is offset by flashy amenities.

10   SNOWMASS CLUB VILLAS
High Line Rd., Snowmass, CO 81615, 800-525-6200
2BR $188–312, 3BR $188–328
Amenities: Golf, tennis, racquet ball, squash, health spa, pools, restaurant, pro shop

These club villas are the most luxurious resort in the Aspen area. Located in its own private valley on a golf course, it's two miles from the Snowmass ski lifts. The main lodge reminds you of Denver's Brown Palace with its mahogany paneled living room and cocktail lounge. The restaurant is on a glass enclosed terrace overlooking a pond and the 18th hole in the summer. The villas are townhouses or duplexes along the fairway, only a short walk from the main lodge. Within the units, you'll find handsome architecture with gabled roofs, oak doors, and tile floors. In some units, the central living area is on two levels. Luxurious, interior decorator furnishings feature style, fantasy, and good taste. There's a patio along the fairway for summertime, and a massive hearth for winter nights. The Snowmass Club has a full health club with indoor tennis courts, pools, massage, racquetball, and a pro shop. It is simply the best.

7   SNOWMASS INN (See Pokolodi Lodge)

9   WOODRUN V
Wood Rd., Snowmass, CO 81615, 303-923-5252
2BR $317–516, 3BR $469–730, 4BR $834–1250
Amenities: Hot tub, pool, sauna

These are among the newest and most luxurious townhouse condos in Snowmass. Off on a cul-de-sac, they enjoy ski-in/ski-out accessibility to the slopes as well as great management and a truly warm reception for guests. Woodrun V and its sister property Chamonix are in their own little world because they are slightly separated from the main part of Snowmass. The condos have designer-decorated interiors, and although there is a range of styles, all are of top quality. The large country kitchens have Jenn-Air grills for indoor barbecues. Each condo also has a lichen rock fireplace and, in the utility room, a private washer/dryer.

RENTAL RESOURCES

Alpine Property Management, 800-543-0839
Aspen Classic Properties 303-925-5759
Aspen Club, 303-920-2000
Aspen Resort Accommodations, 800-727-7369
Aspen Skiing Corp., 303-925-1200
Aspen/Snowmass Care, 800-759-3686
Aztec, 303-925-1441
Boomerang, 800-992-8852
Christiana, 303-925-3014
Coates, Reid & Waldron 303-925-1400, Extensive inventory.
Condominium Rental Management, 303-925-2260
Crestwood, 303-923-2450
Destination Resorts 303-923-2420
Dickerson & Whitaker Rentals 303-925-9080
Interwest Realty Management 303-925-2772
Lift One, 800-543-8001
Little Nell, 800-525-6200
McCartney Properties, 800-433-8465, Many luxury homes.
Mountain Queen, 303-925-6366
Peak Properties of Aspen, 303-920-2300
Prospector, 303-920-2030
Resort Management Company 303-923-4310
Ridge, 800-222-7989
Rocky Mountain Residential 303-925-2526
Shadowbrook Condos, 303-923-2300
Silvertree Hotel, 800-525-9402
Snowmass Central Reservations, 800-225-SNOW
Snowmass Club Villas, 303-923-5600
Snowmass Lodging, 800-365-0410
Stirling Homes Management, 800-642-4210
Stonebridge, 800-323-2577

Top of the Village, 800-525-4200

Village Property Management, 303-923-4350. A leading national
condo chain.

2. BEAVER CREEK / AVON

Beaver Creek and the town of Avon (which services the small noncommercial Beaver Creek resort) are 25 miles to the west of Vail along Interstate 70.
Often viewed as a part of Vail because it was developed by Vail Associates
as an offshoot of Vail's initial success, Beaver Creek today is emerging as a
resort with its own identity. Avon is just a raw little town whose primary
attraction is budget accommodations for those who want to ski in the Beaver
Creek area.

Beaver Creek is a world apart from Avon and distinct from Vail. Access
to the mountain is controlled, and there is a five-mile drive to the ski area
once you pass the security gate. If you are staying in a condo at Beaver
Creek, chances are you have ski-in/ski-out access directly on the mountain.
This gives the Beaver Creek guests a distinct advantage over those staying
in less expensive lodgings in the town of Avon. The control was designed to
limit access to the mountain by day-trippers from Denver who weren't staying in Beaver Creek and were driving in from the other resort areas. If you
are staying at Avon or driving over from Denver, you must take the bus to
get up to the ski area. Once at Beaver Creek, you will find a charming little
village with a square and condos flowing along the hillside.

In summertime, there is a wide range of vacation possibilities, and Avon
becomes more appealing with golf, hiking, and biking possibilities. The
town's new landmark is Bob. Bob is a bridge over the railroad tracks to the
main entrance of Beaver Creek. You can experience the music festival, play
golf, ride the gondola, fish for trout, hike in the Rockies, or go white-water
rafting on the Roaring Fork. The rafting companies will outfit you for a day
and teach you the skills of controlling your boat in turbulent waters. If
smoother sailing is your goal, less than an hour away is Lake Dillon with
25 miles of shoreline and marinas for sailboat rentals.

Transportation to Beaver Creek/Avon couldn't be easier. There are two
options. Fly to Denver and either rent a car or take the shuttle bus for the
two and one-half hour trip along Interstate 70. Or, in winter, you can fly to
Vail/Eagle airport, only nine miles away. Nonstop flights are available from
Chicago, Dallas, Los Angeles, New York, Las Vegas, and Phoenix. Beaver
Creek Village is designed so you won't need a car, but if you're staying at
Avon a car is strongly advised.

WHERE TO STAY

6 AVON CENTER
100 W. Beaver Creek Blvd., Avon, CO 81620, 303-949-6202
Amenities: Exercise room, hot tub

This nine-story highrise is a landmark in Avon because of its height. The condos enjoy great views of the valley because there is no other high-rise structure around. The condos are spacious and handsomely decorated with contemporary furniture and fabrics in light rose and aqua colors. Each unit has a small fireplace and lots of mirrors and picture windows to bring the view indoors. The shuttle bus up to Beaver Creek stops right in front. There's no swimming pool, but this resort has an exercise room and a hot tub that is the social center after skiing.

9 BEAVER CREEK LODGE CONDOS
25 Avondale Ln., Beaver Creek, CO 81620, 303-845-9800
3BR $225–475, 4BR $275–590
Amenities: Pool, restaurant, concierge

Right in the heart of Beaver Creek village, atop this all-suite hotel, you'll find some of the area's most elegant condos. These three and four-bedroom units are huge and are to be distinguished from the studio and one-bedroom suites on the lower floors. Inside, you'll find that these units have spectacular interior decor with wood paneling, oriental rugs and palatial bathrooms with oversized whirlpool tubs, large enough for two. With over $60,000 worth of interior decor in each unit, these are among the most elegant vacation condos you'll find anywhere. Downstairs, in the main lobby, the hotel operation offers a full service front desk with a concierge. Only a few of these units are available, but for a "blow the budget" holiday try this one.

5-6 BEAVER CREEK WEST
360 Benchmark Rd., Avon, CO 81620, 303-949-4840
1BR $79–209, 2BR $99–279, 3BR $119–349
Amenities: Pool, hot tub, tennis

Bargain accommodations are available in the town of Avon, just a half mile from the entrance to Beaver Creek Mountain. These are spacious condos in two four-story towers plus a cluster of townhouses. The townhouses are best with extra privacy and half-timbered gabled ceilings. The furniture is made of sturdy materials and each living room features a stove hearth fireplace. Outside there is a heated swimming pool, hot tub, and in the summer, two tennis courts. This is a good choice for active families or groups of young skiers.

8+ THE CENTENNIAL
1880 Offerson Rd., Beaver Creek, CO 81620
Amenities: Outdoor heated pool, hot tub

Located in the heart of Beaver Creek village and only steps from the high speed Centennial Express ski lift, the Centennial offers a ski-in location. Designed to be a local landmark offering luxurious accommodations, you'll be impressed by the interior decor. Decorators obviously were told "expense is no concern" and they have brought together some of the most imaginative combinations of fabrics and furniture to be found anywhere. Bright floral, oriental-type prints give the living room a rich feel. There's a fireplace in the living room and a gourmet kitchen. The fireplace is complimented by a bookcase and brass andirons. Spectacular is the word to describe the dining area with three gables to permit three arched windows. The four-story atrium lobby is on one side of the building; each condo has a balcony that opens onto the ski slope with magnificent mountain views. The Centennial is truly luxurious.

9+ THE CHARTER OF BEAVER CREEK
120 Offerson Rd., Beaver Creek, CO 81620, 303-949-6600
1BR $145–195, 2BR $220–350, 3BR $325–495
Amenities: Health club and spa, pool, restaurant

Luxury and convenience in an enchanted mountain setting, these French Provincial style condos are in a village cluster within walking distance of the Beaver Creek PGA Golf Club and the skiers' chair lift. Perfectly positioned and designed and operated to radiate a European ski village charm, your accommodations have all the luxury of the U.S. The lobby has a reception area and an elegant concierge desk off to the side. Trimmed in light wood, the feeling is at once casual and stylishly Bavarian. Inside, the condos have thoughtful room design for maximum comfort and privacy, including architectural recesses and Bavarian blond wood furniture. There are nice touches like a deacon's table with two candle-holders at the entrance to your condo and an Austrian letter-writing desk with pigeon holes. Best feature: the leaded glass balcony door. Is your home this elegant? Social life in the evenings revolves around either the lobby or the Spa and Health Club. The exercise room, weights, indoor lap pool, outdoor pool, and bubbling outdoor stone-decked hot tub as well as an in-house masseuse all help to knead away sore quadriceps and biceps.

6 CHRISTIE LODGE
0047 Beaver Creek Blvd., Avon, CO 81620, 800-551-4326
1BR $39–120
Amenities: Pool, hot tub

Right before you begin the two-mile drive up to the lifts at Beaver Creek Ski Resort, you will find the Christie Lodge. It occupies a great location. Although the units are very small, they can accommodate a surprising number of bodies. For example, the one-bedroom units each have a queen-sized bed, two bunk beds in the entrance way, and a fold-out sofa in the living room. To compensate for the small size, the condos have been dressed up with beautiful furniture and lots of mirrors. The kitchen is tiny, with a microwave, half-sized refrigerator and counter for dining. Good hospitality, service, and a concierge make your trip more enjoyable. The Christie Lodge offers an organized activities program for its guests and you have guest membership privileges at Vail's Cascade Club sports complex. The shuttle bus up to Beaver Creek stops right in front of Christie Lodge. This one gets better each time we visit, providing remarkably good value.

9   CORDILLERA
Cordillera Way, Edwards, CO 81632, 303-926-2200
1BR $225–495
Amenities: Spa with pools, saunas, exercise room, restaurant

Today's most talked about resort is in the Vail Valley west of Beaver Creek/Avon. Cordillera is a masterpiece condo/hotel offering European elegance and Rocky Mountain grandeur. Unlike so many resort communities, Vail has never had a truly grand lodge. Now it does, only Cordillera is so far from Vail that it's hard to say this is a Vail-area accommodation. The condos are absolutely spectacular. Designed by a Belgian architect, it makes a bold statement with stone and slate construction. Windows are angled to capture the best view of the Rockies. Inside, you'll find a cozy lounge with a carved wooden oak ceiling, which you would only hope to find in the Tyrolian Alps. The luxury at Cordillera is only matched by the venerable Broadmoor. The condos feature fireplaces, secluded lofts, and balconies. Distinguished from the hotel rooms, the larger ones have kitchenettes. But you'll probably want to enjoy the resort's five-star dining. Cordillera is brand new with many new condos and villas to be added around the main lodge in the next few years.

7+ CREEKSIDE
Village Rd., Beaver Creek, CO 81620
Amenities: Outdoor heated pool, steam rooms, saunas, hot tub

Just down from the main part of the village, overlooking the golf course as it flows down the mountain, you'll find the three-to-five-story Creekside condo buildings. Of different heights to coordinate with the slope of the mountain, Creekside offers superb lodgings without being pretentious—a rarity in Beaver Creek. These two- and three-bedroom condos are perfect for a family vacation as well as for groups of skiers. New and beautifully decorated, the unit we saw looked almost like a New England tap room with

Queen Anne antique reproduction furniture and muted plaids in the fabrics. Designed to appeal to the traditional, there's a friendly outdoor heated pool that is a special treat in winter.

9 GREYSTONE
Greystone Ct., Beaver Creek, CO 81620
Amenities: Pool, hot tub. Tennis and golf privileges

Greystone provides some of the most elegant townhouses in Colorado. Commanding a view at the highest point above the village, these huge three- and four-bedroom townhouses have massive stone and half timbered architecture. Multiple gables in the roof have been covered with slate, a rare touch in the 1990s. Inside, the rooms are oversized and accented by architectural flourishes. Some of Hollywood's most famous are your neighbors here. Each townhouse has its own private hot tub outside on a secluded patio. Perhaps the most prestigious address in a community where *ne plus ultra* is the standard.

8 KIVA
1350 Offerson Rd., Beaver Creek, CO 81620, 303-949-5474
Amenities: Pool, hot tub. Tennis and golf privileges

One of Beaver Creek's largest condo properties, these are just above the Hyatt and the center of the village. They have warm, spacious interiors with a moss rock fireplace as the centerpiece. The third-floor units have vaulted ceilings and a sloping roof line that creates a cozy feeling inside. These units vary from studios to four-bedroom condos and a system of "lock offs" will create the size suited to your group. Personal touches are important at Kiva and each guest receives a special gift basket on arrival. Ski-in/ski-out convenience is here too.

9 THE MEADOWS
Upper Offerson Rd., Beaver Creek, CO 81620
1BR $120–335, 2BR $140–390, 3BR $175–585
Amenities: Pool, hot tub

Called "Beaver Creek's most successful condominium development," these three-bedroom townhouses are unique. The location at the top of the village, just below Greystone, permits ski-in/ski-out accessibility. Unlike Beaver Creek's other condo properties, each unit has a separate entrance and garage. You'll find "river rock" fireplaces and imaginative interior decor in the living room. Each bedroom has its own private bath making this an ideal set up for two or three couples wishing to share a vacation home. Each cluster of townhouses has its own hot tub and there's a central pool. Guests at The Meadows have a shuttle bus on call if they don't have a car.

8   **PARK PLAZA**
46 Avondale Ln., Beaver Creek, CO 81620, 303-845-7700
2BR $175–525, 3BR $190–625
Amenities: Hot tub, pool, sauna

This is built like a grand hotel. Not as elaborately decorated as its neighbor Poste Montaigne, it is elegant nonetheless. The furnishings and ambience are a little more relaxed than at Poste Montaigne. Park Plaza has some of the most lavish suites anywhere. The living room with fireplace and the small library are filled with paintings and art objects. The library is larger than some bedrooms at other condo resorts. This extra room has a plug for your fax or laptop computer, so it can be an office away from the office. The two-bedroom-with-den model has two full master bedroom suites, each with its own hot tub large enough for four people. Could the environment be more luxurious? These condos, with over 2,000 square feet of living space are larger than average. Just off the lobby, there's a small pool and hot tub and the ceiling is two and one-half stories high. An antique "flying machine" is suspended from the ceiling.

8   **POSTE MONTAIGNE**
76 Avondale Ln., Beaver Creek, CO 81620, 303-845-7500
1BR $80–190, 2BR $110–320
Amenities: Hot tub, steam room, sauna

This resort advertises itself as the most expensive in the country because a Christmas week of timesharing has sold for $110,000. Poste Montaigne is like a European lodge; the suites are individual in both floor plans and decorations. The lobby walls are richly paneled with mahogany. The crystal chandeliers are from Venice and the floral arrangements are fabulous. Reportedly, a couple of movie stars own at Poste Montaigne. The only amenity is a hot tub/sauna area in the basement. There is no swimming pool. Condo interiors are romantically furnished; several beds have canopies or are "four-poster" models. All have "romantic fantasy" decor with imitation Laura Ashley prints and some antique furniture. The hotel rooms have no kitchens; only a hot plate and microwave.

7   **RIDGEPOINT**
85 Willis Pl., Avon, CO 81620, 303-949-7150
Amenities: Outdoor pool (summer only) exercise room, tennis

Not in the village of Beaver Creek, these townhouse condos overlook the golf course at the base of the mountain. You have the convenience of being "inside Beaver Creek" without the hassle of being in the village. It's definitely or those who value privacy. In sharp contrast to so many other Beaver Creek properties, these have a fanciful "western-frontier" look with stone fireplaces and raw wood paneling throughout and comfortable skierized furniture. Families or those who want to be alone will appreciate the look of Ridgepoint.

9 ST. JAMES PLACE
Avondale Ln., Beaver Creek, CO 81620, 303-845-7900
Amenities: Indoor pool, hot tub, sauna, steam room, fitness center

Right next to the Hyatt shopping plaza and the village hall, which is the hub of activity, this impressive six-story building has an imposing circular drive entrance. Step inside to a special blend of Colorado hospitality and European elegance. The one-, two-, and three-bedroom condos are huge. Each bathroom is almost the size of many condo living rooms in other communities. Each has a separate shower and a tiled step-up whirlpool bath. Beautifully decorated in Bavarian blond wood furniture and cute Alpine prints, this is better than what you would find in most European inns. Televisions and VTPs have been hidden in carved armoires or behind recesses in the bedroom wall. The top floor units, which are two-story, two and three-bedroom condos, are spectacular with cathedral ceilings and two stories of glass. It has great views, great location and best of all is the management. Quietly efficient, they are always ready to take care of any special request. This is what a ski resort should be.

8 THE SEASONS
Arrowhead Resort, 600 Sawatch Dr., Edwards, CO
Amenities: Golf, pool, tennis

Brand new, these townhouse condos may seem remote this year. They are fifteen minutes away from Beaver Creek in the new Arrowhead ski and golf area. Located at the entrance to Arrowhead with its pond and waterfall, most of the units front the new Jack Nicklaus golf course. Designed for today's pioneers, you'll find elegant accommodations at a reasonable price. Don't expect this value to last. Ten years from now, Arrowhead just might compete with Beaver Creek as the place to be.

7 STRAWBERRY PARK
1280 Village Rd., Beaver Creek, CO 81620
Amenities: Pool, hot tub. Tennis and golf privileges

Located above Beaver Creek village, these condos have easy access to the slopes because they are at the base of ski lift #12. Built in the style of a European hunting lodge, the condos in this five-story building are distinctive and superior. The moss rock fireplaces are imposing. Woodwork throughout the units makes them warm and inviting. Furnished in western or Colorado Mountain style, you'll find that accents such as armoires and stereos make these distinctive.

6   **SUNRIDGE**
110 E. Beaver Creek Blvd., Avon, CO 81620
Amenities: None. Tennis nearby

Located along the Eagle River, these three-bedroom condos are popular as residences as well as vacation retreats. Natural cedar siding both inside and out gives them a rustic look. Reasonable rates and attractive decor makes these condos a sensible alternative to the expensive lodgings in Beaver Creek village.

7   **SUNRIVER**
39377 U.S. Hwy & Rt. 24, Avon, CO 81620, 303-949-1000
1BR $69–119, 2BR $79–129
Amenities: Pool, hot tub

Located about a half mile outside the town of Avon, these rustic condos offer a comfortable alternative to the expensive accommodations at Beaver Creek. Designed for comfortable family living, you'll find handsome interior decor and a warm wood-burning fireplace. Along the Eagle River, the air is fragrant with pines in spring and summer. Sunriver is a sensible value.

RENTAL RESOURCES...Beaver Creek (See also Vail)
Brandess Cadmus, 303-476-1450
Slifer, Smith & Frampton, 303-476-2421
Vail Associates Rentals, 303-949-5750
Vail Realty & Rental Management, 303-476-880

3. BRECKENRIDGE

Rugged individualism is the spirit that built this area. Breckenridge is a Victorian mining town founded in 1859 and named after Vice President, John Breckinridge. Because of the Vice President's sympathies to the southern cause, in 1861 the spelling of the name was changed to Breckenridge. Gold can still be panned from the Blue River and many of the ornate Victorian homes have been preserved. New construction is encouraged to have a Victorian exterior also. The skiing is great with a choice of three peaks, and Breckenridge somehow has succeeded in developing a reputation as both North America's premier "family ski resort" and the top destination for singles.

The area's phenomenal success can be attributed to both the Chamber of Commerce and to the Ski Corporation. Over the past ten years, the infrastructure has been continuously improved and upgraded. Ski lift lines are now shorter than they were, even though the number of visitors has increased by 50%. This is due to technological improvements in the ski lifts, such as high speed quad chairs and gondolas. Additionally, new areas have been added for all levels of skiers and even beginners, after a few days, are able to ski from one area to another. The ski mountains, Peaks 8, 9, and 10, are part of an interconnect system, which now gives Breckenridge the second largest area of ski terrain in the U.S.

Breckenridge is further blessed with a Victorian mining town where the cute cabins have been renovated into an area of shops, restaurants, and million dollar bungalows. Nonskiers have plenty to do during the day. Also, there is a sports center for swimming and ice skating, and a cross-country ski section.

Summer in Breckenridge is beautiful. The days are warm and free of humidity and the evenings are crisp and cool. The surrounding Arapaho National Forest provides 200 miles of wilderness for hiking, mountain biking, fishing, and camping. The Colorado, Arkansas, and Blue Rivers are nearby playgrounds for white-water rafters and kayakers. Guided jeep tours and horseback rides to the abandoned mining communities and ghost towns are available daily. The 40-mile paved bike path from Breckenridge to Vail is perhaps the most exciting bike trail in the U.S.

Breckenridge has several distinct neighborhoods that you should be aware of as location may influence your selection of a vacation home. The old mining town is the core, and today there is an array of shops and restaurants along Main Street. Most of the miner's town is east of Main Street in a 25-square-block area of cute one- and two-story "shacks" that have been renovated into charming homes. You'll find some condos tucked away in this neighborhood. The ski lifts for Peaks 8, 9, and 10 are west of Main Street. Over 20 condos have been built in this area over the past 15 years because the Four O'Clock ski run empties out here. That means that guests staying at Sundowner, Sawmill Creek, Double Eagle, and Blazing Saddles can ski home at the end of the day and not bother with a shuttle bus. Almost none have on-site management, so writing or calling the resort direct is not an effective way to plan a vacation. For Breckenridge, it is best to shop the Rental Resources companies.

A third major area of condo development is around the village plaza. Two mega resorts—The Village and Beaver Run are located in this area as well as half a dozen smaller condo developments, such as The Cedars, Trail's End, and Der Steirmark. The Quicksilver quad chair lift is here as well as the Peak 9 gondola. This area is new, modern, and cute with an array of cafes and sports shops.

Farther to the south, there is the Lower Four Seasons area that is a sea of condos along two roads, Columbine and Broken Lance. The advantage to this area is a community sports center with a covered outdoor heated pool, hot tubs, saunas, and a clubhouse. Guests only at condos located on either of the two streets may use these community recreational facilities.

Farther south around the Falcon lift up to Peak 10, there's another area of condo development where you'll find the luxurious Sunrise Ridge townhouses. Driving up into the hills in the southerly direction you'll find the

Boreass Pass area. Formerly an area of gold mines, you can still see the mine shafts and the old mill. These condos, like Gold Point, are remote and you'll need a car if you stay up there. In an area of fishing cabins along the Blue River six miles south of town, you'll find Blue River condos. These are best in the summer for those who want to enjoy Colorado's outdoor sports.

Finally, due west of town, 1000 feet up a winding mountain road, you'll come to the Peak 8 Village. This is a community of condos in a wooded environment. Great for skiers, many of these condos offer ski-in/ski-out access, although the mountain road up to this area can be treacherous in a snowstorm. Also, this location is inconvenient for nonskiers or those who plan to spend time in the village each evening.

Transportation to Breckenridge couldn't be easier. It's an hour due west of the Denver airport by interstate highway. Only the last nine miles is a secondary road. There are shuttle vans commuting between Denver and Breckenridge every half hour, so if you're staying in town or within walking distance of the lifts you really won't need a car. Even the outlying areas are connected by the town's frequent and efficient local bus service. Breckenridge as a community has for years done everything right and the success is self evident.

WHERE TO STAY

8 **AMERIND**
296 Broken Lance Ln., Breckenridge, CO 80424 (no mail)
3BR $210–425
Amenities: Hot tub, sauna

Located on the south end of town in The Columbine/Broken Lance area of condos, it's a short five minute walk from the Amerind to the heart of town. The Peak 9 gondola terminal is within walking distance for the hearty; other skiers may prefer the shuttle bus. These are among the most attractive townhouses in Breckenridge, being two and one-half stories high and surrounded by fir trees. Each has a large living room with a fireplace, a full kitchen, a washer/dryer, and a whirlpool in the master bath. A few have private saunas. Ask them to specify which one you'll get. Well furnished, you'll enjoy great views of the mountains. An excellent choice for families or groups of skiers who want a home away from home.

6 **THE ATRIUM**
530 French St., Breckenridge, CO 80424 (no mail), 2BR $160–240
Amenities: Hot tub

This is located on the southeast side of town, just above the Victorian miner's cabins that are now million dollar homes. The Atrium condos are in a three-story building overlooking Carter Park. Designed with extra touches to create a neo-Victorian effect, you'll find a beveled-glass entry way and stained glass pieces in the windows. Most have a "themed" interior decor featuring western or the Colorado country look with four poster beds and ruffles. The master bath has a whirlpool. More than just lodgings, there's a little fantasy here.

7   BASE NINE
800 Broken Lance, Breckenridge, CO 80424 (no mail)
2BR $150–240
Amenities: Sauna

Located in the Columbine/Broken Lance area of condominium development, these units have an unobstructed forest view, yet you are within five minutes of the Peak 9 gondola and the village plaza. Built in townhouse style, they were designed to get lots of sunlight. The living room with its vaulted ceiling is bright and cheerful. The master bedroom is extra large and designed to be "locked off" and rented as a studio if so desired. The pleasant decor in these two-bedroom units makes it nice for families or groups.

8+   BEAVER RUN RESORT
620 Village Rd., Breckenridge, CO 80424, 303-453-6000
1BR $453–6000
Amenities: Pools, hot tubs, tennis, miniature golf, restaurants

One of the most popular choices in Breckenridge, this is an eight-story condo-hotel where most of the units are studio rooms or suites with kitchenettes. Larger units are created by opening a door to adjacent rooms. The studio and one-bedroom units are a little bit small. Many of these condos have a whirlpool large enough for two or three, surrounded by a tile bench, plants, and mirrors. Furniture is stylish and sharp. What makes Beaver Run special? In many ways it's the social center for Breckenridge with lots of hospitality and lots of activity. It's great for active vacationers who ski all day and still have the energy to dance all night—and then to relax. Many of the condos have a private hot tub and a VTP.

4   BLAZING SADDLES
200 Washington, Breckenridge, CO 80424 (no mail)
Studio $80–125
Amenities: None

Located along the Four O'Clock ski run overlooking Victorian Breckenridge, Blazing Saddles captures the spirit of funky Breckenridge. The units are all either studio or one-bedroom units in a three-story building. It is designed to appeal to the huge "singles" market in Breckenridge. Spacious units, some are carefully decorated for a fun environment. Many have VTPs. Blazing Saddles is located at the heart of the town's nightlife.

3   BLUE RIVER CONDOS
575 Highway 9, Breckenridge, CO 80424, 303-453-2260
1BR $50–95, 2BR $79–125
Amenities: Hot tub, fishing stream

Located five miles south of town along the Blue River in an area of rustic fishing cabins, you'll find Blue River condos. You have to wonder why anyone built these three-story buildings in the middle of nowhere. Fishing in the spring, summer, or fall is excellent in this area. Otherwise, the location is inconvenient for skiers in winter or shoppers in summer. Many units have tired interior decor and carpeting in the hall needs replacement. Do you really want to stay here?

9   THE CEDARS
505 Village Rd., Breckenridge, CO 80424 (no mail)
2BR $220–450
Amenities: Pool, hot tub, sauna

Next to the Quicksilver high-speed chair lift, these are among the best townhouses to be found in Breckenridge. Spacious, with vaulted ceilings to capture the most of the mountain view from the living room, you'll want to spend your vacation right here at home. The Victorian part of Breckenridge is five minutes away, but this location is close to the village plaza with its ski shops and restaurants. Most townhouses have their own private hot tubs where you can soak in the warm waters while looking out on the mountain. Most have been decorated by interior designers. The Cedars is one of Breckenridge's best.

9   CHIMNEY RIDGE
519 Primrose, Breckenridge, CO 80424 (no mail)
Amenities: Pool, hot tub

Close to town with incredible views, these are some of the most luxurious condos in Breckenridge. The location is across the street from the quad chair lift. They have beautiful interior decorator furnishings in contemporary, almost high-tech style. Chimney Ridge has a wide array of amenities for après ski. The pool becomes a social center in the evenings.

6   CIMARRON
405 Park Ave., Breckenridge, CO 80424
Amenities: Pool, hot tub, sauna

These new condos are just a short hop from the village plaza and an easy five-minute walk from the Peak 9 gondola. In the evenings you can ski home along the Four O'Clock run. Although dark on the outside, inside you'll find modern units with an efficient floor plan. Contemporary decor surrounds the fireplace in the living room. We saw one decorated in the Santa Fe style with art pieces from New Mexico. Although the exterior is foreboding, you can't tell a book by its cover.

7-8 CLAIMJUMPER
877 Airport Rd., Breckenridge, CO 80424
Amenities: Pool, hot tub

You will need a car as the Claimjumper is a quarter of a mile outside of town. Located near the new recreation center, it's convenient for families who still have the energy to swim or ice skate in the evenings. These two-story townhouses have views of Baldy and some glimpse the lights of Breckenridge in the evenings. Each master bedroom has its own fireplace. Some of these condos have private saunas. Generally, these spacious units have superior interior decor. The one we saw was decorated in a southwest Native American theme with Navajo rugs, some lodge pole furniture pieces, and good art reproductions on the wall. Claimjumper offers a very inviting environment for your vacation at Breckenridge.

5 COLUMBINE
700 Columbine, Breckenridge, CO 80424, 2BR $160–320
Amenities: Pool,hot tub

This is a three-story condo building in the Columbine/Broken Lance section of town. Although the location has advantages and some have been dressed up with southwestern decor, these units were poorly built and you can hear your neighbors. It is comfortable, but rentals here should be a bargain.

7 DER STEIRMARK
600 Village Rd., Breckenridge, CO 80424, 303-453-1939
Amenities: Hot tubs

Centrally located, you can walk everywhere from one of the most convenient sites in town. The Peak 9 gondola, the Quicksilver lift, the village plaza, and the Victorian town are each one block away from Der Steirmark. These boxy three-story buildings are unpretentious from the street, but they have elevators for those in the upper units. Some have cute "country Colorado" decor. Others are decorated with durable "skierized" furniture. Each cluster of condos shares a hot tub. Der Steirmark is good for families and friends.

7 DOUBLE EAGLE
500 Four O'Clock Rd., Breckenridge, CO 80424 (no mail)
3BR $145–350
Amenities:Pool, hot tub

Right on the shuttle route in the mornings, you can ski home in the evenings. This three-story building has an enviable location and you are only minutes away from the village plaza or Victorian old town. Well maintained, the condo we saw had just been redecorated in styles reflecting the southwestern desert—potted cactuses everywhere. It is a friendly place with an active pool in the evenings.

8   EAGLE RIDGE TOWNHOUSES
346 Broken Lance, Breckenridge, CO 80424 (no mail)
Amenities: None

These are luxurious two and two and one-half story townhouses located in the Columbine/Broken Lance area of condominiums. Next door to Amerind, they share the same wooded environment. Here you are close to town and the lifts, yet also have the Colorado mountain feeling. These spacious townhouses have an extra recreation room/den for families or socializing. We saw one with a billiard table. Each has its own private hot tub where you can listen to the rushing Blue River nearby.

4   FOUR O'CLOCK LODGE
550 Four O'Clock Rd., Breckenridge, CO 80424, 1BR $140–250
Amenities:Pool, hot tub, sauna

These studio and one-bedroom condos have a convenient location on the Four O'Clock ski run at the end of the day. Then for the evening Victorian Breckenridge just two blocks down the hill. With raw wood exteriors and comfortable interiors it is popular with singles who know that Breckenridge is the place to be.

4   GOLD CAMP II
1173 Ski Hill Rd., Breckenridge, CO 80424
1BR $95–170, 2BR $120–210
Amenities: Hot tub, sauna

Located a mile above town in a village on the side of Peak 8, Gold Camp II has a special flavor because of its remote location. Serious skiers are the ones who stay up here in the winter because of the ski-in accessibility. Here you are in a forest in the evenings with no stores or restaurants in sight. There are six other condo developments up here so a sense of camaraderie develops. It's said that the evenings are a lot more fun up here than down in the bars and restaurants of town. These modest condos are great for groups of young skiers or active families. Although nothing fancy, you're surrounded by the beauty of Mother Nature.

4   GOLD POINT
185 Fuller Place, Breckenridge, CO 80424, 303-453-1910
Amenities: Hot tubs

Located in the hills outside of town, in the Boreass Pass section, this was once an area of gold mines. You can still see the entrances to mine shafts along the hills and there's a mill down below. Gold Point is an unusual condo development. Designed to be a luxury condominium, it had bad market timing. Although beautifully designed with inspired architecture, the interior decor is substandard and the comfortable resort ambiance is somehow lacking. Many units have their own private hot tubs. These three-bedroom condos offer a lot of space and amenities at a low price.

3   INNER CIRCLE
820 Kinnikini, Breckenridge, CO 80424 (no mail), 1BR $95–170
Amenities: Pool, hot tub, sauna

These one bedroom units are brand new and designed for singles or small families. It is a young person's place with a friendly pool area.

6   LANCES WEST
835 Broken Lance, Breckenridge, CO 80424 (no mail)
Amenities: Pool, hot tub

Located in the Lower Four Seasons area of condos, these spacious condos are fairly new. In a two-story building, the units have bright, cheerful interior decor. There's always lots of young people around the pool and hot tub in the evening.

6   THE LOFT
705 Snowberry, Breckenridge, CO 80424 (no mail)
Amenities: Pool, hut tub, sauna

These two-bedroom condos were designed so that one bedroom can be locked off and rented as a studio. Consequently, there's a small refrigerator and coffee maker in the master bedroom as well as a full kitchen. Located on the northern edge of the Four Seasons area, the main part of Breckenridge and the Peak 9 gondola are only steps away.

4   LONGBRANCH
107 Harris St., Breckenridge, CO 80424 (no mail)
Amenities: Pool, hot tub, sauna

Located in the Victorian town section of Breckenridge, Longbranch is close to the shops and restaurants. The condos on the third floor of this building have cathedral ceilings and lofts that can be used as an extra bedroom. Half of these units are occupied by Breckenridge residents, and the other half are occupied by vacationers. There's an interesting mix around the pool in the evening and there's a good chance that you'll pick up some insider tips on where to ski.

6   MILL RUN
1416 Broken Lance, Breckenridge, CO 80424 (no mail)
Amenities: None

A cluster of three-bedroom townhouses, these are located in the Lower Four Seasons area close to town and the Peak 9 gondola. The Mill Run condos face the forest and they offer peace and seclusion in this area of crowded condos. The size of these condos also offers an unexpected spaciousness. These units offer an excellent value considering the size, location, and price.

4   MINER'S CANDLE
805 Broken Lance, Breckenridge, CO 80424 (no mail)
Amenities: Pool, hot tub

These one- and two-bedroom condos are simple and cozy. The all-cedar interior decor provides a rustic, Colorado-mountain feeling. These are for young people as the activity here can get a little noisy. Bargain prices prevail.

4   MOTHER LODE
800 Columbine, Breckenridge, CO 80424 (no mail)
2BR $190–340
Amenities: Pool, hot tub, sauna

Located in the Lower Four Seasons area, these condos have easy access to the main part of town and the Peak 9 gondola. These condos are cute with great wood beamed ceilings and brick fireplaces. Some of these studio, one and two-bedroom condos have been enhanced with stereo systems and VTPs. These are good for groups of young skiers or families. Many Breckenridge residents live here and you'll quickly learn about the area.

6   PARK PLACE
325 Four O'Clock Rd., Breckenridge, CO 80424, 303-453-2262
2BR $160–250
Amenities: Pool, hot tubs

These units were built within the last ten years along the Four O'Clock ski run so you can ski-in, each evening. A three-story building, the units on the top floor are superior because of the lofts, cathedral ceilings, and the views out over the trees. Attractive interior decor show the owner's personal taste. The contemporary furniture is accented by ski posters or mementos from some hometown back East. Well maintained, they provide a good value considering the location.

4   **PEAK 8 VILLAGE**
1100 Ski Hill Rd., Breckenridge, CO 80424
Amenities: Sauna

A short drive from town at the Peak 8 lift area, these condos are in their own little world. At night the restaurants and activities are a mile away down the hill. The location is great for skiers because you're only one quarter of a mile from the Peak 8 lifts. Here residents make their own parties in the evening. These one- and two-bedroom condos have casual furnishings and many have treasures from the attic. Low rental rates and lots of space make these units a bargain for vacationers on a budget and great for those who plan to stay home in the evening.

6   **POWDER RIDGE**
500 French St., Breckenridge, CO 80424, 2BR $140–190
Amenities: Pool, hot tub, sauna

Located across from Carter Park on the fringe of the Victorian old town, these condos are some distance from the ski lifts. This is a quiet location on the edge of the national forest along the side of a hill. Attractive units, the best are those on the third floor with the lofts and the vaulted ceiling in the living room. It offers solid value for those who want a peaceful environment only minutes from the activity of town and the village plaza.

7-8   **POWDERHORN**
745 Columbine, Breckenridge, CO 80424 (no mail)
2BR $160–250
Amenities: Pool, hot tub, sauna

This three-story building has one of the best locations in the Lower Four Seasons area. Located on the river, this is convenient to the village plaza and right next to the Quicksilver lift. Some have been beautifully decorated. We saw one in forest green, which with the plants, brought the outside indoors. On a sunny day in winter, this is a pleasure to the senses. Although it's hard to draw distinctions among the sea of condos in this area, these are slightly superior and it is evident that the owners are trying to make them even better. Powderhorn is good bet for families or those seeking extra quality for the money.

5   **RIVER MOUNTAIN LODGE**
100 Park Ave., Breckenridge, CO 80424, 303-453-4711
Amenities: Hot tub, exercise room, restaurant, bar

Near the bottom of the mountain, you can ski home along the Four O'Clock run and walk the last block to River Mountain Lodge. This complex offers more hotel-style services than other condos in the area and (at last check) Continental breakfast in the lobby each morning. The one-bed-room condos are functional with cozy fireplaces and small kitchenettes. Interior decor is standardized with fairly new contemporary furniture. Although individually owned, these are a cross between the personalized nature of a condo and the homogenized standard of a hotel. The shuttle bus stops here, and Victorian Breckenridge is only a block away. The Fireside Lounge, with its wood paneling and antique decor, is a popular restaurant in the evenings.

7   SAWMILL CREEK
      105 Park St., Breckenridge, CO 80424, 303-453-2222
      Amenities: Sauna, hot tub

This location offers the best of both worlds. Located at the base of the Four O'Clock ski run, Sawmill Creek gives you the luxury of skiing home to your condominium at the end of the day. But you start your skiing at the lifts at the base of Peak #9, located just two blocks away. Main Street is only two blocks from the complex. The condominiums are actually suites in a four-story structure. Each condo has a fireplace as well as a fully equipped kitchen. The units have been decorated for comfortable, casual living.

6   SKI HILL
      250 Ski Hill, Breckenridge, CO 80424, 303-453-2262
      2BR $160–300
      Amenities: Pool, hot tub, sauna

This location allows skiers to ski home in the evening. Here you are on the edge of the mountain, just above Victorian Breckenridge. The shops and restaurants are less than five-minutes away for walkers. In the morning, the shuttle bus to the lifts stops right in front. Ski Hill has a new swimming pool, plus a hot tub and a sauna for those who want to relax in the evening. The condos are generally well furnished with contemporary decor. Some have VTPs or you can just sit by a crackling fire. Ski Hill is convenient, practical, and reasonably priced.

6   SUNDOWNER I AND II
      465 Four O'Clock Rd., Breckenridge, CO 80424, 1BR $110–175
      Amenities: Hot tub, pool

Located at the bottom of the Four O'Clock ski run, this is convenient for skiers. It's also only three blocks away from the shops and restaurants of Victorian Breckenridge. These condos comprise one of the largest condo complexes in Breckenridge. At first glance, it's a collection of two- and-three story boxy buildings with a changing roof line. Sundowner I condos are about ten-years-old, spacious, and with fireplaces. On the other side of the driveway are the newer, more stylish units. On-site pool and hot tub make this choice in Breckenridge.

9 SUNRISE RIDGE
437 White Cloud, Breckenridge, CO 80424, 3BR $300–400
Amenities: None

On the southwestern edge of town, the Sunrise Ridge townhouses enjoy an enviable position right next to the Peak 10 quad chair lift. It has true ski-in/ski-out accessibility. This is a quiet area that is a little bit hard to find. You'll want to drive into town in the evenings, rather than walk. These new units are some of the best in Breckenridge. They have spectacular views of all three Peaks—8, 9, and 10. Spacious and with neat little touches like half-circle windows, these are beautifully decorated. We saw one with over $60,000 worth of new decor to make this the ultimate ski condo. Each unit has a private hot tub and an individual sauna. Check before you rent, these may be the best units in Breckenridge.

7 TANNENBAUM
815 S. Columbine Rd., Breckenridge, CO 80424, 303-453-6380
Amenities: Pool, hot tub

Some of the oldest condos in Breckenridge, these 20-year-old units have an excellent location. Located on the Blue River, on the edge of the Columbine/Broken Lance community of condos, you can hear the rushing river most of the year. Well landscaped, you are surrounded by towering trees that are a buffer between Tannenbaum and all the activity of Breckenridge. The Peak 9 gondola terminal is only a stone's throw away as is the village plaza with its ski shops and restaurants. Victorian Breckenridge is a healthy five-minute walk away. Because they are older, these units are among the most spacious in town. The disadvantage is that the buildings are starting to show their age. The Tannenbaum has its own reputation and attracts a fun-loving clientele year after year. In a town of condos, this one stands out.

7 TRAIL'S END
455 Village Rd., Breckenridge, CO 80424
1BR $130–195, 2BR $190–310
Amenities: Pool, hot tub, sauna

These enjoy a great location in the village plaza area with true ski-in/ski-out accessibility. You are steps away from the Quicksilver Peak 9 quad lift. These one- and two-bedroom condos are slightly larger than most and the sunny balcony is right above the village plaza. For families where one skis and the other stays home, this is one of the best choices in the area because there are so many other things to do here. Trail's End offers great value, in a prime setting.

6   TYRA SUMMITT
644 Four O'Clock Rd., Breckenridge, CO 80424
Studio $90–150, 1BR $105–170, 2BR $150–220
Amenities: Pool, hot tub

Located mid-mountain on the Four O'Clock ski run, you can ski home at
the end of the day. This casual, rustic condo complex enjoys a quiet, serene
location about a mile above town near the Peak 8. Not in the center of town
and not on a strip, the three-story structures offer spacious accommodations.
Lots of windows bring the mountain view inside. They all have quality contemporary furniture and full kitchens. Each condo has a fireplace where you
can roast marshmallows on those dark winter nights.

8   VICTORIAN QUARTERS
310 French St., Breckenridge, CO 80424
Amenities: None

These are among the area's most attractive condos because of the neo-
Victorian architecture with high gables, gingerbread, beveled glass, and
stained glass inserts in some of the windows. Located in the miner's town,
you are steps away from the shops and restaurants. You'll need to take a
shuttle bus to the ski lifts. Inside, interior decor carries through the Victorian
theme with antique reproductions mixed with comfortable contemporary
pieces. Each master bath has a whirlpool and most of these three-bedroom
townhouses have VTPs. You'll find good lodgings as well as a little fantasy.

9+   THE VILLAGE RESORT
535 S. Park, Breckenridge, CO 80424, 303-453-2000
2BR $200–320
Amenities: Health spa, exercise room, hot tubs, saunas,
restaurants, shopping arcade, ice skating

Located at the south end of main street next to the Quicksilver chair lift,
the Village is a self-contained community in Breckenridge's best location.
You'll find this resort right away because its bell tower is one of
Breckenridge's distinctive features. There are 96 condos in buildings named
Plaza I, II, and III. The condos are luxuriously furnished with full kitchens
and fireplaces. The decor is so well done you'll feel like you are in a private
home. The sunny southwest decks wrap around the living room. There's a
full time social director and a summer activities program for children. The
Village takes pride in its conference center and all of the amenities that
attract small conventions.

7   THE WEDGEWOOD
534 Four O'Clock Rd., Breckenridge, CO 80424, 303-453-1800
Amenities: Sauna, exercise room, hot tub

The Wedgewood condos are at the end of the Four O'Clock ski run and are easily spotted because of the blue trim on these townhouse/condo buildings. Inside, the units are modern and they have full kitchens and fireplaces. Some have been decorated in a Victorian style that makes these condos preferable. Many of the condos are in the five-story lodge building with corridors and inside access to the bubbling hot tub pool. Others are townhouses with separate entrances and give a greater sense of privacy. Guests have membership privileges at the North Village Swim and Health Club only a couple of blocks away.

RENTAL RESOURCES
Peak Property Management, 303-453-1723
Alpenrose Condos, 303-453-2288
Alpine Meadows Management, 303-453-1226
Alpine Valley Rentals, 303-453-1762
Asset Management, 303-453-6480
Beaver Run Real Estate, 303-453-1450
Boreass Pass Realty, 303-453-6131
Breckenridge Accommodations, 303-453-9140
Breckenridge Lodging, 303-453-2160
Breckenridge Resort Condos, 303-453-2222
Colorado High Country Rentals, 303-453-1411
Colorado Condo Connection, 804-999-SSKI
Colorado Mountain Lodging, 303-453-2856
Columbine Lodging, 303-453-2856
Executive Resort Rentals, 303-453-4422
Four Seasons Lodging, 303-453-1403
French Ridge, 303-453-1226
Good Earth Management, 303-453-2136
Horizons Unlimited, 303-453-1119
Manor Management, 303-453-6906
Mark IX, 303-453-1724
Panda Bears Management, 303-453-9140
Park Meadows, 303-453-2414
Pine Ridge Rentals, 303-453-6946
Ski Country Resorts Management, 303-453-4474
The Managers, 303-668-3174
Tonti Property Management, 303-453-1800
White Cloud Lodging, 303-453-1018
AMR-Affordable Mountain Rentals, 303-453-0833

4. COPPER MOUNTAIN

Copper Mountain is a world unto itself. Just off I-70, it is just 75 miles from Denver. Of all the Colorado ski resorts you'll be least likely to use chains for driving in the snow when you go to Copper Mountain. Recently voted "number one" in trail and slope design, this is a skiers' mountain whether you are a beginner or a back-bowl expert. There's a village at the base and more than 500 condominiums around the village and at the bottom of the ski trails. It's new, modern, and stylishly contemporary. At the village center there are a number of French, German, Italian, and Mexican restaurants as well as the requisite bars and discos. Copper Mountain has achieved popularity as a family resort as well as a place where singles will find a casual, comfortable atmosphere to relax and play. For that reason, Copper draws a large number of groups of youthful skiers from urban centers. Everything is within walking distance and, although there are streets, this is primarily a village for pedestrians and you won't need a car.

Copper Mountain has a unique geographic design that provides for a natural separation of ski trails. You'll find mild, rolling terrain on the western side and challenging "black diamond" runs on the eastern side. With over 255 inches of snow per year, Copper enjoys some of the best ski conditions in Colorado. Copper is justifiably proud of its ski school, which is world-class. "The Ranch" is where children from ages 4 to 12 learn to ski with instruction from some of the best in Colorado. For nonskiers there is a wide selection of activities including sleigh rides and ice skating.

Accommodations at Copper are mostly in condominiums and few have front-office arrangements. For booking information you'll need to use the Rental Resources section where we have also listed the representative prices. The rental companies here are quite competitive and you should be able to negotiate a deep discount after three or four calls.

Condo rentals in Copper Mountain are handled differently from other resorts. Here, there are several rental management companies and they draw no distinctions between the various condo properties. Rental rates are based strictly on the number of bedrooms so, if you want to stay clear of the expert lifts or believe that one resort is more appealing, you must negotiate to be sure you get the place in the building where you want to be. For Copper Mountain resorts, the quoted rental rates are:

Studio	$105–150
1BR	$135–250
2BR	$180–340
3BR	$250–390

Some vacationers prefer Copper in summer. With few visitors, it's easy to get a tee time or walk on to the tennis courts. The Racquet and Athletic Club is always a popular place with aerobic and ski-ercize classes, weight training, and therapeutic massages. Use of the club is complimentary to guests through some of the condo rental programs. Other visitors, perhaps even staying in the condo next door, will have to pay a small fee. It all depends upon the current policy of each rental agency.

WHERE TO STAY

5 ANACONDA
125 Wheeler Pl., Copper Mountain, CO 80443
Amenities: Hot tub, sauna

The Anaconda condos are in a red barn-like structure near the sports center, a short walk from the main village. If your skiing expertise is a consideration, Anaconda is by the B lift, which accesses the advanced intermediate and expert skiing. Here you are away from the commotion of the ski school and the beginner activities. If this will be your first ski vacation, pick another choice. Come summer, these become popular with golfers. These units are older than most at Copper, but they are spacious and have two-bedrooms, one on each side of the living room. Interior decor generally is cheerful and adequate, but don't expect anything fancy. This is an athlete's choice for golf or skiing.

8 BEELER PLACE
105 Beeler Pl., Copper Mountain, CO 80443
Amenities: Hot tub

These three-bedroom townhouses are surrounded by the woods in the East Village. A true home away from home, these four-level condos are among the most luxurious accommodations in the Copper Mountain area. Great for groups—most units have their own hot tub on the solarium porch, which is truly a sensational touch. Although these are some of the best units in the area, they are five-minutes walking distance from the ski lifts.

6 COPPER JUNCTION
214–230 Ten Mile, Copper Mountain, CO 80443
Amenities: None

This 25-year-old building is the oldest group of condos at Copper Mountain. As such, it has the best location in the village by the high speed American Eagle lift. Also, the condos have excellent views of the mountain and the valley to the west. These have ski-in/ski-out access. There are no on-site amenities but the Copper Mountain Health Club is only five minutes away. Interior decor leaves much to be desired. Although adequate and comfortable, it is uninspired. It is, however, great for skiers and those who want to be in the center of the action.

4 **COPPER VALLEY CONDOS**
    48 Ten Mile, Copper Mountain, CO 80443
    Amenities: Pool, sauna

This is a budget choice right across from the health club. If you have small children or are a beginning skier, these one- and two-bedroom condos are in a perfect location because they are next to the C lift for beginners and Pooh Corner for children. Well maintained, interior decor reflects an inexpensive style from ten years ago. It is a good location for small children or beginners.

7 **FOXPINE INN**
    154 Wheeler Rd., Copper Mountain, CO 80443
    Amenities: Pool, hot tub, restaurant, ski shop

One of the most talked about condo developments at Copper. These condos offer a range of sizes from simple hotel rooms with no cooking facilities, to deluxe three-bedroom units. Striking features are the spiral staircase in the two-story loft units and the cathedral ceilings. These are generally superior in decor, some done in high-tech or ski-chalet style. The location is down by the B lift, so they are great for golfers or those with advanced intermediate skiing ability. This is one of the few properties with on-site management. There's also a restaurant and a ski shop.

8 **THE GREENS**
    82 Wheeler Rd., Copper Mountain, CO 80443
    Amenities: None

Perhaps the most beautifully decorated units at Copper, these units have easy access to the golf clubhouse. In winter, they are best for serious skiers because they are next to the B lift. There are great views from your porch or patio of the Gore or Ten Mile mountain ranges. These deluxe units have extra-high ceilings, interior woodwork, and tiled tubs to create that elegant Roman spa feeling. Lots of silk flowers are in the rooms and each has a VTP.

5 **THE LODGE**
    35 Wheeler Pl., Copper Mountain, CO 80443
    Amenities: None

Originally designed as employee housing, these functional condos have now been usurped by vacationers because of their excellent location by the American Flyer lift. These functional one-bedroom units are perfect for skiers of all levels. Guests here have privileges over at the Athletic Club. The Lodge is a great value in Colorado.

5-7 PEREGRINE
85 Wheeler Pl., Copper Mountain, CO 80443
Amenities: Hot tub, sauna

Although great for golfers, good skiers will also enjoy these because of their easy access to the B lift. The one-bedroom units are small, but the two-bedroom condos are spacious with both a living room and dining area. The quality of interior decor varies widely from "early attic" to elegant interior decorator. Determine what you'll be getting before renting.

5 SNOWFLAKE
104 Wheeler Pl., Copper Mountain, CO 80443
Amenities: Health club next door

You couldn't be closer to the golf clubhouse or the B lift than at Snowflake. Right in the heart of the clubhouse area, these one-bedroom units are a little on the small side with a very efficient design. The kitchen appliances are actually along the wall of the living room. A good location, but close quarters, it is great for a couple or a young family.

6 SPRUCE LODGE
168 Ten Mile Dr., Copper Mountain, CO 80443
Amenities: None

Located in the center of the village, you are right next to either the American Eagle or the American Flyer high-speed lifts. Popular with everyone, there is easy access to ski terrain for all levels of skiers—from young children to advanced. This is one of the most popular places to stay at Copper. All of the afternoon activities are over at the health club or in the village cafes.

7 SUMMIT HOUSE
88 Ten Mile Dr., Copper Mountain, CO 80443
Amenities: Sauna

These are stylish two-story units in the village center. We like these because of the location in the village—yet not the heart of activity. These two-bedroom units are convenient to both the American Eagle lift and the health club. The two-level design makes the living room extra spacious with a cathedral ceiling and, best of all, a spiral staircase to the upstairs bedroom. Although great for a family, it is not very private for two couples. Some of the balconies have been glass enclosed creating an extra den. Summit House does provide good living arrangements.

8 **TELEMARK**
45 Beeler Pl., Copper Mountain, CO 80443
Amenities: None

This European-style condominium building is one of the most stylish at Copper Mountain. The entrance is spectacular with a large moss-rock fireplace in the lounge and a quiet bar nearby. Intelligently designed, each unit commands an outstanding view of the ski slopes and Union Peak. Located in a wooded section, the village and the ski lifts are only a short walk away.

5 **VILLAGE SQUARE**
189 Ten Mile Dr., Copper Mountain, CO 80443
Amenities: Hot tub, sauna

Located just across the wide plaza from the shops and ski lifts, you'll find the Village Square condominiums. One of the older properties, the units in these five-story buildings are comfortable, although a little tired. This is in a convenient location.

7 **THE WOODS**
54 Golf Course Dr., Copper Mountain, CO 80443
Amenities: None

Best for golfers; skiers should think twice. These townhouses are the farthest away from the ski slopes. Deluxe units, they are beautifully decorated and have a "better than home" appearance. Vaulted ceilings and lots of glass make the living room seem extra bright and inviting. The master bedroom also has skylights. These units are completely self-sufficient with their own washer/dryer. They provide a great view over the fairway and the mountains.

RENTAL RESOURCES

Carbonate Property Management, 303-968-6854
CMCR, 800-525-3887
Copper Mountain Lodges & Condominiums, 303-968-2882
Copper Mountain Resort, 303-968-2882
The Managers, 303-453-2829, 800-766-1477

5. CRESTED BUTTE / GUNNISON

Crested Butte offers two vacation experiences in one. There's the western town of Crested Butte, just 25 miles from the airport at Gunnison with non-stop jets to Houston, Chicago, Dallas, and Atlanta. Although the downtown with its Victorian miners' homes has been declared a National Historic District, you'll find everything from T-shirts to T-bones. Two miles away is the skiers' village of Mt. Crested Butte with over 40 separate condominium buildings that radiate from the core village shops and ski lifts. Very few of the condo developments have on-site management, so you'll need to contact some of the companies in the Rental Resources section to arrange a vacation rental. Crested Butte is casual and comfortable. It is clearly one of Colorado's treasures and is just beginning to receive national attention.

In summer, there's golf, white-water rafting, fishing, and hiking in the mountains. This is an unspoiled part of the Rockies and a great destination for family vacations. "Expeditions" are the main industry of the town of Gunnison. This is the center for campers, hikers, back packers, and river rafters. There's a wide choice of outfitters and sporting good shops that can lead you on an expedition or can arrange for the supplies and give you the appropriate trail maps.

WHERE TO STAY

6   **THE CHATEAUX CONDOMINIUMS**
        651 Gothic Rd., Mt. Crested Butte, CO 81225, 303-349-2448
        1BR $85–130, 2BR $130–180, 3BR $160–210
        Amenities: Skiing, pool, hot tub, saunas

This large complex is located 400 yards from the ski lifts. These condos are spacious, have a fireplace, and are conveniently located near the ski mountain. Interior decor is dated, but it is a good choice for value in Crested Butte.

9   **CRESTED MOUNTAIN VILLAGE**
        22 Emmons Rd., Mt. Crested Butte, CO 81225
        1BR $155–210, 2BR $150–245, 3BR $200–400
        Amenities: Indoor pool, indoor and outdoor hot tubs

Located in the heart of the resort area at the base of the mountain, these condos are right next to the ski lifts. Pitched roofs with oak beams and ceilings as high as 12 feet give a great feeling of space. The slopeside wall is made of glass and allows lots of sunlight and great mountain views. There is a hotel-style front desk and a conference center. This is good for families and small executive conferences. The interior decor of the condo we saw was top quality with a moss-rock wall and a "bench" by the fireplace, two queen-sized fold out sofabeds, a glass-top dining table that would seat eight, and lots of flame stitch or Navajo style fabrics. Crested Mountain Village is truly impressive. In many, the master bath has both a private sauna and a whirlpool.

7+ EVERGREEN CONDOMINIUMS
25 Emmons Rd., Mt. Crested Butte, CO 81225, 303-349-2448
Studio $85–105, 1BR $130–185, 3BR $160–210
Amenities: Skiing, ski shop, pool, hot tub

Spacious units and a central location make Evergreen a winner. Located one and one-half blocks from the ski lifts at the base of the mountain, this resort is convenient to skiing as well as to shopping and restaurants. The condo units have large kitchens and airy living rooms surrounding a fireplace. Furniture is comfortable. Some interiors are showing their age. The units surround a covered atrium and indoor pool. A good choice for groups of young skiers or active families, this is one of Crested Butte's larger developments.

8 THE GATEWAY AT CRESTED BUTTE
16 Snowmass Rd., Mt. Crested Butte, CO 81225
1BR $145–260, 2BR $180–350, 3BR $245–430
Amenities: Skiing, hot tub, sauna

The Gateway is a four-story condo project located right on the "High Tide" ski run. It's convenient with ski-in/ski-out access. These luxurious condos have an unusual floor plan set at angles and generally have been decorated with superior furniture. Each condo has a fireplace, washer/dryer and a private balcony. Although convenient for skiers, it's a walk to the Village.

8+ MOUNTAIN EDGE CONDOMINIUMS
11 Hunter Hill Rd., Mt. Crested Butte, CO 81225
1BR $105–145, 2BR $160–195
Amenities: Clubhouse, health club, shuttle bus

Nestled high in the Rockies, Mountain Edge was developed to ensure that each guest enjoys a luxurious, fully equipped vacation home. These condominiums near the Peachtree ski lifts allow easy access in the winter after a full day of skiing. The condos are large and the loft units are spectacular with a unique glassed-in sun deck and a private whirlpool. There's a fireplace in each living room and, as a special touch, there's a fireplace in the loft bedroom. The furnishings are beautiful with lots of wood and special decorator accents.

7+ THE PLAZA
11 Snowmass Rd., Mt. Crested Butte, CO 81225
2BR $160–315, 3BR $215–400
Amenities: Health club, indoor pool, restaurant

These six-story Plaza condominiums are located within 200 yards of the chair lift at Mt. Crested Butte. Offering sharp contemporary accommodations in a hotel atmosphere, some of these condos have oak-beamed ceilings, a fireplace, and a breakfast bar separating the kitchen from the living room. Expect to find "skierized" neutral furniture with snappy tweeds and lots of plants. These condos are a place where you can be comfortable while viewing skiers on the mountain. The Plaza has a health club with indoor swimming pool, exercise/weight room, saunas, and two bubbling hot tubs (indoor and outdoor).

6 PONDEROSA CONDOMINIUMS
17 Treasure Rd., Mt. Crested Butte, Co. 81225
2BR $135–175, 4BR $190–255
Amenities: Ski lift access

Located just one block from the ski lifts, this three-building complex gives you convenient access to the ski lift as well as the resort center. The condos in these lodge-style structures are spacious with furniture groupings around the hearth fireplace. The centerpiece is the private fireplace in each unit. Furnishings are adequate with laminated wood tables and sofas that can double as beds at night. Enjoy great mountain views here.

6 REDSTONE CONDOMINIUMS
35 Emmons Rd., Mt. Crested Butte, CO 81225
1BR $105–165, 2BR $155–220
Amenities: Hot tub, sauna

Located in the main base area, Redstone gives you easy access to the resort center. The condos are compact and starting to show a little wear and tear. These have been designed for comfortable family living. The resort doesn't offer any special activities, but guests can make new friendships at the outdoor hot tub spa, the two indoor hot tubs, or in the sauna area. This is your budget choice in Crested Butte.

8 WOOD CREEK CONDOMINIUMS
400 Gothic Rd., Mt. Crested Butte, CO 81225, 800-821-3718
Studio $90–110, 1BR $110–145, 2BR $160–210
Amenities: Skiing, hot tub, sauna, tennis

Located just a snowball toss from the base of Peachtree chair lift, on the banks of the stream for which it is named, Wood Creek Condominiums feature comfortable units for families or groups of skiers. It has great views of the ski mountain. The loft units with fireplaces are definitely superior.

RENTAL RESOURCES
Alpine Chalet Rentals, 303-349-2800
Cox & Hagen, 303-349-5388
Crested Butte Accommodations, 303-349-2448

Crested Butte Reservations, 303-349-7555
Gateway to Crested Butte, 303-349-2447
High Country Resort Rentals, 303-349-5705, 800-451-5699

6. DILLON / FRISCO

Just over the Continental Divide, on the other side of the Loveland Pass Tunnel from metropolitan Denver, Dillon, and Frisco are two mountain towns that have sprung to life as "bedroom communities" for Denver. Each has a raw-boned Western flavor and most of the condos in this area are weekend retreats. Although neither community has yet developed a resort ambiance that is sustained during the week, there are two major factors that make accommodations in this area popular.

First, is the convenient location, just one and one-half hours from Denver. Once in either Dillon or Frisco, you are less than ten miles away from several major ski resorts. Keystone is to the east, Breckenridge is to the south, and Copper Mountain is due west. Vacationers staying in the Dillon/Frisco area really have their choice of skiing at any of these three major ski resorts. As if that weren't enough, Vail is only 25 minutes away on Interstate 70.

Second, for those who consider price to be important, accommodations in this area are less expensive than those nearby ski resorts, and much less than in Vail.

Dillon is the town that moved. The original town was moved to its present location when the lake was formed twenty years ago. Today, the new Dillon is more attractive and the mountain lakeside area is beautiful in spring, summer, and fall. In winter, many of the condos offer shuttle buses to the ski resorts. However, we believe you will need a car if you stay in this area. Unlike Aspen, Vail, or Breckenridge, there is no cute "pedestrian village" here, but to be lakeside in Dillon means you'll have a spectacular view.

Frisco evokes the frontier spirit. In recent years, development along the main street has been with log cabin or lodgepole style construction. You'll find family style diners as well as Texas or Wisconsin style bars in town. The best condos are those along the river. Those to the west, in the Mountainside area, are of early modular construction—just a step above mobile homes.

For a central location at prices way below what you'd pay in Vail or even Breckenridge, the Dillon/Frisco area offers a wide array of vacation homes, cabins, and townhouse condos for rent.

Air transportation, of course, is by way of Denver. Although there are shuttle buses from the Denver airport to Dillon and Frisco, once here you'll be glad you rented a car.

WHERE TO STAY

7 CEDAR LODGE
99 Granite, Frisco, CO 80443
Amenities: Hot tub. Near lake

Located a few blocks from Lake Dillon and a short walk from Main Street in Frisco, Cedar Lodge enjoys an enviable location. With a futuristic design on the outside, Cedar Lodge strives to create a European ski chalet atmosphere with quality service. Although the units are very small (400 square feet), they are luxuriously decorated with designer fabrics, lots of wood, and all tile entryways. By the lobby, you'll find a greenhouse with a bubbling hot tub for a bit of relaxation.

6 CROSS CREEK CONDOMINIUMS
223 Creekside Dr., Frisco, CO 80443, 303-668-5175
Amenities: Pool

A place apart from daily demands, Cross Creek Condominiums offers you the unique blend of European style with the freshness of Colorado's Arapahoe National Forest. These condos are located on a bluff overlooking Ten Mile Creek. The interiors are light and airy with lots of sunlight and blond wood furniture. Each condo is beautifully decorated with designer furniture, has a fireplace, and features a whirlpool in the bath. Cross Creek strives to create a "country inn" atmosphere in a secluded setting in the Colorado Rockies.

5 DILLON VALLEY EAST & WEST
475–1143 Straight Creek Dr., Dillon, CO 80435
Amenities: Pool, tennis

One of the largest vacation condo developments in Colorado, this condo project contains 28 three-story buildings sprawling along the hillside. Designed so each unit has impressive views of the Ten Mile Range, this resort has the character of Suburban Denver. Although too large to be clubby, many of the owners and guests know each other. Vacationers from other areas may feel they're missing something because they don't live in Colorado. Advertised as inexpensive lodging for families, these fill the bill. Some units are over 25-years-old and have been recently redecorated with superior furnishings and touches of the ski chalet look. Others offer treasures from the attic. Bare bones, it has a location convenient to three ski resorts.

5   LAGOON TOWNHOMES
Box 462, Dillon, CO 80435, 800-525-3682
Studio $55–80, 1BR $70–135, 2BR $100–165
Amenities: Pool, hot tub

Located near the shores of Lake Dillon, this resort is more lively in summer than winter. Nevertheless, these spacious townhomes provide excellent value and they have their own sports center for play in summer or after a hard day on the slopes.

2   MOUNTAIN SIDE RESORT
500–600 Bill's Ranch Road, Frisco, CO 80443
Amenities: Pool, hot tub, sauna, tennis, racquetball

Overlooking the spectacular Ten Mile range and right on the Vail to Breckenridge bike trail, this location has a peaceful atmosphere on the edge of the forest. A dozen three-story condo buildings frame a square and radiate away from this nucleus. Just a few short blocks from Frisco's Main Street, they provide bargain accommodations in the area. Built with modular construction, they are pretty to look at, but noisy because of a lack of sound proofing. You can hear your neighbors. Some have spectacular interior designer decor. There's a pool, sauna, and racquetball center that becomes a busy place on winter afternoons.

6   SPINNAKER AT LAKE DILLON
317 La Bonte St., Dillon, CO 80435, 303-468-8001
Amenities: Pool, hot tub, sauna

This resort is a model of efficiency and overlooks Lake Dillon. Enjoying a spectacular view of the lake and mountains, across the street you can rent a sailboat in summer. You are 30 minutes driving time from Keystone, Breckenridge, and Copper Mountain ski resorts in winter. The units are furnished in contemporary style and provide ample space for a family on vacation. Expect a warm reception from management as well as attention to detail. The indoor pool is popular in the evenings when skiers return with tales of ski conditions on the various mountains. This resort offers great value considering the price, accommodations, and location.

5   TENMILE CONDOS
200 Granite St., Box 543, Frisco, CO 80443, 303-668-3100
2BR $69–138, 3BR $80–164, 4BR $90–196
Amenities: Indoor pool, hot tub, sauna

This offers a spacious budget choice in downtown Frisco. Not a cute resort community, this is a raw western town where the cowboy spirit thrives. These units are comfortable with fireplaces and solid Victorian reproduction furniture. These large units will appeal to groups of skiers because the bathroom/bedroom layout provides maximum privacy. When you realize that a four-bedroom accommodates 8 people and the price is $196 in high-season, you can not afford to miss out on this opportunity for your ski vacation.

RENTAL RESOURCES
Americana Resort Properties, 303-468-8363
Buffalo Village, 303-468-1465
Chateau Claire, 303-468-2760
Coeur du Lac, 303-696-6962
Coldwell Banker, 303-468-9300
Columbine Rentals, 303-468-0611
Hansen Management, 303-468-1465
Lake Dillon Condotel, 303-468-2409
Mountain Condo Management, 303-468-0566
Orofino, 303-468-5484
Cross Creek Condos, 303-668-5175
Tenmile Creek, 303-668-3100
Wildernest Lodging, 303-468-7851
MC2 Property Management, 800-525-3682
Summit County Central Reservations, 800-365-6365
SC Lodging Resource, 303-468-7851

7. DURANGO / PURGATORY

Born during the uproarious days of the gold and silver mining boom, Durango has only recently discovered that its future is with tourism. Unlike most other Colorado resort areas, high season in Durango is summer.

Durango is a natural gateway to some of the most spectacular scenery in the United States. Because they are geologically younger than other Colorado mountain ranges, the San Juans present a more jagged, precipitous appearance. U.S. 550 runs north from Durango to Silverton and Ouray. This part of the road is known as the Million Dollar Highway. It was cut from nearly vertical cliff sides and constructed on top of hundreds of gold and silver claims, now sealed beneath the asphalt. The Purgatory ski area and alpine slide are 25 miles north of Durango, just off U.S. 550 in the San Juan National Forest.

Because it is so difficult to get to this Purgatory, most visitors stay for a week or more. There's a good spirit of camaraderie and this is one of those places where close friendships are formed.

WHERE TO STAY

4 BRIMSTONE AT PURGATORY
400 Sheol St., Durango, CO 81301, 303-259-1066, 1BR $75–130
Amenities: Pool

This is the budget choice in the area and you'll need a car to go into the town of Durango. Brimstone is located at the base of Purgatory. The condos are in a motel-style, two-story structure, and are furnished simply for the casual lifestyle or for groups of young skiers. These one- and two-bedroom units are spacious and have a full kitchenette. The couple that manages the property is friendly and helpful. There is a genuine, warm hospitality here.

8 CASCADE VILLAGE
50827 Highway 550 North, Durango, CO 81301, 303-259-3500
1BR $59–79, 2BR $79–129
Amenities: Hot tub, pool

The Cascade Village shuttle will take you from this self-contained resort village to nearby Mt. Purgatory for skiing. Durango is 25 miles away. The condos are in a three-story building. They are new, spacious, and well decorated. There is a whirlpool in each bath, so you can have your own spa. There's a lot to do around the Benchmark building, which contains the Cascade Village clubhouse. Socializing becomes quite natural. The guests here quickly get to know each other and discover common interests in skiing or horseback riding. There's a lively western cocktail lounge and the Meadows restaurant is where many guests gather each evening in a clublike atmosphere. All in all, this is a great choice for families or groups of skiers.

6 EAST RIM CONDOS
Purgatory Ski Village, Durango, CO 81301, 303-247-5528
1BR $60–120
Amenities: None

Enjoying quick access to the slopes and to the village, this has a great location. The condos are spacious and pleasantly furnished. The couple that manages this resort wants your business, and the rental rates here are very attractive.

7 THE FERRINGWAY
Ferringway Cir., Durango, CO 81301, 303-247-0441
1BR $90–145
Amenities: Pool, hot tub, sauna

Unlike the other properties located 25 miles north of town around Mt. Purgatory, these condos are located in the town of Durango next to the

Hillcrest Golf Course. They are a great choice for summertime and an alternative for skiers in the winter. It's a great choice for seniors because it is quiet and many residents have retired here from other parts of the country.

5   THE NEEDLES
Highway 550 North, Durango, CO 81301, 303-259-5960
1BR $70, 2BR $145
Amenities: None

Just off the highway, a half mile from Purgatory, these condos are a budget choice. Although the location should attract skiers, this property is most popular with summertime visitors seeking the western mountain experience for fishing, horseback riding, or hiking.

9   PURGATORY VILLAGE HOTEL
175 Beatrice Dr., Durango, CO 81301, 303-247-9000
1BR $49–95, 2BR $89–190
Amenities: Pool, hot tub, steam baths

Located at the ski area 25 miles from Durango, these ski-in/ski-out condos have great views of the ski slopes in winter or the Needles Mountains in summer. The condos are modern and comfortable. Each unit has a fireplace and a private balcony. Downstairs, the restaurant, bar, and cafeteria are the center of the skiers' village, You couldn't have a location more convenient in Purgatory.

10   TAMARRON RESORT
40292 U.S. Highway 550 North, Durango, CO 81301
303-259-2000, 1BR $85–150, 2BR $125–210, 3BR $165–260
Amenities: Restaurant, shuttle bus, pool, health club, golf, tennis, horseback riding, conference center

Located 17 miles north of Durango and eight miles south of Purgatory, Tamarron is a world of its own. This is a major, established Colorado resort lodge. Condominiums have been added in recent years. It's the sister resort to Florida's Innisbrook. Tamarron is an exclusive destination for golfers in the summer, and little known to most tourists. The summertime beauty is incredible and it's a great place for parents to introduce their children to western sports like horseback riding, fishing, and rafting, or to the more civilized sports like golf and tennis. You can even rent an ATV to roam the countryside if you prefer motorized riding to going horseback. Programs are also available for you to hike on Rocky Mountain trails. The area abounds in sightseeing opportunities including the Ute Indian reservation with its pueblos and the Anasazi ruins located in Mesa Verde National Park. The condos are well furnished and many provide a sophisticated environment you wouldn't expect to find in the San Juan Mountain forest. Tamarron offers a full range of recreational activity and a unique experience for a family. The resort also features special package rates for the golf institute and the Australian Tennis Institute. The best feature of this resort is its unpretentious high quality without the hustle or glitz. It has a "confident" environment.

RENTAL RESOURCES
Alpine Purgatory Management, 303-259-6600
The Wells Group, 303-247-9000

8. KEYSTONE

This is perhaps the best example of planning and development in Colorado. Located only 75 miles west of Denver, Keystone Mountain was created 25 years ago beginning with a lodge, small village, and condominiums arranged around Keystone Lake. Beautiful in the summer, the lake forms a natural ice-skating rink in winter. Keystone includes two mountains: Keystone Mountain, which is great for intermediates and the older, more challenging A-Basin. A-Basin sits at the top of Loveland Pass (the old road before the highway was built) and commands a view of the Continental Divide. After skiing, social activity often centers around the Keystone Lodge Pool and Health Club. There are eight other pools, saunas, and even more hot tubs strategically positioned throughout the resort community They are convenient to the separate condo developments, but the Lodge's pool seems to be the focal point.

Keystone is a complete, planned resort community and there has been no uncontrolled growth here. The resort has been carefully developed to create an excellent overall environment for skiers as well as for small conferences. The ski lifts are among the most modern in Colorado and the trails are perfectly groomed.

In summer, Keystone offers its own 18-hole golf course with a rustic log cabin style clubhouse surrounded by geraniums and more alpine than you would find in Switzerland. The John Gardiner Tennis Ranch is also open during the summer with 19 courts and a host of clinics and instructors. The warm sunshine and cool mountain air make conditions just right. Jeeping, biking, hiking, fly-fishing, and horseback riding are popular activities arranged through the Keystone Sports Desk. Keystone has its own network of biking and hiking trails close at hand. There are a variety of programs for children ranging from child care to ski classes or tennis instruction.

Keystone's Conference Center, however, may be the main draw. The main lodge has won a much coveted five-star rating that has boosted the resort's conference center as a popular destination for executives from the East or doctors from the South. As most guests stay in the condos surrounding the lodge and conference center, housekeeping and interior decor in the units is superb. Nothing is out of place and all appliances work perfectly.

These condos are carefully graded by management before the resort will allow them to be rented out.

Keystone's condo accommodations are in two major areas: the central village plaza with the sprawl of condos down the hillside to the lake below, and the West Keystone area where three new high-speed lifts whisk skiers up the mountain.

Almost none of the condos have a front-desk operation to receive mail or to book reservations. Instead, you must contact Keystone Resort (800-222-0188) or else try one of the rental resources we have listed. Keystone Resort has provided solid management and has kept the owners happy. They control most of the inventory in the area. The prices they charge for condo rentals are in alignment with the prices for their five-star hotel rooms, and they do not reflect the market for condos in the neighboring Dillon/Frisco area. The rental rates quoted for condos in the Keystone area are not based upon the complex or the location but, rather, on the number of bedrooms:

Studio	$110–230
1BR	$125–315
2BR	$165–515
3BR	$190–750
4BR	$340–650

As you can see, these are among the steepest condo rental rates found in Colorado and, in our opinion, they approach those stratospheric rates charged in the movie star communities of Aspen and Telluride. For the value-conscious, Keystone offers a lot, but we think you might be able to negotiate a better rate through one of the off-site rental resources.

Transportation to Keystone is easy as it's only one and one-half hours from Denver and shuttle buses leave Denver's Stapleton airport every 30 minutes.

WHERE TO STAY

8 ARGENTINE
175 Argentine Rd., Keystone, CO 80535
Amenities: Pool, hot tub, sauna

Located in the very heart of Keystone village, these condos are tops in popularity with guests attending conferences at Keystone. The one-bedroom units are spacious, handsomely decorated, and each has a fireplace. Argentine permits great views of Keystone Lake and the snowcapped mountains of the Continental Divide.

10 CHATEAUX D'MONT
1203 Keystone Rd., Keystone, CO 80535
Amenities: Hot tub

These three-story wood condos are located in the newer area of Keystone West. Perfect for skiers, they are only 50 yards from the new Peru Express quad chair lift. Among Keystone's most luxurious condos, these have stylish touches such as oak woodwork or beveled glass windows. Large kitchens, cathedral ceilings, and friendly fireplaces provide a convivial atmosphere for families or groups of skiers. Some units have their own private hot tubs in a glass enclosed "greenhouse" overlooking the ski slopes. Everyone likes this one.

8   CINNAMON RIDGE
23062 Highway 6, Keystone, CO 80535
Amenities: Hot tub

Some of the newest condos at Keystone, these two-bedroom units are in the West Keystone area, only a short distance from the lifts. Because it is relatively brand new, special rental rates have been promoted.

7   DECATUR
22340 Highway 6, Keystone, CO 80535
Amenities: Pool, hot tub, sauna

These ultra-modern condos can be rented for some of the most reasonable rental rates in Keystone. On the west shore of the lake, this is right next to a shuttle bus stop. The village plaza is only a few minutes away by foot and the conference center is just across the highway.

7   EDGEWATER
105 Keystone Rd., Keystone, CO 80535
Amenities: Pool, hot tub, sauna

This modern five-story building is right in the heart of the village and is a popular choice among conference attendees.

8   ENCLAVE
13072 Highway 6, Keystone, CO 80535
Amenities: Pool, sauna, steam room, tennis, racquetball

Located at the far end of West Keystone, this is a little inconvenient for skiers. However, the inconvenient location is easily compensated for by the large units with fanciful interior decorator decor. Expect southwestern themes with the pastel paintbrush colors of the desert or the darkly wooded forest cabin interior complete with horseshoes on the furniture frames. Enclave is a romantic setting that is quiet and peaceful.

7 **FLYING DUTCHMAN**
1937 Soda Ridge, Keystone, CO 80535
Amenities: Outdoor pool, hot tub, sauna

These new two and one-half story condos enjoy a quiet location just south of the main village. The main activities of Keystone village are accessible by shuttle bus or a healthy hike up the hill. Reasonably priced, these condos are contemporary in style with windows at an angle to provide the best sunlight. Guests here have their own pool/hot tub center, so a clubby atmosphere slowly evolves as you see the same people each evening. This is a pleasantly quiet resort.

7-8 **FROSTFIRE**
Oro Grand, Keystone, CO 80535
Amenities: None

Frostfire condos are in the West Keystone area, and are within walking distance of the Argentine and Peru ski lifts. The one-bedroom units are on the ground level, the two story two-bedroom units are like little townhouses upstairs. Some are luxuriously furnished. We saw one with a bearskin rug by the fire. Most of the two-bedroom units have whirlpools in the master bath and some have a small private steam room. Frostfire provides great views and it is good for families or two couples.

6 **KEYSTONE GULCH**
1944 Soda Ridge, Keystone, CO 80535
Amenities: Pool, hot tub

Located just south of the main village, these townhouses are across the street from the shuttle bus stop. The advantage here is that these units offer lots of space at a reasonable price. With its own pool center, guests often make friends here rather than up at the main Keystone sports center.

6 **LAKE CLIFFE**
160 E. La Bonte Dr., Dillon, CO 80435, 303-468-2301
Amenities: Pool, hot tub

Featuring excellent views of the Ten Mile Range, these solid units feature stone walls in the living room. Creating a Rocky Mountain experience, these units seem to be mainly occupied by Denverites out for an unusual living environment—try this one.

6 **LAKESHORE**
22174 Highway 6, Keystone, CO 80535
Amenities: Pool, hot tub

These are among the most popular units at Keystone because of the location right on the pond. These condos are closest to the Keystone Conference Center. The studio and one-bedroom condos are contemporary in design and decor. Furnished with contemporary style, you'll find accents like brass andirons in the fireplace, carved ducks on the mantle, and framed ski posters on the walls. Warm, pleasant, and convenient, you'll enjoy Lakeshore.

7   LIFTSIDE
      23024 U.S. Hwy 6, Keystone, CO 80435
      Amenities: Pool, hot tub

At Liftside, you are just steps away from Keystone Mountain and access to North Peak and the new Outback area. These modern units are well designed and attention has been paid to detail in order to make the most of the setting. For example, the southern exposure takes advantage of the warm, golden Colorado sunshine and the spectacular mountain views. The living room is attractive and decorated with contemporary furnishings with soft pink and blue colors. Each has a VCR and a fireplace. In the master bath, you'll find private whirlpools. In winter, you'll be impressed by the heated underground parking.

4   MARINA PLACE
      210 E. LaBounte Dr., Dillon, CO 80435
      Amenities: Pool

Located in the heart of Dillon, the condos in this four-story structure are a budget choice and convenient for those who want to ski Keystone, Copper, or Breckenridge. A little on the small side, but they are fully furnished and each has a fireplace.

RENTAL RESOURCES
Keystone Property Management, 303-468-4155
Keystone Resort, 303-468-4226
Snow Country Resort Properties, 303-468-7755

9. STEAMBOAT SPRINGS

The name "Steamboat Springs" comes from a geologic curiosity. When white trappers entered the area, they were startled to hear the sound of a steamboat chugging down the Yampa River. Further investigation revealed a mineral hot spring where the water bubbling between rock formations created the sound of the mysterious steamboat. The Yampa Valley, where Steamboat is located, is one of the West's major cattle areas. Steamboat was primarily a cattleman's town, until the late 1970s, when the community awakened to the promise of tourism. Rather than add to the Western town, a new area of development sprang up five miles away. The Western cattle-man's town is still intact, and the condo growth has been concentrated in an area around Mt. Werner.

The resort community centers around Ski Time Square and a second area, Gondola Square. The 82 condo developments radiate from this core—up and down the mountainside. Most are small with between 12 and 24 units. Not many have pools, but all have a large hot tub/spa area. Steamboat is a community where the athletic go to the popular central Steamboat Health Club, built around one of the area's natural "chugging" hot springs. Therefore, you won't find the small poolside congregations typical of après-ski life at other resort communities. One of the most notable features of Steamboat is its "Kids Ski Free" program.

Transportation to Steamboat has become easy. Only a few years ago trav-elers overlooked Steamboat because it was a four-hour drive from Denver across the Continental Divide. Today, there are nonstop flights from Chicago, Dallas, Los Angeles, San Francisco, Phoenix, and Minneapolis. The airport at Hayden is 25 miles away, an easy route for rental cars or shut-tle buses. Convenient air transportation is a key factor in making Steamboat Springs one of North America's hottest vacation real estate markets.

WHERE TO STAY

9+ **BEAR CLAW CONDOMINIUMS**
2420 Ski Trail Ln., Steamboat Springs, CO 80487, 303-879-6100
1BR $190–280, 2BR $280–380, 3BR $340–470
Amenities: Heated pool, hot tubs

One of the few condominiums with ski-in/ski-out convenience. These are Steamboat's most elegant condos. A private, clubby enclave where the concierge knows each guest by name, it's located about 3/4 of a mile from the main lifts. Put your skis on in the morning and ski down to the lifts. Then ski home at the end of the day. Generally, the units are decorated in understated good taste with a preference for expensive woods. Many units are decorated in rich greens or tan-colored fabrics. Others are lighter and perhaps more contemporary. But, as with everything at Bear Claw, you can always expect quality. Each condo has its own private hot tub overlooking the mountain. There's also a heated pool, which is the resort's social center.

8 **BRONZE TREE**
2050 Storm Meadow Dr., Steamboat Springs, CO 80487
2BR $325
Amenities: Hot tub

This modern five-story, high-rise condo resort is located near the Christie chair lifts and is convenient for skiers in winter. The location seems urban because you are surrounded by small shops and restaurants. The condos are fairly new and attractively furnished to provide a comfortable, quality atmosphere for skiers. Bronze Tree has superb management and a neat appearance. Each unit has a stone fireplace that is great for evening fireside chats and marshmallow roasts. There is a great view of either Mt. Werner or the Yampa Valley from each balcony. Bronze Tree is a good choice for well-heeled travelers or groups of skiers.

8+ DULANY CONDOMINIUMS
Village Dr., Steamboat Springs, CO 80487, 2BR $325, 3BR $415
Amenities: Hot tub

"Good taste" defines the atmosphere here at this small, private, 25-unit, five-story condo complex nestled discreetly on the banks of Burgess Creek. The location is just slightly removed from the skiers village. It's a short distance to the Ski Time Square area of shops, restaurants, and ski lifts. The condos are large and spacious, especially those on the fifth floor, which have cathedral ceilings. Some are very well decorated with the 1890s frontier look or southwestern casual decor. These are high quality condos. One real benefit is the complimentary guest privileges at the Steamboat Athletic Club. Management is available 24 hours a day, a luxury for a small condo resort.

8 GOLDEN TRIANGLE CONDO RESORT
2400 Pine Grove Cir., Steamboat Springs, CO 80487
303-879-2931, 1BR $160, 2BR $220
Amenities: Pools, hot tubs, steam room, racquetball

This resort has luxurious condominiums just off the highway. One of the few condo resorts in Steamboat with its own sports center, it includes an indoor and an outdoor pool. There are also two racquetball courts. Management is attentive. The concierge wants to help you enjoy your vacation. The units are beautifully furnished with good use of colors, art objects, and all electrical appliances including VTPs. The loft units are well designed and give you lots of space in the living room. There is a cute balcony that children will enjoy.

8 LA CASA
Village Dr., Steamboat Springs, CO 80487, 2BR $275, 3BR $350
Amenities: Outdoor hot tub

La Casa consists of spacious mountain townhouses in a new development on the edge of the skiers village. Great condos away from the congested core area, they are new, modern, and bright. Each has a private fireplace. The units have a pantry with a laundry room. This is a good choice for a longer stay.

8+ THE LODGE

2700 Village Dr., Steamboat Springs, CO 80487, 303-879-6000
1BR $190, 2BR $225–325
Amenities: Hot tubs, tennis

Centrally located next to Gondola Square, the Lodge is in a prime location. This three-story condo complex offers some of Steamboat's most deluxe accommodations. Add high quality services to the equation and you'll understand the pricing structure. The condos are large with pine-paneled walls, wood trim, full kitchens, and private fireplaces. Wooden beams cross the living room ceiling adding character. You'll find great views from each unit and some have private balconies. The social center of this complex is at the two hot tubs. It is a great place to go in the evening after skiing. In summer, there are two tennis courts. One special feature here is a complimentary guest membership at the Steamboat Athletic Club, which has pools and two indoor tennis courts.

8+ THE MORAINE

Clubhouse Dr., Steamboat Springs, CO 80488
2BR $280–330, 3BR $330–380
Amenities: Pool, tennis. Golf nearby

The Moraine provides some of the largest condos you'll find anywhere, they are located on the outskirts of the skiers' village, so you'll need a car. There is a shuttle bus stop in front of these units, however. Many of these 3000-square-foot condos (we told you they were large) have private saunas and private hot tubs. Interior decor is highly personalized and many of the condos reflect the touch of a professional designer. These condos are not recommended for families with little children because the living room on the second floor has a balcony with a "cutaway" area. Children could fall to the floor below. The Moraine is very popular for those seeking a long-term rental in the summer because they are so spacious.

8 THE PHOENIX

2315 Apres Ski Way, Steamboat Springs, CO 80487
303-879-7654, 2BR $230, 3BR $330
Amenities: Outdoor heated pool, hot tub

The Phoenix has two-bedroom condos as well as some spectacular four-bedroom units with massive moss-rock fireplaces and cathedral ceilings. This is a great choice for groups of skiers because of the spaciousness and deluxe decor. Each condo comes complete with a private washer/dryer and a heated garage. Some of the units have been decorated with a touch of whimsy. For example, some bedrooms have painted rough oak and wicker furniture with lots of pastel fabrics and a quilt over the bed. Others exude a western feeling with lots of wood and good, sturdy furniture. The Phoenix is very attractive. Guests gather at the heated outdoor pool and the hot tub area for relaxation after a hard day of skiing.

5   PINE GROVE VILLAGE
Pine Grove Ln., Steamboat Springs, CO 80487
1BR $130, 2BR $150
Amenities: None

These condos are your budget choice in Steamboat. Formerly an area of employee housing, these were recently converted to resort condos offering short-term rentals. They are simple and unpretentious. They are located down by the highway, about two miles from the skiers village, but across the street from Safeway.

6   PTARMIGAN HOUSE
2322 Apres Ski Way, Steamboat Springs, CO 80487
303-879-6278, 1BR $155, 2BR $220–275
Amenities: Hot tub

This is one of the first condominium properties built in the skiers' village at the base of Mt. Werner. Because of it's central location, Ptarmigan has retained its favored status with knowledgeable Steamboat visitors. The condos have comfortable furnishings. Each condo has a private balcony for a breath of fresh air in winter and relaxation in the summer. This resort has a busy lobby area and the bar is a place everyone visits at least once.

8+   THE RANCH AT STEAMBOAT
1 Ranch Rd., Steamboat Springs, CO 80487, 303-879-3000
2BR $285, 3BR $305
Amenities: Heated outdoor pool, tennis, conference center, ranch van

A great value, this resort is also an example of quiet efficiency and good taste. Located about a half mile from the resort center/ski lifts, the Ranch offers a unique on-call transportation system to take you to the ski lifts, skiers village, or "Old Town" Steamboat Springs. The condos are in three-story buildings spread over 36 hillside acres. These are spacious full size condos ranging from "country" to "sophisticated" with lots of wood and interior decorator furnishings. The front desk is open 24 hours a day and there's a tasteful living room/card room with a billiards room next door. The Ranch is one of the best values in Steamboat.

6-7+ THE ROCKIES
Steamboat Springs, CO 80488, 1BR $100–125, 2BR $155–185
Amenities: Outdoor heated pool, hot tubs

This is located just far enough away from the main skiers' village that you'll want a car or you'll rely upon the shuttle bus. This three-story condominium development offers reasonably priced accommodations for skiers and families. The units have eight different floor plans and are now about 12 years old. Many show their age. Others have just been redecorated. It is very well managed. The maintenance engineer takes great pride in his "home" and his helpful presence gives this resort a special atmosphere.

7+ THE SCANDINAVIAN LODGE
Steamboat Springs, CO 80477
Amenities: Restaurant

This resort is located up the mountainside, about two miles away from the skiers village. It is Steamboat's only European-style condo resort. An unusual bit of Scandinavia right here on the western slope of the Rockies. The Lodge offers studio condos in the main wing and two- and three-bedroom townhouse condominiums nearby. The townhouses are the best choice because they have private saunas! Some also have individual hot tubs along with a full kitchen and fireplace. Best feature: the very charming "Swedish country inn" dining room in the main lodge.

6-7 SKI TIME SQUARE
1920 Mount Werner Rd., Steamboat Springs, CO 80477
303-879-3700, 1BR $130–150, 2BR $140–220
Amenities: Hot tub

One of Steamboat's largest and liveliest condo developments, located across the parking lot from the ski lift center. It consists of a cluster of three-story buildings dating from the 1970s. The condos are spacious, but some look worn. Although there are no on-site hospitality services, everything is happening across the street in the skiers village. The location is a big plus for this property.

6+ SKI TRAIL CONDOMINIUMS
Steamboat Springs, CO 80488, 1BR $137, 2BR $167, 3BR $197
Amenities: Ski-in/ski-out access

Few of the condos in Steamboat are on the slopes or have ski-in/ski-out accessibility. Those that do are in the expensive category. This is a real find because Ski Trail condos are slopeside just above the village and they have some of the lowest rental rates to be found in Steamboat. The units are on the small side and they are a little dark because the three-story, motel-style building has functional architecture. Each condo has full features including a kitchen and a fireplace in the living room—rare in Steamboat. They have clean, new, comfortable furniture. If you want one of Steamboat's best values, this is it.

7   **SUBALPINE CONDOS**
Steamboat Springs, CO 80477, 800-872-0763
Amenities: Outdoor heated pool, hot tub

Subalpine is one of those small, well-maintained, comfortable resorts that give you more than you bargained for. Located about a half mile from the ski slopes, Subalpine offers an outdoor hot tub and heated pool, plus shuttle service to the slopes in the winter. Every one of the two- and three-bedroom units offers a view of the scenic Yampa Valley.

6   **SUNBURST**
3325 Meadow Ln., Steamboat Springs, CO 80477
Amenities: Hot tub, indoor pool

Sunburst has twenty-one condominiums in the area of new development, about one mile from the ski lifts and two miles from the main part of the town. The units are stylish and modern on the inside.

7   **TIMBERS CONDOMINIUMS**
31500 U.S. Highway 40, Steamboat Springs, CO 80477
303-879-6183
Amenities: Hot tub, saunas

These condos are located near the west base of Rabbit Ears Pass, about eight miles from the Steamboat Ski Area. The Timbers is a favorite of those looking for a quiet, homey atmosphere after a busy day of skiing, hiking, or sightseeing. The Timbers offers a hot tub, saunas, a large common area, and beautiful views of Lake Catamount, the Yampa River Valley and surrounding mountains. Accommodations include units from studios up to two-bedrooms plus loft. Rustic charm and breathtaking views best describe the feeling here.

8+   **TORIAN PLUM**
1855 Ski Time Square Dr., Steamboat Springs, CO 80487
2BR $280, 3BR $365
Amenities: Heated outdoor pool, hot tubs, saunas

One of Steamboat's premier resorts, this eight-story, high-rise structure dominates Ski Time Square and is right next to the chair lifts. The condo interiors are generally luxurious, with a fireplace and oak woodwork. Generally, most have contemporary furniture with soft green and dusty rose fabrics. Each spacious unit features a private spa in the master bathroom. This is a pleasant, first-class environment. And you'll be equally pleased by the warm lobby/reception area and the fine service from the staff and concierge. Torian Plum is an active, social resort and offers one of Steamboat's most central locations. This is a great choice for the first-time skier because each morning the ski school meets at the Torian Plum. It's also a great choice for families with children because there are children's activities here and the concierge will make arrangements for baby sitters. In summer, the 18-hole Robert Trent Jones golf course is only a short walk away. You just couldn't ask for more than this in Steamboat.

RENTAL RESOURCES

Big Country Management, 303-879-0763
Colorado Resort Services, 303-879-7653
Harbor Hotel, 800-543-8888, Downtown location.
Hillsider, 303-879-7900
Johnson Shipley Management, 303-879-5151
Maxwell Management, 303-879-0720
Mountain Castles, 303-879-1311
Mountain Resorts, 303-879-1035
Pine Real Estate Management, 800-235-5571
Sable Management, 303-879-3000
Snowflower Condos, 303-879-5104
Special Places, 303-879-5417
Steamboat Home Management, 303-879-1982
Steamboat Lodging, 303-879-5104
Steamboat Management, 303-879-5555
Steamboat Premier Property, 303-879-8811
Steamboat Resorts, 303-879-8000

10. TELLURIDE

Located in a remote box canyon, Telluride was nicknamed the "City of Gold" by the miners who worked in claims at 12,000 feet above sea level. They came down into town to celebrate and created what is now called Telluride's "wicked past." It was in Telluride that Butch Cassidy robbed his first bank. Today, some of those rough buildings still house restaurants and saloons that attract a quieter group of celebrants. Many of the old homes have become shops and restaurants, and there's a certain spirit in Telluride town which is often called "funky." A special place which, until recently, had managed to avoid the "push" of 20th century America. The "Cicely" of the Rockies. Now there's a new part of Telluride; four miles from town, the Mountain Village has eight new condo developments that offer a level of luxury previously unknown.

Today, Telluride has become one of the most exciting resort communities in the U.S. Some say it all began with the Telluride Film Festival. Others say it attracted attention when Ralph Lauren began inviting friends to his nearby ranch. This town has long been a hangout for nonconformists and it was just what the creative types who "discovered" it had been looking for. Then the boom was on. In just the past three years, prices for some of the more exclusive mountain homes have doubled; and with good reason, for where else can you find 14,000 foot peaks and waterfalls falling from the clouds? Many say that Telluride's present cachè comes from being carefully preserved. The town's authentic Main Street has been designated a National Historic District. Less commercial than other resorts, the most appropriate description is "Telluride is a town that's neither too big for kids, nor too small for parents, and friendly enough for the whole family."

Transportation to Telluride has always been difficult. In fact some say the name came from train conductors telling passengers "To Hell you ride." (The truth is that the town was named for the telluride ore mined in the early years.) The trip is torturous no matter how you do it—unless you have a private plane. Telluride is easily a 10 hour drive from Denver, assuming there are good weather conditions. The airport at Durango is at least two hours away via the scenic Million Dollar Highway (so named because it is paved over more than a million dollars in gold and silver veins). The runway at Telluride is short and approaches are difficult in this box canyon. It was widened during the summer of 1991 but little can be done to increase the length. As a result, there's a good chance that your wintertime commuter flight from Denver or Los Angeles may be diverted to Montrose, fifty miles away. So unless you have your own plane, plan on a long journey to Telluride.

WHERE TO STAY

5 BOOMERANG VILLAGE
Aspen St., Telluride, CO 81435, 303-728-4405
Amenities: Next to the ski lift

These 60 condos in a three-story structure are as close to the Oak Street ski lift as you would want to be. These one-bedroom units are good for a couple or a small family on a budget.

4 BROWN HOMESTEAD
Highway 145, Telluride, CO 81435, 303-259-6580, 1BR $120–230
Amenities: None

Located outside of town, these futuristic two and two and one-half story townhouses have floor plans varying from two to four bedrooms. Comfortable interior decor, but the rustic feeling prevails. What these offer is lots of space for a group or an extended family. These are among the most inexpensive condos in Telluride.

7   CIMARRON LODGE
300 S. Mahoney Dr., Telluride, CO 81435, 303-728-3803
1BR $55–140, 2BR $95–240, 3BR $135–315
Amenities: Hot tub

Located at the base of the Coonskin lift, these new condos are some of the best in the area. The upper-story units have cathedral ceilings with two rows of plate glass windows for the sunlight. Light and airy, these have the decor you would expect in Florida: pale pastels in pink and violet with beige carpet and blond ash wood. Each has a fireplace and some have a bench in front so you can warm up after a day of skiing the canyon. Behind the lodge, there's a hot tub area overlooking a snow-fed trout stream. In this cowboy town, these are among the most feminine condo interiors to be found.

9+   DORAL TELLURIDE
Country Club Drive, Box 2702, Telluride, CO 81435
800-22DORAL, 1BR $540–720

Enjoying the ultimate ski-in/ski-out location, all 177 of the suites have outstanding panoramic views. Doral is one of the snazziest timeshare developments ever to be created. Offering some of the most luxurious accommodations in Colorado (with prices to match), you'll be impressed by all the special touches added to these suites, including oversized bathrooms with dual marble vanities and hair dryers, plush terry robes, and VCRs. Lacking full kitchens, each unit has a mini bar, fridge and coffeemaker—adequate for fixing breakfast or late-night snacks. The raison d'etre is the 42,000 square foot spa, featuring Roman pools, hot tubs, and a cardiovascular fitness center. For those weary ski muscles, there is a staff of masseures/masseuses and 44 personal treatment rooms. Other services include a concierge, a "vacation planner," daycare center, and 24-hour room service. The Plunge offers breathtaking views and is a convivial center for après-ski activities.

8   ETA PLACE CONDOMINIUMS
Mahoney Dr., Telluride, CO 81435, 303-728-4405
2BR $199–450, 3BR $325–518
Amenities: None

Located at the base of the Coonskin lift, this postmodern building is a rare exception to the strictly enforced Telluride building code. These are some of the most luxurious units to be found in town. Comfortably decorated, you'll find lots of wood and woven fabrics. Many owners have personalized their units with art and impressive reproductions. You may find New York sophistication or Hopi weavings from Taos. Some of these condos have private hot tubs by the window, so you can soak in the sunlight and view the mountains.

7 ### LULU CITY CONDOMINIUMS
Mahoney Dr., Telluride, CO 81435, 800-LETS SKI
1BR $55–175, 2BR $65–300
Amenities: Pool, hot tub, skiing

One of the most popular choices in Telluride because of its location at the base of the Coonskin lift and the pool/hot tub area. These attractive, spacious condos were professionally decorated by an interior designer to blend the local Southwestern culture into contemporary styles. Many two-story units have a spiral staircase to the loft upstairs. Some units have private hot tubs enclosed in a solarium. One of the more luxurious condos in town, you'll like it here.

MOUNTAIN VILLAGE
Mountain Village Blvd., Telluride, CO 81435, 303-728-8000
Studio $99–144, 1BR $122–207, 2BR $288–500, 3BR $356–575
Amenities: Golf, tennis, pool, sports center

These are among the most attractively furnished condos that you'll find in Colorado. There are several different developments and private homes within this enclave. Mountain Village is four miles away from the town of Telluride. Located on a different side of the skiers' mountain, there is a separate approach to the ski area than from the Telluride "town" lift. In summer, a brand new championship golf course is available at Mountain Village. This master development is entirely different from Telluride in style, and with over 1000 acres it has retained its forested environment. There are eight separate condo developments within Mountain Village. Most have been built as three- or four-story buildings resembling Austrian-style chalets. Some of the three-bedroom condos are larger than most homes. One advantage of Mountain Village is its location outside of town and wood-burning fireplaces are allowed. There's a shuttle bus to town, but you will probably be content to stay in this skiers' village and enjoy the social life. The following is a thumbnail sketch of these condos:

Aspen Ridge (8) These huge townhouses are conveniently located with easy access to the ski lifts, the golf course, tennis courts, and the small shoppers village. Each unit has cathedral ceilings, fireplaces, a slopeside spa, and incredibly decorated interiors. Several models are candidates for *House Beautiful*. All have fireplaces in the living room.

Kayenta Legend (9) These are luxurious condos with private whirlpool tubs and vaulted cathedral ceilings in the living room. Interior decor offers lots of fantasy with Bavarian blond wood furniture and very stylish fabrics.

The Telemark (9) This is yet another luxury condominium offering two- and three-bedroom condos in a neo-Victorian structure. These units are larger than most homes and the interior decor is straight from a designer's showroom.

Two others worth noting are **Le Chamonix (8),** which are condominium homes and **Columbia Place Lodge (7),** which offers the warmth of a country inn at an affordable price.

8 TELLURIDE LODGE

Pacific St., Telluride, CO 81435, 800-662-8747
2BR $75–300, 3BR $95–450
Amenities: Pool

Located right across from the Coonskin lift, these rustic condos have been built in a staggered townhouse style, so only part of the unit borders its neighbors. Most have been recently redecorated with sharp styles and fabrics, although you'll find a hint of the Old West in some. Others have opted for a comfortable ski-chalet style. Each has a gas log fireplace that makes the evenings cozy.

7 THE VIKING LODGE

Davis St., Telluride, CO 81435, 800-446-3192, 1BR $55–210
Amenities: Hot tub, glass-enclosed solarium. Next to lift

Viking Lodge offers hotel-style service combined with the convenience of a condominium. The location is next to the "town" lift that is convenient for skiers. The view of the mountains from each private balcony is spectacular. The condos are spacious and decorated with light-colored neutral furniture. The kitchens are "minis" with only a small refrigerator, sink, and microwave. There are no fireplaces. Telluride is surrounded by mountains and in order to keep the clean mountain air, wood burning fireplaces are prohibited in town.

RENTAL RESOURCES

Clark Taylor Associates, 303-728-3435
Coldwell Banker/Shaw Co., 728-4466
Resort Rentals Inc., 303-728-4405
Telluride Accommodations, 303-728-3803
Telluride Lodging, 303-728-4311
Telluride Real Estate, 303-728-3111
The Lodges, 800-446-3192

11. VAIL

With over 350 inches of annual snowfall each year and the largest area of ski terrain for any single area in the U.S., Vail is guaranteed to please all skiers. Cold and dry in winter, summer is even better with sunny skies, cool alpine breezes, and fragrant forests surrounding the village. In the mountains of Colorado there's an expression, "If you don't like the weather, stick around for an hour" because it's constantly changing. Nowhere is this expression more true than at Vail Village, just over the Continental Divide and Vail Pass. In summer, bring a bathing suit, shorts, a sweater, a rain jacket for the 4 P.M. showers, and maybe a parka for the occasional summer snowstorm. In winter, get out your diamonds and your best furs because Vail can be ultra posh.

The goal at Vail is to make you feel like you are in Europe. All the best of Switzerland and Austria was replicated here when the village was planned. The zoning commission enforces the original concept, so everything appears to be like the Tyrolean Alps. The European themes are carried through in hotels, restaurants, and shops. With incredible attention to detail, exemplary of Vail, each year the town chooses a "color" for all the flowers in the window boxes and bordering the buildings. One year it's pink, another it's purple. Where else besides Disneyland would you find such planned perfection? Vail is a charming town, and it is an attraction in itself even for those who don't ski. For those who do, Vail offers some of the best skiing in Colorado. The closest thing to European "off track" skiing can be found in the bowls behind Vail Mountain. Experts and advanced intermediates can enjoy the vast open spaces and the challenge of skiing in fresh, unpacked snow.

Part of Vail's success can be attributed to good planning and carefully controlled growth. Development began over 25 years ago and for the past 15 years little has changed in the core village. Heading west there's the Lionshead area—a ten-minute walk from the village center. Lionshead is a second "village" with its own shops, cafes, and dozens of condos. Not as expensive as those in the core village, the units in these five- and six-story Austrian chalets and modern mid-rises all have spectacular views of the mountain. Heading farther west there's the Cascades area around the Athletic Club. Eight years old, this is the newest area that can still be considered Vail proper.

Most of the condos in East Vail are for local residents, although there are a few exceptions such as the ultra luxurious Vail Golf Course Townhouses. For bargains in the area, take the pedestrian foot bridge across the interstate highway and you're in an area of newer condominiums, which are much less expensive than those in the village, yet you're only a five-minute walk away across the bridge.

Transportation to Vail is a breeze. The resort is two hours due west of Denver airport along Interstate 70. An easy drive, the only potential problem area is Vail Pass (just before you descend into Vail Valley) where chains are required during a snowstorm. Recently nonstop jet service into Vail's Eagle Airport (18 miles away) has been available during ski season from Chicago, New York, Dallas, Phoenix, and Los Angeles. Commuter flights between Vail/Eagle and Denver are frequent. If you are staying in the village of Vail you won't need a car.

WHERE TO STAY

5 **ANTLERS AT VAIL**
680 W. Lionshead Pl., Vail, CO 81657, 303-476-2471
1BR $120–290, 2BR $160–475, 3BR $175–575
Amenities: Pool, saunas, hot tubs

This eight-story condo complex is a good choice for the young and active. You'll find pine paneling, contemporary, free-standing fireplaces, Western country quilt bedspreads and of course, antlers on the wall. Each condo has a full kitchen and VTP. The condos overlook Gore Creek, just a short walk from the Lionshead lift. After skiing, there are always lots of people around the pool and hot tub. Hospitality and housekeeping could be better here.

3 **APOLLO PARK AT VAIL**
442 South Frontage Rd., Vail, CO 81657, 303-476-0079
1BR $49–79, 2BR $79–135
Amenities: Pool

Formerly, this was employee housing until Vail real estate became too expensive. Today, it is an economy choice in Vail. It is a large condo-minium/timeshare complex, within walking distance of the lifts for the hearty or right on the shuttle bus route. The units are functional, but lack the glamour one associates with Vail. There is a small pool. Every condo has a fully equipped kitchen and private balcony. These condos have seen lots of use but the furniture is sturdy. The loft on the second floor is small.

8 **COLDSTREAM CONDOMINIUMS**
1476 Westhaven Dr., Vail, CO 81657, 303-476-6106
1BR $100–195, 2BR $135–260, 3BR $185–290
Amenities: Pools, tennis, racquetball, saunas

The Coldstream is located just outside town in the Cascade Village area. Set along Gore Creek about a mile from Vail Village, Cascade Village is in its own little world. The centerpiece is the Cascade Athletic Club with rac-quetball courts, tennis facilities, swimming pools, and therapeutic massages. For dining, you'll find several small restaurants as part of the Cascade Village complex.

Aspen, pine, and spruce surround the townhouses, which have contempo-rary, inspired architecture. Inside, the condos are well-furnished with soft peach colors and modern, clean-line designs. Each condo has a private fireplace and there is an outdoor pool area with saunas next to it. Designer accessories complete the picture. It's quiet and refined. We recommend it most for those looking for a sophisticated atmosphere.

9   FIRST BANK
656 Lionshead Cir., Vail, CO 81657
Amenities: None

Located above the bank, this spacious two-bedroom condominium has a cathedral ceiling and the master bedroom overlooks the living room in a loft like setting. There's a great view of the ski slopes from the balcony. Unusual in design, this is for a special vacation to Vail because it's like having your own private home.

6-7 HOLIDAY HOUSE
13 Vail Rd., Vail, CO 81657, 303-476-5631
Amenities: Pool at the Holiday Inn

Managed by the Holiday Inn, these condos occupy a central location in Vail. This eight-story Austrian chalet-style structure was one of the first built when Vail was developed more than 25 years ago. It's right at the Vail exit from the Interstate and the main part of Vail begins at the back door to Holiday House. These condos have seen lots of use. Presently decorated in neutral beige colors, the style is southwestern ranch, with comfortable couches and a breakfast bar separating the kitchen. This resort is great for families because of all the services from the Holiday Inn, including child care and supervised activities for children after skiing. It provides lots of activity for all, a central location, and guaranteed good service.

5   INN AT VAIL
2211 N. Frontage Rd., Vail, CO 81657, 303-476-3890
Amenities: Pool, hot tub, steam room, sauna

This was formerly the Raintree Inn. It's on the north side of the interstate, so you must take the shuttle bus or drive over to the ski lifts. The Inn at Vail was a popular place in 1989 during the World Cup Championships and you may recall seeing the Inn at Vail frequently on television. Why? ABC News used this condo resort as home base for its reporters and film crew for six weeks. The condos are furnished in a contemporary California style with durable furniture. These condos are great for two couples sharing a unit.

6   THE LANDMARK
610 W. Lionshead Cir., Vail, CO 81657, 303-476-1350
Amenities: Heated outdoor pool, hot tub

This is a landmark, but for the wrong reason. It's the only eight-story building in Vail that doesn't conform to the Swiss/Austrian style building code. Although it looks like an apartment building at first, management compensates by providing lots of hospitality and amenities. The condos, which are spacious and attractively furnished, are decorated in natural wood and off-white fabrics. The light colors make the condos seem even more open and spacious. The windows give you a great view and bring the bright sunlight and green forest inside. The resort is good for families because the large pool/sun deck/hot tub area becomes a social center in summer. There's lots of dashing between the two pools in winter.

7   LIFT HOUSE
555 East Lionshead Cir., Vail, CO 81657
Amenities: Hot tub, restaurants

Located right by the Lionshead lift, this four-story building houses newly redecorated studio condos with cute rooms with wood paneling and neutral, "skierized" furniture. Each has a private fireplace and kitchenette. Eager to attract visitors, the staff tries hard to make you feel welcome and comfortable so that you'll return again. Lift House offers a high level of hotel-style services.

7   LION SQUARE LODGE
660 W. Lionshead Pl., Vail, CO 81657, 303-476-2281
1BR $80–229, 2BR $140–362, 3BR $160–436
Amenities: Heated pool, saunas, hot tubs

This lodge is a top choice in Vail. Right on Gore Creek, the well-developed property offers beautiful views of the mountains from each condo. The interior decor is tasteful and modern with southwestern fabrics and a cozy fireplace/hearth arrangement. Although the units are a little small, a homey environment has been created. The location is excellent because it's next to the Lionshead ski lift. Don't worry about the commotion, the property has been designed in such a way that you'll never be aware of skiers coming and going. The pool is popular after skiing, but the best amenity is the hot chocolate offered to each guest upon returning from the ski slopes.

8   THE LODGE AT LIONSHEAD
380 East Lionshead Cir., Vail, CO 81658, 303-476-2700
Amenities: Heated outdoor pool, hot tub

These two-story, townhouse condos enjoy a great location close to the Lionshead gondola, perhaps the fastest way to the top of Vail mountain. Yet the lodge is just far enough removed so that the crowds of skiers don't create congestion at your condo home. The condos are "homey" with wallpaper and lots of knickknacks that personalize each unit. You'll find cozy living rooms with private fireplaces. The units are "stacked" or built into the side of a hill, which creates the impression that this is a small, personal resort. The outdoor pool is surrounded by flowers in summer and, as you are on a small promontory right above Gore Creek facing the pines; it's an enchanting setting.

6-8 THE LODGE/LODGE TOWER
200 Vail Rd., Vail, CO 81657, 303-476-5011 (Lodge)
303-476-9530 (Lodge Tower)
1BR $125–325, 2BR $180–465, 3BR $235–565
Amenities: Shopping arcade, hot tub. Next to lift

When Vail opened in 1964, The Lodge was one of the first establishments. Then the Lodge Tower condos were completed in the early 1970s and this became one of Vail's most popular resorts because of the central location. Due to the market timing of the condo sales program, a majority of the condo buyers/owners are from Texas. The Lodge has been dubbed "River Oaks North." In the heart of the village, the Lodge Tower is next to the Vista Bahn lift and just steps from the best restaurants and shops the village has to offer. Each of these condos is privately owned and the management does not enforce a uniform standard for interior decor. All are well decorated but some much better than others. In some, the owners have invested money to create a European atmosphere or perhaps a "northwoods chalet" ambiance. In others you'll find the standard convertible sofa, with Naugahyde or some other durable fabric. Ask about the unit you'll be renting.

The lobby at The Lodge is always bustling and the resort offers lots of services for its guests. If you travel with children, this is a great choice because The Lodge has a group of baby sitters on call. On the other hand, if you want a social weekend for two, this is also a great choice because the best of Vail's night life—which goes until 4 or 5 A.M. in season—is within a block or two. If you plan lots of skiing, the lift is outside your door. The Lodge is recommended because of its location and the hospitality services provided.

8+ L'OSTELLO (includes Enzian condos)
705 W. Lionshead Cir., Vail, CO 81657, 303-476-2050
Amenities: Heated outdoor pool, hot tub, restaurant, exercise room, room service

One of Vail's oldest establishments. L'Ostello is an eight-story, Austrian-style chalet that offers bright, spacious condos. The location is great because it's only a few steps away from the Lionshead gondola. Each spacious condo has a private fireplace as well as a full entertainment center including stereos and VTPs. The large kitchen also has a washer/dryer. These units have three and four bedrooms, some of the largest you'll find in the village. It is really a home away from home. Within the past year, this property has undergone a complete change. Previously, it was called the Enzian and was just a sleepy condominium development in a spectacular location. New management has capitalized on the location and the luxurious size of the units to create one of Vail's most spectacular European-flavored resorts. With the five-star Italian restaurant as the centerpiece (with chefs from some of the most critically acclaimed restaurants in the U.S.), service has become the hallmark of this resort. Pleasing to the eye, easy on the body, even those New Yorkers with the highest expectations will be pleased with L'Ostello.

8+ MANOR VAIL
595 E. Vail Dr., Vail, CO 81657, 303-476-5651
1BR $150–250, 2BR $210–400, 3BR $360–500
Amenities: Outdoor pools, hot tub, saunas

One of the most centrally located condo resorts in Vail, this resort occupies a prime spot at the east end of the main village. Manor Vail is right at the Golden Peak ski lifts, and the "pedestrian-only" village begins next door. This is a good choice for families with children because the Children's Ski Center is across the street. Also this has a two-story lobby area with a restaurant, game room and activity center. The Lord Gore restaurant, one of the most popular spots in the area for snacks after skiing, is also located here. Manor Vail offers outdoor swimming year-round, a hot tub, saunas, and an exercise area. In 1992 the resort was completely renovated and redecorated in order to keep pace with demands from discriminating vacationers. The "studios" are huge containing separate living and sleeping areas, fireplaces, fully equipped kitchens, and private balconies or patios. At other resorts these "studios" would qualify as one-bedroom units. The one- or two-bedroom units have a townhouse design. Many of these have a highly personalized interior decor with mementos from skiing in Europe. Others have embraced the German high-tech style. This is a lively, popular choice that is located as close to the lifts as you would want to be.

8+ MARRIOTT'S MARK RESORT
715 Lionshead Cir., Vail, CO 81657, 303-476-4444
1BR $205–450, 2BR $240–575, 3BR $320–700
Amenities: Indoor pool, outdoor pool, hot tubs, saunas, tennis, teaching pro, restaurants

One of Vail's largest hotels and conference centers, it also has a few spacious one- and two-bedroom condominiums. The location is in the Lionshead area, but you can walk to the main part of the village along Gore Creek. All the services of the hotel are available and the recent face-lift has resulted in a beautiful new lobby with a fireplace. These condos are spacious with full kitchens, a fireplace and great mountain views. For those who want the luxury of space as well as the fun of an active pool/hot tub/tennis center this is a good choice.

MARRIOTT'S STREAMSIDE
(See Streamside at Vail)

8   MILLRACE CONDOMINIUMS
1000 S. Frontage Rd., Vail, CO 81657, 303-476-6106
Amenities: Heated outdoor pool, hot tub. Next to Cascade Spa

Millrace contains spacious new condos located outside of town on Gore Creek. This is part of the Cascade Village development. Because it is set in a depression along the creek, Millrace is private. In the summer, if you open your windows, you can hear the brook babbling. You'll also see a fisherman or two each day. This is a good spot for trout fishing. The Millrace condos are contemporary in design and built with lots of natural oak and tile. The condos feature soft-colored designer fabrics and private fireplaces for snowy evenings. There's a heated outdoor pool and a hot tub. The Cascade Spa and Health Club is next door. In summer, lots of good humor surrounds those guests who take the cold-water plunge in Gore Creek—quite a stimulating experience. Although it's over a mile to Vail, there is a Cascade chair lift to take you directly up the mountain from this location. Don't expect lots of activity or hospitality—these are just good quality condo rentals.

8+   MONTANEROS
641 W. Lionshead Cir., Vail, CO 81657, 303-476-2491
1BR $84–278, 2BR $134–365, 3BR $164–455
Amenities: Outdoor pool, hot tub

Ask any local to recommend a condo for a vacation and one of the most frequently mentioned names is Montaneros. Everyone likes this condo resort. *Harper's Bazaar* calls it "one of the town's premier condo hotels." We won't go that far in our estimation. Located right by the Lionshead gondola, the condos are attractive, offering everyone a good view of the mountain. Inside, lots of wood and exposed beams create a rustic environment. Some have cathedral ceilings with two stories of glass wall facing the mountain. Some owners have really invested in the interior decor of their condos. You'll find that some of the units have an Austrian or a southwest collector motif. Others have a highly polished western style with flame-stitched fabrics, hand-crafted paneling, and a mounted moose head over the mantel. All condos have VTPs, stone hearths, and fireplaces. The management offers only limited services: here you make your own fun.

7   MOUNTAIN HAUS
292 East Meadow Dr., Vail, CO 81658, 303-476-2434
Amenities: Hot tub, pool

Mountain Haus is an older condo project right at the east entrance to the pedestrian walking village. It's just been spruced up to provide a contemporary atmosphere for the 1990s. For skiers the location is a seven to ten minute walk through the village to the Vista Bahn ski lift from Mountain Haus. There's a pleasant lobby and it's staffed with personnel to assist you at all times, but there's no restaurant or bar. The condos are large, some are well decorated, while others are waiting to be spruced up. After skiing, this resort offers a real recuperation program. There are saunas, a steam room, and a masseuse to take care of you after an active day in the mountains.

5   PARK MEADOWS
1472 Matterhorn Cir., Vail, CO 81657
Amenities: Hot tub

Budget accommodations in Vail yet within easy walking distance of the newest ski lift. The location is up above Cascade Village so town is a healthy 30-minute walk away along Gore Creek, or it's a five-minute drive. These studio, one and two-bedroom condos have some of the lowest rates we could find with a two-bedroom condo renting for $1300 per week in season. For two couples, that's an incredibly low $46 per night per person. And you are right at the ski lift.

6   RIVA RIDGE SOUTH
Willows Rd., Vail, CO 81658, 303-476-2233
Amenities: Heated pool, hot tub, saunas

Riva Ridge is a small 18-unit condo complex that, although it's quiet and private, enjoys a great location next to the #1 chair lift at the entrance to Vail's pedestrian village. Because of its location, Riva Ridge enjoys great views. The condos are spacious and each has a ceiling-high, moss-rock fireplace. This is what you would imagine a ski condo to look like. Interiors are contemporary and comfortable—nothing special, just a pleasant holiday environment. It is great for two couples or a family. You can use the sauna and hot tub next door at the Willows, which is another condo complex under the same management.

8   RUCKSACK
Bridge St., Vail, CO 81657 (no mail)
Amenities: Next to lift

These two-bedroom condos are located on Bridge Street in the very heart of Vail. Passersby will envy you. They are only steps away from the Vista Bahn lift. In spite of the popularity of the location, inside you'll feel snug and cozy with a fireplace and a lovely living room. The master bath has a whirlpool and a steam shower.

5+   **SANDSTONE CREEK (Sandstone & Sandstone Creek Club)**
1020 Vail View Dr., Vail, CO 81657, 303-476-4405
Amenities: Clubhouse, game room, heated indoor/outdoor pool,
health club, snack bar, racquetball, tennis

Perched on a hillside across Interstate 70 from Vail Village, these condos
all have a view of Vail and the mountains behind. Sandstone Creek Club is a
complete resort and a world unto itself. The condos are large, and they have
every convenience. The interiors are almost overwhelming, with Polynesian
patterned fabrics and patterned carpet. Designed for families, it's a happy
choice with lots of children by the pool, pre-teens in the game room, or teens
bragging about their ski exploits. It is also very popular in summer.

5   **SCORPIO**
131 W. Meadow Dr., Vail, CO 81657
Amenities: None

Located on the Frontage Road just above Vail Village, it's only a five-
minute walk along Gore Creek over to the main part of town. You'll find
handsome two-bedroom condos in this five-story building where everyone
has a spectacular view of Gore Creek and Vail Mountain from the balcony.
One of Vail's older condo buildings, there's a wide range of quality here.
Interior decor varies from contemporary modern to fancy western. The centerpiece is the moss-rock fireplace. Scorpio is well suited for a family or two
couples. The Vista Bahn and Lionshead lifts are a short walk away.

6-7   **SIMBA RESORT**
1100 North Frontage Rd., Vail, CO 81657
Amenities: Indoor pool, health club, racquetball, tennis

Located on the north side of the Interstate highway, you need to have a
car because it's a long walk over the pedestrian bridge to the center of Vail.
Of course, shuttle buses run frequently. Although the location is not the most
desirable, this resort compensates by providing a full private health club.
Simba enjoys interesting contemporary architecture and lots of "extras." The
condos are nicely decorated with lots of oak furniture and natural colored
fabrics. The interiors have a warm, comfortable feel to them. You'll enjoy
sitting by the fire drinking hot chocolate after skiing. Then go down to the
health club and enjoy the full-length indoor pool, hot tub, saunas, steam
rooms, and exercise area. There's even a full health club and a masseuse to
loosen up your muscles. If you want activity there are two racquetball courts
and three tennis courts. See what we mean about Simba being blessed with
lots of extras? And, it's reasonably priced.

7+   STREAMSIDE AT VAIL
2264 South Frontage Rd. West, Vail, CO 81657, 303-476-6000
Amenities: Pool, gym, racquetball, health club, shuttle

Located about a mile from the Lionshead lift, this resort has its own shuttle buses constantly en route to the center of Vail. There are four separate buildings, two of which are on the creek. If you like to listen to the rushing stream at night, ask to be in the Aspen building. The buildings are three-story condominium structures. Their interiors are very attractive, with bright colors, professionally decorated, and lots of glass to bring in the view and sunshine. There is a full kitchen, and everything has been provided for. Primarily a family resort, you'll find a very active pool/hot tub center. Management by Marriott, but no restaurant services.

4   SUN VAIL
605 N. Frontage Rd., Vail, CO 81657
Amenities: Outdoor pool (summer only)

These budget accommodations across the highway from the village enjoy a great view of town and Vail Mountain. Furnished for comfort and efficiency, the units are a little small, but then so is the price. Each has a fireplace and a balcony where you can drink up the mountain view.

8+   VAIL ATHLETIC CLUB
352 E. Meadow Dr., Vail, CO 81657, 303-476-0700
Amenities: Pool, saunas, hot tub, rock climbing wall

This is the latest statement on luxury in Vail. This hotel/condo club is actually a fantastic health spa. It's not a sweat shop, but an elegant retreat with marble, leather, and Old World charm. In addition to the swimming pool, the saunas, aerobic classes, hot tubs, nursery and child care programs, the VAC has a ROCK CLIMBING WALL. That's right! Learn to scale the Rockies with indoor professional instruction, and find out about all that expensive mountaineering equipment. It's unique and it provides a genuine physical and mental challenge. The VAC has masseurs and professionals to teach you the "inner game" of racquetball as well as lifetime physical fitness. Most of the 38 rooms are studios with full kitchens. Some have one bedroom. All have elegant interiors with grass cloth wallpaper and luxurious furniture. The lobby looks like the finest in the Bavarian Alps. The restaurant, 352 East, is one of the most expensive in Vail, with exquisite nouvelle cuisine. The VAC is very sophisticated—one of the most glitzy addresses in Vail.

8   VAIL GOLF COURSE TOWNHOUSES
Vail, CO 81657 (no mail)
Amenities: Golf

Located along the golf course in East Vail, these luxurious townhouses are a mile away from Vail Village. Spectacular in summer (except during the week of the Gerald Ford Golf Classic), the location is also lovely in winter when snow blankets the fairways. These spacious three-bedroom townhouses feature a two-car garage, fireplace, large modern kitchen, and a laundry room. In all there's over 2000 square feet of living space on three levels. Most have a private hot tub off the master bedroom. These are truly luxurious year-round.

5   VAIL INTERNATIONAL

300 E. Lionshead Cir., Vail, CO 81657, 303-476-5200
Amenities: Heated pool, hot tub, saunas

Situated between Vail Village and Lionshead, many of these condos enjoy a good view of Gore Creek and the mountain. It's close to all of the town's restaurants and shopping without being in a congested area. It's a short walk to the Lionshead gondola and the Vista Bahn ski lift. The interior decor here is a little bit below average—small units with sturdy, "skierized" furniture. As there are over 100 condos in this six-story resort complex, there's always a lot of activity and it's a good place to develop new friendships. Vail International is a good choice for ski groups and those looking for value.

7+   VAIL RACQUET CLUB

4690 Vail Racquet Club Dr., Vail, CO 81657, 303-476-4840
Amenities: Tennis (including three covered courts in winter), indoor lap pool, fitness center, aerobics classes

This is located in the town of East Vail, four miles away from Vail Village. To get to the ski areas you must either drive or take the shuttle bus, which runs frequently. The Vail Racquet Club is one of Vail's most complete, self-contained resorts. At other resorts, you are staying in a condo and will probably play in Vail Village. Here the fun is self-contained and you'll get to know others who are staying here with you.

The reason to choose this resort is the extensive athletic facilities. It's a great place for children because there are activities, child care programs, and a baby pool. The condos are bright, spacious, and beautifully decorated. The three-bedroom townhouses have fireplaces and cathedral ceilings. If you don't feel like cooking, the Racquet Club has a popular restaurant. As long as you understand you are not in the village of Vail, this is a great choice because of all the activities available.

7+   VAIL SPA

710 W. Lionshead Cir., Vail, CO 81657, 303-476-2700
Amenities: Indoor and outdoor pool, weight room, sauna

The condos here provide home-like living accommodations that are well-suited for families or small groups of friends. One of the newer condo developments in Vail, everything here is modern and very up-to-date. The main reason for choosing this resort is the spa, which has heated indoor and outdoor pools, steam and dry heat saunas, indoor and outdoor hot tubs, and a fully-equipped exercise room. The location in Lionshead is only a short walk from the Lionshead gondola. The condos are well-decorated, but very few have been personalized and most have the comfortable, casual furniture that skiers expect to find in the Rockies—blond wood and plaid fabrics. In each of the condos, you can stretch out in front of the fireplace after an active day.

5   VAIL TRAILS
605 N. Frontage Rd. West, Vail, CO 81657
Amenities: None

These pleasant, two-story buildings are located in the Gold Peak area of Vail Village. All have two bedrooms, spacious kitchens, fireplaces, and great views of the mountains from the balcony and patio. Interior decor ranges from superior "skierized" furniture to units which have a southwestern look, or a "European ski-town" ambiance.

5   VAIL VILLAGE INN
100 E. Meadow Dr., Vail, CO 81657, 303-476-2700
Amenities: Heated outdoor pool, sauna, hot tub, restaurant

The condos at the Vail Village Inn are some of the oldest in Vail, yet this prestigious location has been beautifully maintained as the town continues to grow from the core. There is a picture-postcard view of Vail Mountain. Interior decor is luxurious and shows the work of a professional designer. There's a full kitchen, and there's also a popular restaurant downstairs. Some of Vail's best shops are located in this arcade.

8+   THE VILLAGE CENTER
Willow Bridge Rd., Vail, CO 81657
Amenities: Outdoor pool

Located in the heart of Vail Village, you are steps away from some of Vail's best restaurants and only a short walk from the Vista Bahn ski lift. All units overlook Vail mountain and Gore Creek. The one, two and three-bedroom condos are spacious and have full kitchens. Giant wood-beam ceilings and stone fireplace hearths create a warm, cozy feeling. This is a great location and worth the price.

6 VORLAUFER
385 Gore Creek Dr., Vail, CO 81657
Amenities: Sauna

This is a great location for skiers in Vail just one block from the Gold Peak and the Vista Bahn lifts. These three-story Austrian chalet buildings are handsome and the units on the third floor have vaulted ceilings and sweeping mountain views. Each has a full kitchen and a fireplace.

9 WALL STREET
225 Wall St., Vail, CO 81657
Amenities: None

Right across from Vail's unique Children's Fountain, you'll find the exquisite Wall Street condos. Only the most successful traders and investors can afford this location and level of luxury. These one and two-bedroom condos are luxuriously decorated. There are small kitchens, but beautiful brick-wall fireplaces. The one we saw successfully blended French country with southwestern geometric patterned fabrics. Most of these condos have either a private sauna, a whirlpool or both. Located in the heart of Vail, Wall Street is only steps away from the ski lifts.

5 WESTWIND AT VAIL
548 S. Frontage Rd., Vail, CO 81657, 303-476-5031
Amenities: Pool, tennis

Built in 1969, the Westwind is starting to show its age. It's a good budget choice for those who want to ski in Vail but not spend a lot of money. This is in the Lionshead Mall area, only a five-minute walk from the Lionshead gondola. The interior decor is rustic early American. Each unit has a full kitchen and a fireplace. It's a good choice for groups of skiers because with three or four bedrooms and so many people sharing the cost, the price of a Vail vacation can be quite reasonable.

RENTAL RESOURCES...VAIL (See also Beaver Creek)
Big Horn Rentals, 303-476-5532
Brandess Cadmus Realty, 303-476-1450
Cascade Village Properties, 303-476-6106
Destination Resorts, 303-476-1350
East Vail Rentals, 303-476-6636
Miller Real Estate, 303-476-1766
Property & Rental Management, 303-476-4400
Ruder & Assoc., 303-476-0640
Slifer, Smith & Framptom, 303-476-2421

Vail Associates Rentals, 303-949-5750
Vail Realty & Rental Management, 303-476-8800

12. WINTER PARK

One of Colorado's earliest ski areas, Winter Park is not a classic resort community like Vail or Aspen. In 1939, It began as a one-day destination for Denverites who would ride the morning ski train and return home at the end of the day. Therefore, it was slow in developing the resort community "feel." However, this is a major mountain with 1300 skiable acres and 117 trails and eventually developers realized its potential. In 1993, the Parsenn Bowl expansion was completed with high-speed lifts to take skiers to a summit of 12,000 feet overlooking 200 acres of treeless ski terrain.

During the 1980s, Winter Park experienced a condo building boom and the related restaurants and night spots quickly developed. Now it is a bona fide resort community with a brand new central lodge and one of the largest children's ski schools in the U.S. Winter Park not only enjoys the advantage of being close to Denver (many would call this a disadvantage on week ends) but it has two connecting ski areas, Winter Park and Mary Jane, with a small town in between along the highway. In recent years the skier mix has flipped from day skiers to more destination visitors, including many from Texas and the Midwest. Winter Park offers numerous special programs in order to compete with the other Colorado ski areas. It has the largest and most comprehensive ski program for the disabled in the world.

In the town of Winter Park and in the surrounding region, there's a great choice of accommodations and enough restaurants that skiers will have to think about where they want to go in the evening.

Silver Creek is a new ski area master condo resort development spread over 2300 acres just north of Winter Park and south of Granby, the western entrance to Rocky Mountain National Park. Conceived as a family resort where you can ski, play golf, or improve your tennis game, it is one of Colorado's largest real estate developments and its history is only beginning. In the summer you will be hard pressed to find a better location as a center for camping, hiking, and fishing expeditions.

Rocky Mountain National Park has been a celebrated mountain retreat since the days of Kit Carson. You may have read about this area in James Michener's *Centennial,* which was based in part on the true story of the Irish Earl of Dunraven who built a fabulous hunting lodge near Grand Lake. In the summer, two of Colorado's best driving and biking trails are Trail Ridge Road and Bear Lake Road in the park. Granby is a town built to service Rocky Mountain National Park, but the really good accommodations are at the timeshare condo developments in Silver Creek, midway between the park and Winter Park.

WHERE TO STAY

8   BEAVER VILLAGE CONDOS
50 Village Dr., Box 349, Winter Park, CO 80482, 800-824-8438
1BR $85–130, 2BR $115–180, 3BR $150–240
Amenities: Clubhouse, hot tubs, sauna, pool

Here you are in a beautiful wooded area just far enough off the beaten track that all you see around you is the beauty of nature. The condos are clustered here and there in a campus-style setting. On-site management (a rarity in Winter Park) has created a country-inn atmosphere here and you'll notice the difference upon arrival when you walk in and smell the fragrant potpourri provided to each guest. Unlike many Winter Park properties, this one has its own recreation center so you can walk over and soak in the hot tub or play with your children after a day of skiing or hiking in the wilderness. The condos are new and well-decorated with southwestern fabrics to create a true vacation atmosphere. You won't need a car if you plan to stay here because there is a bus with frequent service to the ski lifts; town and the ski slopes are both a short ride away.

8   CRESTVIEW PLACE
Vasquez Rd., Winter Park, CO 80482
1BR $80–132, 2BR $132–240.
Amenities: Hot tub

You couldn't have a better location than this in Winter Park. It's in the heart of town, across the street from the Transit Center and the shopping plaza. Each condo overlooks the town of Winter Park and the Continental Divide. The condos are spacious and beautifully decorated, not just furnished. There's a private fireplace in each unit and in the master bathrooms, whirlpool tubs turn a bath into an experience. Across from the Transportation Center and the heart of town, this is one of the few resorts where you won't need a car. For a family on vacation, or a group of skiers or summer visitors looking for mountain air, this is a great choice.

7+   HI COUNTRY HAUS
78737 U.S. Highway 40, Winter Park, CO 80482, 800-228-1025
Studio $76–120, 1BR $80–144, 2BR $88–198
Amenities: Pool, hot tubs, recreation center, restaurant, shuttle

Located on the edge of town, this resort enjoys the advantage of being close to restaurants and night life without being in an area of congestion. It's close to the Park Place shopping center, which is a shuttle bus stop for skiers. All of the condos, from studio to three-bedroom units, feature moss-rock fireplaces that add immeasurably to the warmth and enjoyment of an après-ski party. In summer, there's a stream that flows behind the building. It is a good choice for families and groups of skiers. You'll find good hospitality and spacious condos here.

6 THE INN AT SILVER CREEK

U.S. Highway 40 North, Silver Creek, CO 80446, 303-887-2131
1BR suites $71–169
Amenities: Lake, pool, golf, tennis, sauna, racquetball,
exercise room, children's programs

This is a special place in the Colorado mountains and we wish we had better news to report. This has tremendous potential and could be another Keystone, but each year it just seems to slip. Not yet discovered by the crowds, the Silver Creek area where the Inn is located, north of Winter Park and just south of Estes Park, offers everything you could want in a Colorado mountain vacation. The Inn at Silver Creek is the social center of the area and guests at the Inn's condos can enjoy the pools, golf, tennis, and windsurfing on the lake in the summer. In the winter, there is skiing, saunas, racquetball courts, an exercise room and an indoor pool to keep you active and healthy. There is a children's playground and an activities program for kids, including child care during the day while you ski. The interiors were recently decorated with attractive colors and lots of flowers. The loft units have spiral staircases. The master bath is an experience with both a whirlpool and a separate steam cabinet. Third floor rooms and suites have vaulted ceilings, skylights, and lofts. All, except standard rooms, feature a wet bar (with refrigerator, sink and microwave oven) and a dining area. The living rooms have fireplaces. There are no full kitchens.

9 IRON HORSE RESORT

257 Winter Park Dr., Winter Park, CO 80482, 800-542-4253
Studio $85–140, 1BR $125–305, 2BR $185–370
Amenities: Pool, hot tub, racquetball, gym, restaurant,
ski-in/ski-out access

Clearly the best in Winter Park, this is the only ski-in/ski-out resort around. It's a short downhill trail away from the base of the mountain. It has its own history, too. It was the former worker's campsite when the historic Moffat Tunnel was built under the Continental Divide. Today's resort is completely different. This six-story modern condominium is operated with full hotel services. The accent here is on hospitality; it's not just a place to stay. There are cozy "sports suites" for two as well as one and two-bedroom condos. Each condo is nicely decorated—Southwest style, with lots of wood and tweedy fabrics. The upper units have cathedral ceilings and rows of glass skylights that create a "greenhouse effect" on sunny days. Each condo has a cozy fireplace for winter and a sun deck or balcony for summer. Facing the woods, this is a pleasant spot. Some condos have loft bedrooms; these are the ones that also feature overly large living rooms. Most of the condos have private whirlpools (large enough for two) in the master bath. The best feature is the sports complex with racquetball courts, exercise and weight room, and indoor/outdoor pool (the favorite spot for children), hot tubs, and saunas.

6   MOUNTAINSIDE AT SILVER CREEK
96 Mountainside Dr., Silver Creek, CO 80446
Amenities: Hot tub, pool

This is one of the best bargains in the Rockies. The units are new and beautifully decorated for use by a family. The master bath has a whirlpool.

5   SUMMIT AT SILVERCREEK
207 Lake Dr., 3095, Winter Park, CO 80482
Amenities: Pool, steam bath, sauna. Next to lift

Located at the base of the Silver Creek ski area, next to the Summit chair lift, this new condo project sits all alone. It's great for those who want to be near the lifts and in uncrowded conditions. This condo complex is a real find because they are all high quality condos, each with a private hot tub for two. The prices are low because there's nothing else around. The Inn at Silver Creek is about two miles down the hill. For night life, you might want to drive six miles into Winter Park. This is a great choice for those who want to be alone or those groups who have their own self-contained fun.

7   THE SUMMIT AT WINTER PARK
100 Bryant Blvd., Winter Park, CO 80482
Amenities: None

A brand-new complex in the Meadow Ridge development two miles north of town, the Summit is completely set apart. There are no special facilities, programs or activities, nor is there an on-site, check-in office. The project is new and the atmosphere is serene. The units are beautifully decorated and in great condition, but the place is a ghost-town.

7   TIMBER RUN
265 Forest Trail, Winter Park, CO 80482
Amenities: Hot tubs, tennis, sauna, shuttle

This enjoys a nice, central location on the outskirts of Winter Park. You can walk to restaurants and shopping without being in the congestion of Winter Park during peak season. The condos are fairly new and spacious and have private fireplaces. Some condos have private hot tubs and private saunas. This resort offers an escapist's home-away-from-home atmosphere. Timber Run offers a complimentary shuttle bus to world-class skiing nearby at Winter Park or Mary Jane mountains. This resort is a "sleeper" tucked away in the woods just outside Winter Park.

1   TWIN RIVERS
       300 Sterling Way Rd., Winter Park, CO 80482
       Amenities: None

Partially vacation rentals and partially residential, this place is unremarkable. Some of the residents are groups of young workers from the Winter Park ski area. You'll see laundry hanging on the balconies. Do not expect a resort atmosphere. Twin Rivers is for a young skier who would like to meet "the locals" and find the good bars at night. If you want a rental at a low price, this might be a suitable vacation destination.

8   THE VINTAGE
       Box 1369,Winter Park, CO 80482, 800-472-7017
       Studio $85–185, 2BR $195–290, 3BR $230–360
       Amenities: Outdoor pool, hot tub, restaurant , sauna, gym

This condo hotel is one of the newest additions to Winter Park and reflects the community's desire to attract vacationers from beyond Denver. The accommodations would best be described as European style suites. Many have private jacuzzi whirlpools and fireplaces. More sociable than most properties in the area, you'll find the restaurant and bar to be a popular spot for singles after skiing.

RENTAL RESOURCES
All Seasons Vacations, 303-586-3748
Coldwell Banker, 303-726-8831
Colorado Country Properties, 303-627-3425
Condo Management Co., 303-726-9421
Grand Realty, 303-627-3905
Lakeview, 303-887-2461
Prescott Agency, 303-586-3331
ReMax Grand Lake, 303-627-8001
Silverado II, 303-726-5753
Soda Springs Ranch, 303-627-8125
Windcliff, 303-586-2181

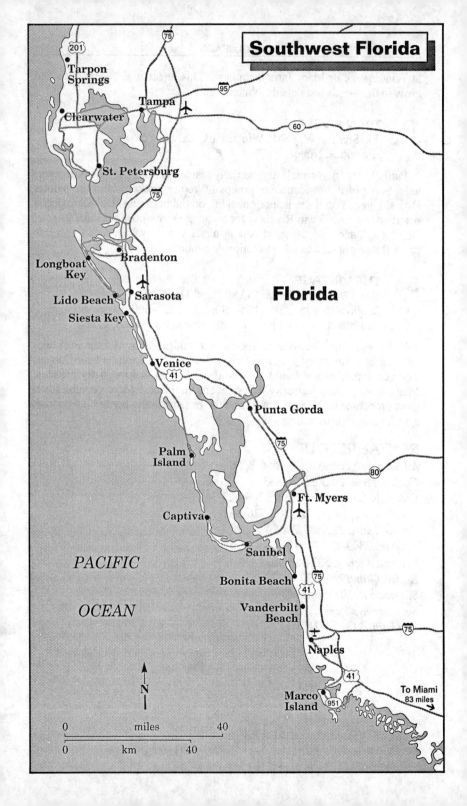

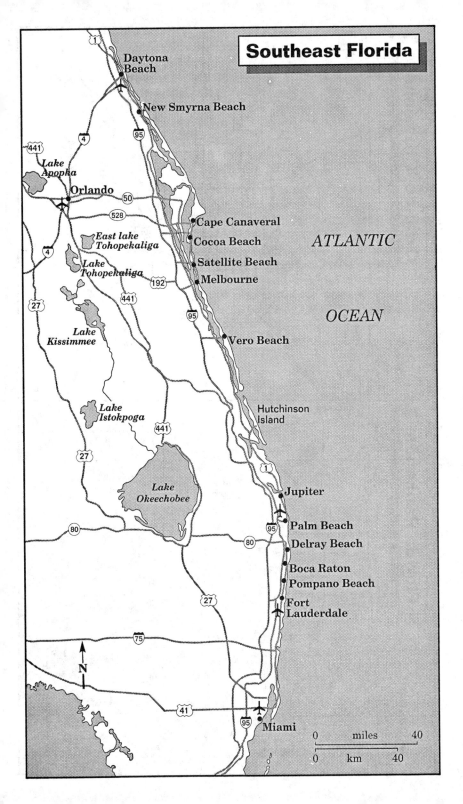

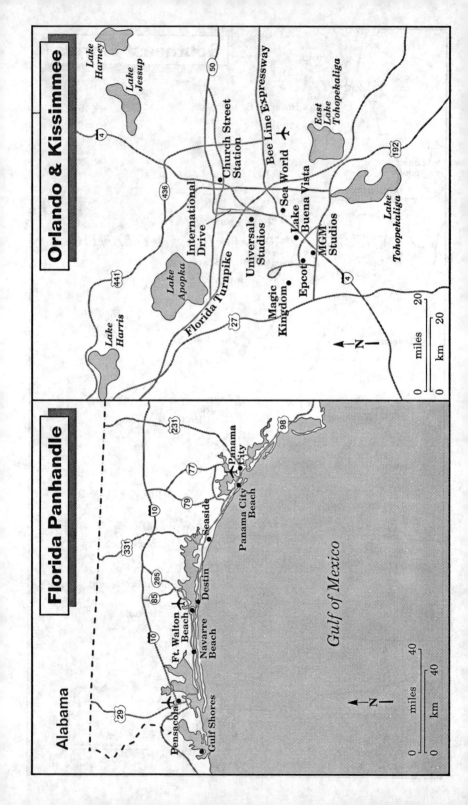

FLORIDA

The most important characteristic of any guidebook is the organization of material so the reader can find relevant information efficiently. Florida presents our greatest challenge, since 22% of the estimated resort condo and villa inventory in North America (available for vacation rentals) is located in this state. We have seen, visited, and inspected over 1200 resort condos in Florida and have discovered that in several instances there are two unrelated resort developments with the same name in different parts of the state. In short, there is no simple, systematic way to review all of the condos in Florida.

We have organized our Florida chapter into eleven separate regions, starting with Orlando in the center, and then dropping down to the southwest corner before progressing around the state's beach resort areas in a clockwise fashion. When planning a vacation, it's best to know what's available in the vicinity of your destination. Therefore, we focused on small areas in order to keep the number of condos under review limited to a small, manageable number. Unlike most other chapters, we have included a map of each separate area as well as of the state.

Many visitors plan their vacation to Florida based upon assumptions about the climate and often upon the recommendations of friends. This guide to Florida is different because we tell you about the area you have focused upon, and we give a glimpse of nearby neighborhoods for comparison. For example, visitors to Collier County know there is a world of difference between Naples, Marco Island, and Vanderbilt Beach. All three are within a 15 mile radius of downtown Naples, but development has created communities with entirely distinct senses of purpose.

Because Florida has so many part-time residents, there are special customs that have developed among local condo resorts. Many have restrictions imposed by the condo homeowners associations that limit or restrict short-term rentals. You'll find some condominiums that may only be rented three times a year. Others have restrictions prohibiting rentals for less than 30 days—in order to attract a more mature clientele that intends to spend part of the winter in Florida. We've even found the very confusing situation in which two separate rental companies cite two different sets of rental restrictions for the same resort. What's a consumer to do? Our advice is to investigate what the rental agents tell you. In every community (except Palm Beach) we've found that short-term rentals for a week or less do exist. It may take a couple of phone calls to ferret them out, especially around the time of Christmas vacation or Spring Break. You'll also find situations in which rental agents bend the rules and do rent out exclusive condominiums for the short term, in spite of the local HOA restrictions. St. Petersburg Beach, Orlando, and the Northern beach communities are quiet, relaxed and receptive to short-term rentals. The rental restrictions we described above are most prevalent on the Southeast Coast, and especially in the exclusive communities of Palm Beach County, Indian River County, and in the town of Naples (on the West Coast).

If yo have trouble arranging a rental, be patient and persistent. Make several calls. Find out about the varying price quotes (and you'll be shocked by the gulf between what rental agency A charges compared to what rental agency B is asking for the same condo resort!) The reward for just a little effort will be an exceptional vacation that will be the envy of your friends and neighbors.

Our goal is to help you find the right resort in the community that's right for you. With this in mind, here's a quick overview of Florida's eleven vacation areas:

1. **Orlando and the Magic Kissimmee**—This region bursts with elaborate, imaginative attractions. Many of the resorts in this area are timeshares that are equally competitive in design and fantasy. Golf resorts with villas along the fairway are also popular and there is a trend toward vacation home rentals where visitors can spend a week or two in a house with three bedrooms and a private pool. Although the homes don't have the activity or fantasy of the timeshares, they are attractive to visitors who plan longer stays.

2. **Collier County (Marco Island, Naples and Vanderbilt Beach)**— Located on Florida's southwestern tip it includes Marco Island, a beach resort offering some excellent values and a warm winter climate. Missing the commercialism of many of Florida's small cities and providing an island life, Marco has a sense of detachment from the worries of the mainland. Naples is rapidly developing into one of Florida's most exclusive resort communities and there is a prejudice here against short term rentals for less than a month. Vanderbilt Beach, on the other hand, caters to both the vacationer with just a week to spend as well as to the pre-retiree planning a month in the sun.

3. **Lee County (Sanibel, Captiva, and Ft. Myers Beach)**—Long established as one of Florida's favorite playgrounds, today Ft. Myers is becoming a small city. Sanibel and Captiva Islands have a uniquely preserved ecological heritage while Ft. Myers Beach offers a host of high-rise towers.

4. **Sarasota (Longboat Key, Lido Beach, and Siesta Key)**—Like Ft. Myers, Sarasota is emerging as a small city, but the three offshore islands cater to seasonal and resort visitors. Longboat Key was developed with a string of towers and townhouses, each of which is surrounded by manicured landscaping. Longboat is popular with the affluent and active. Lido Beach has a strip of budget accommodations as well as solid condo towers, popular with older travelers. Siesta Key is both a resort area, with its fabulous six mile long Crescent Beach, and a residential area popular with artists, writers, and the self-employed.

5. **Tampa Bay and the Northwest Coast (Tarpon Springs, Clearwater, and St. Petersburg)**—Most of the condo resorts are along the strip from Tarpon Springs in the north, through Clearwater and St. Petersburg, down to a couple of islands in the Bay such as Isla del Sol and Isla Verde. Although a few are in the luxury category, many are reasonably priced and offer the convenience of a big city as well as lots of sunshine and a very healthy climate.

6. **The Panhandle (Panama City Beach, Destin, and Pensacola)**—This is also called the Emerald coast and covers a massive number of condo resorts. There are over 150 resort property developments in just Panama City Beach alone. Heading west there are Sandestin and Destin, which are a little more expensive than Panama City Beach, and finally there is the strip of condos between Ft. Walton Beach and Pensacola. Although primarily beach oriented, there are some excellent golf course communities along this 80 mile stretch. Located on the northern end of the state, winter is the low season here, summer is the high season, and we think spring and fall are the best times to visit.

7. **Northeast Florida (Amelia Island, Sawgrass/Ponte Vedra, and St. Augustine Beach)**—This area just north and just south of Jacksonville was the last to be developed, but it may be the best of all. Shunned for decades because the climate is cooler than the rest of the state, the Amelia Island development awakened the state to the potential for ecologically planned resorts. Coexisting with a wetlands environment on the south end of the island are seven championship golf courses and over a hundred tennis courts. Ponte Vedra has been an exclusive resort area since the 1930s, but this is another area that came to life with the introduction of the master planned Sawgrass resort and the TPC golf course. Just twenty miles south you'll come to the new resorts along St. Augustine Island, set back from the ocean in order to preserve the ecology of the dunes. Another twenty miles farther south of St. Augustine, you'll find Palm Coast, a master-planned 42,000 acre resort/retirement community.

8. **The Space Coast (Daytona, New Smyrna, Cocoa, and Vero Beach)**—The east central coast of Florida, from Daytona to Cocoa Beach to Vero Beach, offers a string of beach resorts for all pocketbooks—punctuated by the Kennedy Space Center at Cape Canaveral. Daytona has a wide range of modest to inexpensive condo resorts, many of which are starting to show their age. New Smyrna Beach is quieter, less urban, and growing in popularity with visitors in the spring, summer, and fall. Cocoa Beach is known for its surfing, and Vero Beach has a fifteen mile string of private-gated "enclave" resorts where most vacation rentals are for a month or longer. Hutchinson Island has a host of attractive condo and townhouse resort developments along the beach that are quiet, neat, and appealing to those who prefer the slow lane.

9. **Palm Beach County (Jupiter, Singer Island, Delray, and Boca Raton)**—With Palm Beach as the focal point, the new development has been in the northern part of the county near Jupiter. This town has wisely required that all development be across the street from the beach, leaving a beautifully preserved state beach for all to enjoy. Singer Island has equal numbers of resorts and retirement condos. Nearer the city, the resort areas value their privacy. Boca Raton was a playground twenty years ago. Today more and more resort properties are becoming full time residences.

10. **Broward and Dade Counties (Pompano, Ft. Lauderdale, and Miami)**—The cities of Ft. Lauderdale and Miami have swallowed up many of the resort properties as the year-round population now exceeds four million. There are still vacation homes and condos in the enclave communities of Deerfield and Pompano Beach however, as well as on the islands in Biscayne Bay.

11. **The Florida Keys (Key Largo, Islamorada, Marathon, and Key West)**—Surprisingly there are few beaches, but lots of romantic settings along this 90 mile stretch of coral islands. Key Largo and Islamorada cater to fishermen while Key West enjoys a culture all its own.

As you can see, the southern parts of the state are a little warmer than the northern parts. Draw a line from Tampa to Daytona Beach; this is the dividing line for winter resorts. The areas south of this line have beach weather even in January and February. However, north of this line around Destin or Amelia Island, people don't usually start thinking of the beach until April. Keep this in mind when choosing the part of the state which you wish to visit.

1. ORLANDO AND THE MAGIC KISSIMMEE

Orlando is entirely different from any other resort destination. Walt Disney World, first opened 20 years ago, is the engine driving tourism. Since then other attractions such as Universal Studios, Sea World, and Church Street Station have given vacationers a reason to either stay longer or to come back again. Kissimmee lies between Orlando and Walt Disney World. This was a small agricultural community until a few years ago. With the opening of the Magic Kingdom in 1972, the area was transformed into a strip of motels, restaurants, and convenience stores. Currently it's going through its second generation of construction. The local motels are being replaced by quality condos or upgraded hotels.

Perhaps the most distinguishing feature of the resort properties in the Orlando area is the high concentration of timeshares. Offering short-term accommodations for a week or even less, the Orlando timeshares have set high standards for the community that the hotels now follow. Ten years ago resorts were judged by their proximity to Disney World. Today, that has changed and accommodations are judged by the extra luxury—such as a private whirlpool or the number of VTPs/televisions in each unit. You'll find themed resorts that are among our favorites anywhere, including Bryan's Spanish Cove, the alluring Isle of Bali, and the Parkway Adventure, which has a jungle walk attraction all its own. Some of the timeshares promote sports. For example, Vistana has 26 tennis courts and teaching clinics. Others like Marriott's Sabal Palms or Orange Lake Country Club have a golf course setting.

For those seeking less active and more residential resort areas, we have augmented our list with golf course communities and condos that are good for long term stays. Bay Hill is probably the resort community that comes closest to the benchmark standards we have followed in other communities. Bay Hill, designed by and home to Arnold Palmer, is at once a golf resort community, a retirement community, and increasingly a residential community. With the growth of metropolitan Orlando, the demand for permanent residential housing has increased dramatically. The story here is similar to San Diego and Newport Beach, California. Although prices are low by comparison with the rest of the U.S. (average home prices in Orlando are $80,000 vs a $96,000 national average), many condos or townhouse communities that once were "vacation homes" have become permanent residences. These also include the Parc Corniche condos, Cypress Creek townhouses, and Fortune Place.

Finally, a whole new range of vacation accommodations is emerging in the Orlando area thanks to the influx of European visitors. Beginning as a trickle a few years ago, British visitors first came because, with the fall of the U.S. dollar against the British pound, prices in Florida seemed so very low. Then others came because of recommendations from their friends. Now Orlando has nonstop flights to London, Amsterdam, Frankfurt, and Luxembourg. Scandinavian and Italian air charters are also pouring in. Many of these overseas visitors, impressed to find a four-bedroom house with a pool selling for under $100,000, purchased homes in the Orlando area for investment or retirement purposes. Some of the most popular communities for European home ownership are Sand Lake Point, Sand Pines Estates, Deer Creek Village, and along the golf courses at Metrowest, Ventura, or International Country Club. These vacation homes are used by their owners perhaps for one month each year and then they are rented to other vacationers through local realtors who specialize in this market. With monthly rental rates as low as $1400 for a three-bedroom home with a screened-in patio surrounding a pool, these are a special treat for visitors to the Orlando area. We have reviewed examples of some of these properties and briefly mention those rental agents specializing in Orlando area vacation homes.

Transportation to Orlando is easy with nonstop air service by Delta, United, American, and U.S. Air to many major cities and connections that are available through the airline hubs.

WHERE TO STAY

8+ BAY HILL CLUB
9000 Bay Hill Blvd., Orlando, FL 32819, 407-876-2429
2BR $250–310
Amenities: Golf, tennis, marina, pool

Arnold Palmer was instrumental in the design of the condos and town-houses surrounding the Bay Hill Club and he still maintains a condo there. Basically there are two "lifestyles" for the four-hundred and forty condos here: either along the lake front/marina or along the golf course fairways. Architecturally, you'll find townhouse-style condos with separate ground level entrances or apartment style condos in two or three-story buildings. Constructed in the late '70s, these lack the glitz and glamour of many newer Orlando-area accommodations. But socially this is one of Orlando's most prestigious addresses. Each unit is tastefully decorated and almost all have golfing memorabilia along the walls or on the coffee table. This is for those who want the country club lifestyle as well as access to Disney World and other area attractions. After all, on a one or two-week vacation, just how much time can you spend at amusement parks? Rentals here include the option of club membership privileges, greens fees, and cart rentals at a discount during your stay. The management is by Arnold Palmer.

8 BRYAN'S SPANISH COVE
13875 S.R. 535, Orlando, FL 32819, 800-634-3119
2BR $130–175
Amenities: Beach, pool, hot tub, playground, fishing

Yo ho, a pirate's life for me! This themed resort on the shores of Lake Bryan features the best of a pirate's world for vacationers (not to mention a treasure laden beach!). But we doubt most pirates ever had it this good. Beautifully designed and decorated, this property is meticulously managed. Nary a wadded-up pirate's map nor a piece of trash to be found on the manicured lawns. Everything has been designed to create a "pirates of the Caribbean" adventure. Each of Cap'n Bryan's Villas is decorated with Caribbean pinks and many leafy plants. They are also characterized by a private fireplace, a stereo sound system and a whirlpool in the master bath. The pirate's theme has been carried out with an 8-foot pirate character in the resort lobby. The resort is on a large lake surrounded by a small sandy beach and picnic area. The swimming pool overlooks the beautiful lake. There's a shuttle over to Disney World as well as to Universal. You don't need a car if you plan a pirate's vacation at Bryan's. This is a desirable vacation destination, especially with young children.

4 **CLUB SEVILLA**
4646 W. Highway 192, Kissimmee, FL. 32741, 407-396-1800
2BR $105
Amenities: Pool, hot tub, tennis

Don't fall for the slick advertising, this is one group of timeshare condos in need of a good housecleaning. Located just south of Kissimmee's main drag, you can walk to numerous restaurants and shops in the area that gives Club Sevilla a big plus for location. The development of these twin two-story condos, with red tile roofs, blend with the surrounding pines so aesthetically that the location is very pleasing to the eye. But step inside and you'll find reclining loungers in need of new fabric as well as ovens that are temporarily on the blink. Although the economy lodgings may look good in pictures, you'll find the actual experience may be less than enchanting.

 CONCORD CONDOMINIUMS
3199 W. Vine St. (Route 192), Kissimmee, FL 34741
800-251-1112
Studios $69, 1BR $105, 2BR $155
Amenities: Pool, tennis, Disney shuttle

Each year, this one gets better and better—a special find in the Orlando area. Concord Condominiums is in four separate condo/villa complexes, each offering a different level of quality and price. Concord offers a collection of three and four-bedroom homes, most of which have private swimming pools. The pools are often within cavernous screened porches, and in fact provide an extra room. Located within three golf course communities, you'll have your choice of Montego Bay, Buena Ventura Lakes, and the Meadow Woods Villas. These homes are 25 minutes away from Disney World. Great if you have a car; otherwise Concord provides complimentary shuttle bus service.

Chelsea Village (6) provides comfortable condo accommodations in single-story villas in a park-like setting. There's a full kitchen, living room and dining area. Each condo has two full bathrooms. The contemporary hotel-style furniture includes extra touches, such as silk flowers and plants. Next in quality/price rating are Chelsea and Somerset. What's the difference? At **Somerset (7)** the units are newer than **Chelsea (7)** and the furnishings are more stylish. **The Shadow Bay (8)** units are newer yet and even more attractively furnished. **The Concord by the Lakeside (9)** units are luxurious and these spacious duplexes will meet the expectations of the most discriminating traveler. One of Orlando's better values is getting better each year.

6 **CYPRESS CREEK GOLF TOWNHOUSES**
Cypress Creek Dr., Orlando, FL 32819, 2BR $700/wk
Amenities: Pool, hot tub, golf course location

The Cypress Creek golf course community enjoys an outstanding location at the intersection of the Florida Turnpike with Interstate 4. Just on the other side is the sprawling area of Universal Studios and Disney World is only ten minutes away. These one- and two-story condos overlook the golf course fairway. Some of these two-story condos have unimaginative interior decor with ash wood furniture and vivid fabrics. Others are more sparsely decorated with deck chairs and poster art. There's a wide variation in decor. Each cluster of a dozen condos has its own pool. Still you have easy access to area attractions and you can walk to the golf clubhouse for a game, lunch, or tennis. This is definitely for those who prefer residential privacy as an alternative to most of Orlando's active, family resorts.

 DISNEY RESORT ACCOMMODATIONS
P.O. Box 10–100, Lake Buena Vista, FL 32830, 800-W DISNEY
1BR $175, 2BR $300

For years you've known that Disney operated the theme parks and a couple of themed hotels nearby. But you are probably not aware that Disney also has condo accommodations. The Village Resort and Wilderness Homes have been available since the park opened. They were joined last year by the Vacation Club Resort, Disney's entry into timeshare.

8   DISNEY'S VACATION CLUB RESORT
Amenities: Lake, marina, golf, tennis, pools, fitness center, game room, restaurants, shops

These studio to three bedroom condos are located along The Buena Vista Golf Course between the Village and Epcot areas. All except the studios have full kitchens, a washer and dryer, VTP, and master suites with whirlpool. The architecture is Key West with pastel exteriors, tin roofs, porches, and large windows. The interior design continues the style with vaulted ceilings and fans, hardwood floors, window blinds, and country casual furnishings in pastel colors. Although a great place to stay for families, be advised that they are trying to sell club memberships.

7   DISNEY'S VILLAGE RESORT
Amenities: Golf, tennis, pools, health club, bike paths, restaurant

These townhouses and pedestal villas are next to the Disney Village marketplace (for shopping), Pleasure Island (for entertainment), and they overlook the Buena Vista Golf Course. Along with the timeshares, these are the most spacious accommodations within Disney's 42,000-acre kingdom. The decor—traditional hotel-style furniture and institutional blue or green carpeting—is sadly lacking in imagination, but each condo is equipped with a full kitchen, a private patio, and a private golf cart for traveling to the Golf Club or other parts of the resort. The condos are located in a wooded setting, and you can tee off here or at one of the adjacent new courses; Osprey Ridge by Tom Fazio and Eagle Pines by Pete Dye. If golf isn't your game there are three tennis courts, two pools, bike and boat rentals, and shops. The Disney Village Resort is the best choice for those who want to enjoy golf as well as the parks at Walt Disney World.

7   DISNEY'S WILDERNESS HOMES
Amenities: Lake, pool, tennis, horseback riding, restaurants

These permanent trailer homes are in the Fort Wilderness Resort area, but separated from the campground area. The River Country and Discovery Island attractions are adjacent and the popular Hoop-Dee-Doo Musical Review takes place on site. Comfortable but cute country decor is standard. These are all one bedroom but could accommodate up to six persons and are best for a young family or chaperoned youth groups. There's a grill and picnic table for more of a camping experience. Special features include all the lake activities, horseback riding, petting zoo and pony rides, nature and campfire programs, and nightly Disney movies. There is also a heated pool, tennis courts, and volleyball and basketball courts.

6   THE ENCLAVE
6165 Carrier Dr., Orlando, FL 32819, 800-457-0077
Studio $79–99, 2BR $125–160
Amenities: Indoor and outdoor pools, tennis, playground

Just off International Drive you'll find these three huge condominium towers with distinctive architecture. Built in a giant 90° triangle shape, the jagged roof line is a series of step terraces for each floor overlooking the lake. These studio and one-bedroom suites have mini-kitchens, living rooms, screened porches and (sometimes) a separate bedroom. They are decorated with a casual contemporary style with blond wood furniture and occasional splashes of bright floral fabrics. Although this is a condominium where the units are individually owned, there's an overriding commercial hotel flavor. There's an outdoor pool and an indoor pool with hot tub. Subjected to heavy use it's often either crowded or messy with lots of dirty towels. One advantage here is the children's playground. An improvement in management/housekeeping here would yield a better rating.

5   FANTASY WORLD CLUB VILLAS
2935 Hart Dr., Lake Buena Vista, FL 32830, 407-396-1808
2BR $125
Amenities: Pool, hot tub, restaurant

Close to Disney World, these are located just off Highway 192— Kissimmee's corridor of motels and restaurants. Over two hundred condos are in this village of pink townhouse-style condos surrounding a large pool.

Very commercial in appearance and operation, this has been a favorite of tour groups. With all the activity in the evening and the doors constantly opening, shutting, and echoing in the courtyard, you'll feel like you're in a rabbit warren. Lacking the quiet and distinctive flavor of so many condo resorts, this is a good place for young families or groups of teens. The pool and the video game room are popular gathering places and there's a Bennigan's in the resort where the good times roll.

6 **FORTUNE PLACE**
1475 Astro Dr., Kissimmee, FL 32743, 800-624-7496
2BR $139, 3BR $149, 4BR $159
Amenities: Pool, tennis

Hidden in an area of residential condos, you'll find Fortune Place, a development of cute two-story townhouse condos. These are some of the most spacious condos in the Orlando area and they are ideal for a family with several children of different ages. Well decorated, this is an exceptional value in the Orlando area because of the spacious residential quality of the units. This resort is geared towards relaxation. A social center is near the swimming pool and tennis court. It is good for those visiting the area attractions as well as for those who want a residential retreat in the evenings.

8+ **GREENLEFE RESORT & CONFERENCE CENTER**
3200 State Rd., Greenlefe, FL 33844, 800-237-9549
Studios $95, 1BR $110
Amenities: Golf, tennis, restaurants, pools

Located in the rolling pastureland of central Florida, Greenlefe is only 30 minutes away from all the kids and fun of Disney World. This resort is all together different from most of the other properties in this chapter. You'll recognize this immediately when you enter the property and see split-rail fences and rolling green fairways spread over 6400 acres. Resort life revolves around golf amid the peaceful wildlife of central Florida that is graced by herons and gators. The condo villas follow the contours of the three 18-hole golf courses. Some villas have private pools. You'll find a range of styles from townhouses to detached single bungalows. Interior decor varies in the 900 units, but in general expect to find tropical fabrics (often with floral designs) and all the electronic and cooking conveniences you could want in a vacation home. Many of these condos are rented for only a week; others have long term rentals for three to six months. Rates drop with long-term rentals.

9 **HEATHROW**
1275 Lake Heathrow Ln., Heathrow, FL 32746
Amenities: Golf, lakes, pool, tennis, restaurant

Located north of Orlando, this completely planned residential community has eight separate villages spread over 300 acres; so large that Heathrow has its own private school system for residents. Currently many homes are owned by nonresidents who want to spend part of the year in the Central Florida sun. When not used by the owners these two, three, and four-bedroom vacation homes are available for 30 days or more. Many have private pools. Spacious and attractively furnished, this is an hour away from Disney World. Heathrow appeals to those vacationers who like the Orlando area but who don't want to be in all the commotion of southwest Orlando/Kissimmee.

8 ISLE OF BALI
1777 Bali Blvd., Orlando, FL 32830, 800-634-3119
2BR $130–175
Amenities: Pool, tennis, putting green, small lake

Bali-Hai and all its fantasies brought to Florida! Visitors are initially charmed by the leis and fruit punch reception. The Balinese wood carvings, paintings, and tropical plants create an impressive entrance area. The condos are richly decorated with fabrics, silk flowers, and tropical plants. This is what you would hope to find in Hawaii or Bali. During the length of your stay, you will constantly be impressed by the South Seas Island Fantasy. Management strives to keep their guests entertained with several parties during their stay as well as planned activities. Isle of Bali's efficient and courteous management provides great value for the guests and creates a very successful resort. Dollar for dollar, you can't beat this one.

2 LIFETIME OF VACATIONS
7770 U.S. Highway 192 West, Kissimmee, FL 32741,
407-396-3000
1BR $65–85, 2BR $75–95, 3BR $103–145
Amenities: Pool, hot tub, lake

Formerly a motel, this was one of the earliest timeshares in the area. The motel units were remodeled to make studio, one and two-bedroom models, each with a kitchen or kitchenette. Completely remodeled in 1989, these are some of the most inexpensive accommodations in the Orlando area. One great advantage is the lakeside location with the shade from the cypress trees. This revives the old "central Florida" feeling which has almost been bulldozed away.

5 MAGIC TREE
2795 S.R. 545, Kissimmee, FL 32741, 407-396-2300
Amenities: Pool, hot tub, restaurant

Lots of bubbling youthful activities are in evidence at this resort. Formerly a motel, it was renovated as a timeshare ten years ago. Today the interiors look a little worn, but this resort is always full. Lots of vacationers choose Magic Tree because of the nearby shops, restaurants, and it has easy access to Disney's Magic Kingdom.

8   MARRIOTT'S RESIDENCE INN
       8800 Meadowcreek Dr. Orlando, FL 32821, 800-331-3131
       $100–135
       Amenities: Pool, hot tubs, tennis. Golf nearby

This all-suite hotel, formerly Hawthorn Suites Villa Resort, is located only one mile from Disney World. These Mediterranean two-story buildings are set amid fifty acres of lush landscaping and palm trees. The one and two-bedroom suites have full kitchens and are handsomely decorated in pinks and Florida pastels. The interior decor is standardized and practical in typical hotel fashion. There's a magnificent super pool with a "rock" bridge. In addition, there are two hot tubs and a children's playground by the pool. For the sports minded, there are two tennis courts and a golf course next door.

10   MARRIOTT'S ROYAL PALMS OF ORLANDO
       World Center Dr., Orlando, FL 32821, 800-228-9290
       2BR $175–220
       Amenities: Golf, restaurant, pool, tennis, hot tub

Royal Palms, located in a three-story building with exterior walkways, is a larger development than its sister, Sabal Palms (also on the grounds of Marriott's World Center master resort development). Guests may use the deluxe and intimate facilities at Royal Palms. Or, if desired, the hotel offers a huge free-form pool, water slide, and waterfalls. The interiors of the condos are furnished with soft colors and boldly printed fabrics. This creates an "English country house" effect. The interior decorations are among the finest at any resort anywhere. This resort is designed to offer every advantage to a wide spectrum of vacationers. Royal Palms is convenient to Disney World and is surrounded by a championship golf course.

10   MARRIOTT'S SABAL PALMS
       8805 World Center Dr., Orlando, FL 32821, 800-228-9290
       2BR $175–220
       Amenities: Golf, lake, restaurant, pool, tennis, hot tub

The Sabal Palms condos are located on an island surrounded by the mammoth Marriott Orlando World Center Hotel. Guests staying in hotel rooms look down upon this small condo village and assume it is an executive retreat. The condos are arranged as duplex townhouses with two flats per building. Each has a view of the lagoon and golf course. This project is beautifully designed and decorated. The best designer fabrics, art objects, VTPs, and stereos surpass your expectations of a vacation condo. Most of the activities are at the hotel, which offers a complete array of services, dining, and recreation facilities. A tennis pro shop is next to the condos and the golf course. This is an exclusive golf/country club destination resort just as much as it is an Orlando attractions resort.

8   MISSION INN GOLF & TENNIS VILLAS
Highways 19 & 48, Howey in the Hills, FL 34737, 800-874-9053
2BR $290
Amenities: Golf, tennis, marina, pool, conference center

Located only 45 minutes north of Disney World and other Orlando-area attractions, the Mission Inn is a secluded destination resort for golfers seeking a week on one of Florida's best courses. The main lodge is the Mission Inn; the condos are actually the Mission Santa Cruz Villas. These are individual two- and three-bedroom bungalows with private courtyard patios. Very well decorated, they exude the country-club style of living. The Spanish architecture and arched walkway create the impression that you're in Southern California.

8+   ORANGE LAKE COUNTRY CLUB
8505 W. Space Coast Pkwy., Route 192 West,
Kissimmee, FL 32741, 800-327-4444; 1BR $130, 2BR $165
Amenities: Golf, lake, restaurant, pool, movie theater,
video game room, tennis, health club with exercise room

Orange Lake is spectacular because of its country club village atmosphere. It was designed, created, and is operated by the family who created the Holiday Inn chain. Even if it were not close to Disney World, Orange Lake Country Club would be a major vacation destination. No other property combines golf, water sports, and country club living within the proximity of the Orlando attractions. Orange Lake is beautifully maintained, and the quality and variety of the activities programs are among the highest in the resort industry. The property occupies a 350-acre site located on Orange Lake and offers studio and one-bedroom apartments in a hotel style building. Avoid this building if possible; the townhouse villas along the golf course are more spacious and a much better value. Along the fairways there are over 120 two-bedroom townhouse villas that offer privacy and fairway views. In addition to the 18-hole golf course and 16 tennis courts which you would expect at a country club, the resort offers unlimited water sports. There is a marina where power boats for water-skiing may be rented on the 80 acre lake. Small sailboats and wind-surfing boards are also available for rent. At the clubhouse there is an Olympic-size swimming pool and the resort offers organized baby-sitting services so parents can play golf while the children enjoy the pool. The condos are decorated in neutral colors with furniture you have seen before at Holiday Inns. To enhance the "at home" feeling, there are many knickknacks and pictures.

6   PARC CORNICHE
     6300 Parc Corniche, Orlando, FL 32821, 800-446-2721,
     1BR $92–152, 2BR $127–197
     Amenities: Pool, golf

Located on the golf course of the International Country Club, these condos are popular with both short-term visitors as well as those who want to spend a month or more in Orlando. The flavor here is entirely different because there's a mixture of fun-loving resort guests and owners who are part-time Orlando residents. Therefore, you'll get a different perspective on your vacation when you talk with others by the pool. In very few places will you pickup so much inside information and tips on the best values in the area.

8   PARKWAY INTERNATIONAL ADVENTURE
     6200 Safari Trail, Kissimmee, FL 32746, 800-634-3119
     2BR $130–175
     Amenities: Hot tub, pools, playground, snack bar

This is one of the best values in Orlando right now. Although the name is uninspired, this resort offers a vacation you'll never forget. It is another of those fantasy-theme resorts you'll find in Orlando. At this resort, the theme is African jungle adventure. You'll find 15 acres of pine and palmetto forest with a planked walkway bypassing a safari hunter's jeep and whimsical-looking giraffes and zebras. But when you step inside your condo, you'll find anything but the "roughing it" atmosphere. This family-oriented resort designed the condos with Mom in mind—she won't spend much time cooking or cleaning. The living room has patterned wallpaper, which on close examination shows monkeys watching you. Carved tigers and sculptured zebras give the glass and bamboo furniture in the living room an African safari style. The color scheme is cinnamon and forest green. Hiding in the bamboo cabinet is an oversized television. The master bedroom has, again, the fine pattern wallpaper: this time with leopards. Canopied beds with mosquito netting for whimsy, and a whirlpool tub in the large master bath provide great fun for everyone.

4   POLYNESIAN ISLES
     3045 Polynesian Isles Blvd., Kissimmee, FL 32741
     407-396-2006, 1BR $100–130, 2BR $130–165
     Amenities: Pool, hot tub, restaurant, tennis

These attractive Polynesian long house style buildings have a different flavor. There are four condos in each building, but the upstairs units are best because they have vaulted ceilings. Decorated island style with rattan furniture, you'll have the feeling of the Philippines or perhaps Hawaii in these one and two-bedroom condos. They are very low key and unpretentious. New units under construction promise to break the mold with a luxurious new style. Check before you go.

3-5 RESORT WORLD OF ORLANDO
2758 Poinciana Blvd., Kissimmee, FL 32741, 800-423-8604
Amenities: Health club, tennis, racquetball, pools

Potentially a great resort—if only guests weren't pursued to buy timeshare. Resort World now has two entirely different sections; the deluxe **Spas (7)** as well as the units in the older buildings named **Villa Tahoe (4)** and **Villa Rio (4)**. At these older buildings, you'll find one and two-bedroom apartments where efforts have been made to enhance appearances with designer fabrics and whirlpool tubs. The Spas are quite different. They have a subtropical ambiance with wicker furniture, soft pastels, bright Caribbean fabrics, a stylish dining area, and a mirrored bedroom. Each unit has its own VTP and wet bar in the living room. At the Spas, each condo has a private whirlpool tub large enough for two in the master bath. The health club is a brand new addition, featuring six tennis courts, six racquetball courts, and three new swimming pools. With a little more hospitality service from management, this could become a great choice in Orlando.

8 SONESTA VILLA RESORT
10000 Turkey Lake Rd., Orlando, FL 32819, 407-352-8051
1BR $140–170, 2BR $205–265
Amenities: Pool, tennis, exercise room, hot tub, paddle boats,
playground, game room

You would not expect to find this lakeside resort merely ten minutes from Disney World. Sonesta Village is a popular place for small conventions or meetings. You'll find just as many people here for business as for the Orlando attractions. In the townhouses and villas you will find spacious condos, vaulted ceilings, and kitchenettes. You can enjoy the convenience of the central hotel building or entertain in your own vacation home. A hot tub large enough for six is located outside on your private walled and landscaped patio. The environment is delightful. A large pool, sauna and an exercise room are available at the main hotel buildings and conference center. This resort's social director organizes activities for children at the pool and the resort's private beach on Sand Lake.

8 SUMMERFIELD SUITES
8400 International Dr., Orlando, FL 32819, 407-352-2400
1BR $139, 2BR $159
Amenities: Pool, tennis, hot tub, exercise room

This all-suite hotel may provide just what you're looking for in Orlando. These studio, one and two-bedroom suites are brand new and beautifully decorated with blond woods, rose carpets and drapes, and distinctive tropical fabrics. Each has two televisions and a VTP for your entertainment. There's a full kitchen, even with a microwave, but you'll probably want the complimentary breakfast served each morning. In the evenings there's a cocktail party in the lobby with complimentary hors d'oeuvres. Lots of European and Brazilian visitors have discovered this resort, so there's a friendly "Made in the USA" feeling combined with the spice of getting to know people from other countries around the pool. One advantage to this location is all the great restaurants within walking distance, or for those who've had a long day at the parks, there's catering "in room" from many nearby restaurants. you'll find excellent value here.

7   VENTURA
    3100 Raper Dairy Rd., Orlando, FL 32822
    Amenities: Lake, golf, tennis, pools

Just north of the airport and five miles south of downtown, this country club community has been popular with investors from overseas. Many British and Continental European investors have bought condos or homes along the golf course which they use for a month each year. Local realtors then rent these resort properties to vacationers who plan to spend two weeks, a month, or even longer in the Orlando area. It's a good half hour to the area theme parks, but for those who enjoy an active vacation as much as the Disney attractions it's a great choice.

5   THE VILLAGE OF ORLANDO
    Rio Grande Ave., Orlando, FL 32819
    Amenities: Pool, tennis, lake

This community of townhouses is just twenty minutes away from Disney World and Universal Studios. Located on a small fishing lake, there's a residential atmosphere here. For those who don't want to be in the hubbub or overwhelmed by bus loads of tour groups, these units provide a quiet, relaxing atmosphere at a reasonable price and good value.

10   THE VILLAS OF GRAND CYPRESS
    One North Jacaranda, Orlando, FL 32836, 407-239-4700
    1BR $225–335, 2BR $295–400
    Amenities: Pool, lake, tennis, golf, restaurant

Villas of Grand Cypress, a resort for the discriminating, is a top choice in the Orlando area. You will discover a total community with the Jack Nicklaus 45 hole golf course, lakes, and the ultra-elegant Grand Cypress Hyatt Hotel. These villas are even better than the expensive penthouses at the hotel—honestly. Hardly advertised and hidden from Main Street Orlando, these golf villas have a country club atmosphere. Many overlook the lake. The well designed units feature Old Florida style furnishings with French doors that open onto patios, wicker furniture, and shades of lime green and coral pink—high style with good art and management by Jack Nicklaus Hospitality Services. Also provided is a daily maid and nightly turn-down service (complete with a chocolate left on your nightstand). For sports enthusiasts or corporate executives who have to go to Disney World because of the children, this one's for you.

8 THE VILLAS OF SOMERSET
3187 W. Vine St., Kissimmee, FL 32741, 407-396-8044
Amenities: Pool, hot tub, sauna, exercise room

Professional management and customer service are the hallmarks here. Located in a residential area of Kissimmee, you are fifteen minutes from Disney World and 25 minutes from Universal. But here you'll find brand new units built of brick and wood. Interior decor is the same for each: neutral beige and pink fabrics and functional hotel-style furniture. Everything here is spiffy so you'll be glad you chose this as a place to stay in the area.

VISTANA RESORT
S.R. 535, Lake Buena Vista, FL 32830, 407-239-3100
2BR $125–275
Amenities: Pools, restaurant, health club, tennis

Many call this resort the most successful timeshare project in the world. It lives up to its reputation. Staying here is like being on a cruise or attending a party for a week. It begins at arrival on Sunday with the Sunday Sundae extravaganza at the restaurant named Zimmie's. This condo resort has established new standards of excellence in the resort development industry. Each year, additional efforts have been made to improve the property. So today, there probably is no other resort like it. There are 458 condo units spread over 60 acres. You will also find four pools including the super pool—one of the largest swimming pools in Florida. Another pool features a rock slide. Vistana offers five separate condo developments.

The Courts (7) These condos are the oldest but the most spacious. Some are characterized by cozy lofts and huge floor-to-ceiling windows that allow plenty of sunlight.

The Falls (8) The Falls condos are flat apartments in two-story buildings. They are grouped around a series of lagoons, fountains, and picturesque gazebos. Each condo is equipped with a private whirlpool in the master bath and a screened porch that can double as a den.

The Spas and the Springs (8) Successively newer variations on the same theme.

The Palms (9) The newest phase of development, these condos are designed in a contemporary fashion with interiors in light pastel colors.

The Vistana resort is next door to a golf course and many of the condos have views of the fairways. There is a series of ponds between the buildings and gazebos for quiet Florida evenings. Everyone will enjoy staying at Vistana. You can't miss with this one.

7   WESTGATE
     2770 Old Lake Wilson Rd., Kissimmee, FL 32741, 800-768-2341
     1BR $99–195, 2BR $125–250
     Amenities: Pools, tennis, hot tub, sauna, gym

The flavor of the Caribbean triumphs at this mega resort. Spread over 60 acres, Westgate is a huge development. Yet the condos are designed in groupings so you'll be able to identify with a specific neighborhood. Some are ten years old, some were finished only last year. Expensively decorated, you'll find a luscious pink color used throughout with variations in mauve or tan that create a "designer" decor. Silk flowers and mirrors are every-where—even in the master bath where there's a private, tiled whirlpool built for two. The new Caribbean pool area with its white cabanas is a pleasant place to catch the local sun when you aren't busy visiting area attractions. This one gets better each year.

RENTAL RESOURCES
Adair Lake Villas, 800-882-4844
Balnee Vacation Condos, 407-843-0703
Caribbean Villas & Condos, 407-846-4405
Condo Care Rentals, 800-633-9474
Condotels, 407-847-6007
Epoch Management, 407-425-2552
ERA Property World, 800-999-1825
Fahnie's Homes, 407-348-7663
Feel Like Home, 800-726-0434
Florida Condominiums 407-682-9091
Florida Holidays, 800-328-6262
Florida Rent-a-Home, 800-344-9578
Galaxy Management, 800-634-3119
Holiday Homes of Orlando, 800-421-2187
Phoenix Properties, 800-828-7127
Preferred Properties, 407-872-1717
Vacation Villas USA, 800-633-1053

Vacation Villas/Bermuda Palms, 800-866-2660
The Villas, 800-633-1405

2. COLLIER COUNTY

Florida's Collier County enjoys one of the warmest winter climates in the Continental 48 states. Real estate development here has already had its share of boom and bust cycles, so today the areas of Marco Island and Vanderbilt Beach offer some of the lowest-priced vacation homes and condominiums that you'll find on the shores of South Florida. With bungalows only five minutes from the beach selling at $60,000 and luxury high-rise condos on the beach as low as $49,000, is it any wonder why these areas have been called "paradise at half price?" Just compare this with real estate in the city of Naples next door where beachfront condos start at $200,000. If you're looking for warm weather, unique real estate, and an opportunity to acquire value for personal use or investment, start with Marco.

MARCO ISLAND

Marco Island is a tropical hideaway that deftly blends a touch of Old Florida with modern glass and concrete towers. The site of one of the most important Calusa Indian archeological discoveries, Marco has been occupied for over 2,000 years when its settlers traded with the Mayans of the Yucatan and worshiped a cat-like god whose statue resembles the Egyptian goddess Bastet. Just north of the Tropic of Cancer, enjoying summertime breezes from the Gulf, and having deep fresh-water wells, Marco possesses all the key elements for good living. Add to that six miles of white beaches, a wetlands ecosystem (stretching 100 miles east to the Everglades), and the rich waters of the Gulf teeming with migratory schools of fish, you have a vacation paradise sure to please 9 out of 10. For some unknown reason, and this is good for you the consumer, Marco has never really captured the imagination of the traveling public or the serious real estate investors. You can still buy vacation homes and resort condominiums at prices which are reasonably low when compared with nearby Sanibel Island to the north, or Key West to the southeast.

The entire island is a master planned real estate development by the Deltona Corporation. Forecasts for the island in 1969 indicated a dramatic growth in real estate development, population increases, and business expansion. But in the mid 1970s change in the public's attitude toward the environment slowed the growth rate and caused Deltona to scale back its master plan.

Although it had acquired about 23,000 acres, Deltona only developed about half that amount because the company's holdings consisted largely of wetlands and the fringing mangrove forests. In the last two decades, innumerable state and federal laws imposed tight restrictions over such areas because of their importance to the health and life of fish and animals.

Transportation to Marco Island is at once both easy and difficult. If you plan to stay for a week or more and have a car, fly to Miami. It's an easy two hour drive along the Tamiami trail over to Marco, and Miami is so convenient with nonstop flights to most U.S. cities. Most of the resorts will recommend that you fly into the Naples airport (45 minutes away by car) or into Ft. Myers' Southwest Regional airport (75 minutes away by car). Both Ft. Myers and Naples have frequent flights to Orlando, Atlanta, Raleigh, and Charlotte. Otherwise you'll have to change planes at one of the hub airports which can add an extra hour to flight times.

WHERE TO STAY

5   BEACH CLUB OF MARCO
901 S. Collier Blvd., Marco Island, FL 33937, 813-394-8860
1BR $100, 2BR $135
Amenities: Pool, hot tub, game room

Located across the street from the beach, this resort makes up for the slight inconvenience of its location by offering lots of activities. When you walk in, you'll find a warm reception. The condos in this five-story building have better views of the island and of the Gulf in the distance than they do of the high-rise towers across the street. The apartments are a little small. Each has a screened terrace. Furnishings feature grasscloth wallpaper and sturdy laminated furniture. There are kitchenettes in the single bedrooms and small kitchens in the two-bedroom. Convenient and practical, it is reasonably priced.

8   CHARTER CLUB OF MARCO BEACH
700 S. Collier Blvd., Marco Island, FL 33937, 813-394-4192
2BR $1100–1800/wk
Amenities: Beach, sailboat rentals, pool, tennis, exercise room

One of south Florida's best vacation choices if you like the residential space of a condo and the service of a superior hotel. The location is great and the beach is wonderful. This high-rise complex on the beach at Marco Island has beautiful facilities, including on-site Hobie cat rentals. There are two tennis courts and an attractive landscaped pool area. The available units are two-bedrooms models and are beautifully decorated with soft pastels and that casual "South Florida" look. The structure is ten-stories high so all condos have Gulf views. The swimming pool is surrounded by palms and hibiscus. The resort has a landscaped tropical garden, should you need a break from the beach and the ocean. You'll find a surprising assortment of tropical flowers and landscaping spread over six acres, a fountain and a goldfish pond. The Charter Club offers lots of activities for adults and at vacation times, supervised social programs for children. Great value!

9 EAGLE'S NEST BEACH RESORT

410 S. Collier Blvd., Marco Island, FL 33937
1BR $115–195, 2BR $120–230, villa $140–250
Amenities: Tennis, racquetball, exercise room, sauna, pool, hot tub, sailboat rentals, gift shop

Eagle's Nest combines the spacious comfort of a private luxury condominium suite with the exciting services of a bustling hotel. Eagle's Nest provides one of the best welcomes you'll ever receive at a resort. Most guests stay for a week, and arrive on Saturday for a welcome cocktail party. There are contests and drawings where one out of eight or ten is a winner. Lots of goofy prizes and banter about the gifts provides a lively social mixer. There are two types of accommodations here: one and two-story villas clustered around a tropical garden and swimming pool; and a twelve-story, high-rise tower where the condos have a dazzling view of the Gulf or the islands. You'll discover luxurious decor and solid appointments. There are French doors which open onto screened terraces, terra cotta tiles, wood cabinets, tropical prints, and wicker furniture. The villas are much more expensive but you'll enjoy the convenience of being able to step outside right onto the beach.

7 GULFVIEW

58 N. Collier Blvd., Marco Island, FL 33937, 2BR $2400/mo
Amenities: Beach, heated outdoor pool, tennis

On the beach, this is where you want to stay. Located next door to the private "Residents Beach" in the very heart of the six-mile stretch of Collier Avenue beach, this twenty-one-story tower dates from 1974 when Deltona's land development was in its heyday and before the ecological movement began. Although the style is a bit dated, you can't beat this location. Because the building was designed so each of these two-bedroom units would have the best view of the Gulf, the walls are at an angle, adding surprise on first impression. But outside on your balcony, when you gaze at the Gulf, you'll forgive this minor transgression. These superior units have furniture and color schemes that are a bit dated. Interior decor offers lots of different styles ranging from "My decorator just finished this—don't touch" to "early attic." Check before you rent, they have monthly rentals only.

7+ RADISSON SUITE RESORT

600 S. Collier Blvd., Marco Island, FL 33937, 813-394-4100
Amenities: Beach, pool, tennis, restaurant

Designed and built to be a condo resort, the sales program was never completed. Owning all of the units, the developer decided to have it managed as a hotel. Although these aren't privately owned condos, the property comes so close to falling within our definition, that we decided to include it. Each unit has a spacious living room and full kitchen. The decor is hotel style with institutional fine blue prints and durable wall-to-wall carpet. Each unit has a private screened porch which is really a third room. The strong point here is the service provided by management, such as a full-time activities program for adults and children. Volleyball games and round robin tennis matches occur frequently. Bluebeard's Restaurant, located outdoors, overlooks a small lagoon and the beach. It is a convivial place for snacks and attracts visitors and locals from other parts of Marco Island. Inside, Tradewinds Restaurant offers more formal dining. If you want all the services of a good hotel, and the space and convenience of a condo, this is a good choice.

8   ROYAL SEAFARER
300 S. Collier Blvd., Marco Island, FL 33937, 2BR $3300/mo
Amenities: Beach, heated pool, tennis, game room. Next door to
water sports center

Located just north of (and right next door to) the Marriott Hotel, this may be the most fun part of the beach. Along this six-mile expanse of beach, some parts are very quiet and some are very active. The watersports center at the Marriott is where everyone goes to rent sailfish, Hobie-cats, or paddle boats. The Royal Seafarer is right next door, so you have the best of both worlds, condo convenience and space right next to the buzzing activity of a hotel. The Royal Seafarer is a ten-year-old, twenty-two-story tower with unusual, sculpted architecture. Most units have three sides of window space (instead of the usual one-sided flat picture window or the two-sided corner). Most units have been decorated with superior furniture, some in neutral tones designed for vacation rentals, others with personal or decorator touches. You're right on the beach here with a wonderful view of the beach, Gulf, and the island. Sunsets here are dramatic. You'll remember this one.

8   SANDCASTLE I AND II
720–730 S. Collier Blvd., Marco Island, FL 33937; 1BR $3400/mo
Amenities: Beachfront, heated pool, hot tub, sauna, tennis,
exercise room, game room

Located on the beach, these twin fifteen-story towers feature extra privacy as each unit is staggered so you can't see your neighbors. Wrap around balconies afford views of the Gulf, beach, and the island. These two bedroom units are luxurious and most have been professionally decorated by interior designers. You'll find modern kitchens with microwaves, Jenn-air grills, and trash compactors. Many units have VTPs in the living room. The Sandcastle is located down at the southern end of the beach, where the shelling is best early in the morning. Quiet and superior, this complex offers monthly rentals only.

6 SEA WINDS
890 S. Collier Blvd., Marco Island, FL 33937
Amenities: Beachfront, heated pool, hot tub, tennis. Marina nearby

Located at the southern tip of the island, Sea Winds is a sixteen-story tower next door to the public beach park. These units have great, unobstructed views of the beach and the Gulf. Many of these boxy, two-bedroom units have interior decorator packages where lots of mirrors have been used to bring the Gulf view inside. Built only a few years ago, most of the units are new and exhibit a contemporary style. This is a convenient location for a family because this is one of the few places where you'll find other children around the pool to play with. Watersports and equipment rentals are just around the bend at the harbor, which is also the starting point for many fishing charters. Sea Winds provides good value and is ideal for families.

7 SOUTH SEAS RESORT (North, East & Towers Buildings)
380 Seaview Ct., Marco Island, FL 33937, 2BR $2300/mo
Amenities: Beach, heated pool, boat dock, tennis, exercise room

These are probably the most popular condominiums on Marco Island for vacation rentals. The beach here has been aptly named "Unexcelled" and that's true. Wide, with white sand, it's next door to Tigertail beach park and its dunes. South Seas offers its own center of activity or you can venture over to the quiet of the dunes next door. The North and East buildings are on Clam Bay; the nineteen-story Towers are on the sand facing the Gulf which explains their popularity. If you want to stay in a quality condo in an unexcelled location at a reasonable price, the North and East buildings are probably the best value on the island. The Towers are clearly more luxurious and this is where you'll find units recently furnished by interior decorators. These units have stunning views and spacious oversized rooms.

5 SOUTHERN BREEZE GARDENS
1141 S. Collier Blvd., Marco Island, FL 33937
Amenities: Heated pool

Located at the southern tip of the island, across the street from the beach and a stone's throw from the marina, these brand new units offer an excellent value for those looking for a vacation on the beach at Marco. The design of the units in this five-story building is such that each unit is staggered so you don't look at your neighbor. Each condo has a private screened patio which captures the island breezes and amounts to an extra room. Children will want to "camp out" here. Each condo has a view of Caxambas

Pass and the Ten Thousand Islands. It is a pleasant place for couples or families with monthly rentals only.

RENTAL RESOURCES

Bluebill Properties, 800-525-2745
ERA Sea Coast Realty, 813-394-0589
Flagship Realty, 813-394-7515
Marco Beach Realty, 813-394-2505
Marquis Reservations, 800-237-8906

NAPLES AND VANDERBILT BEACH

With seven miles of sugar white sand along the Gulf of Mexico, 140 miles of waterways, and an average year round temperature of 74°, the Naples area is blessed with all the fundamentals necessary for one of North America's premier resort communities. Naples is a community of millionaires, with estimates placing 10% of the population in that category, and also the fastest growing small town (pop. 21,000) in Florida. This area is one of the last real villages left in a state where development previously has gone mostly unchecked. There are no beachfront honky tonks, T-shirt shops, or fast food joints. Mostly there are well-tended homes and stylish condominiums along the beach. There are bridges over sand dunes to protect the fragile sea oats and buildings are set back from the beach to decrease the chances of erosion. Vanderbilt Beach, just north of the Naples townline, may offer more condo accommodations, but it lacks the exclusivity of its neighbor.

Development in Naples got under way as an exclusive enclave for wealthy Kentuckians. Finding the weather in Naples to be slightly warmer than the rest of Florida in winter and cooler in summer due to the ocean breezes, this community was founded as a Garden of Eden away from the bigger towns of Pensacola and Tampa to the north. Over the years, development has been strictly controlled and, since the '60s there's been a tendency to initiate tight regulations in order to imitate the architectural style of Bermuda. Naples not only has distinctive neighborhoods with tightly controlled zoning laws, but it also has additional ordinances to keep the city neat and orderly. For example:

- no garage doors may be open for more than 20 minutes
- no boats or RVs are allowed in driveways
- no posting of gasoline prices except in small letters
- no clotheslines are to be visible to the public
- all commercial trash containers are to be done in decorative materials

Naples is a city of neighborhoods like Los Angeles, only much smaller. This has been a deliberate part of the city's planning since 1886 and the benefits are evident today. You'll find a wide range of resort properties to choose from when planning your vacation and that includes high-rise condominiums, Bermuda-style garden apartments, and spacious patio homes that are probably larger than your permanent residence. There are inland golf course communities and fabulous tennis resorts with over 20 courts and attractive two-story condominiums spread over acres of land. Beginning with Olde Naples as the core, we will review the various neighborhoods and their attributes.

Olde Naples — This was the first established residential neighborhood. Here early Florida architectural èlan has been preserved. There's a similarity with Key West since parts of both communities were built at the same time. The cottages, guest houses, and estates have been renovated to stay current with expectations for today's lifestyle. Consequently, real estate values have soared for bungalows along these narrow streets lined with leafy palms.

Lely/East Naples — Five miles inland from the water, this area just east and southeast of Olde Naples is currently being developed with a dozen or so enclave golf course communities. With courses designed by Arnold Palmer and Pete Dye to anchor the development, each has several clusters of condos surrounding the course. Most are for retirees or full-time residents, preferring seasonal rentals over short-term vacation rentals, but short-term rentals for a week or two can be arranged. Undoubtedly these are the most inexpensive condo accommodations in the area, yet with the landscaping and fairway views, you'll find them quite attractive.

Port Royal — On the southern end of town, this is an exclusive neighborhood where the most inexpensive home is priced at $925,000. There are no vacation rentals in Port Royal (unless you are the friend or guest of an owner).

The Moorings — This area is just north of Olde Naples and development lines The Moorings bay as well as the sandbar strip along the ocean. This area along Gulf Shore Boulevard North was built in the 1960s and 1970s. Condo communities encompass beaches, inland waterways, sailing opportunities and a splendid golf course. The high-rise condos are no more than twelve stories, although most are much smaller. Painted in pastel shades of pink, yellow, orange, and brown, there's more than a hint of Bermuda style. Nothing is out of place and the beach is carefully cleaned each morning. This exclusive area is choice and very few condos allow short-term, transient rentals. To maintain the club-like tone, vacation rentals here generally are for the season of three months or more. We have noted a few that allow daily or weekly condo rentals, and we have also included a superior all-suite hotel where many residents encourage visiting relatives to stay.

Park Shore — In this area, along Gulf Boulevard North and Park Shore Drive, you will find stunning mid-rise condos (four to nine stories) situated on the edge of the Gulf of Mexico. These superior two-bedroom condominiums have prices beginning at $140,000. Park Shore's best feature is the Venetian Village on the bay. Often photographed, this is a popular area for socializing as well as shopping.

Pelican Bay — Here you'll find a mix of mid-rise condos, townhouses, single-family homes and a few high-rise condominiums surrounding a championship 18 hole golf course. The area's unique feature is the 200 acre wildlife preserve which buffers the area of condominium development from the beach. Each end is anchored by an ultradeluxe resort: The Registry on the south end (which also has 50 garden villa condominiums) and the Ritz Carlton on the north end (which is strictly a hotel). Many of the condo developments have private security gates that keep each of these enclave resorts private and exclusive. Again, only a few properties within Pelican Bay allow short term rentals for a month or less.

Beachwalk — Located at the northern end of Naples, these condo communities are located inland. Less developed and not nearly as exclusive as the other areas, there are three good golf courses here, so this appeals to those seeking a country club lifestyle.

Vanderbilt Beach — This strip of beach along Gulf Shore Drive and Bluebill Avenue is home to a string of high-rise condos and motels. Due east is the Beachwalk section with the golf clubs while the Pelican Bay nature preserve is due south. Monthly rentals in this area generally range between $1800 to $2200. Weekly rentals should be in the $750 to $900 range for a beachfront, two-bedroom condo.

Naples is a city made for the genteel and those who love the good life. Vanderbilt Beach and East Naples are for those who also appreciate the good life, but who just don't want to pay high prices for all the advantages nearby. With 36 golf courses and over 100 tennis courts there are ample opportunities for the active. Or you can just laze in the rich Florida sun.

Most visitors who plan to stay longer than a week will drive to Naples/Vanderbilt Beach. Those who fly can use the convenient Naples airport which has commuter flights from Orlando, Miami, and West Palm Beach. Ft. Myers' Southwest Regional is the main airport for travelers to Naples and the driving distance is only 45 minutes away from Naples' prime vacation areas, and only 30 minutes from Vanderbilt Beach.

WHERE TO STAY

6   **BAREFOOT PELICAN**
210 Commerce St., Vanderbilt Beach, FL 33963, 2BR $850/wk
Amenities: Pool, dock

These bayfront condos are in the Beachwalk section at the north end of Naples, just east of the strip of high-rise condos known as Vanderbilt Beach—nothing fancy, just a good location, a five minute walk way from the beach. These spacious two-bedroom condos overlook the waterway and there's a pool which children will enjoy. The Barefoot Pelican is one of the few condos in the area that allows short-term, weekly rentals at around $850 per week in season.

7 BEACHWALK
Vanderbilt Beach Rd., Vanderbilt Beach, FL 33963
2BR $2800/mo
Amenities: Pool, hot tub, tennis

Located in the Beachwalk section of Naples, this is an attractive community of one- and two-story detached bungalows, townhouses, and condo apartments surrounding a lagoon. This walled community has a 24-hour security gate (you'll feel like you're in a club) and is unique in this part of Naples because the units are set in a spacious, parklike setting. These condos and villas are comfortable for long-term as well as short-term stays. Architectural design has blessed the townhouses with lofts and vaulted ceilings. Furnishings are superior to what you'll find in the rest of Vanderbilt Beach. The beach is only a few minutes away by foot or bike. This has an attractive country club style in a neighborhood just behind the Ritz Carlton.

6 BEAU MER
River Point Dr., Naples, FL 33942, 1BR $650/wk, 2BR $750/wk
Amenities: Pool, hot tub, tennis

Right on the eastern edge of Olde Naples, the Beau Mer condos are located on a lagoon. The beach is across town, just five minutes away by car. The one and two-bedroom condos in these four-story buildings are simple and functional. Children are only seen at Christmas and spring break when visiting grandparents. Rentals are available for a week, a month or more. This is the only condo development in Olde Naples that offers weekly rentals. If you want to be near Olde Naples or are dependent upon public transportation, then this is a good choice.

9 THE COMMONS
Pelican Bay Blvd., Naples, FL 33963
Amenities: Pelican Bay beach shuttle, pool

Located within the Pelican Bay master resort, The Commons condos are among the few in this exclusive community that allow vacation rentals. Minimum stay requirements are for three months, but sometimes realtors can arrange a monthly rental. Pelican Bay is an exceptional development because 200 acres of coastal land has been set aside as a wildlife preserve. This acts as a buffer between the beach and the dozen or so condo developments within the Pelican Bay community. Access to the beach is by boardwalk or an attendant waits to take you over in a golf cart. The units at The

Commons are spacious patio homes, built with only one wall in common. There's a pool that is rarely used except during Christmas and spring vacation when the grandchildren come to visit. Beautifully decorated, many retained professional designers to create an upbeat tropical or Caribbean look. For those who want to spend the winter in a peaceful south Florida community, The Commons is what you've been looking for.

5   EAGLEWOOD
Augusta Blvd., East Naples, FL 33962, 2BR $2000/mo
Amenities: Golf, pool, hot tub, tennis

On the southwestern edge of Naples, a dozen new condos have recently been constructed in the Lely area. Eaglewood condos offer vacation rentals in a country club environment. Surrounded by a pine forest, these cute two-story condos have a touch of Bermuda in the architecture and the tropical flavor of the Caribbean on the inside. Great for groups of golfers.

8   EDGEWATER BEACH HOTEL
1901 Gulf Shore Blvd. North, Naples, FL 33940, 813-262-6511
1BR $190–260
Amenities: Beach, pool, hot tub, restaurant, bar

This all-suite hotel is one of the few condo-style properties in this section of Naples that permits short-term rentals. You can stay for a day, a week, or a month. Drawing upon Bermuda style to set the tone, these one-bedroom suites have full kitchens and a convertible sofa in the living room. The lobby and public areas use lots of pink accented by white gingerbread and wicker furniture. The Edgewater was recently renovated from the ground up to give it a luxurious lobby as well as stylish interior decor for the suites. Apparently the decorators had free rein, because now the units border on being overfurnished with satins and fresh Florida prints. Plants and silk flowers are everywhere. What you'll like most is the view from your patio at this twelve-story high-rise. The pool area is lushly landscaped and you'll see the pink-and-white Bermuda theme carried throughout. This is in the fashionable Moorings section of Naples Beach where the beach is wide and the cute boutiques of the Venetian Village shopping center are close at hand. This all-suite hotel is good for couples, romance, seniors and even families with children—a "find" in this area.

8   GLENCOVE
Glenview Dr., Naples, FL 33963
Amenities: Pelican Bay beach shuttle, heated pool, tennis

Located within the exclusive Pelican Bay community, Glencove is the only condo development which permits rentals for as short as a month. Pelican Bay is unique because the condo developments are buffered from the beach by 200 acres of wildlife sanctuary. There's a boardwalk or an attendant with a golf cart to shuttle guests over to the beach. These condos are new and well built in a series of two-story buildings. The Glencove condos were designed to look like Bermuda. These two-bedroom condos are in coral pink buildings with cute, Bermuda-style roofs. For those who want to stay close to home there are tennis courts and a heated pool landscaped with palms. This is an exclusive community where your vacation experience will be different from anything else in the Naples area.

6+ NAPLES BATH & TENNIS CLUB
4995 Airport Rd. North, Naples, FL 33942, 813-261-5777
1BR $90–130, 2BR $115–170
Amenities: Tennis, health club, pool, bike trails

For tennis buffs, this is a special treat. Taking advantage of the mild year-round climate, the Bath & Tennis Club has a unique character. This is both a private country club and a vacation resort where tennis is the dominant theme. Enjoying the area's most effective security, this enclave insures a private, privileged world. Spread over 40 acres, the one-, two-, and three-bedroom villas are clustered in a series of two-story buildings, each containing four condos. Some enjoy the serenity of a lakeside setting, others are by the tennis courts and clubhouse. We saw most units furnished with a casual island style, lots of rattan furniture and tropical fabrics. For a resort that has developed an image of exclusivity, you'll be surprised by the relative informality. The clubbiness of a sports center pervades this resort and provides a break from the formality of surrounding Naples. There are 37 tennis courts and includes the celebrated NBTC Tennis Academy where adults as well as children can learn to play up to their potential. This is an exceptional find in Naples, not only because of the sports atmosphere, but also because this is perhaps the area's most upscale resort offering daily rentals as well as catering to weekly or monthly guests. Although a great idea 20 years ago and still a unique resort, the time has come to spruce up some of the units to keep up with the demands of some of the stylish guests.

8 NAPLES CAY
90 Seagate Dr., Naples, FL 33940
Amenities: Beach, pools, hot tubs, sauna, tennis, boat dock, health club

Nestled between the Pelican Bay and Park Shores sections of Naples, you'll find Naples Cay. You can't miss the three, fourteen-story towers which dominate the skyline. Set on 33 beach to bay acres, Naples Cay offers six different condominium buildings ranging from the three-story Villas Raphael to the fourteen-story Club Residence towers. The centerpiece is the country club that is available only to owners and guests. Inside, the condos are brand new and deluxe. Some have been decorated with over $30,000 of new furnishings to create a smashing environment, all with a view of the ocean. Naples Cay is a social resort where the owners are developing their own clubby atmosphere. Minimum rentals are for 30 days. It is great for those looking to spend the winter season in Naples.

5   NAPLES GULF POINTE
9439 Gulf Shore Dr., Vanderbilt Beach, FL 33963
Amenities: Pool. Beach across the street

Located on the bay side of the Vanderbilt Beach area, this three-story, fifteen-unit condo building provides a comfortable place to stay. Furniture is superior with island-style rattan furniture and bright tropical Florida fabrics. Each condo has a screened porch and some have a view of the Gulf. This is better than expected for economy lodgings in the Vanderbilt Beach area.

8   PARK SHORE
Gulf Shore Blvd., Naples, FL 33940
Amenities: Beach, pool, hot tub

This is an exclusive high-rise condominium located in the prestigious Park Shore section of Naples. The on-site manager doubles as a concierge giving you tips on sightseeing or arranging guest cards at some of the private country clubs.

7+   PARK SHORE RESORT HOTEL
600 Neapolitan Way, Naples, FL 33940
Amenities: Pool, hot tub, tennis, restaurant

As none of the condos in this exclusive part of Naples permit rentals for less than a month, we have included this deluxe all-suite hotel. Although it lacks the charm of a condo resort where individual owners are also part-time residents of the area, it is beautifully decorated and does have that Bermuda style charm that is so often associated with this part of Naples. Each one and two-bedroom suite is beautifully decorated with Bermuda pinks, soft greens, and pastel floral designs. The units are in a two-story building so you either have a patio or a balcony with a garden view. The beach is five minutes away. You will find that genteel, clubby feeling that so many expect from a Naples vacation.

10   REGISTRY RESORT
475 Seagate Dr., Naples, FL 33940, 813-597-3232
Villas $155–360
Amenities: Beach, golf, tennis, heated pools, hot tubs, health club, supervised children's activities

Located at the southern edge of a 200-acre beachfront nature preserve, the Registry offers a combination high-rise hotel tower and 50 two-story tennis villas. This is one of the best parts of the beach in all of Collier County because it is wide and relatively uncommercial. The Registry occupies a 15-acre site and the villas are behind the tower in a landscaped vacation village setting. Inside are some of the most luxuriously decorated rental units in all of south Florida using themes, designs and fabrics to suggest Florida, contemporary or traditional styles. We saw one that looked more like suburban New York than Florida because of all the art work, potted palms, and indoor ficus trees. There's a full kitchen, but you also have the option of room service. The advantage is a high level of service and lots of available amenities. The disadvantage is that it can be dominated when a convention or conference occupies the hotel tower.

5   ST. REGIS
Augusta Blvd., East Naples, FL 33962, 2BR $2000/mo
Amenities: Golf course, pool

On the southeast edge of Naples, a series of championship golf developments have recently been created. The St. Regis condos are on the fairway of the Lely Golf Estates. The condos are in a cluster of two-story, wood frame buildings shaded by the pines. These spacious two and three-bedroom condos are just perfect for groups of golfers.

5   VANDERBILT BEACH & HARBOUR CLUB
9301 Gulf Shore Dr., Vanderbilt Beach, FL 33963, 800-331-4941
1BR $645/wk, 2BR $1300/wk
Amenities: Pool, beach

One of the few timeshares in the Naples area, the Beach and Harbour Club offers weekly rentals at reasonable rates. This resort is in two sections divided by Vanderbilt Beach's Gulf Shore Drive; half is on the beach and half is on the bay. The two-bedroom units are functional and a little bit on the small side. Decorated in an attractive island style, you'll also find all the necessary appliances such as a washer/dryer and a microwave. One of the busiest pools anywhere; you and your children will make friends quickly.

6   VANDERBILT TOWERS I, II AND III
1–5 Bluebill Ave., Vanderbilt Beach, FL 33963
Studios $1600/mo, 1BR $2200/mo, 2BR $2600/mo
Amenities: Beach, pool

These modern twelve-story, high-rise towers on the north end of Vanderbilt Beach are clustered into their own little world. Each two-bedroom unit is spacious and has a wide balcony. Some face the ocean and some face the bay. Some units are residential and others have rentals by the week. This appeals most to older vacationers who want a beachfront vacation, just slightly removed from the hustle and bustle of the rest of Vanderbilt Beach. The swimming pools are beautifully landscaped and sometimes you'll find a card game in the shade of the palms.

6   VANDERBILT VACATION VILLAS
        9467 Gulf Shore Dr., Vanderbilt Beach, FL 33963, 813-597-1141
        Amenities: Pool, beach

These beachfront villas are a rare find among the high-rise towers of Vanderbilt Beach. Each studio and one-bedroom unit is in a two-story building arranged around a landscaped pool area. Quiet and content, you can walk out your door and be on the ocean (not in an elevator) at any time. Cooking facilities are limited to a two-burner range and mini-fridge in the studios. The one-bedroom apartments are on the ground floor and have full kitchens. Rentals are available here by the day, week or month in this quiet garden community.

7   WORLD TENNIS CENTER
        4800 Airport Rd., Naples, FL 33942, 813-263-1900
        1BR $75–145
        Amenities: Tennis, pools, hot tubs, saunas, restaurant

Bringing a bit of southern Europe to southern Florida, the World Tennis Center features dramatic Mediterranean-style architecture set on an 82-acre site. Built townhouse style, these two-story structures are in clusters. White stucco exteriors, graceful archways, and beautiful tropical landscaping will remind you of the Greek Isles. Each unit has two-bedrooms, a full kitchen, and there's a private pool to go with each cluster of condos. Decor, unfortunately, is casual Florida style. Too bad, because just a little flourish on the inside would have complimented the sophisticated appearance of the exterior. All American conveniences are included and whether you play tennis or not, this is one of the friendliest resorts in the Naples area. Tennis players will appreciate the 11 clay and 5 hard tennis courts, the 2500 seat stadium court, and the full-time staff of teaching pros. Round Robin tennis games are available for players of all levels of skill. Daily, weekly and monthly rentals are available.

RENTAL RESOURCES
Bluebill Properties, 800-237-2010
Kersey Quade, 800-334-4909
Park Shore Properties, 813-261-6161
Phase III, 813-597-9111
Workman & Assoc., 813-262-8992

3. LEE COUNTY

The condo resorts in this area are among the world's trendsetters in resort design, operations, and prices. It is such an idyllic setting that some visitors won't want to leave, but don't expect to vacation here on a budget. These resorts, in many cases, offer more activities than a Club Med vacation. We have organized this section into two subsections: Sanibel and Captiva Islands and Ft. Myers Beach.

SANIBEL AND CAPTIVA ISLANDS

Perennially voted one of the top vacation choices in the U.S., these two islands off the southwest coast of Florida combine quality real estate development with preservation of the environment. Over half the islands' acreage has been set aside as a wetlands wildlife preserve and each morning there's a new crop of colorful shells that wash up on the beach. First settled in the 19th century after the Civil War, Sanibel was a quiet place for fisherman and pioneers. Prior to 1960 the islands' largest industry was a small clam cannery. The laid back environment of Victorian Florida was about to change forever when environmentalists intervened in one of the earliest anti-development movements in Florida. The central issue involved land use when construction of the bridge to the mainland from Sanibel would be completed in the 1960s. The environmentalists prevailed and today visitors from North America and Europe come to Sanibel to see the Ding Darling Wildlife Preserve.

Real estate development on Sanibel and Captiva islands has been done with a strong respect for the sea. With only a few exceptions, most buildings have been constructed of wood and concrete with the first floor open for garage parking or vegetation, in the event of tidal waves. There are numerous clusters of condos ranging in size from 12 to 45 units. Only a few developments have more than 45 units. Very few have on-site management. Therefore, each has a quiet, almost cozy personality that reflects the desired lifestyle of the condo owners. Most developments are on the beach along the southern shore of Sanibel. One, Blind Pass, is all by itself on the northern end of Sanibel Island in the least commercial area. Several developments are on quieter Captiva Island, including the impressive South Seas Plantation with the only golf course in the area.

A word of advice on Sanibel/Captiva real estate. The market here is "built out." That is, all land available for development has already been developed. As more "new product" can not be created, the real estate market here has more and more dollars chasing the same number of condo or villa units. This has caused real estate prices on the island to escalate. For example, just look at these figures:

	1987 Avg. Price	1988 Avg. Price	Percent Increase	1989 Avg. Price	Percent Increase
Condos	206,000	238,000	15.5%	264,000	9.8%
Villas	248,000	297,000	19.5%	341,000	12.9%

Transportation to Sanibel/Captiva is through Southwest Regional Airport in Ft. Myers. There's a parkway from the airport leading to the bridge over to Sanibel and the drive takes about 20 minutes. For those who don't rent a car, shuttle bus service is available. Once on the island, you may be so content that you'll never use your car during your stay.

WHERE TO STAY

8 **ANGLER'S KEY**
2639 W. Gulf Dr., Sanibel Island, FL 33957
Amenities: Pool, tennis, beach

A special place on Sanibel, it has only six units in three buildings surrounded by a lush private garden. There's only one unit per floor. These duplexes are very spacious, each having three bedrooms and a den. They are fairly new and stylishly furnished by an interior decorator. This is privacy in paradise.

6 **THE ATRIUM**
2929 W. Gulf Dr., Sanibel Island, FL 33957, $925–1600
Amenities: Beach, pool

Located right on the beach, the two and three-bedroom condos in this building are extra spacious and comfortable. Each has a large living room with a screened balcony overlooking the Gulf. Over 17 years old, there's a range of furnishings from "early attic" with poster art to serious professional decor. This is a comfortable place for beach walkers or to just listen to the surf.

8 **BANDY BEACH**
1214 Buttonwood Ln., Sanibel Island, FL 33957, 2BR $770–1470
Amenities: Beach, pool

Bandy Beach offers a quiet retreat on Sanibel Island with nary a child in sight. Located on the beach, these duplexes are in five two-story buildings. These spacious condos offer two bedrooms and a den. Each has a screened porch where you can watch the gentle waves lap the shelling beach. Paddle fans in the living room underscore that "Old Florida" style.

7   BLIND PASS
5117 Sea Bell Rd., Sanibel Island, FL 33957
2BR $500–950/wk, 3BR $575–1200/wk
Amenities: Beach, pool, tennis

Enjoying its own quiet corner of the island, Blind Pass condos are up at the northwest end of the island away from most of the development on the east end. Blind Pass offers limited beach frontage and is surrounded on two sides by a wildlife refuge. This is a nature lover's choice, and be advised this property is fifteen minutes away from most of the restaurants or other social activities on Sanibel. The condos in these long two-story buildings are spacious, but drab on the inside. The building exteriors have just been renovated and now it's time to do something about the inside. Generally we found heavy, tired furniture covered in scotch-guarded tweed and tan fabrics. The kitchen appliances are in the gold and avocado colors popular in the late '60s. For such a great location (appealing to those who want unspoiled Sanibel) we were disappointed with the interiors.

  CAPTIVA COTTAGE
Captiva Rd., Captiva Island, FL 33924, 3BR $1100–2500/wk
Amenities: private pool

This is an example of one of the many private villas available for rent on Captiva. Condos are popular, but a villa on Captiva is exclusive and even more in demand. Located between the Gulf of Mexico and Pine Island Sound, this three-bedroom house is only minutes from the bay. The yard is sand with natural vegetation and a wooden swing is positioned for great views of the Gulf and sunset. The private pool is inside a screened-in patio area. Interior decor is handsome with stately English floral prints, an elegant sofa, and traditional wood furniture rubbed with a whitewash. Rates can be substantial, but for a family or a group of friends this is a superior choice.

7   CAPTIVA HIDEAWAY
P.O. Box 850, Captiva Island, FL 33924, 813-472-4398
Amenities: Dock, heated pool, sauna

This intimate eight-unit condominium overlooks Pine Island Sound and the mainland in the distance. Each two-bedroom unit has a living room, kitchen, and a screened porch which is where you'll want to spend most of your time. Although handsome in decor, it's been some time since this was decorated. Never advertised, this has a clubby atmosphere and the first question asked around the pool is "How did you find out about this place?" Prior to this directory, you had to have a friend or owner tell you about this hideaway. The secret is out!

9   CAPTIVA SHORES
Captiva Rd., Captiva Island, FL 33924
1BR $725–1300/wk, 2BR $775–1400/wk
Amenities: Beach, pool

This is Old Florida. Here you'll find a cottage community of neo-Victorian homes, each with a two-bedroom unit and a three-bedroom unit. Simple in design, the interior decor is a study in fabrics and colors well blended. Yellows, greens, and an occasional streak of blue provide an exceptional ambiance for a vacation experience. This nine-acre, well-landscaped compound stretches from the sound to the beach.

9   CASA YBEL
2255 W. Gulf Dr., Sanibel Island, FL 33957, 813-472-3145
Amenities: Pool, activities program, tennis

This is one of the premier resorts in southwest Florida. The centerpiece is the Thistle Lodge and restaurant which was built in a striking Florida Victorian style, highlighted by a rotunda. Casa Ybel lays legitimate claim to the Victorian style, as it was built on a site occupied by Sanibel's pioneers over 100 years ago. There are six tropical colonial-style buildings that are more suggestive of South Carolina's Low Country than of traditional Florida. A touch of romance is in the architecture. There are 115 one and two-bedroom condos in two-story buildings, each with a view of the Gulf. The furniture is island style with rattan covered in light pink and blue fabrics—very smart for the 1990s. Best feature is the swimming pool. You'll find friendly pool attendants, as well as a spacious layout attracting couples and families. This is certainly the most congenial pool area on Sanibel. There is a water slide and an activities program designed for small children as well as teens. Not only is the resort stunning to the eye, but the operations are a model of good service and hospitality. Low key and unobtrusive, yet so efficient. Truffles Restaurant, located in the Thistle Lodge, is one of the best in the area by any standard. Hobie cat rentals are available for sailors and there are six tennis courts for older "children." If you have the money, Casa Ybel offers a great family vacation on Sanibel Island.

8   COMPASS POINT
1299 Middle Gulf Dr., Sanibel Island, FL 33957
1BR $625–1250/wk, 2BR $850–1550/wk
Amenities: Beach, pool

Built eleven years ago on a prime section of the beach, the 45 condos in these four-story buildings are some of Sanibel's most modern. Functional in design, each is well decorated and has a screened balcony. Some condos have the extra feature of a whirlpool in the master bath while others have private rooftop sun decks. The pool area has a large patio and is a pleasant place to soak up the winter sun.

9   COQUINA BEACH
625 B Nerita St., Sanibel Island, FL 33957
1BR $550–1250/wk, 2BR $1000–1400/wk
Amenities: Beach, pool, tennis

Vacation splendor abounds. Regarded by many locals as one of Sanibel's "best" condominiums, this complex of 40 two-bedroom condos enjoys a landscaped garden setting. The two-story buildings have loft units upstairs which are our favorite. They have individual ground level entrances, cathedral ceilings, and a spiral staircase up to the loft which is a small den. Each of the two bedrooms is on the ground floor and has its own bath. Coquina Beach is a good choice for two couples vacationing together. The landscaped pool is romantic with the shade of the palms and there's a tennis court for those who have the energy.

8   CYPRINA BEACH
695 E. Gulf Dr., Sanibel Island, FL 33957
Amenities: Pool, beach for shelling

This community of townhouses is unique on Sanibel. Each can be your own private residence on Sanibel, with the living room, dining room and kitchen on the second floor, and two-bedrooms on the third floor. There's an open space on the third floor that gives the living room ceiling an added dimension. Comfortably furnished, it may be time for some owners to redecorate. This is one condo property that truly creates the "private island" experience. The landscaping here is sand with occasional palms or clumps of bushes.

8   DOSINIA
3339 W. Gulf Dr., Sanibel Island, FL 33957
Amenities: Beach, pool, tennis

These are spacious three-bedroom units right on the beach. These are some of the more expensive condos on the island, and they generally have superior furnishings. The one we saw had the sophistication of Washington D.C. with European period furniture pieces and Japanese art on the wall. Mirrors bring the Gulf view inside and the screened porch can be an extra breakfast room.

7   GULF BEACH
W. Gulf Dr., Sanibel Island, FL 33957, $650–1225/wk
Amenities: Beach, pool

Overlooking an area of sand dunes and vegetation, this cluster of ten two-bedroom condos is often overlooked. If you want peace, privacy, and a beachfront location, these condos are for you. The floor plan is efficient and the rooms are on the small side.

8 **JANTHINA**
3025 W. Gulf Dr., Sanibel Island, FL 33957, $1100–2200/wk
Amenities: Beach, pool

For the select few, these seven unique condos offer privacy and an elegant beach house environment on Sanibel Island. The best feature is the panoramic view of the Gulf from the living room and the master bedroom balconies. Each three-bedroom unit has two bathrooms, so these are best for families or groups of friends. The second floor units have a spiral staircase up to individual roof sun decks. It is a quiet and private environment.

8 **JUNONIA**
W. Gulf Dr., Sanibel Island, FL 33957, $850–1700/wk
Amenities: Beach, pool, tennis

With only eight condos, Junonia is a quiet low-key place. The rooms in each of the units are on the small side and interior decor is generally island style with rattan furniture and fabrics faded since the '70s. There's a path over to the beach that is good for families.

7 **KING'S CROWN**
2721 W. Gulf Dr., Sanibel Island, FL 33957, $750–1500
Amenities: Beach, pool

Although this is a beachfront location, these condos are set back from the beach so they overlook a grassy parklike area and the Gulf beyond. Some are right on the beach, others are inland and overlook the pool. These 54 two and three-bedroom condos are very spacious and the rooms have extra large dimensions. Some are well decorated; others have casual island style rattan furniture with well-preserved fabrics from the '70s. Best of all, these units have been situated to capture the best evening views as the sun sinks into the Gulf.

6 **LIGHTHOUSE POINT**
200 Periwinkle Way, Sanibel Island, FL 33957
1BR $560, 2BR $960–1100
Amenities: Beach, heated pool, sauna, tennis

Enjoying a unique location on the southernmost tip of the island—"where the Gulf meets the Bay"—this secluded location is surrounded by palm trees. These condos are twenty years old and some have interior decor that is attractive, but not stylish. Most have neutral themes emphasizing beige or sky blue colors. The beachfront units are spectacular and well worth any extra price premium. However, most of the units are inland overlooking a lagoon with the Gulf off in the distance.

8 LOGGERHEAD CAY
666 Beach Rd., Sanibel Island, FL 33957
1BR $600–1200, 2BR $800–1500
Amenities: Beach, pool, tennis

These modern four-story concrete structures are set within a three-acre landscaped garden environment. The end units are on the beach, otherwise the views are of the grassy parklike setting and pool. New and stylishly decorated, Loggerhead Cay possesses the largest swimming pool on Sanibel and the tennis courts invite the active sportsman. Located on the beach, this is just what the doctor ordered for the parents who need a week away from their children. (And we know you love them, but sometimes...) This place is quiet and a good choice for energetic corporate executives who need to relax.

7 MARINER POINTE
760 Sextant Dr., Sanibel Island, FL 33957, 813-482-7766
Amenities: Fishing and boat dock, pools, tennis

Mariner Pointe offers a unique location on Sanibel. Right after you cross the causeway to the island, turn left. Mariner Pointe occupies a small finger of land surrounded by water. Sorry, this is canal front so there is no beach. To compensate, Mariner Pointe offers a fishing dock that can accommodate small boats. These are well furnished condos in sturdy two-story concrete structures strung along the shore line. Each unit has a waterfront view from the screened porch. This condo complex is equally divided between vacation rental units and residential units that are quiet, confident, and in style.

7 PINE COVE
2501 W. Gulf Dr., Sanibel Island, FL 33957, 813-454-1400
$900–1800
Amenities: Beach, pool, hot tub

Nestled amid the pines and palms, these are some of the newest condos on Sanibel. Recessed from the beach, each of these 19 two-bedroom units overlooks an area of vegetation with the beach just beyond. The rooms in these units are on the small side but each bedroom has its own bathroom. It's a good choice for families or two couples. It is quiet and secluded.

7   **POINTE SANTO de SANIBEL**
         2445 W. Gulf Dr., Sanibel Island, FL 33957,
         1BR $750–1500, 2BR $1000–1500
         Amenities: Beach, pool, hot tub

Pointe Santo is unique in that it sits on 18 acres of lush tropical landscaping with a spring fed lagoon, visited by many rare and beautiful species of birds. Located in the center of the island, these beachfront condominiums overlook the lagoon and the pool with the beach and the Gulf just beyond. You can walk the beach for two miles in either direction. These modern four-story concrete buildings have units with efficient floor plans. There's a screened porch and the master bedroom is at an angle so you can lie in bed and see the Gulf. With 140 condos this complex is one of the largest developments on the island.

7   **SAND POINTE**
         2737 W. Gulf Dr., Sanibel Island, FL 33957
         1BR $625–1225, 2BR $725–1400
         Amenities: Beach, pool

Each of the 45 two-bedroom condos at Sand Pointe has a view of the beach and the Gulf. There are two three-story buildings arranged so some units overlook the pool and have a northern view of the island along the beach; others overlook the pool and face directly west. The screened porch makes an extra room. It is pleasant and well decorated.

6   **SANDALFOOT**
         671 E. Gulf Dr., Sanibel Island, FL 33957, 813-472-2275
         Amenities: Beach, pool, tennis

This is a cluster of five three-story buildings grouped around a pool. The units are beachfront and have screened patios. Twenty-five years old and with construction style from the 1960s, these are missing that upbeat contemporary feeling. Time has passed this one by, maybe you should too.

8   **SANDPIPER BEACH**
         1919 Olde Middle Gulf Dr., Sanibel Island, FL 33957, $650–1250
         Amenities: Beach, pool, tennis. Racquetball available next door

Located on a dead end street, these deluxe units offer a sense of seclusion on the beachfront. There's an area of sand dunes and vegetation buffering this building from the beach and the early morning shellers. These spacious units have superior decor and most were decorated by interior designers, albeit twelve years ago. Quiet, great views, and pleasant company make this a superior choice on Sanibel.

SANIBEL ACCOMMODATIONS
1149 Periwinkle Way, Suite D, Sanibel Island, FL 33957,
813-472-3191
and
SANIBEL REALTY
1630 Periwinkle Way, Sanibel Island, FL 33957, 813-472-6565
$445–1566

These two rental agencies offer a selection of the island's private homes located on the beach, the golf course, or in total seclusion. When movie stars like Danny DeVito or Glenn Close want the "private island" adventure, this is where they turn. Both of these agencies offer a range of cottages up to private beachfront homes with their own swimming pools. Minimum stays may be required and you might be asked for references. But these island hideaways can make some very special vacations.

8+   SANIBEL COTTAGES
2341 W. Gulf Dr., Sanibel Island, FL 33957, 813-481-3636
Amenities: Tennis, heated pool, beach for shelling

Sanibel Cottages creates an "Old Florida" atmosphere. The 28 condos are in seven two-story buildings. You'll find a landscaped tropical environment on the beach. Victorian style architectural touches, such as ginger bread latticework separating the kitchen from the living room are special characteristics. The furniture is unique: Victorian reproductions done in a light "Old Florida" style. There is white wicker furniture with deep blue fabrics, carved oak kitchen cabinets and glass globe light fixtures from the turn of the century. The style is old, but you are provided with modern conveniences such as a VTP and whirlpool in the master bath. Set back in a forested environment far from the mainland, Sanibel Cottages have their own private ambiance.

7   SHELL HARBOR INN
937 E. Gulf Dr., Sanibel Island, FL 33957, $725–1550
Amenities: Beach, pool, putting green, restaurant, tennis

One of Sanibel's larger condo complexes, there are 101 units in seven three-story buildings grouped around the pool. Beautifully landscaped, this has a true resort atmosphere with a pool bar and a restaurant in the back. Nicely decorated and you can expect to find casual island style decor or perhaps a smart contemporary look. With all the amenities, this is for someone who expects "service" when on vacation.

7   SHELL ISLAND BEACH CLUB
300 Lighthouse Rd., Sanibel Island, FL 33957, 813-472-4497
Amenities: Beach, pool, hot tub, sauna. Tennis nearby

This is a landscaped condo community with three-story wooden structures on stilts spread over 13 acres of parklike beachfront property. Separating the development from the ocean is an area of dunes, sea grass, and boardwalks. The ecology surrounding this resort has been preserved, in spite of the high density of Sanibel Island. The two-bedroom condos are rather small, but have been recently redecorated with classic island-style rattan furniture covered with designer print fabrics. The interior decor displays understated good taste. There's a quiet, landscaped pool area which is good for sunning, watching children at play, reading, or simply day dreaming. If you must have exercise, the beach offers some of the best "shelling" to be found.

7 SNUG HARBOR
W. Gulf Dr., Sanibel Island, FL 33957, $850–1600
Amenities: Beach, pool, tennis

Snug is the word for the 14 condos here. The lot is long and narrow but eight units are in a two-story building so they overlook the dunes and the beach. Six other units are inland. Casually decorated with island style or contemporary decor, this was designed to have a cozy feeling. You'll feel like the guest on a private estate when you sit by the pool. It is pleasingly private and snug.

7 SONG OF THE SEA
863 E. Gulf Dr., Sanibel Island, FL 33957, 813-472-2220
Amenities: Beach, pool, hot tub, tennis club guest pass

Seafarers once believed they could be seduced by the song of the sea, never to return home again. This beachfront resort was aptly named, as you'll not want to leave this languid, subtropical environment of an old world inn. This three-story resort has Spanish or Mediterranean architecture and you often forget you are in Florida. Maybe it's because of the courtyard entrance, the white stucco buildings, and the red-tile roofs. Inside, the condos are like hotel-suites with limited kitchen facilities but they have been professionally decorated with wing back chairs, traditional furniture, and green and cotton candy pink fabrics. Many of the condos are on the beach and you can hear the luring call of the surf at night.

10 SOUTH SEAS PLANTATION
South Seas Plantation Rd., Captiva Island, FL 33924,
813-472-5111, 1BR $775–1200, 2BR $1335–2200
Amenities: Golf, marina, pools, tennis, beach

Wow! This is a fabulous resort property and what a contrast to the other sleepy little cottages on the island. On first approach you are confronted with towering Australian pines. Inside the plantation, you will feel like you are on one of the Hawaiian islands as you are surrounded by a grove of coconut palms. There's no other Florida resort like this. There are 62 two-story buildings spread over 330 acres of well-preserved plantation land and golf course. The only noise is the occasional ping of a tennis ball. Development has been handled with loving respect for the environment and steps have been taken to preserve the vegetation and maintain the natural ecology. It's called "Florida's Tahiti."

There's a wide range of condo accommodations to choose from. Seven separate condo developments exist within this one resort. Our favorite is **Land's End Village** at the northern tip of Captiva Island. These spacious two and three-bedroom condos are found in two-story buildings. The penthouse three-bedroom condos have a master bedroom in the top loft with a private hot tub outside on the deck. The interior decor is smashing. You can walk to the beach or the nearby South Seas Club in only two minutes. At Land's End Village, you are a little over a mile from the main part of the resort. The **Marina Villas** and **Harborside** are well decorated units overlooking the marina. Harborside condos are hotel rooms or junior suites. There are no kitchens. Harborside Villas enjoy a strip of sandy beach where Hobie cats are available for rent. The **Tennis Villas** are at the tennis club. Surprisingly, the **Beach Villas** and **Cottages** are most affordable, yet these condos in three-story buildings are right on Sanibel's famous shelling beach. Great value is found here.

This resort is the best of "Old Florida"—maybe "Old Florida" was never this good.

9 SUNDIAL

1451 Middle Gulf Dr., Sanibel Island, FL 33957, 813-472-4151
1BR $550–1000, 2BR $900–1600
Amenities: Pools, tennis. Golf nearby

Sundial is one of the largest, most active, and most polished resorts you'll find on the very relaxed island of Sanibel. The resort is so complete, you'll find no reason to go anywhere else. There are five swimming pools and 13 tennis courts. By staying at Sundial you have golf privileges at the nearby Dunes Golf Course. This is a great resort for families because there is an activities program for children during major school vacations. Sundial also features two of Sanibel's better restaurants—Morgan's for fresh seafood and a Japanese restaurant named Noopie's. The condos are designer decorated, Florida style with light blue and pink colors emphasizing the seashell motif. Because the suites have entrances off a central hallway, you'll feel like you're staying in a luxurious hotel, but you have the convenience of a condo with a living room and kitchen. A beautiful lobby and cocktail lounge overlooks the dunes.

8 SUNSET CAPTIVA
Captiva Dr., Captiva Island, FL 33924
1BR $650–1200, 2BR $850–1650
Amenities: Beach, pool, tennis, boat dock

This is a colony of privately owned cottages running the width of the island from the beach to San Carlos Bay. These 59 bungalows have two or three bedrooms plus a small loft. Just off the living/dining room, there's a wrap around screened porch. Well decorated, expect to find rattan or wicker furniture (appropriate for a beach house) covered in stylish designer fabrics. Some are older with earth tone colors. Newer ones sprout lots of white and very pale pastels. Designed for comfortable family living, these condos are a superior choice on Captiva Island.

9 TANGLEWOOD
Seagrape and Buttonwood, Sanibel Island, FL 33957
Amenities: Beach, pool

These nine condos are some of the most luxurious on Sanibel Island. Beautifully decorated, each has the touch of an interior decorator. The furniture almost seems too formal for this intimate arrangement of beachside villas. Each building has only two units—one on the ground level and one upstairs. The upper level units have a spiral staircase down to the swimming pool area. It is truly luxurious.

8 TARPON BEACH CLUB
2475 W. Gulf Dr., Sanibel Island, FL 33957, $630–1175
Amenities: Beach, pool, tennis

The thirty units here are in three three-story buildings designed so each looks directly over to the beach and the Gulf. There are great sunsets in the evening. These condos are beautiful on the inside with superior furniture and mirrors to bring the view inside. Nothing overdone, just understated good taste. These condos are recessed from the beach, but there's a boardwalk through the grassy dunes over to the Gulf. This is a great choice on one of America's favorite islands.

7 TENNISPLACE
1250 Tennisplace Ct., Sanibel Island, FL 33957, $425–700
Amenities: Pool, tennis

These one- and two-bedroom condos are along the Deepwater Canal, not on the beach. There's a lovely landscaped pool area which is a pleasure by day and the focal point for cocktail parties in the evening. A little bit small, furnishings are simple with lots of wicker or rattan. Close to the mainland bridge, this is convenient for families where one has to work while the spouse enjoys a Sanibel vacation.

8+ TORTUGA BEACH CLUB
959 S. Gulf Dr., Sanibel Island, FL 33957, 813-481-3636
Amenities: Golf, pool, tennis

The design of this resort features homes on stilts spread over two acres of tropical landscape. The environment has been preserved and the effect creates a sense of privacy and that comfortable "home" feeling you can never get at a hotel. The resort is located on the southern end of Sanibel Island, a great location for "shelling." Guests at this resort have free golf privileges at the Dunes Golf Course nearby. There are eight spacious units in each of the three-story buildings. These are luxurious vacation homes. The condos are tastefully decorated in shades of coral and sky blue in order to create a tranquil Florida beach house effect. Management is attentive but so unobtrusive you'll never feel that you are sharing "the compound" with any more than a few select guests.

6 VILLA SANIBEL
2321 W. Gulf Dr., Sanibel Island, FL 33957, $600–1150
Amenities: Beach, pool, tennis

These three buildings contain twenty private condominiums in a beachside location. The lot is long and narrow, so only four of the 20 units have Gulf views. Here the ambiance is clubby and secure, much like being at a small guest house. The upper level units are truly superior with cathedral ceilings and small lofts. Each two-bedroom condo has the bedrooms downstairs; the loft can either be used as an area for kids with sleeping bags or an area to get some reading done while on vacation.

6+ WHITE CAPS
2407 W. Gulf Dr., Sanibel Island, FL 33957
Amenities: None

Close your eyes and imagine what you would hope to find on Sanibel Island. White Caps is a cluster of nine separate villas that are very cute and cozy. There's no grass surrounding these buildings, only sand and palms. White Caps villas are a little on the small side with tiny kitchenettes. Snow White would have loved these little cottages. There are no amenities and it's a bit isolated, but maybe you'll find a neighbor to talk to. Perhaps you'll feel like Robinson Crusoe. No other property on Sanibel offers this relaxed "cottage by the sea" feeling.

5   **WHITE SANDS**
        W. Gulf Dr., Sanibel Island, FL 33957, $775–1425
        Amenities: Beach, pool, tennis

   These are among some of Sanibel's older beachfront condos. The fourteen
units here are on the small side. Interior decor needs to be spruced up. This
is, however, a good location, with older units. Rentals here should be reasonably priced.

RENTAL RESOURCES
Bluebill Properties, 813-472-0440
Century 21 AAIM Realty, 800-237-3342
Fantasy Island, 800-237-5146
Gulf Coast Vacations, 800-237-6285
Marquis Reservations, 800-237-8906, Mainly quality timeshares
Priscilla Murphy, 813-472-4113/800-237-6008, Largest selection
Prudential Florida, 813-472-4000
Sea Shells of Sanibel, 813-472-4634
Vacation Shoppe, 800-237-7370, Moderate timeshares
VIP Realty, 813-472-1613

FT. MYERS BEACH

Ft. Myers Beach, also called Estero Island, was developed during the first
half of the 20th Century. It is an established resort community with 11 miles
of beaches. Separated from the mainland by a bay, the island, like Sanibel,
has been built out. Unlike Sanibel, the marshlands and barrier dunes were
not preserved. Although not as environmentally conscious, Ft. Myers Beach
offers the most reasonably priced condos in this part of Florida.

   Transportation to Ft. Myers Beach is similar to Sanibel. Fly to Ft. Myers
and take the parkway down to the bridge over to Ft. Myers Beach/
Estero Island.

WHERE TO STAY

7   **MARINER'S BOATHOUSE**
        7630 Estero Blvd., Ft. Myers Beach, FL 33931, 813-481-3636
        Amenities: Pool, hot tub, social director

   From its "dock" on Ft. Myers Beach, the Boathouse creates a nautical
environment. This is different, and the romance of the sea pervades the air.
The units are cabins and decorated as such. You'll see a lot of teak and
brass—such as can be found on a ship. The second bedroom has bunk beds.
The atmosphere around the pool is like a yacht club. The social director

insures that guests are introduced quickly, and friendships form just like on a cruise ship. At noon there is often a potluck luncheon. Nature played a trick here; the beach is actually separated from the property by a shallow gulf of water. The Boathouse provides little boats for rowing to the "island." This development successfully converted a potential obstacle into a big plus. This is perfect for families and is a good choice on Estero Island/Ft. Myers Beach.

8+ PINK SHELL

250 Estero Blvd., Ft. Myers Beach, FL 33931, 813-463-6181
Studios $70–128, 1BR $95–138, 2BR $125–215
Amenities: Beach, heated pool

This resort is a community of elevated pink cottages on the beach. It is spread over twelve sandy acres at the northern tip of Ft. Myers Beach. Pink canopied golf carts cruise the property, delivering new arrivals. You can choose one of the beachfront cottages or stay in the three-story building. All of the units were stripped and completely redecorated in late 1989 with a comfortable tropical look. There is grasscloth wallpaper and, of course, a few splashes of pink for color. Inside you'll find all new modern kitchen appliances and cabinets. The result is an unparalleled vacation environment which will make you think of cottage colonies in Bermuda.

9 POINTE ESTERO

6640 Estero Blvd., Ft. Myers Beach, FL 33931, 813-765-1155
1BR $78–140, 2BR $100–170
Amenities: Beach, pool, hot tub, tennis

Luxury and quality in a modern fourteen-story tower on Ft. Myers Beach. The building was designed so that each condo has a view of the Gulf. These spacious condos have designer furnishings, using lots of pink and beige colors for a romantic tropical environment. Each condo has a marble whirlpool large enough for two and a screened porch, which in Florida amounts to an extra room. The penthouse suites are the best accommodations on Ft. Myers Beach. A spiral staircase connects the first floor to the glass walled "turret." Outside there's a private rooftop sun deck. Good management makes this a friendly resort, but you won't find many children underfoot. There's a landscaped garden with streams, foot bridges, and a little gazebo for private conversations. You'll find this one of the most romantic resorts on Ft. Myers Beach.

8 SEA WATCH

6550 Estero Blvd., Ft. Myers Beach, FL 33931, 813-481-3636
1BR $105–150, 2BR $135–170
Amenities: Activities program, pool, tennis

Perhaps the most luxurious vacation accommodations on Ft. Myers Beach are to be found at this seven-story condo complex. The units here seem new. Everything is "fresh." Sea Watch is an eight-story building with an atrium. Beautifully decorated in a casual Florida style, this resort gives everyone ocean views and a chance to hear the surf at night. Mirrors bring the view inside. There is a full-time social director in charge of the activities program. The resort offers a heated pool, tennis courts, and shuffle board. Sea Watch is an outstanding vacation choice on Estero Island/Ft. Myers Beach.

10 SONESTA SANIBEL HARBOR RESORT
17260 Harbour Pointe Dr., Ft. Myers, FL 33908
813-466-4000, $525–1100
Amenities: Pools, sauna, hot tub, tennis, spa/health club,
racquetball, restaurants

One of the finest spa and tennis resorts in the U.S. The spa has been compared to California's La Costa Resort, where your body can begin the reshaping process in only a week. The Jimmy Connors U.S. Tennis Center features a 5,300 seat stadium court. The Sonesta resort is spread over 80 acres along San Carlos Bay. It is not on Sanibel Island, rather it is at the entrance to the causeway over to Sanibel. There is a hotel tower and two twelve-story condominium towers facing the sound with a view of Sanibel. The two-bedroom condo apartments in the towers are individually decorated. These condominiums cost between $250,000 to $350,000, so you can imagine the quality of furnishings the owners have selected for their vacation homes. Rental rates are surprisingly modest when you consider the high quality. Jimmy's Courtside Restaurant and Bar is a popular place at all times of day and night. Guests here have full use of the facilities at the bustling Sonesta Hotel, including use of the spa. There you'll find exercise programs, beauty programs and nutrition counseling. All of these offerings are available to guests at a discounted rate.

6 WINDWARD PASSAGE
418 Estero Blvd., Ft. Myers Beach, FL 33931, 813-463-1194
1BR $65–125, 2BR $85–150
Amenities: Beach, heated pool, hot tub, tennis

Located on a lovely stretch of beach, this five-story condo complex was designed so every unit faces the Gulf and enjoys the beautiful sunsets. Inside, the units are richly decorated with lots of mirrors and designer fabrics. The resort has a heated swimming pool, a hot tub, and tennis court. A children's playground and sailboat rentals are available on the beach. Good management provides a comfortable and friendly place where you can relax and enjoy your time in the sun without social pressures. This is, indeed, a bargain choice for the area.

RENTAL RESOURCES

Bluebill, 800-458-2766
Century 21 AAIM Realty, 800-237-3342
Gulf Coast Vacations, 800-237-6285
Hussey Company, 813-463-3178
Lahaina Realty, 813-463-5703
Loffreno Realty, 800-741-2986, Competitive prices
Marquis Reservations, 800-237-8906, Timeshare
Kathy Nesbit Vacations, 813-463-4253
Vacation Shoppe, 800-237-7370, Timeshare

4. SARASOTA and its KEYS

Sarasota County on the southwest coast of Florida has been one of the nation's prime vacation areas ever since John Ringling put it on the map in the early part of the 20th century. A sleepy backwater part of Florida, Mr. and Mrs. Ringling were searching for a winter home for their circus when they stumbled upon Sarasota. With a wintertime temperature averaging in the sixties and summertime thermometers rarely rising above the mid-eighties, Sarasota is indeed a wonderful place to live. Even better are its three off-shore islands which in the spring, summer, and fall really are quite pleasant, enjoying continuous Gulf breezes.

We have divided the Where to Stay section into the three major island destinations (Longboat Key, Lido Beach, and Siesta Key) plus one mainland resort.

During the '70s and '80s, vacationers discovered the charms of this part of Florida. The once sleepy ambiance of Siesta and Lido Key slipped away as twelve-story condo towers began to dominate the skyline. Today you'll find a solid strip of high-rise towers mixed with former motels that are now converted to condos. It may seem like high density, but there's also a care-free social atmosphere in this area. It is favored by young families as well as the semi-retired. Siesta Key and Lido Key are more residential than Longboat Key, and not as commercial as Sarasota. Siesta is home to many artists and writers. Technically, Siesta Key is part of the city of Sarasota, as many mailing addresses for resorts which read Sarasota are actually on Siesta Key.

Longboat Key has been fortunate in its development. Building has been carefully controlled and everything is perfect—you'll be among the select few who are able to enjoy this polished environment. Some of the best golf courses and most beautiful condos in Florida are located here.

Transportation to Sarasota is either through the Sarasota airport with service by American, Delta, United, and U.S. Air. Some may prefer to fly to Tampa, which has more nonstop flights and is less than an hour away by car.

WHERE TO STAY... LONGBOAT KEY

8   COLONY BEACH RESORT
1620 Gulf of Mexico Dr., Longboat Key, FL 34228,
800-237-9443, 1BR $205–345
Amenities: Beachfront, restaurants, tennis, racquetball, health club.
Golf nearby

This resort provides formal "high style" on Longboat Key. Yet, it's a
great resort for families and everyone should feel comfortable here. The
Colony, one of the largest and most successful condo resorts in this part of
Florida, enjoys one of Florida's widest white sand beaches. The Colony is
one of the most popular condominiums for purchase in the area. At prices of
$200,000 to $300,000 for a condo, you can be assured that the clientele is
mostly hard-working, prosperous Northerners who want a few weeks under
Florida's winter sun. The condos have been individually decorated. Some
are elegantly decorated with French Bergère chairs and bright orange and
yellow floral print fabrics. Others are more serene and designed with cool
blue and gray colors and futuristic touches. Additionally, the architecture
enhances the Gulf view. The one-bedroom units in the clubhouse are for
adults only, the rest are for families or couples. The social atmosphere
around the health club, cafes, and the swimming pool is a positive benefit of
this resort. There's fun in the sun for all.

9   FAIRWAY BAY
1932 Harbourside Dr., Longboat Key, FL 34228
Amenities: Boat docks, pools, tennis. Golf next door

This is what you would hope to find on prestigious Longboat Key. This
development includes two sections—a six-story high-rise and clusters of
townhouse condos set in a rolling palm-shaded garden. The landscaping is
spectacular and evokes the tropics, although the manicured care given to the
lawns, flowers, and hibiscus bushes is better than the tropics. The condos in
the main building are spacious and luxurious. With panoramic bay views
and vistas of Sarasota over the water there's an openness and a sense of
escape from the nearby city. Even better are the townhouses: two-story
cathedral ceilings in the living room and picture windows on the second
story to allow the sunlight to pour into the living room. This area is laced
with canals and many of the condos have their own private boat docks.
Enjoy a cocktail on your patio and watch the yachts pass by. Clearly one of
the best choices on Longboat, but one you never hear about, this is treasure.

9   ISLAND WEST
2525 Gulf of Mexico Dr., Longboat Key, FL 34228
Amenities: Beach, pool, sauna, tennis

This is what you think of when you hear of the Longboat Key Club. This luxurious eighteen-story high-rise on the beach is stunning in every detail, with twenty-four-hour security and a resident manager to take care of your needs. Step inside the cool marble and glass two-story lobby. It's impressive. Cliff-dwellers understand elevators and hallways but once inside your unit you'll never want to leave. There's a breathtaking view of the Gulf, beach, island, and the landscaped pool area. It's as though each window had been "placed" to frame a picture. Most have stylish professional interior decoration. Although we saw families at the pool, this interior decor is expensive and says "Grandchildren, look but don't touch." There are always great sunsets in the evening from the living room or balcony. Each has a separate breakfast room and dining room. This is one of Longboat's most impressive condos. Just across the street is the cute Avenue of the Flowers shopping center with bayside restaurants and shops.

5 LITTLE GULL

5331 Gulf of Mexico Dr., Longboat Key, FL 33548,
813-383-8818
Amenities: Beach, pool, dock, clubhouse

Little Gull provides a bit of Bermuda with easygoing comfort. The duplexes and cottages are elevated on the bay. Wooden "beach houses" are beautifully furnished with English furniture. Attractions include a bay beach, a dock, and swimming pool. Palm tree landscaping creates a British colonial, subtropical atmosphere. This resort offers good value for the price.

4 LONGBOAT BAY CLUB

3200 Gulf of Mexico Dr., Longboat Key, FL 34228,
813-383-9561
Amenities: Marina, fishing dock, pool, hot tub, tennis

This quiet resort is located on a lagoon cove. There is no beach, but access is across the street. Attractions include a pool, marina, and fishing dock. This resort is good for families as well as grandparents. It is a quiet vacation retreat and there is enough space so guests don't intrude on eachother's privacy. The condos are larger than average and beautifully decorated. The main drawback is that management aggressively promotes timeshare sales, which can be disturbing in the vacation environment.

8+ LONGBOAT KEY CLUB

Box 1500, 301 Gulf of Mexico Dr., Longboat Key, FL 34228
800-237-8821, 1BR $220, 2BR $340
Amenities: Golf, restaurants, country club, pool, hot tub,
health club, tennis, shops

This resort is for the active vacationer. A beautiful master development created 15 years ago, these high-rise condo towers line the beach on a semitropical island. Beautiful landscaping adds a lot to the picture and distinguishes this refined, clubby resort from others in the neighborhood. The palms and pines are perfectly placed by the pool and along the golf course. An area of barrier sand dunes has been preserved with its vegetation, crossed only by a boardwalk that leads to the sugar white sand. The parcourse jogging and fitness trail offers a great opportunity to enjoy the golf course, landscaping, and beach. Life on this extraordinary island resort is active and almost seems like an aging yuppie-heaven. You'll notice many corporate professionals on vacation reading papers by the pool. For relaxing, there's always shelling on the beach or snorkeling in the clear Gulf waters.

There are many condos to choose from on Longboat Key, but the only ones with short-term rentals are on the southern end of the island near the Inn. The **Golf Course Villas, the Atrium, Fairway Bay,** and **Seaplace** only offer condos on a monthly rental basis. The short-term rentals we describe are in the towers next to the Longboat Key Club Inn.

Some of the condos overlook the golf course and the lagoon. Most have a view of the beach and the Gulf. The apartments are fully equipped as longer-term vacation homes, or merely for a short stay. The kitchens offer more appliances than you could ever want, including blenders and cuisinarts for serious cooking. The deluxe two-bedroom units have an oversized living room and extra large balcony.

9   **PROMENADE**
         1211 Gulf of Mexico Dr., Longboat Key, FL 34228
         Amenities: Beach, pool, exercise room, tennis, putting green

One of Longboat's most expensive condos, this solid eleven-story tower dates from the mid-'80s and was carefully crafted to create a luxurious living environment for vacationers. Twenty-four-hour security, and beautifully maintained, there's not a piece of paper or a blade of grass out of order. Lavishly furnished by professional decorators, expect to find solid woods or chrome and glass pieces. Lots of books and art are placed in the units by the owners. Promenade is top of the line on Longboat Key.

4   **SHOREWALK**
         4601 46th St. Ct. West, Bradenton, FL 34210, 800-926-9255
         Amenities: Pools, tennis, exercise and card room

Your best choice in Bradenton is not on the beach. Shorewalk is located in the town of Bradenton across the causeway from the beach. These modern two-story villas are spread over 30 acres in a residential neighborhood and are surrounded by pine and palmetto landscaping. They are well designed with an efficient floor plan. You'll find superior furnishings in these condos. Some have the touch of an interior decorator. You'll find semiformal traditional furniture in some units and island style rattan furniture in others. This is not really a resort atmosphere, but rather a home away from home in the Bradenton area.

9 SUNSET BEACH
2101 Gulf of Mexico Dr., Longboat Key, FL 34228
Amenities: Beach, pool, hot tub. Golf nearby

One of Longboat's most exclusive condos, located at the north end of the Longboat Key, with golf next door, this appeals to active vacationers. The condos in this six-story structure have magnificent views overlooking the pool and the Gulf.

9 VERANDA BEACH CLUB
2509 Gulf of Mexico Dr., Longboat Key, FL 33548
813-383-5511
Amenities: Beach, pool, tennis, squash, racquetball, health club

Wow! We can't think of anything to add or improve at this resort. The outdoor pool extends under the building to create a grotto effect—great for windy days. The beach is beautiful and the property is recessed to preserve the dunes and sea grass (which is hard to find in this part of Florida). The use of tile, glass, and mirrors creates striking units. Art pieces provide the accents. Management is friendly, but doesn't intrude on your privacy. There is a tennis court hidden by an ivy-covered fence. A private whirlpool in the master bath is available. The resort offers full athletic facilities including a health club, racquetball court, and squash court. The condos are arranged in a square around a courtyard atrium with statuary and bubbling fountain. Flowers are everywhere. The landscaping and groundskeeping departments deserve an award for excellence. What could be added?

8 WHITE SANDS OF LONGBOAT KEY
5114 Gulf of Mexico Dr., Longboat Key, FL 33548
813-383-2428
Amenities: Beach, pool, fishing dock

Is this Bermuda? A cluster of pink and white stucco Bermuda-style cottages under shady oak trees composes White Sands. This is Bermuda at half price. The resort is tastefully furnished and carefully maintained in a timeless atmosphere. Everything is immaculate. The kitchens are small, but adequate for a vacation home. The beach is beautiful and there is a dock on the sound side for fishing. Other features include two pools, a putting green, and lots of palm trees. There are a few apartments in the main building.

WHERE TO STAY... SIESTA KEY

7   BOCA SIESTA
5911 Midnight Pass Rd., Siesta Key, FL 34242
Amenities: Pool, sauna, tennis. Across from beach boat dock

One of Siesta's most prestigious condominiums, this seven-story structure sits on the bay side across the street from the six-mile beach. Solid concrete construction, spacious floor plans and professional decoration add up to create a comfortable vacation environment. Most of these condos are owned by part-time residents who spend two to three months in Florida each year. For a vacationer this is a genuine opportunity to get some area insights while sitting around the pool. Many of the condos have private boat slips on the bay in back and for a small additional fee, you can also have a boat included in your condo rental. This place is solid.

7   CRYSTAL SANDS
6300 Midnight Pass Rd., Siesta Key, FL 34242, 349-7007
1BR $345–465/wk, 2BR $800/wk
Amenities: Beach, pools

Located on the Crescent Beach section of Siesta Key, where the water is clear, this uniquely designed condominium has two twelve-story curving towers. Built a dozen years ago with solid concrete construction, you'll find Crystal Sands provides a comfortable environment for a family vacation. Most of the one and two bedroom units have been decorated with a coordinated furniture package: nothing lavish and certainly nothing "early attic." The focus is on the ocean view and you'll spend many hours on your screened balcony or down at the pool. For those who want to be right on the beach, Crystal Sands offers a few private villas on the beach for a price premium.

7   HARBOUR TOWNE (also Dockside Place)
Midnight Pass Rd., Siesta Key, FL 34242
Amenities: Marina, pool, hot tub, tennis, clubhouse

Just across the street from the six-mile beach on Siesta Key, in a more subdued area, Harbour Towne is a master real estate development that includes prestigious $700,000 homes and clusters of condominiums (Dockside Place). Dockside Place is a select condo development because of its location on the water, right next to where the private homes begin. For those who like to know they paid less than 1/3 of what their neighbors have spent, Dockside represents good value. The bay here is the best "sailboat water" on Siesta Key and each of these two-bedroom condos in this three-story building have an excellent view of Riegel's Harbor from their screened porches. Bring your binoculars to watch the boats. Many condos have the touch of the professional interior decorator. Others have been decorated by the owner's loving hands. Most of these condos also include their own private boat slips and sometimes a vacation rental can be arranged so that the boat is included at a small additional charge. This is a sailor's delight.

7   HOUSE OF THE SUN
6518 Midnight Pass Rd., Siesta Key, FL 34242, 813-349-4141
$539/wk
Amenities: Beach, pool, tennis

Located on Crescent Beach, this is one of the few condos in the area that promote short-term rentals for a week or less. These five-story concrete structures have staggered balconies and the beach front building is only three-stories high, affording most units a glimpse of the beach and the water. A pleasant place to stay, you'll find the units to be a little boxy, but most have superior interior decor. As with the name, the emphasis has been to be light and invite the sunlight inside. Built at an angle, the floor plans are cockeyed, but you'll soon adjust. Evenings are charming with the murmur from the water, sunsets, and perhaps a child playing on the lawn under the palms. Here is solid comfort on the beach.

6   JAMAICA ROYALE
5830 Midnight Pass Rd., Siesta Key, FL 34242, 813-349-1800
$300–650/wk
Amenities: Beach, three pools

Located right on the Crescent Beach section of Siesta Key, this six-story building offers casual, contemporary style. Palms and landscaping have been added to frame the beauty of the beach and the Gulf. These spacious condos were built eight years ago and still seem new. Decorated island style with lots of rattan furniture, glass-top tables, and subdued Florida fabrics, these units are comfortable. For those who eschew the high-rise, there's an older section of two-story garden apartments.

7   MIDNIGHT COVE I and II
6302 Midnight Rd., Siesta Key, FL 34242, 813-349-3004
2BR $500–750/wk
Amenities: Pool, tennis

One of the few spots in the Sarasota area that promotes short term rentals. Located on the bay or on Crescent Beach, you are minutes from the mainland as the causeway bridge is almost next door. These two-story plus loft structures are surrounded by a landscaped garden with pools and views of the harbor and bay. Many of the condos have private boat slips and you may be able to arrange a "condo plus boat" package. Although the condos have efficient floor plans and may be a little bit smaller than those on Longboat

Key, the interior decor is superior. Decorator touches and wallpaper accent the wicker and rattan furniture. This is a comfortable condo complex with a friendly resort ambiance where you'll make friends quickly.

6 OUR HOUSE AT THE BEACH
1001 Beach Rd., Siesta Key, FL 34242
Amenities: Beach, pool, tennis

One of the most popular family resorts on Siesta Key, there's always something going on here. Next door to the Siesta Key Public Beach, these two-bedroom condos feature Gulf and island views as well as all the appliances necessary for easy living. With wintertime prices as low as $695 per week for a family of four to six, is there any wonder why this resort is often full?

6 PALM BAY CLUB
5960 Midnight Pass Rd., Siesta Key, FL 34242
Highrise plus-view, 3-story apts, 1BR $400–600/wk,
2BR $500–785/wk
Amenities: Beach, pool, tennis, dock

The Palm Bay Club straddles Midnight Pass Road, so some condos are in garden apartments on the quiet bayside and some, the club apartments, are on the beach side. Then there's the panoramic thirteen-story tower right on the beach with sweeping views of Crescent Beach, the island, and the Gulf. At 15 years old, the decor is somewhat dated in the garden and club apartments. The tower units are much more impressive with sharp colors and decorator touches. There's something to be said, however, for the convenience of a low-rise building where you can walk right in and don't need an elevator. The Palm Bay Club is one of the few condos in the Sarasota area that promotes short-term rentals of a week or less. Although alright for families, it is even better for retirees.

5 SANDPIPER BEACH CLUB
6414 Midnight Pass Rd., Siesta Key, FL 34242
Amenities: Beach, pool, tennis, hot tub, exercise room

This is a large five-story concrete condominium complex on Siesta Key Island. The condos are spacious and each of the two-bedroom suites are well decorated. The resort successfully combines casual beachfront living with quiet sophistication and flair. Some condos are situated directly on the beach and have great views. A pool, health club, game room, and a roof-top tennis court are available. A Monday morning brunch and Tuesday night cookout are offered. The Sandpiper Beach Club keeps children, teenagers, and adults happy by providing activities for everyone.

5   **SARASOTA SURF & RACQUET CLUB**
5900 Midnight Pass Rd., Siesta Key, FL 34242, 800-237-5671
1BR $325–700/wk, 2BR $385–900/wk
Amenities: Beach, pools, tennis

Located on the sand at Crescent Beach, the condos in these five-story
structures are popular with vacationers of all ages. Pleasant units with casual
island style decor, you'll make friends quickly here. There's often a list of
visiting tennis players looking for a partner and the pools are always busy.
The units are a little small and drab. Fully furnished, some of the original
decor has been supplemented by treasures from the attic. This is one of the
few properties in the Sarasota area which encourages short-term rentals for a
week or less.

8   **SIESTA GULF VIEW**
420 Beach Rd., Siesta Key, FL 34242
Amenities: Pool, sauna, exercise room, tennis

Located in the Crescent Beach section of Siesta Key, these luxurious condos command imposing views of the beach and the Gulf. Evening sunsets
are fantastic and once here, you'll wish you too were an owner. Inside the
floor plans are spacious for these two bedroom units—quite livable. Most
have been decorated by professional designers. These are at the top end of
the scale in Siesta Key. Expect to find contemporary furniture styles and soft
pastel Florida or Caribbean fabrics. The tropical ambiance is carried out in
the landscaped pool area. For a one- or two-month stay in the Sarasota area,
this is an excellent choice.

WHERE TO STAY... LIDO BEACH

6   **LIDO BEACH CLUB**
1212 Benjamin Franklin Dr., Lido Beach, FL 34236
Amenities: Beach, pool, hot tub, sauna, tennis

Located at the southern end of Lido Key, where the beach becomes quiet
and the water is dotted with sails and Hobie cats, the Lido Beach Club
exemplifies what you find in the inventory of quality condos. This thirteen-
story high-rise tower was built 17 years ago in an era of quality concrete
construction. They have spacious but functional units that are popular with
grandparents. You'll only find little children at holiday periods, and then
under close parental supervision. The condos open out to the Gulf with great
views of the beach, island, and water. Many have been decorated with mirrors to bring the outside in. Comfortable furniture, although we hear some
owners haven't redecorated in 17 years. There's nothing fancy here, just a
practical place to stay in the sun. There's lots of youthful activity on the
beach nearby and it is convenient to several restaurants on the island.

7   **LIDO SURF & SAND**
1100 Benjamin Franklin Dr., Lido Beach, FL 34236
Amenities: Beach, pool, hot tub, exercise room

Perhaps the most prestigious address on Lido Key, this five-story concrete tower was designed so each unit has sweeping views of the beach,
island, and Gulf. Many owners have decorated their units with mirrors to
bring the view inside. Right on the beach, you'll find two miles of firmly-
packed white sand right out your door. Because the building has wraparound balconies (some as long as 90 feet!), many owners have elected to
enclose part of the balcony. This creates a screened-in porch that doubles as
an extra room. Overall, the furnishings are a bit dated but some have brand
new contemporary decor. This condo building is popular with retirees,
although children are benignly tolerated. If you're looking for a lively family resort, think twice.

5   **LIMETREE BEACH RESORT**
1050 Benjamin Franklin Dr., Lido Key, FL 34236, 813-388-2111
Amenities: Pool, hot tub, tennis, exercise room

Limetree Beach Resort is a cheerful family resort right on the beach at
Sarasota's Siesta Key. Originally built as a motel, the units were completely
redesigned and rebuilt. The two-story building is a U-shape that surrounds
the swimming pool. Therefore, most units have a view of the Gulf. Inside
you'll find an unusual wooden wall where the planks are placed diagonally
instead of horizontally. The brightly colored condos have shag carpeting and
many mirrors. This resort is great for families with children of all ages with
a wide variety of activities available.

3   **SARASOTA SANDS**
2150 Benjamin Franklin Dr., Lido Beach, FL 34236
813-388-2138
Amenities: Beach, pool, health club, racquetball, tennis

Management at this timeshare clearly wants you to have fun. The activity
here makes this a good choice for young families. This is a large converted
hotel complex built around a courtyard and pool. Most units have a view of
the Gulf. The condos are very attractive and designed for beachfront living.
You'll find Polynesian fabrics and rattan furniture. Each week there are two
in-house cocktail parties/barbecues. The resort offers an indoor sports complex with a racquetball court that doubles as a basketball court. This is a
good resort for a family vacation because of the informality, community
activities, and the beach.

WHERE TO STAY... SARASOTA MAINLAND

8 **TIMBERWOODS**
7964 Timberwood Cr., Sarasota, FL 34238
813-923-4966, 1BR $500/wk
Amenities: Golf, pool, tennis, bicycles

For golfers, Timberwoods is choice. Located next to the prestigious PGA owned Tournament Players Club and the Prestancia, Timberwoods mixes the comforts of home with the luxurious amenities of a world class resort. Each single-story villa has a red-tile roof and is nested in the pines. Elegantly furnished by professional decorators, you'll find the size of the living room and bedroom to be extra spacious. Each casita has a private screened patio that doubles as an extra room when the temperature's right. It's over ten miles to the beach at Siesta key, so water-lovers gravitate to the large, pine-fringed pool area. Timberwoods is good for families as well as retirees.

RENTAL RESOURCES... SARASOTA and its KEYS

Arvida, 800-237-8821
Bowyer & Assoc., 813-383-9502
Century 21, Paradise Realty, 800-237-2252
Holmes Beach Property, 813-778-5549
Kevin Levins Realty, 813-383-5577
Kings Crown Realty, 813-383-5502
Longboat Key Realty, 813-383-3840
Prudential Boomhower, 813-366-8070
Michael Saunders & Co., 813-383-5521
Neal & Neal, 813-383-5886
Schlott Realty, 813-388-3966
Taylor & Assoc., 813-388-4457

5. TAMPA BAY and the NORTHWEST COAST

Tampa Bay includes the bustling commercial centers of Tampa and St. Petersburg. St. Petersburg was once known as a haven for the nation's retirees. Now it is one of Florida's fastest growing cities. The American Medical Association hailed St. Petersburg as one of the healthiest places to live in America, but there is much more to the Bay Area than just St. Petersburg. Clearwater, located on the northern end of the coastal strip, is a year-round vacation destination due to the beaches of Sand Key. Clearwater is also the Spring training home of the Philadelphia Phillies. Belleair Beach and Bluffs provide exclusive residential neighborhoods. Indian Rocks and Indian Shores are areas lined with resort motels and mid-rise condominiums. Reddington Beach features "John's Pass Village," a rustic nautical enclave similar to a New England fishing village. The shops and restaurants attract tourists. Madeira Beach is another strip of motels and mid-rise condominiums. Treasure Island prides itself on being distinct and aims for the affluent vacationer who will pay extra for landscaping and larger condos. St. Petersburg Beach is the most commercial section of the shore and the activity gravitates around the Don CeSar Hotel built as a pink stucco fantasy in the 1920s. The Bay Area also has some of the best resorts in out-of-the-way places. Isla del Sol is an island in Tampa Bay just off the southern tip of St. Petersburg Beach that is popular with semiretired snow birds.

WHERE TO STAY

6   BAY SHORES YACHT & TENNIS CLUB
        19415 Gulf Blvd., Indian Shores, FL 34635
        Amenities: Dock, pool, tennis, hot tub, sauna

This huge condo project is located on the Inland Waterway, not on the beach. There are two eight-story buildings with 200 condos. The beach is a short five minute walk across the street. This project is well built and the condos have basic, comfortable furnishings. There is a pool on the grounds and a dock for fishing. Pelicans come by, and across the water there is a mangrove forest. In the evenings families gather round for poolside barbecues. This resort has a congenial family atmosphere. Children and adults will make friends quickly.

7   CLEARWATER BEACH RESORT
        678 Gulf View Blvd. S., Clearwater Beach, FL 33515
        813-441-3767, $65–136
        Amenities: Beach, pool, tennis

This three-story resort is ten years old. Some of the condos are being redecorated, so there is a discrepancy between the new "light" units and the older ones where the furniture is a little heavier in tone. Whirlpool tubs are in the master bath. The special feature here is the resort's own cruiser for deep-sea fishing. Clearwater Beach Resort welcomes families with children as well as teenagers. This is a good choice in the Clearwater Beach area in the mid-price range. The one-bedroom units are basically long studios and the two bedrooms are like two motel rooms which have been joined.

5   CORAL REEF
        5800 Gulf Blvd., St. Petersburg Beach, FL 33706, 813-360-0821
        Amenities: Beach, pool, hot tub, racquetball, tennis

Coral Reef is composed of three large buildings bustling with activity. The condos in the high-rise tower have Gulf views. The other condos located further away from the beach are two-story, motel-style suites. The pool area, located near the condos, features two pools and a snack bar. Children and teenagers will make friends quickly in this active resort that is strong on hospitality services.

9+ INNISBROOK

P.O. Drawer 1088, Tarpon Springs, FL 34688-1088
800-456-2000, Studios $80–160, 1BR $111–207, 2BR $154–324
Amenities: Golf, tennis, racquetball, pools, restaurants,
conference center

Innisbrook is located on 1,000 acres of rolling Florida countryside, about 30 miles north of Tampa and six miles from the Gulf beaches. It is a classic golf/tennis resort community. Developed within a forested area, the community revolves around three separate country clubs and rolling fairways that add up to 63 holes of golf. The Island, Copperhead, and Sandpiper courses are designed around lakes and woodlands alive with peacocks and herons. The landscaping is different from what you would expect to find in Florida. You'll find azaleas, palmetto, flowering hibiscus bushes and Spanish moss on pine trees. There are 27 buildings with condo suites and townhouses spread over 1,000 acres. The interior decor of the condos features quality furniture, contemporary color and design, and an ambiance for a golf-oriented vacation.

Although each condo has a full kitchen, you'll probably spend your days at one of the country clubs or in the pro shops. Although golf is the main draw, the Racquet Club is equally impressive—it boasts 18 tennis courts and four racquetball courts. There are six swimming pools scattered throughout the estate. Although Innisbrook sounds formal, it offers an excellent children's program with the "Zoo Crew"—a nationally known program for vacationing children between the ages of four and 12. Almost no one rents a condo by the night because the rental rates for the all-inclusive golf and tennis packages are so attractive. This is a beautiful estate and great resort.

8 ISLA DEL SOL

Boca Ciega Bay, St. Petersburg, FL 33715
Amenities: Golf, tennis, marina, restaurants

Isla del Sol is a master resort community situated on a 340-acre island in Boca Ciega Bay just off the tip of St. Petersburg Beach. Several of the condo developments line the golf course. Most of the condos are for part-time residents spending several months in the St. Petersburg area, but short-term rentals are also available. We highly recommend this resort area because it is a self-contained golf/tennis center on its own island. Built to look like a Spanish-Mediterranean village, you'll instantly recognize the California style. Vista Verde is a cluster of two-story townhouse condos with white-washed walls and red tile roofs. Spacious enough to be year-round residences. Bahia Vista condos are apartments in a four-story building. Each cluster surrounds a pool and has a view of the bay.

8+ LANDS END

7500 Bayshore Dr., St. Petersburg Beach, FL 33706
800-382-8883, 1BR $425–685/wk, 2BR $465–870/wk
Amenities: Beach, boardwalk, tennis, hot tub, security gate
(no public access to this resort)

Wow! This is what we were looking for. Located at the southern end of Treasure Island, Lands End comes closest to creating a "tropical island paradise" feeling. It is located at the tip of the island near the widest part of the beach. It is possible to walk to the beach on the planked walkway. A buffer area of sea oats and sand dunes gives this resort an extra degree of privacy. Here you can leave the real world behind, yet you are only minutes from all of the Bay Area's activity. The gazebo is a perfect place to sit and watch the sunset. An oversized heated pool and two tennis courts are available. This is a perfect environment for families because of the open space, gardens, beach walk, and beach. The interiors of the condos are handsomely decorated with sturdy contemporary furniture such as overstuffed couches, track lighting, plenty of plants, and an overhead paddle fan to catch the Gulf breezes.

6 NORDVIND

12700 Gulf Blvd., Treasure Island, FL 33706, 813-360-7037
Amenities: Beach, pool

Nordvind offers a little bit of Scandinavia nestled among the Florida pines. The location is quiet in a cul-de-sac off the main beach road at the northern end of Treasure Island. A rolling berm has been created to shelter the landscaped pool and garden area from the beach. The resort consists of a six-story concrete structure with ten sides. There are six units on each floor, so everyone gets a slice of the pie. Decorator furnishings are characteristic of the condo interiors and Nordvind strives to give you a pleasant, casual environment. Most of the units have Gulf views, although some face Boca Ciega Bay.

5 RAMSEA

17200 Gulf Blvd., North Reddington Beach, FL 33708
Amenities: Pool, hot tub

One of the largest properties in the North Reddington Beach area is Ramsea. The resort is composed of a pair of quiet condominium towers on the beach. The condos are maintained well and are professional in appearance. Spacious quarters are also provided for lengthy stays. Many semi-retirees live here part of the year.

7   SAILPORT
2506 Rocky Point Dr., Tampa, FL 33607, 800-255-9599
Amenities: Bay beach, pool, health club, tennis, racquetball nearby

What a location! This new resort is located on Rocky Point Island just west of the Tampa Airport. It is a private island in the bay only minutes away from the airport or downtown Tampa. The beaches of Clearwater/St. Petersburg are 30 minutes away to the west. These one-bedroom suites are designed for the business traveler as well as for vacationers. The furniture in the condos is contemporary, but not fanciful. It feels like you're staying at a hotel—not a condo resort. Maybe this is because of the proximity to Tampa or maybe it's the corporate types who have chosen this resort over a downtown hotel. There is a good mix of business and pleasure here. You will be provided with all the services you would expect at a hotel such as valet, laundry, 24-hour switch board, concierge, etc. The sports center includes a pool and tennis courts. A health club is the most outstanding feature. The management is helpful.

7   SAND PEBBLE RESORT
12300 Gulf Blvd., Treasure Island, FL 33706, 813-360-1845
Studio $50–95, 1BR $90, 2BR $100, 3BR $125
Amenities: Beach, hot tub, pool

You must see the interiors of some of these condos. Imagine a beautiful Florida beach setting with a few pine and palm trees. Add some sand dunes and a landscaped pool area. A six-story building surrounds a landscaped atrium. Then, step inside the units and be overwhelmed by black Chinese lacquer furniture and Chinese red fabrics. Silk flowers are everywhere in addition to a few art objects which suggest the Orient (in case you hadn't noticed). One warning, though—not all of the condos are decorated this way; some have neutral environments. This resort successfully preserves the Florida environment and gives you a fantasy as well. Management is helpful, courteous, and efficient. There is an all-purpose social director who is a favorite with the children. Rentals are reasonably priced considering all that you receive. Try it, you'll like it.

8+   TRADEWINDS
6500 Gulf Blvd., St. Petersburg Beach, FL 33706, 800-237-0707
1BR $143–225, 2BR $300–395, 3BR $399–494
Amenities: Beach, canals with gondolas, pools, exercise room, playground, tennis

Tradewinds creates a magic, romantic environment on 13 acres at the southern end of St. Petersburg Beach. You will discover tropical Florida villas, palm-shaded courtyards and a network of canals with small boats. You'll catch the Victorian sentiment of the gazebos, the soothing sway of hammocks and the romance of gondolas drifting on the waterways. A beach with a buffer zone of sea oats separates the buildings from the beach. There are four swimming pools including one large pool (which is the resort's social center), hot tub, sauna and exercise room available. The condos are cheerfully decorated. Many units lock off into separate hotel rooms. The kitchens are equipped with a toaster, coffee maker, refrigerator, and wet bar. Some units face courtyards and others the ocean. Expect to find lots of blond wood, glass-top tables and soft neutral fabrics. Food can be obtained through a popular restaurant/bar or room service. The deli will pack a picnic lunch for a day's outing.

RENTAL RESOURCES
Coral Resort, 813-446-3711
Great American Holidays, 813-393-6005
Metro Leasing, 813-785-8887
Plumlee Real Estate, 800-521-7586
Provident Management, 813-530-7557
Rentarama, 813-786-7368
Suncoast Resort Rentals, 813-393-3425
Tarpon Wood Management, 813-785-7414
T. C. Management, 813-397-0441

6. THE PANHANDLE

Some call it the Emerald Coast because of the clear blue-green water. Actually it's the fine white sand and the blue sky reflected in the water that give the Gulf waters this special color. The surf is perfect for playful adults and children. The Yucatan current brings with it big game fish like dolphin and blue marlin. So why did it take so long for this area to develop? Because it's just a few hundred miles north of the tropics and the distance causes the weather to be just a little cool for those desiring a winter break. It is primarily a spring, summer, and fall area. Florida's Panhandle offers some of the best beaches and sports opportunities in Florida. People can enjoy a variety of activities including fishing, sailing, and even waterskiing in the Gulf. In the summer, you'll find lots of teens on the beaches playing volleyball, and families jumping in the waves. Winter is considered the off season but don't tell that to all the snowbirds from the northern states and Canada who flock here because of the year-round golf and brisk sweater weather. It's a great place for a vacation because you can choose between active sports or relaxation on the beach.

Transportation to this area is primarily by car and it's less than six hours from destinations as diverse as Texas and Tennessee. Due to easy transportation, the Emerald Coast is a popular destination for visitors from those areas. Panama City and Ft. Walton Beach have airports, but service is limited primarily to flights from Memphis, Nashville, Atlanta, and Miami. If you do fly, please consider renting a car during your stay. The Panhandle strip contains so many recreational areas that you'll be glad you have a car.

With so many resorts clustered in this area, we have divided this section into three subsections: Panama City Beach, Destin, and Ft. Walton Beach to Pensacola.

It may be called the Emerald Coast, but don't expect to pay the same prices as you would down on the Gold Coast. Although this area has recently been "discovered" on a national basis due to the tremendous success of *The Firm,* prices here are less than half of what you would pay for a vacation on Sanibel Island. Just remember, though, that the winter weather in January can be cold and the restaurants are not as fancy.

PANAMA CITY BEACH

The gleaming star of the Emerald Coast, Panama City Beach used to be described as Florida's best kept secret. Not any more. According to the Florida Bureau of Tourism, Panama City Beach is currently the state's number one destination after Orlando based upon the number of visitors to this area. Many of these visitors are children. The Emerald Coast provides a gentle slope and thereby the the safest beach area in Florida. You can walk out as far as 50 feet and still not be in water over your head. This partially explains why Panama City Beach has become a major family vacation area. Two amusement parks, eight golf courses and over 100 tennis courts are also available in this area, so activities appeal to children of all ages.

Most of the condos are on the beach. A 17-mile strip begins on Thomas Drive, passes along Miracle Strip Parkway, and extends west along Alternate Highway 98 (the beach road) almost half way to Destin. Over 150 resort condominium developments are located in this area, so a choice is difficult. We have reviewed and rated the resorts that have something special to offer such as a complete resort environment, a "theme," or the best vacation value for the consumer.

WHERE TO STAY

BAY POINT
100 Delwood Beach Rd., Panama City Beach, FL 32411
904-234-7692, 1BR $159–179, 2BR $200–260
Amenities: Golf, tennis, pools, hot tubs, exercise room,
restaurants, marina

Shades of Bermuda on the Gulf Coast of Florida with Bermuda style architecture and roofs. Bay Point was designed to be the premier golf resort on Florida's panhandle. It is not a beach resort like others in the area. Rather, it is a self-contained golf and tennis resort set on 1,100 acres.

There's a yacht and country club, a hotel and five of the area's best restaurants. Although there's no beach, the resort offers a paddle wheel steamer that travels to Shell Island twice daily for two hours in the mornings and afternoons. Bay Point caters to families with children. For example, it offers a daily supervised activities program for children called "Alligator Point Gang."

Bay Point contains six separate condominium developments, as well as over 250 private vacation homes. Expect a comfortable, nonextravagant environment perfect for a week or two at Bay Point.

Bay Town (9) These condos are the most luxurious, located above the shops of Bay Town. These second-story suites have been decorated by interior designers with expensive furniture and lavish use of fabrics. It is not recommended for families.

Harbor Villas (9) These villas have a sophisticated environment next to the tennis center and marina. These two-story townhouses are one-bedroom units and are perfect for a couple.

Lagoon Towers (7) It is perfect for families because of the swimming pool and health club at this location. The construction is top quality. You'll find spacious one, two, and three-bedroom condos in this seven-story tower, the tallest structure for miles around.

Turtle Grass (7) These villas are one- and two-story townhouse style structures. Each villa has its own private walled patio or courtyard. They're great for parents who want to allow their children to play outside and not have to worry about them roaming away. Turtle Grass condos are the oldest at Bay Point and are now nine years old.

3　　**CASA BLANCA**
　　　1115 W. Highway 98A, Panama City Beach, FL 32407
　　　904-234-5245, $175–500/wk
　　　Amenities: Beach, pool, exercise room, sauna

Casa Blanca is a budget choice. It is located about a mile from the center of town at the junction of Highway 98A to Pensacola. The white stucco walls and red tile roof buildings convey a Mexican look. The three-story building is a converted, motel-type structure located across from the beach. Most of the rooms have a Gulf view, but the units do not face the water. The building is perpendicular to the Gulf, so each unit has an angular view from the private balcony. There is a pool with a hot tub and an indoor exercise room with sauna. This resort welcomes families and is not far from two amusement parks in Panama City Beach. The condos are a little small but the decor and kitchen facilities are modern and upbeat. This is a quiet, well run property where families can have fun on vacation. They provide weekly rentals only.

4   THE COMMODORE
4715 Thomas Dr., Panama City Beach, FL 32411, 904-234-7099
1BR $65–85, 2BR $75–100, 3BR $100–135
Amenities: Beach, pool, sauna, card and game rooms

The Commodore is a huge condo development right in the heart of Panama City Beach. The building is fifteen-stories high, and the spacious units either face the Gulf or the sandbar island and lagoon. There are five floor plans to choose from. The condos have been recently redecorated with island-style light colors and rattan furniture. There are separate adult and youth recreation centers that include saunas, billiards, exercise, and card rooms.

9   EDGEWATER
11212 Alt. Highway 98, Panama City Beach, FL 32407
904-235-4044, 1BR $75–110, 2BR $80–125, 3BR $110–190
Amenities: Beach, golf, tennis, pools

The Edgewater is one of the largest resorts in Panama City Beach, partially located on the beach and also across the highway where the Edgewater has its own golf course. This resort tries to be Caribbean in style, but just doesn't make it. You'll find the twelve-story high-rise **Towers** on the beach. Across the street, along the fairway, there are two-story **Golf Villas** with red tile roofs. Edgewater Beach has a pedestrian overpass connecting the two distinct parts of this bustling resort community. The condo apartments in the Towers have sweeping views of the Gulf and the free form lagoon pool right below. There's a restaurant and landscaped garden by the pool, as well as a children's playground. The Golf Villas are for more sophisticated travelers. Golf and tennis facilities are immediately accessible. There is a pool by the Golf Villas but it's much quieter than over by the Towers. Interior decor in the Towers concentrates on standardized themes of coral pink and seafoam green. Comfortable and classic, the decor within the Golf Villas is more personalized and ranges from kelly green plaids on traditional furniture to casual island style with rattan furniture.

7+   INN AT ST. THOMAS SQUARE
8600 Thomas Dr., Panama City Beach, FL 32407, 904-234-0349
Amenities: Pool, hot tub, sauna, tennis, lagoon beach,
complimentary breakfast buffet

With its oyster stucco walls and red tile roofs, the Inn at St. Thomas Square evokes the spirit of a Mediterranean village. This all-around resort is one of our favorites. The condo suites in this two and three-story village have been designed with a central foyer and lock off doors so you can occupy a studio, a whole three-bedroom condo or any combination in between. Several different floor plans prevail, depending on how many of the suite "pieces" you require. All units have kitchens or kitchenettes. Some have Murphy beds to make a studio living room more spacious. Others are mainly designed as a bedroom and are equipped with an extra sink and refrigerator. Put these two together and, voila, you have a one-bedroom unit.

The Inn is meticulously maintained, well managed, and provides some of the area's most gracious hospitality. The Inn offers a complimentary breakfast buffet and a weekly manager's party. There's an attractive pool area with an adjacent children's playground. Created with imagination, the resort's lagoon beach reminds you of a pirate's landing. Across the street is Panama City's famous wide, white sand beach. This is a great choice in the area.

7   LARGO MAR
      5717 Thomas Dr., Panama City Beach, FL 32408, 904-234-5750
      1BR $60–94, 2BR $75–116, 3BR $90–190
      Amenities: Beach, pool, hot tub, golf, tennis

These down to earth townhouse condos and low-rise flats are a true discovery at Panama City Beach. While other accommodations are in high-rise towers, Largo Mar offers condominiums in cute three-story buildings grouped around a landscaped free-form swimming pool. Largo Mar is right on a great section of the beach, so you can enjoy both the garden environment and beach front living. Stylish and well maintained, Largo Mar bills itself as "A Family Place." Actually its country club environment has a strong appeal to the golf and tennis crowd because of the nearby golf facilities. The interior decor is snappy and features contemporary blond woods and neo-Art Deco style. Soft colors are used in the living room and they also have a full kitchen. Most condos overlook the courtyard swimming pool.

4   LANDMARK HOLIDAY RESORT
      17501 W. Highway 98, Panama City Beach, FL 32407
      904-235-3100; 1BR $90–140, 2BR $100–200, 3BR $120–230
      Amenities: Beach, indoor pool, hot tub, sauna, tennis

Located about four miles away from the center of Panama City Beach, Landmark Holiday Resort is jumping with activity. It is a sixteen-story high-rise located on the beach with lots of amenities and facilities. This high-rise dominates the skyline of the surrounding area. The condos are apartments and have various sizes to meet the needs of couples, as well as families. The units are being redecorated, so some condos have modern, upbeat furnishings. All enjoy a spectacular view of the Gulf. Each week there is at least one potluck supper and the resort offers a complimentary breakfast each morning. It's like taking a cruise because of the size of this resort, the number of vacationers, and the high level of folksy hospitality services. For those seeking a week at the beach, this resort offers real vacation value.

7 **PELICAN WALK**
8815-A Thomas Dr., Panama City Beach, FL 32407
904-234-5564; 1BR $65–100, 2BR $100–165, 3BR $125–180
Amenities: Beach, pools, hot tub, racquetball. Golf privileges

Stylish Pelican Walk is a ten-story condo tower on the beach that has some of Panama City's best decorated units. The condos are spacious and designed to bring in the sunlight. The architect designed it so each condo is a corner unit that has the best light and views. Each condo has a balcony. On the higher levels, though, it is windy. An attractive pool area is popular with adults, as well as children. A glass enclosed hot tub is a special feature. This resort is pleasant.

5 **THE SUMMIT**
8743 Thomas Dr., Panama City Beach, FL 32408, 800-824-5048
1BR $67–93, 2BR $76–108, 3BR $94–144
Amenities: Beach, pools, tennis, exercise and game rooms, hot tubs

The Summit is a very big condo complex composed of 600 separate apartments on 15 floors. Sometimes the facilities are crowded, although the resort occupies one of the best positions on Panama City Beach. Management works hard to keep you busy during your vacation by providing many activity programs. The condos are nicely decorated with rattan furniture that creates an island style. Teenagers often use the exercise room, saunas, and pool-side snack bar. There are kiddie pools and a game room for teenagers.

RENTAL RESOURCES
Aquatic Realty, 800-528-4466
Beachside One Realty, 800-654-6052
Condo World, 800-232-6636
Endless Summer, 904-234-9205
John Davidson Realty, 904-235-4190
Judy Keeton Real Estate, 904-234-3665
Lawrence Travel, 800,633-5171
Mann Resort Properties, 904-234-0676
Richmond Management, 904-234-5064
Sand Dollar Surf & Sand, 800-821-2042
Seagrove Beach Realty, 904-231-4851
St. Andrew Bay Resort Management, 904-235-4075
Sunspot Realty, 800-423-8367

DESTIN

Destin is perhaps the most attractive spot on the Emerald Coast. It boasts one of the finest snow-white beaches to be found in North America. It's texture, like sugar, is a natural phenomenon found only in this part of Florida. Add to this the clear warm waters which take on the emerald green color and you have a setting for a spectacular resort community. Sandestin (east of town) and Holiday Isle are two sections of the beach where there are heavy concentrations of condos. The newer developments are farther east near Seagrove Beach. The newer areas have been carefully developed with respect for the sand dunes and the sea oats. Sandestin is a master development focusing on its twin golf courses. Entry is restricted to guests and owners of Sandestin condominiums. Holiday Island is not restricted, but you'll find many attractive condos in these high-rise towers.

WHERE TO STAY

7 **BEACH CREST**
County Rd. 30-A, Seagrove Beach, FL
Amenities: Beach, pool

Located 24 miles east of the town of Destin, on the beach road heading toward Panama City and tucked away from all the activity of Destin, this is just the place for a quiet vacation at the beach or where children can play without the constraints of neighbors. As one of only two high-rise condos in Seagrove Beach, the condos in this twelve-story building have unobstructed views. It has contemporary, stylish decor.

7 **CORAL REEF CLUB**
Highway 98 East, Destin, FL 32541
Amenities: Indoor heated pool, beach

The Coral Reef Club is located to the east of Henderson Beach Park, in the area of new development. The architecture is reminiscent of Bermuda. The building is a long pink structure overlooking the beach with balconies and a white roof. The condos are attractively decorated and can accommodate up to six people. There are two bunk beds in the hallway entrance to each unit.

7+ **CRYSTAL VILLAS**
2850 Highway 98 East, Destin, FL 32541
Amenities: Beach, pool

One of the best values in the Destin area, it is not cheap, but very attractive and comfortable. The location is away from the clutter and activity in other locations. The soft white sand beach is dazzling white and the water is true aquamarine because it is so shallow and clear. It is a perfect location for families with little children. There are even tidal pools for very small children. Most of the units have attractive decor; some are deluxe. This is a special spot along Destin's beaches.

7   DESTIN POINTE
480 Gulf Shore Drive, Destin, FL 32541, 904-837-4800
1BR $75–115, 2BR $85–145
Amenities: Beach, pool, hot tub, tennis. Golf nearby

This is a new six-story condo development out on the point of Holiday Isle where each condo has a view of the dunes and the Gulf. These condos are a stunning surprise. The interiors are attractive and professionally decorated. Expect to find soft green and peach colors offset by the view of the vivid white sand and blue Gulf. This appeals to young professionals from the cities on family vacation. You'll see baby-sitters with kids while Mom and Dad play tennis.

8   HUNTINGTON BY THE SEA
Highway 98 East, Destin, FL 32541
Amenities: Beach, pool

One of the best choices in this area, this four-story condo resort has a flavor evocative of tropical island living. It enjoys a serene setting on a beautiful strip of the beach where the sand is white, the water is shallow, and the building is buffered from the ocean by an area of sand dunes and sea oats. The condos here are relatively new and have fairly stylish interior decor and a wonderfully serene environment.

6   JETTY EAST
500 Gulf Shore Dr., Destin, FL 32541, 904-837-2141
1BR $600–900/wk, 2BR $600–1200/wk
Amenities: Beach, pool, tennis

Spacious accommodations on Holiday Isle. The interior decor is inspired with designer wallpaper, fabrics, and several styles of furniture ranging from traditional to "African safari." Lots of mirrors bring in the Gulf view. Jetty East is separated from the beach by a buffer zone of sea oats. With more service and hospitality, this would draw a higher rating. It does, however, provide good value for accommodations.

8   MAINSAIL
5100 Highway 98 East, Destin, FL 32541
Amenities: Beach, tennis, pools, exercise/weight room

Located eight miles east of the town of Destin, Mainsail occupies 15 acres along a beautiful stretch of beach where the sand is white and the water is a vivid blue-green. The condos in this eight-story building are larger than most in the area and a few are in ground level townhouses. Many have superior interior decor; some are downright luxurious. Lots of amenities, lots of activities make this a great spot for an active vacation.

8-9 SANDESTIN
Emerald Coast Parkway, Destin, FL 32541, 904-267-8000
1BR $120–195, 2BR $180–275, 3BR $180–300
Amenities: Golf, tennis, pools, beach, fitness center, restaurants

Sandestin was created with loving care for the environment and a desire to create a premier resort community. Located five miles east of Destin, development at Sandestin has lived up to this promise. There are ten separate condominium projects within the 2,600 acres of Sandestin. In several, rentals are handled through a central office that will assign a villa, townhouse, or beachfront apartment to you depending upon your expectations. We saw three of the different condo developments and found them all similar in design and decor. Accordingly, we saw attractive solid condos with rattan furniture, glass-top tables, and lots of emerald green and blue fabrics.

Beachside I and II are two modern high-rises handled by outside rental agents. Again, these have superior construction and decor. The only distinction from the Beachside units is different management and a separate check-in area.

Sandestin has been called one of the most sports active resorts in the U.S. There are two 18-hole championship golf courses and The Links has been rated as one of the Top 50 in the Southeast. Sandestin has 16 tennis courts including two manicured all grass courts. The pro staff will give instructions to experts as well as amateurs. One of the best features is the resort's complete program of supervised activities for children and sports instruction programs for preteens.

6 SANDPIPER COVE
775 Gulf Shore Dr., Destin, FL 32541, 800-874-0448
Studio $50–70, 1BR $60–125, 2BR $120–150
Amenities: Pools, golf, tennis, restaurant

This sprawling 43-acre condo village is on both sides of the beach road in Destin's Holiday Isle section. Some of the units are on the beach, but the majority are in a village clustered around a nine hole, par three golf course. You'll find the units in these two-story wooden buildings to be attractively decorated hotel style. It's a comfortable environment for discriminating travelers. The resort is friendly, but look elsewhere if you are a family with little children.

10   SEASIDE COTTAGES
Route 30A, P.O. Box 4730, Seaside, FL 32459, 904-231-1320
Amenities: Beach, pools, tennis

This resort has received a great deal of publicity during the past few years because of its exceptional architecture. At a time when increased profits seemed to be the primary motivation for most real estate developers, this exceptional resort was created with a town center and a visually exciting collection of Victorian and early 20th century beach cottages. The architectural styles are a combination of Key West, Nantucket, and Cape May. The cottages have porches with swings, widows' walks, cupolas, latticework, and gingerbread everywhere. Attractive decor on the inside emphasizes quality, quality, quality. Lots of polished wood and touches of bright cheerful fabrics bring these beach houses to life. The "Colors" and "Rainbow" phases were purposely designed with children in mind. Prices range from $750 per week for a couple to $2000 for a group of eighteen. It's a great spot for a honeymoon or a family reunion.

8   SUN DESTIN
1040 Highway 98 East, Destin, FL 32541, 800-874-8914
1BR $75–125, 2BR $90–175, 3BR $130–215
Amenities: Pools, health club, hot tub, restaurant

Brand new sixteen-story, high-rise towers on the beach in the Holiday Isle section of Destin. Each condo has a view of the Gulf. You'll find the condos to be cheerful with light colors, butcher block tables, and lots of mirrors to invite the Gulf view inside. These condos offer extra opportunities for the sports active—a real health club with exercise equipment, steam room, and saunas. There's an indoor and outdoor pool for lap swimming or just playing. During the summer there's a social director who runs an activities program for children and adults.

7   WATERVIEW TOWERS
150 Gulf Shore Dr., Destin, FL 32541
Amenities: Pool, beach, tennis

Located in the Holiday Isle section of Destin, the condos in this seven-story concrete structure have views of Destin's East Pass Harbor as well as of the beach and the Gulf of Mexico. It has handsome decor.

RENTAL RESOURCES
Abbott Realty, 800-336-4853
Shoreline Realty, 800-874-0162

FT. WALTON BEACH TO PENSACOLA

This is a beautiful strip of Gulf coast shoreline and wooded pine forest in the shadow of two of the U.S. Military's largest installations: Elgin Air Force Base and the Navy bases ringing Pensacola Bay. Ft. Walton is more of a "regional" resort area than a "national" destination resort. It doesn't attract visitors from around the U.S. as do Panama City Beach and Destin. Instead you'll find over 50 beachfront condo developments here that primarily cater to frequent weekenders from Pensacola or Alabama. Therefore, the condos resorts with a Ft. Walton address generally don't have all the hotel services that guests taking an annual vacation might want.

WHERE TO STAY

8 **BLUE WATER BAY**
2000 Bluewater Blvd., Niceville, FL 32578
Amenities: Golf, tennis, exercise room, pools, marina

This is a full service golf resort located on the beach about six miles from the center of Ft. Walton Beach. Spread over 1800 acres, the resort offers very attractive accommodations set within the pine forest and lots of jogging and bicycle trails. You can choose from the stand-alone villas or the townhouses lining the golf course. The individual condo groupings have names such as **Gleneagles Greens** or **Villas of St. Andrews.** Over on the water there are the **Bay Villa** condominiums that have good decor but nothing fancy. This is a quiet, comfortable resort for families. There are many activities for adults and during Easter break and the summertime, there's a supervised activities program for children. The golf pros, tennis pros, and social director make this resort an outstanding choice.

6 **ISLAND ECHOES**
676 Nautilus Ct., Ft. Walton Beach, FL 32548
Amenities: Beach, pool, tennis

Located on the snow white sand beaches of Okaloosa Island, this seven-story condominium complex offers one of your best bets in Ft. Walton Beach. Casual decor, this is the sort of spot you could pick for a comfortable week at the beach.

RENTAL RESOURCES
Barrs Realty, 800-874-9010
Century 21 Island View Realty, 904-939-2774
Century 21 Lieb & Assoc., 800-553-1223
Gulf Breeze Realty, 904-932-3539
Gulf Properties, 800-821-8790

Joseph Endry, 904-932-5300
Key Realty, 800-325-3272
Navarre Beach Realty, 904-939-2020
Pensacola Beach Realtors, 800-874-9243
Pensacola Beach Realty, 800-874-9243
Realty Marts Int'l, 800-874-9245
Saints Realty, 904-433-1563
Sandcastles & Cottages, 904-932-9723
TME Realty, 800-554-3695

7. NORTHEAST FLORIDA

This section is divided into four subsections: Amelia Island, Sawgrass/ Ponte Vedra, St. Augustine Beach, and the Palm Coast.

Starting in the North with Amelia Island, you'll find the southern part of the Golden Isles remains to a large degree a forest primeval of moss-laden live oaks, marshlands, and sand dunes. Located just 22 miles north of Jacksonville and its airport, Amelia Island is an exclusive resort community where the condos have been designed to blend into the environment. But don't be misled—the interior decor of some of these vacation homes is sophisticated and visually stunning—better than what most of us have at our permanent homes.

Sawgrass at Ponte Vedra beach, located 30 miles south of Jacksonville's airport, is another example of ecologically planned development. This community is home base for the Tournament Players Association ("TPA"). Real estate and condo purchase prices may be steep. However, if you only want a week's vacation, you'll never forget this "emerald city" of manicured fairways and gardens. Farther south, St. Augustine Beach (also called Anastasia Island) has recently been developed into a 15 mile strip of condo resorts during the past ten years. The rolling barrier dunes remain intact and these resorts are generally recessed from the ocean. Condo rentals in this area are reasonably priced, and we believe this area provides one of the best vacation values in Florida. Heading south, halfway between St. Augustine and Daytona Beach, you'll find ITT's master-planned Palm Coast development. This is one of the most ambitious real estate developments in Florida, and it still has more condominiums and vacation homes on the drawing board.

The Northeast Coast from Amelia Island to Palm Coast is beautiful but not quite as warm as the southern part. Henry Flagler started the era of resort development in Florida with a resort in St. Augustine. After a couple of seasons of harsh chills, he was forced to turn south to Key West and Palm Beach. In other words, beach lovers might want to avoid December, January, and February in this part of Florida, but it's great for golf, tennis, or just getting out of the cold northern Midwest or New England. The golf/tennis season is a genuine twelve months of the year and snowbirds from Ohio, Canada, and the northeast revel in the winter "sweater weather."

Transportation to this part of Florida is much easier than you would imagine. Jacksonville is the major airport and when the airport's reconstruction is finished, this promises to become a major destination for Florida-bound travelers. Shuttle buses to Amelia Island and Sawgrass/Ponte Vedra are frequent. St. Augustine is an hour from Jacksonville airport and for those heading to the beach or Anastasia Island, as it is sometimes called, tack on an extra thirty minutes driving time. Palm Coast is two hours due south from Jacksonville or an hour north of the airport at Daytona. Watch for all the *Garfield* "Palm Coast" signs along Interstate 95.

AMELIA ISLAND

The island is divided into two halves as a result of development. The southern half is Amelia Island Plantation. It is an exclusive area of development that is sensitive to the ecology. The northern half, including Fernandia Beach, is still an area of natural beauty but it has been commercially developed. Shopping centers and condominiums are now tucked in between beach and forest. Therefore, you'll notice a difference between staying on the southern half of the island ("on plantation") and staying on the northern half. "On plantation" means you are within the master community of Amelia Island Plantation.

Rolling sand dunes bordered by fields of sea oats, a "sunken forest" between the barrier dunes and the golf course, moss-draped live oak trees and glimpses of herons and cranes—these are images of Amelia Island Plantation which occupies half of Amelia Island. Access through the security gate is restricted to owners and guests staying in the condos "on plantation." There are 17 separate condo developments within the 1,250-acre plantation. In addition, there are another 18 condo developments on the northern half of the island. Condos located outside the plantation do not have access to all the clubs services and golf provided "on plantation."

Amelia's beach as been rated as one of the ten most beautiful in the world. Wide white sand leads to dunes, sea oats, and a "sunken forest" thick with wild azaleas and palmettos. A second row of barrier dunes gives way to the golf course; active people can jog or walk through this area. Others staying "on plantation" may prefer to view the magnificent landscape from the cocktail lounge at the Amelia Island Inn.

"On plantation" there are two championship golf courses (one 18-holes and the other 27). There are two additional golf courses "off plantation" and Summer Beach Golf course is developing its own exclusive reputation. "On plantation" the Tennis Center has 25 courts including a stadium court surrounded by magnolias and moss-laden oak trees. "Off plantation" there are 36 additional courts including the private courts at each condo resort.

Fishing is available at the island's beaches or through one of the charter boats at the Fernandia Beach marina.

Children will find unsurpassed programs on Amelia Island. The Plantation offers the best collection of playgrounds we have seen. You'll find a real tree house with a ladder, rope nets, and gang planks by the Beach Club. Supervised activity programs are offered for children during spring and summer at the Plantation's Beach Club and the Tennis Club.

WHERE TO STAY

AMELIA ISLAND PLANTATION
Amelia Island, FL 32034, 800-874-6878
Amenities: Beach, golf, tennis, paddle boats, youth program
in the summer

Amelia Island Plantation offers a symphonic resort environment with everything you could want. It was designed so that you won't want to go outside the gates during your entire vacation. Upon entering the gates, your first stop will be the reception center. You will receive a gate pass, a club membership card, and directions to the condo of your choice. There are 17 separate condo developments, each with a unique identity. All of the developments are superior or deluxe and well decorated. In general you'll find **Lagoon Villas** and **Fairway Oaks** have forest or lagoon-view locations. Near the ocean, there are **Beachwalker, Beachwood, Shipwatch,** and **Courtside.** Those with ocean views or close to the Beach Club are **Captain's Court, Sandcastles, Shipwater,** and **The Pool Villas.** Finally, those on the beach (and the most expensive) are **Windsong** and **The Dunes Club.** Our selections are based upon the individual location and layout, so you can choose whether you want to be on the beach, marshside by the golf club, in a high-rise, or near the social activities of the Amelia Island Inn.

No matter which condo you choose within the plantation, you can enjoy the Tennis Club and its 25 courts, aerobics studio, and weight-training room. One special feature of Amelia Island Plantation is the conference center and the unique "management communications adventures." These are organized expeditions for executives that involve teamwork and planning in the outdoors. The "ropes course" is the most challenging of these expeditions involving a 25-foot high wire, a fourteen-foot wall, an electric fence, a human spider web, river crossing, and a "nitro" crossing. This is one executive retreat you won't forget.

Beachwalker Villas (8+) Enjoy a golf course location overlooking the ocean. The villas are a two minute hop across a fairway to the beach. They are also close to the "sunken forest" and about a ten minute walk away from the restaurants at the Amelia Island Inn. These are Amelia Island's most casual condos. You'll mainly find young couples and young families occupying these two-story wood and stucco townhouse structures. The furniture is attractive and comfortable. Beachwalker Villas is just what you dreamed a Florida beach vacation could be.

Courtside (7+) The two-story townhouses of Courtside are located in a heavily wooded area. They are only a short walk from the Tennis Club and the separate health club. Each cluster of townhouses surrounds its own swimming pool. The interior decor consists of rattan furniture and quality designer fabrics. The glass-top tables, grasscloth wallpaper, and occasional art pieces create a comfortable "clubby" environment. The townhouses are located away from the beach and a five minute drive from the Beach Club.

Sandcastles (8) Sandcastles' architecture will remind you of a dream from the plains of Spain. This cluster of condos ranges from three to eight stories in height. Sandcastles is located on the beach near the center of the Plantation. The location is convenient and only a short walk from the beach club. Sandcastles' architect created several unusual floor plans. The foyers are tiled and the woodwork is top quality. Teal carpets set the color scheme for most of the condos here and the master bedroom has an extra sitting room. This is superior for these who want to be near the seashore.

Windsong Villas (9) The most expensive condos on Amelia Island are the Windsong Villas that can be purchased for $300,000 to $450,000. As you would expect, these "vacation toys" are elegantly furnished. Unwind from business world pressure in your oceanfront living room furnished in crisp, inviting traditional "country club" decor. The condos are actually townhouse structures that border the beach. Additionally, there is a six-story Mediterranean style building behind the pool. It overlooks the townhouses, the ocean, and the surrounding golf courses.

7+   **AMELIA SURF & RACQUET CLUB**
        800 Amelia Pkwy. S, Amelia Island, FL 32034, 904-261-0511
        Amenities: Pool, tennis, sailboat rentals

Located on Amelia Island, but not within Amelia Island Plantation, you'll find the Surf and Racquet Club. This is an active resort with plenty of social life and a sporting atmosphere. Six eight-story mid-rise towers are located on the beach and overlook the ocean. True to its name, there are nine clay and True-Hard tennis courts, and a teaching pro for assistance. This resort is popular with young families from Atlanta. The condos are comfortably decorated with contemporary decor and lots of personal extras.

SUMMER BEACH
5000 Amelia Island Pkwy., Amelia Island, FL 32034,
904-277-2525
Amenities: Golf, tennis, pool, clubhouse

Summer Beach is a complete golf course community located on Amelia Island (not within Amelia Island Plantation). Summer Beach enjoys a beachfront location as well as a golf course that takes advantage of the gently rolling dunes and marsh ponds.

The Outrigger Villas (8) are some of the most expensive condos on Amelia Island with prices starting at $300,000. They are composed of two-story townhouses with tiled foyers, fireplaces, and woodwork such as moldings and chair rails. This is an ideal spot for a golf foursome or two couples. Children are welcome although these condos aren't geared towards families.

SAWGRASS / PONTE VEDRA

This area borders metropolitan Jacksonville but in spirit it is a universe away. Ponte Vedra Beach is actually 20 miles south of downtown Jacksonville. It's been an exclusive resort community for over 50 years. Beautiful homes line the beach and high walls protect the exclusive estates. Sawgrass is a master community developed by Arvida (of the Boca Raton Hotel and BocaWest fame) and is the prestigious home for the Tournament Players Association (formerly the PGA). This top quality development offers second homes and condos to corporate executives from northern cities such as Hartford and Detroit. Everything about Sawgrass is as meticulous as the neighborhoods of Simsbury or Grosse Pointe.

Ponte Vedra is an exclusive, established beach resort community. Although there is an abundance of homes and condos available for rent, most condos are available for three month minimums and only a few offer one month rental options. Inside the Sawgrass development there are several that offer short-term vacation rentals. The condos listed below are available for short-term vacation rentals of a week or so.

WHERE TO STAY

SAWGRASS
5 TPC Blvd., Ponte Vedra, FL 32082
Amenities: Golf, pools, jogging trails, tennis, horseback riding

Like Amelia Island Plantation, Sawgrass is a master community in northeast Florida. Unlike other parts of Florida, Sawgrass/Ponte Vedra Beach is an area of rolling sand dunes covered with sea oats, saw grass, and palmettos. Forty-eight thousand acres of Ponte Vedra Beach have been turned into the master golf resort community of Sawgrass. Sawgrass features 13 tennis courts and three golf courses including the famous 17th hole with its island green designed by Pete Dye. The whole area of carefully planned landscaping and manicured fairways shines like an emerald.

Ponte Vedra (9) Within Sawgrass there are 21 pools, several jogging trails, two tennis centers, and stables for horseback riding. For children there's the Grasshopper Gang—a program of supervised activities and "Kids Night Out"—an evening of pizza or pool parties. A large part of Sawgrass has been dedicated to residential homes. With all the activities, Sawgrass sounds like it's another fountain of youth. This is true to a certain extent, but there's another side of Sawgrass. It is private and occupied by part-time residents.

Sawgrass offers eleven separate condo developments to choose from. Windmere and Spinnaker's Reach are located on the beach and The Fairways is a two-minute walk away. Deer Run condos, located near the tennis courts, is only a five minute drive to the beach. Players Club Villas are next to the Marriott Hotel and the TPC Stadium Course, farther inland and about ten minutes from the beach.

Player's Club (9+) The Player's Club is a golfer's dream. Located just steps away from the Tournament Players Club, these two-story townhouse condos and three-bedroom villas feature spacious sun rooms. This is where you'll want to enjoy morning coffee or play cards in the afternoon sun. The condos are luxuriously decorated in a country club style. You'll find traditional hardwood furniture covered with classic fabrics in primary colors such as red, green, or yellow (there are no muted pastels in these condos). Since the condos are managed by Marriott, it is possible to use the hotel facilities located a short walk away. If needed, room service is available, otherwise there are kitchen facilities in the condos. The villas were designed as part-time homes for members of the Sawgrass Club. If you are fortunate enough to find a rental, you'll enjoy this for your vacation.

Spinnaker's Reach (9) Spinnaker's Reach condos are located on the beach, about ten miles away from the TPC Clubhouse and five minutes from the tennis center. For a family vacation, these offer the best choice at Sawgrass. The beach club is nearby and features an activities program called The Grasshopper Gang. The condos are quite luxurious. They are beautifully decorated and have marble foyers and a skylight in the living room. They have the touch of a professional interior designer. The condos aren't ostentatious, though. This resort is perfect for anyone looking for an exceptional beach vacation at Ponte Vedra.

RENTAL RESOURCES
Stockton Realtors, 904-285-4884, Largest selection in the area.

ST. AUGUSTINE BEACH

St. Augustine Beach is actually Anastasia Island, a sixteen-mile sandbar connected to the mainland at both the northern and southern ends. The drive to St. Augustine takes 30 to 45 minutes. On the island, you'll find everything from supermarkets to a host of activities involving golf, tennis, boating, and fishing. St.Augustine Beach is most popular in summer when children are on vacation, unlike nearby Sawgrass which is most popular with golfers during the long spring and fall seasons.

One of the last major beach areas of Florida to be developed, St. Augustine Beach offers modern condo accommodations in generally low-rise townhouse villa or condo developments clustered around a pool.

WHERE TO STAY

7+ COLONY REEF CLUB
4670 A1A South, St. Augustine Beach, FL 32084, 800-624-5965
Amenities: Beach, tennis, racquetball, pools

At the Colony Reef Club you'll find seaside fun and fitness in a resort setting. This attractive condo village was created for the young at heart. Located on the beach, it is composed of two groupings of condos. One group consists of two-story townhouse buildings overlooking a garden, a pool, and the ocean. The decor, featuring light woods and solid colors, is modern and upbeat. The second group is near the eight tennis courts and full service health club. The exercise room is equipped with a full range of Nautilus equipment. Additionally, two racquetball courts and an indoor heated lap pool are available. The beach is great for long walks, jogging or renting a sailboat. This resort is good for singles, groups, or families. Management provides front office check-in services; for activities you make your own fun.

8 OCEAN GALLERY
4600 Highway A1A South St. Augustine Beach, FL 32084
904-471-3665, 1BR $100–325, 2BR $475–525, 3BR $600–650
Amenities: Beach, pools, tennis, racquetball, weight room

Ocean Gallery is a large self-contained condo village spread over 44 acres of beachfront property. Built in several phases over the past six years, some condos are brand new. About one-third of the condos are on the ocean, the other two-thirds surround the central lagoon in hub fashion. The beach area is protected by an area of dunes, saw grass, and sea oats. The beachfront condos are in a series of three-story buildings. The other condos surrounding the lagoon are townhouse villas with two levels of living space. The resort has been created with the emphasis on quality accommodations at a reasonable price. Accordingly, the interiors are spacious, well designed, and comfortable (nothing fancy). This resort has a relaxed atmosphere and is great for vacationers seeking a quiet and pleasant spot at the beach.

8   OCEAN VILLAGE CLUB
4250 S. Highway A1A, St. Augustine Beach, FL 32084
Amenities: Beach, pools, hot tub, tennis, racquetball

This resort is a good value. The brand new condominiums are located in
ten three-story buildings on the beach. This is a real condo village spread
over 16 acres and includes four tennis courts and two pools. An area of sand
dunes and saw grass separates this condo village from the beach, and there's
a boardwalk over the dunes to the beach. This is a high quality real estate
development, yet reasonably priced. Expect to find comfortable and stylish
interior decor—almost Art Deco. The furniture is sturdy and the fabric has
been Scotch-guarded, so you need not worry about being too neat. This is a
great choice for families and adult vacationers looking for quality vacation
villas in northern Florida.

6-7 PONCE DE LEON
4000 U.S. 1 North, St. Augustine Beach, FL 32085, 904-824-2821
Amenities: Putting course, tennis, pool, restaurant. Golf nearby

For 40 years, the Ponce de Leon has been a traditional choice for vacations in the St. Augustine area. Unlike the other properties in this section,
Ponce de Leon is not on St. Augustine Beach. It is in the modern city of St.
Augustine. It's approximately six miles away from Anastasia Island and
three miles from the charming streets of Old St. Augustine. The Ponce de
Leon has a traditional main hotel lodge with the expected Spanish architecture and furniture. The condos were developed in the '70s at a time when the
resort enjoyed popularity as a leader in north Florida. The tennis villas are in
two-story condos built in a U-shape around a lagoon. Many of the condos
feature private hot tubs or upstairs sleeping lofts that are great for kids.
Unlike the hotel, the interiors are modern and use Florida's pinks and
greens. This part of the resort is beautifully landscaped with centuries-old
oaks dripping Spanish moss. You'll find six tennis courts and a hopping
cafe/cocktail lounge called "Bogie's" only a short volley from the villas. The
Ponce de Leon is the only resort in the U.S. that provides an 18-hole championship putting course. Tee times for regular play can also be arranged at
the neighboring Ponce de Leon course.

8   ST. AUGUSTINE BEACH & TENNIS
4 Ocean Trace Rd., St. Augustine Beach, FL 32084
904-471-9111, 2BR $68–84
Amenities: Tennis, beach, pools, health club

Tennis magazine calls St. Augustine Beach & Tennis "...the finest new
tennis resort in North Florida." Located on 16 acres of beachfront property,
this resort offers the best of competitive tennis and family beach activities.
The condos have been furnished according to the owners' individual taste,

but in general expect to find comfortable contemporary furniture. What we saw would have been called "Danish modern" in style with lots of wood, well placed lamps, and burnt orange colors. The tennis program alone is reason enough to visit this resort. It offers ten courts and reasonably priced professional instruction. Many other guests look for a game in the Player's Club Lounge. Also provided is a complete health club with exercise room for those who really want to stay in shape.

PALM COAST

Midway between St. Augustine and Daytona lies the 42,000-acre Palm Coast master community. Development by ITT began in 1970 and is so ambitious the U.S. Postal Service created a new zip code for the emerging town of Palm Coast. There is a balance between part-time vacationers and full-time residents. ITT created a college here to be one of the area's major employers. There are 54 holes of golf including Matanzas Woods, rated as one of the 30 best courses in Florida. The Belle Terre Swim and Racquet Club includes a 25 meter pool, 16 tennis courts, and Nautilus exercise room.

In the past, Palm Coast has been neglected by vacationers. Most of the condos are for part-time residents or the semiretired. A policy encourages condo rentals for a month or more. However, this is an unspoiled section of Florida's Atlantic coast and vacationers are increasingly turning to Palm Coast as a place for great fun in the sun where golf, tennis, and boating are the main activities.

WHERE TO STAY

6   HARBOR CLUB VILLAS
     300 Clubhouse Dr., Palm Coast, FL 32037, 904-445-1809
     $150–225
     Amenities: Pool, golf, exercise room, tennis, restaurant

These condos are located at the Palm Cost Marina next door to the Sheraton Hotel (which also manages and rents these condos). The two-story condos surround Pleasure Island. Pleasure Island is bordered by a lagoon and features a pool, sauna, hot tub, and an exercise room filled with Universal gym equipment. The condo interiors are a little disappointing. For example, the furniture is hotel style, the carpeting (for hiding dirt?) is unattractive, and the paint on the screened porch is not only dreary, but also peeling. With a name like Pleasure Island you would expect a little more. It is a good location but it definitely needs to be spruced up.

6   LAKE FOREST VILLAS
     Palm Coast Pkwy W., Palm Coast, FL 32151
     Amenities: Golf, tennis, swim club

The Lake Forest condos are most popular for vacation rentals. The condos are all on one level and there are six condos in each building. This is a quiet location. You'll need a car for the five minute drive to the country club, the Belle Terre Swim Club, and the beach.

8. THE SPACE COAST

This section covers five resort communities along 120 miles of Florida's East Coast. Those communities are Daytona Beach, New Smyrna Beach, Cocoa/Satellite Beach, Vero Beach, and Stuart/Hutchinson Island, Jensen Beach.

Daytona is famous for the riotous carnival atmosphere that prevails around Easter break or during race weekends. If you're looking to party on the Florida beaches, Daytona is where you want to go. Surfers and shapely coeds are everywhere. New Smyrna is only a few miles away, but it is altogether different. It is very popular with the semiretired in winter and becomes a bustling family resort in summer. This is where the citizens of Orlando and workers from Disney World come to escape from all the tourists. We heartily recommend that you investigate and consider New Smyrna Beach for your vacation because of the clean beaches and wholesome atmosphere. Also, you should know that the beach at New Smyrna slopes at a very slight angle so the water is shallow and the surf is very gentle. It is known as "one of the safest beaches in the world" and it is great for children.

Daytona's high season is summer when families, students, and residents of inland Southern towns flock here to escape the heat. This is one of the widest beaches in Florida, yet the Pier is packed solid with bodies on Sunday afternoons. Teenagers love this area. It's a healthy environment and the amusement parks are a major attraction. The resort accommodations are not deluxe; the lodging industry in Daytona competes to offer the lowest prices. You'll find good value in the condos we've selected and even lower prices at the condos in our index. When making reservations, be sure to ask about the races. During the Daytona 500 and the Firecracker race weeks, hotels and condos are usually fully booked and the prices double. The city is at its most festive and everyone becomes a participant in the celebration at "Florida's biggest beach party!"

Only a few miles from Daytona, New Smyrna is a world apart. The environment is quite family-oriented. Daytona has been a popular destination for nearly seventy years, but resort development at New Smyrna has mostly taken place in the past ten years. The central part of the beach consists of a few resorts that primarily cater to families. Farther south, the condos resorts are more private. Guests do their own thing without much socializing around the pool.

Farther south, toward Cocoa Beach, the beach narrows and there are many condo communities with one and two-story buildings along the beach.

Cocoa Beach is as much Florida's high-tech center as it is a resort community. Cape Canaveral and the Kennedy Space Center dominate the economy of this area. The condos are partially residential as many scientists have succumbed to the lure of living at the beach. Cocoa Beach is also known as Florida's surfing center. The beach slopes at a steep angle giving birth to some of the bigger waves in Florida—great for surfers. All types prevail in Cocoa Beach—young professionals with children in tow who have come for a week of surf; older couples who appreciate Cocoa's mellow "beach town" ambiance; and lots of hard-working people who happen to live here.

Vero Beach is another story. Surrounded by the orange and citrus groves of Indian River County, Vero Beach has been one of Florida's primary agricultural centers for decades. Fifteen years ago, however, large sections of beachfront property were walled off to create private "enclave" resort communities of condos and villas where the main occupation is golf and tennis. These are some of Florida's most private golf communities and vacation condominiums. These resorts discourage short-term rentals as the condos are really part-time residences. Vero's atmosphere, though, appears to be on the verge of change as the Disney Corporation has recently acquired a large parcel of oceanfront land to build a super beach resort, geared to families and those who need a vacation after a trip to Walt Disney World.

The Stuart/Hutchinson Island area is still emerging as a tourist destination. The town of Stuart has seen some dramatic ups and downs in real estate. Hutchinson Island (Stuart's beach) has been carefully developed as a community of mid-rise condos, that have been recessed from the beach to save the sand dunes and prevent erosion. With the ecology movement in the public eye, Hutchinson Island will become more and more attractive in the years to come.

Transportation to this area offers a wide range of airport options: Daytona Beach, Melbourne, and West Palm Beach all have convenient air service to Atlanta, Raleigh, Miami, Nashville, New York, Chicago, Dallas, Charlotte, and Memphis.

WHERE TO STAY... DAYTONA BEACH

9 INDIGO LAKES RESORT
P.O. Box 10859, Daytona Beach, FL 32020
904-258-6333, 1BR $180–249
Amenities: Golf, tennis, restaurant, pool, health club with spa

Only five minutes away from Daytona's airport is this 600-acre sprawling golf and tennis resort community. Here you'll find the native vegetation of Central Florida's wooded marshes and lagoons. This seems a world away from the high-rise strip lining Daytona Beach. The 64 condos are clustered in the village next to the conference center. The units in these two- and three-story buildings are comfortable with a full kitchen, screened porch, and a whirlpool in the master bath. The units can be locked off, giving conference attendees the choice of a bedroom or a living room/kitchen unit. Conferences are big business at this resort and you'll find immaculate housekeeping. For golfers, the Indigo Lakes course has been rated by Golf Digest as one of the ten best courses in the state.

7   MARINE TERRACE
1018 N. Atlantic Ave., Daytona Beach, FL 32018
Amenities: Beach, pool, gym, saunas

Marine Terrace is a beautiful eight-story mid-rise on the north end of the beach. The city's redevelopment efforts have brought this part of town back to life. The units are well decorated and management deserves good marks for hospitality and professional service. A social director is on hand during the summer months to help plan lots of activities, so both you and your children will have a great vacation. The units are spacious and there's also a full kitchen. If you choose not to cook thee is a small restaurant on site.

6   MAVERICK
485 S. Atlantic Ave., Ormond Beach, FL 32074, 904-672-7120
Amenities: Beach, pools, restaurant, playground

This is one of the better choices at Daytona Beach because it is clean, attractive, and the units are well decorated. They have sturdy furniture, track lighting, and a movie-star-style, lighted mirror in the master bath. The Maverick is a five-story converted hotel structure on the beach with a pub/restaurant, that is the focal point for social life. The condos are a little small, but nicely decorated. The kitchens are small but adequate. This resort is good for families who want the option of dining in or out. The Maverick has some spritely summertime social directors who will organize poolside activities or help you find a baby sitter.

6   OUTRIGGER BEACH CLUB
215 S. Atlantic Ave., Ormond Beach, FL 32176, 904-672-2770
Amenities: Beach, heated pool, hot tub

At first you'll think of Polynesia because of the half-timbered construction and the Hawaiian tapa cloth design in the fabrics. This crescent-shaped oceanfront building offers a romantic atmosphere in Daytona Beach, and is a cut above most other properties. Each unit has a full or partial ocean view and, although a little dark, the Polynesian theme is carried out with grass-cloth wallpaper, louvered shades, and South Seas designs in the fabrics. The kitchens are small. The Outrigger is popular with mature travelers and families with small children.

7   **SUNGLOW**
3647 S. Atlantic Ave., Daytona Beach, FL 32019, 904-756-4005
1BR $69–99, 2BR $89–139
Amenities: Beach, heated pool, hot tub, video game room

Sunglow is your best choice in Daytona Beach for beachfront peace and quiet. This ten-story high-rise is located at the southern end of the Daytona Beach area, in Port Orange. This is an area of new development. Each condo has a private balcony and three-quarters of the units have an ocean view. Inside, the condos have been furnished with sturdy rattan furniture in an island style. Dark wine colors and brown carpeting set off the bright sunlight steaming in from the glass window. The management is good.

2   **TURTLE INN**
3233 S. Atlantic Ave., Daytona Beach, FL 32018, 904-761-0426
Amenities: Beach, pool

This four-story building along a strip of motels is unpretentious, comfortable, and popular with retirees. There is a morning coffee klatch in the lobby with coffee and pastries where new arrivals will quickly learn the inside scoop on what to do in Daytona. Interior decor has been dressed up with imaginative touches, wall hangings, mirrored headboards in the bedrooms and silk flowers everywhere. Turtle Inn is very reasonably priced.

RENTAL RESOURCES

Atlantic Properties, 904-760-8000
Beachview, 904-441-8028
Erdman Realty, 904-788-2250
Ocean Properties & Management, 904-428-0513
Rent-A-Condo, 904-788-8555
Southport Condos, 904-788-3550

WHERE TO STAY... NEW SMYRNA BEACH

7+   **ISLANDER BEACH RESORT**
1601 S. Atlantic Ave., New Smyrna Beach, FL 32069
904-427-3452
Amenities: Beach, pool, snack bar, activity rooms

This eight-story high-rise is one of the most popular resorts on new Smyrna Beach because of the good hospitality and management. Islander Beach Resort is quiet, efficient and someone is always there to help answer a question or plan an excursion. Sometimes volleyball games just get started at the pool. For a family on vacation, this is one of your best choices at New Smyrna. The condos are just a little small but well-designed for comfort and privacy. The interior decor includes comfortable pastel colored furniture. You'll enjoy the balcony overlooking the ocean for peace, and the pool for activity.

8 OCEANVIEW TOWERS
5205 S. Atlantic Ave., New Smyrna Beach, FL 32069
904-427-8555, 1BR $375, 2BR $475, 3BR $600
Amenities: Beach, pool, tennis, video game room

This is a modern mid-rise condominium on the quiet end of the beach. Oceanview is a perfect choice for families as well as two couples desiring a week or two on one of Florida's best beaches. Twin eight-story towers flank the pool. Each of the one-, two- or three-bedroom units has been designed to maximize the ocean view, that is visible from the bedroom and the kitchen, as well as from the living room. The advantage here is that the rooms are larger than what you would expect, and the double balconies create a sense of extra spaciousness and comfort. Interior decor is contemporary and attractive. Management is quietly efficient and the Southern hospitality adds an unexpected graciousness to the ambiance. Solid and non-commercial, Oceanview towers will make you feel as though you're taking a real breather from the rush of the workaday world. This is also an excellent choice for snowbirds because of the attractive monthly and seasonal winter rates.

7 SEASCAPE TOWERS
5207 S. Atlantic Ave., New Smyrna Beach, FL 32069
904-423-2305, 1BR $400/wk, 2BR $500/wk, 3BR $700/wk
Amenities: Beach, pool, hot tub, saunas, tennis

This is a new, luxury high-rise condominium on the beach at New Smyrna. Two towers are built in a V-shape so that every unit has a balcony overlooking the beach and ocean. The condos are built well and feature a whirlpool large enough for two in each master bath. Tiled foyers, plush carpeting and designer fabrics are some of the design characteristics. Some of the most expensive condos on the market in New Smyrna can be rented at a reasonable price. This resort is one of the best values anywhere.

8 TRADEWINDS
5255 S. Atlantic Ave., New Smyrna Beach, FL 32069
Amenities: Pools, hot tub, tennis

The top choice at New Smyrna Beach, its two, fourteen-story towers flank a large pool, fountain and hot tub. There is a second pool just off the ocean as well. The condos are large and spacious with high ceilings and quality decor. There are sunken bath tubs, wood cabinetry and paneling and Chatahoochee stone terraces. These condos could be permanent homes, but

Tradewinds is primarily a vacation resort especially popular on weekends with owners from Orlando.

RENTAL RESOURCES
Century 21, 904-428-2457
Coldwell Banker, 904-428-3108
Ocean Properties, 904-428-0513
St. Andrews Villas, 904-427-2158

WHERE TO STAY...
COCOA BEACH / SATELLITE BEACH

7+   **LAS OLAS BEACH CLUB**
1215–25 Highway A1A, Satellite Beach, FL 32937, 407-777-3224
Amenities: Beach, pool, children's playroom

This is one of our favorite spots in Florida for a family vacation. It combines good accommodations and exceptional hospitality. This is the older sister resort to Las Olas of Cocoa Beach. The building is a solid five-story concrete structure on the beach just across from the city of Melbourne. The grounds are well landscaped, and the pool is a good gathering place. The condos are decorated with traditional beige and orange furniture. The spacious interiors are done in a modern Danish style. This resort offers you a memorable week in Satellite Beach. Social directors, activities programs, and supervision for children are available.

8   **LAS OLAS BEACH CLUB OF COCOA BEACH**
5100 Ocean Blvd., Cocoa Beach, FL 32931, 407-784-2706
Amenities: Beach, pool

Just like its sister resort, this is an exceptional spot for a family vacation on the beach. Clearly, this resort is the best choice in Cocoa Beach because of the beautiful condos and the high level of hospitality service. This is a bustling family resort located on a good part of Cocoa Beach. The condos are new, luxuriously decorated and designed for families desiring a lengthy stay at the beach. The "show piece" feature is the private whirlpool (large enough for two) in each unit. This resort offers the most complete social program that we saw in the Daytona Beach/Cocoa Beach area. If you are looking for a resort that offers quality and fun (such as a cruise for a week), choose this resort.

5-6   **OCEAN LANDINGS (Caribbean and Dream Buildings)**
900 N. Atlantic Ave., Cocoa Beach, FL 32931, 407-783-9430
Amenities: Beach, pools, exercise room, restaurant, tennis racquetball, aerobics classes

Located on the beach, Ocean Landings comprises a large community of vacation condos and timeshares. The property has been developed in several stages over the years. There are different management groups operating the condos. The older buildings (Baltic and Atlantic) are covered below. The Caribbean and Dream Buildings are newer additions and were built as time-share condos. These are five-story concrete structures with spacious units that have an ocean view. The interiors are furnished with standard hotel-style furniture and there are full kitchens. This is a comfortable spot for a family on vacation. What we like best here is the recent landscaping, a prodigious effort to spruce up this property. In addition to the beach and nearby Kennedy Space Center, this resort offers a full activities program for vacationers. There are organized volleyball games for teenagers, as well as planned excursions to Disney World only an hour away. This resort offers high density living and lots of opportunities to make new friends.

3   OCEAN LANDINGS (Atlantic and Baltic Buildings)

The difference between the Atlantic/Baltic Buildings and the Caribbean/ Dream Buildings described above is significant. The Atlantic/Baltic Buildings are converted motel structures. They are not on the beach and they do not have ocean views. Furnishings are aged. However, management has begun a refurbishment program. At Ocean Landings, you get to use all the athletic facilities described above and participate in the activities programs.

7   OCEANIQUE
2105 Highway A1A, Indian Harbor, FL 32937, 407-777-6512
Amenities: Beach, pool, game room

Oceanique is clean, modern and efficient. It's been there for years, but is so well maintained that it seems brand new. It's on a good strip of beach just north of Melbourne. There's an attractive pool area and game room for chil-dren and teenagers. The resort is strong on hospitality services and there's a fully operational lobby and front desk. Everything except room service is available to make your stay enjoyable. The condos are attractively decorated in a light, modern style. The units are airy inviting the ocean "inside."

7   ROYAL MANSIONS
8600 Ridgewood Ave., Cape Canaveral, FL 32920
800-346-7222, 1BR $80–130
Amenities: Heated pool, hot tub, beach

Clearly one of the best choices for beach resorts in this part of Florida, Royal Mansions is the beach resort closest to Orlando's Walt Disney World. It's designed in the French Caribbean style, and is one of the most distinctive waterfront residences between New Smyrna and Vero Beach. The condos in this three-story building have special flourishes such as arched windows and small patios in the ground floor units. The light and spacious interior decor has been professionally designed. Built around a courtyard, there's a pool in the center.

WHERE TO STAY... VERO BEACH

8 **CORALSTONE CLUB**
9025 N. Highway A1A, Vero Beach, FL 32963
Amenities: Beach, pool, tennis, exercise room

Coralstone Club is composed of Bermuda style cottages on the beach about ten miles north of the main part of Vero Beach (in the town of Orchid). These condos are comfortable, attractive and a good choice for a long vacation.

6 **DRIFTWOOD INN RESORT**
3150 S. Ocean Dr., Vero Beach, FL 32963
Amenities: Beach, pools, restaurant, shuffleboard

The Driftwood Inn began as a beach cottage for one of the early Florida pioneer families in 1910. It's expansion has retained that personal "guest house" atmosphere. Furnishings in the main part of the Inn are Victorian. In the 1930s decor from the nearby former casino was acquired for the Driftwood. Today these condos provide a cozy vacation retreat, arranged in a garden setting. This is one resort where you'll get to know the other guests. It is like a quality bed and breakfast environment, yet the units are full condos with living rooms and kitchens designed for both short and long-term stays.

7 **REEF OCEAN RESORT**
3450 S. Ocean Dr., Vero Beach, FL 32963, 407-231-1000
Amenities: Beach, pool, putting green, paddle tennis

This laid back resort has an infectious charm. Located on the beach, these 36 villas are set amid a garden of palms and flowering hibiscus. The small pool is by the walkway leading to the ocean. A resort like this couldn't be built today because the land would be dedicated to higher density. This is a relic from Florida of 30 years ago. Inside you'll find solid contemporary furniture, grasscloth wallpaper and many mirrors. The bar has memorabilia from the Dodgers (both of Brooklyn and of Los Angeles), since Vero Beach has been the spring training camp for many years. This resort has character and there's a special atmosphere here—sort of "relaxed, but in the know."

8 **SEA OAKS**
8850 N. A1A, Vero Beach, FL 32963, 407-231-5656
Amenities: Beach, pool, hot tub, tennis. Golf nearby

Located about eight miles north of Vero Beach, Sea Oaks is a choice for sophisticated golfers and beach lovers. Just south of Orchid, this area is home to numerous condo developments favored by golfers. However, most other developments are restricted by the original deeds against short-term rentals. In an exclusive area where most of the residents are snowbirds seeking three or four months of winter sun, Sea Oaks is the exception. The attractive condos are tucked away behind a security gate in a secluded, resort, like setting. Families with small children looking for a beach resort would be well advised to stay elsewhere. Sea Oaks is special because of its controlled environment.

WHERE TO STAY...
STUART / HUTCHINSON ISLAND / JENSEN BEACH

9   **INDIAN RIVER PLANTATION**
555 N.E. Ocean Blvd., Hutchinson Island, Stuart, FL 34996
800-444-3389, 1BR $155, 2BR $195
Amenities: Golf, beach, tennis, pools, marina, restaurant

Where the Indian River separates Hutchinson Island from Florida's southeast coast, you'll find a refreshing vacation retreat. Formerly a pineapple plantation, the area has been recently developed into a master golf course/residential community. A marina is located on one side of the island. It's a short five minute drive over the causeway to Stuart on the mainland. On the other side, there's the beach with Atlantic surf. There's a par 61 executive golf course and 17 tennis courts, as well as restaurants and a clubhouse. The resort also has its own cruiser called the Island Princess which is available for two-hour, day or evening cruises. There are several groups of condos within the plantation. The best condo rentals are available in the Spoonhill and Pelican buildings located on the beach. The condos are decorated with pink and green colors and furnished with contemporary glass-top furniture. An overhead paddle fan catches the pleasant year-round breezes.

7+ **PLANTATION BEACH CLUB**
329 N.E. Tradewind Lane, Hutchinson Island, Stuart, FL 34996
813-481-3636, 1BR $805/wk, 2BR $980/wk
Amenities: Heated pool, hot tub, sauna

Serene Hutchinson Island is one of those unexpected surprises on Florida's Atlantic Coast. The Plantation Beach Club is within the larger Indian River Plantation master community, an area of palms, wooded landscapes and a golf course. These condos are luxuriously decorated with the Florida wicker/rattan look and designer fabrics. Special touches and accessories such as ceiling paddle fans create a better-than-home environment. Each condo has a private screened porch that overlooks the ocean. The building is slightly recessed from the sea and there's a wooden walkway leading to the beach.

The area is quiet and refined. The beach location is a desirable retreat for families because of all the sports activities "on plantation."

6+   VISTANA BEACH CLUB
10470 S. Ocean Dr., Jensen Beach, FL 34957, 407-229-9200
Amenities: Beach, pool

Just a couple of miles north of Indian River Plantation on Hutchinson Island (Hutchinson Island is within the township of Jensen Beach), Vistana Beach Club offers a totally different environment. Much more expensive than the neighboring condos, this resort offers lots of extra services. It's the active hospitality that creates the "go go" environment here. The building has been painted hot pink so you can't miss it from the street. Cheerful girls will welcome you and make sure you are set for a fun-filled vacation. The condos are rather small, but they are so well decorated you probably won't notice. You'll discover designer fabrics, vivid colors and glass-top tables. The master bath has a Roman tub large enough for two. Additionally, the condos are equipped with a real entertainment center which includes a VTP. During the day you'll find organized activities and maybe a bingo game around the pool.

9. PALM BEACH COUNTY

Palm Beach County has been one of the nation's playgrounds since the 1920s when the very wealthy built palaces on the sandbar island named Palm Beach. Today that sandbar—the town of Palm Beach—is one of the most exclusive residential areas in the world, with palatial homes such as Mrs. Meriweather Post's Mar Lago and the much smaller estate (albeit more famous) belonging to Mrs. Rose Kennedy. During the 1970s developers looked north from Miami and saw the potential Palm Beach County offered with its sandy beaches and saw grass dunes. Thirty-two communities have evolved in Palm Beach county, each with a distinct flavor. Today the town of Palm Beach remains the exclusive nucleus. However, a much broader segment of the population can afford the area's charms. Temperatures range between 63° and 83°.

Palm Beach County naturally divides into two halves at the town of Palm Beach. There are no vacation condos for rent in the town of Palm Beach and the few vacation homes which are available for short term seasonal rentals are difficult to find, unless you have a knowledgeable friend or a list of references.

NORTHERN PALM BEACH COUNTY
(Jupiter, Singer Island)

Starting at the northern part of Palm Beach County, this is the place to be. The early settlers 100 years ago planted the seeds that have become the area's magnificent landmarks; rows of towering royal palms. This is a golfer's paradise since 43 of Palm Beach County's 100 golf courses are located in the area of Palm Beach Gardens (PGA National), including Tequesta, North Palm Beach, Jupiter, and Singer Island. Many have recently retired to this area, and many of these young retirees in their 50s and 60s still enjoy competing in a host of local amateur golf tournaments. There are townhouses and condos facing the fairway at PGA National as well as some villas affiliated with a major hotel complex. There are several smaller courses with groups of condos available for rent.

Both Singer Island and Jupiter Beach offer an array of oceanfront condos. Singer Island has been developed with high-rise condo towers including one, that at 45 stories, is the tallest in Florida. The style in Jupiter is quite different with numerous clusters of townhouses and condo buildings (no higher than six stories) in beautifully landscaped park-like settings. Whatever your taste, you'll find it in these pages. One important consideration: there is no town of Singer Island. It's merely a geographical designation. The town is technically Riviera Beach, Florida, but all of the Riviera Beach addresses in this chapter are actually on Singer Island.

Again, there is a prejudice against short-term rentals in the Northern Palm Beaches. Only a few condo developments in PGA National, Jupiter Beach and on Singer Island allow condo rentals for a week or so. Many more allow rentals for one month. All have rentals for those planning three months. For those who can only stay a short time, we have included one all-suite hotel because it provides luxurious condo style units that are available for daily rentals as at any other hotel.

WHERE TO STAY

8   **AQUARIUS**
5440 N. Ocean Dr., Riviera Beach, FL 33404, 407-842-7611
Amenities: Beach, heated pool, sauna, exercise room

A true value on Singer Island, this sixteen-story tower has spacious one and two-bedroom condos—most with an ocean view. The Aquarius sits right on the beach for those who want to play in the surf and there's a quiet heated pool area. Interior decor is mostly dated. You'll find treasures from the attic here. The minimum rental is two months at this quiet location.

7-9 THE BLUFFS (Marina, River, Ocean and Ocean South)
101 Ocean Bluffs Blvd., or 101 South Seas Dr., Jupiter, FL 33477, 407-844-3102
Amenities: Beach (some), pools, hot tubs, tennis

This is one of the most handsome condo developments to be found in South Florida. The Bluffs is a major development comprising over twenty five-story buildings on several different parcels of land in a section of Jupiter Beach. Popular with surfers and beach walkers, these condos on the two-mile strip of Jupiter Beach are now referred to as the Bluffs. Two developments are on the Intracoastal Waterway and two are on the ocean. The oceanfront developments, called The Ocean and The Ocean South, are like almost all developments in Jupiter; across the street from the beach. This has preserved a narrow area of sea grass and dunes which helps to prevent the beach erosion common along the east coast of Florida. The Ocean development is a cluster of four, six-story buildings arranged in a semicircle on eight acres of land. A park-like atmosphere prevails because of all the land which has been set aside. In the center there's a pond with a fountain. Inside, the two bedroom condos are spacious and arranged to get the best views of the park and the ocean. Well furnished, some have the touch of an interior decorator. Expect to find rattan furniture with bright pink, blue and yellow pastel colors. Screened porches provide extra room and we'll bet you'll want to have breakfast and lunch on your porch. This is a friendly place. Rentals generally are for a minimum of three months, but most local realtors can work around these restrictions.

8 EASTPOINTE
5380 N. Ocean Dr., Riviera Beach, FL 33404, 407-844-3102
Amenities: Beach, pool, hot tub, billiard room

This is located on a prime section of beach on Singer Island. One of the most luxurious condominiums in the area (and one of the largest), Eastpointe has its own Country Club with tennis and golf privileges for members or guests staying at Eastpointe. Tower I units have over 2,000 square feet of living space in the two-bedroom condos. Tower II units are even more luxurious with over 3,000 square feet each (as large as many homes). The condo association limits rentals to a minimum of three months, but most realtors can work around these restrictions for those planning shorter stays. There's a 24-hour security gate and a quiet sense of confidence here. All the world seems in order here. Older vacationers will be attracted to Eastpointe.

6 GEMINI CLUB CONDOMINIUMS
336 Golfview Rd., North Palm Beach, FL 33408, 407-626-3853
Amenities: Pool, exercise room, tennis. Golf next door

These huge twin twelve-story towers are on Lake Worth. There is an ocean view but the beach is actually a twelve-minute drive from here. The Gemini condos may be the area's best value because a two-bedroom unit can be purchased at prices as low as $70,000. The North Palm Beach Country Club golf course is only a five minute walk away. Since long term rentals of a month or more are the minimum, this is a great find for a retiree on a budget looking for a great location in Palm Beach County.

7   GOVERNOR'S POINT
356 Golfview, North Palm Beach, FL 33404, 407-626-9474
Amenities: Lake beach, pool, jogging trail. Golf next door.

This twelve-story complex overlooks the North Palm Beach Country Club and the Intracoastal Waterway. There is a lake-front beach, not an ocean beach. There are spacious two- and three-bedroom condos, each overlooking the waterway. Popular with retirees, seasonal rentals for a month or more can easily be arranged.

7   JUPITER BAY RESORT & TENNIS CLUB
350 U.S. Highway 1 South, Jupiter, FL 33477, 407-744-0210
Amenities: Pool, restaurant

This is one of two condominium resorts in Jupiter Beach that actively solicits short term rentals. Therefore it has the atmosphere of a resort hotel with a central check-in office and lots of friendly new faces at the pool every day. Jupiter Bay is located perhaps 100 yards from the beach, buffered by a wide grassy area. Covering over 18 acres, there are twelve, six-story buildings in a park-like setting. The architecture is reminiscent of Bermuda with pink stucco and gracefully sloping white roofs. Inside, the condos are new and they have been decorated island style with casual rattan furniture and lots of pastel floral fabrics to further enhance that Bermuda garden feeling. One of the area's most popular Italian restaurants is located here and the Burt Reynolds Theatre is only steps away. This is a popular choice at vacation time.

8   JUPITER DUNES GOLF CLUB
501 N. Highway A1A, Jupiter, FL 33477, 407-746-6654
Amenities: Golf, pool

At the most northern tip of Jupiter Beach, just before it becomes Tequesta, sits the charming Jupiter Dunes development. This is a private, walled-off, nine-hole golf course development wedged between the beach road and the shore. The two-bedroom condos are in attractive two-story buildings, taupe in color and with screened porches. Jupiter Dunes is a golfer's delight since each unit looks out over the fairway. Some owners have used mirrors in the living room to bring the light and the view inside the attractive interiors.

7   JUPITER OCEAN AND RACQUET CLUB
     1605 U.S. Highway 1 South, Jupiter, FL 33477, 407-747-5331
     Amenities: Pools, hot tub, saunas

A massive development just 200 yards from the beach at Jupiter, some of
Jupiter's best priced condos are here. Prices for a one-bedroom unit begin
at $69,000 and at $90,000 for a two-bedroom unit. These garden apartments are in a park-like setting. It's a good choice for young families with
lots of activity around the pool, especially in the evening. For a unique
vacation experience different from staying in a hotel, try the friendly JORC.
You just might join in with a group and learn to surf or take on a competitive golf game.

7   JUPITER REEF CLUB
     1600 South Ocean Dr., Jupiter, FL 33477, 407-747-7788
     1BR $85, 2BR $125
     Amenities: Beach

Jupiter Reef Club is one of the very few properties on the ocean at Jupiter
Beach. Zoning has required that most condo developments in Jupiter be
across the street from the beach but the Jupiter Reef Club is the exception.
An attractive single-story structure, it blends into the sea bluff with a
California ranch look. At first you'll think "This is Carmel" but it's actually
Palm Beach County, Florida. Each of the suites in this main building has a
patio and a view of the ocean. Well decorated with bright, cheerful fabrics,
the decor is enhanced on the outside with landscaping and flowers.

8   MARTINIQUE
     4100 N. Ocean Dr., Riviera Beach, FL 33404, 407-848-8208
     Amenities: Beach, pools, hot tub, tennis

Located on a wide strip of the Singer Island beach, these twin towers provide solid, comfortable value. One oddity of the Martinique is that the units
are two-bedroom in design but each has four bathrooms. This is a quiet
place where many owners come for "The Season" in Palm Beach County.
During school vacations you'll find children at play with their grandparents.
Martinique is solid, carefree, and comfortable. Although the condo association permits rentals only for a three-month minimum, most local realtors can
work around these restrictions for guests who only want to stay for a month
or two.

8   OCEAN TRAIL
     300/400 Ocean Trail Way, Jupiter, FL 33477, 407-747-7407
     Amenities: Beach, heated pools, hot tub, card rooms

At the northern end of Jupiter Beach, next to the Hilton and across from the Burt Reynolds Theatre (a major destination for area visitors), you'll find these four, curving high-rise towers. These are the only high-rise condos on Jupiter Beach. Solidly built, there's an aura of security and confidence. This is not a lively resort. You're likely to find people relaxing by the pool or perhaps some grandparents entertaining children on the beach. Nothing is rushed or out of place. The condos have sweeping views of the beach and the ocean. Most have superior decor designed by a professional. The minimum rental is for three months and, although realtors claim they can work around these restrictions, this is the type of place that really is designed for seniors or those who want to spend the season playing golf at nearby Tequesta or PGA National.

6   OLD PORT COVE
115 Lake Shore Dr., North Palm Beach, FL 33804, 407-626-3411
Amenities: Heated pools, exercise room, marina, shops

Located on its own private peninsula, the condos at Old Port Cove have their own waterfront complex. This is on Lake Worth (not the beach), with views of the ocean across the narrow body of water. Old Port Cove has its own marina for boaters where fishing charters leave early in the morning.

9+   PGA NATIONAL—GOLF AND TENNIS VILLAS
7100 Fairway Dr., Palm Beach Gardens, FL 33418, 305-627-3000
Amenities: Pools. Access to PGA golf and racquet club
with special guest membership

Not to be confused with PGA Sheraton Golf Villas (two-bedroom cottages next to the hotel), these condos are actually apartments in a series of two-story buildings. They are small and more fancifully decorated than their neighbors. They are luxurious, private, and offer a true vacation home atmosphere. The villas are surrounded by a golf course and are close to the 18 tennis courts of PGA National Health & Racquet Club. A few of the condos have been decorated by interior designers with over $30,000 worth of furniture. Expect to find contemporary, overstuffed furniture, textured wall paper, glass-top tables, and lots of designer accents. Except for Christmas and Easter break, this resort isn't good for children.

9+   PGA SHERATON RESORT
400 Avenue of the Champions, Palm Beach Gardens, FL 33418
407-627-2000, Villas from $300
Amenities: Golf, tennis, racquetball, pool

PGA National is a 2,340-acre master resort community located just north of West Palm Beach and about six miles inland from the beach. With five, 18-hole golf courses and 17 tennis courts, it's a sportsman's paradise. The centerpiece is the Sheraton Resort Hotel and Golf Villas surrounded by the lake and fairways. The 80 Sheraton Golf Villa condominiums, under the same management as the hotel, have the best of both worlds since they are spacious, private, and have access to all the hotel services. These are the only condos at PGA National available for daily rental. The Sheraton Golf Villas are ideal for vacationers from all walks of life. They are especially well suited for executives on a corporate retreat and groups of golfers. The hotel is a popular destination for executive sales conferences and as an incentive travel reward. It is not really a family destination, although there's no reason why a family wouldn't enjoy this vacation environment. Each condo has a full kitchen for cooking, and food can be obtained through room service. You'll find attractive interior decor with modern, overstuffed furniture. The "new Art Deco" style would be the operative term here. The setting is superb.

8   THE PHOENIX
     2500 N. Ocean Blvd., Riviera Beach, FL 33404, 407-844-8641
     Amenities: Beach, pool, tennis, putting green

This is the only condo on Singer Island which openly permits short term rentals. There's a lively, friendly resort atmosphere around the pool. Located right on the beach, these two-bedroom condos in the Phoenix's twin towers have magnificent views of the ocean, Palm Beach and Lake Worth. Some are better decorated than others but all in all there's more personal home-like ambiance than you would find in a hotel.

8   PRESTWICK CHASE
     7100 Fairway Dr., Palm Beach Gardens, FL 33418
     Amenities: Pool. Access to PGA golf and racquet club
     with special guest membership

These two-story townhouse condos are the best choice for those seeking extra privacy at PGA National because each has a private walled courtyard and patio. Each building fronts on the golf course and contains four townhouses. They have vaulted ceilings, a formal dining room and a kitchen with a breakfast nook. All of the condos are individually furnished and some have been decorated by interior designers. One condo in particular had a "nouveau French-country" look with lots of blond wood, Bergére chairs and light colored Florida fabrics. Rentals are only available by the month. There is no hospitality other than check-in and maid service.

9   SEA COLONY
     1401 Mainsail Cr., Jupiter, FL 33477, 407-743-5411
     Amenities: Pool. Beach across the street.

This is a colony of luxurious two-story townhouses in the Bluffs section of Jupiter Beach. Across the street from the beach, these townhouses are in a beautifully landscaped setting. A new development, you'll be dazzled by the interior decor of many of these units which have been decorated Florida-style with lots of bright fabrics and glass-top tables. One of the most exclusive properties on Jupiter Beach, rentals are for a three month minimum.

9　TIARA

3000 N. Ocean Dr., Riviera Beach, FL 33404, 407-845-7755
Amenities: Beach, heated pool, hot tub, tennis, exercise rooms

Florida's tallest condominium at 45 stories towers over the other developments along Singer Beach. These condos have a panoramic vista of the Palm Beaches and the ocean. Occupying a nice strip of beach, an area of sea dunes has been preserved with a gazebo. Enjoy an early morning cup of coffee as the world wakes up. There's a landscaped garden and heated pool which is popular yet, somehow, very serene. The condos here are luxurious and most have been decorated by a professional designer. The condo association restricts rentals to a three month minimum, but generally brokers will work around these restrictions for those desiring shorter stays.

6-7　TWELVE OAKS

11353 Twelve Oaks Way, West Palm Beach, FL 33408,
407-626-6878
Amenities: Heated pool, hot tub, tennis, boat dock

Located on an arm of the Intracoastal Waterway, this is a quiet budget choice for boaters and golfers in North Palm Beach. If you don't have a car, the location is perfect because you are right across from the Oakbrook Square shopping mall. Each of the condos in this six-story building is functional in design and decor. Many are full-time residences. Twelve Oaks also has a bevy of cluster homes which can be rented for those who need the extra space.

RENTAL RESOURCES
Campbell & Rosemurgy, 407-395-9355
Gimelstob Realty—Boca Raton, 407-488-3700
Gimelstob Realty—Jupiter, 407-575-4022
Investment Equity Realtors, 407-626-5100

SOUTHERN PALM BEACH COUNTY

In the town of Palm Beach there are no condos or vacation homes available for rent, unless you happen to know one of the owners. This community disdains working class America and unless you're retired or able to take a three month vacation periodically, look elsewhere.

The Polo Club, 13 miles west of Palm Beach has been developed in the past 15 years to become one of the nation's favorite golf and horseback riding playgrounds. This area caters to short term vacationers as well as to those who come down for the season.

Lake Worth, just south of the town of Palm Beach, is an area in transition. This was once the home of many of the workers who serviced the exclusive shops and estates lining Palm Beach. Today many wealthy vacationers are attracted to the new condominiums lining the beaches, and the mile-wide lake for which the town has been named on the Intracoastal waterway. Very few of these new condos permit rentals for less than three or sometimes even six months. However, there are a few older housekeeping apartment communities which rent apartments by the week.

Moving south, Delray Beach continues to exude an exclusive air. Clusters of single-story vacation villas line the beach since Delray has generally prohibited the high-rise condominium towers so popular in Boca and the northern Palm Beach resort areas. Delray has a quiet sophistication and attracts young executives who come for the wealth of tennis and golf activities.

Boca Raton is just north of the southern border of Palm Beach County. Here, development began with the very exclusive pink palace of the Boca Raton Hotel and Club. One of the tonier resort communities in Florida, the Boca Club is still the centerpiece but there are new condos on the shores which sell for prices as high as $1,500,000. Following the familiar pattern on the southeast coast of Florida, short term rentals at most of the luxury condos has been discouraged. Many condo homeowner associations, in order to retain the gracious, almost club-like atmosphere, restrict rentals to a three or six month minimum. There are some exceptions and most realtors will brag about their ability to circumvent the condo board's rules. However, don't be surprised if you call one of the condos listed below and are told unequivocally that vacation rentals are not permitted. They are, otherwise those properties wouldn't be listed in these pages. At Boca, you have a choice of two major types of resorts: high-rise towers along the beach or the low, two-story buildings around the BocaWest golf course.

WHERE TO STAY

4   BERKSHIRE BY THE SEA
125 N. Ocean Blvd., Delray Beach, FL 33444, 407-272-5045
Amenities: Pool, clubhouse with game rooms

Berkshire by the Sea is located across the street from the beach in Delray. Two distinct construction phases exist at the resort: the old section (three, two-story structures with ample size condo suites and fifteen floor plans to choose from) and the newer phase (a five-story building with standardized condos in one- and two-bedroom models). The furniture in the high-rise is in better condition, but all of the units are comfortably furnished. A large club-house/entertainment center with billiards, video games, and other activities for children and teenagers are available.

10 BOCA RATON RESORT & CLUB VILLAS
P. O. Box 225, Boca Raton, FL 33432, 407-395-3000
Amenities: Two pools (one for adults only, one for families),
beach club membership, golf, tennis, marina, restaurants

The Boca Raton Resort & Club is one of the most famous resorts in this section of Florida. Often it's simply called The Hotel. Its history is as legendary as its guests. The Hotel was built in 1926 as a Spanish Rococo "pink palace" and is located on 300 acres next to its own private 315 acre golf club. It's on the inland Waterway about a mile from the beach as the crow flies. The Boca Hotel has its own golf country club and three miles away is the super elegant, modern Beach Club. Both clubs are private for members and condo/hotel guests only and security insures this. The main part of the Hotel called The Cloister has marble passageways, carved wooden ceilings, potted palms and a pool-side setting designed more for entertaining than for swimming.

There are 120 private condo golf villas along the fairways. The two-bedroom villas have full kitchens, and you can also order room service from the Hotel. It is a perfect choice for families (wealthy families) or a golf foursome. Decor is controlled by the Hotel so don't expect the vacation-home atmosphere. The standardized decor is a disappointment. However, if you need extra service, just pick up the telephone and your wish will be granted.

Guests at the Boca Hotel have reciprocal privileges at BocaWest with its four golf courses, 29 tennis courts and superlative golf/tennis clinics. There are excellent programs for children.

9 BOCAWEST
7762 W. Glades Rd., P.O. Box 100, Boca Raton, FL 33434,
800-327-0137
Amenities: Pool, guest privileges at the Boca Hotel

Although the Boca Raton Hotel is geared towards people who enjoy the glamorous life, BocaWest is for those who want an athletic outdoors vacation. BocaWest features four championship golf courses and 33 tennis courts. Behind the private security gates, you enter a world of hushed conversations on the fairway or the rapid ping of an intense tennis match. The road is lined with moss-draped cypress and palms—a whole world away from the activity and traffic of Boca/Deerfield. There are 36 separate condo developments, or clusters, spread over the 1,428 acres of this master planned community. Each separate condo "village" is surrounded by woods, the golf course, or waterway, so you have a sense of individuality and privacy.

Most of the condos in BocaWest are for part-time residents. They are popular with executives from West Hartford, Winnetka, and Grosse Point. A few condos at BocaWest are available for short-term rental. Some of the individual developments have restrictions against rentals for less than three months. The two choices for those seeking to stay for only one month are **Arbor Lake** and the **Hammocks.** At Arbor Lake, the two-story buildings contain four condos: two upstairs and two downstairs. Individually furnished, this is one of the nation's most exclusive resort communities, and the interior decor reflects the taste of the individual owners. The condos each have two-bedrooms, and there is a small pool area for quiet sunbathing. The Hammocks are garden apartments in one and two-story buildings, each with a ground-level entrance. There's a small pool area, but the Hammocks have the advantage of being near the clubhouse and tennis pro shop.

The real advantage at BocaWest comes to those who pay for an additional guest membership at the club. The tennis and golf instruction programs are highly personalized and some of the best in Florida. At BocaWest you become known around the club quickly and lessons could be from the same pro—your choice—for a month or more. BocaWest offers tennis/golf clinics for special groups of beginners, children or juniors, as well as advanced amateur matches.

BocaWest has a reciprocity program with its sister resort, the Boca Raton Hotel, so guests there can use the Hotel's beach club.

9 CORONADO
3400 S. Ocean Blvd., Boca Raton, FL 33487, 407-272-4775
Amenities: Beach, pool

Located in the prestigious Highland Beach area of sleek, high-rise towers, the Coronado is the exception to the rule prohibiting short term rentals. This luxury building has 168 spacious two and three-bedroom condos overlooking the Intercoastal Waterway. The beach is across the street and there's a clubhouse reserved just for Coronado owners and guests. Inside, the condos are superbly decorated. Some have traditional furniture which once graced a home in New England. Others have a Florida look that comes from letting an interior decorator loose with $40,000.

5 DOVER HOUSE
110 S. Ocean Blvd., Delray Beach, FL 33444, 305-276-0309
Amenities: Beach, pool

Dover House consists of a lovely Bermuda-style building and courtyard setting with a Greek revival swimming pool. The condos have recently been redecorated with rose carpet and fabrics. Each condo has a private whirlpool tub. This resort achieves a gracious, peaceful ambiance.

8   INTERNATIONAL TENNIS RESORT OF DELRAY
651 Egret Cr., Delray Beach, FL 33444, 305-272-4126
Amenities: Tennis, pools, racquetball, health club, restaurant

Tennis, tennis, tennis. This resort is a super retreat for tennis players. There are 44 tennis courts spread over 100 acres, and 27 courts are lighted for night play. The USPTA pros offer individual instruction as well as tennis clinics. You'll find programs for beginners, children, and juniors. When you're not on the courts, you'll be able to shape up in the health club's exercise room, racquetball courts, one of the two Olympic-size swimming pools, or by jogging on the trails. The condos are attractive, but guests don't choose this resort because of the interior decor. The interior decor is comfortable with the clean, sleek lines of contemporary furnishings.

6   LA BOCA CASA
365 N. Ocean Blvd., Boca Raton, FL 33432
407-392-0885, $900/wk
Amenities: Pool

This project is a sleeper. It doesn't look like much from the street—just your average two-story condo building. It's not even on the beach; it's on the inland Waterway. But it will surprise and charm you! The condos are arranged in a Spanish courtyard style. Inside the cloister there's a romantic Mediterranean passageway. The condos are beautifully decorated with luxurious furnishings, lovely patterned fabrics, many tropical plants and even a wet bar. What about the beach? La Boca Casa is located across the street from South Beach Park, a county beach preserve that is one of the finest stretches of beach in Boca Raton, or for that matter, in Palm Beach County: it is wide with sand dunes, sea grass and lots of shells.

4   PALM BEACH RESORT
3031 South Ocean Blvd., Palm Beach, FL 33480, 800-424-1943
Amenities: Pool

Don't be fooled by this address. This resort is in Lake Worth, not in Palm Beach. Aside from this small deception, you'll find this to be a pleasant row of one and two-bedroom townhouse condos on a finger of land stretching into Lake Worth. Located right on the Intracoastal Waterway, the beach and the Lake Worth fishing pier is only a five minute walk away. Decor is island-style with rattan furniture and beige or off-white fabrics. Many units have seen their better days and it's time they were redecorated.

10 PALM BEACH POLO CLUB

131 Forest Hill Blvd., West Palm Beach, FL 33414, 407-798-7000
Studio $105–150, 1BR $130–174, 2BR $236–315, 3BR $336–450
Amenities: Golf, tennis, polo, horseback riding, squash,
racquetball, clubhouse, health club, pools

You've read about this resort in winter issues of *Town & Country* that discuss the spectacular parties and gatherings at The Polo Club. You must have seen the pictures when Charles, Prince of Wales, came to play. This is where the trend setters from New York, Saddle River, and Chevy Chase come to relax and be seen. Bring your diamonds and at the first sign of a cold front—unwrap your mink.

In spite of the hype, the Polo Club offers a warm country club environment ideally suited for a family vacation or an unforgettable honeymoon. World class equestrian events are held each season at the Polo Club where instruction in both English and hunt-seat riding styles is available. With 96 acres, there's a wide range of trail rides and this is one of the best riding schools available for children in the U.S. Polo classes are also available for beginners or intermediates. Not only do they really practice and play polo here, but golf may be even more popular on the resort's private 45 hole course. You can choose to play the enchanting Scottish Links course or brave the Dye-abolical new course designed by Pete and P.B. Dye. There are golf clinics, as well as informal "skins games." For people with other interests, a John Gardiner tennis center with 17 courts is available, as well as group or individual tennis instruction. This is a great place for children because during the school vacation periods, there are organized tennis and golf clinics for budding athletes. At the clubhouse you'll also find squash and racquetball courts, as well as a full-service health club. There's a wide range of accommodations to choose from at the Polo Club ranging from the bungalow style hotel rooms to four-bedroom villas along the fairways. The following describes some of the properties within the 2 square miles of this master resort community:

Chukker Cove — A private enclave of luxury two and three-bedroom units with high ceilings, bright open living rooms, deluxe kitchens and large curved patios where you can watch the golfers pass by.

Wimbledon Patio Lodges — These units surround the 17 tennis courts and social life centers around the Tennis Club House and its pool. Young, active and exclusive.

Bagatelle — This is a neighborhood of attractive two-story buildings surrounding a park area with the diamond-shaped pool as the centerpiece.

Polo Island Condominiums — Bordered by a lagoon and close to the Polo Clubhouse, these are convenient for those who want to be near the equestrian center and its training facilities.

Polo Island Estate Homes — These villas are more Californian in appearance than Floridian. Designed for luxury living, these are top of the line with interior designer decor. Each has a private patio and pool.

8 **SEAGATE HOTEL & BEACH CLUB**
400 S. Ocean Blvd., Delray Beach, FL 33483, 407-276-2421
Studio $59–129, 1BR $69–199, 2BR $109–259, 3BR $229–425
Amenities: Beach club, pools

Located across the street from the beach in quiet, upper-crust Delray, this pleasant resort offers condos in a two-story building designed in a U-shape around the swimming pool. This is a peaceful resort where children are seen only at school vacation time visiting grandparents. The attraction here is the private beach club across the street which is available to Seagate guests. There's a freshwater and salt water pool at the beach club. Lots of service is available, including a 24-hour front office and switchboard. One perk: complimentary newspapers in the morning. The interior decor of the condos tends to be pleasant and well maintained in a style popular 25 years ago.

7 **SPANISH RIVER RESORT**
111 East Atlantic Ave., Delray Beach, FL 33444, 305-243-SWIM
Studio $70–90, 1BR $95, 2BR $150–165
Amenities: Beach across the street

One of this year's biggest surprises is the rebirth of this landmark in the heart of Delray. Located on the corner of Atlantic Avenue (the main east-west artery) and Ocean Drive, across the street from the beach park, this is the only high-rise in Delray. Within walking distance of Delray's exclusive shops, this is perhaps your best choice in South Florida if you don't have a car. In past editions we spoke of the need for change and someone surely heeded our advice. The resort is in the midst of a major refurbishment program which began with the lobby and pool areas, and now extends to remodeling many of the condo units.

Check-in is a treat with courteous management that wants you to become a member of the family. The pool, saunas, and tennis court are on the second floor plaza level. Upstairs many of the units have been recently redecorated with crisp, contemporary furniture using blond woods and pastel fabrics. Spanish River's most distinctive feature is the huge arched windows that bring the ocean view inside.

Word of the renovation has spread slowly so this is one of the area's best values—underpriced when you consider all it has to offer.

7 **VENTURA**
2301 S. Ocean Blvd., Boca Raton, FL 33432, 800-323-3001
Amenities: Heated pool, hot tub. Beach across street.

Ventura is composed of Spanish style townhouses arranged in a land-scaped garden which surround a swimming pool. The resort is exceptional because it exists in an area dominated by high-rise development but has maintained ground-level entry. The red tile roofed condos are comfortable and practical for vacationers of all ages. No activities programs are offered.

10. BROWARD and DADE COUNTIES
(Deerfield, Pompano, Ft. Lauderdale, and Miami)

Once upon a time this was America's favorite playground. Wealthy vacationers from suburban New York made plans for the season and of course, the children would come down for Christmas vacation. Frankie Avalon and Connie Francis made movies of the Ft. Lauderdale beach parties at spring break. Later, the Galt Ocean Mile glistened with sleek high-rise towers harboring elegant condos. Low-rise colonies of condos and bunga-lows hovered around the tennis courts and pool activity of the Silver Thatch or the Sea Ranch. In fact, way back in 1929 when the Hollywood Beach Hotel (now a condominium) first opened its doors, this was the statement of elegance for Broward County.

During the 1970s and '80s time seemed to pass this area by. It became a suburb of commercial Miami and many vacationers went off to new resorts. But today the beach is bringing them back. Urban growth is to the west in the Pembroke Pines area and today the beach resort atmosphere is returning to Broward County.

There are three distinct resort areas. The first is that of north Broward County including Pompano and Deerfield Beach. High-rises only recently have crept into this area of single-story beach bungalows. Popular with retirees, this is a quiet area of golf courses and tennis courts. The resort properties are those along the narrow strip of Highway A1A (also called Ocean Boulevard) between the Atlantic Ocean and the Intracoastal Waterway. Even if you are not on the beach, it's only a block away and it's pleasant in the late afternoon to watch the boats parade by and to check the owners in the *Registry of Yachts*.

The second area includes the south Broward County beachfront properties of Ft. Lauderdale and Hollywood Beach. Ft. Lauderdale has a strip of high-rise condos which are now more residential in nature than vacation-oriented. Firm and secure, the condo rentals in Lauderdale generally are superior, with sweeping ocean views. Hollywood Beach is dominated by the pink stucco confection of the Hollywood Beach Hotel condos and its Oceanwalk Mall. Radiating away are a series of motels and inexpensive two-story beachfront condos.

The third area is Dade County. Once upon a time this was one of the most glamorous resort areas in Florida, In the '70s, Miami was bypassed for resort development, and in the '80s it emerged as an urban area. Nevertheless, there still is no place like it. Everything is on Collins Avenue that begins with the lower numbers at the southern end and progresses upward as you move north. Today the southern end is fighting urban decay with a renovation program that brings out the best of the area's Art Deco heritage.

In Broward and Dade Counties there is a strong prejudice against short term condo rentals and most luxury condos only permit the owner to rent the condo once a year for a minimum of three months. The condos we have described in this section all permit short-term rentals for a week, or even less. You'll find all to be reasonably priced although some suffer from poor management, causing you to play hide and seek for service.

Air transportation to this area couldn't be easier. Nearby Miami International is one of the busiest airports in the world and Ft. Lauderdale handles almost as many domestic visitors bound for this area. The distance between these two airports is only 45 minutes. West Palm Beach is a third major airport, one hour and fifteen minutes north of Ft. Lauderdale. Without exception, Ft. Lauderdale is the choice for convenience, but Miami may offer cheaper flights and non-stops direct to your home town.

WHERE TO STAY...
POMPANO BEACH / DEERFIELD BEACH

4   **AVALON**
735 S. Highway A1A, Deerfield Beach, FL 33441, 305-427-6611
Amenities: Pool, putting green

Avalon is an attractive condo complex located across the street from the ocean. The main building is three stories high and surrounds a putting green and swimming pool. The property is located on the Inland Waterway across the street from the beach. The condos were recently redecorated and the clubhouse was just remodeled. Each unit has a private balcony. Designed for couples in need of relaxation, it is as suitable for grandparents as it is for their grandchildren.

6   **BEACHCOMBER HOTEL & VILLAS**
1200 S. Ocean Blvd., Pompano Beach, FL 33062, 305-941-7830
1BR $85, 2BR $120
Amenities: Beach, pool, children's pool, restaurant

Located right on the beach, this family-run hotel also offers studio apartments as well as one and two-bedroom villas for rent. This property is unique because there are so few single-story bungalows in this Pompano Beach area. It has become a popular, almost clubby enclave, where the same guests return year after year. The one and two bedrooms are cozy in design and simply decorated with contemporary furniture. Expect to find lots of pink and cool mint fabrics. The kitchenettes are small but adequate. Best of all is the ambiance around the pool where you'll find "Old Timers" to tell you about the best places to fish or golf in the area.

4 BERKSHIRE BEACH CLUB
500 N. Ocean Blvd., Deerfield Beach, FL 33441, 305-428-1000
$475–500/wk
Amenities: Beach, pool

Located at the very northern end of Deerfield Beach, this property really should have a Boca Raton address. The condo structure is a two-story U-shape that surrounds the swimming pool and courtyard. Located on the beach, this has an established clientele that returns year after year. The units are comfortably furnished, but don't expect anything contemporary or lavish. The golf courses of Boca Raton are a stone's throw away.

5 CANADA HOUSE
1704 N. Ocean Blvd., Pompano Beach, FL 33441, 305-942-8200
$44–99
Amenities: Beach, lagoon, pool

Canada House is located on the beach in a beautiful setting. However, nature played a trick—a small sandbar, separated from the mainland in front of the property, created a small lagoon. The potential problem was solved by building a bridge over the lagoon to the sandbar. Thus, the property is distinct and even romantic. It is possible to fish or paddle around the lagoon. This is a large resort with a high-rise tower and two small wings around the pool. The condos are fully furnished but the furniture is aging. The resort environment is good, but the accommodations are quite small. A nice setting, but after a couple of days, you'll feel the need for more space.

7 DEER CREEK PLANTATION
2345 W. Hillsboro Blvd., Deerfield Beach, FL 33442
(No mail receptacle)
Amenities: Pool

Just over the line from Boca Raton, this master-planned community in Broward County looks and feels like Boca Raton real estate. Deer Creek is a 600-acre master-planned community consisting of eleven condo developments that surround an 18-hole golf course. Most of the condos are part-time residences for Yankees who want some winter sun. Some are available for short-term vacation rentals with a two-week minimum; some are townhouses; and others are apartments in two- or three-story buildings. A few are single-story villas or bungalows. Each condo has been individually decorated by the owner and there is no way to characterize the interior decor. Each condo development has its own private pool. Deer Creek is a golf/tennis community (guest membership costs extra) and offers an attractive setting for a Gold Coast vacation. Deer Creek Plantation provides quiet vacation home where you'll have privacy and be left alone.

6 **EMBASSY SUITES—DEERFIELD**
950 S.E. 20th Ave., Deerfield Beach, FL 33441, 305-426-0478
1BR $85–160
Amenities: Beach, pool, sauna

Located on the beach in Deerfield, this offers good value and an excellent location. Convenient to both Boca Raton and Ft. Lauderdale, this has a tropical ambiance not usually found in a chain hotel. The semicircular drive leads to a salmon building with aqua trim and lots of palms. The Florida-style lobby is tropical also with pictures of polo matches from days gone by. This all-suite hotel lacks the individual character that one associates with private villas or condos. However, it's a good alternative in an area that is short on condos available for short-term rentals of less than a week. We have included this property since there are so few resorts in this area offering short-term rentals.

2 **EMERALD SEAS RESORT**
660 N. Ocean Blvd., Deerfield Beach, FL 33441, 305-427-1300
Amenities: Pool

This resort is located two blocks from the beach and almost next to the Intracoastal Waterway. Emerald Seas is a small apartment hotel tucked away in a cluster of wooden homes dating from the '40s. This is "downtown" Deerfield Beach where the town originally began, but most of the businesses packed up and left years ago. There's a certain wayward charm to this neighborhood that is a quiet testimonial to Old Florida, but it hasn't yet been discovered by the Yuppies who want to renovate and make it cute. Interior decor is very casual; '60s motel style. It remains a good location for an inexpensive holiday.

5 **INN AT DEER CREEK**
9 Deer Creek Rd., Deerfield Beach, FL 33443, 305-421-7800
Studio $59–69, 1BR $69–79
Amenities: Pool, hot tub

The Inn at Deer Creek is a small development consisting of two-story garden apartments. Located over the line from Boca Raton and BocaWest, these are the only condos in this golf/tennis area available for daily rentals. The condos include an upstairs bedroom and kitchen/living room downstairs. They are well designed, and also feature a private whirlpool for two in the master bath. Given the exceptionally good location and golf/tennis resort advantages, the interior decor is disappointing. You'll be overwhelmed by the dark colors, heavy woodwork, and all the mirrors that make the space seem larger. The furniture is a little worn and there are steelcase tables and chairs in the kitchen/dining area. If you can overlook the decor, there are genuine advantages to staying here. Be sure to get a guest membership for the Deer Creek golf or tennis clubs.

5   LA COSTA BEACH CLUB
1504 N. Ocean Blvd., Pompano Beach, FL 33062, 305-942-4900
Amenities: Beach, indoor and outdoor pools, tennis

La Costa is located at the north end of Pompano Beach near the Hillsboro inlet and lighthouse. It is an unusual complex because there appear to be three construction periods. There are twelve different floor plans. Many of the condos are two-story, one-bedroom townhouses with a bedroom upstairs and a living room/kitchen downstairs. They have private entrances on the ground level. The other condos located in the large tower building are similar to suites and have the advantage of ocean views. Take your pick. A beach and three pools (one indoor) are available.

8   LIGHTHOUSE COVE
1406 N. Ocean Blvd., Pompano Beach, FL 33062, 305-941-3410
Amenities: Beach, pool, restaurant, tennis

The Lighthouse Cove is a great resort for couples and young families. It is on the beach and features an expansive pool area, a palm-thatched poolside bar, and a trendy restaurant. The condos are located in a seven-story concrete structure in the form of suites and apartments, that are cheerfully decorated, albeit a little on the small side. Each condo has a private balcony that, usually overlooks the ocean. In addition, there are several night spots nearby for evening entertainment.

7+   ROYAL FLAMINGO VILLAS
1225 Hillsboro Mile, Deerfield Beach, FL 33442
Amenities: Pool, tennis. Beach across the street.

Long favored by Canadians, these red tile roofed, single-story bungalows are cute. Scattered in a garden setting across the street from the beach, this single-story beach house environment is hard to find in South Florida. Some day the Royal Flamingo will be sold and a new high-rise will sprout in its place. Until then, you can enjoy what is at once a romantic and a very convenient vacation spot. Interior deco is very casual with tile floors and simple furnishings. Who cares? You'll want to sit on your patio and watch a chameleon climb a palm, or wander over to the beach and listen to the surf. These villas are a rare find along the Gold Coast.

8   SEABONAY BEACH RESORT
  1159 Hillsboro Mile, Hillsboro Beach, FL 33062
  Amenities: Beach, pool

This quiet, two-story apartment building is right on the beach in the semi-exclusive Hillsboro section. To the south, there are the million dollar homes of the Hillsboro mile. To the north, there's a strip of condos and motels for a mile and then the Palm beach county line into Boca Raton. This suite hotel offers studios, and one- and two-bedroom apartments for rent by the day week or month. Each has a view of the ocean, but the oceanfront units are superior. Several years ago the beach was washed away. It has slowly returned so now there is a pleasant area for adults and children to play in the surf. The only drawback is the interior decor—island style with rattan furniture and fabrics we haven't seen since the '70s. A relaxing place to stay right on the ocean in a prestigious area, you'll understand why this unpretentious resort in a great location is called "Hometown paradise."

9   SILVER THATCH OCEAN CLUB
  510 N. Ocean Blvd., Pompano Beach, FL 33062
  Amenities: Beach, tennis, pool, restaurant

Don't be confused by the name. This is a busy resort with two high-rise towers. Once upon a time this was a seaside inn catering to tennis players. In the 1960s it became a local sensation when a glass wall was built into the side of the swimming pool so guests at the bar could watch the swimmers under water. Much of the old, clubby style remains, but today the Silver Thatch property is graced by twin high-rise condo towers at either end. Now you can enjoy the comfort of a condo with a kitchen and, at the same time, participate in all the activities on the courts, by the pool, or on the beach. These new units are handsomely decorated with blond wood or rattan furniture covered in smart Florida floral print patterns. The soft curves and geometric styles create a new art-deco feeling in some units. Although the condos are superior and the location is superb, the best feature is that "good old times" feeling around the inn. This resort is exceptional.

RENTAL RESOURCES
Andes Realty, 305-427-2700
Campbell & Rosemurgy, 305-427-8686
Deer Creek Real Estate, 305-421-8333

WHERE TO STAY...
FT. LAUDERDALE / HOLLYWOOD

6   **THE BREAKERS**
909 Breakers Ave., Ft. Lauderdale, FL 33304
305-566-8800, Studio $65–85, 1BR $80–115
Amenities: Heated pool, children's playground, restaurant

The Breakers is a seventeen-story tower in the heart of Ft. Lauderdale—a couple of blocks from the beach. Yet, because it is in a cul-de-sac, you are not aware of being in the center of Ft. Lauderdale. Also, there are no problems with traffic or noise. The location seems to be the best of both worlds. It is a good resort for couples, families, and even the business traveler. All of the condos in this high-rise have been set up as suites. Some appear to have more space because of Murphy beds that fold into the wall during the day. Half of the units have ocean views and all have private balconies. The interiors are spacious and modern. All of the condos have been recently redecorated with soft tropical colors, mirrors, and lots of silk flowers. The condos are smaller than average and although the pool is tiny, it draws a lot of use, especially in the afternoons during bingo.

5   **COCONUT BAY RESORT**
919 N. Birch Rd., Ft. Lauderdale, FL 33304, 305-563-4229
Amenities: Pool

A few blocks from the beach and a block from Ft. Lauderdale's McArthur Park, Coconut Bay Resort takes advantage of its location on the waterway. It began as a converted motel structure, but all of the units were rebuilt into condos with kitchenettes. Interior decor is new and trendy with lots of rose and blue hues. The pool is a real social center; Roman columns here create a fantasy effect at night. Coconut Bay has a mixture of short-term vacationing guests and long-term part-time residents. You'll even find a few business executives who have taken a short-term lease.

7   **EMBASSY SUITES—FT. LAUDERDALE**
1100 S.E. 17th St. Causeway, Ft. Lauderdale, FL 33316
305-527-2700, 1BR $79–129
Amenities: Pool, health club, restaurant

So many vacationers want a condo on the beach in Ft. Lauderdale, but most condos in this area restrict rentals to a three-month minimum. For this reason we have included an all-suite hotel as an alternative for those who seek the comforts of home on a vacation. This Mediterranean-style tropical oasis is a mile from the beach and close to the cruise ships of Port Everglades. This "pink palace" has tile floors and a waterfall cascading into a tropical lagoon where swans float gracefully. Lush landscaping makes the picture even more romantic. Built traditionally around a twelve-story atrium, each one-bedroom suite has a small living room, kitchenette, bathroom, bedroom and balcony. Not personalized or distinctive, these suites offer the homogenized benefits which many are looking for in Ft. Lauderdale.

7   **GALT OCEAN CLUB**
3800 Galt Ocean Dr., Ft. Lauderdale, FL 33308
Amenities: Beach, pool, hot tub, clay tennis court

Once the most prestigious address in Ft. Lauderdale, the Galt Ocean Mile was allowed to decay. Recently developers have rediscovered the enduring appeal of this beach front real estate. The Galt Ocean Club is a brand new eleven-story condominium tower where the condos have balconies overlooking the ocean. There is a handsome free-form landscaped pool and a clay tennis court. They've added smashing interior decor with pastel fabrics, potted palms, and all new appliances, even VTPs. The major effort to rejuvenate Ft. Lauderdale's beachfront has worked.

7+   **HOLLYWOOD BEACH HOTEL**
101 N. Ocean Blvd., Hollywood, FL 33019, 800-331-6103
Studio $55–150, 1BR $105–175
Amenities: Beach, heated pool, hot tub, exercise room

This is the Queen of Hollywood Beach. This pink cotton confection was born in 1927. The condo/hotel was recently renovated, remodeled, and reopened in early 1988. The interiors are beautifully furnished with pink and rose designer fabrics. There are several mirrors that bring the ocean view inside each suite. The studios have Murphy beds that are closed in the morning by the maid. In this way, more space is available during the day. The first floor has been converted into the Oceanwalk Mall which is the place to go in Hollywood. A new outdoor heated pool area includes a hot tub spa. This resort is warm, friendly, and an exciting place for a vacation. It combines the right amount of suite space and privacy with the best of Hollywood's beach activities. The management is superlative.

6+   **LAGO MAR**
1700 S. Ocean Lane, Ft. Lauderdale, FL 33316
Amenities: Pool, tennis, putting green, restaurant. Beach nearby

Separated from the beach by a small lagoon, Lago Mar is located on a thirteen-acre peninsula that is an island of peace and calm in Ft. Lauderdale. This area landmark has just been renovated from top to bottom to create a contemporary look. Part is a hotel and intermixed on the floors are studio and one-bedroom condos. A little on the small side, these are perfect for those who plan a lengthy stay in Ft. Lauderdale and who want all the services, amenities, and restaurants of a major hotel. There's a cabana on the beach for Lago Mar guests.

7   OCEAN MANOR
4040 Galt Ocean Dr., Ft. Lauderdale, FL 33308
Amenities: Beach, pool, coffee shop

These beachfront condominiums occupy one of the best sites along the beach at Ft. Lauderdale. Once an exclusive area in the 1950s, time passed this one by. Then in the 1980s someone discovered the value of this beachfront real estate and Ocean Manor was completely renovated. Today this eleven-story landmark offers a quiet and distinctive environment. Not the place for college students, Ocean Manor is where you'll see grandparents playing with young children on the beach or by the pool. The lobby is impressive with a Banana Republic look, glassed-in marble, carved woodwork, and elephant tusks! Don't tell these people about today's "Save the Planet" crusade. Each condo is individually decorated and some are much better than others. They all have spacious living rooms with ocean views. Some have been decorated with colorful coral or canary yellow prints. Others are more sedate. This is a great location for Ft. Lauderdale.

WHERE TO STAY... DADE COUNTY

4   BEEKMAN TOWERS
9499 Collins Ave., Surfside, FL 33121
Amenities: Beach, heated pool

Beekman Towers, located on a wide strip of white, sandy beach offers daily rentals. It is only a block away from the elegant shops of Bal Harbour. A good reception is given by the management, but the condos need new furniture.

7+   CRYSTAL BEACH CLUB
6985 Collins Ave., Miami Beach, FL 33141, 305-865-9555
Amenities: Beach

We hope this is a harbinger of good things to come. Miami Beach has all the potential to regain its former glory as a glittering vacation destination—sun, sand, restaurants, and lots of things to do. The hoteliers here failed to change with the times so Miami Beach was overlooked until a few boutique hotels created today's dazzling art deco fad. Sadly, however, the traditional hotel room remains in vogue with only this new timeshare entry—a four-story pink stucco confection designed for your mind's eye. We saw one unit where the bedroom—bedspread, walls, ceiling, and chairs were all covered in vividly patterned fabric. With all the mirrors, it reminded us of Mardi Gras. The living room, however, is more sedate with a luscious green carpet and watermelon fabrics on the sofas—spritely and exciting. The Crystal Beach Club oozes romance, as well as being a convenient hostelry for a family on vacation. We hope there will be more condo or condo-style resorts like this one!

10 FISHER ISLAND
One Fisher Island Dr., Fisher Island, FL 33109, 800-537-3708
1BR $300, 2BR $500–800, 3BR $975
Amenities: Golf, tennis, pool, hot tubs

This is a unique resort on a 216-acre island in the middle of Biscayne Bay. Only ten minutes from downtown Miami, this is a sheltered world protected from the mainland by tight security. Entrance to this private island is permitted only for owners and renters. Formerly the home of William Vanderbilt, the island has been transformed into an exclusive country club condominium community. Vanderbilt's mansion has been preserved as a clubhouse with a pool, seventeen tennis courts, and a nine hole golf course. Some of the condos are actually buildings dating from the time of Vanderbilt ownership. The servants' quarters and Rosemary's cottage today are splashy condominiums. The elegant interior decors feature both Miami's Art Deco style and the more traditional "floral Florida" look. This is what happens when you turn an interior decorator loose with a per unit budget of $80,000. Each condo has a private hot tub on the patio or balcony. These villas are very expensive, but very deluxe.

7 GOLDEN STRAND RESORT
17901 Collins Ave., Sunny Isles, FL 33160, 305-931-7000
Studio $55, 1BR $100, 2BR $125–200
Amenities: Beach, pool, snack bar, playground

Si vous parlez français, vous devrez aimer cet endroit. A French speaking colony right in the heart of South Florida, Golden Strand Resort stands on a beautiful stretch of sand. The setting is perfect. Two six-story buildings, each with a balcony at an angle, preserve privacy, yet allow ocean views. They surround a courtyard and a swimming pool area that is landscaped with coconut palms. All the condos are attractively decorated with bright colors and fully furnished with all you desire in a vacation home, but the two-bedroom villa units are the best. The resort owners are primarily from Québec, however, a high number of European visitors are attracted to this cosmopolitan atmosphere. Bikini tops just seem to fall off by the pool. This is a beautifully maintained property and convenient to the Gulfstream Race Track, home of the Florida Derby.

4 RONEY PLAZA
2301 Collins Ave., Miami, FL 33139, 305-531-8811
Studio $94, 1BR $136, 2BR $178
Amenities: Beach, pool, sauna, restaurant

Roney Plaza, located at the south end of the beach, is a landmark hotel in Miami Beach that has been converted into full size condominiums. Although close to the convention center and the renovated of Art Deco buildings, we're sad to report that the Art Deco facelift recently bestowed upon Miami Beach has not yet happened at the Roney Plaza. It is a good place for adults, but families with small children would be better off elsewhere. The lobby is pretentiously designed with marble floors and crystal chandeliers. The upstairs interior decor features white and gold styles that were popular in the early '60s. The units are designed well and a pleasant pool area is available. The best feature here is a management that wants you to have an exceptional vacation so you'll return year after year. You'll find this style quite different from the commercialism of today's South Florida. Adults who want the convenience of a condo near Miami's artist community might choose this.

11. THE FLORIDA KEYS

There's no other place in the U.S. like the Florida Keys. More like the Caribbean than the U.S., these islands are connected to the mainland by Highway 1. Life moves slowly here and there's an appreciation for nature's fragile qualities: the pinkish glow in the sunrise, the delicate one-legged stance of an egret, the clear waters and brightly colored coral reefs teeming with fish. First and foremost, this is a divers' paradise. Fishermen also love these waters because just off-shore the Atlantic meets the Gulf of Mexico so there's an abundance of game fish at this intersection. You'll see uninhabited cays and sailboats on the horizon made famous by Ernest Hemingway. A new breed of traveler has discovered this Margaritavilla of Jimmy Buffet's lyrics.

Addresses in the Keys are given in terms of mile markers along U.S. Highway 1, the thread that binds these islands together. The distance from Miami is 120 miles and all reference points in the Keys are from Key West where the center of downtown is zero or "0." Heading north you'll pass Sugarloaf Key, an island out of the mainstream that is favored by bird and nature lovers. Continuing north you'll pass Newfound Harbor Key, 28 miles north of Key West, where guests relish the privacy and seclusion of this location.

Marathon Key with 10,000 residents, is teeming with activity at Mile Marker 48. One look at the DC3's on the runway and you'll think you're in a developing country. Not as sophisticated as Key West, Marathon has its own style and is the center for fishing, diving, and sailing charters. Farther north at Mile Marker 61 there's Duck Key with the famous Hawk's Cay Resort. Here you can actually swim in the lagoon and be a part of the dolphin encounter. Islamorada at Mile Marker 75 to 82 has the only golf course found in the Keys. This is where former President Bush comes for recreational fishing in winter.

Finally at Mile Marker 100 there's Key Largo. A transitional island, it's closest to the mainland in both distance and spirit. Here the tempo is much slower than Atlanta or Jacksonville, but it's positively "rushed" when judged by the standards of a local conch from Key West. Don't miss the John Pennecamp Underwater State Park. Only in Hawaii or the Virgin Islands will you find an experience to compare. Designed for novices as well as experts, there are glass bottom boat trips as well as an underwater snorkeling trail. Many diving and fishing charters also operate from Key Largo which has a friendly harbor.

The Where to Stay portion of this section on the Florida Keys has been organized into three parts, grouped around the nearest major town or transportation "hub." For example, you'll find that two resorts in the southern end of the Keys are private islands where guests can literally escape from the pressures of the 20th century into an ageless time warp. Although not in Key West, the nearest major town selected is the closest center for transportation or serious grocery shopping. The three subsections are: Key West, Marathon, and Key Largo/Islamorada.

Transportation to this area is both easy and difficult. Key West is a tedious four hour drive from Miami where speed limits on the causeway sometimes are as low as 35 MPH. Key Largo is an easy one hour drive from the Miami airport. Islamorada is only an additional thirty minutes farther south, but Marathon, Duck Key, and Key West are another story. You might want to consider the convenience of a commuter flight from Miami to either Key West or Marathon.

KEY WEST

Residents of Key West are called "conchs" and cruising the beaches, bars and bistros is an acceptable way to spend your days here. Although all the Keys enjoy good weather and great diving opportunities, many choose Key West because it offers so much to do. First timers enjoy the Conch train and touring the historic homes. Repeat visitors are more likely to return to some of the Jimmy Buffet style watering holes that give Key West its flavor. The town's sophistication and eclectic style attracts celebrities as well as vacationers from all walks of life. Today, there's a good chance you'll find one of the streets blocked for the filming of some new movie or a segment from the television series, "Key West." The restaurants have an international flavor with lots of spice and the downtown streets often resemble the French Quarter in the evenings when they seem to host a large outdoor party. There are a number of sailing, diving, and fishing excursions offered each day. A trip to an uninhabited island or a dive in the remains of one of the 300 wrecks that dot the coral encrusted ocean floor are typical of the Key West daily offering. But the best part of the day is sunset when the breeze is gentle and the sky slowly turns orange, then pink, then blue. A vacation in Key West is an unforgettable experience and there's a wide range of accommodations from budget to luxury, yet all have an eye to romance and escapist fantasy.

WHERE TO STAY

9 1800 ATLANTIC
1800 Atlantic Blvd., Key West, FL 33040, 800-732-2006
1BR $95–150, 2BR $100–150
Amenities: Pool, health club, racquetball, tennis

This is the perfect choice for those who want comfort and luxury in one of Key West's most respectable environments. Part of the charm of Key West is its offbeat nature but it also accommodates those who prefer to return in the evening to the world from whence they came. These two-bedroom condos are not the fanciest in Key West but they come close. 1800 Atlantic is a tropical paradise island resort located just five minutes away from the commercial atmosphere of Old Key West. It is oceanfront, but like most resorts in the Key West area, only a small patch of hard packed sand exists. The landscaping makes this resort seem like a tropical paradise. You will discover plenty of mangrove trees, palms, and sea oats. The condos are located in a modern five-story building. Each unit has an ocean view and mirrors bring the view inside.They are fancifully decorated with Oriental art pieces and Arabian throw pillows that give each condo an added touch of paradise. The master bath has a sunken whirlpool tub large enough for two. Lots of activities including racquetball, tennis and a teaching pro are offered. This is one of the best all-around, wholesome choices in the Keys. It is just as good for a second honeymoon as it is for spring break with the children.

✆ ACCOMMODATIONS CENTER
816 Eaton St, Key West, FL 33040, 800-732-2006

For villa, guesthouse, or condo rentals, this reservations agency will find just what you need. Extending as far out as Key Largo, their homes include exotic estates as well as family oriented cottage compounds. There is no reason to spend $300 a night for a hotel room when you can save money by renting a luxury home with three bedrooms, a secluded pool, and your own private beach. And don't think you're intruding on someone else's life—all of these properties were designed to be vacation fantasies that take your thoughts away to another world. Some of the homes you can rent range from:

Crisp and Clean — This private estate includes two separate cottages that share a courtyard with pool and hot tub. The large house has three bedrooms. Architecturally, it has been stripped bare so you are alone in a two-story white shell. Trimmed with oak, the effect is spare, simple, and almost Japanese. The Hopi pot, the Navajo jug, and the painting of Taos are the only three objects with a dash of color in the entire house. Otherwise the, simple furniture and beds blend into the outlines of the house so well that you are unaware of the furniture. What an impact upon the eye. The third bedroom is an upstairs loft reached by stepladder—only suggested for the young and the restless. The smaller home again has the same spare simplicity but is much more feminine with its floral fabrics.

Incentra Carriage Houses — These three cottages surround a pool and are hidden by one of Key West's largest private tropical gardens. Our favorite is the Tree House where your deck is built into the heart of an ancient Sopadilla tree. Laze in the hammock surrounded by branches and listen to the call of the wild. This studio unit has two double beds, a large living area, and a full kitchen. The main Bahamian-style house has been carved into a series of one and two bedroom units. Decorated with antiques and special touches like four poster beds, we think this is the "tree house" for those of us who don't want to grow up.

Travelers Palm — A rare find for families and the budget conscious, this collection of five bungalows is tucked away in a lush tropical garden. Each is small and cute with space for two, four, or six. These wooded Conch homes have been brought to life by fresh fabrics and floral prints. On one hand it's a timeless setting; on the other it has contemporary comfort. Cross ventilation has been maximized but each cottage has a unit air conditioner. What makes this stand out is the pool and the children's play area, a rarity in sophisticated Key West. Management offers a complimentary breakfast by the pool in the morning with freshly baked homemade bread. You can always retreat to the privacy of your own kitchen, however.

Villa Casa Roma — This celebrity home has been a guesthouse for political leaders in the Roosevelt, Truman, and Eisenhower eras—as well as a vacation home for Barbara Streisand and Don Johnson. Located on an inlet, there is no beach. But Don Johnson was so enamored with this retreat for his Key West sojourns, that he had the owner create a private sand beach with tropical palms. Retaining that vacation home of the "'40s" style, you'll find alcoves, a sun room, and a well stocked library and video entertainment center. Nothing is ostentatious. Everything is done to perfection and is in balance. The private black bottom pool is a great place to laze and watch the egrets on the other side of the inlet.

The Winter Garden — Remember the opening scene of *License Revoked* when James Bond comes forging over the garden wall, through the banana and hibiscus bushes, to rescue the damsel in distress? Remember the wedding ceremony at the luxurious Key West home? Both of these scenes were filmed on the premises of the Winter Garden that has one of the largest private gardens in Key West. This in-town estate, hidden behind a nine-foot wall, is quite a surprise. It is a collection of cute Conch houses that can be rented separately, or as an entire estate. You'll find a mixture of styles with each room designed to dazzle the eye. The all-black walls of the kitchen are framed by rows of bleached white conch shells. One bedroom looks like a Thai cottage, while another is a blend of Burma and Boston. Cross-ventilation, aided by paddle fans, keeps the rooms cool. Out in back you'll find a landscaped free-form pool, and just off the master bedroom there's a deck and a very private hot tub for two. Designed for the senses, you won't forget this one.

6   THE BANYAN RESORT
323 Whitehead St., Key West, FL 33040, 305-294-9573
Studio $95–125, 1BR $110–160, 2BR $125–180
Amenities: Pools and garden

This resort is set in a residential neighborhood close to the home of James Audubon. It is a five-minute walk from the restaurants or Sloppy Joe's Bar in downtown Key West. It is composed of six three-story "conch" style homes that have been redesigned on the inside to offer striking suite accommodations. The garden is lush, tropical, and hides two small pools. The effect is languid decadence. The Banyan is the place to go if you plan to read a good book by the pool under the shade of bananas and palms. Almost New Orleans in style, the Banyan was designed with a touch of whimsy. The units are each individual. Some have two-story living rooms with a spiral staircase leading to the loft sleeping area. Some have small kitchenettes. The houses in this resort are in the National Register of Historic Places. Children under 18 are not allowed.

7   COCONUT BEACH RESORT
1500 Alberta St, Key West, FL 33040, 305-294-0057
1BR $125–170
Amenities: Pool, hot tub

Brand new in 1991, this three-story Conch-style building exudes Key West from the outside; the snaz of Orlando on the inside. These 30 two bedroom, two bath units are a little on the small side although mirrors and silk flowers have been generously used as a remedy. What surprised us is the lack of both beach and coconuts. The pool area is bordered by a concrete and boulder breakwater. For beach lovers, this is only a five-minute walk from the Monroe County Beach. Although a lovely building with potential, we found the atmosphere marred by an aggressive timeshare sales plan. Otherwise this could be one of the best condo resorts in Key West.

 COCONUTS
Summerland Key, FL (no mail)

Coconuts is one of the most extraordinary vacation homes that we've ever seen. So many of the most exclusive and fabulous residences are hidden among the small keys north of Key West that it's impossible to describe each one. But this rates mention on its own. The entrance is a carved Balinese gate. Once you step inside, you'll think you should make a temple offering. This home consists of three separate pavilions surrounding a 25-meter lap pool. Standing on the beach and looking at the estate with the pavilions reflected in the water, you'll be reminded of the Taj Mahal. Each pavilion has its own carved Balinese gate/archway facing the pool. Let's start with the main house. It has a large modern kitchen, including three ovens, and it's perfect for entertaining. The interior wall is lined with mirrors that bring in the view of the pool, garden, and beach. The living room contains pieces of Thai and Indonesian furniture that enhance the initial romantic impression. Between the living room and the beach, there's a large screened sleeping porch that doubles as a library during the day. The master bedroom, however, is quite a surprise with leopard-patterned carpeting and genuine Queen Anne and Regency antiques—imported direct from the owner's country manor home in England.

The other pavilion across the pool contains two bedrooms. The oceanside bedroom is authentically Balinese with plank wood floors and Balinese garudas for spiritual protection. The second bedroom has air conditioning and is slightly more of this century. Each has skylights, screens, and lattice walls. The bathrooms have been built to appear as separate additions. The glass roofs create the effect that you are bathing outside. To stay in this pavilion is to be at once in a delicately contrived artistic environment—and in harmony with nature. The centerpiece pavilion faces directly out over the pool to the beach and beyond. Here you really will feel as though you are in a Balinese temple because of the custom made Indonesian wood carvings. There is a live palm tree growing right next to your bed and on through the roof. Rentals of all this fantasy are available through the Accommodations Center in Key West.

8 THE GALLEON
617 Front St., Key West, FL 33040, 800-544-3030
1BR $115–150, 2BR $230–300
Amenities: Marina, tiny sand beach, pool, health club

This resort combines an urban setting with a dynamite location on the water. There is a postage stamp-size beach which is a luxury around the coral shores of Key West. This resort, located at the end of Front Street in downtown Key West, looks like the neighboring Hyatt Hotel. One building is pink and the other blue. The blue Galleon's accommodations are much larger and more elegantly furnished. It has been constructed in three separate phases. Some of the condos are brand new. The older condos have been maintained so well that they seem new. The very stylish interiors were designed by a professional decorator who used soft peach and aqua colors. Each condo has an entertainment center that includes a VTP. Florida-style French doors open out onto balconies overlooking the water. The master bathroom has a private whirlpool tub large enough for four. The attractive pool is the place you will want to spend many of your days and the restaurants and bars of Key West are only steps away.

6 KEY WEST BY THE SEA
2601 S. Roosevelt Blvd., Key West, FL 33040, 305-294-7401
1BR $500–800/wk, 2BR $1050–1650/wk
Amenities: Pool, tennis, across from beach

Just across the highway from Smathers Beach, the longest on Key West, you'll find this traditional condo resort. Set on five landscaped acres, there are four four-story concrete buildings. Some units are residential; some are for vacation rentals. The attitude here seems to be "you go your way, I'll go mine." For families as well as seniors, this is a comfortable place to stay and, thankfully, it is away from the commotion of the main part of Key West. Considering the price for a weekly rental, and all that is offered, this presents good value for a Key West vacation.

7 LA BRISA
1901 S. Roosevelt Blvd., Key West, FL 33040, 305-274-4770
1BR $100–150
Amenities: Pool, sauna, tennis

This resort was named La Brisa, the Spanish word for breeze, because the condos were designed to be naturally cooled by trade winds. Nature lovers who want a spot in Key West, this is your choice. La Brisa is located on a quiet part of the island between Smathers Beach and the nature preserve. The condos are luxurious, and just because you like nature doesn't mean you need to give up comfort. The condos in these four-story buildings have ocean views, oversized living rooms, and are decorated with a little style. Each balcony is recessed for privacy. This resort has the atmosphere of a private club and many guests return year after year. This resort is hard to find since La Brisa is not advertised.

10 LITTLE PALM ISLAND
Route 4, Box 1036, Milemarker 28.5, Little Torch Key, FL 33042
800-872-2215, 1BR $395–700
Amenities: Beach, pool, all-inclusive watersports

Little Palm Island takes you back to nature. The only way to reach this resort on its own private island (Newfound Harbor Key) is by a private launch from Little Torch Key. Once there, we'll bet that you won't want to leave. There are islands much farther from the U.S. that would seem to be closer to home than this little hideaway. This legendary island, once the personal retreat for President Harry Truman and his family, was chosen in 1963 for the film *PT109*. Today you can enjoy one of the best beaches in the keys and the most romantic accommodations imaginable. The resort has fourteen air-conditioned, thatched-roof rondevals scattered discretely among tropical palms and lush foliage. Designed for privacy, each villa houses two suites including a living room, mini-bar with a coffee maker, master bedroom and bath with a whirlpool. Surrounded by lattice walls and dense foliage, there's also a private sun deck with a refreshing outdoor shower. Interior decor is plush and tropical, furnished with rattan and wicker. The beds have mosquito netting although this is purely for dramatic effect. There are no televisions or telephones in the villas; if your office needs you, the front desk can field those calls. One other item of interest at this romantic hideaway resort: no children under the age of twelve, and the older ones are quietly discouraged.

8   OCEAN KEY HOUSE
Zero Duval St., Key West, FL 33040, 800-328-9815
1BR $190–265, 2BR $325–350
Amenities: Pool, restaurant, health club

This resort consists of a five-story building in the center of Key West. Streets take their markings from this point. From the pool deck, you can see the geographer's point where the Gulf meets the Atlantic at the tip of the Florida Keys. Such a location deserves an imposing resort. Ocean Key House fulfills the promise and it's beautiful. The lobby is open air and the Key Room Lounge is a popular place in the evenings. The Dockside Bar on the Pier looks beautiful at night with the little white Christmas lights. Quiet Jimmy Buffet style music plays in the evenings while you listen to the palms in the breeze and gaze out over the waters. The condo interiors are luxuriously decorated—no expense has been spared. Most condos have a private whirlpool large enough for two. Lots of mirrors bring the ocean view inside.

8   THE REACH
Simonton St. on the Ocean, Key West, FL 33040, 305-296-5000
1BR $240–350
Amenities: Beach, pier, pool, health club

Priding itself as "outrageously romantic," this resort has 90 suites as well as numerous hotel rooms. Set on the largest natural beach in Key West (100 feet of white powder sand), the atmosphere here is one of island sophistication. All suites have a kitchenette and a small sitting room overlooking the pool and the ocean beyond. Brand new, the units have been designed to cascade down toward the beach in a setting reminiscent of a rambling old plantation house. Architectural flourishes embellish the balconies and roof line to further enhance a neo-Victorian style. There's lots of activity around the pool and a poolside bar, deli, and snack bar out on the pier. The Reach is both romantic for couples and fun for families.

6 **SUGAR LOAF LODGE**
Mile Marker 17, Sugarloaf Key, FL 33040
Amenities: None

Seventeen miles from Key West, this is a unique budget resort that features a dolphin pond with three free shows daily. Primarily a hotel, there are also apartments to rent for those on a budget or for those who eschew the social activity of Key West. This resort is very quiet and is favored by bird or nature lovers. The hotel rooms and studio apartments are in two rustic buildings overlooking the dolphin pond. Furnished island-style this property is more Hemingwayesque than Key West.

RENTAL RESOURCES
Century 21 All Keys Realty, 305-294-4200
Key West Reservation Service, 800-327-4831
Key West Realty, 800-523-2460, xM-721
Knight Realty & Management, 305-294-5155
Property Management of Key West, 305-296-7744

MARATHON

Don't think of this as an island but rather as the geographic designation for a number of islands clustered together. Marathon Key is the largest with two islets branching off: Key Colony Beach and Coco Plum. Key Colony Beach has the distinction of hosting an 18 hole golf course, the longest in the Keys and stiff competition to the nine hole courses to be found on the other Keys. Sombrero Reef Beach also provides one of the longest strands for walking in this part of Florida, but don't expect to find soft sand. Both Coco Plum and Key Colony have marinas. You'll find Coco Plum to be more status conscious. There there's Hawk's Key Resort that occupies the entire island of Duck Key. It is the largest, full service resort in the Keys. Sleepy Marathon was a major destination for retirees before the low prices of North Carolina and Arizona resorts diverted their attention. However, it remains a quiet place and is heavenly for those who like to turn in at 9 P.M. The accommodations do not have the style of Key West but all offer comfort and "value"—an important term in the local lexicon. One observation we made was a general indifference on the part of people in the tourist business. In most communities, management tries hard to please but we got the distinct impression across the board of "just go enjoy your stay and leave us alone." Maybe there was a bad case of island fever, but we've noticed it on each trip. They seem to think that Marathon can best be appreciated by those who know it and who return year after year.

WHERE TO STAY

5   BONEFISH TOWERS
2000 Coco Plum Dr., Marathon, FL 33050, 305-289-0488
Studio $950/2wks, 1BR $1550/2wks, 2BR $1950/2wks
Amenities: Heated pool, tennis, saunas, exercise room

Nestled by the side of the marina on Coco Plum Key, away from the main commercial activity of Marathon, Bonefish Towers offers quiet in the Florida sun and comfortable oceanfront accommodations. More residential than vacation oriented, this is a good choice for those who plan to spend two weeks or more in Florida. Each unit has been decorated differently. We saw two widely divergent decors in Bonefish Towers. One unit was tired and cheaply decorated with rattan and lawn furniture. The other unit was freshly decorated and Indonesian art pieces was strategically placed to create a fanciful environment. Be sure you determine what your accommodations will be like before you go.

7   THE BUCCANEER LODGE (Pirate's Cove Villas)
48.5 Mile Marker, Marathon, FL 33050, 800-237-3329
Cottages $49–79, 1BR $109–149, 2BR $160–200
Amenities: Dock, pool, tennis, restaurant

You know when you walk in the lobby and see stuffed pirate "dummies" sitting on the couch that this is going to be fun. Buccaneer Lodge was one of the leading hotels on Marathon Key: part of the property is devoted to the Pirate's Cove condos; and part contains the hotel cottages. Frankly in our opinion, they let the hotel section go while focusing renovation in the area of the Pirate's Cove condos. The condos are just a short distance from the main lodge. Each condo building is a ten-sided duplex on stilts. The interiors are "nicely" decorated with rattan furniture and tropical fabrics, a disappointment after the initial introduction to fantasy. The resort is neat, clean and above all, management wants you to have fun. Each unit has a full kitchen, although there is a large, popular restaurant in the hotel. Room service is also available. There are activity programs for adults and children and the pool is a good place for new friendships. The environment is relaxed and upbeat—definitely an island escape. The rental rates are reasonable considering the size of the condos and friendly service throughout the hotel.

8   COCO PLUM
109 Coco Plum Dr., Marathon, FL 33050, 305-743-0240
1BR $125–185, 2BR $220–250
Amenities: Pool

Coco Plum is a nifty little hideaway in the Keys. This is an intimate resort that allows you to unwind or to venture to Key West for history and culture.

It's like staying at a little inn. There are 28 octagon villas on stilts and they have been divided into one and two bedroom models. It's obvious that a lot of attention has been paid to the decor in these cute condos. There's a sophisticated flair and fabrics are color coordinated. Popular with visitors from the Northeast, this is the one resort in the area that also captures a number of European visitors. Guests frequently congregate at the pool, and the palm-fringed beach has charm. This resort is on one of the best stretches of sand in the Keys and the efficient management keeps the place humming. They clearly want you to be happy.

6   COCO PLUM BEACH VILLAS
133 Coco Plum Dr., Marathon, FL 33050, 305-289-1102; $950/wk
Amenities: Beach, pool

Don't get your hopes up—this is a six-story tower and not a collection of beach villas. More part-time residential than vacation oriented, this is a quiet place to stay with a mature clientele. The units are solid and comfortable although interior decor has languished. The best adjective would be comfortable, and the desirable Coco Plum isle location makes this a good destination for those who want a home away from home in the Keys.

5+   CONCH KEY COTTAGES
Route 1, Box 424, Milemarker 62.3, Marathon, FL 33050
305-289-1317; Studio $75, 1BR $85–135, 2BR $125–165
Amenities: None

Tucked away on a tiny islet, this cottage community provides romance and privacy. Each of the nine cottages has been named after a species of conch and the seashell-nautical theme has been carried forward on the inside. Offering barefoot simplicity, this is for those who want the Robinson Crusoe experience.

5   CORAL LAGOON RESORT
12399 Overseas Highway, Marathon, FL 33050, 305-289-0121
2BR $100–140
Amenities: Dive shop, dive trips

This diverse resort captures the spirit of the Keys in a way of which Jimmy Buffet would approve. Located on a canal, this tropical garden contains a colony of duplex cottages. There's a sleepy ambiance here and you may want to spend your days in one of the hammocks under the coconut palms. The cottages are simply furnished and chances are you'll spend most of your time outside on your private sundeck or socializing by the pool. For the energetic, Marathon's largest dive shop is located here.

5-7   FARO BLANCO
1996 Overseas Highway, Marathon, FL 33050, 305-7430-9018
Cottages $55–119, Houseboats $75–135, 3BR Condos $198
Amenities: Pool, restaurant, dock

This resort is a landmark because of the lighthouse and you can actually rent accommodations in this structure for your vacation. You can see the lighthouse from five miles in either direction. However, we think you'll be more impressed by the condos, some of the largest in this part of Florida. Each is as large as some permanent homes and the privacy is enhanced by the winding floor plan and hallways. The large screened porch doubles as an extra room. Faro Blanco extends over both sides of the highway. With a marina for sailors, this resort offers a friendly bar area which attracts sailors from all over the Keys. For those so inclined, there are even houseboats for rent on a nightly basis. The garden cottages are more appropriate for divers or folks on a budget. With many diving trips originating from this marina, it is no wonder that there are so many repeat visitors.

9+   HAWK'S CAY RESORT
Mile Marker 61, Duck Key, FL 33050, 305-743-7000
800-327-7775, 1BR $110–190, 2BR $225–295
Amenities: Beach, pool, tennis, dive shop, boat rentals

This private island has retained the laid back lifestyle of the Caribbean, yet it offers the sophistication of Boca Raton and provides an enviable milieu for small conventions. How do they do it? Hawk's Cay began as a hotel in the 1950s and fortunately was blessed with 60 acres of land, a luxury in these islands. Over the years it has expanded slowly so that it now includes some condo villas that were begun in the 1980s and are part of a major building plan extending through the century. The tone is set around the front porch of the main lodge with coral and celadon tile, white wicker furniture and paddle fans overhead. Welcome to paradise. The main hotel has the cool, dark corridors designed for the tropics. Outside, the landscaping is lush with vegetation including hibiscus and bananas. There's a pretty pool area and a sandy shored ocean lagoon. This is where the dolphin encounter takes place each day. For those who reserve in advance, you have the opportunity to swim with the dolphins (under the close supervision of their trainers).The condos are in a series of three-story buildings set away from the main hotel building; these have an orientation toward the golf course and the large, screened porches have a view of the fairways. Interior decor is smart and sophisticated with rich fabrics and the most modern conveniences. Again, the soft tropical pinks and greens of the Caribbean are prevalent, accented by tropical plants. We saw one with an exquisite collection of African art—it belongs in a museum. Hawk's Cay is famous for its activities programs, ranging from sailing and fishing to golf and tennis. There are eight tennis courts and a "starters" program for those who plan to give the game some serious attention. Also, there's a dive shop and divers' certification program. In the summer and around holiday times, there are supervised children's programs. In short, there's nothing else like this in the Keys.

2   HAWK'S NEST
One Kyle Way South, Marathon, FL 33050, 305-743-6711
1BR $700/wk, 2BR $800–850/wk
Amenities: Pool, dock

When there are so many great places to stay, why come here? Located at the southern tip of Marathon Key, this ten-story structure commands an imposing view. Although recently renovated, we were hard put to find where the improvements were. The units we saw were decorated in the lemon and lime colors of the sixties and the tracks in the shag carpet seemed like paths through a forest. A telling feature was the vinyl deck chairs, "so they can be cleaned in a jiffy." That, to us, seemed to sum up management's attitude toward guests.

3   MARATHON KEY BEACH CLUB
4590 Overseas Highway, Marathon, FL 33050, 305-743-6522
2BR $100–150
Amenities: Pool, hot tub

This resort offers a collection of 20 octagon villas on stilts in a tropical garden setting. The garden has grown nicely but the units have seen their better days. What we find so disappointing is that we've made three inspections over four years and each time we were told the resort was on the verge of a major redecoration. Simple in style but overpriced is the best we can say.

5   OCEAN BEACH CLUB
BOX 9, 351 E. Ocean Dr., Key Colony Beach, FL 33051
305-289-0525, 1BR $135–160
Amenities: Pool, hot tub

Located on Key Colony Beach, this has the best "beach" location in the area. More for retirees than young vacationers, you'll find this quiet property offers everything you need. Each has a small living room furnished many years ago with rattan furniture. Although the beach commands a premium, the price here is high for what is offered.

6   ROYAL PLUM CLUB
133 Coco Plum Dr., Marathon, FL 33050, 305-289-1102
1BR $750/wk, 2BR $875/wk, 3BR $1000/wk
Amenities: Tiny beach, pool, tennis

This two-story condo development surrounds the pool so as to give each unit a view of the ocean. Attractive, well designed and well furnished, these units provide a home away from home for those who plan to stay for a week or more. The units don't have telephones but the manager will be sure you get your messages, if you desire.

7+   SOMBRERO RESORT CONDOMINIUM
19 Sombrero Blvd., Marathon, FL 33050, 305-743-2250
Studio $65, 1BR $95
Amenities: Pool, hot tub, saunas, clubhouse, restaurant,marina.
Next to golf club

Wedged between the harbor and the Sombrero Country Club, this resort offers the best of both worlds at a reasonable price. Built in several styles, you'll find two concrete five-story structures plus a series of duplex and quadruplex condos. The heart of the resort is the restaurant and activities center near the junior Olympic swimming pool. Unfortunately, we thought, the interior decor was cheap and reflected an urge to cut costs, with metal doors, plastic chairs, and a rattan sofa bed which already seemed rickety. Otherwise, this is a first class property and management provides more services than you'll find at most other resorts in the Marathon area.

RENTAL RESOURCES
Carico Ral Estate, 800-940-7636
Duck Key Rentals, 305-566-3340 Hawk's Cay area
Land & Sea Vacations, 800-327-4836
Reed Realty, 305-743-7520
Sarah's Island Realty, 305-289-0999 Large selection
Sunwater Vacation Rentals, 305-743-0391

KEY LARGO / ISLAMORADA

Closest to the mainland, there is a world of difference between this area and either Key West or the Marathon area. Key Largo extends for nearly ten miles and is almost as large as all the other Keys put together. Dominated by the John Pennecamp Underwater Park, Key Largo is a destination for divers. The atmosphere here is different largely because most of the visitors are day trippers from Miami. Although Key Largo has almost as many athletic activities as Key West, it lacks the sophisticated restaurants that make Key West an international destination. Following Hurricane Andrew, many Miami residents leased the Key Largo vacation homes while their Key Biscane estates were being rebuilt. Here was a simple community living off the sea when suddenly the economy was changed by an influx of wealthy urbanites. Key Largo has settled down since then but we hear that a whole slew of ethnic restaurants opened up catering to the new residents. Islamorada, another ten miles to the south, has changed little over the years. Its only moment in the limelight came when George Bush chose it for his bonefishing vacations in January. Islamorada has a number of quiet and prestigious condo projects that recently instituted rules restricting short-term rentals. These were some of the best values in the Keys—great accommodations at reasonable prices. The sense of value remains, but the inventory of vacation rentals is now more limited.

WHERE TO STAY

6   ANCHORAGE RESORT & YACHT CLUB
107050 Overseas Hwy., Key Largo, FL 33037, 305-451-0500
Amenities: Pool, hot tub, tennis. Marina next door.

This resort is a good place to visit for a week of fishing in the Keys. Management is strong on hospitality services. The condos are one-bedroom models with ocean views in a five-story, hotel-style structure. The resort is next to the marina, and convenient for sailing or fishing. There is a tropical landscaped swimming pool and hot tub area that is popular at the end of the day. There are also two tennis courts for sports enthusiasts. The large, spacious and well-decorated condos are attractively furnished island style with rattan furniture. Everything is neat, trim and tidy. Guests relax in the club atmosphere. Try it.

8   BAREFOOT POINTE
80581 Old Highway, Islamorada, FL 33036, 305-664-8632
1BR $100–132, 2BR $125–155
Amenities: Pool, tidal pool/aquarium2

Brand new in 1992, this resort was designed in the old-fashioned Key West style. Still under construction, there's a three-story condo building and a couple of Banana Republic cottages under the palms. The coconuts make this resort secluded and there's a charming oceanfront tidal pool, perfect for little children and those who want to laze in the water. There's a patch of sand which passes for a beach but don't expect too much. Service here is rough but we expect to see a major improvement during the 1993 season as this new resort gets going. The units are very attractive, and are among the most well decorated in this part of the Keys. You'll find a plush contemporary style, lots of pink fabric, and silk flowers everywhere. Each unit has a VTP as well as a jacuzzi tub in the bath. This unexpected find is certainly a far cry from the "barefoot" style.

4   BREEZYPALM
BOX 767, Milemarker 80, Islamorada, FL 33036, 305-664-2361
1BR $75, 2BR $110
Amenities: Pool

This motel was recently remodeled to create condo-style one and two bed-room units. Very reasonably priced, this budget find will appeal to divers as well as those who just want to cruise the Keys. For those less ambitious, you can laze on a large, private screened porch.

4   CALOOSA COVE RESORT
73801 Overseas Hwy., Islamorada, FL 33036, 305-664-8811
Studio $85–105, 1BR $105–155
Amenities: Marina, pool, tennis

This is a beautiful resort with some of the most spacious accommodations on Islamorada. You can snorkel right off the beach in clear, warm waters. The condos are attractively decorated with tile floors and modern Danish furniture. Last summer Caloosa Cove was completely refurbished with new carpets everywhere, new furniture in some units and an overhaul of the com-mon areas and swimming pool. The management is good, but some guests/owners report indifference. You decide. The "Moosehead" bar is surrounded by the ocean and offers good fun.

9   CHEECA LODGE
Mile Marker 83.5, Box 527, Islamorada, FL 33036, 800-327-2888
Amenities: Golf, 6 tennis courts, 2 pools, 525 ft. fishing pier,
restaurant, water sports center, hot tub

George Bush stays here when he goes bonefish fishing in Florida. Primarily a resort hotel, there are private villas with kitchenettes. This is one of the most sophisticated resorts in the Keys, catering to golfers and tennis players as well as to fishermen. This is the only golf course in this part of the Keys. The villas are beautifully furnished to reflect the navigational history of the area. Small kitchenettes have microwave ovens and each villa has a VTP. A children's playground adds an unexpected touch

6   CHESAPEAKE RESORT
83409 Overseas Highway, Box 909, Islamorada, FL 33036,
305-664-4662; 1BR $79, 2BR $99
Amenities: Pools, hot tub

Offering relaxed tropical rhythms in the Florida Keys, the Chesapeake is a new all-suite hotel. Each unit overlooks the pool area with a view of the ocean beyond. Interior decor is new, light and stylish. Although the units are a little small, this can be easily overlooked since the Chesapeake provides good value.

6 **HOLIDAY ISLE / EL CAPITAN**
Milemarker 84.5, Islamorada, FL 33036, 800-327-7070
1BR $55–130
Amenities: Marina, restaurants, pool

Holiday Isle is one of the largest resorts to be found in the Keys. It has annexed the El Capitan resort next door and converted it to an all-suite hotel. Holiday Isle's Tiki Bar is one of the most popular watering holes for sailors, fishermen, and singles. The Tiki Bar sets the tone for this resort. Interior decor does not have a high priority with management. You'll find dull wood paneling, dark colors, and lumpy mattresses. But creature comforts are not what Holiday Isle is about. A swinging place, it's as popular in summer as winter.

5 **MATECUMBE RESORT**
76261 Overseas Highway, Islamorada, FL 33036, 305-664-8801
Studio $55, 1BR $75, 2BR $90
Amenities: Pool

Matecumbe Resort is definitely on the upswing. Once upon a time this resort promised the world. Then management changed and decay set in. New Management has been working to reverse that trend and we are happy to report that the improvements are visible. It's the extensive garden that makes this resort in the first place. This is a collection of octagon villas on stilts set amid six acres. Inside, you'll see a variety of styles that, if you're open minded, gives this resort character. The wallpaper may be torn here and there, and don't expect all the chairs to match. But all in all, it's comfortable and the price is right.

7+ **OCEAN POINTE AT KEY LARGO**
500 Burton Dr., Tavernier, FL 33070, 800-882-9464
1BR $85–120, 2BR $95–150
Amenities: Pools, children's pool, tennis, gym, restaurant.
Next to marina.

This ambitious condo resort opened in 1990 with the first of four, three-story buildings. Located on the ocean (read: no beach) it sets a new standard of quality for Key Largo. This is clearly the most modern and attractive resort in the area. Interior decor is comfortable and stresses the Caribbean in color and style. There's a large clubhouse and a junior Olympic pool. There is a patch of limestone which has been cleared and covered with sand to make a beach. As with so many beaches in the Keys, it's not a place for walking in the sand. Divers will love the many dive shops nearby, and the opportunities for dive trips.

RENTAL RESOURCES

All Vacation Condos, 305-882-7777
Freewheeler Vacations, 305-664-2075
Keys Country Realty, 305-664-4470

GEORGIA

G is for golf. Georgia offers some of the best golf resorts to be found any-where. Start with the weather. Georgia enjoys a warm temperate climate in winter and cool breezes from the Appalachian foothills in summer. We have divided the state into two sections; the islands and the mountain resorts. Starting with the islands, the hands-down favorite for vacationers is the rela-tively compact area around Brunswick, called the Golden Isles, which includes 170 miles of coastline. Sea Island, St. Simons Island, and Jekyll Island have for generations attracted vacationers from all over the U.S. and Canada. The citizens of the Georgia mountains, however, have been fiercely resistant to yankee carpetbaggers since the Civil War. Only recently have they sought to attract outside visitors to the charms of the Chatahoochee National Forest and the surrounding mountains. Channeling their energy toward golf resorts, some unbelievable courses have been created around Callaway Gardens and Helen.

1. GEORGIA'S ISLANDS

Sea Island set the tone for the area when The Cloister, part of a crop of neo-Spanish colonial pleasure palaces, was built in the late 1920s. The "Old World" traditions have survived although a concession to modern taste was made when the condos were added in the 1970s. This exclusive resort has been a favorite among presidents and the very wealthy. However, Sea Island has no community apart from The Cloister. As The Cloister attracted so many visitors to the area, development spread to St. Simons Island in the 1950s.

St. Simons has its own prestigious, yet mellow, ambiance. Since it is an island, it is a world apart from life on the mainland. The island is graced with beautiful natural landscaping such as forests of live oaks, magnolias, barrier dunes, and the seemingly unlimited Marshes of Glynn. Beautiful beaches are just over the hill and the golf courses see lots of play. Everyone will want to visit Ft. Frederica and the tabby ruins (tabby is a local building material native to coastal Georgia; oyster shells are its principal ingredient). Ft. Frederica was Britain's outpost against Spanish Florida. Most of the development on St. Simons has come within the past decade. You'll find stylish beachfront condos as well as plantation-style golf course communi-ties. The island is six miles long and three miles wide, so no matter which resort area you choose, you're never far away from other options.

Jekyll Island is altogether different. Originally developed as "The Millionaire's Club" in the 1890s, Jekyll is dotted with extravagant man-sions. As the twentieth century progressed, the island lost its glamour and the mansions fell into disrepair. Today the mansions are operated under the care of the historical society. Jekyll has turned to retirees instead of millionaires. The beachfront is lined with motels and only a couple of condo resorts have been developed.

St. Simons and the Golden Isles offer a choice of airports. Commuter flights go to Brunswick, only thirty minutes from each of the isles. Jacksonville, Florida may be more convenient because it has nonstop jet service to cities such as Raleigh, Charlotte, St. Louis, Dallas and Washington, DC. Only a little over an hour away, the convenience of a nonstop flight and the cost savings of competitive airfares makes Jacksonville a winner. Savannah is another airport option, just under two hours away from the Golden Isles.

WHERE TO STAY

8+ THE BEACH CLUB
1440 Ocean Blvd., St. Simons Island, GA 31522, 912-638-5450
1BR $70–115, 2BR $80–130, 3BR $130–200
Amenities: Beach, outdoor pool, hot tub, tennis

These oceanside condos are slightly separated from the beach by an attractive area of sand dunes and sea oats. This is a luxury, four-story condo development, arranged in a long U-shape around a fountain and swimming pool. Some of the condos have great ocean views while others have courtyards and partial ocean views. The interiors are beautifully furnished with quality furniture and contemporary light woods. Glass-top tables and sliding glass windows bring the sunlight inside these spacious, airy units. The dimensions of the living room, bedrooms, and kitchen are larger than average. A few of the condos are occupied by part-time residents, creating a quiet, established ambiance at the resort. This is one of the best choices on the island.

9 THE CLOISTER
Sea Island, GA 31561, 912-638-5112, 3BR $1500–2800/2 weeks
Amenities: None. Optional guest membership at the Beach Club for a fee.

Established in 1928, The Cloister has long been a vacation retreat for the nation's leaders. It offers a number of villas for seasonal or weekly rental, as well as a small collection of condos. The Cloister has maintained the historic charm of years gone by while providing guests with all the services that the most demanding expect. Sea Island is a small barrier island separated from St. Simons Island by a salt marsh. Since The Cloister resort occupies the entire island, necessities such as groceries must be acquired on the main island. The Cloister, built in the 1920s in classic Spanish colonial style, seems to be in its own world. As you may imagine, the homeowners and island guests like it that way.

Within The Cloister master resort there are homes, bungalows, villas, and condo apartments. All rentals are handled through The Cloister's administrative office. Renting can be difficult unless you are a regular guest or have the proper introduction. The homes, bungalows and villas are collectively referred to as "the cottages." Each is its own entity and is personalized since the residences on Sea Island were designed and built by the individual home owner over the years since the late '20s. These cottages are available on a weekly rental basis.

The "condos" are the River Club apartments which were built in a Spanish style 25 years ago and overlook the lagoon and the Village Creek. When you enter the condos you'll feel like you've passed through a time warp due to the presence of solid stucco walls, parquet floors, and inlaid wood and tile work. You just won't find craftsmanship like this in contemporary America. The rooms are overly large, there is wasted space, and some of the furniture dates from the 1950s. Again, great effort has been made to preserve the memory of years gone by. The bedrooms are upstairs. The third bedroom (in the three-bedroom units) is actually a very small room and is just right for a study or two bunk beds.

There are no amenities such as a pool, but you can pay $120 for guest privileges at the Sea Island Beach Club and Spa. There you'll find a pool, exercise room, and spa therapy programs including massages.

KING AND PRINCE
Arnold at Downing St., St. Simons Island, GA 31522, 912-638-3631
2BR $159–219, 3BR $219–279
Amenities: Tennis, golf, beach, restaurant, pools

The King and Prince Resort Hotel was built in 1939 and retains the gracious ambiance of days gone by. Located on the beach, it offers a comfortable vacation environment. Over the years the hotel has expanded by adding the Beach Villas on each side of the hotel's oceanfront setting. During the 1980s the King and Prince's expansion took place at Hampton Plantation on the opposite end of the island near the Marshes of Glynn and the intercostal waterway.

The hotel provides a social center for the condos. Guests staying in the condos at Hampton Plantation can drive thirty minutes across the island to use the beach club facilities. Similarly, guests in the Beach Villas can drive to the golf course at Hampton Plantation. Check-in for all condos takes place in the hotel lobby. This lobby is notable for its colonial styling, tile floors, wrought iron grill work, and huge portraits of England's King Edward VII and Prince Albert (for whom the resort was named). The hotel offers a large pool, restaurant, and tennis courts that the condo guests may use. There are additional private facilities at each condo development.

Beach Villas (8+) In two locations flanking the hotel, the villas are similar in style and design. The condos in these four-story buildings are all situated directly on the beach, enabling you to hear the surf at night. These contemporary condos are spacious and some have been beautifully decorated by interior designers. Each has a private terrace overlooking the beach and a fireplace in the living room for chilly evenings. The quality furniture is built of solid woods with striped satin and raw silk fabrics. The style of the sample condo we saw is timeless, for it is at once traditional with ball and claw legs on the tables and chairs, yet contemporary, displaying peach and pale blue colors. Wet bars in the living room are convenient for entertaining. Each cluster of condos has its own pool.

Plantation Point River Villas (9) Set within Hampton Plantation and overlooking the Hampton River and marina, these two plus-story condos have been created in a "Low Country plantation style" with decks, screened porches and dormer windows upstairs. The condos are connected by oak-shaded walkways. You know you are in Dixie from the crickets and the languid air. Inside, the architectural design features cathedral ceilings and a two-story-high wall of glass overlooking the marsh and the river. Designer interiors create that southern "hunt club" atmosphere. You will find comfort and quiet luxury. The geometrically shaped pool has a sundeck, but is primarily shaded by moss-laden trees. This is the new "Old South."

8   NORTH BREAKER CONDOMINIUMS
213 Driftwood Dr., St. Simons Island, GA 31522, 912-638-5450
2BR $85–140, 3BR $185–280
Amenities: Beach, pool, hot tub

This five-story oceanside structure is separated from the beach by sand dunes and vegetation. A boardwalk allows for easy barefoot access to the beach. This is a quality vacation condominium where many of the units are occupied for a month or two at a time by some of the island's part-time residents. The area is quiet and undisturbed. You will only see children during the summer months. Inside you'll find large, spacious, and well-decorated rooms. Some are personalized by the use of wallpaper and quality designer fabrics. All condos are modern, comfortable, and offer a wet bar in the living room. The pool area (including a hot tub) overlooks the beach and is a great place for reading and sunbathing.

SEA PALMS
5445 Frederica Rd., St. Simons Island, GA 31522, 912-638-3351
1BR $96–115, 2BR $140–206
Amenities: Golf, tennis, health club, heated pool

Sea Palms is a master resort and residential community designed around its 27-hole championship golf course. Located in the center of the island, development has carefully preserved much of the forest located on Sea Palm's 800 acres. Sea Palms offers a country club, a recreational center, and a tennis club with 12 courts. There is a wide variety of condo accommodations to choose from. Those designed as luxury vacation homes are the most attractive rentals. Others are more residential in tone. All prices, however, are based upon the number of bedrooms, not upon the quality of the condos. Be sure to choose what's right for you.

Sea Marsh Villas (8) Sea Marsh Villas are in the center of the action. Located along the fairway, the condos in these three-story buildings also have a view of the endless Marshes of Glynn. Located right behind these villas is the golf pro shop, the bike shop, Oglethorpe's restaurant, and the Sea Palms general store. Inside, the condos are spacious and handsomely furnished with contemporary furniture. A sunroom connects to the master bedroom, and a screened porch to the living room. You will want to spend the evening watching the island's rose-colored sunsets from either of these pleasant spots.

Courtside Villas (7) A wide variety of two and one-half story townhouses are available at Courtside Villas. They are located next to the Health & Racquet Club which features 12 tennis courts, a weight room, saunas, a hot tub, and a tennis pro shop. This is a convenient place to schedule a match or find a fourth. The condo interiors are marked by a casual, contemporary style. You will find wicker and rattan furniture, neutral colors and views overlooking either the tennis courts or golf course. A pool is located right outside the door and a jogging path passes Courtside Villas.

Cedar Walk Villas (7) Cedar Walk Villas are two-story pedestal homes with two bedrooms and a loft. More private than the others, they are also great for families because of all the space. Located at the edge of the marsh, it's a short walk to the pro shop.

6 VILLAS BY THE SEA
1175 N. Beachview Dr., Jekyll Island, GA 31520, 912-635-2521
1BR $69–89, 2BR $94–109, 3BR $114–149
Amenities: Pool, beach

This is a village of 170 condos lining the shore of Jekyll Island. Cradled by lush natural landscape and windswept oaks, Villas by the Sea offers a vacation environment secluded from mainland cares. Rustic boardwalks wander within the landscaped 17-acre setting through the dunes to the beach. The condos are practical and spacious with several different floor plans. Some have loft bedrooms, and these are superior because of the living room's cathedral ceiling and two-story wall of glass. Most units have an ocean view, and all are close to the beach and pool. The decor is practical. You will find sculptured carpets, tweed fabrics, and color schemes designed for durability. A few owners have enhanced their condos with superior decor and personal touches. Villas by the Sea is considered a vacation resort, but some condos are occupied by Snowbird part-time residents.

RENTAL RESOURCES
Glenn Lewis Associates, 912-638-8229

Jekyll Realty, 912-635-3301
Parker Kaufman Realty, 912-635-2512 (St. Simons)
Sea Palms Realty, 912-638-5450, St. Simons
THE Management, 800-627-6850, St. Simons, The island's largest and
   a leader

2. GEORGIA'S MOUNTAINS

On the other side of the state, the Appalachian Mountain chain ends in northern Georgia, creating the natural splendor of the Peach State's rolling hill country. Northern Georgia will surprise you. It has been graced with shining lakes, countless streams, dense forests, and numerous waterfalls. As you admire the sylvan beauty of a glade, however, don't be too surprised to suddenly confront a group of laughing "tubers" floating down the stream on a lazy afternoon. Tubing is a sport that epitomizes this languid countryside marked by refreshing mountain waters.

There are several resort communities in the northern part of the state that take advantage of the mountains and the rolling foothills. Due to its elevation, the Georgia mountains have a milder summertime climate than you would find in neighboring states, such as Alabama or southern Georgia. Helen is the most exciting of these communities because it has been transformed over the last twenty years into a Tyrolean village. Gingerbread architecture and geraniums are everywhere. Cobbled alleyways and outdoor fresco paintings on the sides of buildings are other characteristics of the community. The town even has a bell tower with a glockenspiel that plays music just like they do in Austria and Switzerland. It also has the largest selection of Alpine imports available in the U.S. The resorts around Helen are faithful to this theme and everything is done to perfection.

Transportation to the Georgia mountain resorts is easy; all are within two hours of Atlanta. Vacationers heading to Calloway Gardens from the west don't even have to think about passing through Atlanta as Calloway is only 30 miles north of Atlanta.

WHERE TO STAY

10 CALLAWAY GARDENS
   U.S. Highway 27, Pine Mountain, GA 31822, 404-663-2281
   1BR $144–219, 2BR $238–333, 3BR $431–651
   Amenities: Golf, tennis, pools, hot tubs, trap shooting range,
   gardens, greenhouses, restaurants, shops

Perfect for nature lovers, Callaway Gardens is one of the largest botanical gardens in the world. It prides itself on its 2,500 acres of woodlands and lakes, containing some of the finest botanical greenhouses in the United States. Thirteen miles of road wind past the John Sibley Horticultural Center with a two-story indoor waterfall and the Cecil Day Butterfly Center. Special outdoor plots have seasonal displays of flowers, azaleas, and rhododendrons interconnected by crushed brick winding paths. Throughout the year, Calloway Gardens offers horticultural seminars for adults and children on gardening, preservation of dried plants, or the manufacture of natural dyes. Callaway Gardens though, is equally famous among golfers, due to its 63 holes of golf and the fact that it is the site of the Chet Atkins Country Gentleman Golf Classic. The developer was an avid golfer and these courses are certainly challenging. Mountain View is the toughest course followed by Lake View, Garden View, and Sky View. Two separate country clubs are available as well as the All-American Tennis Sports Academy and the tennis center, consisting of 19 courts. As if this weren't enough, Callaway Gardens also offers one of the finest summer programs for children in the U.S. Tennis, golf, horticultural, and watersports instruction are available. In addition, instructors from Florida State University's "High Flying Circus" work as counselors, and perform once a day.

The Mountain Creek condo villas are, by far, the most desirable accommodations at Callaway. These condos are within walking distance of the inn, the tennis center, and the Lakeview golf course. The condos are spacious and comfortable. You will discover living room fireplaces and screened porches, which serve as an extra room. Although they are individually owned, Callaway encourages standardized decor for the condos that is contemporary, but not ostentatious. For decor, you'll find preplanned furniture packages with color coordinated ensembles, but don't expect silk flowers or many personal accessories. Don't confuse the condos with the cottages that are also available at Callaway Gardens. The cottages are rustic while the condos have a romantic, sophisticated ambiance.

7   FAIRFIELD PLANTATION
1602 Lakeview Pky., Villa Rica, GA 30180, 404-834-7781
800-241-0792, Studio $90, 1BR $125, 2BR $140
Amenities: Lake, pools, restaurant, golf, tennis

This master community rests on 2,400 acres and is only 45 minutes away from Atlanta. The area is composed of retirement homes, vacation condos, and timeshares surrounding a small lake and golf course. There are two Olympic-sized swimming pools, a golf course, and five tennis courts. Small power boats or sunfish are available for rent at the marina. Horseback riding is available at the stables, and sometimes there are organized trail rides. The condos are 8 to 15 years old, and there are several floor plans to choose from. A few of the older units are decorated in gold and orange colors, while the new ones are decorated with soft earth tones. These condos are spacious enough to be a home away from home for a week or two. This is a self-contained, very social resort. You'll be sure to make friends whether your interests lie at the pool, the golf course, or the yacht club.

7+ IGLS AT INNSBRUCK RESORT
P.O. Box 845, Helen, Georgia 30545, 404-878-2400, 3BR $90–140
Amenities: Pool, tennis, golf, hot tub

The Igls condominiums are within the Innsbruck master community development located just two miles away from the neo-Austrian town of Helen. Want to know what the area looks like? Just recall the first few scenes of the *Sound of Music.* You will be surprised by the steep gumdrop hills from which a golf course has been carved. Rated by *Golf Digest* as one of the most challenging golf courses in Georgia, it is also one of the most scenic. The Igls condos are perched on a promontory while the Innisbruck golf course is wrapped around down below. Igls is fairly new. The condos are fully detached houses and are larger than a villa. They consist of two bedrooms and a loft. You'll find them to be beautifully decorated with oak and glass furniture, stone fireplaces, and attractive pastel fabrics. Each condo has a private balcony with a spectacular view. There is a small pool at Igls and, for a nominal fee, you can use the Innsbruck Country Club facilities.

5+ LORELEI
1 Bruckenstrasse, Helen, GA 30545, 404-878-2238
1BR $65, 2BR $100
Amenities: Weight room, tennis, hot tub

Lorelei is a condo village consisting of Alpine chalets that are located across the street from the Innsbruck Golf Resort. The condos are furnished with Bavarian furniture, fine floral prints, and lots of wood. Also present is a large hot tub which, at first glance, appears to be an indoor swimming pool. Guest memberships for golfers are available because Lorelei and Innsbruck have the same management.

4 SKY VALLEY
P.O. Box 1, Dillard, GA 30537, 404-746-5301
1BR $125, 2BR $150, 3BR $175
Amenities: Tennis, golf, skiing, hiking, horseback riding, pool

Located in the Chatahoochee National Forest, this resort's hospitality programs are exceptional. Skiing, golf, fishing, and horseback riding are available. This vast 2,400-acre area has enough space for many of the sports you can't enjoy in your backyard. Wilderness trails, lakes for boating, streams for fishing, and skiing in winter are other features. In addition, there is a Munchkin Day Camp for children and a recreation center for adults. The condos are fully equipped and furnished in styles popular in the '70s. Most of the condos are in large lodge-type structures with high gables and loft bedrooms. Some of the units are private, detached chalets. Sky Valley condos have seen lots of use over the years.

IDAHO

Idaho offers some of the most rugged outdoor beauty in the U.S. The Sawtooth Mountains have discouraged settlers, leaving Idaho a pristine wilderness for fishing and hunting. The flavor and spirit of the Old West is alive and well in this land of sagebrush and ghost towns that date from the mining days. Sun Valley sits in the middle of this as an island of glamour with manicured golf courses, private corporate jets lined wing to wing at the airport, and a scintillating social life like no other. Visit Sun Valley on a summer day in July and you'll think you are in Newport, Rhode Island with all the yachtsmen attire and preppie pink sweaters.

Sun Valley, spread over a 15 mile-wide area, offers a full range of accommodations for skiers, golfers, fishermen, and equestriennes. Founded in the 1930s by Averell Harriman, chairman of the Union Pacific Railroad, Sun Valley was created to be a sensation to attract tourists to Idaho and thereby sell railway tickets. It far exceeded his ambitions. Harriman hired Austrian Count Felix Von Schaffgotch, who spent over two years studying the area's geography before selecting Sun Valley as the site. This area has an exceptional climate offering sun in the daytime and snow at night (a little fog in the mornings, too!).

The topography offers great skiing, from challenging expert runs at Bald Mountain slopes to miles of groomed intermediate trails to the gentle slopes of Dollar Mountain, a perfect place to learn. All along this area, whose correct geographic designation is the Wood River Valley, the terrain offers the gentle bump and turn, just perfect for four championship golf courses.

The area's appeal goes way beyond physical appearances. There's a genuine warmth and a level of sophistication that's a bit surprising for this remote slice of the Old West. The area has a synergistic blend of urban culture and rural calm, a retreat from city pressures that offers such surprises as a Swiss tea room. Mild weather, ample snowfall, inspiring scenery, and some indefinable magic blend into a compelling vacation environment.

Lodging in Sun Valley is just as remarkable. This is an area of multimillion dollar homes in the wilderness within a stone's throw of the $38,000 studio on the manicured golf course. Real estate prices vary widely. Yet strangely, vacation rental rates are stable and not reflective of the asset's underlying value. For example, there's a good chance that you'll spend $100 per night for a one-bedroom condo that cost the owner $185,000. A lot depends upon which neighborhood you select to enjoy your vacation.

The condos in Sun Valley can be divided into four groups: those which are part of Sun Valley Resort and have access to the resort's amenities; those which are part of Elkhorn Village with its golf and sports facilities; those which are part of Warm Springs Village; and those in the town of Ketchum. Sun Valley Resort was one of the first ski resorts to develop condominiums as part of the total village plan. The older condos are close to the center of Sun Valley Village, but they generally don't offer the luxury of newer resort developments which have private saunas, VTPs, and other extravagances. Sun Valley's appeal is both the social aspect and the setting. No other ski resort except maybe Aspen has the special caché associated with its name. Perhaps it's the fact that Sun Valley is relatively difficult to reach that so many of the vacationers fly their own planes or jets to the airport in Hailey. The setting is lovely with a pedestrian village of shops and restaurants around a large green with swans floating on the pond. The pond mirrors the mountains and creates a dreamlike setting. The Sun Valley master development encompasses many individual condo developments (Atelier, Cottonwood, Dollar Meadow, The Lodge Condos, Snowcreek, The Villagers, and Wildflower) which are located on the golf course or Sun Valley Lakes. For those staying in these "Sun Valley Condos," you have the use of the Sun Valley sports facilities, the concierge, and the shuttles.

Elkhorn Resort is similar to Sun Valley in that it also is a master real estate development with a ski mountain, golf course, and recreation center just for those staying in Elkhorn Resort condos (Bluff, Bonne Vie, Elkhorn Village Inn, Fairway Nine, Indian Springs, The Ridge, Sagehill, and Sunburst). Elkhorn has been developed within the past 20 years and, although the quality of accommodations is superior to Sun Valley and the walking village is almost as cute, Elkhorn does not have the same social prestige as Sun Valley. Consequently, prices are much lower in Elkhorn so, in our opinion, it offers the best value in the area.

Warm Springs is not a master resort development. In many ways it's like staying in any other ski town. Warm Springs is for skiers in winter and golfers in the summer. The main chair lift to most of the skiing on Bald Mountain is at Warm Springs, so guests at Sun Valley or Elkhorn have to take a four to five mile shuttle bus over to the ski lifts at Warm springs. Compare this to some condos and townhouses at Warm Springs which have ski-in/ski-out convenience and you can draw your own conclusions. One point about Warm Springs is that most of the condos were built 15 to 20 years ago when expectations may have been lower. In general, you won't find the luxury accommodations you would expect in Sun Valley's Warm Springs area. There is one exception, Greyhawk, and we hope this will lead the way to redevelopment of this area.

Ketchum, once home to workers at Sun Valley Resort, today is developing into a resort community on its own. This is where most of the shops, restaurants, bars, grocery stores, etc., are located. The 25 square blocks of Ketchum are teaming with gourmet shops and real estate offices, but snuggled in here and there are a couple of condo developments. Most of Ketchum's condos are just south of town along Trail Creek or over by the River Run ski lift. Sun Valley's master plan calls for a new high speed quad chair lift to be built here during 1992-1993 which will transform this area to the center stage for skiers. Instead of fighting traffic congestion and the shuttle busses over to the Warm Springs lift, River Run will become an area with the best and fastest access to Sun Valley's super skiing. Definitely, Ketchum is an area to watch.

There are two developments which are not in any of these four neighborhoods. The first, just north of Ketchum, is Big Wood, a golf course community of multimillion dollar homes and a few condos by the clubhouse. The second is south of town in an area of individual three- and four-bedroom vacation homes called Weyakin. Each has its own pool and sports center so there is some similarity to the master resort communities of Sun Valley and Elkhorn, yet the flavor is not so much like a resort center and more like Warm Springs or Ketchum.

Renting a condo in the Sun Valley area must be done almost exclusively through one of the Rental Resources companies, as hardly any developments have on-site management. Once you determine where you want to be, call an agency for rentals at Elkhorn, Warm Springs, Sun Valley Lodge, etc. The rental rates for those condos within the Sun Valley master development are based on the size of the unit:

Studio	$65–85
1BR	$90–180
2BR	$110–235
3BR	$150–425

As for the Warm Springs area, prices should run:

Studio	$35–65
1BR	$65–150
2BR	$75–230
3BR	$100–385

As you can see, these posted rack rates demonstrate differences in price but a lot of it has to do with the social prestige of staying within the Sun Valley master development. Prices are very negotiable, although many rental companies require a three-night minimum stay.

Transportation to Sun Valley presents several options for those who plan to fly. The Sun Valley airport handles private planes and commuter flights from Salt Lake and Seattle. Convenient, but with limited service and high airfares. For a better perspective see the Idaho map on page 426. You may be better off flying to the jet airport at Twin Falls or Boise which offers many more flights. Another option is Idaho Falls. Although it appears to be farther away on the map, the actual driving experience is quite easy since this is desert landscape and a straight route across the plains. An extra bonus on this trip is the incredible landscape of the lava fields at Craters of the Moon National Park.

WHERE TO STAY

5   ALPINE VILLA
Cottonwood Rd., Ketchum, ID 83340
Amenities: None

These townhouse condos in a quiet, residential section of Ketchum have unusual architecture. Built in a row, the backside is a solid two and one-half story wall as if another building were planned to be adjacent. Due to their one-face design, all look out over Wood Creek and Bald Mountain. These are within walking distance of the River Run ski lifts. Spacious, most of these units are occupied by full-time Ketchum residents, although some are available for vacation rentals. There is really no resort feeling here. These would be good for groups of skiers who want a spacious three-bedroom home in the area at a bargain price.

6   ANDORRA VILLA
U.S. Highway 75, Ketchum, ID 83340
Amenities: None

Located on the main highway, these condos are in a quiet residential section of Ketchum, only a five-minute walk away from the center of town with its shops, restaurants, and night spots. Each unit faces out over Trail Creek and the fir trees for a view of Bald Mountain. The hearty can walk to the River Run ski lifts, others will want to take the shuttle bus. You'll enjoy this a quiet, comfortable place.

6   ATELIER
Sun Valley Resort, ID 83353
Amenities: All Sun Valley Resort golf, tennis, and pool privileges.

These were the first condos to be built in the area. Convenient to the main lodge, they have shuttle bus transportation to the ski slopes a mile away. These condos are showing 15 years of use. Although Sun Valley Management generally does an outstanding job of maintenance, these just lack the design and style which we've come to expect in the 1990s. Interior decor is fairly standardized although we saw condos where replacements came from discount stores instead of design showrooms. Although a great location, don't expect too much.

9   BIG WOOD
U.S. Highway 75, Ketchum, ID 83340
Amenities: Golf, clubhouse, pool, tennis

Located just north of the town of Ketchum, Big Wood is its own separate community, distinct from Sun Valley, Ketchum, or Warm Springs. Some of the area's most luxurious homes with price tags between $1,000,000 and $3,000,000 are on the fairways of this 9-hole golf course. Just across from the clubhouse, you'll find the Big Wood condominiums. Designed for luxurious living, these condos have extra high ceilings, curved windows, and cabinet work in the living room, which gives a personal home touch. The centerpiece is the hearth fireplace for cozy winter evenings, but in the summer, you'll want to be out on the deck overlooking the golf course and Bald Mountain in the distance. Skiers will enjoy the luxury, but tennis and golf players in the summer will especially appreciate this location.

8   THE BLUFF
Elkhorn Resort, ID 83353
Amenities: All Elkhorn Resort golf, tennis, and
swimming privileges.

These two and one-half story wood frame condos are situated on the hillside overlooking the main part of Elkhorn Village. The tennis center and pool complex are close by and accessible by a hillside path, which makes The Bluff condos a highly desirable choice during the summer months. Skiers will probably want to take the shuttle over to Bald Mountain, but the lifts to Dollar Mountain are less than five minutes away by car. On the inside, these condos are handsomely decorated with lots of wood trim, cabinet work, and hearth fireplaces. Luxuriously decorated, many have themed interiors drawing upon the ski or golf course location. The Bluff is very attractive for families, children, and seniors.

7   BONNE VIE
Elkhorn Resort, ID 83353
Amenities: All Elkhorn Resort golf, tennis, and
swimming privileges.

Just across the street from the center of Elkhorn Village, these condos are along the fairway of the 9th hole. Two and one-half stories in height, some are townhouses including two bedrooms and a loft. Built 15 years ago, most have been recently redecorated. This community exudes solid comfort (nothing flashy), and a sense of well-being in the world. In the summer, these have the advantage of being next to the pool and across from the tennis center. It's a great location for families with young children who want to swim or take lessons. In winter, the shuttle to Bald Mountain stops across the street and the lifts up Dollar Mountain are only a short walk away.

7   CHRISTOPHE CONDOMINIUMS
351 2nd Ave., Ketchum, ID 83340, 208-726-0999
Amenities: Athletic club membership.

Near the River Run lift in Ketchum, this condo building has undergone name changes so regularly in the five years since it was built that it's been difficult to keep track. Known most recently as Stovall's Spa Suites (formerly The Tyrolean Condominiums), the Christophe Condos have recently undergone a major refurbishment. The new developer has created an innovative, contemporary package that includes membership in the Sun Valley Athletic Club (just two blocks away), on-site property management, and heated underground parking. The exterior has been redesigned to reflect the stylish interior renovations. Upbeat contemporary furnishings, such as wing chairs paired by the fireplace and a VTP are in each living room. Upgraded baths with marble tubs and mirrors add a touch of elegance. All in all, this does have a uniquely advantageous location since it is both in town (within walking distance of all the shops and restaurants) and next to the ski lift up Bald Mountain.

8   COTTONWOODS
Sun Valley Resort, ID 83353
Amenities: All Sun Valley Resort golf, tennis, and pool privileges.

Some of the older units in Sun Valley, these two-story wooden condos have views of the golf course and Mt. Baldy. The focal point of each one and two-bedroom condo is the wood burning fireplace in front of which is a good spot for drinking wine. There are a few free standing three-bedroom units that are great for a group of skiers. These are as large as many homes and some have private saunas. With lots of space, they are perfect for families just as they are well designed for one or two couples on a ski or golf vacation. The interior decor varies with the owner's interests. Some units look like "home" while others fit into the mold of resort accommodations with neutral colors, wood end tables, and a cowboy-style dining table with rawhide covered chairs. Some have full entertainment centers where widescreen TVs have been supplied for everyone's enjoyment. Conveniently located, they are just across from the ice skating rink or above Trail Creek/Sun Valley Lake. Within a five minute walk you are at the Sun Valley Art Center or at the equestrian center. Cottonwoods is casual and Sun Valley chic.

6   DOLLAR MEADOW
Sun Valley Resort, ID 83353
Amenities: All Sun Valley Resort golf, tennis, and pool privileges.

Just a two minute walk from the Sun Valley Lodge, with its green and village shops, lie the Dollar Meadow condominiums. These two-story buildings were built 18 years ago and the trees have grown up around the units, so each has a forested environment. They are simple in design and decor. Remember this is Sun Valley real estate where guests may use the sports facilities of the Lodge and all the extra services. The two-bedroom-plus-loft units are far superior because of the vaulted ceilings, and many have converted the little loft into a sleeping area that is perfect for children

6 ELKHORN VILLAGE INN
Elkhorn Resort, ID 83353, 208-622-4511
Amenities: All Elkhorn Resort golf, tennis, and pool privileges.

Although these are technically condominiums, they are more like hotel suites since they are upstairs at the Elkhorn Lodge. Built 10 years ago to resemble a European ski village, Elkhorn Village is four stories high and has French/Italian/Austrian architectural touches. The apartments are beautifully decorated like deluxe hotel rooms with neutral colors, lots of plants, and a pleasant environment. All right for families, these are much better suited for sophisticated couples who want to walk upstairs after a night of lively dancing.

8+ FAIRWAY NINE
Elkhorn Resort, ID 83353
Amenities: All Elkhorn Resort golf, tennis, and pool privileges.

Deluxe and top-of-the-line Fairway Nine is located within the Elkhorn resort area. These are duplexes or triplexes in a parklike setting overlooking the fairway of Elkhorn's ninth hole. New and beautifully designed, most are professionally decorated with lots of fabric, wallpaper, and silk flowers. They include all conveniences—VTPs, microwaves, and indoor heated garages. Guests here may use the pools and facilities at Elkhorn Village

9 GREYHAWK
Ritchie Dr., Warm Springs, ID 83340
Amenities: Pool, hot tub, tennis. Near Warm Springs golf course and ski lift.

These classy condos are just what the Warm Springs area needs. Many of the Warm Springs properties are now 15 years old and although considered an exclusive area for vacationers, many of the buildings and unit interiors appear "down at the heels." Greyhawk is new and the condos have style and extra features. Lodgepole timbers on the outside, accentuating the normal two-story gabled roof structures, give the first clue that these are a treat. Inside, there's lots of wood in the entrance way and along one of the living room walls. Some have decor using American Indian designs in the fabrics and good reproduction art. All have full kitchens with microwaves. At Greyhawk, you have your own pool, sauna, and hot tub at the clubhouse. Clearly Greyhawk is the best in Warm Springs.

5 HABITAT 2000
Leadville Ave., Ketchum, ID 83340

Amenities: Pool, hot tub

With such a striking name, you would expect a little more. This quiet cluster of 20 two-story condos are in angular wooden buildings on Trail Creek. They are on the far side of the highway with only Trail Ridge condos and the fire station for neighbors. Interior decor is superior for what you would expect to find in this price range, but the futuristic style, which the name implies, is sadly missing.

5   HORIZON IV
Third Ave., Ketchum, ID 83340
Amenities: Pool, hot tub

Located in a quiet residential section of Ketchum, these condos are surprisingly cute. Although they are some of the area's most inexpensive, the two-bedroom loft units have cathedral ceilings and a sense of space. They provide great views of Bald Mountain and these units are within walking distance of the River Run chair lift. It is a good place for groups of skiers or young families.

7   INCLINE VILLAS
Warm Springs, Ketchum, ID 83340
Amenities: None. Warm Springs Golf and Tennis Club
almost next door and guest memberships are available.

Brand new at Warm Springs, these are some of the best in this area. Well built and decorated in a contemporary, casual style, you'll enjoy the overall ambiance. These units were designed with lots of glass to make the most of the view and bring the sunlight inside. Great for golfers in summer, skiers will want to take the shuttle bus to the Warm Springs lift in winter.

9   INDIAN SPRINGS
Elkhorn Resort, ID 83353
Amenities: All Elkhorn Resort golf, tennis, and pool privileges.

The location is the advantage here. These deluxe one and two-bedroom condos are located at the Elkhorn ski lift, which will take you up Dollar Mountain. Just a stone's throw from the village with its shops, many of the Indian Springs condos overlook the golf course. The tee for the first hole is right out your doorstep. What could be more convenient? Although these condos are now 17 years old (some of Elkhorn's oldest), they have been well maintained. All have superior interior decor, generally with a motif such as golf, the Old West, or American Indian. Perhaps the best feature is the scale of the units. All of the rooms are overly large. Very comfortable, it is one of the area's best values.

6   THE INN AT TRAIL CREEK (Ptarmigan Condos)
Wood River Dr., Ketchum, ID 83340
Amenities: Pool, hot tub

These modest condos have a great angle over the competition: ski-in accessibility from the River Run area in the winter. These two-bedroom condos are along low-lying Trail Creek, so all views are up Bald Mountain. Interior decor is neutral with "skierized" furniture for comfortable vacations. The jolly manager will give you a warm welcome.

5   INTERNATIONAL VILLAGE
Warm Springs, ID 83340
Amenities: Pool, conference room

Located right by the lifts in the heart of the Warm Springs area, these one-bedroom condos enjoy an excellent location. The conference center in their advertisements, in reality is a meeting room adequate for groups of 25 or less. Sadly, the maintenance at these units has slipped. Several have threadbare interiors and they do not represent the standard of quality you'd expect to find in Sun Valley's Warm Springs area. Most of the units are one-bedroom models although there are a few two-bedrooms.

7   KNOB HILL RIDGE
Sixth at East Ave., Ketchum, ID 83340
Amenities: None

These two-story townhouse condos have the most central location in Ketchum that you could want. Near the intersection of Main Street and Sun Valley Road, these two-bedroom units are close to the area's restaurants, bars, and shops. You won't need a car as the bus stop for the Warm Springs ski lift is nearby. The three-bedroom units are some of Ketchum's finest with superior decor and as many appliances as you probably have at home. These can be expensive, but the space and solid comfort make the price worthwhile. Knob Hill Ridge provides an "in town" choice that is best for groups of skiers.

9   THE LEGENDS
Elkhorn Resort, ID 83353
Amenities: All Elkhorn Resort golf, tennis, and pool privileges.

Elkhorn's newest and most elegant townhouses, these three-bedroom patio homes only have one shared wall with their neighbors. They would otherwise be individual single family homes. The exterior design with stone and lodgepole construction make these some of the most attractive in the entire Sun Valley area. Inside, you'll find stone fireplaces and oversized rooms. Many have been decorated by interior designers who have a proclivi-

ty for the Pacific Northwest or Native American designs. Some have imaginative lodgepole beds. Truly, top-of-the-line-for style and decor in the area,
yet rental rates are quite reasonable.

7+   **THE LODGE CONDOS**
         Sun Valley, ID 83353, 208-622-2151
         Amenities: All Sun Valley Resort golf, tennis, and pool privileges.

Right next to the swimming pool the Lodge Condos are actually a part of
the luxurious Sun Valley Lodge. On the outside, these look like three-story
college dormitories, but this is where Cary Grant and Lucille Ball stayed
when they took their kids skiing. At Sun Valley, low-key comfort is in
vogue because many of the guests are the true elite and have no need for pre-
tense. These condos are straightforward and comfortable. Everything is there
in a standardized cookie cutter mold to make sure you enjoy your stay.
Colors are forest green and beige. Absolutely nothing is out of place, but it
does not have the customized luxury which you would expect to find at a
deluxe condo. Use of all of the hotel facilities, including swimming pool and
saunas is included. Also, kids ski free when their parents stay here. Although
the appearance to the naked eye wouldn't tip you off, the lodge condos are
considerably more expensive than the other condos in the Sun Valley area.
Why? It's the Lodge itself, with its imposing air of 1930s elegance. You'll
find Bavarian blond wood carved furniture where you take afternoon tea and
watch the ice skaters. There's a refined luxury here. The nicest advantage is
the atmosphere. You might be vacationing next to one of today's TV stars.
Don't plan on using the sofa as a bed—Sun Valley Lodge is just not where
guests sleep on a sofabed.

6   **PINNACLE CLUB**
         Elkhorn Resort, ID 83353, 208-622-4511
         Amenities: All Elkhorn Resort golf, tennis, and pool privileges.

Part of the condos at Elkhorn Village have been set aside for those who
prepaid for the right to use this resort. If you're planning a timeshare
exchange to Sun Valley, this is by far the best choice.

7   **THE RIDGE**
         Elkhorn Resort, ID 83353
         Amenities: All Elkhorn Resort golf, tennis, and pool privileges.

Probably the most popular condos in Elkhorn Resort, they offer solid
comfort, great location, and excellent value. These one- and two-bedroom
units are in a series of two-story buildings along the hillside, across the street
from the main part of Elkhorn Village with its shops, restaurants, and sports
facilities. The dimensions of the rooms in the units are overly large, which
immediately creates a sense of luxury. Step inside to a large living room and

dining area. The kitchen is probably larger and perhaps better equipped than what you have at home. Many have been decorated with that Northwest woodsy look where woven fabrics compliment polished wood. Even the one-bedrooms have their own washer/dryer and you'll find a small alcove that can easily be converted into an extra sleeping area for a child. Not pretentious, The Ridge condos make a wonderful vacation home.

6   RIVER RUN LODGE
P.O. Box 1298, Sun Valley, ID 83353, 208-726-9086
Amenities: Pool, hot tub. Ski lift next door

Located on the outskirts of Ketchum, tucked away at the bottom of Bald Mountain's ski trails, is River Run Resort. This is a great location because you can walk to the River Run lift. Ski-in/ski-out convenience is a rarity in Sun Valley and the value of this location will only improve when the high speed quad chair goes in. Sadly, however, the units are a little bit small. It may not be quite the vacation home that some are looking for. Fully furnished, you'll find the centerpiece to be the wood-burning fireplace in the living room. The "skierized" furniture that has been treated to withstand use and each sofa converts into a bed. It's a great location and it is reasonably priced.

1   SADDLEVIEW CONDOS
Ketchum ID 83340
Amenities: None

These two-story wood ranch-style buildings look as though they've seen better days. Contrary to the area's quality image, cheap construction has made these best suited for groups of college students.

7   SAGEHILL TOWNHOUSES
Morningstar Rd., Elkhorn Resort, ID 83353
Amenities: All Elkhorn Resort golf, tennis, and pool privileges.

Unlike most of the condos at Elkhorn, Sagehill is located far away from the village, over by Harker Center and the Willows tennis courts. These very spacious two- and three-bedroom units are quiet and appeal to those seeking privacy. The village is five minutes away by car. Vaulted ceilings heighten the sense of space. Well furnished, some show the work of interior decorators who have imported traditional upholstered furniture and brass beds to this otherwise rustic setting. It is good for large families and groups of skiers or golfers.

6   SMOKEY PLAZA
Warm Springs, ID 83340
Amenities: Hot tub

One of the most popular choices in the Warm Springs area, it is located in an area dense with vacation condos. Smokey Plaza offers quiet townhouse-style lodgings close to the Warm Springs lift. Superior in space and decor, these units are great for families or skiers who have brought their own fun with them. The living room with its fireplace and open breakfast bar to the kitchen provides a good setting for entertainment.

8   **SNOW CREEK**
Sun Valley Resort, ID 83353
Amenities: All Sun Valley Resort golf, tennis, and pool privileges.

Located within the Sun Valley resort area, guests here are able to use the pool and facilities up at the Lodge. However, it's easily a five-minute drive over to the Lodge. These condos sit at the edge of Sun Valley on a hill with views of Dollar Mountain. We like these units. They are new, well designed and most are beautifully decorated with lots of soft green and beige fabrics. Snow Creek has its own heated swimming pool, saunas and clubhouse. These two and one-half story condos have loft bedrooms on the second floor that are perfect for children while parents sit by the fireplace downstairs. Snow Creek is a good choice in Sun Valley.

4   **SUN CHATEAU**
Warm Springs Rd., Ketchum, ID 833440
Amenities: None

These unpretentious condos are a good healthy half-mile walk away from the Warm Springs chair lift. Not especially for skiers, these studio and one-bedroom condos overlook the Warm Springs golf course. Designed so each has a southern exposure, sunlight streams into the living room. Sun Chateau provides economy lodging in the Sun Valley area.

9   **SUNBURST CONDOS**
Elkhorn Resort, ID 83353
Amenities: All Elkhorn Resort golf, tennis, and pool privileges.

Some of Elkhorn's finest condos, they have vaulted ceilings in the living room and skylights for warm winter sun. Located on the golf course in summer, they are within walking distance of the Elkhorn chair lift in winter. All have private fireplaces, attractive quality furniture, and little lofts or nooks where a member of the family can go off for a little privacy. Decor is generally in the Southwest Indian or desert style. Guests here can use the facilities at the Elkhorn clubhouse. Or, step into your tiled bath, the whirlpool is large enough for two.

4   **TRAIL CREEK CONDOS**
Leadville Ave,, Ketchum, ID
Amenities: Hot tub

Located in a residential section of Ketchum, the main part of town is a ten-minute walk away. These newish wood and stone units overlooking Trail Creek, the valley and Bald Mountain, are spacious and adequately finished for those looking for a bargain price. Many of the units are occupied by local residents, and guests here will soon learn the inside scoop on the Ketchum/Sun Valley area. These condos are more residential in flavor.

7   **VILLAGER I AND II**
Sun Valley Resort, ID 83353
Amenities: All Sun Valley Resort golf, tennis, and pool privileges.

Located on the backside of Sun Valley resort, guests here have the right to use the Sun Valley swimming pool and lodge facilities. It's a five-minute drive over to the Lodge or a very short walk to the nearby tennis club and the Olympic swimming pool. These condos see lots of use in the wintertime. The two-story wood and stucco buildings are attractive on the outside and well furnished on the inside. The Villager is for people who want to ski or play at Sun Valley; not for those who come because of the social life.

4   **WARM SPRINGS VILLA**
Warm Springs, ID 83340
Amenities: None

This cluster of four buildings has only 36 one- and two-bedroom units. Within walking distance of the Warm Springs ski lift, each unit has a view of Pioneer Mountain. Interior decor is comfortable and homey. You'll find occasional pieces obviously removed from someone's attic. It is, however, comfortable for skiers.

7   **WEYAKIN**
Highway 75, P.O. Box 1710, Ketchum, ID 83340
Amenities: Sports center, racquetball court, sauna, hot tub,
heated pool

Weyakin is a village of individual houses, which are part of a condo project where owners and guests enjoy use of the swimming pool and clubhouse. Weyakin is located on Highway 75 about three miles south of Ketchum/Sun Valley. The houses are large and the furnishings are simple. Each house has two fireplaces: one in the living room and one in the master bedroom. Each house has 2,500 sq. feet of space. But this can be a lonely area and you won't get to know your neighbors. At the clubhouse there is a sports center with a racquetball court, sauna, hot tub, and heated pool.

9+ WILDFLOWER
Sun Valley Resort, ID 83353
Amenities: All Sun Valley Resort golf, tennis, and pool privileges

These are the most expensive condos for rent in Sun Valley. They surround the tennis club and are on the fairway of the 10th hole. It's definitely your best location for summertime fun. These two and one-half story condos are in duplexes and the combination of wood, masonry, and stucco bring to mind Japan's Osaka Castle with the carved wooden entryway. Inside, the condos have been furnished to individual taste without a standardized color theme. However, be assured that these $400,000 plus condos have deluxe furnishings in accord with their owner's finances. Guests here have the use of the Sun Valley Olympic pool, the tennis club in summer, and the Lodge's heated pool all year round. These are Sun Valley's most prestigious condos.

RENTAL RESOURCES
Alpine Resort, 800-251-3037
Bitterroot Property Management, 800-635-4408 (large selection in all areas)
Elkhorn Resort, 800-635-9536
Mountain Resorts, 800-635-4444
Premier Properties, 208-726-1569
Professional Management Services, 208-622-3510
Resort Reservations, 800-635-8242
Sun Valley Resort, 800-635-8261 (the genuine original)
Warm Springs Resort, 800-635-4404
White Cloud Properties, 208-726-0110

LOUISIANA

New Orleans is the vacation attraction in Louisiana. "Laissez les bons temps roulez" or "let the good times roll" is your introduction to this city of self-indulgence. Nowhere else can you find the combination of European history, French architecture, Southern hospitality, and spicy Cajun food. The reason to come to New Orleans is the French Quarter and environs. During the day, you can enjoy the mystique of the side streets and the lush, tropical gardens tucked away in the courtyards. At night, when the temperature has cooled off, the city comes alive with jazz halls, crowds roaming the narrow streets in one of the world's greatest year-round outdoor parties and, of course, some of the finest dining in the world.

The French Quarter is the original section of the city and is about 400 years old. Everywhere you turn in the quarter, you'll find the ghost of some historical person, many of whom had questionable reputations like pirate Jean Lafitte or the infamous Voodoo Queen, Marie Laveau. After seeing the architecture, the museums, the shops and just walking the lovely streets with their flowering trees and graceful palms, your mind will be refreshed. The homes of the French Quarter have an unassuming look from the street. Following the 18th and 19th century French style, these are four-story town-houses with high ceilings and inviting courtyards called "maisons." You would find this architecture in some sections of Paris, but here with the 20th Century embellishments, the style is all New Orleans.

The food of New Orleans is superb. Some of the best restaurants in the U.S. are located here. Lots of seafood, especially shrimp and oysters with Cajun spices or "blackened" abound here. The French cuisine is rated tops and the prices in the established restaurants are surprisingly low for all that you get. Enjoy strolling the French Market for fresh sugar cane and other surprising delights. Drinking is noteworthy, too. You can begin with a Hurricane at Pat O'Brien's, where introductions come quickly, and soon your group will be off to a series of bars or jazz houses. The smallest bar in the country is located on Bourbon St., in a three foot wide closet. They serve a great Hurricane too. New Orleans prohibits glass bottles or glasses on the street but, because of the custom of outdoor partying, you'll see locals and visitors alike mingling with their drinks in plastic cups.

Accommodations in New Orleans are short on space and long on style. The few condo/timeshare properties in this area offer primarily suites with mini-kitchens. Only the Hotel de la Monnaie is family oriented. Transportation to New Orleans is a snap with nonstop jet service provided by most of the major carriers to cities all over North America.

WHERE TO STAY

6 **AVENUE PLAZA/EUROVITA SPA**
2111 St. Charles Ave., New Orleans, LA 70130, 504-566-1212
Studio $125
Amenities: Health club spa, heated outdoor pool, hot tub

Avenue Plaza/Eurovita Spa is a converted apartment building located in the (garden) district. It is only 15 minutes away from the French Quarter. The advantage of this resort is the large size of the condo suites and the cosmopolitan atmosphere. The focal point is the health spa. It occupies most of an entire floor and features a pool, exercise equipment, beauty treatments, and massages. When you enter, you'll feel as though you've stepped into a hotel. But this is one of those residential hotels that were common before World War II. Many guests have lived here for as long as 15 years. Upstairs, a few floors were set aside for vacation ownership accommodations. This is the Eurovita Spa part. The units are actually suites filled with early 20th century-style decor (heavy rosewood) along with new upbeat contemporary styles—a comfortable mix. All units have kitchens. Avenue Plaza is one of the best choices for an extended stay because the resort isn't in the hubbub of the French Quarter, yet transportation is easy; the St. Charles streetcar stops right in front of the building to take you to the French Quarter or the parks and zoo in the Garden District. The area is convenient to Tulane for football or college weekends.

8+ **HOTEL DE L'EAUX VIVES**
315 Tchoupitoulas St., New Orleans, LA 70116, 504-942-3700
1BR $125–155
Amenities: Pool

Located near the World Trade Center and the central business district, Hotel de L'Eaux Vives is only a stone's throw away from the French Quarter and the Moonwalk. This maison is a series of three buildings remade into a four-story condo hotel. Formerly warehouses and a hotel, the buildings now sport an elegant lobby done in an oriental style with marble floors and many gilt-edged mirrors. The potted palms, oriental carpets, and reproductions of Charleston furniture create a romantic ambiance. The living room in 16 of the 20 units can be partitioned off to create a second bedroom. There's a quiet, landscaped pool area. The Hotel de l'Eaux Vives welcomes children although we didn't see any.

8+ **HOTEL de la MONNAIE**
405 Esplanade, New Orleans, LA 70116, 504-942-3700
1BR $125–155
Amenities: Pool, hot tub, sauna

Hotel de la Monnaie is located right across the street from the Old U.S. Mint on the eastern edge of the French Quarter. Formerly a hotel, it was totally rebuilt in 1980 as timeshare condominiums. While the other properties in the French Quarter are small maisons, this is a five-story building which, on first impression, looks like a hotel. It is a suite hotel with 24-hour, front-desk and concierge service and a small restaurant where Hotel de la Monnaie provides a complimentary Continental breakfast to all guests.

Step inside the ornate lobby and you'll be surrounded by elegance from the liveried doorman to the gilt-edged mirrors. The condos are spacious and are filled with English and French antiques as well as antebellum reproductions. If you had a rich uncle, this is where he would pass the time in New Orleans. Almost unique to this city, there's an indoor pool which is popular with children. For service and a touch of romance, this is your top choice in New Orleans. Also far and away, this is the best choice for children because of the pool area.

5   MARDI GRAS MANOR
619 Governor Nichols St., New Orleans, LA 70116, 504-524-0370
$925/wk
Amenities: Pool

Attractive, but Mardi Gras Manor has no on-site management. It is located in the French Quarter, a stone's throw from the French Market. They are brick houses that have a connecting wooden balcony surrounding a charming courtyard. Sit under the shade of the live oak trees and enjoy serenity. One minute away, outside this cloister, you are in the bustling Quarter. There is a small pool. The condos are small with kitchenettes, but who needs to cook in New Orleans? The quiet setting and the location convenient to evening attractions make this a recommended property. On our visit we didn't see children, but they say they are welcome here.

6   QUARTER HOUSE
129 Chartres St., New Orleans, LA 70130, 504-525-5906; $950/wk
Amenities: Courtyard pool, hot tub

Quarter House is located in the heart of the French Quarter. This residence is a cluster of four restored Victorian warehouses. Times have changed, and the central location is within easy walking distance of Jackson Square, the French Market, and Bourbon St. The four continuous buildings that comprise the Quarter House complex date from 1831 through 1835. Shops facing the street on the ground floor were interconnected to create a residence with condo suites. At one time it housed Martin's, the largest and longest running bookie palace in the city. While the building exteriors have been restored in a manner that maintains their historic appearance, the interiors were gutted and totally modernized. Each condo includes a mini kitchen with two burners, a microwave oven, a dishwasher, and a whirlpool tub in the bathroom. There is a charming landscaped brick courtyard and pool. Always in residence are Veaux, a blue Amazon parrot, and Barrett, a brown and gold macaw. Inside the condos, the decor is traditional, with mauve and blue hues, exposed red brick walls, and mahogany furniture in the bedrooms.

MAINE

Resorts in Maine can be divided into two categories: the coastal resorts from Ogunquit up to Bar Harbor, and the ski resorts of Sunday River and Sugarloaf. There's a special allure to the coastal resorts owing to the fresh breezes, the craggy shore, and the towering firs. No other seaside areas offer the same drama as the Maine resorts along the East Coast. For skiers, Sugarloaf and Sunday River offer some of the steepest vertical drops and best snow conditions to be found in New England. Not as popular as the resorts of Vermont or New Hampshire, the ski areas of Maine offer shorter lift lines and less crowded conditions. The one drawback is the remoteness of these ski areas, especially Sugarloaf. They are fairly distant from the population centers, so transportation is unquestionably difficult. Also, take warm clothes. Temperatures in upstate Maine on a winter evening can drop to 20° below zero.

In this chapter, we describe over 70 resort properties: condominiums, cottage colonies, and lakeland cabins. There are many, many more vacation homes available for rent, but on an individual basis. We have included collections of vacation properties in all price ranges. This chapter is divided into four parts:

1. The Maine Coast
2. Sunday River
3. Sugarloaf Mountain
4. Lakeland Cabins

Vacation Rentals in Maine require a real estate broker. Therefore, the most private resort condos and vacation homes will not have telephone numbers. Cottage compounds or motels that have added condominiums *will* have telephone numbers. Like North Carolina and Massachusetts, the list of rental agencies in the Rental Resources section is of utmost importance. For individual vacation home rentals, there is also a "900" telephone number where individuals list their vacation homes for a fee (900-97-MAINE).

1. THE MAINE COAST

If you could choose any resort for a summer vacation, where would you go? President George Bush chose Kennebunkport, Maine, as the spot for his private family vacations. Kennebunkport is a charming Victorian town with picturesque homes, a dramatic strip of shoreline, and a fishing village that serves as the focal point with shops and restaurants. For years, Bostonians and industrialists from the New England mill towns traveled to Maine for summer vacations because of the pristine forests and lakes, within a stone's throw of the rugged coast. Artists also love this area of the Maine coast because the natural beauty lends itself to creativity. Whatever your profession, you're bound to have reasons to choose a Maine vacation. The Maine coast is legendary for its craggy beauty, the picturesque light-

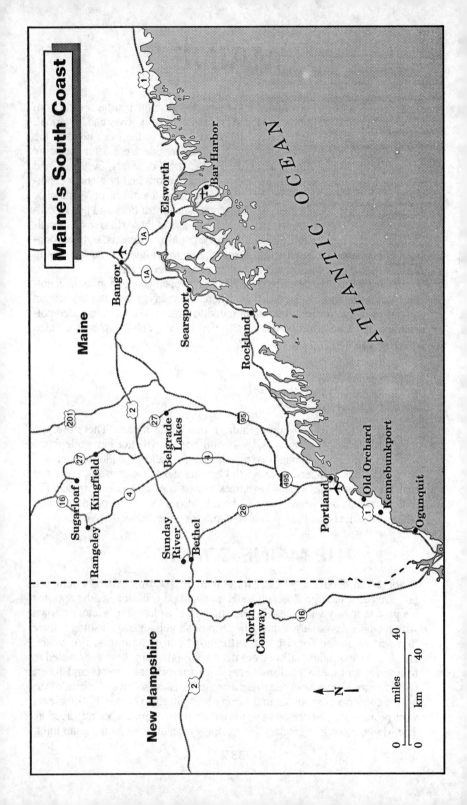

houses, and a way of life that hasn't changed much since the seafaring days. Although the Age of Sail has passed, sailors and fishermen still go down to the sea in small boats to explore the coves or perhaps to search for lobsters.

One of the primary reasons for coming to Maine is a love of the sea, and resorts in this area offer sailing instructions as well as sailboat rentals. Rockport and Kennebunkport are names you know. Ogunquit is a surprise farther down the coastline. Visiting Perkins Cove and the Marginal Way is like taking a trip to the English coastal areas of Cornwall or Devonshire. The Marginal Way is a walking trail along the cliffs. Perkins Cove offers the unspoiled atmosphere of a fishing village with little tea shops and boutiques.

We have divided this coastline into four geographic subsections:

1. Ogunquit to Kennebunkport
2. Old Orchard Beach
3. Penobscot Bay to Booth Bay
4. Bar Harbor

Transportation to the Maine coast is generally by car from other New England towns or Boston airport. Portland airport offers frequent jet service to Boston, New York, Washington, and Atlanta. Bar Harbor Airlines has commuter flights from new York, Hartford, and Boston. Driving within Maine is a pleasure because the state has a system of well-maintained roads.

WHERE TO STAY...
OGUNQUIT TO KENNEBUNKPORT

5 **CAPTAIN THOMAS RESORT**
Route 1, Box 1670, Ogunquit, ME 03907, 207-646-4600
Motel Suites $560–700/wk
Amenities: Indoor heated pool

Located just five minutes away from Ogunquit's Footbridge Beach, this is a motel cum condos. Operated as a condo hotel, these one-bedroom units are modern and efficient. Inexpensive laminated furniture in the living room, there is also a comfortable sleeper sofa. The bedroom has two double beds. The Pullman kitchen is adequate for light meals.

4 **EASTWIND**
261 Route 1, Ogunquit, ME 03907 (no mail)
Amenities: None

This is a colony of cute little redwood cottages spread over seven wooded acres. Each is individually owned and decorated. It is a quaint spot. Contact local realtors for rentals.

5   HILLCREST INN

P.O. Box 2000, Shore Rd., Ogunquit, ME 03907, 207-646-4524
Studio $52–88, 1BR $88–126
Amenities: Indoor pool. Golf nearby at Cliff Country Club

You'll find the Hillcrest Inn located just above Perkins Cove and the artists' colony at Ogunquit. This is a large four-story Victorian structure that has seen many vacationers in its day. Hillcrest has some of the charm of an English seaside resort. A musty drawing room with overstuffed sofas and wing chairs are characteristic. Yet with all the children at this family resort, the image fails. The studios have a refrigerator and coffee maker. The one- and two-bedroom suites have limited cooking facilities. What could be a charming inn with a great location turns out to be a disappointment because of dowdy furniture and indifferent housekeeping.

5   INN AT GOOSE ROCKS

Box 935, Dyke Rd., Kennebunkport, ME 04046, 207-967-5425
1BR $80–140
Amenities: Pool

The Inn at Goose Rocks is a beautiful 32-suite country inn surrounded by marsh lands. It is located about a half mile from Goose Rocks Beach. It is similar to what you've seen on the "Bob Newhart Show" except these timeshare condos are privately owned. You can rent from owners through the condo reservations services of the Inn itself. You'll find the warmth of a traditional New England Inn in the lobby, the library, and the dining room (which is popular during breakfast and dinner). The suites are nicely decorated and have parlors and sleeping areas with plaid fabrics, four-poster beds, and antique reproduction furniture. Most units include a hot plate, coffee pot, and small refrigerator. A small outdoor pool is available, but generally the guests spend their time sailing, hiking, or playing golf.

6   LOOKOUT RESORT

Israel Head Rd., Ogunquit, ME 03907 (no mail)
Amenities: Indoor pool

A huge barnlike Victorian Hotel, it enjoys great views of the ocean, Perkins Cove, and Ogunquit Beach. This is what you'd expect to find on the Maine Coast. It is very private and has no on-site management. These condos are true summer homes. Many families return here each summer while other first-time visitors choose this because of the location. Interior decor varies from contemporary to collegiate maple. Rentals are through Seeley & Ames Realty.

6   MARSHVIEW CONDOMINIUMS
Goose Rocks Beach, Kennebunkport, ME 04046 (no mail)
Rentals: 914-476-0898
Amenities: None

These ten individual cottages overlook a nature-filled marsh, yet they are in walking distance of the sand at Goose Rocks Beach. Quiet and private, this is an understated retreat.

5   MISTY HARBOR RESORT
Mile Road, Box 367, Wells, ME 04090, 207-646-8373
1BR $55–95, 2BR $80–125
Amenities: Indoor pool, restaurant, pub

Located just off Route 1, this is across the street from the Rachel Carson Wildlife Sanctuary and only a short walk from the beach. There are both one- and two-bedroom units in this condo hotel. The two-bedroom units are far superior because they are on two levels and offer twice the space with skylights and architectural flourishes from an angled roof line.

3   OCEAN DUNES
Ocean Ave., Moody Beach, ME 04054, 207-646-2946
1BR $60–200
Amenities: None

This is a cluster of three wood buildings of different heights. It houses twelve condominiums of various sizes, ranging from studios to a three-bedroom unit with a full kitchen. It is a quiet spot.

7   OCEAN VIEW APARTMENTS
72 Beach Ave., Kennebunk Beach, ME 04043, 207-967-2750
Amenities: Beach, restaurant

These apartments enjoy an in-town location and are actually an extension of a quaint bed and breakfast establishment. Each apartment has two bedrooms and a full kitchen.

7   OROTINO
Israel Head Rd., Ogunquit, ME 03907 (no mail)
Amenities: None

A rambling Victorian Hotel, it is located just steps from the Marginal Way and the Lighthouse. Converted into condos several years ago, the units on the upper levels have sweeping views of Ogunquit beach on the other side of the bay. Rentals are only through local realtors.

7 **SANDDOLLAR CONDOMINIUMS**
RR2, Box 920, Goose Rocks Beach, Kennebunkport, ME 04046
207-967-3421, Studio $80–110, 1BR $100–140
Amenities: Beach

Just a stone's throw from the white sands of Goose Rocks Beach, these condos don't look like much from the outside, but inside you'll find charming, personalized decor accented by knickknacks from the days of whaling captains.

6 **SEA CASTLES RESORT**
50 Shore Rd., Ogunquit, ME 03907, 207-646-6055, 800-648-6055
Studio $65–115, 1BR $85–150
Amenities: Indoor pool, outdoor and indoor hot tubs

The location of Sea Castles Resort is undistinguished, yet the condos are among the most beautifully decorated in Maine. These new townhouses are located in an old neighborhood of Ogunquit where there are a mix of country inns and private residences. Sea Castles has two sections: old suites and new townhouses. A full kitchen and a breakfast nook in the bay window are included. Contemporary furniture, potted palms (in Maine!), and designer fabrics are other characteristics. There's an indoor pool for exercise, but your best bet is the picturesque walk to Perkins Cove.

3 **SEAFARER**
Route 1, Ogunquit, ME 03907
Amenities: Pool, restaurant

A popular motel where some of the rooms have been converted into studios and sold as condos. This is a far cry from a vacation home at the beach.

4 **SEA MIST**
Route 1, Box 1524, Wells, ME 04090, 207-646-6044
Studios $55–135
Amenities: Pool

Built five years ago to cash in on the condo hotel boom, these studio units are small, practical, and efficient. It's great for Boston-area weekenders. It's a long walk over to the beach.

5 **THE SEASONS**
171 Route 1, Ogunquit, ME 03907, 207-646-6401; 1BR $55–135
Amenities: Heated outdoor pool

The Seasons is a new condo hotel within walking distance of the Marginal Way. These small units are decorated with sterile laminated furniture. There are studios, one-bedrooms, and townhouses. We saw two, and the dimensions of the rooms were small, although they had a cheerful contemporary decor with lots of pink, blue, and grey colors. They are efficient for a weekend, but you'd be cramped for a longer stay.

6 SHOREWAY
Shore Rd., Box 589, Ogunquit, ME 03907, 207-646-2040
1BR $110
Amenities: None

Well located in the quaint residential area surrounding Perkins Cove, these twelve modern Bauhaus townhouses stick out like a sore thumb. They are unattractive in a quaint neighborhood. But they are spacious and comfortable on the inside. In spite of appearances, these are choice accommodations (because of the size) for area vacationers.

5 VILLAS BY THE SEA
RR 3, Box 552, Route 1, Wells, ME 04090, 207-646-1100
800-762-5600, 2BR $75–150
Amenities: Indoor pool, restaurant

Villas by the Sea, a cluster of new three-story yellow clapboard buildings with condo suites, is located just over the line from Kennebunkport. The resort is located at the edge of the Rachel Carson Wildlife Refuge, and you can see the ocean about a quarter of a mile away across the marshlands. The resort is suited for people with a car who want to make the most of the Ogunquit-Kennebunkport area. Bird lovers will like it, but beach lovers should probably look elsewhere. The suites have a small kitchen, and a living/dining area. What's missing is a fireplace for spring or autumn. An indoor swimming pool and a coffee shop restaurant are provided. The management is helpful and genuinely friendly.

RENTAL RESOURCES
ABC Realty, 207-985-7987, Kennebunkport
Atlantic Coast Rentals, 603-887-4905, Wells
Beechwood Realty, 207-967-4336, Kennebunkport
Downing Agency, 207-985-3328, Kennebunkport
Drown Agency, 207-985-6176, Five offices in the Kennebunkport-
    Wells area
Garnsey Bros. Rentals, 207-646-8301, Wells
Jean Knapp Agency, 207-646-4546, Extensive list of vacation rentals
Kennebunk Beach Realty, 207-967-5481
McKeon Realty, 207-985-3345, Kennebunkport
Ogunquit River Properties, 207-646-6062
Perkinds Real Estate, 207-646-5535, Ogunquit
Sanddollar Agency, 207-967-3421, Kennebunkport

Seaside Rentals, 207-363-1825, Ogunquit
Shore Realty, 207-646-9345, Upscale cottages in Ogunquit

WHERE TO STAY... OLD ORCHARD BEACH

4   BEACHFRONT
       1 Walnut St., Old Orchard Beach, ME 04064, 207-934-7434
       Studio $50–120, 2BR $85–175
       Amenities: None

This two-story condo hotel is located right down in the heart of Old
Orchard, near the Boardwalk and the pier. Small and tidy, each studio has a
kitchenette. It is good for weekenders.

8   DANTON TOWERS
       207 E. Grand, Old Orchard Beach, ME 04064, 207-934-0511
       Amenities: Beach, indoor pool, hot tub

Clearly the best in terms of size and quality of construction. It is located
on the north end of the beach, about a mile from the Boardwalk area with its
carousel. The condos in this eight-story structure have ocean views and
some have spiffy interior decor with contemporary style, deck chairs, and
splashes of bright fabrics to offset the blue-grey sea. The old Danton home
has been preserved as part of the property.

6   GRAND BEACH INN
       198 E. Grand, Old Orchard Beach, ME 04064, 207-934-4621
       800-926-3242, Studio $55–95, 1BR $65–105
       Amenities: Heated outdoor pool. Beach across the street.

This condo hotel has the accent on the word "hotel." Brand new, these
studio and one-bedroom units are modern, efficient, and cheerful. You'll
find Pullman kitchens in the studios and slightly larger kitchens in the one-
bedroom models. Interior decor uses modern light woods, Bentwood chairs,
and coordinates of pink, grey and blue fabrics. It is comfortable for a weekend with good, attentive management who contribute substantially to the
vacation flavor.

5   GRAND VIEW CONDOMINIUMS
       189 E. Grand Ave., Old Orchard Beach, ME 04064, 207-934-4837
       207-934-5600, 1BR $55–120, 2BR $75–175, 3BR $95–195
       Amenities: Beach

Originally these condos were meant to be part of a quarter-share project
where four families would jointly own the unit. As such, these second-rate
condos were dressed up with luxurious interior decor: bright designer fab-

rics, videotape players, and lots of silk flowers. That program was abandoned, so today these condos are available for rent at very reasonable prices, considering the beachfront location and all they offer. Three cheers for good value.

6   OCEANSIDE
225 E. Grand, Old Orchard Beach, ME 04064
Amenities: Beach

Another concrete high-rise on a quiet section of the beach.

6   PINE POINT VISTA
205 E. Grand, Old Orchard Beach, ME 04064
2BR $200
Amenities: Beach, indoor heated pool

This eight-story, high-rise of recent vintage has walls of pre-stressed concrete. Rumor has it that you can hear the building creak in a strong gale. They are spacious one- and two-bedroom condos, generally, with neutral contemporary decor, tweed sofas, Bentwood chairs, and nautical accessories.

6   SEA SCAPE
221 E. Grand, Old Orchard Beach, ME 04064
Amenities: Beach, heated indoor pool

This is a quiet, eight-story concrete building on the north end of the beach where a few of the condos are available for summer rentals. It has no resort flavor, but it is solid and comfortable.

6   SEAWATCH
181 E. Grand, Old Orchard Beach, ME 04064, 207-934-0760
1BR $550–770/wk, 2BR $650–840/wk
Amenities: Beach, heated indoor pool

The condos in this five-story building are a little on the small side. They enjoy a great beachfront location and one real distinction over most of the competition: on-site management that wants to help newcomers to the area. It is a friendly, family resort where you'll find lots of children on the beach, playing volleyball, or by the pool. The interior decor is more like a motel than a condo with laminated tables, tweed sofas, and inexpensive fabrics. Each condo has its own washer/dryer unit.

RENTAL RESOURCES
Beach Realty, 207-934-5768
Cloutier Property Management, 207-934-4837
Seashore Realty, 207-934-4391

Wright Agency, 207-934-4576

WHERE TO STAY...
PENOBSCOT BAY TO BOOTH BAY

7   **HOMEPORT INN**
Box 647, Searsport, ME 04974
Amenities: None

Searsport is a quiet fishing village that has only reluctantly responded to the call of tourism. Most accommodations here are in privately owned homes that have been used by some families for several generations. It's an authentic, unspoiled "summer place." Homeport Inn is actually a former estate offering a cluster of Victorian cottages on the quiet ocean frontage of Penobscot Bay. Each two-bedroom cottage has an upstairs loft and is fully equipped for a getaway vacation. You'll enjoy Penobscot Bay and Acadia National Park is only an hour away.

9+   **SAMOSET RESORT**
Waldo Ave., Rockport, ME 04856, 207-594-2511
800-341-1650, 1BR $75–205, 2BR $99–245
Amenities: Golf, tennis, racquetball, health club
indoor and outdoor pool, saunas, hot tub, game room

Samoset is one of Maine's premier year-round resorts. It is an oceanside resort that overlooks Penobscot Bay and covers 230 acres. Vacationers come to this resort because of the variety of sports activities offered such as golf (18 holes), tennis, racquetball, and skiing at Ragged Mountain. Unlike other resorts in Maine, Samoset eschews traditional "Down East" for an almost California contemporary lifestyle. The new condos are housed in four-story buildings. They are nicely designed with lots of glass walls. They are also luxuriously decorated; no spindly New England furniture here. Surprisingly, the condos do not have fireplaces. Small kitchenettes are provided for breakfast or light meals, otherwise food is available at the on-site dining room and snack bar. The two-bedroom condos have a private two-person whirlpool in the master bath. The service here will please children as well as adults. In addition to all the sporting activities for adults, there are courses of tennis instruction for juniors and supervised summertime activities programs for children (Camp Samo). Samoset has one of the best restaurants in this area and at night people come from all around for the dancing. This is a unique resort in craggy Maine.

7   **SPRUCE POINT INN CONDOMINIUMS**
Boothbay Harbor, ME 04538, 207-633-4152
Amenities: Dock, pool, restaurant, cocktail lounge

This Inn is a relic from another era, yet the condominiums offer modern, oceanfront luxury. Here you have the best of both worlds. Boothbay Harbor's rocky shoreline has an array of summer houses, that are truly private; passing from family member to family member through the generations. The Inn has been this community's focal point for weddings and special events. Over the years, there has been a devoted following which has resulted in the creation of these modern luxurious condos. The Inn occupies a quiet, wooded peninsula, that is tucked away just far enough from the activity of the Inn.

RENTAL RESOURCES
Colburn Realty, 207-882-4020
Ethelyn Giles, 207-633-4350, Offers over 70 vacation homes
    from cottages to Victorian estates
Tindal and Callahan Real Estate, 207-663-6711, Exclusive properties
Waite Realty, 207-633-4062

WHERE TO STAY... BAR HARBOR

5 **ACADIA VILLAGE RESORT**
    U.S. Routes 1 and 3, Box 1105, Ellsworth, ME 04605
    207-667-6228
    Amenities: Pool, exercise room, tennis

Aggressively promoted as luxury townhouse rentals in the Acadia National Park/Bar Harbor area, these condos are a long stretch from Acadia. They are actually located in the town of Ellsworth which services Mt. Desert Island 15 miles away. You are easily 30 minutes away from the activities of Acadia National Park or Bar Harbor. Promotions aside, however, they represent an excellent vacation rental value as you are close to the "real world": Ellsworth shopping mall, and only minutes away from the Bar Harbor golf course in Trenton or the natural beauty and beach of Lamoine State Park. With 450 acres of land, privacy is assured and each modern two-story townhouse has a full kitchen, washer/dryer, microwave, and a VTP for your entertainment. In the master bath, which has an ambiance created by the cathedral ceiling and skylight, there's an oversized whirlpool. Definitely not Acadia or Bar Harbor, but these condos have their own unsung advantages.

8 **ALBERT MEADOW CONDOS**
    17 Albert Meadow St., Bar Harbor, ME 04609
    Amenities: None

Formerly the old schoolhouse, this white elephant from the 19th Century has been recently remodeled to contain eight condo units. Well located next to the park overlooking the harbor, the main part of Bar Harbor is a three-minute walk away. Stylishly decorated, these units are meant to be a home away from home with efficient kitchens and modern luxuries. The decor is far above the standard of most area vacation rentals.

4   BAR HARBOR TOWNHOUSES
Route 204, Trenton, ME 04605
Amenities: Golf

Located on the Bar Harbor Golf Course, do not for one minute imagine that these townhouses are in Bar Harbor. The golf course is six miles from Mt. Desert Island at Trenton on the mainland, and twelve miles from Bar Harbor. Brand new, these three-story units overlook the fairway, but the location is lonely and it's a surprise to find them punctuating the windswept landscape. Lamoine Beach Park, one of the best kept secrets of the downeast area, is on the other side of the golf course.

8   BAYVIEW MEADOW TOWNHOMES
111 Eden St., Bar Harbor, ME 04538, 207-288-5861
800-356-3585, 1BR $95–250
Amenities: Pool, restaurant

Located next door to the former Oakes estate, these three-story white townhouses have an excellent new of Frenchman's Bay, and the Porcupine Islands. The main part of town is a half mile away so this is a peaceful residential area. These two-bedroom units are the most spacious condos in the area and each has a full kitchen. On the lawn in front there's a picnic set-up for private entertaining. Otherwise, guests may use the recreational facilities of the Bayview Hotel next door (one of the area's most prestigious). These townhouses are Bar Harbor's only offering and are well suited for two couples travelling together and, of course, they are perfect for families.

6   EMERY'S COTTAGES
Sand Point Rd., Bar Harbor, ME 04609, 207-288-3432
1BR $60–78
Amenities: None

An old fashioned New England cluster of cottages by the sea, these little Cape Cod style cottages have decor from the 1950s including kitchenettes and aged televisions. The location is Salisbury Cove, a mile from downtown Bar Harbor. There is a picturesque view of Frenchman's Bay.

NR **HARBOR RIDGE**
Freeman Ridge Rd., Southwest Harbor, ME 04679, 207-244-7000
Amenities: Indoor pool, exercise room, game room, tennis

Currently under development, Harbor Ridge clearly is the largest project in Southwest Harbor. Scattered over 19 acres, this forested location is inland, very close to Acadia National Park. These three-story townhouses are in a series of three-unit buildings. Interior decor promises to set a new standard for elegance in Bar Harbor. Each two-bedroom townhouse can be rented on a weekly basis only. They are being sold as timeshares. This has more activities available than any other resort in the area.

6 **MT. DESERT CONDOS**
49 Mt. Desert St., Box 536, Bar Harbor, ME 04609, 207-288-4523
Studio $625/wk, 1BR $750/wk, 2BR $975/wk
Amenities: None

Looking like a large Norwegian mansion, these condos are in a brand new rambling yellow wooden structure in downtown Bar Harbor. The arches of the roof line have a Scandinavian angle and have been trimmed in green. The location is two long blocks away from all the activity of Main Street, so don't worry about noise. This is where Bar Harbor's streets become tree-lined avenues of gracious homes. These condos are among the area's most luxurious. The three-bedroom model, for example, has a private whirlpool and a private deck where you can read under the shade of the tree. Rare for condos along the shore, each has a private fireplace.

6 **STONE HAVEN**
Eagle Lake Rd., Bar Harbor, ME 04609, 207-288-3401
Cabins $560/wk
Amenities: None

This typifies rustic living. This hideaway of small houses set on 20 mountaintop acres has all the benefits of being within Acadia National Park. Close to the park entrance, these vacation cottages are only four miles from downtown Bar Harbor. Each cottage is surrounded by birches, pines, granite ledges, and blueberries. Inside, you'll find two-bedrooms, living room, bath, and kitchen. The living room has pine cathedral ceilings, a fieldstone fireplace, and tweed furniture. Close and accessible to town, it's private and secluded up here.

8 **WESTERN WAY CONDOS**
Robinson Ln., Southwest Harbor, ME 04656
Amenities: Dock and pier

Formerly the site of a picturesque Victorian home overlooking the bay, the old has made way for a new generation of condos. Handsome in design, this is one that the conservative villagers applauded. These three-story buildings have been designed to follow the natural contour of the hillside and the weathered wood exterior—with green trim as an outline, blends in with the local area architecture. Western Way is superior to its neighbors. Light airy interiors, polished blond wood, sky lights, and designer fabrics create an environment that would please any urban sophisticate. Some of these three-story, two-bedroom-plus-loft units have a built-in sauna on the ground floor where the garage is. The living rooms are upstairs and the bedrooms are on the third floor with an extra loft above. The pier across the street is for the exclusive use of Western Way guests.

RENTAL RESOURCES
Island Realty, 207-288-9778, Best bet for condo rentals
L.S. Robinson Realty, 207-288-9784
Lynham Agency, 207-288-3334

2. SUNDAY RIVER

Operating on the premise that some of the 13 million skiers in the Northeast would go the extra distance to find a ski area with virtually no lift lines, Sunday River has seen more construction within the past five years than any other ski area in North America. Lacking the terrain of Killington, the style of Stowe, and the accessibility of Stratton, Sunday River nonetheless is a destination resort where you'll be busy for a week. There are five mountain peaks that all interconnect, and it boasts the most extensive snow-making equipment in the Northeast.

The condos at Sunday River are in nine separate developments on the mountains. There are two off-mountain developments along Route 2, at the Bethel Country Club seven miles away. These were designed to appeal to summertime golfers as well as to skiers. There are 800 individual condo units on the mountain, and after a day of inspection we honestly couldn't remember which was which. The condo developments are almost all the same in three- or four-story, barracks-style structures. Interior decor is pleasant and comfortable, generally displaying the individual owner's personality. Although there are many rental agencies in the area, Sunday River Real Estate (207-824-3000) seems to have a lock on most of the properties. Very few of the individual condo properties have a telephone number and almost everyone checks-in at the Condominium Welcome Center.

Transportation to the area is relatively easy. It's a four-hour drive from Boston and eight hours from the New York suburbs, all along interstate highway except for the last 40 miles. From the Portland airport, the drive can be done in less than two hours.

WHERE TO STAY

8+ **BETHEL INN AND COUNTRY CLUB**
Bethel, ME 04217, 207-824-2175, 800-654-0125
1BR $85–130, 2BR $130–200
Amenities: Golf, tennis, restaurant, health center, pool

This rambling white inn surrounded by towering maples dates from the beginning of the 20th Century. Management has not rested on its laurels and over the past fifteen years has added an 18-hole championship golf course and 80 two-story townhouse condos overlooking the fairway. You'll love the view. The condos are on a ridge overlooking the valley. These are the most luxurious lodgings in the area with a spacious living room and fireplace for those cold winter nights. Ceiling fans will keep you cool during the summer. Snack in your kitchen or walk over to the inn's dining room for your meals. Rates are set by the inn and rental rates are per person, not the customary per unit charge. Located in the heart of Bethel, the Sunday River is seven miles away.

6 **CASCADES CONDOMINIUMS**
Sunday River Resort, Bethel, ME 04217
Studio $84–120, 1BR $128–170
Amenities: Pool, sauna, hot tub

This barracks-style building houses a bevy of studio and one-bedroom condos. Popular with youthful skiers, there is ski-in/ski-out access on the lower Broadway run and a host of après-ski activities, including an indoor pool, health club, and video game room. The condos are functional and we've heard that studios can be purchased for as little as $30,000.

5 **CHAMBERLAIN RESORT**
Route 2, Bethel, ME 04217, 207-824-3090; 2BR $80–150
Amenities: Pool, sauna, hot tub

This is a modern four-story structure just outside of town. The two-bedroom units are stylish, but a little on the small side.

5 **EDEN RIDGE CONDOMINIUMS**
Paradise Rd., Bethel, ME 04217
Amenities: None

These new two and a half-story townhouse condos could be full-time residences as well as vacation homes. Located on the edge of the town of Bethel, the setting commands an impressive view of the fields of the valley and Sunday River mountain off in the distance. Each two-bedroom unit has a fireplace for wintertime warmth and ceiling fans for the summer. The Bethel Inn golf club is only ten minutes away by foot for those who want to play in the summer. The Sunday River ski area is seven miles away.

7 FALL LINE CONDOMINIUMS
Sunday River Resort, Bethel, ME 04217; 1BR $128–170
Amenities: Indoor pool, game room, restaurant

Located just a stone's throw from the ski lifts at the South Ridge Base Area, this is one of the most popular and social condo clusters at Sunday River because of all the après-ski amenities they offer and the popularity of the restaurant in the evening. You are right on the lower Sundance ski run, so there is ski-in/ski-out accessibility. These one-bedroom units are reasonably priced.

7 LOCKE MOUNTAIN TOWNHOUSES
Sunday River Resort, Bethel, ME 04217
2BR $112–206, 3BR $256–373
Amenities: None

Overlooking the Roadrunner ski trail, these spacious townhouses are just a little removed from the main South Ridge Center. These are spacious three-bedroom units with over 1900 square feet of living space.

8 MERRILL BROOK VILLAGE CONDOMINIUMS
Sunday River Resort, Bethel, ME 04217
Amenities: None

These condos are superior in construction and decor to most of the lodgings at Sunday River. Each one-, two- and three-bedroom condo has its own fireplace. There are private hot tubs where you can soak in the afternoon and look out over the mountain. Interior decor includes basic tweed furniture accented by pillows and perhaps framed ski posters on the walls. These are the most convenient condos in Sunday River because they are next to the South Ridge Base Area.

4 PLEASANT RIVER CONDOS
Route 2, West Bethel, ME 04217, 207-836-3575; 1BR $50–125
Amenities: None. Restaurant and pool next door

These new condos are a mile or so outside the town of Bethel when heading south toward Poland Spring. Simple and efficient, this is a pleasant cluster of second homes, but first time visitors will miss that resort feeling. These reasonably priced one-bedroom units are perfect for a young family.

4   **RIVERVIEW**
Route 2, Bethel, ME 04217, 207-824-2808; 1BR $65–125
Amenities: Sauna, hot tub, game room

This is a three-story Victorian inn. Several years ago a wing of modern clapboard condos was added on in order to accommodate the growing demand for lodgings in this area.

8   **SOUTH RIDGE TOWNHOUSES**
Sunday River Resort, Bethel, ME 04217
1BR $128–170, 2BR $192–256
Amenities: Sauna. Use of the Brookside facilities

Clearly the most spacious and the most private units at Sunday River, these two-story duplex townhouses are scattered through the woods overlooking Ridge Run. There is ski-in/ski-out access and you can walk to the South Ridge Base Area. Decor includes "skierized" tweed furniture and lots of wood tables and paneling. The fireplace is the centerpiece. Some have a finished family room or game room on the ground level.

6   **SUNRISE CONDOMINIUMS**
Sunday River Resort, Bethel, ME 04217; 1BR $128–170
Amenities: Pool, sauna, hot tub

Sunrise offers one-bedroom units adjacent to the intersection of the lower Broadway and Easy Street trails. There's a popular game room, health club, and an indoor pool.

RENTAL RESOURCES
Manhoosuc Realty, 207-824-2771
Riverbend Associates, 207-824-2078
Scott Management, 207-824-3090
Sunday River Realty, 207-824-3000, 800-543-2-SKI

3. SUGARLOAF

The Sugarloaf tale can be sad or it can be fortuitous, depending upon your perspective. Sugarloaf is clearly the best skier's mountain in Maine and for that matter, maybe in all of New England. There are 45 miles of skiing on 75 groomed trails. Snow making covers 80% of the mountain, which on its own, receives one of nature's heaviest snowfalls in the Northeast. Summer is even better when the air is fragrant with pines, and meadows of wildflowers are a visual feast. The pinkest glow of sunrise will inspire you and it can only be matched by the lingering mountain shadows in the evening. This is a beautiful area with all the right ingredients: natural beauty and sparse population.

Unfortunately, the area's remoteness is at once an advantage and its nemesis. Ask any skier and you'll hear that Sugarloaf is just too remote. The condo development at the base has been carefully planned and would normally draw hordes of skiers, but Sugarloaf is a solid five hours from Boston and twelve hours from New York. The nearest airport is in Lewiston, nearly an hour away and not on any airline's frequent flight schedules.

You can enjoy the forest primeval, just don't be surprised if its a little more lonely than you expected. There are a couple of restaurants and night spots at the resort, but the nearest town, Kingfield, is a long 19 miles away. The condos are attractive and you'll be stunned by how low the prices are. As recently as November 1991, it was estimated that 40% of the area's resort condos had been repossessed by banks or currently were in some stage of the foreclosure process. Condo asking prices are 30% lower than just a year ago and, for the few sales that actually do take place, the price may be 40% below the original purchase price. We hear that some are even selling for less than the construction costs.

In short, Sugarloaf is a beautiful place with excellent facilities and ski conditions. Well developed, it offers a handsome village, but social life is very limited. Condo rental rates are low, the prices for resort condos are among the best bargains in North America. But the question is how do you get there.

For first-time visitors, it is wise to know that the area has been designed so the main road is the spine with dozens of side roads branching off. Each is located directly on the mountain so almost all units, except those down near the highway and the Gondola village, have ski-in/ski-out access. The rule of thumb is that you want to be closest to the village for après-ski and evening social life. However, the condos closest to the village are twelve to twenty years old. Sometimes it can be noisy in the area. The units also rely upon a dumb waiter system for luggage and groceries. They are the least attractive with gold and avocado color schemes or burnt orange shag carpet. The newer condos, which are the most attractive and luxurious, are farther away from the village. There is a resort shuttle, but we've heard complaints about the frequency of its runs. Perhaps it's better to rely upon your own car.

All of the units we describe are within Sugarloaf Village, so we have dispensed with the mailing addresses because they are all the same. Just write to either Sugarloaf Resort Rentals, Carabassett Valley, Maine 04947 or to the largest off-site competing rental service, Mountain Valley Property, P.O. Box 281, Kingfield, ME 04947, 207-265-2560.

WHERE TO STAY

8 BIGELOW CONDOMINIUM
3BR $160–328, 4BR $228–402
Amenities: Sauna, hot tub

Bigelow is one of the best choices because it's only a two-minute walk to the village, yet you are away from the center of commotion. These units are huge with three or four bedrooms, over 2,000 square feet of living space, and most have either a private sauna, a private hot tub, or both.

7 BIRCHWOOD
2BR $150–235, 3BR $160–328
Amenities: None

Birchwood is just a hop from the Sugartree Health Club, one of the most active places in the evenings. These new two- and three-bedroom units have vaulted ceilings and lofts for an extra spacious feel. The location is a little inconvenient for skiers, and this is one of the few complexes without ski-in/ski-out access.

7 THE GLADES
Studio $108–167, 1BR $108–173
Amenities: None

Architecturally inspired, these condos are superior to most of the condos at Sugarloaf. Sizes range from studios to four-bedroom units. Antique reproduction wood-burning stoves are popular. The location is remote on the west side of the ski area.

4 GONDOLA VILLAGE
Studio $108–173
Amenities: None

Although popular with young skiers on a budget, because of the central location at the base of the mountain, the cheap construction, and the generally poor maintenance of the common areas this one of the least desirable spots in the area.

7 MOUNTAINSIDE
207-237-2200, 2BR $150–235
Amenities: None

Located at the intersection of Mt. Blue Road and the Buckboard ski trail, this is close to the center of the village. These are some of the older condos in the area. The boxy architecture is more functional than aesthetic. These two-story condos generally have faded decor from the late '70s. Some have been accented with touches of nostalgic New England, such as wood-burning stoves and framed posters on the walls of ski resorts.

7 SNOWBROOK
1BR $120–190
Amenities: Indoor pool, hot tub, tennis

Among some of the newer condos at Sugarloaf, these are located at the bottom of the mountain just off the highway next to the Snubber chair lift. The units have a modern boxy design, and many have lofts that make the interiors spacious. Each has an attractive fireplace. Snowbrook has its own recreational center with an indoor pool, hot tub, and tennis courts in the summer.

8+ SUGARTREE
Studio $108–167, 1BR $108–173
Amenities: Health club, pool

The attraction here is the health club, which is a center for all the village after skiing. The location is on the far side of the parking lot so it's a good five minute walk uphill to the village and the ski lifts. These studio and one-bedroom units seem to be most popular with the first-time visitor to Sugarloaf. The units are handsome with customized cherry cabinetry, fireplaces, and quality furnishings.

5 VILLAGE CENTER
1BR $108–184, 2BR $150–264
Amenities: Next to ski lift

These are some of the oldest condos at Sugarloaf and if you are young and plan to be up part of the night anyway, you won't mind the noise. Cheap construction means you can hear your neighbors as well as party-goers at night. The location, however, is perfect because you are right next to the ski lifts and close to restaurants.

8 VILLAGE ON THE GREEN
3BR $160–388
Amenities: None

Clearly, the best around, these deluxe duplex townhouses and homes are stunning with high arched windows, lots of sunlight, and superior interior decor. Overlooking one of Maine's best golf courses, these units have a year-round appeal.

RENTAL RESOURCES
Mountain Valley Properties, 207-265-2560
Sugarloaf Homes, 207-237-2100
Sugarloaf Mountain Condos, 800-527-9879
Sugarloaf Resort Rentals, 207-237-3500

4. LAKELAND CABINS

This section covers a large and magnificently scenic section of Maine from the New Hampshire border over to Rangeley in the middle of the state. Created by glaciers, the landscape has shallow, warm lakes that were gouged from the land eons ago. One of the area's sights is Daggett Rock—a boulder left by the glaciers that measures over 100 feet in length. This is wide open country and not the place for condominiums. But it is thick with vacation homes and cabins that attract summertime visitors from Florida and California, as well as the expected groups from Boston and Connecticut. We have identified a couple of the larger vacation home rental agencies for you, and we have summarized a few of the properties they offer for rent. This is not even one-half of one percent of the cabins and cavation homes in this area, but it will give you some direction and sense of whom to call.

WHERE TO STAY

 DASCHUND HOLLOW RENTALS
Box 520, Rangeley, ME 04970, 207-864-5666

Another large vacation rental agency, this group specializes in cute country homes. An example would be the **Greenvale Cove House,** which is a cute bungalow enjoying a private out-of-sight location on the shores of Rangeley Lake. Carefully decorated with Yankee and antique touches, this one also has a private hot tub. Others include log homes over by Saddleback Ski Mountain.

 HIGH COUNTRY RENTALS
Box 173, Rangeley, ME 04970, 207-864-3446

This agency seems to concentrate on the upscale properties in the area such as the **Hylenski House** featuring views of both Saddleback ski mountain and Rangeley Lake, or the **Zambranski House** with just two bedrooms, an interior decorator living room, and a private sauna.

 MAGNUM DEVELOPMENT
Box 189, North Windham, ME 04062, 207-892-2732

This rental agency accommodates the sophisticated golfers as well as those who want the "Backwoods Maine" experience. Many of the vacation homes are located close to the Mingo Springs golf club. Our favorite was **Conifer,** a four-bedroom house with a small dorm and den upstairs. It is perfect for two families traveling with lots of children.

MOUNTAIN VIEW AGENCY
Box 1100, Rangeley, ME 04970, 207-864-5648

One of the largest rental agencies in the area, they have lakefront homes, such as the **Connaugton Lodge,** which is built in the style of a modern log cabin, and the **Shapiro Cabin,** which is more rustic.

7 **ROCK POUND CONDOMINIUMS**
Saddleback Ski & Lake Preserve, Box 490, Rangeley, ME 04970
207-864-5671
Amenities: Skiing

Located at Saddleback Ski Mountain, these deluxe condos are huge and compete favorably with the highly stylized vacation homes nearby. Although they don't offer the log cabin architecture, many have cute country French or New England Yankee decor. These are three-, four-, and five-bedroom condos and most have a private hot tub. Some also have private saunas.

5 **WHITE BIRCH CONDOMINIUMS**
Saddleback Ski & Lake Preserve, Box 490, Rangeley, ME 04970
207-864-5671
Amenities: Skiing

These simple one- and two-bedroom condos are great for families who want to ski. In summer, they are often overlooked because most vacationers want to be on the Lake, not in a sublimely quiet, closed ski resort. The rental rates are very low here. In our opinion, these offer a better value than most of the area's vacation homes.

RENTAL RESOURCES
Belgrade Rental & Management, 207-495-2525, Belgrade—Paland Springs
Cabin Condo Care, 207-647-5241, Rangeley
Foster Property Management, 207-647-8093
White Church Associates, 207-864-5979

MARYLAND

Maryland's playground is Ocean City on the Eastern Shore. This barrier island has one season, summer, when the population swells from 7,000 to well over 100,000. It's a beach resort and one of the most popular spots for deep sea fishing. Summer days are sunny with temperatures in the 80s, evenings in the 70s. Spring and fall are refreshing and the island is a quiet place for beachcombing. Winter can be cold and blustery.

Ocean City is a strip of high-rise hotels and condominiums. Town begins at 1st Street, where the Amusement Park is located and the Boardwalk begins. The older part of town extends from 1st to 24th Street. Paradoxically, it enjoys the best and safest beach. the shallow waters and sand are gradually increasing each year. The streets north of 24th have areas of quiet low-rise and townhouse condos. There is no on-site management. All have condo rentals, but there isn't full-service resort hospitality because most of these condos are for weekenders from Baltimore and Washington. Weekenders already know the area and generally don't need a local manager to give them some orientation.

Around 80th Street the buildings have grown taller maturing into a series of high-rise towers. Antigua, the Pyramid and the Plaza are the most outstanding because of their height. A few of these high rises have on-sight management and all have pools, hot tubs, and decks for sunbathers wishing to avoid the sand. The Carousel at 118th Street is the busiest with a hotel and a condo tower as well as a conference center. Ironically, this part of the beach is where the sand has eroded creating a sharper drop and stronger surf. You'll see Boogie boards and an occasional surfer here, but not many swimmers. The height of the buildings, and the activity, decreases on up to the end around 145th Street.

There's also the Bayside with low-rise condos and many shingle-sided wooden structures that are no more than three or four stories high. The Bay is quieter and vacationers on this side of the island tend to be more interested in fishing and water sports.

Ocean City is a regional resort area for the most part. Most of the condos do not have on-site management, an office, or even a telephone number. Rentals, with few exceptions, are in the hands of realtors who have developed local reputations in handling the thousands of condo vacation rentals in Ocean City. You'll find the names and telephone numbers in our rental resources section. Rentals generally are for a one week minimum and prices are all over the board. The following chart should give you a ballpark figure for summer rentals.

Shoulder Season	July/August
1BR $300–550/wk	$600–800/wk
2BR $350–675	$650–900

The rental agents have agreements with the individual owners, and generally there's no on-site rental program, so there's no one to enforce consistent interior decorating standards at these condominiums. After visiting and inspecting these condos we found most of our selections to be clean and furnished with superior taste. However, you won't find many with the professional interior decorator decor we've described here in other condo properties in this book.

Ocean City is a relaxed and friendly place. Families can enjoy activities together. Young travelers revel in the social life, which in summer, can continue until 1 a.m. Mature travelers can find a quiet place to relax and enjoy the sunshine and fresh ocean air.

WHERE TO STAY

6 ANTIGUA
86th St. and the Ocean, Ocean City, MD 21842
Amenities: Oceanfront pool

A new high-rise, 12-story condo tower, Antigua has unusual architecture. There are ten sides to this building and a donut hole atrium in the center. Some condos have bay views, some have ocean views. You'll find attractive furnishings in most condos with lots of blues, greens, and orange colors. Some have very casual rattan furniture; others show an effort to decorate; still others look like surplus from the Holiday Inn.

5 BOARDWALK ONE
P.O. Box 762, 1st St. and the Ocean, Ocean City, MD 21842
410-289-3161
Amenities: Pool, beach. Guest membership at health club.

This is one of the very few condo buildings on the southern end of the beach with on-site management. Boardwalk One is on First Street, just north of the Pier and the Amusement Park. In addition to the advantage of being close to the center of activity, Boardwalk One also enjoys perhaps the best portion of the beach. At this southern end of the island, the beach is at its widest and the water is shallow, permitting small children to play in the gentle surf. Unfortunately, although it enjoys a good location, the condos at Boardwalk One are dreary. The one-bedroom units are actually studios with two Murphy beds built into plywood pine paneled walls. It's time to replace the striped plush fabric on the sofas. There's a swimming pool, and guests may use the Ocean City Health and Racquetball Club. Boardwalk One enjoys a good location, offers fair accommodations and is reasonably priced.

8+ CAROUSEL
118th St. and the Ocean, Ocean City, MD 21842
Amenities: Beach, outdoor and indoor pool, exercise room, hot tub, tennis, ice skating rink

This is Ocean City's most exciting resort. Operated like a hotel rather than vacation condo, Carousel offers a carnival of activity for children and adults. Located on a prime section of the beach, these twin 21-story towers were designed so all have an ocean view. Pleasant, spacious interior design with blond wood furniture, seafoam green and pink fabrics are found throughout. They've added lots of mirrors to bring in the ocean view and glass-top tables to keep it light. All have kitchenettes. Everything is in perfect working order and there's even a little basket of soaps and shampoo. The Carousel has a conference center and atrium meeting hall that is popular with small conferences or receptions, and makes the resort seem much busier. There's a huge indoor pool, a large rock-bordered hot tub, and an outdoor pool. This is where you'll find most of the activity. You'll also find a game room arcade, ping-pong, and tennis outdoors. In winter, there's an indoor ice-skating rink. The Carousel social directors run a supervised activity (building sand castles) for children in the summer.

4 DIAMOND BEACH
39th St. and the Ocean, Ocean City, MD 21842
Amenities: Beach

Here is your standard, mid-rise condo on the beach in mid-town. Not down near the pier (1st Street) or up in the dense area of high rises (95th St.). A quiet, no-nonsense place at the beach, all condos are either oceanfront or there is a view from the wing running toward Atlantic Avenue. There are no standardized furniture plans; each unit reflects the owner's style. The location is across from the convention center.

8 GOLDEN SANDS
109th and the Ocean, Ocean City, MD 21842
Amenities: Indoor and outdoor heated pools, saunas, snack bar, exercise and game rooms, tennis, paddle ball

These are among the most spacious and luxurious condos that Ocean City has to offer. A small studio with a Murphy bed becomes an attractive living room in the day. There are five plans to choose from and the deluxe one- or two-bedroom has an extra nook or den which can be used as an extra bedroom. Golden Sands offers lots of amenities—extra large outdoor and indoor pools, a 24-hour security guard, and a small gift shop in the lobby. The beach is steep here, so small children tend to congregate around the kiddie pool. Older children play with their Boogie boards in the surf.

6   LIGHTHOUSE POINT VILLAS
      14409 Lighthouse Ave., Ocean City, MD 21842

A slumbering location on the northern end of the Ocean City island. These townhouse condos aren't on the beach, merely a short block away in a quiet location. You'll see young families by the pool. Each condo has a fenced in courtyard where there's a private hot tub.

7   MARIGOT BEACH
      102 St. and the Ocean, Ocean City, MD 21842
      Amenities: Indoor pool, hot tub

Well-decorated condos overlooking the ocean Marigot Beach is a mammoth new high-rise tower. Spacious and luxurious, these are some of the most expensive condos to be purchased in the Ocean City area. Decor is highly personalized but you should expect tasteful and quality furniture. They are filled with lots of soft pastels and the newest styles. Marigot offers a popular indoor heated pool. Even in summer in good weather families like to gather here. The beach is at a steep slope here and the ocean is a little rough for small children.

2   OCEAN VILLAGE
      78th St. and the Ocean, Ocean City, MD 21842
      Amenities: Beach

It's a bad sign for a supposedly modern two and one-half story row of townhouses to have peeling paint and weathered wood on the exterior. Surely maintenance could do better! These spacious three-bedroom townhouses offer generally superior interiors although, unfortunately, there are no standards in furnishings. Each unit reflects the owner's individuality. There are only ten units here.

8   THE PLAZA
      98th and the Ocean, Ocean City, MD 21842
      Amenities: Indoor and outdoor pools, sauna, game room

Some of the most desired condo rentals in Ocean City are at The Plaza. With an established reputation, rental agents report that The Plaza is one of the first condos to be fully booked each summer. The Plaza even has its own on-site rental and front office check-in. In this 17-story high-rise you'll find larger than average condos. Most have been decorated by an interior designer with some of the best interior decor in the area. A light tropical look has been encouraged with rattan furniture, glass-top tables, seafoam green and peach colors. Each has lots of mirrors and full kitchens. There's a popular outdoor pool and an indoor pool. Unfortunately, this section of the beach is at a steep slope so the water may be too rough for little children. Fortunately though, there's also a pool for children.

7 PYRAMID

95th St. and the Ocean, Ocean City, MD 21842
Amenities: Beach, outdoor pool, hot tubs

This is the landmark structure in Ocean City because of its architectural design. It is shaped like a steep pyramid, ranging from six stories on each side to 19 stories at the center. Not only are there steps from each side, but it's arranged in an arch surrounding a swimming pool area. Each unit has an ocean view. These are some of Ocean city's more expensive condos to own and the interior decor reflects a high level of decor. Unfortunately, hospitality is limited to one person in an office, so this resort lacks the service that you would expect at a landmark. Too bad, though, because this is a special building with better than average units.

6 THE QUAY

107th and Beachfront, Ocean City, MD 21842
Amenities: Indoor pool, sauna, game room, card room

One of the tallest buildings among this strip of high rises. They are spacious condos, but have tacky interior decor with inexpensive fabrics and lots of artificial flowers. It's all the activities that distinguish this one. The entire second floor is a recreation area with game rooms, card rooms, billiards, and video games. Indoor pool and saunas are included here.

5 SALTY SANDS

46th St. and the Beach, Ocean City, MD 21842
Amenities: Beach

Up around 46th Street the beach starts to slope steeply into the ocean. What began as gentle surf around 1st Street has become a series of rolling waves that crash on shore. Here at Salty Sands, you can hear the surf. This five-story wooden condo structure has two wings: one along the beach (oceanfront) and one heading toward Atlantic Avenue (oceanview). There is a peaceful atmosphere here and the condos are comfortable. There is no standardized furniture plan, so each unit reflects the taste of the individual owner.

6 SANDPIPER DUNES

58th St. and the Ocean, Ocean City, MD 21842
Amenities: Sheltered pool

The first high-rise you come to heading from the southern end of the beach is Sandpiper Dunes. This ten-story high-rise has no rental or administration office on site. You will find a clutter of luggage carts in the drive way to help you move in. Everything is self-service here. Spacious condos, but no standardized furniture packages. The advantage here is a swimming pool in the rear; desirable on those windy days along the shore. Some condos face the ocean; the others face the bay.

3 SUNRISE EAST
75th St. and the Ocean, Ocean City, MD 21842
Amenities: Beach

These are efficiently designed modern oceanfront condominiums. There are only 15 units here in this three-story buildings in the mid-town section of Ocean City. Here, you are on your own. You have a place to stay at the beach and that's it. There are no standardized furniture plans.

5 WHITE MARLIN
Somerset St., Ocean City, MD 21842
Amenities: Pool, marina

A brand new four-story wood condo structure on the bay with its own marina and boat dock. It's at the very southern tip of Ocean City island, down below first street. It is a great location for those planning fishing expeditions. You can bring your own boat or cruiser and tie up at the marina. These condos have an efficient floor plan for the one-bedroom units that are a little bit smaller than average. Many have beautiful, modern furnishings. We saw several decorated by professionals with peach or aqua fabrics and blond wood furniture. There's an attractive swimming pool overlooking the marina. As these are on the bay, they enjoy beautiful sunset views.

RENTAL RESOURCES

There are two mega rental agencies here, Moore, Warfield & Glick and O'Connor, Piper & Flynn. These two companies each have rental listings at over 120 condo developments in the Ocean City area, plus additional listings for condos over the line in the Bethany Beach, Delaware, area.

Antigua, 410-525-1116
Atlantic Condominium, 410-524-9100
Carousel Hotel/Condo Resort, 410-524-1000
Club Ocean Villas, 410-524-5241
Colonial Property Management, 410-524-5241
Golden Sands Club Condominium, 410-524-5505
Marigot Beach, 410-524-2442
Moore, Warfield & Glick, Inc., 800-437-7600
O'Connor, Piper & Flynn, 800-633-1000
Ocean Realty, 301-524-7800
Ocean Time Condos K & W Mgmt, 410-524-5577
Plaza Condominium, 410-723-3300

Pyramid, 410-525-6003
The Quay, 410-524-0204
Resort Reservations, 800-346-3834
Sea Watch, 410-524-4003
Sewell Matthews, 410-228-5673
Shoreline Properties, 800-492-5832
Waves, 410-250-2262

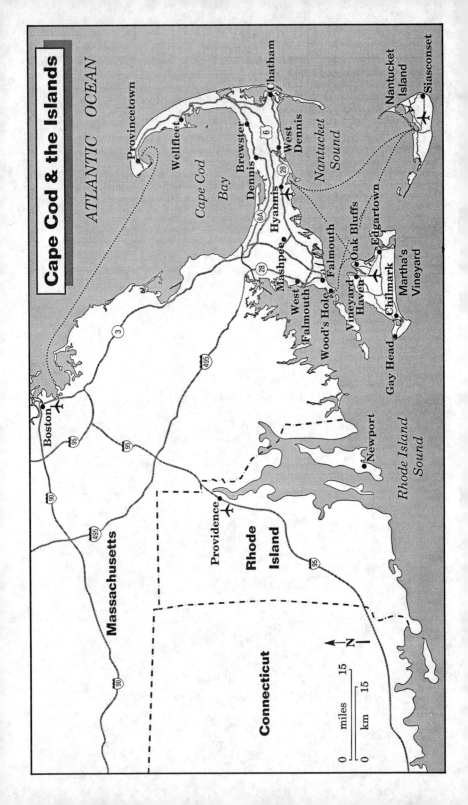

Cape Cod & the Islands

MASSACHUSETTS

Although Massachusetts is a small state, it has a lot to offer vacationers. The climate varies and there are several resort areas to choose from. The main centers are Cape Cod, Martha's Vineyard, Nantucket, and the Berkshire Mountains of western Massachusetts. Cape Cod has a mild climate because of the nearby warm gulfstream waters. The ocean water can actually be warmer around Cape Cod than at the beaches further south. The temperatures are mild and range between 65 and 78 degrees in the afternoons during the months of May through October. A sweater will probably be necessary in the morning, but in the afternoon the weather is usually warm and great for playing at the beach. What are the chances of a dry day? A surprising 84 percent of the days between June and September are classified as sunny, according to the Cape Cod Visitors and Convention Bureau.

Martha's Vineyard and Nantucket are two unique offshore islands. Each has developed its own personality and clings strongly to tradition. Martha's Vineyard is easily reached by frequent ferry service from Woods Hole. The charge for taking your car over can be quite reasonable; the problem is getting a reservation. Nantucket is a full two hours away by ship and the cost of ferrying a car over to the island exceeds $80. Some condo/villa rental agencies on Martha's Vineyard and Nantucket include ferry reservations and tickets with the rental. If you've ever waited in a ten hour line to take your car aboard, you'll understand the priceless value of those ferry reservations.

Once on the islands, you'll discover a wonderful vacation area. Martha's Vineyard has several distinct communities and can be quite exclusive. Nantucket is more democratic in spirit, but it can be almost as expensive. There are no other summer resorts in North America like these two islands and each should be visited at least once in a lifetime.

The Berkshire Mountains have a climate similar to the neighboring Vermont mountains. Snow is prevalent in the winter and summer temperatures are mild. There are about ten hot days each summer, otherwise the afternoon temperature hovers around 75°. For a look at the resort areas of the Berkshires, see the map of western Massachusetts on page 448.

Before taking a look at the vacation areas in Massachusetts, you need to understand that resort property accommodations in Massachusetts are handled differently than in most other states. To begin with, most of these properties are cottages and only in the western part of the state, in the Berkshires, will you find traditional condominium resorts. We say that cognizant of two huge condo complexes on Cape Cod; Ocean Edge and New Seabury. Second, in the Yankee tradition, furnishings are not generally as plush as in other parts of the country. There's a respect for hard wood floors and wicker chairs that eschews contemporary notions of soft fabrics and lots of accessories. Third, and most important, condos and vacation homes are defined as "real estate" and rentals must be through a real estate broker. Unlike veterans of the hotel industry, realtors are more likely to negotiate prices and less likely to quote a "rack rate" which in turn can be discounted. Therefore, in very few cases were we able to even obtain a ballpark figure for vacation rental rates. Many, many of these properties do NOT have front desk operations for rentals or check in, so you must use an off-site realtor.

Travel agents abhor doing business with real estate agents in Massachusetts because they don't pay the agents commissions. But the truth is that many Massachusetts realtors will pay an advertising fee to the agent that will closely approximate a commission. It's too bad that both sides have to play games when all the consumer wants is to go on vacation in accommodations better than a motel. Nevertheless, if your travel agent discourages you from booking resort property in Massachusetts, be firm. Either call the realtors and do it yourself or tell your agent that the realtor should pay the agent an advertising fee. Suddenly, doors will open and you'll get exactly what you want at no extra charge.

With four distinct vacation areas in Massachusetts, this chapter has been divided into four sections:

1. Cape Cod
2. Martha's Vineyard
3. Nantucket
4. The Berkshires

1. CAPE COD

Cape Cod has been a summer resort area for over 150 years. For example, Cape Cod was known as "the Summer White House" a century ago when President Grover Cleveland announced he was escaping Washington's summer heat to do some work in a more hospitable climate. The resort areas of Cape Cod have been developed and redeveloped to suit the changing tastes of vacationers. Individual summer homes have always been popular with the wealthy. During the 1960s and 1970s, a trend toward communities of cottages and bungalows began. These are individual villas on land where the owners collectively pay for maintenance and winter caretaking.

The trend to "condominiumize" has never been strongly developed on the Cape. Rather than apartments or townhouses, there are so many cute little Cape Cod three room houses or "saltbox" cottages in competition that there has been no need for congregate housing. What you'll find is a large number of cottages and villas in different neighborhoods having distinctive social characters. In order to fully describe the vacation accommodations on the Cape we have divided the Where to Stay section into the following sections:

Brewster — On the north shore of the Cape these properties border Massachusetts Bay and not the Atlantic Ocean. Due to the trend-setting influence of Ocean Edge, there are many cottage communities that are more than just beach resorts, because they appeal to golfers and sailors. Well-manicured, this is one of the Cape's most attractive areas.

Chatham — At the outward hook of the elbow facing the Atlantic Ocean, this is the Cape's most exclusive residential area. The homes appear to be weathered cottages, but inside you'll find many to be richly decorated and appointed with antique reproductions. Clearly the most "preppy" section of the Cape, this area will be most enjoyed if you have friends whose families have maintained summer homes here for the past 100 years.

Falmouth/Mashpee — Falmouth at the western end of the Cape has a heritage dating back to the whaling days, and has a unique charm. Mashpee, which is inland, used to be an area of cranberry bushes and inexpensive accommodations. Not so any more. With New Seabury leading the way, a host of modern new cottages have been built here in imitation Nantucket style. This is emerging as one of the Cape's most attractive neighborhoods.

Hyannis — The commercial center of the Cape, this is home to numerous motels and restaurants. Some new condos have been constructed here and others have rebuilt existing motels as timeshare units.

Provincetown — Once upon a time this former whaling village at the furthermost tip of the Cape was cute with its New England charm combined with eclectic accents from the New York theatrical crowd. But today the Gay culture shouts its presence and on a summer evening you might think many in town were dressed for Halloween.

Truro/Wellfleet — This is a neglected area of the Cape on the forearm extension just south of Provincetown. Truro has long catered to vacationing college professors and today the beach is noteworthy for some of the "clothing optional" areas. This economical area is for the young. Neighboring Wellfleet has elements of New England charm and many homes were developed as an extension of Chatham.

Yarmouth — Just east of Hyannis, Yarmouth has the best beaches, but many of its resorts are older. We have focused on two which have been completely rebuilt during the past few years and offer lots of activities to compliment your stay at the beach.

As you can see, Cape Cod offers something for everyone. With this overview of the neighborhoods, we have organized the resort accommodations accordingly.

WHERE TO STAY... BREWSTER

3   **BREWSTER GREEN**
South Pond Rd., Brewster, MA 02631
Amenities: Pool, tennis, racquetball, whirlpool spa

Brewster Green is composed of lovely little cottages on the north side of Cape Cod in a quiet wooded area complete with cranberry bushes. The location is great, but the units are not. Unfortunately, maintenance and housekeeping are a little too relaxed. There is a sports center but it, too, is in need of a good scrubbing.

7+   THE COLONY
Snow Rd., Brewster, MA 02631
Amenities: Indoor and outdoor pools, sauna, hot tub, tennis

Modern bungalows nestled together in the woods make up the Colony. Architecture is a two-story "saltbox" style with a roof line that slants 35° from the top of the second floor to the top of the first. Modestly decorated, these are comfortable with the young "Crate & Barrel" glass, wood and deck-chair look. Great for families, these have an indoor recreation center that will substitute for the beach for those days when the weather turns. The Colony is attractive and a very good value.

8   OAKWOOD
Snow Rd., Brewster, MA 02631
Amenities: None

Just a short drive from the ocean, these townhouses offer spacious vacation accommodations in a forested setting. The bike trail passes nearby and you can be deep within the Nickerson wildlife sanctuary in minutes. Fairly new, these condos have been carefully maintained and stylishly decorated. We saw one with a country charm: white wicker furniture, blue cushions, Waverly fabrics, white ruffled curtains, and a large patio. A little on the formal side, this is one of the quietest properties on the Cape.

10   OCEAN EDGE
Route 6A, Brewster, MA 02631, 508-896-9000, 800-343-6074
Amenities: Indoor and outdoor pools, beach, dock, golf, tennis
health club, restaurants, children's program

This is one of the most exceptional resorts in New England. This mega-resort was originally a private estate for Sam Nickerson, founder of the First National Bank of Chicago. Built in 1912, the main house, Fieldstone Hall, serves as the central reception and entertainment area. Immediately upon entry you'll be struck by the intricately carved oak staircase leading up to the second floor. Polished oak floors, oriental carpets and fabulous floral arrangements fill the home. Downstairs the restaurant has stone walls from the days when it served as a pantry and wine cellar. In 1930, 1600 acres of the property was donated to the state and today that tract is known as Nickerson State Park. The remaining 2400-acre parcel has been carefully developed since 1980 as a golf course/conference center resort.

The property is divided into two parts by Highway 6A. The bay side of the property has a private beach and dock where you will witness some of the most beautiful sunsets to be found in New England. The property is right at the inside cusp of the Cape's elbow so you see the beach heading north and west. This has long been a nature preserve and the resort's management is quick to train guests that the ecology (i.e. nesting birds) is more important than they are. This pays untold dividends for all who visit Ocean Edge.

Bay Side Villas — These are two- and three-bedroom condos just a short walk from the beach. Decor is controlled by the conference center management so you know what you'll find. Carved Bavarian blond wood furniture and lots of pink and pale blue fabrics. Chinese lamps and small bouquets of flowers complete the picture. These units are close to the conference center and the sports center with the Olympic-size indoor and outdoor pools, exercise room and tennis courts. A lot of celebrity jocks own condos here and don't be surprised to find your heroes working up a sweat.

Golf Course Villas — These are nearly two miles away, surrounded by the fairways and having views of the ponds and woods across the fairway links. Interior decor picks up on these colors so expect these one-, two-, and three-bedroom condos to have traditional decor, lots of green and beige fabrics, and accents of kelly green country club plaid. In many ways these condos are best for families with children because the "conference center crowd" usually stays on the other side.

8 SEA PINES
Route 6A, Brewster, MA 02631
Amenities: Beach, tennis, children's playground

Next door to Ocean Edge, this is a much smaller version that will appeal to those who want something a little more residential than its famous neighbor. This is a cute village of two-story duplex condos with sharply angled roofs. The architectural style can best be described as modern combined with Cape Cod. Spread over 19 acres, a large part of the natural wetlands has been preserved with mallow and cranberry bushes. There is a large children's playground with modern, "natural wood" equipment and a tennis court sunken to avoid the ocean breezes. These condos feature their own private beach. Inside we saw one decorated in a Williamsburg style with a tiled foyer, chair rails and molding, and wing chairs by the fireplace. Rentals are restricted to a two week minimum. Sea Pines is very well done.

9 SEARS POINT
Sears Point Dr., Brewster, MA 02631
Amenities: Beach, pool, tennis

These 62 condos are spread over 33 acres in a forested environment yet there is a boardwalk to your own private beach. Built in 1985, these are some of the most deluxe units to be found on this part of the Cape. Some have unobstructed views of Massachusetts Bay. Interior decor tends to be

"American Heritage" with brass eagles as a popular item. Some units have private whirlpools. We saw one with a large screened porch that seemed to be the main living/dining area. Sears Point is great for families or friends vacationing together but is rather expensive.

RENTAL RESOURCES
Bay Village Realty, 508-896-7001
Baywood Cottages & Homes, 508-852-6572
Great Vacations, 508-896-2090
Peter McDowell Associates, 508-385-9114
Silver Sands, 508-385-5020

WHERE TO STAY... CHATHAM

9 **CHATHAM BARS INN**
Shore Rd., Chatham, MA 02633, 508-945-0096
Amenities: Beach, golf, pool, tennis, restaurant, dancing

This is the Grand Dame Hotel of the area and enjoys a superb beach-side location, just north of the lighthouse at the Cape's "elbow." Popular with the gentry and for small conferences of senior executives, the Chatham Bars has a number of cottages available for rent right on the beach. Superbly furnished as befits a truly first-class hotel, these cottages are available for "villa rentals" at astronomical prices. One night here could equal the cost of a week at other nearby cottages in Chatham. But if you want the blend of residential privacy with the bubbling atmosphere of a hotel, this is the choice for you. There is no other offering in Chatham that combines gracious service, private "residences" with kitchens, a beachfront location, and a package of recreational amenities.

7 **COCKLE COVE CONDOMINIUMS**
46 Cockle Ridge, Chatham, MA 02633
Amenities: None

Located in the woods, a mile from Cockle Cove Beach, these are attractive two-story, brick colonial townhouses. Chatham is an exclusive, expensive neighborhood, but rentals here are at the low end of the spectrum—expect a seasonal rental to be $500 a week in the summer for a two-bedroom unit. Quite a bargain considering the location and the cost of nearby accommodations. Decor is simple. The one we saw was a mixture of Early American with contemporary "Crate & Barrel" and spindly Bentwood chairs with canvas deck chairs. This is a bargain in one of the Cape's nicest areas.

9   LIGHTHOUSE VILLAGE
4 Lobster Ln., Chatham, MA 02633
Amenities: Private beach

These are condos in name only. Actually they are individual three-bedroom Cape Cod-style villas sharing the same parcel of land. The only difference between them and single family homes is that the gardener takes care of all the units on this six-acre parcel. These are among Chatham's best condos. They have water views and a private beach. The one we saw had an Early American-style living room with hooked rugs, nautical accents, and a china cabinet for pewter mugs and plates that recalls the "Tap Room" look. The bedrooms upstairs had polished wood floors, ceiling fans, and fancy "country French" linens. Although modern, it reflects Chatham's timeless charm.

8   OYSTER POND CONDOS
1235 Main St., Chatham, MA 02633, 508-945-1095
Amenities: Boat dock, pool, tennis, recreation center

This villa colony of cute two-bedroom, single-story Cape Cod-style bungalows have some of the best saltwater views in Chatham. Boaters will also appreciate the dock on Oyster Pond. These cottages have the best of both worlds: the privacy of individual units and the setting on 16 acres of resort community with a pool and tennis court. You can stay in and relax while the kids go outside to play with the active set. This balanced arrangement is not easy to find on Cape Cod where the resort is either commercial with activity or a collection of homes with no amenities. The one we saw was beautifully decorated with large floral-designed fabrics and natural woods that provided a sort of "English-country-home-comes-to-the-shore" look. They have tiny kitchens.

7   STAR FISH LANE CONDOS
11 Starfish Ln., Chatham, MA 02633
Amenities: Private beach, pool

These contemporary condos are actually a cluster of single-story duplexes on the beach. You can walk to the lighthouse, the outermost harbor marina, and the Morris Island bird sanctuary. Simply furnished in a beach house style, these two-bedroom condos are popular with quiet families in the summer.

8   SWAN HILL CONDOS
444 Old Harbor Rd., Chatham, MA 02633
Amenities: Boat dock

These four-bedroom cottages are among the largest condos you'll find in Chatham. Located on Pleasant Bay, some of these are actually occupied year-round. They have solid, winterized construction. These two-level cottages are beautifully decorated with a mix of contemporary and Early American styles. Boaters will enjoy the private dock here.

 SYLVAN REALTY
2469 Main St., Chatham, MA 02633, 508-432-2344

With over 1100 vacation homes for summer rentals in the area, Sylvan is the leader in villa rentals with over 200 properties to choose from. Many of these vacation homes are claimed a year in advance by guests who have been returning to Chatham for years. The following reviews examples of what you can expect if you rent a separate vacation home:

Hardings Beach House — From the outside, this weathered cedar-shake house doesn't appear to be much but once inside you'll change your mind. This four-bedroom home has a 180-degree view of the water because the architect designed numerous corners with large picture windows to capture the view. Three sides of the house are surrounded by decks. This is truly designed for outdoor summertime living. White wicker furniture and neutral colors on the inside focus your attention on the smashing views of the sea oats, sand, and the blue ocean. It has a tiny kitchen, but a large outdoor barbecue area.

Forest Street Guesthouse — This two-bedroom home is actually the guesthouse on the grounds of a larger estate. Rare for Chatham (even New England) this villa has a private swimming pool and a large deck area where you have sweeping views of Nantucket Bay.

Whaler's Watch — This two-story Georgian residence has a widow's walk on the third floor where wives of whaling captains could pace in the fresh air while watching for the ships to come in. Although in town and reasonably priced, this has gorgeous interior decor with English country home fabrics, moldings and chair rails, and a private whirlpool in the master bedroom.

RENTAL RESOURCES
Chatham Real Estate, 508-945-0044
Oceanfront Townhouses, 508-771-3838
Pine Acres Realty, 508-945-1186

WHERE TO STAY... FALMOUTH / MASHPEE

6   BRIARWOOD
Pine Valley Dr., Falmouth, MA 02540, 508-540-4366
Amenities: Pool, sauna, tennis

Briarwood is located two miles from the beach in Falmouth at the southwestern end of Cape Cod. These 67 two-story condos are spread over twelve acres. The resort is like a village: not too dense and not too spread out. Each spacious condo has a full kitchen, a private patio, and two bedrooms upstairs. They are casually decorated with comfortable furniture. Briarwood is for those who want to enjoy a week at the Cape in comfortable surroundings without the nuisance of going out for meals. The management is helpful. The recreation center includes a pool. You'll make friends and share your vacation stories with other vacationers around the swimming pool or at the tennis courts. Briarwood provides good value.

7   CAPE COD HOLIDAY ESTATES
Four Season Dr., Mashpee, MA 02649, 508-477-3377
Amenities: Pool, tennis

This resort has been reborn. This is a collection of one and one-half-story Cape Cod cottages scattered through the woods, two miles from the beach. Each unit has a whirlpool. The decor shows imagination—durable furniture with contemporary design in keeping with the New England spirit. Next door to New Seabury, you may want to use its restaurants and golf club. Congratulations on the improvements.

10   NEW SEABURY
P.O. Box B, New Seabury, MA 02649, 508-477-9111
Amenities: Golf, tennis, pools, boating and fishing charters
jogging trails, health club

New Seabury is one of the finest resorts in New England. It claims 2700 acres of a private peninsula on the south shore of Cape Cod. It is a total resort community. You won't want to leave it after you arrive. The twelve separate condo villages range from cute Nantucket-style Maushop Village to private villas with private pools. The resort offers programs for children and a full fitness/activities program for adults. Younger children will enjoy Kids Kapers and older children will enjoy the junior athletics program. The Cabana Club on the beach features pools, restaurants, and a happy crowd. The Popponset Inn, the Country Club, and the casual Marketplace Cafe are the area's dining choices. One of the two golf courses has been rated among the top 100 in the U.S. by *Golf Digest*. The following is representative of some of the condos and villas available for rent at New Seabury:

Maushop Village — This is clearly the most popular place to stay. As they advertise, it is "a Nantucket fishing village perfectly recreated." It consists of grey Cape Cod cottages with brick patios and white picket fences. The cottages are fancifully decorated in an Early American style with polished plank floors, bentwood chairs, comfortable sofas, and decorator touches. Skylights, full kitchens, and fireplaces add to the comfort. The beach is only a short walk away.

The Mews — This is another popular choice. It has townhouses that usually include private swimming pools. The interiors have a decided California look, enhanced by a modern design, blond woods, and patios bordered by flowers.

Sea Quarters — This cluster of townhouses has its own recreation center with swimming pool and children's playground. The condos are designer decorated with striking fabrics. They include a private whirlpool in the master bath.

Tidewatch — These are the "economy" condos at New Seabury. Built in a saltbox style, these are right off the green at the 18th hole and only a short walk away from the Cabana Club. Spritely decorated, they have a special appeal for golfers.

7   SOUTH CAPE RESORT
Route 28, RFD 1, Mashpee, MA 02649, 800-228-2968
Amenities: Health club, indoor pool, indoor/outdoor tennis

These two-story townhouses are in a wooded setting, two miles from the beach. Completely rehabbed and redecorated in the past year, these units are beginning to show their potential. Spritely contemporary decor has changed these units and seemingly created additional space. There's a large indoor pool and health club.

WHERE TO STAY... HYANNIS

7   THE BREAKWATERS
432 Sea St., Box 118, Hyannis, MA 02601, 508-775-6831
Amenities: Beach, heated pool.

The Breakwaters is a small vacation retreat in a residential neighborhood on the beach in Hyannis. Twenty condos are available in nine weathered, wood-shingled cottages. The decor is impressive. Inside the decor includes colonial reproductions, Laura Ashley-style "country house" fabrics and wall paper in fine patterns of white and blue. There is plenty of space between the cottages. Each unit has a private patio with a table and umbrella. Families are welcome, but we did not see (or hear) any children on the lawn or by the pool during our visit. This resort is a special find on Cape Cod.

4   **CAPTAIN GOSNOLD**
230 Gosnold St. Hyannis, MA 02601, 508-775-9111
Amenities: Pool, children's playground

These are an example of bargain basement accommodations on Cape Cod. Primarily a motel, some of the one-bedroom, saltbox cottages have been sold as condominiums. Prices to buy hover near $25,000 and vacation rentals are accordingly priced. You'll find imitation walnut paneling, pullman kitchens, daybed sofas, two brass beds and "collegiate maple" furniture. Simple and practical. They are great for young families because of the company around the pool and there's a large children's playground. There are a couple of three-bedroom cottages. It is an excellent value for Hyannis because you are near several restaurants and the ferry to Nantucket. The beach is also within walking distance.

5   **IYANOUGH VILLAGE**
1029 Iyanough Rd., Hyannis, MA 02601
Amenities: None

These two-story, two-bedroom condos are just off Route 132 near the Hyannis airport. The shops of the Cape Cod Mall are within walking distance. Too far to walk to the beach, these are budget offerings on Cape Cod. The second-story units have skylights that make them brighter than the ones downstairs. Interior decor varies, but generally can be summed up as "collegiate maple" with wall-to-wall carpeting, maple tables, club chairs, and fabrics that were discontinued a dozen years ago. They have good prices, for the Cape. For those who are interested, you can buy a two-bedroom here for $45,000.

5   **SEA MEADOW**
720 Pitchers Way, Hyannis, MA 02601
Amenities: None

Practical and efficient two-story, two-bedroom condos in a multi-unit building that is hidden in a quiet residential neighborhood.

7   **YACHTSMAN**
500 Ocean St., Hyannis, MA 02601, 508-775-5049
Amenities: Pool. Beach within walking distance

This is one of the most popular condo complexes in Hyannis because management is so attentive to the property and the guests. Nearly 20 years old, these weathered cedar-shingle townhouses have recently been refurbished with contemporary decor. The units are on three levels with a sunken living room with a fireplace in the corner, a kitchen and dining area, and two bedrooms. The one we saw had lots of pink and pastel blue fabrics in the bedrooms. The pool is a great place for first time visitors to meet other owners who are familiar with the area. Veteran's Beach is just a stone's throw away.

RENTAL RESOURCES

Cape Cod Connection, 800-445-4125
Cape View Rentals, 800-924-9300
Coldwell Banker, 508-775-1404
Dacey Homes, 508-771-4400
Poyant Realty, 508-775-0079
Realty Executives, 508-445-4125
Walsh Realty, 508-775-7330

WHERE TO STAY... PROVINCETOWN

6   **CAPTAIN JACK'S WHARF**
West End Wharf, 73A Commercial St. Provincetown, MA 02657
508-487-1450
Amenities: None

Formerly home to Portuguese fishermen, these shacks have been improved and are now cute studio and one-bedroom condos available for rent. Like living on a boat, the space is compact, but with the location, you are only steps from town.

8   **DELFT HAVEN**
7A Commercial St., Provincetown, MA 02657
Amenities: Beach

Perhaps the cutest cottages in all of Provincetown. Right on the beach just west of the main part of town, these Cape Cod cottages have been converted to studio and one-bedroom units. Individually decorated, we saw one that was stark white except for gilded reproductions of funereally models from Pharaoh Tutankhamen's tomb. It's a classic.

6   **FISHERMAN'S COVE**
145–147 Commercial St., Provincetown, MA 02657
Amenities: Beach

A three-story cedar-shingled building in the west end within easy walking distance of the main part of town. Simply decorated, these are reasonably priced. The quiet setting makes them one of Provincetown's best values.

7   **HARBOR HILL TOWNHOUSES**
Route 6A, Provincetown, MA 02657
Amenities: Beach, pool

Brand new, these three-story units cascade down the hillside at land's end. There's nothing further west except the sand dunes of the National Seashore Park. Quiet and private, they are handsomely decorated with sturdy blond wood decor, Waverly fabrics, and lots of silk flowers.

5   ICE HOUSE CONDOMINIUMS
451 Commercial St., Provincetown, MA 02657
Amenities: Beach

This aging icehouse from the early part of the 20th Century has recently been converted into an unusual collection of loft condominiums. The brick and concrete exterior seems so out of place in this village of cedar-shingled homes. This is the New York lifestyle brought to the Cape.

RENTAL RESOURCES

Associates Real Estate, 508-487-9000
Beachfront Realty, 508-487-1397
Binnacle Real Estate, 508-487-0092, Properties in N. Truro
In Town Reservations, 508-487-1883
Pat Schultz Associates, 508-487-9550

WHERE TO STAY... TRURO / WELLFLEET

6   BILLINGSGATE
2 Mayo Beach, Wellfleet, MA 02667
Amenities: Beach

Located right across from Mayo Beach, these condos enjoy an excellent location. These simple one-bedroom condos are tastefully furnished with wicker and contemporary fabrics. Each has a patio overlooking the beach. For a couple that wants a relaxed vacation on a picturesque Cape Cod beach, this is an excellent choice.

8   CORN HILL COTTAGES
Corn Hill Rd., North Truro, MA 02667
Amenities: Beach

This is a community of individual Cape Cod cottages on a bluff overlooking Cape Cod Bay. Quiet, they exude a sense of Old Cape Cod, before the area became commercial. Each condo is individually furnished and each rental here gives you access to its private beach. More like Martha's Vineyard than Cape Cod—a real find.

7 **WELLFLEET HARBOR**
Commercial St., Wellfleet, MA 02667
Amenities: None

Located on a knoll just above the salty flatlands at Wellfleet harbor, these condos enjoy an impressive view. Mayor Beach is only a short walk away. Tastefully decorated, these seem casual and belie the underlying real estate value. It provides a quiet place in a community that is removed from the crush of the 20th Century.

RENTAL RESOURCES
Cape Cod Realty, 508-349-2245
Meadow Marsh Realty, 508-255-1500

WHERE TO STAY... YARMOUTH

8+ **COVE AT YARMOUTH**
Route 28, P.O. Box 1000, West Yarmouth, MA 02673
508-771-3666
Amenities: Indoor/outdoor pool, health club, indoor/outdoor tennis squash, racquetball, restaurant. Golf nearby.

The Cove at Yarmouth offers something for everyone. The property is located on over 25 acres and stretches from the highway to the ocean. There are two huge sports complexes. One has a large indoor pool in an atrium with skylights and condo units surround it. The other is a health club with racquetball, squash, and indoor tennis facilities. The health club provides a professionally supervised exercise program that will put you back into good physical shape during your vacation. Nearby are 14 tennis courts, golf, and fishing. Some of the condos are suites and are located in the main building around an indoor swimming pool. The units are spacious and beautifully decorated with lots of fabric, designer accents, and VTPs. Also included is a private whirlpool large enough for two. Kitchen facilities are minimal but there is an on-site restaurant. This resort is one of the best choices for active families who want a reasonably priced Cape Cod vacation.

6+ **OCEAN CLUB ON SMUGGLER'S BEACH**
329 S. Shore Dr., South Yarmouth, MA 02664, 800-228-2968
Amenities: Health club, library, beach, indoor/outdoor pool

The Ocean Club is composed of a two-story converted motel structure with some of the best interior decor on the Cape. The resort was opened in 1988 after a complete renovation that created small one- and two-bedroom units with fireplaces and kitchen areas including a refrigerator, microwave, and coffee maker. You'll be impressed by how much can be done by a professional designer—nautical brass work and a lantern made into a lamp;

duck decoys over the fireplace mantle; a full entertainment center including VTP that is hidden behind a sailor's chest; satin stripe materials and just the right number of throw pillows. Truly, you'll be surprised when you walk into your condo. Its almost sad to see the expense of such high quality decor on units that are so small they are substandard in size. The ground-floor units have private walled patios away from the sea; the upper level condos have balconies facing the sea. There's a private hot tub large enough for two in each condo. You'll find a game room just off the lobby level.

RENTAL RESOURCES
Cranberry Real Estate, 508-394-1700
D & B Realty, 508-771-3731
James Mischler Realtors, 508-394-3300
Les Campbell Realty, 508-394-0971
Mueller Real Estate, 508-394-9494
Waterfront Rentals, 508-778-1815

2. MARTHA'S VINEYARD

The distance from Woods Hole on the mainland over to Martha's Vineyard island is just an hour, but this is a world away. The ferry pulls into the island's commercial center, Vineyard Haven, which is at the foot of a cove. Tempting for a walking tour, but we advise you to first go out and see the island.

Like Bermuda, Martha's Vineyard has been divided into several distinct sections. More than mere geographic boundaries, these lines of demarcation separate distinct and very private communities. Heading down the east coast of the island, you'll first come upon the Victorian town of Oak Bluffs where the mansions facing the park have been trimmed in vibrant pinks and blues—nothing gaudy, just a spritely touch.

Then there's Edgartown. Edgartown was the capital of the whaling industry in the days of square-rigged clipper ships. Over 110 sea captains built the massive and ornate homes with their earnings from what was a lucrative business. To wander the streets of Edgartown is a unique experience. This trim district has been preserved from the abuses of commercialism. Edgartown is the island's social center and the venerable Harbor House has witnessed many a celebrity wedding. Over by the harbor you'll find a row of Victorian homes, one of which formerly belonged to James Cagney, and the exclusive Edgartown Yacht Club. Just to the east there's the ferry over to Chappaquiddick Island, the setting for numerous exclusive vacation homes.

Although the New England spirit tends to be thrifty, Martha's Vineyard truly is a national playground for the elite. Hollywood celebrities and New York socialites have homes hidden in the hills of Martha's Vineyard. This is where Wall Street lawyers come to play in an environment sheltered from the harsh realities of the 20th Century. South Beach has a number of private beaches where admission is restricted to owners (and rental guests) at selected vacation properties. Many of these homes are in Gay Head, on the western end, or inland in the Chilmark section. From a distance Chilmark appears to be serene pastureland for sheep and painted Jersey cows, but in fact this is the most exclusive section of this island of vacation homes.

Menemsha Harbor is a favorite of Carly Simon who owns a home on either side and who filmed a special concert at this picturesque harbor. Heading farther north along the west coast of the island you'll come to the quiet Sengekontacket Village and the backwaters of Lambert's Cove. Then you're only a short hop from Vineyard Haven and the ferry back to the real world.

WHERE TO STAY

7+ HARBORSIDE INN
3 S. Water St., Box 67, Edgartown, Martha's Vineyard, MA 02539
800-627-4009, Suites $65–210
Amenities: Pool, sauna

Strangely enough, in spite of the island's exclusive and carefully cultivated image, this is a timeshare within sight of the Yacht Club and the Harbor View Hotel. Originally a group of Victorian and Greek revival sea captains' homes, these residences have been joined to create a unique establishment. It's quite a surprise to be solicited for a sales tour on the cobblestone streets of Edgartown where candy wrappers and cigarette butts are quickly whisked away. This development has a quiet appeal not usually associated with most timeshares. The units are essentially single hotel rooms with a refrigerator and coffee maker; not a spot for families with children. This is an impressive setting on an historic dockside. Katama Beach is within walking distance and golf is available up by Oak Bluffs.

8 HARBOR VIEW HOTEL VILLAS
N. Water St., Martha's Vineyard, MA 02539, 508-627-7000
Cottages, $75–225
Amenities: Pool, tennis, restaurant

Located on the dividing line between South Beach and the public Katama Beach, the Harbor View has been the island's grand old hotel for generations. Many years ago the cottages were added. They have been renovated and are now superlative vacation homes for those who want the privacy of a residence plus the activity of a hotel setting. Bordered by roses, each is exquisitely decorated in the style of an English country cottage. Cooking facilities are limited to a refrigerator and coffee maker. You are encouraged to dine at the inn.

5   **ISLAND INN**
Beach Rd., Box 1585, Oak Bluffs, MA 02557, 508-693-2002
800-462-0269, Studio $65–125, 1BR $75–145, 2BR $95–185
Amenities: Pool, tennis, exercise room. Beach across the street.
Golf next door

Perched near the sea on the quiet outskirts of Oak Bluffs, the Island Inn offers compact studio and one-bedroom condos. When we say compact, we mean two beds, a room divider, a living area, and a Pullman kitchen. Boat quarters might be more spacious. But the location is wonderful across from Sylvia Beach and next door to the Farm Neck Golf Club. The inn's conference center is the focus of attention and during the season this is popular with many groups. The Island Inn is great for a budget weekend, but for a longer stay, you'll be cramped.

4   **KATAMA SHORES CONDOMINIUMS**
Katama Rd., Edgartown MA 02539
Amenities: Beach, pool, tennis

Right across the street from the beach, these were the first condos to be built on the island in 1965. After 25 years the location remains wonderful, but these units are showing their age. Simple in design, each is a one-bedroom model. Decor varies greatly from "early attic" to new "Crate & Barrel" with blond wood, deck chairs, and campy accessories. These condos are reasonably priced and popular because there are so few condos in this price category. If this is going to be your one trip to the Vineyard, think twice. It is great, however, for Bostonians on weekends.

_Ⓒ_   **MARTHA'S VINEYARD VACATION RENTALS**
51 Beach Rd., P.O. Box 1207, Vineyard Haven, MA 02568
508-693-7711

No matter what you've read or heard, nothing will prepare you for the fabulous vacation accommodations made available to you through Martha's Vineyard Vacation Rentals. Despite over 1,000 vacation homes available for rent on Martha's Vineyard every summer; the best homes are those often claimed a year in advance by families who have been summering on Martha's Vineyard for generations. Therefore you need all the expertise you can get in order to match your expectations with just the right summer house on this island. From Chilmark to Vineyard Haven to South Beach, this agency knows the details on each property and how to get it for you. Plus, as an extra advantage, ferry tickets are purchased eight months in advance so you'll be able to get on and off the island when you want. There will be no need to spend seven hours in the "stand by" line.

Vacation homes on the island are not cheap and prices can be as high as $50,000 a month. After all, this small island is the summer home for a host of celebrities when New York and Beverly Hills converge for summer on the island. Some of the vacation homes available for rent are:

Island Retreat — Located on exclusive South Beach, this rambling shingled-beach home appears unpretentious. The layout of this five-bedroom home, however, is anything but. There's a separate studio for visiting artists. The living room is a masterpiece of traditional design with the "Vineyard" look accented by oils of whaling ships and replicas of treasures from Spanish galleons. The dining room can comfortably seat twelve. It is perfect for entertaining or a small corporate retreat. Best of all, you have your own private beach protected by dunes and a barrier of picturesque sea oats.

On Walden Pond — This idyllic retreat was photographed for *House Beautiful* several years ago. The sylvan setting is on a small, private pond that leads out to your own private beach on Lambert's Cove. Listen to the birds and catch the light through the trees. Inside decor is Vineyard style. A pair of wing chairs guarding the fireplace, and a sea captain's chest doubling as an end table. Polished oak floors and off-white summer rugs. There's a large screened porch where you'll spend many evenings listening to the crickets by the pond.

She Sells Sea Shells — Located in Menemsha, these two cottages are cute with an authentic island style. The main house has three bedrooms and the guest house has two. Varnished pine walls and planked wood floors give that boathouse feeling—or maybe it's the view of the boats in Menemsha Harbor. Interior decor is imaginative with new uses found for old items. Bookshelves and sea shells line the living room walls while the hallway contains a straw hat collection from around the world. Two quaint bedrooms are guarded by an imaginative upstairs loft. In spite of the rustic aura, the gourmet kitchen has every appliance you could ever want.

Flying Nun — This "hippie house" from the '60s has expanded with a new addition each year. Located on a private beach in Gay Head, flying buttresses extend from the second floor to provide shade, at just the right angle, for the first floor windows. The beach is down below and the smell of the surf is ever present. Interior decor is eclectic as the hippies turned professional and made a fortune during the Roaring '80s. Expect to find nautical gear, priceless Oriental rugs, deck chairs, and a ceiling fan to catch the island breezes. Although small, it is an exceptional spot.

Lagoon Beach — This rambling summer home with bachelor's quarters is what you would hope to find on the Vineyard. Built in the upside down style with the main living room upstairs to catch the views, it is impeccably decorated in a style befitting Greenwich, Great Neck, or Potomac. Downstairs there's a large rec room with billiards table and wet bar. Best of all, this home has a private beach on the shores of the quiet lagoon.

6   MATTAKESSET VILLAGE
Katama Rd., Edgartown, MA 02539
Amenities: Pool, tennis, playground. Beach nearby

Right across the narrow bay from Katama Beach, this development encompasses 25 acres of ocean and bay frontage where you'll find vacation homes, bungalows, and condo townhouses. The townhouses offer spacious accommodations in a prime location. Built 20 years ago the style is quite contemporary with a happy blend of modern angles and Vineyard woods. These two-story structures are "upside down." The living room and kitchen are upstairs while the bedrooms are downstairs. We saw one decorated in sturdy wood furniture covered in neutral off-white fabrics. Pillows added splashes of color. Ceiling fans capture the island breezes. Appliances in the kitchen are showing the effect of salt air. In the individually owned homes, there's a wide variety in quality, interior decor, and maintenance. Some are definitely showing their age.

7   MEETINGHOUSE VILLAGE CONDOS
Meetinghouse Way, Edgartown, MA 02539
Amenities: Pool

The location makes you wonder why these were built. Located in an emerging residential area of Edgartown near the Great Pond, it is a long walk from the historic part of Edgartown. These condos are the newest on the island and they have architectural flourishes to capture the sunlight. Beautifully furnished, you'll find white wicker in the living room mixed with new art deco, polished oak floors, and Berber area rugs. The octagonal dining room table can expand to meet the crowd. Bedrooms are upstairs. You aren't near a beach nor are there any beach club rights. Guests here can use the pool or drive to the beach at Katama or Sylvia. A spacious residence, but you're missing part of the reason for coming to Martha's Vineyard when you stay here.

6   SEA VIEW
Beach Rd., Oak Bluffs, MA 02557
Amenities: Beach across the street.

On the edge of Oak Bluffs, this postmodern building somehow blends into this neighborhood of classic Victorian homes. Five-stories high, these units have large bay windows overlooking the beach and Nantucket Pond. Each two-bedroom condo has solid contemporary decor in the living room, a full kitchen, and brass beds in the master bedroom. The town of Oak Bluffs is in easy walking distance and the island's best beach is across the street.

7   **SENGEKONTACKET VILLAGE**
Sengekontacket Rd., Oak Bluffs, MA 02557
Amenities: Clubhouse, tennis, boat dock

Located just off County Road, on the western edge of Sengekontacket Pond, this is a great choice for bird watchers. The Audubon Society's forest preserve and the state forest are both nearby. This is one of the island's newer residential areas. Every home is on a two-acre lot. These townhouses are on the edge of the Sengekontacket residential area in a serene forest environment. Pale sunlight streams through the trees and the air is alive with singing birds. For years these have been among the island's most popular vacation rentals because you get a lot of space for a relatively low price. Decor varies, but we saw one with white wicker furniture and a blue sofa. Some personal poster art and ruffled pillows on the beds provide country charm in a gracious environment.

RENTAL RESOURCES
Alden Moore Real Estate, 508-627-9401, Edgartown
American Real Estate, 508-627-3734, Edgartown
Linda R. Bassett Real Estate, 508-627-9201, Edgartown
Conover Real Estate, 627-9883, Edgartown
Conroy and Company, 508-693-0033, Vineyard Haven
Flanders Up-Island Real Estate, 508-645-2632, Chillmark / Gay Head
Harborside Realty, Inc. 508-627-3721, Edgartown
Howell Real Estate, 508-645-2255, Chillmark / Gay Head
Island-Wide Realty, 508-693-3700, Vineyard Haven
Beverly King, 508-693-0499, Chillmark / Gay Head
Landmarks Real Estate, 508-693-6866, Vineyard Haven
Lawrence Realty, 508-693-3302, Oak Bluffs
Macomber Real Estate, 508-627-8030, Edgartown
Martha's Vineyard Properties, 508-693-4820, Chillmark / Gay Head
Martha's Vineyard Real Estate, 508-627-4737, Edgartown
Martha's Vineyard Vacation Rentals, 508-693-7711
Mattakesett Properties, 508-627-4432, Edgartown
Muskeget Associates, 508-693-7044, Chillmark / Gay Head
Barbara Nevin Real Estate, 508-627-7174, Edgartown
Margaret S. O'Neill, 508-627-4886, Edgartown
Sandpiper Realty, 508-627-3737, Edgartown
Sea Gull Realty, 508-693-5739, Vineyard Haven
Segekontacket, 508-693-2810, Edgartown
Tea Lane Associates, 508-645-2628, Chillmark / Gay Head
Towne and Country Realty, 508-693-1100, Oak Bluffs
Wallace and Co. Realtors, 508-627-3313, Edgartown
Waterfront Associates, 508-693-7188, Vineyard Haven

3. NANTUCKET

To fully appreciate Nantucket it is necessary to understand that Nantucket is history and history is Nantucket. This cozy elbow of sand offers a unique charm among the premier vacation home communities of North America. Benefiting from an enlightened and thoughtful planning commission, the island's history has been carefully blended with modern comfort and above all, style.

Neat and trim, nothing is out of place on this sandbar island two hours off the coast of Cape Cod. The ferry voyage can be rough as you plow through the open sea to this former capital of the whaling industry. The wharf area is the only commercial-looking district on the island. Immediately you'll be plunged into the 18th Century with the cobblestone streets and stone storefronts. The sidewalks are still adorned with hitching posts and wooden casks (for trash).

Unlike Martha's Vineyard, Nantucket has only one town and the rest of the island is residential. With eighty miles of beaches and the warm Gulf of Mexico current, Nantucket is a prime vacation destination from June through October. Spring may come a little late, but that is more than compensated for by the lingering Indian summer and sunny days of September. Recreational activities include sailing, golf, tennis and, of course, fishing the rich waters that abound with striped bass and bluefish.

There are several distinct neighborhoods outside the town of Nantucket. Tristram's Landing is an exceptional 250-acre development of vacation homes and condos near the Madaket Yacht Club. This is the most modern section of the island and has the quiet confidence of the Norman Rockwell era of Americana. For history buffs, there's Siaconset (pronounced "S'conset") Village where some homes date from the 17th Century. Simple with low ceilings, these cottages were built to last by our Puritan ancestors. Today, most of Siaconset has modern homes that are built to look like the originals on the outside and to blend in with the character of the village.

Brandt Point is an area of cedar-shingled homes and cottages surrounded by extensive plantings of roses, peonies, and hydrangeas. Nashaquisset is a modern recreation of 360-year-old Siaconset Village where doctors from the midwest have built fabulous homes, which on the outside appear to be in the modest Nantucket style.

Nantucket's airport has a bevy of commuter airlines offering frequent flights to Boston, Hartford, Washington, and New York. Others who come by sea need to call in advance for ferry reservations for their car, otherwise waiting times may be lengthy.

WHERE TO STAY

 BARQUE
Ocean Ave., Nantucket, MA 02554

A single vacation home, this is one of the cutest cottages you'll find on Nantucket. The owner is an amateur horticulturist, so this weathered gray cottage is surrounded by spritely colors from springtime pastels to the deep colors in fall. Not to be overlooked are the vines of climbing roses. This one-bedroom cottage has a window seat in the living room where you can look out over the beach to the yachts out at sea. Rentals are not cheap but this honeymoon cottage will provide memories forever. Rentals are available through Nantucket Real Estate only.

5 BEACHSIDE
North Beach St., Nantucket, MA 02554, 508-228-2241
Amenities: Pool, complimentary breakfast

Beachside is located in the Brandt Point section of town, just a couple of blocks from the historic downtown area. It's only a short walk over to Jettis Beach. At first blush, the Beachside appears to be a motel. It is and it isn't. Some of the units have been turned into condos and sold to private owners. A few have tiny Pullman kitchens; some are just hotel rooms. A major redecoration program has just transformed these units into fluffs of fantasy with the Laura Ashley look: English floral fabrics, white wicker furniture, bleached wood tables, small floral arrangements, and maybe a couple of library books between bookends. Brass beds complete the picture. Although tiny, it is well decorated.

7 BRANDT POINT COURTYARD
Swain St., Nantucket, MA 02554
Amenities: Pool

Located in the picturesque Brandt Point area, within walking distance of both downtown and Jettis Beach, these two-story units are tidy and well decorated. Previously known as "Suitcase Simpson's," this property was completely renovated and converted to condos several years ago. Tastefully decorated, you'll find an attractive loveseat in the living room and a Nantucket hooked rug. Small floral arrangements and decorator accessories make this a charming picture. Not the lively spot it was in Suitcase's day, these units are pleasant and conveniently located for a week-long stay.

8+ CLIFFSIDE BEACH CLUB
Jefferson Ave., Box 449, Nantucket, MA 02554
508-228-0618, Suites $145–335
Amenities: Beach, restaurant

This is one of the most picturesque spots on a very photogenic island. It is one of those rare properties in Nantucket that sits directly on the beach. The weathered cedar-shingled building is arranged so each unit looks directly out to sea. Sit on your white Adirondack chair and gaze past an array of yellow, blue, and green beach umbrellas. Each has a small bricked courtyard patio where you'll want to be on sunny days. Inside, the units represent the best in New England craftsmanship and wood work—custom-milled cedar and heart pine reclaimed from Boston's South Station. Vaulted ceilings create a New England boathouse effect. They have tiny Pullman kitchens but who cares. If you're traveling across the country for something special, consider Cliffside. It's perfect for beach lovers.

6 **MONOMOY VILLAGE**
6 Federal St., Box 217, Nantucket, MA 02554, 508-228-9559
Amenities: None

This community of bungalows was formerly a cottage motel before its conversion to condo-bungalows. Each little cottage has its own name (for some part of the island) just as in Bermuda. These one-bedroom units are unquestionably cute—Nantucket style on the outside, charming on the inside. There is nothing fancy and the ceilings are a little low. Nevertheless, this is the quintessential "beach house" that one expects in New England.

ℭ **NANTUCKET VACATION RENTALS**
P.O. Box 426, Nantucket, MA 02554, 508-228-2530

Nantucket has over 7,000 residential dwellings, 60% of which are owned by "off-islanders." Of these possible 4200 second homes, approximately 2800 are made available by their owners for vacation rentals in the summer. Many visitors return year after year, so in truth the supply of vacation homes which are available to first time Nantucket visitors can be quite limited. For this reason you should be aware of Nantucket Vacation Rentals. This agency has a knack for finding just the right place, even in the height of the season. Some of the properties available are described below:

The Mother-in-Law — Extended families that vacation together often find that a little extra privacy can add a lot to the value of a vacation. So it was when the Mother-in-Law was built in the exclusive Brandt Point area, close to town yet within walking distance of Jettis Beach. These are actually two homes joined as one on the upstairs level. These are "upside down" houses where the kitchen/dining and living areas are upstairs. The main house has a California feeling to it with polished hardwood floors, comfortable off-white furniture, crisp white walls, and impressive art work as accents.

The Square Rigger — An exclusive beach house with its own private beach. Simple on the outside in a Nantucket way, the interior is a sight to behold. The oak-beamed living room dates from the 19th Century whaling village while the newer addition has a vaulted ceiling. There's a sea captain's chest for a coffee table, wing back chairs covered in crewel-work, and model whaling schooners complete the picture. Upstairs, you'll find a four-poster bed in the master bedroom and handmade quilts cover all the beds. Very few whaling captains ever had it this good.

Stilldock — Located right in the heart of downtown, on one of the wharfs, these one-bedroom units are handsomely decorated in a Nantucket style. Great harbor views and prices that compete favorably with local inns. Stilldock provides good value.

10 NASHAQUISSET
7 Nashaquisset Ln., Nantucket, MA 02554
508-228-0625, Houses $950–1400/wk
Amenities: Pool, clubhouse, hot tub, tennis

The village of S'conset is 360 years old and over the centuries an inimitable charm has evolved. Nashaquisset is a modern attempt to capture the spirit of S'conset village in a cluster of modern accommodations. The effort has succeeded far beyond general expectations to the point where even local cynics are proud of this development. Spread over 20 acres there are 105 two-story cottages in a recreation of an 18th-Century fishing village. The Siaconset cottages have cedar-shingled siding and some have a wraparound porch. Inside you'll find two-story living rooms with some of the most impressive decors of any vacation homes in the U.S., much less New England where the understated is a way of life. Some have an extra loft sitting room on the second floor as well as two additional bedrooms. The windows are strategically placed so the interiors are light and airy. Decor ranges from the Nantucket style with painted white wicker and lots of pastel fabrics, offset by a collection of Portuguese porcelains on the walls, to urban New York. In one, the interior decorator was unleased to blend French Empire elegance with the simplicity of New England. Another was "underdecorated" to accentuate the few quality art pieces over the mantle and hanging from the two-story wall. Each one of these homes has been individually decorated and there seems to be a keen sense of competition among the owners. There's a quiet pool area and the tennis courts always seem to be in use. For those who want Malibu luxury transported to the quaintest of New England shore side villages, this is a "must see."

6+ OLD NORTH WHARF COTTAGES
Old North Wharf, Nantucket, MA 02554
Amenities: None

These cottages are very simple but unforgettable, and you would be amazed to know who some of your celebrity neighbors are. Located on the

Old North Wharf just steps from downtown Nantucket, these twelve cottages date from the 19th Century and have been named for whaling ships of the period: Mary Slade, Lydia, and The Independence. Sizes range from studios to three-bedroom units. Staying here is like being on a boat. You are in a small, simple wooden space surrounded by water. Decor is very simple; some only have a pair of twin beds. Others have varnished knotty pine walls and an open-loft sleeping area. Expect a hooked rug for the living room and a pair of deck chairs. Plumbing fixtures are from the 1940s. Each cottage has its own identifiable china. Rustic, but authentic, when you stay here, you're staying at a "site."

Some of those units were severely damaged during the storms and high tides. We urge you to consult with a local rental company regarding their status.

9 SANKATY
Towaddy Ln., Nantucket, MA 02554
Amenities: None

Located just three blocks from Siaconset Village, these Cape Cod bungalows capture the true flavor of Siaconset village. Weathered shingles on the outside and painted planked wood floors on the inside set the low-key beach house tone. Two of these cottages, **Ibid** and **Avec des Fleurs,** are across the walkway from each other and have identical floor plans (hence the name Ibid). Immediately, your attention is riveted to the low ceiling and the oak beams of the living room that were the core of the house before "modern" additions; all to the satisfaction of the Historic Preservation Board. These cottages are very well decorated with a combination of Early American antique reproduction furniture and modern appliances, including cable television and a microwave. There's a brick fireplace in the living room for those foggy mornings, a kitchen, dining room, and two separate bedroom suites on the first floor. Upstairs, via the spiral staircase, there's a twin bedroom and a large old-fashioned sleeping porch with four single beds. This is great for two families sharing a place at the beach. Welcome to S'conset: the low-key beach area that so many of today's quality developers are now trying to imitate. Ask a realtor about renting one of the cottages. Rates are as low as $1600 a week in season for one of the houses that will accommodate ten.

7 STONEBARN INN CONDOS
North Beach St., Nantucket, MA 02554
Amenities: None

Yuppie Heaven, it was formerly an old stable within walking distance to downtown, that was converted to a vacation apartment complex in the 1930s. Then came the 1980s and with approval of the town's planning board the old building was once again gutted. This time it was converted to luxury condos to satisfy the desires of Wall Street's young brokers. Today, several of these condos are available for vacation rentals and they are gorgeous. Berber rugs and brick fireplaces set the basic tone. Sumptuous sofas where you can sit and contemplate how the model ship was ever inserted into that glass bottle.

TRISTAM'S LANDING
Nantucket, MA 02554, 508-228-0359
Prices vary from $79–400/wk; Monthly rates are best
Amenities: Private beach, pool, tennis, health club

It's rare to find any property located right on the beach at Nantucket. Tristam's Landing has over a mile of private beach. Located on the western end of the island, just off Madaket Road, this 250-acre community of vacation homes, townhouses, and condos is one of the most popular destinations on the island. Slowly developed over the past 25 years, there's a great deal of variation among some of these properties. A lot depends upon the individual owners interest in maintaining and redecorating the property. There are four distinct models to choose from:

Deluxe Condos (8) These are single-story detached houses each with two bedrooms, a loft, a living room, and kitchen. Expect to find the charm of Nantucket combined with Laura Ashley country fabrics—hard-wood floors, track lights, oak beams, and vaulted ceilings, large kitchens and dining rooms with tile floors, and a brick fireplace. Colors, fabrics, and wallpaper with dark blues and Swiss patterns, along with bookshelves, add a warm, homey touch.

Standard Condos (7) These are handsome and spacious and have similar space, but lack the extra decorator touches of the deluxe condos.

Towne Houses (6) Although, the most disappointing of the properties, these are spacious and have three levels. The first floor has a bedroom and the living/dining areas are on the second floor. There are two more bedrooms on the third floor.

Private Homes (9) These are a real treat. The three- or four-bedroom homes are scattered throughout the property, but the majority are by the beach. Some even have a beach view. We saw one that had a first-floor plan as large as many homes. They all have plank wood floors, modern kitchens, and again the superior Laura Ashley-style fabrics. Open the door to the closet and—surprise—there's a hidden staircase. Upstairs, the huge loft has a "boathouse" look with open beams and pine paneling.

Tristam's not only has the beach, but it also has a large swimming pool and a game center with billiards and electronic video games. Exceptional in the northeast, Tristam's is a rare treat.

8+ **WHARF COTTAGES**
Swain's Wharf, Nantucket, MA 02554, 508-228-1333
Amenities: Marina, concierge services through the
Harbor House Hotel

Similar to the Old North Wharf Cottages, these enjoy a unique "on-the-water" location, but a style that is entirely different. Managed by a major hotel company, each cottage has been homogenized with contemporary, upscale interior decor. Bedrooms are downstairs and the living room/kitchen are upstairs under the vaulted ceiling. The views of town, the island, the harbor, and the yachts are incredible. A carved Bavarian, blond-wood armoire in the living room hides the 20th-Century television set. Named after ships such as Orion, Zenu's Coffin, Willet, and the Young Hero, these studio, one-, two-, three-, and four-bedroom accommodations are modern and very comfortable. Hotel services are available including a concierge who'll take care of personal errands, including grocery shopping.

8 **WHITE ELEPHANT INN COTTAGES**
Easton St., Nantucket, MA 02554, 508-228-2500
Cottages $210–550
Amenities: Concierge services through the White Elephant Hotel

Not at all what you would imagine. The White Elephant Hotel is one of the premier resorts on the island that dates from an earlier era. The island's elite come here to celebrate weddings and other special events. The Spindrift cottages are in a garden community, hidden behind a forbidding hedge. Although not privately owned, these tiny one-bedroom cottages have all the accouterments of a private residence; only you're in an enchanted rose garden setting. Interior decor is standardized, but nevertheless inspired with plank floors, bentwood chairs, and Early American pine furniture. Little bouquets of flowers make these cottages appropriate for a honeymoon or a romantic getaway.

RENTAL RESOURCES
Heaven Can Wait, 508-257-4000
Nantucket Accommodations, 508-228-9559
Nantucket Breeze Vacations, 508-228-4889
Nantucket & Martha's Vineyard Accommodations, 508-693-7200
Nantucket Vacation Rentals, 508-228-3131
Still Dock Rentals, 508-228-9480

4. THE BERKSHIRES

The Berkshire mountains of Massachusetts, just south of the Vermont border, (see map on page 448) have come alive in recent years to the sound of music. In wintertime, the area is promoted for skiing although it lacks the mountain ruggedness and elevations associated with ski country. The serene countryside is dotted with proverbial New England-style villages, each having a white church spire in the center. In between, there are rolling forest, brooks, and ponds. Old Stockbridge Village is a living museum of how life was lived 150 years ago in this part of New England. We doubt life in Massachusetts was this pleasant at that time, otherwise there wouldn't have been the push for western migration. Today, Stockbridge is a town of tea shops, New England inns, and preserves the image of small-town America that local artist Norman Rockwell made famous.

Of course, the main reason for visiting the Berkshires is the summertime music festival. The importance of this annual series of concerts has fostered the growth of small art, music, and drama festivals. Several theaters provide excellent summer stock.

Resorts in the Berkshires have discovered the latest trend toward European style spas. Today, several exceptional "wellness" spas are in operation attracting vacationers who want light classical music, tennis in the fresh air, and exquisitely prepared, low-cholesterol dining. Nearby, other resorts still cater to those who want to return to a less complicated rustic lifestyle. Biking, hiking, fishing, and antiquing are sports that are actively pursued in the hills during the day. There's always music at night.

Air transportation is convenient through nearby Bradley Field serving Springfield, Massachusetts. Bradley Field is less than an hour from most resorts in the Berkshires.

WHERE TO STAY

7   BEAVER POND CONDOMINIUMS
Jiminy Peak Mountain Resort, Hancock, MA 01237.
Amenities: Pool, tennis, exercise room, restaurant

Beaver Pond Condominiums are located in a secluded, rustic area approximately one mile from the Jiminy Peak Village Center. The condos are actually two- and three-bedroom townhouses with a deck or a patio. A fireplace is located in each living room. Beaver Pond features a private clubhouse and tennis center with a pool, hot tub, and saunas. This resort is ideal for vacationers seeking privacy.

JIMINY PEAK MOUNTAIN RESORT
Hancock, MA 02137
Amenities: Golf, pool, sauna, hot tub, tennis

This is the story of the resort that grew and grew. Jiminy Peak was an undistinguished ski resort in western Massachusetts a dozen years ago, but extensive development has transformed it into the finest resort condo community in western Massachusetts. Summer is now the most popular time to visit; urbanites pour into the Berkshires for fresh air and culture.

Country Inn (6) The Country Inn condos are located at the base of the ski slope, where all the activity is concentrated. The pool or hot tub is the social center depending upon the time of the year. The Country Inn condos are in a series of large, lodge-style buildings that are all interconnected, so you need not walk outside during bad weather. These one-bedroom condos are functional with kitchenettes and hotel-style interior decor. Although no fireplaces, there are whirlpools in the master bath.

Country Village (7) These condos are located behind the Country Inn. They are two-story townhouses that include loft bedrooms, cathedral ceilings in the living room, private fireplaces, full kitchens, and private patios.

Mountainside Condos (8) Mountainside Condos, off the left bank, are clearly the best choice in the area. They have ski-in, ski-out access to the ski slopes. These two-bedroom townhouses have architectural flourishes such as vaulted ceilings, skylights, and half-circle windows over French doors that create a Federalist look. Expect to find stylish, upbeat contemporary decor—bleached wood chairs with designer fabrics, a pair of cozy loveseats in front of the fireplace, and lots of designer fabrics for the curtains, and full kitchens that open to the living room if the cook wants to continue a discussion. During the winter, Jiminy Peak has an exceptional Ski Wee program for children learning to ski.

7 LAKECREST CONDOMINIUMS

Hancock Road, Lake Pontusuc, MA 012##
Amenities: Lake, lakefront lodge, fitness center, pool, tennis.
Golf Nearby

The lakefront location is inviting and after a full day of sailing or golf, you'll be weary. This condo resort is only minutes away from Tanglewood and its evening performances. These new condominiums are solid and comfortably furnished in contemporary decor that is accented by poster art reveling in the area's "antiquing" heritage. The best features beyond the lakefront location are the fitness center and the Olympic-sized pool. Such amenities are rare in Massachusetts. These condos are best for families or groups as they range from two- to four-bedroom floorplans.

5 OAK N'SPRUCE RESORT

Meadow St., South Lee, MA 01260, 413-243-3500
Amenities: Pool, hot tub, tennis, game room, restaurant

Oak N'Spruce Resort is located amid the mountains and offers a traditional New England-inn environment. Renovated twelve years ago and converted to condo suites, it's now time to spruce up the resort again. They have attractive suites with contemporary decor. The new garden apartments have full kitchens; the suites simply have a parlor area. This is a convenient resort for those who enjoy spring, summer, and fall in the Berkshires.

8+ PONDS AT FOX HOLLOW
Route 7, Lenox, MA 01240, 413-637-2000
Amenities: Pool, tennis, jogging trails, spa and fitness center with lap pool, restaurant, library

What a surprise! During the past two years this former Vanderbilt home improved sharply with the opening of the full-service spa. The Ponds now bills itself as "an adventure in wellness." Special features include aerobics, cardiovascular testing, herbal wraps, saunas, sunken whirlpool spas in the locker rooms, and massages. It combines wellness and hedonism. They serve light California cuisine in the spa restaurant and New England fare in the dining room. Attractive suites in the surrounding new two-story, town-house-style buildings. You'll find tiled entrance hall and a tiled area around the fireplace, neutral colors, potted palm trees, and designer touches. Most are less than two years old, and all units have VTPs.

7 SOUTH POND FARM
1136 Barker Rd.. MA 012##, 413-443-3330
Amenities: Lake

Located midway between the town of Pittsfield and the restored 18th-Century Hancock Shaker Village, this has a peaceful setting. You can sit on the deck in the sunshine, smell the pines, and watch a canoe silently glide by on the lake. Well built, they are furnished with a Nantucket style—lots of wicker and Waverly fabrics

RENTAL RESOURCES
Berkshire County Properties, 413-623-5776
Charlotte Isaacs, 413-298-3300
Cohen & White Real Estate, 413-637-1086, A favorite for vacation rentals
Evergreen Realty, 413-499-4610
Gile Real Estate, 413-269-4048
Harsh Associates, 413-458-5764
Mole & Mole Real Estate, 413-637-0096, An area tradition for 95 years
Ramon Rustic Real Estate, 413-528-9175
Reinholt Realtors, 413-637-1251
Rose Agency, 413-443-7211
Ruffer Real Estate, 413-445-5661

MICHIGAN

Often overlooked, Michigan provides several romantic vacation areas along the Great Lakes as well as some of the best skiing in the Midwest. Instead of resting on their laurels, the local business interests became active a dozen years ago in developing and promoting a number of new championship golf courses. Today, Michigan is the golf capital of the Upper Midwest as well as a prime destination for sailors, skiers, and persons who like to fish. Although the weather may not always cooperate, Michigan has some of the most beautiful white sand beaches found anywhere—but don't think of it as another Ft. Lauderdale. What we think you'll most appreciate is the craggy coastline that compares favorably with Maine.

For purposes of condo and villa resorts we have divided this chapter into two subsections: Traverse City Shoreline, an area extending 40 miles in either direction from Traverse City, runs along the northwest of Michigan's Lower Peninsula. Starting with Sleeping Bear Dunes National Seashore and running up past Traverse City and Petosky to Harbor Springs, this is emerging as one of America's must popular vacation destinations. Recently, Michigan's unspoiled forest and lake communities have been attracting large numbers of retirees. This in turn has created demand for new construction and a boom in local real estate prices. But take heart. The prices were already so low that a 100% increase in real estate values would equal a 5% increase in California. Nevertheless, the infrastructure is there and this area is ready for national recognition.

The Upper Peninsula is much more of an adventure. Unlike the civilized area around Traverse City, this area has an enduring horizon of wide open spaces. The social life reflects this, as you'll find a number of eclectic Moosehead bars and hamburger joints instead of candlelit restaurants. The ski resorts here are inland, away from the lake, so it does get cold. Persons planning ski trips in December and January should also be advised that it starts to get dark around 3 P.M. and sunrise may come at 9 A.M. The ski resorts of the Upper Peninsula are good for the Midwest, but don't imagine they compare with the mountains of Vermont. Snowmobiling and cross-country skiing are just as popular, however. When you've got your family and friends gathered around the fire in the evening, you'll find a sense of satisfaction big enough to warm everyone's heart. The best time, actually may be in the summer when 1.5 million acres of forest preserve are alive with ecological surprises.

1. TRAVERSE CITY SHORELINE

Surrounded by the Great Lakes, Michigan's harbors and shoreline offer access to one-fifth of the world's fresh water supply. Michigan's shoreline encompasses over 1,000 miles of beaches plus rocky coasts and fog-shrouded harbors. Due to the moderating influence of the lakes, Michigan's

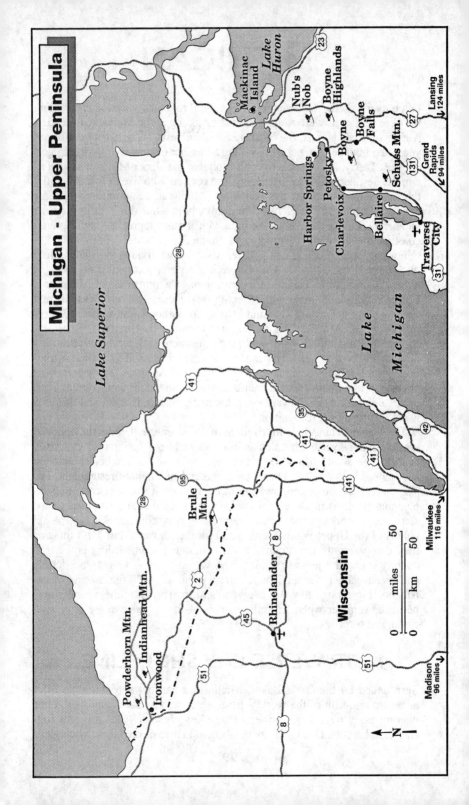

summer is a little cooler and its winters a little milder than in other parts of the Midwest.

The northwest corner of Michigan, between Sleeping Bear Dunes National Seashore and Harbor Springs to the north, is emerging as one of America's most popular vacation destinations. Recently, Michigan's unspoiled forest and lake communities have begun attracting large numbers of retirees. Known for the Midwest's best skiing in winter, the area is really at its height of popularity during the summer. In summer, this is the golf capital of the Midwest. There are 16 major courses in the small strip between Traverse City and Harbor Springs. And, of course, there is always boating. Whether you desire sailing or cruising in a power boat, Michigan's waters provide limitless opportunities.

The condos in northwest Michigan are in several communities. Starting with The Homestead in Glen Arbor and stretching up to Boyne Highlands, there are a series of ski resorts:

The Homestead — a private ski hill

Crystal Mountain — popular with Midwest skiers

Sugarloaf — some of Michigan's best

Shanty Creek/Schuss Mountain — two distinct areas 5 miles apart

Boyne Mountain — Michigan's most famous ski area

Nubs Nob — an uncrowded hill

Boyne Highlands — as popular with Canadians as Detroiters

Along this coast you will find other groupings of condos in yachting centers such as Mackinac Island. For golfers, some of America's top-rated courses are to be found near Traverse City, Bellaire, and Harbor Springs. Michigan attracts those seeking outdoor sports and the increasing number of visitors is testimony to its popularity.

With one exception, all of the condo resorts in this section are within one hour's drive of the Traverse City airport. Most vacationers in this area drive from Midwestern cities such as Flint, Southfield, or Midland. If you choose to fly, Traverse City has numerous flights on commuter carriers from Detroit, Chicago, and Milwaukee.

WHERE TO STAY

8   **BIRCHWOOD FARMS COUNTRY CLUB**
6789 S. Lakeshore Dr., Harbor Springs, MI 49740, 616-526-2156
800-433-8787; 2BR $475–1275/wk, 3BR $575–1425/wk
Amenities: Golf, tennis, pool, clubhouse

As the golf capital of the Upper Midwest, it is no surprise that one of the newest developments of vacation homes is along the fairways of an 18-hole championship course just above the shores of Lake Michigan. Each house is architecturally different and models vary from two to five bedrooms. Each has a fireplace and a deck for outdoor enjoyment in the summer. Guests are allowed the use of the club facilities, which is a major plus.

5   **THE BEACH CONDOMINIUMS**
1995 U.S. 31 North, Traverse City, MI 49684, 616-938-2228
Suites $39–110
Amenities: Pool

Only three years old, these attractive condominiums are small and practical. Located on the edge of town, along the beach, they do qualify as resort area accommodations. Each has a private jacuzzi whirlpool.

6   **CRYSTAL MOUNTAIN RESORT**
12500 Crystal Mountain Dr., Thompsonville, MI 49683,
616-378-2000, 800-968-7686
Studio $54–169, 1BR $79–205, 2BR $120–314
Amenities: Indoor pool, gym, lodge

Located just 30 miles southwest of Traverse City, this is one of the four mountains that makes the corner of Northwest Michigan the ski capital of the Midwest. Not as steep as Boyne, nevertheless, there is substantial terrain to keep you busy. There are two condominium developments here, **Pinehurst** and **Winter Green.** Both are similar in design and decor. Each is a three-story-plus building surrounded by a thick grove of pines. The second-floor condos are actually on two levels. The top floor is a loft bedroom and opens onto an extra-spacious living room. Cheerfully furnished, we think the property would benefit if the owners were allowed to express a little more individuality in the decor. You'll find light maple woods and tweed fabrics. Each condo has a private jacuzzi whirlpool for two. This is a good spot for a family vacation especially if you want to play and socialize in the snow country.

7   **DEER LAKE EXECUTIVE VILLAS**
Boyne Falls, MI 49713, 616-549-2441, 800-632-7174
1BR $89–105, 2BR $110–140
Amenities: Lake, pool, clubhouse

Hidden on the far side of Boyne Highlands, these condos are great for golfers or boating enthusiasts. Too bad they are only open in the summer. These villas are two-story eight-sided buildings with lots of glass windows and sliding doors to bring in the view. The buildings are duplexes with a condo on each floor. Staying here is like staying in a family compound because of the remote location. You make friends and many of these families return year after year as their children grow. Patio barbecues are frequent, operated by the staff from the main lodge at Boyne Highlands. Here you have a private lake, streams, a golf course, and congeniality. What more could you want!

7 EDGEWATER INN
100 Michigan Ave., Charlevoix, MI 49720, 616-547-6044
Studio $59, 1BR $79
Amenities: Marina, indoor and outdoor pool, restaurant

In an area where most of the hotels or condos promote their lake or beachfront locations, it is a little unusual to find a condo development on the harbor. Even more so, these are some of the best condos in the Charlevoix area. Compact, but beautifully decorated, the loft units are superior because of the high ceilings and harborview. The real advantage of the Edgewater Inn is a central location. Yet, because you are on the harbor, you have the privacy of an open view toward the yachting harbor. The pools, spa, and sauna are true assets here.

8-10 GRAND TRAVERSE RESORT
M-72 at U.S. 31, Grand Traverse, MI 49610-0404, 616-938-2100, 800-678-1308; Studio $75, 1BR $105, 2BR $150, 3BR $210
Amenities: Golf, health club and spa with racquetball, squash and handball courts, saunas, indoor and outdoor tennis courts, beach club, cross-country skiing

Located just six miles north of Traverse City, this is an unforgettable resort covering 900 acres of rolling hills along Lake Michigan. The core is a high-rise hotel tower. At 16 stories, it is an area landmark. The condos are in three separate areas; on a hill by the main tower, along the fairway, by the pro shop, and across the highway by the beach. Around the tower, **Valley View (8)** condos are apartments in a three-story building. Older than most of the other condos at Grand Traverse, they have a ho-hum decor package. If you like standardized hotel room decor, you will like these. **The Terrace (9)** condos are larger and have the personalized interior decor you would expect to find in a vacation home. Great views of the valley and Lake Michigan can be seen in the distance. By the golf club, **Hilltop (10)** condos are townhouses designed for golfers with the country club lifestyle in mind. Very attractive, they are located over at the beach, **The Shores (10)** condos have a different feeling because they are surrounded by the woods, far enough away from the main center of activity to be truly private. The true charm here is the list of activities. A destination in and of itself, many visitors find no reason to leave the resort.

7   HAMLET VILLAGE CONDOMINIUMS
     5484 Pleasantview Road, Harbor Springs, MI 49740,
     616-526-6651, 800-678-2341
     Amenities: Pool, gym, saunas, Nubs Nob chair lift

Here you are less than five minutes away from skiing at Boyne Highlands
or Nubs Nob. The unobstructed view of the countryside is spectacular. Well
designed, the condos feature cathedral ceilings in the living room and stone
fireplaces. All have private, tiled hot tubs, set in a corner of the unit so you
look out on the virgin forest or the carpet of snow. There's a community
center with an indoor pool, saunas, and tennis courts.

6   HARBOR COVE
     Page Hill Rd., (No mail receptacle), Harbor Springs, MI 49740
     Amenities: Beach, indoor pool, tennis

Located on a sheltered bay, these spacious townhouses are at their best in
summer, yet they are only 15 minutes away from skiing in winter. There is
no on-site management, but there is a clubhouse for guests with keys.

8   HEATHER HIGHLANDS AT BOYNE MOUNTAIN
     c/o Heather Highlands Realty, 1755 Heather Dr., Harbor Springs,
     MI 49740, 616-526-6206, 800-462-6963
     2BR $175, 3BR $200, 4BR $225–275
     Amenities: Heated pool, tennis, putting green

These condos are huge. Located at the base of Boyne Highlands Mountain, it is a two mile drive through the woods over to the village and ski lifts.
This would not qualify as a ski-in/ski-out resort. Each condo is either a
duplex or fourplex that is two stories high with a basement and enclosed
garage. A few have private saunas in the basement. The living room is
expansive and leads to a view of the forest. They have full kitchens and two
fireplaces. Furniture styles vary from comfortable to decorator design.
Expect to find all the little amenities a family could want (games, books,
stereo, etc.) in a vacation home.

6   HEATHER HIGHLANDS INN
     600A Heather Highlands Dr., Harbor Springs, MI 49740,
     616-526-2171, 800-562-3899
     Amenities: Next to lodge with indoor pool and restaurant

Located across the circle from the main skiers' lodge at Boyne Highlands,
these condos are the most convenient lodgings for skiers in the area. Wake
up in the morning, have breakfast, and walk over to the ski lifts. The units
themselves are disappointing, considering the strategic advantage of this
location. They are relatively small and boxy. Nicely decorated, the furnish-

ings that you will find in most units are a little institutional. Interior decor has all the ambience of staying at one of the hotel chains. For convenience or for a couple or a small family, you can't beat it.

7 HIDEAWAY VALLEY
Clayton Rd., Harbor Springs, MI 49740
Amenities: Outdoor pool

Designed with the golfer in mind, these spacious condos are available by the week or month. The one we saw had a collection of framed prints of great golfing scenes.

10 THE HOMESTEAD
Woodbridge Rd., Glen Arbor, MI 49636, 616-334-5700
1BR $140–225, 2BR $180–265, 3BR $215–300, 4BR $295–375
Amenities: Private ski hill, beach club, restaurants, village shops, tennis, cross-country ski trails

One of the Midwest's finest resorts, the Homestead is a private waterfront resort community made up of 14 separate condo clusters. The Beach Club is the focal point in summer with a pool, snack bar, and "lodge dining room" restaurant. The Homestead is spread over 220 acres along the shoreline of Lake Michigan, where the Crystal River meets the lake. This is a dramatic area with hills, a private ski area and bluffs 350 feet above Lake Michigan. The land has been lovingly developed to create an atmosphere that is reminiscent of Stowe or Aspen. The other major point of interest is The Village with its boutiques and restaurant.

There are four main areas of condo development within the Homestead. All are equally well done. **The Village** is new and is the first area you will encounter once you pass the reception area; a good spot for those who want a social atmosphere. **Hawksnest** is on a remote bluff overlooking the lake. Hawksnest condos have ski-in access to the ski hill. **Rivermouth** is an area of condos overlooking the beach club and shore, not to mention the convenience for families with children. **South Beach,** the fourth area, is also remote. It is tucked in between the woods and sand dunes on the beach.

Reservations for the summer season open on a particular day in February. Within two to three hours, certain time periods become fully booked with flocks of returning visitors.

8 LAKESIDE CLUB CONDOMINIUMS
2310 M-119, Harbor Springs, MI 49740
2BR $85–170, 3BR $140–205
Amenities: Beach, indoor pool, tennis

These are some of the most luxurious townhouse condominiums in the area. Located on the shores of Round Lake, some units are built around the pool but the best ones face the beach and the lake. Cross-country ski trails pass by here in winter.

5   ON A BAY RESORT CONDOMINIUMS
1773 U.S. 31 North, Traverse City, MI 49684; 1BR $59
Amenities: Restaurant

Located on the East Bay's Miracle Mile Beach, this is a resort motel that added some condominiums. They have the space and convenience of a condo, and the amenities of a hotel next door, if you need them. Recently redecorated, this is a budget choice.

5   POINTS NORTH INN
101 Michigan Ave., Charlevoix, MI 49720, 616-547-0055, 800-678-2422; Studios $59–126
Amenities: Pool

Identical to its sister property in Traverse City, this snug little all-suite hotel offers cheerful studios—better decorated than most of the area hotels and many of the condos. Well done, it is cheerful, romantic, and inexpensive.

5   POINTS NORTH INN
2211 U.S. 31 North, Traverse City, MI 49684, 616-938-9191, 800-678-1267; Studios $59–135
Amenities: Pool

Located right on the beach in Traverse City, these new units are convenient for vacationers, as well as those on a business trip, or those planning an extended stay in the area. The units are very compact. Angles in the design and clever use of mirrors help create a better sense of space. Each unit has a private balcony and view of the lake. They have a bright, cheerful decor with lots of pinks and silk flowers to create a feeling of romance. Convenient, functional, and well priced, Points North is a reasonable choice.

6-7+ SHANTY CREEK/SCHUSS MOUNTAIN
RR3, Box 1, Bellaire, MI 49615-9555, 616-533-8621, 800-632-7118
Studio $100–125, 1BR $145, 2BR $20–220
Amenities: Golf, convention center, clubhouses, restaurants, skiing, health club, indoor/outdoor pools, hot tubs, tennis

This resort has been called America's Summer Golf Capitol. Nestled in the heart of northwest Michigan's forest is this dual resort complex of Shanty Creek/Schuss Mountain. Schuss Mountain is a skier's village with a main lodge (sports complex, dining room, shops) and a dozen large chalet-style buildings. Radiating away from the lodge, Shanty Creek is the much larger resort center five miles away at the other end of this sprawling property. In between there are two 18-hole golf courses, forests, nature trails, and paths for cross-country skiing.

At Shanty Creek Lodge, there is an indoor pool, an outdoor pool, full health club and a clubhouse restaurant with some of the best food you will find in Michigan. The condos are in several different buildings (with different styles representing the various phases of development). Primarily, you will find suites with a small refrigerator or one-bedroom units. There are some new two- and three-bedroom condos which are gorgeous with contemporary-style decor.

At Schuss Mountain, the units are a little bit older and show years of active use. This is a well-planned village with a central lodge and condos designed for easy access to the ski lifts. Each condo has a private fireplace and its own view of the mountain or meadows.

7   SPRING LAKE CLUB
1575 Konle Rd., Petosky, MI 49770; 2BR $79–149, 3BR $99–179
Amenities: Boat dock, indoor pool, hot tub

These large condominiums are set on the shore of spring lake. Each has a deck to enjoy the summer weather and a fireplace for those nippy evenings the other eleven months of the year.

SUGAR LOAF RESORT
4500 Sugar Loaf Mountain Rd., Cedar, MI 49621-9755,
616-228-5461, 800-632-9802
1BR $80–140, 2BR $120–160, 3BR $160–210, 4BR $210–260
Amenities: Skiing, golf, restaurant, indoor and outdoor pool, tennis

Sugarloaf may offer some of the best skiing in northwest Michigan, but the condominium accommodations are limited to two choices: the townhouses attached to the main lodge and the new, large Winged Foot duplexes just a five-minute walk away.

Sugarloaf resort is now 25 years old and beginning to show its age. The **Townhouses (5)** next to the lodge look a little worn inside and out. Interior decor seems to have been planned many years ago, now supplemented by treasures from the attic. They are adequate accommodations and have the convenience of hospitality from the lodge next door.

Winged Foot (7) is an altogether different story. Brand new and sumptuously decorated, these have been done with style. Each condo has a private fireplace and most have a private hot tub large enough for two or four persons to soak among the bubbles. Expect to find a contemporary interior designer decor with lots of mirrors and silk flowers. Color themes run in dusty pink and sky blue. These are well done condos.

8   SUNSET SHORES
250 Water St., Petosky, MI 49770
1BR $100–129, 2BR $150–189, 3BR $175–232
Amenities: Beach, tennis court

Long established as a prestigious address, these condos appeal to a clientele that returns year after year. Each condo has a fireplace in the living room and a private hot tub. Considering the prime location on the bay, each of the units has an excellent view and the beach is right out in front. In the evenings you can walk to Petosky's famed Gaslight District.

7   TANNERY CREEK
1231 U.S. 31 North, Petosky, MI 49770
Amenities: Heated outdoor pool

Located next door to the state park's beach, this is a water-lover's dream. Each of the units has extra large dimensions in the rooms and most living rooms have cathedral ceilings.

8   TROUT CREEK CONDOMINIUMS
4749 Pleasantview Rd., Harbor Springs, MI 49740, 616-526-2148,
800-748-0245; 1BR $70–110, 2BR $80–160, 3BR $110–185
Amenities: Tennis, recreation center, indoor and outdoor pools

Located less than five miles from Boyne Highlands and a mile from Nubs Nob, Trout Creek Condominiums are a special find in this area. There is a Western or California feeling at this village of two-story townhouses. The Boyne Highlands golf course is across the street and the condos have an open, expansive view from their position on the ridge. Inside, each unit has a fireplace, spacious living room with cathedral ceilings, loft and whirlpool. The recreation center offers a popular indoor pool, hot tub and a small outdoor pool. The furnishings are contemporary in style and of good quality. You'll find this a good value in the Boyne Highlands area.

7   WEATHERVANE TERRACE
111 Pine River Ln., Charlevoix, MI 49720, 616-547-9955,
800-552-0025; Studio $59–110
Amenities: Outdoor pool, hot tub, restaurant, conference center

Blending the old with the new, this resort offers a unique atmosphere for those seeking a Lake Michigan vacation in the summer and fall. For the traveler in the other seasons of the year, this is an exceptional value. Starting with the stone European-style Castle Lodge (and its gothic towers topped with weather vanes), this resort has grown over the years. Today there are modern, stylish condominiums surrounded by trees overlooking "Charlevoix the Beautiful" and Round Lake Harbor. They have an attractive, smart interior decor with private fireplaces and kitchenettes. The real advantages are a private condo and the use of the Castle Lodge facilities next door with the hearth fireplace in the lobby, conference center, and swimming pool.

7   WINDWARD CONDOMINIUMS
West Lake Rd., Harbor Springs, MI 49740
1BR $52–81, 2BR $78–115, 3BR $97–147
Amenities: Heated outdoor pool, clubhouse, tennis

These luxury condominiums overlook the bay. There is a private beach club for owners and guests.

RENTAL RESOURCES
Alpine Resort, 616-347-8501, Petosky
Atrium Inn, 616-582-6220, 800-748-0160, Boyne
Crystal Rentals, 616-378-4229
Harborage Condos, 800-456-4313, Boyne
Heather Highlands Realty, 616-526-6206
Holiday Accommodations, 616-348-2765, 800-432-7680, Conway
Land Masters, 616-526-2641
Little Traverse Accommodations, 616-526-7540, 800-968-8180,
    Harbor Springs
Northern Michigan Property Management, 616-547-4501, Charlevoix
Resort Property Management, 616-348-2500, 800-968-2844,
    Harbor Springs
Sylvain Management, 800-678-1036, Harbor Springs
Vacation Properties Network, 616-582-6724, Boyne
Vacation Properties Network, 616-547-9905, Charlevoix
Wildwood on Walloon, 616–582-9616

2. MICHIGAN'S UPPER PENINSULA

This area is a surprise for vacationers. It is often overlooked because of its out of the way location on the north central border of the U.S. The waters of Lake Superior moderate the climate so in summertime, the temperatures range in the 70s and 80s. In winter, the guaranteed snow makes the local mountain resorts some of the most popular destinations for Midwest skiers. Perhaps the best time of year, however, is the fall when the changing colors of the trees rival New England— yet the area is devoid of the hordes of leaf peepers. The 1.5 million acre Ottawa National Forest is one of the largest expanses of virgin forest found in the U.S. and the opportunities for fishermen and hikers are limitless.

Surprisingly, there are several concentrations of condos in the area as well as the isolated country cabins that you would expect. The condos are concentrated around the ski resorts of Brule, Big Powderhorn, Indianhead, and

Whitecap Mountains. For those who want to vacation on the shores of the lakes of the Upper Peninsula, contact some of the rental agencies listed in the rental resources section.

Transportation to this part of the country must be by car. The most convenient major airport is Duluth/Superior, but all flights into that airport involve connections in Minneapolis.

WHERE TO STAY

 ### BIG POWDERHORN LODGING
Powderhorn Rd., Bessemer, MI 49911, 906-932-3100,
800-222-3131

There are over 300 chalets and condos clustered around the base of this ski resort, or hidden in the woods. There is no one name to cal this aggregation of condos and cabins; the tie that binds is that they are all handled by the central reservation service. We saw one cabin which, although it was in the remote part of the north woods, reminded us of the sophisticated suburbs of Minneapolis. There was a massive stone hearth fireplace and coordinated plaid and deep green colors. Accented by duck decoys and a teddybear with a matching plaid bow, the interior was far better than the simple exterior would suggest.

 ### BLACKJACK SKI RESORT
Blackjack Rd., Bessemer, WI 49911, 906-229-5115, 800-848-1125

This small ski mountain has over 80 condos along the slopes. It has the added advantage of being only a mile from the larger Big Powderhorn Mountain. These one-, two-, and three-bedroom condos have ski-in/ski-out access in the winter and many have private saunas. In summer, the area is deserted, but this is wonderful for those who want to enjoy nature and do not want to be disturbed by their neighbors.

BRULE MOUNTAIN
397 Brule Mountain Road, Iron River, MI 49935, 906-265-4957,
800-338-7174
Amenities: Skiing, indoor pool

Located just east of Iron River, Michigan, or a little over an hour north of Rhinelander, Wisconsin, this is one of the finest ski resort in the Midwest. Brule is one of the most well-groomed mountains here with an abundance of natural powder, snowmaking, and, of course, packing and molding the snow at night. Socially, life revolves around the lodge where Pig Roasts are a local tradition. The condos are in walking distance of the central lodge area and they include:

Pampering Pines (9) single-unit chalets with private hot tubes and saunas. These are the best accommodations in Brule. Some have been decorated with country antiques, brass beds, and quilts. Rentals from $105 to $190.

Brule Fever (8) These are chalets ranging in size from two to four bedrooms. Each duplex building has a hot tub and a sauna to be shared by the two groups. Rentals from $95 to $160.

Alpine Attitude (8) Similar in design to Brule Fever, and each has a private sauna. Rentals from $75 to $120.

Nordic Nites (7) Older duplexes, again with private saunas. $75 to $115.

Snow Clouds, Warm Winds, and **Pioneer Lodge (6)** Three separate groups of condos. Pleasantly decorated, you can expect rental woods and tweed fabrics. These do not have the private saunas described above.

 INDIANHEAD MOUNTAIN CONDOMINIUMS
500 Indianhead Rd., Wakefield, MI 49968, 906-229-5181, 800-3-INDIAN

One of the largest ski resorts in the Midwest, most of the accommodations are in a series of condos built around the mountain. We saw one condo that was drab to say the least. It had "skierized" furniture and carpeting that had seen better days. But the advantages here are the health club with the large indoor heated pool, racquetball courts, gym, and aerobics classes to name only a few. For summertime visitors to the area, the restaurant and health club are distinct advantages.

7 **INDIANHEAD VALLEY CONDOMINIUMS**
Route 1, Box 5, Wakefield, MI 49968, 906-229-5113
1BR $59–99, 2BR $79–125
Amenities: None

Located at the base of Indianhead Mountain, these are the best accommodations in the area. As an added advantage, Blackjack Mountain ski area is only a mile away. These condos offer skiers the opportunity to enjoy two resort areas. The modern two and one-half story buildings have been built of cedar and stone. Lofts, cathedral ceilings, and skylights are architectural embellishments. Interior decor generally is uninspired. The one we saw was newly decorated but it looked as though someone had just purchased this week's bargains at the local furniture store. Most of these condos have private saunas and/or hot tubs.

7+ **POWDERMILL INN RESORT CONDOS**
N11330 Powderhorn Rd., Bessemer, WI 49911, 906-932-0800,
800-882-0888; Studio $60–125, 2BR $100–170
Amenities: Indoor pool, sauna, restaurant

Nestled at the base of Big Powderhorn Mountain, these condos are an outgrowth of the local lodge and a response to the consumer's demand for condo accommodations. The studios are a step above hotel accommodations with a bed, kitchenette, and a sleeper sofa. The loft units have an additional bedroom upstairs and are much more inviting because of the space created by the cathedral ceiling. The Inn's pool center and restaurant are a real bonus here.

 RIVER ROCK RETREAT
N10675 Junet Road, Ironwood, MI 49938, 906-932-5638
3BR $200–350/night

This is an example of one of the better cabins available for rent in this neck of the woods. Built of logs, the owners had fun designing and decorated so that every creature comfort would be fulfilled. The cabin has its own sauna and a hot tub large enough for six. There are three bedrooms, one of which is like a dorm with four bunkbeds. The best feature is the little loft accessible by a cast iron spiral staircase spacious and romantic, just staying here is enough of an adventure.

RENTAL RESOURCES
Black River Lodge Condos, 906-932-3857, Ironwood
Hedgerow Lodging, 906-663-6950, Bessemer
The Real Estate Store, 906-932-5416, Ironwood
Kathy Richards Management, 906-932-5500, Ironwood

MISSISSIPPI

The Mississippi Gulf Coast has been a vacation area since before the Civil War. The antebellum homes lining Beach Boulevard, in some places right next door to a modern condo development or motel from the 1960s, are testimony to the area's proud past. Today, many vacationers have overlooked this area, but you'll find that broad white sandy beach unchanged with stately magnolias, and the water shimmering with phosphorous at night.

Many of these condos are annexed to larger hotels. A few are timeshares. This is a quiet, pleasant area with a mild year-round climate (except January) which attracts Yankee snowbirds in winter and visitors from Mississippi or New Orleans in the summer.

Most visitors to this area drive. If you plan to fly, there is a regional airport at Gulfport/Biloxi with nonstop flights from Memphis. Or try New Orleans, only ninety minutes away.

WHERE TO STAY

7   **CHATEAU DE LA MER**
1410 Beach Blvd., Gulfport, MS 39507, 601-896-1703
1BR $750/wk
Amenities: Pool, tennis

Your best bet for condo rentals along the Mississippi Gulf Coast. Chateau de la Mer is a three-story wooden structure with landscaped pool. Across the street from the beach, each condo was designed with the balconies at an angle, giving you some privacy and a view of the Gulf. The interior decor is attractive. Expect butcher block table and chairs and tweed fabrics on the couch. In addition to the queen-sized sleeper sofa, there are two bunk beds in the hallway. Pleasant and relaxing, these condos are convenient to the town and across from the beach.

3   **MARINER'S HARBOR**
715 Beach Blvd., #164, Biloxi, MS 39530, 601-375-2124
1BR $550/wk
Amenities: Small pool, hot tub

Located at the marina on the site of the former Biloxi Yacht Club, Manning Harbor is about a five-minute walk along the shore from the beach. These are quiet, well-furnished condos suitable for a day, a week, or a month in the heart of Biloxi. They do have hotel style furnishings, however.

6   **ROYAL HOLIDAY BEACH RESORT**
40 Royal d'Iberville Hotel, 3420 W. Beach Blvd., Biloxi, MS 39531, 601-388-7553; 1BR $850/wk
Amenities: Pool, hot tub, hotel restaurant

Perhaps the most attractive beachfront condos in Mississippi, these two-story townhouses are in the backyard of the Royal d'Iberville hotel (formerly the Sheraton) across the street from the beach. The condos are all on two floors with a spiral staircase. They face the hotel's pool and hot tub. There's a private whirlpool in each master bathroom. Handsomely decorated, this is a gracious environment and far superior to the hotel rooms across the way.

5   SHORELINE OAKS
1130 E. Beach Blvd., P.O. Box 6823, Biloxi, MS 39530,
601-868-1916; 1BR $95
Amenities: Pool

A two-story motel-style condo resort across the street from the beach. Located next to a college and close to the pier, this resort provides a gracious atmosphere in the heart of Gulfport. The condos are adequately furnished, almost over decorated, with plush velour chairs, patterned wallpaper, and lots of personal, at-home touches.

MISSOURI

The bumpy Ozark Mountains with their forests and twisted roads have hindered the economic growth of the southwestern part of this state, but the barriers may have preserved a natural asset. The term Ozarks came from the French explorers who referred to the bumpy mountains as "the arcs"— "aux arcs" which was corrupted to Ozarks. The area enjoys an eight-month, spring-fall season with two hot months in July and August. The dead season is December and January. Originally a regional resort area for Kansas City and residents of metropolitan St. Louis, Missouri, the Lake of the Ozarks area now attracts vacationers from all over the U.S. who've discovered the dogwoods and azaleas in spring, and the changing colors of the foliage in fall.

Resort properties accommodations in Missouri represent two extremes— luxury and rustic. The Lodge of the Four Seasons and Tan-Tar-A are two master-planned developments, each on over 2,000 acres of lakeside land. These two are among the top 50 resort developments in the U.S. There are only a few resorts in the middle range. Unfortunately the quality of Missouri resorts drops sharply. Off-site management is the norm here with most resorts having an office to hand out keys and perform business accounting services. Unlike the two leaders, hospitality is weak in this region as a general rule. It is too bad because the land is beautiful, the sporting opportunities are outstanding and usually not crowded, and Branson's Country Music Hall Strip is well on its way to becoming a national entertainment center. We have divided this chapter according to the major resort destination areas:

1. Lake of the Ozarks
2. Table Rock Lake/Branson

To help you become more familiar with the area, we have a map of the Ozarks including Arkansas, on page 22.

Missouri is emerging as a major vacation destination on a national level, but the state has yet to comprehend the significance of this development. First of all, Missouri state law requires that all condo and vacation home rentals be handled through a realtor. This means that there are very few condo/villa resorts with on-site, front-desk operations, and you must endure a fair amount of confusion in order to rent a condo or vacation home. The benefit, however, is that there are a number of condo rental agencies that offer the same units at very competitive prices.

1. LAKE OF THE OZARKS

This lake was created in 1931 by the construction of Bagnell Dam on the Osage River. The shore line of this lake alone (1,375 miles) exceeds the California coast. The lake is in the central part of the state, 175 miles from both Kansas City and St. Louis. The local airport has only two commuter flights, and the real air fare bargains are to the two major cities where weekly car rentals are reasonably priced. The best approach to the lake is by Highway 54 from Interstate 70. Be careful to determine your exact destination. There are only two bridges across the lake, and it can be over an hour of driving time around the lake. There are three major commercial centers here: the first is the Lake Ozark/Osage Beach area, a community that has been booming for years and is now upgrading the quality of restaurants and entertainment for tourists. This is on Highway 54 on the east side of the lake. The second community consists of Gravois Mills/Laurie/Sunrise Beach on Highway 5 on the western side of the lake. These are sleepy towns just awakening to vacationers' needs and expectations. The third area is Camdenton, where Highways 5 and 54 intersect on the southern border. The town is older, with construction dating from the 1920s. Remember, these short distances take longer to travel because of the twisting mountain roads.

Summer is the most popular season, with lots of visitors from Midwestern cities. The spring is a beautiful season. The hills are pink with dogwood and green with new leaves. Autumn is a special time, and the foliage here rivals New England and the Rockies. The advantage to the Ozarks is that you won't have to fight the crowds, and you can enjoy the natural beauty. Winter is a time to snuggle by the fire or play golf on clear, sunny days.

Most of these resorts have no on-site office. Do not write to the resorts for reservations. Your letters will be returned because most resorts do not have mail receptacles. For reservations, use the Rental Resources unless there is a telephone number indicating that someone is there at the resort working in an office, ready to handle your request. This area offers some of the best vacation values in the U.S. It doesn't have the reputation of Florida or California for water sports, but it's all here except for the surf and deep-sea fishing.

WHERE TO STAY

6 **BAY POINT**
State Road H.H., Osage Beach, MO 65065
1BR $60–85, 2BR $90–125, 3BR $130–185
Amenities: Pool, boat docks

Do not confuse these simple condos with those at Bay Point Village; there is a big difference between these two developments. The units in these two-story brick buildings are older and the decor is very simple. Centrally located near Horseshoe Bend, these older units have seen better days.

7 **BAY POINT VILLAGE**
State Road K.K., Lake Ozark, MO 65049
1BR $60–85, 2BR/Loft $95–135
Amenities: Pool, tennis, boat dock

Overlooking the water, these new condominiums are spread over 25 acres near the Tan-Tar-A resort. This is one of the few "gated" communities located on a point of land jutting out into the lake. Some units have lofts and cathedral ceilings. Interior decor is light and modern, generally with neutral tweed fabrics and lots of light contemporary woods. Each has a fireplace for winter and ceiling fans for summer. Pleasant and modern, these units are superior to many accommodations in this area.

6 BREAKWATER BAY CLUB

Baydy Peak Rd., State Road K.K., Osage Beach, MO 65065, 314-348-4337
Amenities: Pool, tennis

Located near the Tan-Tar-A resort area, these brand new condos appeal to both water enthusiasts and golfers. These units are crisply modern and efficient with lake views, fireplaces, and large kitchens.

7 BRIDGE POINTE

Highway 54, Osage Beach, MO 65065, 314-348-5512; 2BR $90–135
Amenities: Pool, boat dock

Located just before the bridge over the lake, this is one of the most convenient locations for those who don't want to drive. Many of the area's better shops and restaurants are located on the surrounding hills. These new condos look nice from the street, even better from the water, but on the inside they come up a little short. We found them to be in need of a good housecleaning. Each has the extra amenity of a screened porch.

5 COPPER RIDGE

Lake Ozark, MO 65049
Amenities: Pool, dock

These spacious duplex condos literally flow down the hillside. Large and spacious, they are choice for extended families.

7 GOLDEN REEF

Lake Road 54-29, Osage Beach, MO 65065
Amenities: Pool, dock

Centrally located in Osage Beach, this is one of the area's most popular condo resorts. These two-story buildings almost blend in with the slope of the hillside, and each unit has a breathtaking lake view from the living room and deck. Large and spacious, each has oversized rooms and ceiling fans to catch the lake breezes. Furnishing tends to be older. After all, some of these units were last decorated fifteen years ago. Golden reef is a popular, comfortable choice.

3 **HAWK HARBOR**
State Road H.H., Osage Beach, MO 65065
Amenities: Swimming platform

This has simple, dark units on a quiet corner of the lake. Instead of a pool there's a swimming platform anchored in the lake.

4 **HERON BAY**
Lake Road 54-56, Osage Beach, MO 65065
1BR $50–75, 2BR $75–110
Amenities: Pool, boat dock, clubhouse, tennis

Some of the newer condominiums on the lake, these units are distinguished by vaulted ceilings and skylights. Each has a breakfast bar that separates the kitchen and preserves an open airy feeling. Ceiling fans circulate the cool lake breezes in summer. This is a huge complex where over 300 families can be accommodated. Children are sure to find playmates and there are lots of activities.

3 **HOLIDAY SHORES**
Highway 54, Lake Ozark, MO 65049, 314-348-3438
Amenities: Pool, lake, boat dock

Holiday Shores has interesting "glass-walled" tree houses overlooking a cove of the lake. The condos are on a hillside that slope down to the lake.

7 **INDIAN POINT**
Osage Beach, MO 65065; 2BR $85–120
Amenities: Pool, boat dock

Centrally located near Osage Beach, this lakeside setting seems far removed from the crush of civilization. There's a collection of four-story buildings here, all of which are relatively new. Interior decor is modern and sleek, although the actual furniture pieces are inexpensive.

7 **THE KNOLLS**
Route 1, Box 435, Osage Beach, MO 65065, 314-348-2236,
800-648-0339; 1BR $59–99, 2BR $79–110, 3BR $99–139
Amenities: Tennis, indoor and outdoor pool, hot tub

The Knolls condominiums offer some of the finest accommodations to be found in the rustic Ozarks area. These one, two, and three-bedroom condos are spacious and well decorated. Expect to find neutral, earth-tone furnishings, bentwood chairs, and lots of personal touches reflecting the hill country heritage. Each kitchen has an open breakfast bar and the fireplace is the focal point of the living room. Beautifully landscaped, this is an inviting setting on the shores of the Lake of the Ozarks.

6   LAKE CHALET
Route 1, Highway 54, Osage Beach, MO 65065, 314-348-4718
1BR $120–154
Amenities: Pool, restaurant

Management at Lake Chalet wants you to enjoy this cozy resort located on an arm of the lake. The sloping hillside and sparkling waters make this an attractive destination. This is a small resort that emphasizes personal attention. The condos are newly decorated with mirrors, leather chairs, and lots of solid wood. This is right behind the Best Western, and check-in is at the hotel's front desk. Children will enjoy the swimming pool.

LODGE OF THE FOUR SEASONS
Road H.H., Lake Ozark, MO 65049, 800-727-0717; 2BR $145–290
Amenities: Golf, tennis, racquetball, pool, sports center and spa, beach, marina

Clearly one of the finest resorts in the Midwest and one of the best in the U.S. The scope of Lodge of the Four Seasons is far reaching. It is a master-planned community on 2,800 acres of rolling Ozark landscape on a long, skinny peninsula that is surrounded by water. Manicured landscaping and well-positioned trees enhance the view. Beginning with a European style hotel on a grand scale, the master resort community now encompasses two separate condominium developments, acres of residential and vacation homes, as well as the central core lodge. Surprisingly, there are Japanese-style gardens surrounding the lodge. The design blends well with the rough Ozark terrain. Unlike other Ozark resorts, this one effuses polished refinement.

Racquet Club Villas (10) There are 125 of these Mediterranean-style condos located next to the sports and social center. Lodge of the Four Seasons has incorporated the best from cultures like Spain, Mexico, and Japan to create this rare environment. The Mediterranean villas have whitewashed walls and red tile roofs, similar to what you would expect in San Diego. Elegantly furnished in soft beige and peach colors, you'll find the living room dominated by a stone fireplace, and a screened porch that serves as an extra room during eight months of the year. Glass-top tables, designer fabrics, and brass accessories create a sophisticated environment. About the only thing suggestive of the outside architectural style that you'll find inside these condos is the Mexican woven bedspread.

Treetops (9) Treetops is another group of condos on a sloping hillside that cascade down to the lake. Entirely different, there's a hint of Frank Lloyd Wright in the architecture, perhaps because of the use of stone, natural wood, and well-positioned windows that capture the view. Perhaps it's the well-tended, Japanese-style landscaping. Treetops condos are on stilts. Each condo has four plate-glass walls, with contemporary decor on the inside and just a hint of the Pacific Northwest and a touch of Mexico. It is beautifully decorated and beautifully maintained. Treetops has its own pool and clubhouse/exercise center. In addition, an impressive new sports and social center is available.

The Lodge offers an 18-hole Robert Trent Jones golf course and is one of two campuses (the other in California) of the University of Golf. This is a training program for amateurs that combines clinics, private instruction, and videotape critiques in intensive five- or seven-day sessions. The Van der Meer Tennis University is one of two such tennis centers (the other is in Hilton Head, SC). Lodge of the Four Seasons is unique for having both types of centers. The main lodge building is the popular social center, but you'll also make friends around the impressive sports center. A true European spa with figure-control counseling, exercise machines and muscle building weight lifting programs for men is provided. You'll find lots of activity. Simply put, this is a good example of how man can transform nature into a total vacation environment.

3   PARKSIDE PLACE
Highway 54-29, Osage Beach, MO 65065
Amenities: Pool, dock

Modern, simple, and efficient are the adjectives to describe the condos in these three-story buildings. Pleasant and contemporary in style, the only drawback is the construction. It is so poorly insulated, that you can hear your neighbors.

7   PORT ELSEWHERE
1018 Bagnell Dam Blvd., Lake Ozark, MO 65049, 314-365-4077
Amenities: Boat dock, pool

Port Elsewhere injects a nautical fantasy into the resort atmosphere. There are 14 condos in this resort and it is still growing. When complete, it will be a major development at the Lake of the Ozarks. Management tries hard to please guests, and you will be impressed that everything in the condos is "shipshape." There are two small pools and a dock for boats. Small sailboats are available for rent. Plans exist for a full-service marina adjacent to the property. Rentals are a good value through the resort.

7   SOMERSET
State Road H.H., Lake Ozark, MO 65049
Amenities: Pool

There are just ten of these duplexes along the lake at Horseshoe Bend. Each one has been custom built and decorated. One big plus—there's no unit on top or below you. Great views from a quiet backwater are provided. Hospitality is limited to a key drop, so bring your own fun.

8   SOUTHWOOD SHORES
Horseshoe Bend, 790 State Road H.H., Lake Ozark, MO 65049,
314-365-4644, 800-331-0965
Studio $69, 1BR $84, 2BR $109, 3BR $139
Amenities: Tennis, boat docks, indoor and outdoor pool

This is one of the area's most popular condo developments because of all the recreational facilities and superior hospitality. Southwood is one of the lake's largest developments. It is located on a point of land that juts into the lake. Everything is available here, from indoor and outdoor pools to a hot tub, tennis courts, and a clubhouse. It is tailor made for small conferences. In the Horseshoe Bend area, you'll find many boat charters available.

10   TAN-TAR-A
State Road R. R., Osage Beach, MO 65065, rentals c/o Duenke
Development, Box 1020, Osage Beach, MO 65065, 314-348-2706
Amenities: Golf, marina, tennis, racquetball, bowling, ice skating,
indoor pool, health club, restaurants

Located on 420 acres along the shores of the Lake of the Ozarks, this resort offers a variety of accommodations and activities. The main lodge is a timbered, rambling structure that follows the contours of the hillside. Elevators go down from the lobby. A short walk away from the main hotel are stone and wood one-bedroom townhouses on the lakeshore, next to the marina and beach. Part of the hotel complex, they are decorated in a neutral hotel style that is unremarkable. They have fireplaces, kitchens, and a private patio with an umbrella table.

Across a footbridge and a rivulet from the main hotel and marina, is the area of vacation homes and beautiful condominiums. Shaded by trees, you know you are in the Ozarks with the rocky outcroppings and stone and rustic wood-faced buildings. Furnishings are generally in a sophisticated country style. Some homes are more sophisticated than others, but all in all the quality is excellent; only the style differs. Beveled ceilings, exposed beams, stone fireplaces and lots of glass doors and windows frame the view.

The resort features an 18-hole golf course. It is a mile away from the main resort center. For tennis buffs, there are nine tennis courts and a sports complex (housing an indoor pool, racquetball court, and tennis pro shop). The best feature is the two marinas with 64 slips for boats and a variety of "user-friendly" boat rentals including sailboats, water ski boats and equipment, flat-bottom pontoon boats, and fishing boats with trolling motors. There are great restaurants. This resort takes pride in hosting small conferences and medical seminars. Everything is perfect and well run and this resort provides an inviting environment.

8+ **THREE BUOYS HOUSEBOAT VACATIONS**
Route 71, Box 1870, Camdenton, MO 65020, 314-873-5202,
800-423-7021
Amenities: Boat

Condominium houseboats! These boats provide exceptional vacations that you'll never forget. Pontoon boats with flat bottoms for cruising the lake are available. These spiffy "winnebagos of the waves" are excellently maintained and trouble-free. After a short, one-hour briefing on operations and the maps of the lake and its coves, you'll be at the helm for three days, four days, or a week. A hospitality director will help you plan your vacation. The quarters are efficient and a little small, but who cares. You have the freedom to enjoy the entire lake. Find a private cove or spend the day fishing. A waterslide is even attached to the stern! All boats are fully equipped for ten passengers with complete kitchens, dining areas, bedrooms, and baths. The dining room table converts to a bed at night. These "marine resorts" provide lots of fun for groups or families.

2. TABLE ROCK LAKE / BRANSON

The Southern Missouri Ozarks, right along the Arkansas border, are more mountainous than the Lake of the Ozarks area. Driving through the hills, you'll catch glimpses of views that, as you twist and turn, are spectacular. Sometimes however, you'll be glad there's a guard rail. The commercial areas center around Branson, Silver Dollar City, and Kimberling City. The recreational areas are primarily Table Rock Lake and Lake Tanneycomo.

This is the area of Harold Bell Wright's *The Shepherd of the Hills*. The novel has been turned into an outdoor drama about the true grit displayed by the area's inhabitants around the turn of the century. This is the original attraction that drew tourists to this area. Subsequently, Silver Dollar City was created in the 1950s as a replica of an Ozarks pioneer settlement. Today, the most famous attractions may be the country music halls and the emergence of an entertainment center rivaling Nashville.

None of the resorts here offer sophisticated lodgings. This area is where people come to return to an earlier, simple era. The healthy climate promotes relaxation. Summer is the most important season. The music halls and outdoor theater are in full swing. Many attractions close after September and reopen in May.

The weather is hot in the summer with little rain. In the spring and fall, lengthy seasons here, the climate is mild and inviting for outdoor sports. Winter lasts only two months, and sometimes there can be snow in the mountains.

WHERE TO STAY

8+ BASS' BIG CEDAR LODGE

c/o Bass Pro Shops, 1935 S. Campbell St., Springfield, MO 65898,
417-335-2777
Amenities: Lake, tennis, pool, restaurant

Whether or not you enjoy fishing, this is one of the most distinctive resorts in the booming Branson area. Located on an inlet of Table Rock Lake, there is a main lodge and a bevy of rustic cabins that are spread over 12 acres. Each of the cabins has a boat slip. There's also a 92-slip marina where you can rent a boat. The cabins are better than most and were among the first to capture the romance of the Ozarks. Expect to find a stone fireplace, a hooked rug, rockers, and comfortable furniture. The real draw is the collection of paraphernalia about fish, fishing, and the ecology. The youthful owner of the Bass Pro Shops has great respect for fish and the ecology, and his attitude is reflected at this resort. It is pleasantly different.

6 KIMBERLING INN CONDOS

Highway 13, P.O. Box 159, Kimberling City, MO 65686,
417-739-4101; Studio $49–56
Amenities: Marina, pool, tennis, restaurant

The Kimberling Inn sits on a peninsula surrounded by the waters of Table Rock Lake. A popular resort hotel, condos were added in the '70s for families desiring to stay a week or so. The furniture is no longer stylish, but the location remains popular because of the main hotel facilities—the pool, tennis courts, restaurant, and boat docks. The condos are in a two-story brick and wood colonial-style structure. It is behind the main hotel and overlooks the lake. It is spacious and comfortable for a family.

6 OZARK MOUNTAIN RESORT

Route 3, Box 910, Kimberling City, Missouri 65686, 417-779-4131
2BR $79–102
Amenities: Beach, boating, lake, swimming pool, tennis

About a mile away is Ozark Mountain Resort. It has a completely different atmosphere. There are 100 rustic cabins and condos spread over 120 wooded acres. There is an attractive clubhouse and recreation area. One hundred yards away, there is a separate clubhouse and administration building.

5+ ROARK RESORT

403 N. Business 65, Branson, MO 65616, 417-334-1430
Studio $45–70
Amenities: Lake, pool

Roark Resort, located on the shores of Lake Tanneycomo, was originally a motel resort. Chalet condos have been added to its parklike setting. These two-story, steep-gabled buildings are actually duplexes with condos attached. The second-story units have extra loft bedrooms and cathedral ceilings. Each has a deck for enjoying the fresh outdoors and the lake. There's a large pool area that is popular in the summer.

RENTAL RESOURCES... MISSOURI
Alpine Lodge, 417-338-2514, Branson
Bentree Lodge, 417-338-2218, Branson
Brokers Club Realty, 314-365-6200, Lake Ozark
Century 21 Lake Realty, 314-348-3101, Osage Beach
Duenke Development, 314-348-2706, Tan-Tar-A and others
Al Elam Co., 314-365-2311, 800-356-2311, Wide selection at Lake Ozark
Eleven West Condos, 314-374-9378, Lake Ozark
John Farrell Realty, 314-348-2121, Lake Ozark
Four Seasons Realty, 314-365-5303, Lake Ozark
Gundaker Better Homes, 314-348-1727, 800-451-LAKE, Osage Beach
Lakeshore Resort, 417-334-6222, Branson
Osage Realty, 314-348-2010, Lake Ozark
PMG, 800-238-3434, 800-237-3434 (MO), Largest rental agency.
   Handles Three Seasons, Heron Bay, Golden Reef, Wrenwood, Bay Point,
   Bridge Point, Harbor Point, Robin Wood, and Pelican's Bay
Pointe Royale, 417-334-0079, Branson
Riverpoint Estates, 417-334-6721, Branson
Ed Sanniger Realty, 314-365-0007, Lake Ozark
Southwood Shores Realty, 314-365-4644, 800-331-0965, Lake Ozark
Sunrise Ridge, 314-374-7711, Lake Ozark
Welek Realty, 314-365-5356, Lake Ozark

MONTANA

Images of Montana usually begin with the Marlboro man herding cattle across an open prairie with majestic purple mountains in the distance. Perhaps this tradition began a hundred years ago with the vigorous cowboy art of Charles Russell, but the Montana of today needs to be painted with quite a different brush. The absence of major cities and the transportation distances have combined to create natural obstacles to development. Therefore Montana remains a land of wide open spaces and "the big sky." But increasingly you hear the locals say that they are going to get out and roam the wide open spaces while they can. Although Montana has heretofore escaped the attention of developers and masses of tourists, it's only a matter of time before it changes.

There are two major resort areas, each with it's own distinct personality. Whitefish/Big Mountain is located 500 miles from Big Sky; each has been designed to capture Montana's best. Near Butte there is one large resort built around a natural hot spring, so we have included it in a section of its own. After all, it's a very long full day's drive from Whitefish to Big Sky and there are many states that could easily fit within this distance. You'll find Whitefish on the map on page 678, just over the border from Canada; while Big Sky is on the map of Montana, Idaho and Wyoming.

1. WHITEFISH / BIG MOUNTAIN / GLACIER NATIONAL PARK

It's been our experience that none of the commercial images ring true about this area. The Whitefish/Big Mountain/Glacier National Park area is certainly the state's most spectacular location, and well it should be, as it is the southern extension of the Rockies that bring fame to Canada's Banff National Park. There are several peaks that could have been the prototype for the Paramount Pictures emblem and Disney didn't have to go all the way to Switzerland's Matterhorn to find a majestic peak. With peaks towering up to 12,000 feet and sharp angular faces striated by eons of glacial action, this is a dazzling area of awesome natural beauty. Glacier National Park features 50 ice-age glaciers and over 200 sparkling lakes for summertime adventures. The main town is Whitefish, a raw railroad town with a new funky overlay, recently introduced by California refugees. Kalispell is the nearest airport and in the summer, the shores of Whitefish Lake (any of the condos along Wisconsin Avenue) is where you'll want to be. Six miles away, Big Mountain ski resort offers some of Montana's finest skiing and ski lift prices are some of the most reasonable. When the winds bluster, take heart at the Great Northern cafe in Whitefish or one of the local watering holes. Nowhere else will you feel as though you are actually "living" TV's "Northern Exposure." Although there is a shuttle bus between the town of Whitefish, the condo strip outside of town along

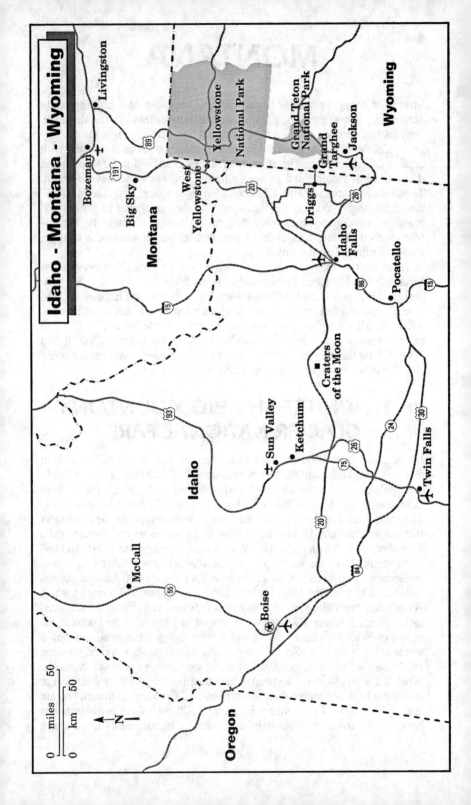

Wisconsin Avenue, and the Big Mountain ski area, service is infrequent. When planning a vacation, you need to know the local conditions ahead of time because driving the icy roads at night can be treacherous.

Recently the Whitefish/Big Mountain area has emerged as "Malibu North." Among the celebrities who have purchased vacation homes in the Whitefish area you'll find Carol Burnett (who is selling her home on Maui for $3.5 million) and fellow Mauian Jim "Gomer Pyle" Nabors. Other celebrities you might see are the San Francisco 49ers owner Edward DeBartolo Jr, young actors like Emilio Estevez and Kiefer Sutherland, director Michael Cimino and "Entertainment Tonight" anchorwoman Mary Hart and her producer husband Burt Sugarman. Yet the towns of Big Fork, Columbia Falls, Whitefish, and West Glacier are still raw cowboy towns where wages run $4 to $5 an hour for honest work.

The Big Mountain is where most of the condos and vacation homes are concentrated. Unlike other ski resorts, the condo complexes usually have no more than 6 to10 units and since very few have on-site property managers, those who are interested in condo or vacation home rentals usually go straight to one of the rental agencies which will have a couple of units at each of the complexes. Where possible we have held true to our format of reviewing each condo/vacation home complex, but in the Whitefish area we must go with the flow and describe some of the leading rental agencies that have units within each of the complexes.

Big Mountain has two subdivisions, the flats and "on the mountain." All of the Big Mountain condos we have reviewed are on the mountain. The flats is primarily an area of vacation homes. If you wind up staying in the flats, there is a shuttle bus over to the lift. Otherwise, be prepared for a rigorous uphill walk in the morning.

Transportation to Montana is where the rub comes. Air transportation to the Whitefish/Glacier National Park area is terrible unless you own your own plane. The best connections are through Salt Lake or Minneapolis and even those flights make an extra stop after you've already made a connection. An alternative would be to fly to Calgary and drive south for three hours. Most of the route is divided highway across the prairie and Calgary has some of the lowest air fares of any city in North America. The other alternative is Amtrak, a method of transportation promoted by the resort, although those on a week's vacation may be reluctant to spend four days travelling back and forth by rail from either Minneapolis or Seattle.

WHERE TO STAY

 ALPINE VILLAGE HOMES
Big Mountain,Whitefish, MT 59937, 406-862-3511
1BR $110–$165, 2BR $140–$215
Amenities: All have use of the Big Mountain sports center which includes a pool.

One of the two large rental agencies in the Big Mountain area, this group offers as many vacation homes as condos for rent. Some of the homes have a touch of romance as reflected in names such as Chickcharney Lodge and Blarney's Castle. In addition to the full furnishings, fireplaces, and occasional jacuzzi hot tub, these units often are equipped with games, special facilities for entertaining, and many are decorated with antiques celebrating Montana's past. Ask about the various possibilities and your vacation will definitely be enhanced

 ANAPURNA PROPERTIES
3840 Big Mountain Rd., Box 55, Whitefish, MT 59937
800-243-7547, 1BR $90–$175, 2BR $145–$245
Amenities: All have use of the Big Mountain health club which includes a pool.

Anapurna is one of the two large rental agencies servicing skier condos in the Big Mountain area. With over 60 condos and 25 vacation homes Anapurna can find accommodations for groups of young skiers as well as that private chalet on the hill.

The **Anapurna (7)** condos, which are right behind the check-in office, consist of eight condos in a two-story, lodge-style building. Decorated with contemporary furniture, these were designed more for durability than aesthetics. There is a hot tub just for the use of Anapurna guests. For a central location and quality better than most, these are perfect for families. **Bitteroot Condos (7)** are just up the hill from Anapurna and are brand new for 1993. This four-story blue wood structure is pleasant because it's new, but the opportunity for design was missed. Cheery and functional, Anapurna has a 24-hour staff that makes using this service truly advantageous.

6-8 BAY POINT ESTATES
300 Bay Point Dr., P.O. Box 35, Whitefish, MT 59937
406-862-2331, 800-327-2108, 1BR $68–105, 2BR $100–150
Amenities: Beach, pool, hot tub, clubhouse with gameroom.
Golf nearby

Bay Point Estates is located on the shores of Whitefish Lake across from the 27-hole golf course. Unique to the resorts in the area, Bay Point has its own beach. The resort almost has a clubby atmosphere resulting from the large number of returning guests and owners. These people like this resort and have no desire to search for greener pastures elsewhere. This is a community of large cabins and condos, many of which have been eclectically decorated. We saw one that reflected the opulence of one of the timber barons with crystal chandeliers and a gilded mirror. We suspect the owner inherited grandma's priceless antiques and just didn't know where to store them. For a vacation home, this was really different, but that was the exception. Most of the condos are fully furnished with fireplaces and comfortable skierized furniture. Oriental rugs and Native American art are common accents. They are maintained well, but there is nothing glamorous about them. A supervised activity program is available for children in the summertime. This resort offers a good value.

7   CHAMONIX
The Big Mountain, Whitefish, MT 59937 (no mail receptacle)

These spacious three-bedroom condos are some of the most attractive units in the Big Mountain area. New, architecturally inspired with a two-story-high living room ceiling and large expanses of glass, and well decorated, count yourself as fortunate if you can rent one of these beauties. Located right next to the No. 3 chair lift, you have ski-in/ski-out convenience. There is a private glass-enclosed hot tub on the front deck, where you can overlook the slopes. Designed for entertaining, there are two bedrooms upstairs and one down.

6   CRESTWOOD RESORT
1301 Wisconsin Ave., P.O. Box 1000, Whitefish, MT 59937
800-766-1181, 2BR $85–125
Amenities: Pool, hot tub, tennis, health club membership

Crestwood Resort is a village of townhouse timeshare condos surrounding an outdoor pool. It is only a short two-minute walk from the beach at Whitefish Lake and less than ten minutes from skiing at Big Mountain. The spacious units are good for families as they are equipped with fireplaces and skierized furniture. In our opinion, decor has been on a gradual downhill slide. The resort emphasizes both summer and winter seasons. Guests have membership privileges at the Downtowner Health & Racquet Club in town, just five minutes away. Racquetball, aerobics classes, weight room, and sauna are provided at the health club. Crestwood, in our opinion, seems to lack the "Northwest woods" feeling which abounds elsewhere. A little romance would go a long way toward boosting this resort's rating.

8   EDELWEISS
P.O. Box 55, Whitefish, MT 59937, 406-862-5252
Single $65, 1BR $150–180, 2BR $190
Amenities: Hot tub

Located at the top of the Big Mountain "village," this 50-unit condo complex offers studio, one- and two-bedroom units. Edelweiss claims a great location—it is at the base of the lifts at the Big Mountain. There is no other resort in the area like it because it is run like a hotel-condominium with full services for guests and an on-site check-in office. The condos are contained in three-story buildings and each condo has a private fireplace. The loft units are the most attractive, due to the vaulted ceilings and skylights. The units are fully furnished in a casual, contemporary style. This resort is ideal for skiers.

8   KANDAHAR LODGE
The Big Mountain, Whitefish, MT 59937, 406-862-6098
1BR $160, 2BR $280

This sets the standard for luxury in the area. Primarily a hotel, Kandahar bows to consumer demand and now offers "kitchen loft" and two-bedroom suites in condo-style accommodations. With its own sports facilities, Kandahar offers more amenities than some of its neighbors, but you'll lose your privacy and the adventure of staying in a unique home.

8   MARINA CAY
180 Vista Ln., P.O. Box 663, Bigfork, MT 59911, 406-837-5861
Amenities: Pool, hot tub, restaurant, canoe and boat rentals

The Marina Cay Resort offers attractive condos in three-story buildings and is located on the west side of Bigfork Bay where the Swan River empties into Flathead Lake (the largest body of fresh water west of the Mississippi). This is a great place for watersports and fishing, plus it's close to Big Mountain ski resort. The 85 condos are spacious and have contemporary decor with attractive earth tone colors, grasscloth wallpaper, brass end tables and sharp lamps. Marina Cay is a superior family resort with lots of activities for every age group.

6   MEADOW LAKE SKI RESORT
415 Tamarack Lane, Columbia Falls, MT 59912,
406-892-7601, 800-321-4653
Amenities: Golf, tennis, pool, hot tubs

For those who want to be near the park, Columbia Falls may be the answer for you. More of a western supply town than a resort community such as Whitefish, Columbia Falls does have the advantage of proximity to the Park. The Meadow Lake Ski Resort is a smaller version of the Big Mountain and the appeal is to those who really want to be away from it all.

9   PTARMIGAN VILLAGE
3000 Big Mountain Rd, Box 458, Whitefish, MT 59937
406-862-3594, 1BR $50–95, 2BR $95–155, 3BR $115–200
Amenities: Pool, hot tub, tennis

Although other critics give kudos to the Kandahar Lodge, we think Ptarmigan Village is the best choice in the area. Just 5 minutes away from the Big Mountain and 10 minutes from Whitefish Lake, this is the only resort in the area that captures the quintessential reason for making the journey to Montana in the first place—the romance and fantasy of being at the end of the line. This village of modern wooden duplexes are scattered over 40 acres of forested mountainside. Each has a sense of privacy where you can commune with nature. Here, the brightest lights at night are the stars. Each of the condos is decorated with style to incorporate modern convenience with the rustic past. Two- and three-bedroom units have cathedral ceilings in the living room, great mountain views, and an iron spiral staircase up to the loft. For larger groups, there are individual mountain cabins for rent. A complete resort, you'll find indoor and outdoor heated pools, tennis courts and a trout-stocked fishing pond. You'll love this place and like so many of the owners and guests, you'll surely choose to return here year after year.

6   ROCKY MOUNTAIN LODGE
6510 Hwy 93 South, Whitefish, MT 59937, 800-862-2569
Amenities: Indoor pool

This resort hotel, just south of the town of Whitefish, offers a series of completely equipped cabins for rent. Modern and well maintained, this doesn't have the personal touch which you would find at most condo/vacation home resorts.

8   WHITEFISH LAKE LODGE CONDOMINIUMS
1399 Wisconsin, Box 2040, Whitefish, MT 59937, 800-735-8869
1BR $70–160, 2BR $130–200, 3BR $190–260
Amenities: Beach, outdoor pool,

This new four-story condo development sits on the shore of Whitefish Lake, just 15 minutes away from skiing at the Big Mountain. At its best in summer, this is also a lively spot during winter. The dimensions of the units are larger than average and the furniture is superior to most of what we've seen in the area. The Phase II condos are even larger and are priced at a premium. Each has a gas fireplace and the cathedral ceilings/lofts in the three-bedroom units make them nicer than many private homes.

C   WHITEFISH PROPERTY MANAGEMENT
128 Central Ave., Whitefish, MT 59937, 406-862-2578
Condos $75–125, Homes $65–175

Offering a selection of vacation homes in the Whitefish/Flathead Lake area, this service also handles many of the **Wildwood Condos** which are on Wisconsin Ave. on the road up to the Big Mountain. If you stay at any of these properties, you'll need a car due to the distances. Each one of the homes is individually designed and reflects the owners' personal taste.

RENTAL RESOURCES

Alpine Village Homes, 406-862-3511
Anapurna Properties, 800-243-7547
Big Mountain Alpine Village Homes, 406-862-3511
Big Mountain Reservations, 800-858-5439
Flathead Travel Service, 406-862-3597
Lake & Mountain Accommodations, 406-862-2535
Whitefish Property Management, 406-862-2578

2. BIG SKY / WEST YELLOWSTONE

Going to the south central corner, just about where the state border makes
that big hook so that Wyoming remains a perfect square, you'll find the area
of West Yellowstone at the northern entrance to Yellowstone National Park.
West Yellowstone is another frontier town but it was corrupted years ago, so
today it has a tawdry face of T-shirt and souvenir shops. But just north
we've saved the best for last. Big Sky is a marvelous development with
wonderful skiing in winter and easy access to Yellowstone in summer. Why
stay in one of the crowded campgrounds or motels near the park when you
can rent a luxurious condo at Big Sky for the same price and be only 20
miles farther up the road? Big Sky has two mini-villages; one at the base of
the ski lift and the other on the golf course in the flats just six miles down
from the ski center. The scenery here compares favorably with its more
famous neighbor to the south, Yellowstone National Park. Big Sky was
developed as a resort for intermediate skiers from the big cities who ski for a
week or two each year. This is a comfortable place to learn to ski as well.
Great instruction programs and lots of little touches insure your comfort and
safety during the day.

Transportation to Big Sky/Bozeman is pretty much the same story as trying to get to the Whitefish/Big Mountain area. Northwest offers flights to
Bozeman from Minneapolis and Delta flies in from the south. An overlooked alternative is to fly to Jackson Hole, Wyoming. Big Sky is two miles
north along the eastern front of the Grand Tetons. You'll drive through both
Yellowstone National Park and the Grand Teton National Park, past some of
the most spectacular scenery in North America.

WHERE TO STAY

9+ **ARROWHEAD CONDOMINIUMS**
Big Sky, MT 59716, 406-995-2121; 3BR $390
Amenities: Private hot tub, sauna and porter

Although many will try to tell you that other condos in this area are better,
we've seen them all, and Arrowhead is the best. These cute little chalets facing the mountain are three stories high with a personal sauna and mud

room/laundry in the basement. These are huge condos with over 2,000 square feet of living space and all are beautifully decorated. Arrowhead offers the special advantage of its own private porter with an electric cart. Just call before driving up the mountain and when you reach the Big Sky parking lot, you'll be met. You can walk to your vacation house while your luggage or groceries are whisked away for you. Arrowhead has a great location, beautiful homes, and is a very good value.

9   BEAVERHEAD
P.O. Box 430, Big Sky, MT 59716, 406-995-4584
2BR $340, 3BR $390, 4BR $450
Amenities: Pool at main lodge, hot tub

Beaverhead features top-of-the-line condos with spectacular designs. The condos are huge, luxurious, and cover over 2,000 square feet. Located just above the Huntley Lodge, these condos have ski-in/ski-out access and fabulous views of the mountains. Lots of stonework and wooden beams accent the interior of the units. You won't find any standardized furniture here—only the best is provided. A great feature is the fireplace designed for sitting by the fire and enjoying the view. Every condo is equipped with a hot tub large enough for five.

5+   GOLDEN EAGLE LODGE
P.O. Box 6, Big Sky, MT 59716, 800-824-7767
Amenities: Tennis, pool, restaurant. Next to golf course

Economy lodging in the Meadows Village, these compact three-room suites can accommodate up to eight people and are very popular with young skiers. But, it's the ambiance here that is outstanding—almost like a European youth village where teenagers and college students make friends. It is good for families as well.

6-7   HIDDEN VILLAGE CONDOMINIUMS
Big Sky, MT 59716, 800-548-4488
2BR $150–195, 3BR $190–220
Amenities: Pool, hot tub

Hidden in its own private world midway between the skiers' village at Big Sky and the golf resort area of Meadows Village, these condominiums are one mile from the golf course. They are located on the cross-country ski-trail system, six miles from the downhill ski area. These newer condos have two-, three-, and four-bedroom floor plans (up to 2,200 square feet of living space) with private garages. All have completely furnished kitchens, fireplaces, and some have whirlpools and/or saunas, and washers and dryers. The recreation building has an outdoor heated pool that operates during the summer, and an indoor whirlpool and sauna available year-round. For the price, these rental units are one of the best vacation values in Big Sky.

7 **SHOSHONE CONDOMINIUM HOTEL**
Box 1, Big Sky, MT 59716, 800-548-4486
1BR $240–280, 2BR $365
Amenities: Full health club, saunas, hot tub, shops, restaurant

Just completed in 1991, this is what Big Sky needed for a long time, but never had. This conference center condo hotel is the center of the resort with a slew of shops and activity centers. These 94 units were designed to be deluxe, and are priced accordingly, but frankly, we thought construction was a little flimsy and you can hear your neighbors. Decor is new and splashy, but it also misses the mark. Rustic in style, yet comfortable, the quality just isn't up to par with that of the neighboring condos. A large man will think twice before sitting down hard. For convenience and fun, however, this is your best bet.

7 **SKYCREST CONDOS**
Big Sky, MT 59716, 1BR $180, 2BR $285, 3BR $340
Amenities: Underground parking

These condos are about six blocks from the lifts. This new complex has an underground parking garage and laundry facilities on each floor near the elevators. The spacious, luxurious units have one, two, and three bedrooms—some with private whirlpools and all with a spectacular view of Lone Peak.

8 **STILLWATER CONDOMINIUMS**
P.O. Box 1, Big Sky, MT 59716, Studio $120, 2BR $215
Amenities: Pool, hot tub

Stillwater Condominiums is located two minutes away from the ski lifts at Big Sky and is part of the Mountain Village. The condos are spacious apartments that are ideal for groups of skiers and young families. The design creates the ambiance of cute little chalets with a variety of floor plans and lock offs. They are fully furnished, but you'll be too busy skiing or enjoying Huntley Lodge to notice the decor. This resort is Big Sky's best value.

© **TRIPPLE CREEK REALTY**
Box 160219, Big Sky, MT 59716, 800-548-4632

This real estate and rental company is a good bet for condo rentals, along with Golden Eagle. Both of these off-site agencies are very competitive and work hard to give you more value for your money. Becky and Jerry Pape at Tripple Creek provide hands on management and closely supervise their condo inventory. This agency is notorious with owners for forcing them to frequently improve, upgrade, and redecorate their units. On our inspection, we were pleased to note that all of the Tripple Creek condos were much better than average at each of the Big Sky complexes and several had taken Becky's hint to add a little fantasy. With either company, you can't go wrong and it's always a pleasure to report when management has gone the extra mile to provide customer satisfaction.

6   YELLOWSTONE CONDOMINIUMS
Big Sky, MT 59716
Amenities: Golf, indoor pool, sauna, hot tub

Located in Meadow Village on the Arnold Palmer golf course/cross country trails, these condos have an indoor heated pool, sauna, whirlpool, and laundry facilities. The units range in size from a one-bedroom, one-bedroom plus loft and two-bedrooms. All have kitchens and fireplaces.

RENTAL RESOURCES
Arrowhead, 406-995-4847
Biggerstaff Co., 406-995-4875
Big Sky Chalet Rentals, 406-587-4107
Big Sky of Montana Vacation Property, 800-548-4486
Big Sky Real Estate, 406-995-4060
Big Sky Ski & Summer Resort, 406-995-4211
Big Sky Vacation Properties, 406-995-4891
Blue Grouse Real Estate, 406-995-4318
ERA Real Estate, 406-995-4433
Golden Eagle Lodge, 406-995-4800
Gold Key Realty, 406-995-4110
Mountain Lodge Condo Rentals, 800-822-4484
Mountain Village at Big Sky, 406-995-4550
Park Condominiums, 406-995-4132
The Real Estate Agency, 406-646-9523
Russ Estes Realty, 406-995-4132
Tripple Creek Realty, 800-548-4632
Westfork Properties, 406-995-4255
Yellowstone Village, 406-646-7335

3. HOT SPRINGS

Located in the mountains just west of Butte, there's a natural hot springs resort which was first patronized by the Native American tribes several hundred years ago.

8 FAIRMONT HOT SPRINGS
1500 Fairmont Road, Anaconda, MT 59711
406-797-3307, 800-443-2381
Amenities: Hot springs, spa, pools, waterslide, golf, tennis
cross-country skiing

First discovered by the Indians, these hot springs enjoy an isolated location about 40 miles from Butte, just off Interstate 90. Surrounded by mountains and the Deer Lodge Valley, it's easy to get lost in time here. This area remains relatively untouched by Western mankind. The hot springs and the pools were the original attraction, but it's the golf course that has emerged as the main attraction today. In winter, there is cross-country skiing. The main hotel has 130 rooms but the resort also has 30 condo accommodations. The upbeat contemporary decor is a real surprise in this remote corner of the Rockies. This resort is particularly well suited for families with children as there are a number of organized activity programs in the summer.

NEVADA

Nevada is a state of sharp contrasts. Las Vegas is one of the most vibrant cities in the U.S., with the dazzling neon lights and flashy cars along the Strip, yet is only twenty minutes away from the open desert where the only sounds are from the wind and rolling sagebrush. Up north around Lake Tahoe, you can ski in some of the deepest snow anywhere and overlook the stark desert floor below. This chapter is divided into two sections reflecting the state's major regions: Las Vegas and Lake Tahoe/Reno. Las Vegas has a warmer climate and more glamour, but Lake Tahoe/Reno offers the variety of a lake, the mountains, and desert. Las Vegas is fun for the warm weather golfer or tennis player, and Tahoe has special opportunities for more invigorating exercise in winter as well as a six month golf season. Because half of Lake Tahoe is in California, for additional listings beyond the Nevada side Tahoe properties, you should turn to the Lake Tahoe section of California. The map of Lake Tahoe can be found on page 48.

1. LAS VEGAS

Las Vegas has a reputation as the gambling capital of the U.S. but deserves one as the entertainment center of the U.S. Nowhere else will you have the opportunity to see live performances by so many celebrities.

The climate is dry and temperatures are mild most of the year, with warm days and cool nights. Bring a sweater not only for the evenings, but for the overly-air-conditioned casinos as well. Although the reputation of Las Vegas is predicated upon glitz and glamour, the city also has a perfect climate for sports enthusiasts. On either side of the Strip, the city is green with golf courses. There are over 240 tennis courts in the area and only during hot summer afternoons, due to a cooling thunderstorm, will a match be called on account of rain. Twenty-four miles away, you can water ski or sail on Lake Mead. The lake is the largest manmade lake in the world, and in many places you can see the waves lap against the former canyon walls.

Increasingly, Las Vegas is trying to promote itself as a family resort. Many of the casinos have large game rooms with Nintendo and Sega for teenagers and others have started to promote wholesome family shows as well as the legendary burlesque and chorus girl revues. With families in mind, there are now several attractions just outside of town which feature the western or desert experience.

Transportation to Las Vegas couldn't be easier with interstate highways and nonstop flights from most major U.S. cities. One of the secrets to the success of Las Vegas is the abundance of inexpensive airfares.Las Vegas is on of the hubs for America West Airlines offering nonstop flights to over 60 cities each day. Las Vegas is an easy place to reach. All of the major airlines such as United, American, Delta, USAir, Northwest, and Continental have several flights a day to Las Vegas. Hawaiian Airlines now offers nonstop flights from Honolulu.

WHERE TO STAY

7   **CARRIAGE HOUSE**
105 East Harmon Ave., Las Vegas, NV 89109, 702-798-1020
Studio $65, 1BR $98
Amenities: Small pool, hot tub, tennis

The Carriage House is a nine-story high-rise located near the Strip. The condos are decorated in a contemporary style and use pastel colors, indirect lighting, and lots of pillows. They are similar to hotel suites. A few units have a kitchenette, but others have only a hot plate and refrigerator. Since the resort is operated like a hotel, plenty of services are offered. The Carriage House is one of the best choices in the area for families.

4   **GRAND FLAMINGO CLUB**
100 Winnick Ave., Las Vegas, NV 89109, 702-731-6100
Studio $95, 1BR $145
Amenities: Pools, health club, tennis

The Grand Flamingo Club has a great location; it is just behind Bally's Hotel and Casino in the most central part of the Strip. It is closer to the biggest casinos than are many hotels on the Strip. This property is an exception to the usual high-rise hotels in the area. One part was built as a three-story motel structure, and across the street there are clusters of eight villas, each surrounding a private pool or patio. The Grand Flamingo Club is recommended for its location and facilities. The condos are nicely furnished and were recently redecorated with sharp gray and maroon designer fabrics. There is a heated main pool and health club with an exercise room and sauna. A Continental breakfast is also available every morning in the clubhouse, which is a nice place to congregate.

7   **JOCKEY CLUB**
3700 Las Vegas Blvd. South, Las Vegas, NV 89109, 702-739-8686
Studio $89, 1BR $119
Amenities: Pool, health club, tennis. Golf next door

The location of the Jockey Club is great; it is across the street from Bally's and Caesar's Palace. Step outside and you are surrounded by the action of the Strip. The rear units face a golf course and have a mountain view. A pool, tennis courts, and full health club are provided. The project has been built in three phases and the newest units are handsomely decorated. All have comfortable furniture and full kitchens. This is one of the few properties in Las

Vegas that caters to the family vacationers as well as adults. Lots of organized activities for children are offered during vacation times.

4   SHEFFIELD INN
3970 Paradise Rd., Las Vegas, NV 89109, 707-796-9000
Studio $66
Amenities: Pool, hot tub, tennis

Although this resort is located a quarter mile from the Strip, it features
many compensations. Three four-story buildings are surrounded by a Spanish
courtyard and fountain, plus a quiet outdoor pool is provided. The condos are
newly decorated with contemporary furniture, lots of fluffy pink pillows,
pink fabric, and silk flowers for accents. About half of the units are just large
hotel rooms, and the other half are studios with mini-kitchens, complete with
microwaves. A Continental breakfast is served in the party room every morning. The friendly and efficient management sets this resort apart from the rest.

2. LAKE TAHOE

The Lake Tahoe experience is constantly changing with the skies and the
seasons. Clouds, sunlight, trees—they all contribute to the reflective quality
of the lake, taking it from bright blues and greens to deep shades of grays
and purple. Situated at 6,225 feet above sea level, Lake Tahoe has been a
vacation retreat for centuries since the bubbling hot springs were first
discovered by the Washoe Indians.

In the 1950s, the gambling industry discovered Lake Tahoe. Today,
you'll see shows with Sinatra and any name as big as you'll find on the Strip
in Vegas. In 1960, the VIII Olympic Winter Games were held at nearby
Squaw Valley, and after that, the name Lake Tahoe became a name synony-
mous with sports and recreation. Each year thousands of visitors come to
Lake Tahoe. Most accommodations are clustered around either the north
end (Incline Village, Crystal Bay, or King's Beach) or Stateline, South
Lake Tahoe, and Zephyr Cove in the south. As the state line runs down the
middle of the lake you'll find equally as many vacation condos on the
craggy western shore, which is the California side where the towering
redwoods meet the sky. For a map of Lake Tahoe, please refer to page 48.

Looking at the neighborhoods of the Nevada side in more detail, let's
begin with Crystal Bay on the north end of Lake Tahoe. Lacking beaches,
nevertheless this setting along the bluff offers some of the most picturesque
lake and mountain views imaginable. There are a couple of casinos here but
they are small and understated. Crystal Bay is a prestigious neighborhood
and not one for neon signs. Heading east there's Incline Village, a master-
planned community developed by Boise Cascade twenty-five years ago.
Today, it's in its prime with the Diamond Peak ski area, two Robert Jones
golf courses, and a 2.5 mile jogging trail along the lakeshore overlooking

some of the lake's best beaches. Incline has a wide range of accommodations to choose from. Some have a lakeside setting close to the discrete Hyatt Regency Casino. Others are along the golf course or in a central wooded area. Then there's a third concentration along Ski Run Boulevard as you head toward the Diamond Peak ski lifts.

Heading south there's an area of forest, private homes, and cabins. Near the south end, Zephyr Cove has a little marina, but the condos are in the mountains overlooking the Nevada side of Heavenly Valley Ski Resort. Accordingly, these hillside accommodations are most popular in winter. South Lake Tahoe is an area of high-rise casinos butting up against the California state line. For lakefront or summertime accommodations in the South Lake area, see our California Lake Tahoe section.

Transportation to Lake Tahoe is relatively easy. Located 120 miles by freeway due east of the San Francisco Bay area, the drive over Donner Pass and the 10,000 foot Sierra Mountains takes about 3 hours. Air service to Reno is the best bet. Al of the major airlines offer air service to Reno with United and Southwest offering the most flights. Recently a new airfare, RenoAir, has emerged with an array of low budget fares to California, Seattle and Minneapolis. Travelling from those cities will find not only competitive service, but reduced airfares as well. Once in Reno, you can rent a car and it's easy to get to Lake Tahoe. These are three roads leading to Tahoe City, Incline Village, or South Lake Tahoe. You can drive or take a 45 minute shuttle bus ride over to Tahoe. There is an airport at South Lake Tahoe which has flights by regional carriers to the Bay Area and continuing on to Los Angeles in the south.

WHERE TO STAY

5   ALL SEASONS RESORT
        807 Alder Ave., Incline Village, NV 89450, 702-831-2311,
        800-322-4331; 2BR $125, 3BR $140
        Amenities: Clubhouse, indoor pool, gym

All Seasons Resort is very economical and is located in a great area. Close to the golf course, it is surrounded by woods at Incline Village and overlooks the lake. Unfortunately, maintenance slackened and the resort has decayed. A new management team has literally rebuilt some of the units though, and there has been dramatic improvement. The two-story townhouse condos have some architectural flourishes. The new interiors are beautifully decorated with soft green and rose colors and each has a private fireplace. The clubhouse has a heated indoor pool, spa-whirlpool, universal weight center and sun deck. Casinos are nearby for glamorous nightlife and gambling. When we rated the physical structure, the new units scored a seven and the old units scored a three, so be sure to check on what vintage you are getting before you go. Of course, hospitality is also an important part of the ratings.

Since renovation is in process and the resort is trying to make a comeback, the price quotes are below market. Be sure to rent a deluxe condo.

4-6 BITTERBRUSH
400 Fairview Blvd., Incline Village, NV 89450; 2BR $125
Amenities: Pool, tennis, hot tub

Cascading down the hillside, with the Diamond Peak ski area off to one side and the lake down below, you'll find the Bitterbrush condominiums. In many respects, this is two separate resorts in one because of the gap in quality between the building phases. The lower condos have sweeping lake views but the design makes them dark. Some haven't been redecorated in fifteen years, but others have cute modern interior decor. Avoid the lower units unless you know what you'll be getting. The brand new Bitterbrush units have the highest mountaintop location in Incline. They have wide decks. Some have private hot tubs, where you have sweeping mountain views. This is a rare "top-of-the-world" sensation. Interior decor generally has a fanciful ambiance created by interior decorators. Some are sparse and ultra-high tech so that nothing detracts from the natural beauty. Others have been decorated with a sophisticated country look—lots of fabrics and wallpaper to create a better-than-home environment. As we said, this is an inconsistent resort complex.

6-7 BURGUNDY HILL/SKI WAY RIDGE
333 Ski Way, Incline Village NV 89450
Amenities: Pool

Located above Incline Village on the road to the Diamond Peak ski lift, these three-story wooden condos were situated to capture views of the Lake below. This complex was built in two phases: some call it Burgundy Hill and others call it Ski Way Ridge. Either way, it's the same complex under the same management. Surrounded by fir trees, the air is fragrant in this forested environment. These one-, two-, and three-bedroom condos, built a dozen years ago, are spacious and have extra touches such as stone fireplaces and a double wide whirlpool in the master bath. Interior decor varies a great deal. We saw one dressed up with Indian artifacts, a featured medicine ball, and carved totems over the mantle. The effect was truly like "Twin Peaks." These condos enjoy a popular location, especially if you enjoy outdoor walks, winter or summer.

6 CLUB TAHOE
914 Northwood Blvd., Incline Village, NV 89450, 702-831-5750, 800-527-5754; 2BR $120
Amenities: Racquetball, tennis, pool, restaurant

The location couldn't be more central: next to the golf course and close to the lakeshore or gambling at the Hyatt casino. They provide great on-site amenities. This resort may have more on-site activities than any other at Incline Village with two racquetball courts, two tennis courts, exercise room, lap pool, hot tubs, sauna, pool room, and a large game room for teenagers. Each two-story building contains identical two-bedroom condos with neutral, handsome decor and a wood burning stove fireplace. You can walk everywhere or take a shuttle bus to the slopes in winter.

6 COEUR DU LAC
Juanita Dr., Incline Village, NV 89450, 702-831-3318
1BR $90–105, 2BR $105–120, 3BR $120–135, 4BR $135–150
Amenities: Heated pool, hot tub, sauna

Coeur Du Lac is a nice condo project just a short walk from the beach in Incline Village. The quiet and private duplex condos are scattered in a parklike setting and shaded by tall pines. The air is fragrant and although this spot is good for skiers, it is even better for golfers. The warm, roomy interiors have rustic beamed ceilings, redwood-paneled walls, and wood-burning fireplaces. The decor relies upon earth tones and naturally colored fabrics. A heated swimming pool, hot tub, and sauna are provided. The resort is small, private, and nice.

3 CREEKSIDE
835–837 Southwood, Incline Valley. NV 89450
Amenities: Pool

Enjoying a central location only two blocks from the lake and along the side of a wooded creek, these poorly maintained condos are more like college dormitories than vacation homes. They offer economy lodgings that are popular with young skiers and college students.

7-9 CRYSTAL SHORES (EAST AND WEST)
525 Lakeshore, Incline Valley, NV 89450
Amenities: Beach, tennis, pool

Enjoying spectacular lake views from its bluffside location, this condominium development was built in two distinct phases. The Crystal Shores West units are in a large "rowhouse" building running parallel to the shore below. They enjoy good views and comfortable interior decor. The Crystal Shores East units are new and much more stylish. Built as split levels, there's lots of glass and imagination in the design that make the most of the gorgeous location. Along with new interiors, many have upgraded amenities, such as tile floors, whirlpools, and VTPs. Ask before you rent.

8   **FAIRWAY PINES**
908 Harold Dr., Incline Village. NV 89450, 702-831-1307
1BR $95–125, 2BR $105–155, 3BR $120–180
Amenities: Golf, pool, tennis

Located on the 12th Tee of the championship Incline Village golf course, this is a small condo development with a series of modern two-story buildings. The living room has open-beamed ceilings and the upstairs loft units are superior because of the cathedral effect and all the sunlight. Decorated to match the golf course and the country club lifestyle, these are popular rentals with businessman in the summer on corporate golf outings.

7   **FOREST PINES**
123 Juanita, Incline Village, NV 89450, 702-831-1307
1BR $95–125, 2BR $105–155, 3BR $120–180
Amenities: Pool, hot tub, recreation center

One of Incline's most popular condo complexes for families, the location is less than two blocks to the beach and the casino at the Hyatt. Set amid a forested environment these modern, boxy condos have two to four units in each building: an upstairs unit and a downstairs unit. Designed to be open and full of light, there are beamed ceilings and windows angled to capture the most sun. Some are well decorated with casual furniture accented by ski posters or touches from the early West. Some are one bedroom units good for a couple; some are two-, three-, or four-bedroom models good for a larger family. What makes Forest Pines special? The attractive pool area and the manicured central green, which is the core of the complex. In summer, you'll see sunbathers on one side and children across the way splashing in the pool. Excellent management delivers a high level of personalized attention. The units are private, and there's a friendly amenities area. There is no request too big nor too small for Lucy, the Manager, to take care of for you.

3   **LAKESIDE TENNIS & SKI RESORT**
979 Tahoe Blvd., Box 5576, Hwy 28, Incline Village, NV 89450, 702-831-5258
Amenities: Pool, hot tub, tennis

Although this resort is just off the main highway near the center of Incline Village, it is completely surrounded by ponderosa pines. You can walk to the village, the lake, and the golf course. The resort was built in 1972, and is beginning to show its age. It's a wonderful place for tennis players because 12 tennis courts and a Van der Meer teaching center are available. The instructors work one-on-one, or with classes that require a maximum of six players. The clinic combines active drills with video analysis to help improve your game. There are several different buildings at this lakeside resort, including a two-story, motel-style building and townhomes. The interior decor is dated and marked by brown and blue hotel-style furniture designed for durability rather than beauty. The townhouses are the best choice. On last inspection we learned that the resort is now under new management and has plans for improvements.

8   999 LAKESHORE
999 Lakeshore, Incline Village, NV 89450; 3BR $225
Amenities: Beach, pool, tennis

A reasonably priced beachfront property, 999 Lakeshore enjoys a great, central location. The Hyatt casino is across the street, the shopping plaza is a block away, and the boat launch is just up the beach. This is a group of cute two-story wooden buildings set within a landscaped setting. Painted green, they blend with the trees to reflect the surrounding forested area. Fresh on the inside, these are well decorated by the owners who enjoy coming here whenever possible. Some have wonderful lake views. This property offers an excellent location in Incline.

8   McCLOUD
Village Blvd., Incline Village, NV 89449, 702-831-3318
1BR $130, 2BR $175
Amenities: Hot tubs, saunas

These deluxe condominiums are nestled among pine and fir trees in a parklike setting with bright splashes of landscaped flowers. The condos are brand new with stone chimneys, red brick hearths, and oak-beam ceilings that create a harmonious blend of texture and style. Blond wood, sunken living rooms, and vaulted ceilings are additional characteristics. The interiors are professionally designed and rely upon natural fabrics, area rugs, and woodsy accessories. It's just a short walk down the hill to the beach.

8   MOUNTAIN SHADOWS
321 Ski Way, Incline Village NV 89450; 3BR $125–150
Amenities: Pools, tennis, hot tub

This sprawling complex of 300 condos hugs the mountainside just above the village on the road to the Diamond Peak ski area. These handsome two-story buildings were constructed of cedar to blend in with the forested environment. There's a wide range of one-, two-, and three-bedroom units to choose from. All have great views; some overlook the lake, others view the forest. The location is excellent. You have a private location, yet the village is only a short walk away and you are less than a half mile from the lakeshore and the Hyatt casino. This is one of Incline's best mid-priced ski condos. Each has been decorated differently. We saw one where most of the rooms had wallpaper with geometric or floral designs, monotone-colored fabrics on the furniture in shades of beige and green, and accent pieces or silk flowers that are almost oriental in effect. In the summer, the complex offers two outdoor pools.

7+ THE RIDGE SIERRA
Quaking Aspen Ln., Box 5790, Stateline, NV 89449, 800-648-3391
2BR $135–205
Amenities: Shuttle and access to Ridge Tahoe facilities

Located outside the security gates and about a mile form the main Ridge Clubhouse is the Ridge Sierra. These condos are next door to Ridge Tahoe Resort's world class condos. Superficially, they don't look that different on the outside, but inside, what a difference. Everything has been perfectly placed to create an inviting, luxurious environment. The interiors are marked by pine paneling, wooden beams, and nubby tweed fabrics that create a rustic north woods environment. Each condo has a VTP as part of the entertainment center. Take the shuttle bus or drive up the hill to the main clubhouse where everything awaits you, including a full spa, herbal wraps, swimming pool, and fine dining. If you want the benefits of the Ridge at a lower price, consider the Ridge Sierra. For more action, the casinos of Stateline, like Harrahs and Caesars Palace, are only six miles away down the hill. Frequent shuttle bus service is offered. The chair lifts at heavenly valley are only about a mile away.

10 THE RIDGE TAHOE
10 Ridge Club Dr., Stateline, NV 89449, 800-648-3391
Studio $110–130, 1BR $125–175, 2BR $195–265
Amenities: Tennis, indoor/outdoor pool,spa, gym, restaurant

The Ridge Tahoe, one of the finest resorts in the U.S., offers "the peak of perfection." You will not believe the location. It is on top of a craggy notch and overlooks the windswept plains of Nevada. You will feel as though you are on top of the world. Step inside the reception center and you'll enjoy light classical music. The bar and restaurant are elegant and have breath-taking views. The Health Club offers the most in hedonistic experiences, such as herbal wraps and professional massages. There's an indoor/outdoor pool, full gym with an instructor for a week-long training program, and a tennis center. The Ridge Tahoe is located less than 100 yards away from Heavenly Valley Ski Resort. If you're up to it, drive or take the shuttle bus to the casinos and shows. Stateline/Lake Tahoe draws top name entertainers from Frank Sinatra to the Beach Boys. Some of the condos are in architecturally intriguing five-story structures that are known for the dramatic views from the round or square windows. Others are in the 18-story tower, which is the pinnacle of perfection. The condos are beautifully decorated in mauve and burgundy colors. The tower units have fully mirrored entrance halls that make for a dramatic introduction. Each condo has an entertainment center with video tape player. Lots of wood and private fireplaces give each condo a warm, at-home atmosphere or maybe home was never this good. It doesn't get any better than this.

10 STILLWATER COVE
120 Highway 28, Crystal Bay, NV 89402
Amenities: Beach, pool, tennis

Some of Lake Tahoe's finest condos are offered at Stillwater Cove. It is located at the northern end of the lake, just before the California state line. With price tags of over $1,000,000 for some of these lakeside beauties, you know they have to be good. Inside the security gate, you enter a world of perfection. Stone walkways bordered by flowers and manicured grounds in summer; a festive Christmas village in winter. These two-story redwood buildings at once have a sense of community and a sense of privacy because of the trees and landscaping. Inside, the interior decor is spectacular. First, you'll notice the views of the Lake and the snowcapped mountains in the distance. This isn't a postcard; this is real. Interior decorators had fun with these. We saw one with a planked wood floor entrance and a medley of blue, green, and Scottish plaid fabric. The garage had a special annex for the golf cart. Located above the lakeshore, there's a private cable car down to the beach where the pool and hot tub are in a dramatic setting. The Cal Neva casino and several showplaces are only steps away. Stillwater Cove is truly memorable.

8 THIRD CREEK
Northwood Blvd., Incline Village, NV 89449
Amenities: Tennis, pool, gym. Golf nearby

Third Creek is architecturally interesting with lots of windows that bring in the view. The handsome and spacious condos are located across from Incline's Championship Golf Course. Convenient for skiers, too, this is the perfect corporate getaway (meeting room on site) or hideaway from family and business. These units are expensively furnished and enjoy vaulted ceilings, river-rock fireplaces, and cathedral windows that create an unmatched feeling of solid, spacious luxury. Some of the four-bedroom condos have private indoor saunas. They are more expensive, but certainly worth it.

7-8 TAHOE TYROL
Pine Hill Road, Incline Village, NV 89449, Rentals c/o Vacation
Station, Box 14441, So. Lake Tahoe, CA 95702, 916-541-2355,
800-841-7443; 2BR $140–190, 3BR $175–225
Amenities: Pool, clubhouse, sauna. Golf and skiing nearby

Located on the road to the Incline ski lift, this 22-acre complex sports 45 Austrian chalets. These individual vacation homes each have a common Tyrolian exterior although interior decor varies. Cute on the outside, each has the Tyrolian half-timbered look, painted flowers on the wooden shutters, and flower boxes in summer. Wide open decks overlook the forest, the ski slopes, and the lake in the distance. Inside, the European look prevails with beamed ceilings. Many owners have embellished this theme with lots of Old World European furniture and accessories. We saw one that just benefitted from a $60,000 refurbishment. Light and serene, the stone fireplace inside was offset by the view of the vivid blue lake and green forest. Great for two couples or families, these are designed for entertaining. Some have private saunas or private jacuzzi whirlpools. Others are showing their age. Check with management to determine the one you will get. The only drawback is that the noise from the snowmaking equipment permeates part of this neighborhood in winter. Also, there's a good chance that you'll need a car to drive to the Tyrolian pool and recreation center tennis courts.

RENTAL RESOURCES

Abella Properties, 702-831-5335
B.R.A.T. Realty, 702-831-3318, 800-869-8308
Coldwell Banker, 702-831-1515
Dean Miller Realty, 702-831-9000
Delores Bell Realty, 702-831-8882
Ed Malley Realty, 702-831-0625
Incline Sales, 702-831-3349
Incline Village Realty, 702-831-1515, 800-572-5009
Inn at Incline, 702-831-1052, 800-468-2463
Jacobson Realty, 702-831-0205
Lakeside Sales, 702-831-0752, 800-487-0616
Northshore Properties, 702-831-0606
OMNI Properties, 702-832-3003
Sugar Pine Properties, 702-831-7803
Tahoe Management, Co., 702-588-4504
Tahoe North Realty, 702-831-1169, 800-829-1269
Timberlake Realty, 702-831-1166
Vacation Station, 702-831-3664, 800-841-7443
Wheeler & Assoc., 702-831-8333

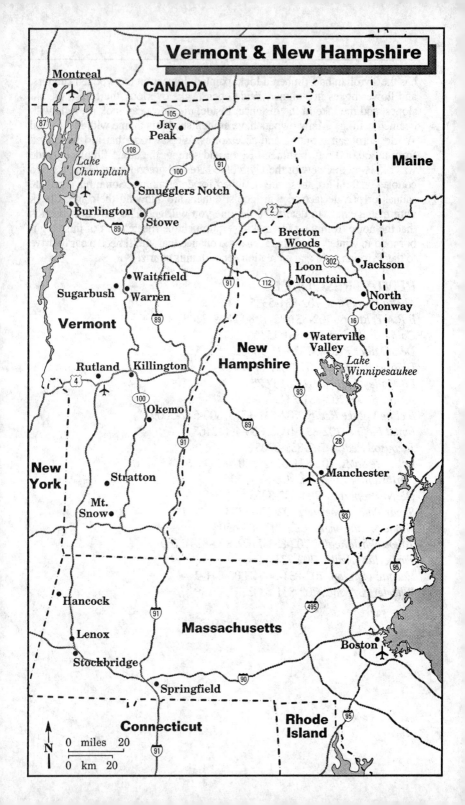

NEW HAMPSHIRE

After years of watching urbanites pour into Vermont and spend their city dollars on country lodgings and fresh air, New Hampshire has awakened to tourism. Many of the New Hampshire resorts were sleepy places along the lakes or around the ski mountains. Development during the past decade has seen the addition of numerous golf courses to ski resorts as they now seek to become year-round "alpine recreation" destinations. Formerly, New Hampshire was a local resort for families and sports enthusiasts from Boston. Now that is changing. New resorts have begun to offer luxurious condominiums, gourmet restaurants, and nightlife that no longer ends at 10:30 P.M.

The resorts of New Hampshire are situated around the ski mountains and along the lakes to attract boating enthusiasts. Windsurfing has become popular and the lakes are now dotted with hot-colored sailboards as well as the traditional white mainsails. Some of the small lakes have quiet coves for fishing and canoeing. Golf is becoming increasingly popular and although the season is short in the White Mountains, you'll find an abundance of challenging courses.

New Hampshire offers a long list of ski resorts to choose from in the northern part of the state. Waterville Valley offers a planned village of condominiums and shops near the base of Mt. Tecumseh. The Mt. Washington valley is perhaps the state's most famous ski area with four separate ski centers that include Mt. Cranmore, Wildcat, Attitash, and Black Mountain. The condos servicing these areas are located in the towns of North Conway (Mt. Cranmore), Jackson (Black Mountain and Wildcat), and Bartlett (Attitash). Glen sits right in the center between the four mountains. This is also the site of some of New England's best cross-country skiing with 40 miles of interconnecting trails starting from the village of Jackson.

Lower in elevation, but featuring a resort village with some of New Hampshire's best social life, is Loon Mountain. The condos around Loon set the standard for luxury in New Hampshire. Nearby, Bretton Woods offers gentle, intermediate slopes but at a lower elevation. Cannon Mountain, at Franconia Notch, offers some of the most challenging skiing in the east.

Farther south and almost in the middle of the state is a lake region. Mountain-rimmed Lake Winnipesaukee has been a vacation destination for nearly 100 years. It is less than two hours from downtown Boston. The resorts have capitalized on the area's natural beauty by offering golf courses that follow the contours. Although the resort is best in the summer, it also offers skating and cross-country skiing in the winter.

WHERE TO STAY

5   **ATTITASH**
Route 302, Bartlett, NH 03812, 800-223-SNOW
Studio $85–129, 1BR $125–190, 2BR $151–209, 3BR $191–289
Amenities: Indoor pool, exercise room, hot tub

A whole world unto itself, Attitash claims its own mountain base lodge, and five surrounding condo developments. The core condo development is Attitash Mountain Village. It is the largest and most well known group of condos and consists of ten, two-story buildings across the street from the base lodge. Each building contains eight condo apartments. The upstairs units have loft bedrooms and spacious living rooms. Generally you'll find basic furnishings and full kitchens. Some look a little worn. Most condos have fireplaces, wood-burning stoves, and a few condos have private whirlpool tubs large enough for two. Attitash has its own recreation area with an indoor heated pool, exercise room, saunas, and hot tub. Here, you'll find lots of families, lots of children, and a very social environment. In the summertime, the outdoor environment takes on a special appeal because Stoney Brook runs through the property and the rushing Saco River, rife with fish, is the property boundary.

6   **ATTITASH WOODS**
Route 302, Bartlett, NH 03812
Amenities: None

This cluster of 54 townhouses is located just two miles from Attitash ski resort and offers breathtaking views of Mt.Washington. Spread over 56 acres of wooded hillside, these two-story structures have two bedrooms, cathedral ceilings and lofts, and wood burning stoves. The rooms have modern contemporary decor, accented by personal touches, such as antique nostalgia or framed ski posters. Spacious and private, this is good for families or two couples who want to sample the area's resorts. Call local realtors in Bartlett or Glen.

7   **BLUEBERRY VILLAGE**
Route 302, Bartlett, NH 03812 (no mail)
Amenities: None

Located along the hill at Attitash, hidden by the woods, you'll find these modern three-story condos. Built of wood, they have been painted blue. The windows are placed at angles to capture the best views. One advantage is the ski-in/ski-out access to the unit. Quiet and private, each has a fireplace in the living room.

7-8 BRETTON WOODS

Route 302, Box WB, Bretton Woods, NH 03575
603-278-4000, 800-334-3910, 1BR $70–115,
2BR $140–185, 3BR $180–225, 4BR $220–265
Amenities: Golf, cross-country ski trails, pool, tennis

Bretton Woods is famous for the International Monetary Agreement settled in this tiny village in the late 1940s. Bretton Woods offers scenic White Mountain beauty, summertime golf, and cross-country skiing in winter. There is a small ski hill with five chair lifts.

Some of New Hampshire's newest and best vacation condos are in this community. They are located around the golf course or clustered near the skier's village with the indoor health club. All the condos are new and provide full kitchens and private fireplaces.

Forest Cottage (8+) These condos are the best. Each unit is on the ground level with a sleeping loft upstairs. Special features include a wood-stove fireplace, a whirlpool in the master bath, and outdoor wood plank deck. These are close to the Bretton Woods ski area.

Rosebrook Townhouses (7) These two-story condos are located in a forest glen and are only a stone's throw from the golf course.

Mt. Washington Place (7) Mt. Washington Place offers two-story condos near the base of the cog railway that goes up to Mt. Washington. Tasteful interior decor is achieved with that Laura Ashley sophisticated, country-style wallpaper and woodsy furniture.

Fairway Village (8) At this location you will find single-story duplex townhouses on the fairway. These condos have vaulted ceilings, casual California furnishings, and bentwood chairs. These are private and highly desired during the summer.

5 CATHEDRAL LEDGE

Route 16, North Conway, NH 03860, 800-258-4708; 2BR $120
Amenities: Indoor and outdoor pools, sauna, tennis

This is located in one of the most scenic areas of New England. You have to visit the Rocky Gorge Scenic area early in the morning to know just how beautiful daybreak can be. Cathedral Ledge is a small condo complex nestled in the woods. The units are all two-bedroom, three-story models. Well furnished a dozen years ago, the units need to be redecorated today. But if you are here for the winter or summer sports, who cares! There is an indoor pool, an outdoor pool, a sauna, and a tennis court. This is a good resting spot for those who want to enjoy the beauty of the outdoors, but do not expect a resort where you will be entertained.

6 **COLD SPRING RESORT**
White Mountain Country Club, Plymouth, NH 03264, 603-536-4600
Amenities: Golf, tennis, pool, children's pool, hot tub

This resort has promise. Located in south central New Hampshire, Cold Spring is on the fairway of the White Mountain Country Club. You are also less than one hour away from skiing at Loon Mountain, Cannon, and Waterville Valley. This is a quiet, secluded location on the Pemigewasset River. An ambitious golf course and recreational community development, the project went bankrupt in the mid 1980s. Recently rejuvenated, this resort has been brought back to life, but visitors just haven't discovered it yet.

One advantage: there are readily available tee times in the summer for all the golf you want. During the winter, the area is popular for cross-country skiing. The condos are actually townhouses positioned along the fairways in several different clusters. Modestly furnished, they provide an adequate environment for a family on vacation. Full kitchens and private fireplaces make each condo a home away from home. The advantage here is that you'll find no crowds on the golf course, and reasonable prices to boot.

5 **DANA PLACE INN**
Pinkham Notch, Route 16, Jackson, NH 03846, 603-383-6822
800-537-9276, 1BR $60–125, 2BR $90–165
Amenities: Pool, restaurant, library

This Yankee inn has recently grown a cluster of timeshare condos hidden in the woods across the street. While the inn is charming with antique reproductions and ruffles, the condos are modern and functional. The best features are the restaurant and pool over at the inn, about four minutes away by foot.

8 **DEER PARK RESORT**
P.O. Box 175, Lincoln, NH 03251, 603-745-9040, 800-637-8380
1BR $70–115, 2BR $140–185, Houses $180–265
Amenities: Pool, health club, racquetball, shuttle to lifts

Deer Park is an attractive, four-story structure in a landscaped setting with spacious condo apartments. These condos are different from the others around Loon Mountain in that they are away from town. Located just outside the village, Deer Park features a pastoral lakeside location and 65 acres of White Mountain forest. The condos have deluxe interiors with exposed wooden beams, stone fireplaces, and lots of glass for views of the lake and mountains. Furnishings tend to be natural with lots of wood, glass, and rustic fabrics for the furnishings. No boisterous colors, it is just simply inspired by nature's best.

6 **EASTERN SLOPE INN**
Main St., N. Conway, NH 03860, 800-258-4708
Studio $84, 1BR $112, 2BR $189
Amenities: Indoor pool, spa, cross-country skiing, tennis

This historic 100-year-old Victorian hotel is one of the most famous resorts of the Mount Washington Valley. In addition to an indoor pool, spa, and sauna, there is a restaurant and cocktail lounge featuring live entertainment, which attracts not only the guests, but other vacationers in the North Conway area. Eastern Slope Inn has all the advantages of staying in a hotel, including room service, except the rooms were converted to privately owned timeshare suites. Some are two-story suites with a stairwell. You'll find lots of young families. Although good property, there is an indifferent management/service with lackluster hospitality.

5 **ELLIS RIVER VILLAGE**
Route 16, Jackson, NH 03846 (no mail)
Amenities: None

If you want to ski Wildcat, these townhouses are about as close as you can be. The actual ski mountain is on federal land in the White Mountain National Forest. Quiet and unpretentious, the townhouses are in a forested setting and you can hear the babbling brook. Wildcat is 20 minutes north; the village of Jackson is ten minutes to the south. Rentals can be obtained through realtors in North Conway or Jackson.

8 **FOREST RIDGE**
Route 112, P.O. Box 477, Lincoln, NH 03251, 603-745-2115
800-533-3651
Amenities: Indoor pool, exercise room, racquetball

Set on 285 private acres, this is a community of brand new townhouses surrounding a central sports club complex within two miles of the skiing at Loon Mountain. The architecture at these brand new condominiums is striking with gabled roof lines, vaulted ceilings, and unexpected windows. The Sports Club has an indoor pool as well as an exercise room and racquetball courts.

8+ **JACK O'LANTERN**
Route 3, Woodstock, NH 03293, 603-745-8121; 1BR $74–160
Amenities: Golf, tennis, pool, hot tub, cross-country skiing
inn dining room

This is an oasis of relaxation. Operated as an inn as well as a condo resort, Jack O'Lantern offers accommodations in condo townhouses as well as the traditional inn rooms. This family-run resort has been lovingly planned and developed over the past 40 years. The different groupings of accommodations reflect a catering to the vacationer's changing tastes over the years. Initially conceived as an inn, Jack learned that vacationers wanted space and the convenience of condo living arrangements. The townhouse condos are the newest addition. They are spacious with full kitchens. In the living room you'll find lots of oak woodwork creating a crisp, Scandinavian environment. Best feature: the stone fireplace in each unit with a tiled hearth area. Most condos have been decorated with casual, contemporary furniture including a few designer touches in some units. Jack reaches the height of popularity in summer when the heated outdoor pool bubbles with splashing children and golfers arranging tee times. Winter offers the opportunity for cross-country skiing and you're only an hour or so away from New Hampshire's ski areas along Interstate 93.

7 **LINDERHOF**
Route 16, Box 126, Glen, NH 03838, 603-383-4334; 1BR $68–177
Amenities: Restaurant, indoor pool, sauna

Centrally located between Mt. Cranmore, Wildcat, and Attitash, the tranquil village of Glen offers no ski resorts as such. The Linderhof is a cute Alpine motel that expanded with a community of spacious condominiums across the street. Set in a small park, each building has Alpine trim, red Austrian shutters and cute flower boxes with geraniums in the summer. These condos are large, with from two to four bedrooms. Interior decor is a disappointment with inexpensive pine and maple furniture and lots of fabrics to cover up years of use. There's a pleasant restaurant across the street at the main motel building where you'll also find the pool.

9 **LOON MOUNTAIN—MOUNTAIN CLUB**
Route 112, Lincoln, NH 03251, 603-745-8111
Studio $69–129, 1BR $99–195, 2BR $129–209
Amenities: Health club, pools, racquetball, restaurant

The most luxurious accommodations in this part of New Hampshire, they are located at the base of the mountain. Skiers won't have to take a shuttle bus. The condos are spacious suites in a cluster of four-story buildings. Completed in 1989, everything is stylishly new. Furnishings include an imaginative color scheme with deep green carpet, boxy overstuffed chairs covered with cherry or chocolate colors, light woods, and indirect track lighting. The impact is almost Scandinavian. These condos have full kitchens and most have a fireplace or wood-burning stove. Best feature: the full service health club with racquetball, exercise equipment, indoor pool, hot tub, and saunas. Mountain Club has the best gym in the area. You will also be treated to good service and a friendly restaurant (or room service if you feel like dining in). There's a casual, sophisticated environment here.

6   **MITTERSILL**
Route 18, Mittersill Rd., Franconia, NH 03580, 603-823-5511/5536
Amenities: Indoor and outdoor pools, spa, skiing, tennis.
Golf nearby

This is an Austrian village recreated in New Hampshire. Everything is done in Austrian style, including the exterior of the surrounding chalets as well as the Mittersill Lodge. Downstairs, there are two restaurants and cocktail lounges decorated in Tyrolean style with antlers and beer steins. During the ski season, this is the focal point of the community. There are indoor and outdoor swimming pools as well as a small health club. The units are really hotel rooms or suites in the lodge. Decorations are Austrian in style, perhaps a little dated by U.S. tastes. Every unit has a kitchen, but it is probable that you will want to dine in one of the restaurants or grill rooms. There's a small ski hill at the resort, but the challenging skiing is five minutes away on Cannon Mountain. Management is friendly and wants you to have a good vacation.

9+   **NORDIC VILLAGE**
Route 16, Jackson, NH 03860, 603-383-9306, 800-472-5207
Amenities: Pools, tennis, hiking trail

Located three miles from Jackson, this beautifully planned resort community has 14 small clusters of townhouse condos spread over 100 rolling acres. It is a village with its own pond and recreation center. During the winter, this resort is like a scene from Currier & Ives. Even better, at night the snow covered gazebo seems a winter wonderland as it is outlined with hundreds of tiny white lights. In the summer, these cedar condominiums are hidden by the landscaping. Inside, the condos are light and airy with vaulted ceilings, lofts, and heatilator fireplaces. Each has a private whirlpool large enough for two. Decor emphasizes natural oak and ash accents. A spiral staircase leads to the second floor. The townhouses can be locked off to create two separate units. Nordic Village is situated on a 100-mile Nordic cross-country ski trail that circles Jackson. Best of all, you can hike a mile to Nordic Falls within the property where on many winter nights a crackling bonfire lights up the sky. Guests gather by the fire or skate under the stars. In the summer, there are three rowboats available for guests to use at the falls area.

6   **RIVER RUN**
Route 302, Bartlett, NH 03812
Amenities: Guest privileges at Attitash Sports Center

Located across the street from the base of Attitash, on a branch of the Saco river, the condos in this barklike, three-story building are cute and compact. Guests can use the Attitash Sports Center that is next door with its indoor pool, exercise room, and tennis courts.

8+ RIVERGREEN
Route 112, P.O. Box 1056, Lincoln, NH 03251, 603-745-2450
Amenities: Pool, hot tub, sauna

Comfort, luxury, and convenience are the key ingredients to Rivergreen's design. This four-story structure has architectural flourishes including what looks like a bell tower to inspire images of Austria. This is part of the Millfront Marketplace complex, a popular area of shops and cafes for the après ski life at Loon Mountain. Millfront is the tourist center of town in the evenings. You'll find a mall, restaurant, an inn, and condos that are all part of one complex. The studio condos are just a little on the small side, but designed well enough to make efficient use of the space. There are small but adequate kitchens. The one-bedroom has a full living room and kitchen. Best of all, it has a whirlpool large enough for two. The two-bedroom condos are made by combining a studio and one-bedroom unit. There's a recreation center just for Rivergreen guests. Because of its location at the central, social Millfront Marketplace, this is one of the top choices in the Lincoln/Loon Mountain area.

7 THE SEASONS
Attitash, Rt. 302, Box 415, Bartlett, NH 03812, 800-332-6636
2BR $125–149
Amenities: Pool, hot tub, saunas

The Seasons is located a mile away from Attitash Mountain and the ski center. This development of townhouse condos offers slightly better accommodations than at Attitash Village. The condos offer vaulted ceilings, a downstairs master bedroom, and an upstairs loft with bunk beds or twins. The focal point of the living room is the brick fireplace. The condos have been decorated with boxy but sturdy "skierized" furniture for active families. You'll find butcherblock tables and sofas covered in nubby fabrics. Bouquets of artificial flowers have been placed here and there as accent pieces.

6-8 STEELE HILL RESORT
RFD #1, Laconia, NH 03246
Amenities: Indoor and outdoor pools, health club, tennis
restaurant. Golf nearby

Steele Hill is an attractive resort on the top of the mountain that is designed in a rustic style. The views from the units, pool, and restaurant are spectacular. The restaurant and cocktail lounge are attractive and the food is good. There is a rustic, romantic feeling here. The atmosphere of a weekend-in-the-woods has been preserved. Just up the hill is the modern new Steele Hill West with a spectacular glass enclosed swimming pool and a three-story enclosed atrium that overlooks the valley. Although more modern and better decorated, there's a lot to be said for the charm of the older structure at Steele Hill. There is no organized rental program at the resort, but they do have an introductory program for prospective buyers. If you rent a unit through one of the local realtors, we believe you will find this a great place to vacation.

8 STONEHURST MANOR TOWNHOUSES
P.O. Box 1900, North Conway, NH 03860, 800-525-9100
2BR $150
Amenities: Pool, tennis, restaurant

Set on the 33 acres of Stonehurst Manor, this is a former country home that was converted to an inn in the 1930s. During the '80s the townhouses were added as a surprise tucked away in the woods. These three-level homes have brick hearth fireplaces, cherry paneling, a spiral staircase, and wooden furniture with lots of cushions. Overall, this is an excellent resort and the appeal may be stronger in the summer than in winter for ski lodgings because you can use the pool and play tennis.

6 SUMMIT AT FOUR SEASONS
RFD #3, Box 111-67, Laconia, NH 03246, 603-366-4896
Amenities: Pool, lake, marina, horseback riding, tennis

This is a cozy condominium complex overlooking the lake and nestled in the woods. Management is friendly and runs a clean, neat property. There is no organized activities program, nor is there an organized rental program. Rentals are available by calling the resort periods of for times when the owners are not planning to use their units.

7 TOPNOTCH AT ATTITASH
Route 302, Box 429, Bartlett, NH 03812, 800-762-6636
Amenities: Privileges at Attitash Sports Club

Located high on the mountainside, these two-story townhouse structures feature an eclectic architectural design with greenhouse window boxes, sky-lights, and surprising mountain views. Generally interior decor is a disappointment and doesn't blend with the stylish architectural flourish of the exterior. Expect to find tweed fabrics, lots of wood end tables, and a brick fireplace. The rooms are furnished for function, not for style, and it is too bad because the location is superb.

6   **VILLAGE AT MAPLEWOOD**
Main St., Bethlehem, NH 03574, 603-869-2911
Amenities: None

Not a skier's retreat, this is geared more for those who want to enjoy the White Mountains and the nearby golf courses. Bethlehem is at one of the highest elevations in New Hampshire and it is one of the two resorts most convenient to Cannon Mountain. Bretton Woods is also within an easy 15-minute drive. These townhouses are simple in design, and while furnishings may be inexpensive, they have style. Bentwood chairs carry the day and there's a freshness from the carnation pink carpeting.

6   **VILLAGE AT WINNIPESAUKEE**
Route 3, Weirs Beach, NH 03246, 603-366-2272
Amenities: Pool, tennis, beach

Lake Winnipesaukee has been a popular New Hampshire resort for over 50 years. Weirs Beach is the center of the action. As a result, there is an abundance of restaurants and area attractions to keep vacationers busy. The Village is a large condo complex of more than 200 units that overlook the lake. They are fully equipped for a family on vacation. Furnishings are functional and vary with the owner's level of interest and finances.

8   **VILLAGE OF LOON MOUNTAIN**
P.O. Box 508, Lincoln, NH 03251, 603-745-3401, 800-258-8932
Amenities: Skiing, golf, tennis, sports complex

One of the most established and successful timeshare resorts in the United States, everything has been done with professionalism and meticulous attention to detail. This is not just a ski resort; it is a genuine four-season resort as a result of planning and commitment to service. This large development is across the highway from the recreation center at the Mountain Club (developed by the same company) and the Loon Mountain ski lifts. Well maintained, the units are a little on the dark side, and a good spring housecleaning would be helpful. Marriott has recently taken over management and we expect to see major improvements.

WATERVILLE VALLEY RESORT
Waterville Valley, NH 03215, 603-236-8371, 800-GO-VALLEY
Amenities: Golf, ski mountain, sports center, indoor pool

This is becoming New Hampshire's most popular ski area because good ski conditions are almost guaranteed between Thanksgiving and the end of March. Waterville Valley is a self-contained skier's village. What began as a small ski area has been developed into a genuine resort village with a Sports Center, shops, restaurants and a wide range of accommodations. Eight of the

19 condo communities have been developed and managed by the Waterville Valley Resort that operates the ski area. Guests at the Black Bear Lodge, the Golden Eagle, the Silver Squirrel Inn, and the Snowy Owl Inn have privileges at the Sports Center.

Waterville Valley is designed like a broad bowl that is rimmed by 4,000-foot mountains. The resort occupies about 600 acres and no building in the village looks more than ten years old. Everything has been created with architectural style and respect for the environment. This is clearly New Hampshire's best skier village.

Many of the condo resorts have a common developer and are next door to each other, so it's hard to draw distinctions among them. We have reviewed the Black Bear, Golden Eagle, Inns of Waterville Valley, and Mountain Sun Quarters. Others, such as Windsor Hill, are operated by different management, but have features such as mountain locations and nice views.

Black Bear Lodge (9) Black Bear may offer the finest accommodations in the village, since it combines the advantages of condo lodgings with the convenience of a professionally staffed hotel. The condo suites have Murphy beds in the living rooms as well as a sofa bed. Some have additional sleeping lofts while others have second bedrooms. Expect to find comfortable to luxurious furnishings, contemporary styles, maple dining tables with bentwood chairs, and earth colors in the fabrics. The lobby emotes an Alpine-lodge romance feeling. You'll notice wood paneling and exposed wooden beams everywhere. In addition to privileges at the Sports Center, Black Bear has its own indoor/outdoor pool, hot tub, and sauna. It is a convenient walk to the ski slopes.

Golden Eagle (8) Brand new in 1989, Golden Eagle sits at the edge of Corcoran Pond close to the Sports Center. This luxurious ten-story resort has a grand lobby with a massive fireplace. The condos have been designed to make the most efficient use of space. They are professionally decorated in a modern, contemporary, neutral style, with understated good taste. Guests have privileges at the Sports Center as well as the use of Golden Eagle's own indoor pool, hot tub, and sauna.

Mountain Sun (9) The most spectacular interior decor of any condos at Waterville Valley, each spacious townhouse has been professionally decorated. You'll find cathedral ceilings in the living room, oak trim, designer accents, art pieces, and woodwork throughout. Each condo is three stories high with the master bedroom on top. Other features include a walk-in closet and a whirlpool that is large enough for two. In the two-bedroom with loft units, the loft is accessible by ladder for older children or teens only.

8-9 WENTWORTH HOTEL
Route 16A, P.O. Box M, Jackson, NH 03846, 800-637-0013
1BR $150–250, 2BR $200–300
Amenities: Golf, cross-country skiing, tennis

This is an integration of the old with the new. Formerly a 100-year-old rambling summer home converted into a hotel, the Wentworth offers some of the area's finest townhouse condos. They are located behind the main hotel building along the golf course. This resort appeals to cross-country skiers since it is situated on Jackson's famous 100-mile, cross-country circuit. In the summer, the Wentworth's 18-hole golf course attracts sophisticated vacationers seeking a different form of exercise. The townhouse condos are new, spacious, and luxurious. Designed as modern split levels with lots of glass windows, the living rooms feature vaulted ceilings and a brick fireplaces. The country kitchens are huge and there's a little study on the third floor, next to two bedrooms, that is a great place for escape from family activities. Each is individually decorated. We saw one that had new blond wood cabinetry combined with Queen Anne antique reproduction furniture. The result, a comfortable home environment that has the "Chestnut Hill" look rather than the sterility of a hotel or the planned design of a resort condo. Then there is the "Santa Fe" look that has been incorporated into the design of several condos. The Southwestern cottonwood furniture is painted in white or in pale desert colors. Accents include carved Native American masks and "stuffed" reproductions of cactus, bobcats, and snakes made from silk. Unique and truly a vacation fantasy, these condos are next to the heart of the village of Jackson. You can walk across the covered bridge for shops or après ski activities.

8   WHISPERING BROOK
Route 16, Jackson, NH 03846
Amenities: Cross-country skiing

Just outside the village of Jackson, these townhouse condos enjoy a serene wooded setting straight from a Currier & Ives engraving. The back door is on the 60-mile Jackson cross-country ski circuit. These spacious three-bedroom units each have their own private hot tubs, that are large enough for two. Decor is neutral, attractive, and contemporary with tweed fabrics, lots of wood, ski posters, and a wood-burning stove. This appeals most to New England types who enjoy good books, the outdoors, and eschew conspicuous consumption.

6   THE WINDRIFTER
South Main St., Wolfeboro, NH 03897
Amenities: Lake, golf, indoor pool, cross-country skiing, tennis

This resort revels in its history that dates back to 1778. The Inn is furnished with antiques in the open areas, but the rooms were furnished in the 1970s. The development is on the grounds of the Kingswood Golf Course just across from Lake Winnipesaukee. The units are suites and accommodate either two to four people. The kitchen is small, so this is designed for vacationers who would rather eat in some of the restaurants in the area.

7 **WINDSOR HILL**
Route 49, Waterville Valley, NH 03215
Amenities: Pool (summer only)

The largest condominium complex in Waterville Valley, Windsor Hill is located about one mile from the village in a grove of mountain pines. The townhouses are attractive and spacious. Each includes its own fireplace. The two- and three-bedroom units have bunk beds and are great for large families or groups of skiers. Some of the condos first built at Windsor Hill have Waterville Valley Sports Center privileges that can be passed along to guests; others don't. It all depends on the specific unit is assigned to you, so be sure to inquire when making reservations.

RENTAL RESOURCES

Apre's Tour Townhouses, 800-232-5177, Bretton Woods
Badger Realty, 603-356-5757, North Conway
Century 21 Keewayden Properties, Lake Winnipesankee
Coldwell Banker, 603-524-2255, Lake Winnipesankee
Cranmore Lodging, 800-543-9206
Crossroads Property, 800-448-3798, Bretton Woods
Franconia Lodging, 603-823-5661, Cannon Mountain
Franconia Notch Vacations, 603-823-5536
Lincoln Woodstock Reservations, 603-745-6621
Loon Mountain Lodging, 800-227-4191, 603-745-9976
Meredith Bridge Garden Condos, 603-366-5744
Mt. Sunapee Accommodations, 800-258-3530
Mt. Sunapee Reservations, 603-763-2495
Preferred Properties, 603-253-7341, 800-253-4345, Lake Winnipesankee
Preferred Vacation Rentals, 603-476-5767, Statewide
Resort Realty, 608-383-9800, Mt. Washington Valley
Samoset at Winnipesankee, 603-293-8068
Select Real Estate, 603-447-3813, Conway
Top Notch Vacation Rentals, 800-762-6636, Bartlett
Townhome Rentals of Bretton Woods, 800-334-3910
Twin Mountain Lodging, 603-846-5407
Valley Vacation Condos, 603-356-3960, Intervale
Waterville Estates Realty, 603-726-3716, Waterville
Wright Realty, 603-447-2117, North Conway

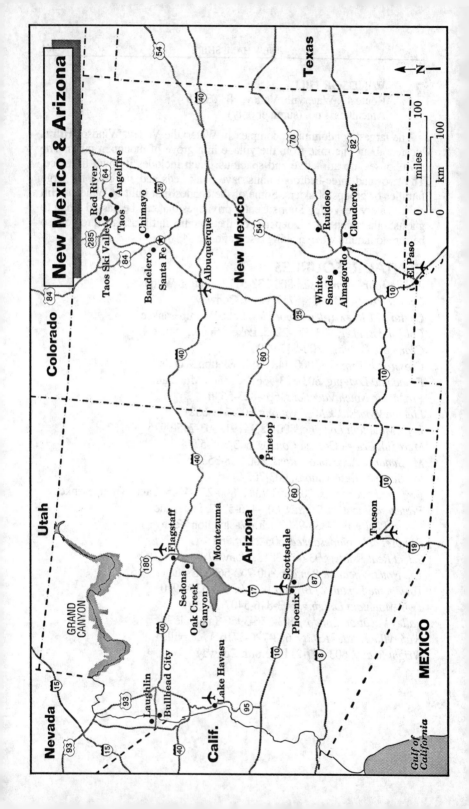

NEW MEXICO

No other state, not even Hawaii, can compare with the rich cultural diversity that awaits visitors to New Mexico. History plays a large part in this. When the Spanish Conquistadors came in the 16th Century, the "Pueblo Culture" was the most sophisticated and established in the area that was to become the United States. This was the only Native American group to successfully rebel against the Spanish in the 17th Century and as a result, the population enjoyed a certain degree of autonomy and integrity not bestowed upon other Spanish subjects. Today, the Eight Northern Pueblos still survive and the 145-mile circuit—from Taos to Tesuque—is a major visitor attraction. Each Pueblo has district art forms including pottery, weaving, jewelry, dances, and festivals.

Santa Fe is the oldest continuously, occupied capital in the U.S., dating back to 1610. The architectural style is unique—adobe with lodgepole ceiling supports and rounded kiva fireplaces. All new construction has been in accord with the original city plan—designed 380 years ago—so at first sight the city is a massive sprawl of brown punctuated by clumps of green chamisa trees. In winter, the snow adds a second color and wisps of smoke climb up against the bright blue sky. An artists' colony, recent polls reveal that this has become the nation's "most desired" resort destination. Fortunately, however, the number of tourists are a fraction of those visiting Williamsburg or the French Quarter in New Orleans. Warm for nine months of the year, the sports of golf, horseback riding, fly fishing, and river rafting attract enthusiasts of all ages. The Santa Fe Ski Bowl—23 miles away offers challenging skiing, but there has been no resort development around the base of the lifts.

Taos is a smaller version of Santa Fe without the careful cultivation. More rustic, you'll be constantly reminded of the Native American culture. Prices in Taos are generally lower and hospitality is much less commercial. Culturally relaxed, many of Taos' residents have moved here from other parts of the U.S. because they heard a different drummer. The Taos Ski Valley is one of the finest ski mountains in the U.S. and also is 23 miles away from town. Unlike the Santa Fe Ski Bowl, Taos Ski Valley is different because it is a fully developed resort community and the theme is Swiss. Only Vail seems more European than Taos Ski Valley.

Farther north, just 40 miles from the Colorado border, you'll come to the resorts of Red River and Angel Fire. Red River as the name implies, is a town that talks Texas. A cowboy town which revels in its Texas roots, you'll find the spirit of the Old West alive in a zesty, youthful way. The ski area is smaller than Taos or Santa Fe, but don't tell its devotees that. With over 15 condo resorts, a dozen hotels, and six RV parks, this area has a wide range of accommodations to choose from. Angel Fire, yet another ski resort, is 25 miles east of Taos. It's a mega-real estate development from the '70s that is still awaiting discovery. The ski mountain is excellent, the accommodations are plentiful with over 30 resorts to choose from, and Angel Fire's bars and restaurants reflect a California style.

South of Albuquerque, halfway to El Paso, there's a fourth vacation area centering around Ruidoso. This alpine community rises 7,000 feet above the White Sands desert floor and nearby Almogordo. Promising Camelot and a new era of recreational enjoyment, this too is awaiting discovery by large numbers of tourists. The Ski Apache area is better than what you'll find in the East but it pales by comparison with Taos Ski Valley. For fun in the snow, tennis, golf, or just a day's adventure, head over to Cloudcroft. Although the Cloudcroft ski area can best be described as quaint, this Victorian resort has character and charm. With a mild climate for nine months of the year, and low prices, the Ruidoso-Cloudcroft area is attracting growing numbers of early retirees.

Air travel to New Mexico is through Albuquerque. That's it. Yes, there are a couple of commuter flights to Santa Fe and Taos, but you can drive the distance in about the same time. As for those heading to the Ruidoso-Cloudcroft area, you'll find the El Paso airport to be most convenient. The drive to Ruidoso is less than two hours from the Rio Grande.

1. SANTA FE

Santa Fe calls itself "La Ciudade Differente." Even the city's motto is different; it's in a foreign language. The Santa Fe area was originally settled by the Anasazi Indians over 1,500 years ago. Even as recently as the '60s, Santa Fe was a sleepy community where the main business was state government. But as an art center, it attracted the smartest from New York and California. In the '70s, Liz Taylor came to town, followed by the press, and the place hasn't been the same since. Today, the art galleries of Canyon Road rival the government for economic importance. Santa Fe has some of the best restaurants to be found anywhere, with a warm intimacy rivaling New Orleans. Accommodations reflect the local interest in art and we know of no other community where interior decor has gained a similar level of importance.

Transportation to Santa Fe usually comes through the airport in Albuquerque, although Mesa and Aspen Airlines offer commuter flights directly into Santa Fe's sleepy airport.

WHERE TO STAY

9   **CAMPANILLA COMPOUND**
334 Otero, Santa Fe, NM 87501, 505-988-7585, 800-828-9700
1BR $155, 2BR $205
Amenities: None

Campanilla Compound is an unusual, high-quality development. The original structure is on the state Register of Historic Properties. Starting with the original home as a base, new townhouse units were constructed on the grounds of the original estate. Built in the Territorial style with adobe walls, the resort offers the finest in New Mexico architecture, and the project was designed so that each unit would have a view of the mountains. The interior decorations are also different from what you would expect in a condo. Whitewashed walls, tile floors, wooden beamed ceilings, and a kiva fireplace. Art objects are placed throughout. Many little nooks have katchina dolls, "gods eyes," and mandillas on the walls. The result is stunning. There is no pool or activities program, but who cares when the units are this attractive.

8+ CIELO GRANDE
750 N. St., Francis Dr., Santa Fe, NM 87501, 505-982-5591
1BR $120–160, 2BR $145–195
Amenities: Hot tub, plunge pool

Quality craftsmanship in the Santa Fe style Cielo Grande overlooks downtown Santa Fe and has great views of the city. These modern condos were designed in the traditional Pueblo style (for those who want a home away from home in Santa Fe) with kiva fireplaces and beamed ceilings. Inside, you'll find neutral interior decorator decor with fabrics in varying shades of pink and tan. Accents include Indian paintings and a sturdy ranch dining table and chairs.

6 527
527 E Alameda, Santa Fe, NM 87501; 1BR $82–112
Amenities: None

Located only 7 blocks from the Plaza and across the Santa Fe River from the art galleries of Canyon Road, these 12 one-bedroom condos enjoy a quiet residential setting. Each condo has been professionally decorated with Southwestern decor. Expect to find furnishings with neutral fabrics, nooks housing carved trasteros, color TVs, and compact disc players. It is more residential than resort oriented, and there is no on-site management.

9 FT. MARCY COMPOUND
320 Artist Rd., Santa Fe, NM 87501, 505-982-9480, 800-745-9910
1BR $98–165, 2BR $140–198
Amenities: Indoor heated pool, hot tub

Situated on the hillside marking the northern limits of Santa Fe, Ft. Marcy Compound is only 4 blocks from the historic plaza. Of all of Santa Fe's accommodations, this in the one which makes the most of the view of the range. This location is excellent because it's both private and very convenient. Ft. Marcy Compound wants to be your Santa Fe home and management tries hard to make each visitor's stay exceptional. We think they succeed in their effort and other guests such as Lily Tomlin, Kim Basinger, Adam West, and the Judds agree. There are two styles of condos here—the three-bedroom units are townhouses with two up and one down. They also have one- and two-bedroom condos which are flats. We like the two-story townhouses the best not only for space but also because the townhouse owners tried to dress their units up more. Expect to find the Territorial style blended with touches from the Pueblo culture. We saw two condos with lots of personal touches, such as electronic toys to play with and lovely coffee table books on local art or culture. It's the homey touches that make this a special place, yet nothing is too personal.

6   LA POSADA DE SANTA FE
330 E. Palace Ave., Santa Fe, NM 87501, 505-986-0000
Studio $98–130, 1BR $145–205, Cottage $255–390
Amenities: Restaurant, pool

This hotel in the heart of town is a series of 22 adobe-style buildings spread over 6 acres. It includes cottages as well as duplex suites. Not a condo, the garden setting and the fact that many of the units have kitchenettes make this a viable all-suite alternative to regular hotel lodgings. Casual and a bit on the faded side, this is a home away from home for art dealers during the summertime Indian markets.

7   LAS BRISAS DE SANTA FE
624 Galisteo St., Box 1770, Santa Fe, NM 87501, 505-982-5795
1BR $120–150, 2BR $150–200
Amenities: None

What a long way we've come over the years. Las Brisas can now take its place among the finest condo accommodations of Santa Fe. Architecturally, these are truest to the Pueblo style with alcoves, adobe geometric walls, surprising windows, and a kiva fireplace. Inside, you'll find Saltillo tile floors and brick half walls that offset the traditional whitewashed stucco. The lodgepole beams and the hand-crafted wood ceiling in the kitchen enhance the romantic feeling. Each has a private patio. Recently we visited and found tremendous improvement in interior decor and resort services. Located just six blocks from the Plaza, this is very convenient for those who want to browse the shops or walk home from the restaurants in the evening.

8   PUEBLO HERMOSA
501 Rio Grand Ave, Santa Fe, NM 87501, 800-274-7990
2BR $145–175, 3BR $185–260
Amenities: Tennis, pool

Located on the hillside that traditionally marks the northern border of Santa Fe, you'll find this sprawling condo development convenient to town but not in the middle of the congestion. You can walk to many shops and restaurants, and you're at the head of the highway heading north to Taos, skiing, and the Pueblos. Pueblo Hermosa is built around the historic Kopp House, dating from the 1880's and in the National Register of Historic Places. This former home is the reception area and where you can enjoy a complimentary breakfast served each morning, if you don't feel like doing it yourself. Built in the Territorial style, you'll find that interior decor exemplifies the best of Santa Fe and its indigenous cultural heritage. You'll find kiva fireplaces, southwestern wood, and rawhide chairs. The walls have been adorned with Native American artifacts or treasures from local galleries. Spacious and comfortable, this is well suited for families or friends traveling together. Not too splashy, this offers the best of residential condos with resort services.

10 QUAIL RUN
3101 Old Pecos Trail, Santa Fe, NM 87505, 968-2222
800-548-6990, 1BR $150, 2BR $205, 3BR $245
Amenities: Nine-hole golf course, tennis, pool, health club,
restaurant

This is what Santa Fe has needed for so long—and when it finally arrived, it was better than expected. For nearly 50 years, Santa Fe has been favored by the nation's art admirers, who also happen to be very wealthy. But there never was a country club community that was a center for social activities without involving the arts—until Quail Run came along. Borrowing the best from country club communities in Palm Springs and Boca Raton, Quail Run occupies 103 landscaped acres just ten minutes from the historic Plaza, which is the heart of Santa Fe. The centerpiece is the clubhouse with its restaurant, pool, and full health club. The clubhouse is the social center as well as the starting point for the nine-hole golf course. Clustered near the clubhouse are the two-story condo buildings—the larger casitas line the fairways.

Quail Run has a Pueblo design for the exterior and the condo interiors are jewels to behold. Soft-lined adobe walls, open-beamed ceilings, and kiva fireplaces are some of the architectural frills that are fundamental to all units. With this as a starting point, some owners have indulged in flights of fancy with painted Indian furniture, Saltillo tile floors, carved oak doors, and bright weavings from the Inca Empire of South America. Others have opted for a more subdued style, using Navajo rugs and lodgepole furniture. All in all, in most cases you should expect the Santa Fe style refined to its highest potential. Don't forget to make arrangements to use the Quail Run Country Club. The golf course is private and you'll need a guest membership.

10 RANCHO ENCANTADO

Route 4, Box 57C, Santa Fe, NM 87501, 505-982-3537
1BR $175–335, 2BR $215–415
Amenities: Conference center, pool, tennis, stables, cantina,
entertainment center

Rancho Encantado is an experience—and one which is savored by the
rich and famous. Guests range from Princess Anne to Whoopi Goldberg—
from Jimmy Stewart and Henry Fonda to Dan Fogelberg. You may have
seen photos of "the rancho" in *People Magazine* where they covered a story
on Princess Caroline of Monaco. Or perhaps you saw Robert Redford's film
of the "Milagro Beanfield War"—parts of which were shot here. Rancho
Encantado was the setting for the television series "Westward Ho," based
upon the innkeeper's book *Guestward Ho*. Originally developed as a guest
ranch in the 1930s, it took the arrival of the Egan family in 1968 to transform this setting into a state of mind. Situated on 168 acres of scrub country,
this offers an unpretentious ranch house from the outside, but inside you'll
notice the difference when you gaze at the Santuario and Katchina statues in
the hallway, the kiva fireplace in the library, and the oak-beamed ceilings.
Accommodations are in two sections: Rancho Encantado which has the hotel
rooms and junior suites on the hillside above the main lodge; and Pueblo
Encantado on the other side of the road, which is where you'll find the one-
and two-bedroom condos. The condos at Pueblo Encantado, are extra luxurious with 12-foot high ceilings, large fireplaces, and kitchens with hand-
painted tiles. The dimensions of the rooms, including the kitchen, are extra
large and they are great for entertaining or for the family that wants to
reunite while on vacation. The master bedroom also has a kiva fireplace
which has a hand painted border. Interior decor is elegant and perhaps a little
on the spare side, by comparison with other condos in the Santa Fe area—
sometimes less is more. The pool is a place to congregate in summer; in winter you'll find celebrities working puzzles in the game room by the fireplace.
It's the social caché at this resort, carefully cultivated for 25 years, which
makes this unique and outstanding.

SANTA FE CASITAS

Box 2805, Santa Fe, NM 87501, 505-982-3332
Amenities: Conference center, pool, stables, cantina,
entertainment center

For the truly residential villa experience in Santa Fe, contact this rental
agency. They represent a number of vacation homes tucked away in quiet
residential neighborhoods, or hidden among the mountains outside of town.
Fully furnished, these vacation homes are popular with celebrities seeking a
little privacy.

7   **ZONA ROSA**
Calle San Francisco, Santa Fe, NM 87501 (no mail)
2BR $1100/wk (rentals only through realtors)
Amenities: Hot tub

Centrally located just 4 blocks from the main plaza, these condos are more residential in flavor. Comfortable and well-furnished, you'll find these have contemporary decor and are furnished more for comfort than the romance of Santa Fe. But the surprise is each light, open airy unit does have a touch of Santa Fe. And the art in the units is all for sale. Surprise...you're living in a gallery.

RENTAL RESOURCES
Frontier Property Management, 505-984-2192
The Management Group, 800-283-2211
Proctor Property Management, 505-988-1782
Santa Fe Accommodations, 800-745-9910
Santa Fe Properties, 505-982-4466

2. TAOS

Located just 130 miles north of Albuquerque and 40 miles south of the Colorado border, Taos is a unique destination in North America and one which is often overlooked because of the competition with Santa Fe just 70 miles to the south. Whereas Santa Fe is the heart of government and culture in New Mexico, Taos retains the ramshackle quality of a frontier town and the reality of living Native American culture. There is no better Native American Pueblo to visit than Taos. You'll recognize it immediately because it has been so often painted and photographed that it has become the symbolic Pueblo of the mind's eye. Visitors can enjoy the smell of the frybread and strike up conversations with the tribe members as they go about their daily chores.

Westernized by Kit Carson and the Texans who followed in his footsteps, the town's destiny was changed in the early 20th Century when it became an artists' colony. Then came the wealthy cognoscenti from New York and Europe in the '20s and '30s including British author D.H. Lawrence. In the '60s, Taos became a haven for flower children. Just about this time Ernie Blake created the ultimate sports fantasy at Taos Ski Valley. The mountain at Taos Ski Valley tops out at 12,000 feet and on first impression, you'll think you've just arrived in the Swiss alps with the pedestrian streets, fresco paintings on the outside of buildings, and more Engadiner paraphernalia than actually remains in some Swiss villages.

Taos area accommodations fall into two distinct categories—in town and out at TSV, the way locals refer to Taos Ski Valley. If you want the Native

American experience, the mystical romance, and look forward to savoring six varieties of chili peppers, then you should stay in the town of Taos. If you want to be near the slopes and in a fantasy of gemütlichkeit, then stay out on the mountain. A few condo resorts, such as the Quail Ridge Inn, offer a compromise as they are along the road between town and the mountain.

One observation about lodgings at the mountain: we find it amazing that so many other vacation areas have gone to great lengths to recreate the architecture and designs of the Santa Fe look, yet here where it should be, we have a recreation of a Swiss village. Another observation about accommodations is the area in general: the quality of the decor is no match for what you'll find in Santa Fe but then that reflects this community's efforts to avoid commercialism and to be casual and loose.

You can reach Taos by first flying to Albuquerque and then taking either the airport bus or renting a car for the drive north. You can fly to Taos from Albuquerque but it's in a small 5 passenger Cessna 310.

WHERE TO STAY

7   ALPINE VILLAGE
Box 2719, Taos, NM 87571, 800-322-8269
1BR $78–130, 2BR $120–200, 3BR $150–260
Amenities: None

You couldn't have a more central location at Taos Ski Valley. These units are a stone's throw from the main lifts, above the sporting goods shops and restaurants. Modern and compact, the units are well designed, beautifully decorated, and have kitchenettes which are a little on the small side. None have fireplaces. These are better suited for discriminating adults who demand style and convenience—and can do without the trappings of a traditional family resort.

5   COTTAM'S COTTAGES
Box 2719, Taos, NM 87571, 800-322-8267, Chalets $60–120
Amenities: None

These rustic ski chalets are two miles from the village at Taos Ski Valley and can be locked off into studio and one-bedroom units. Alternatively, you can rent the whole chalet as a two-bedroom unit. This is for those who want to be alone and who don't need to be near the restaurants or nightlife.

7   EL PUEBLO LODGE CONDOMINIUMS
412 Paseo del Pueblo Norte, Box 92, Taos, NM 87571
800-433-9612, 1BR $80–100, 2BR $120–150, 3BR $100–200
Amenities: Outdoor pool, hot tub

For those who want the experience of the Native American Southwest, this is your choice. Located on the north of Taos town (and 4 blocks from historic Taos Plaza), these condos offer a unique environment, reasonably priced, in a parklike setting shaded by cottonwoods and pines. The one- to three-bedroom condos combine modern Southwest charm with early Taos architecture. One unit has a kiva fireplace, lodgepole ceiling beams and ristras of hanging red peppers. Others have more of a ranch look with stone fireplaces and lots of wood paneling. Each unit has a private comfortable feeling. Taos Pueblo, the reservation, is less than two miles away and the historic Taos Plaza is only a short stroll down the street.

6 HACIENDA DE VALDEZ
P.O. Box 5651, Taos, NM 87571, 505-776--2218
Studio $60–95, 1BR $85–155, 2BR $105–195
Amenities: Hot tub

For those who can't choose between being out in the ski valley or in the town of Taos, there's Hacienda de Valdez located halfway between the two. This secluded environment in the foothills has a personalized atmosphere, almost like a bed & breakfast. This is a great spot to make new friends. Because it's so quiet, you'll turn around when you hear a neighbor come or go. You must have a car if you plan to stay here. Each unit has been designed in the Southwestern style with Spanish tile entrances. Decor emphasizes Native American fabrics, furniture, and poster art. Each condo has its own fireplace.

8 HONDO LODGE
Box 89, Taos Ski Valley, NM 87525, 800-322-9815
1BR $120–175
Amenities: Bar and Restaurant

Some would call this the center of town and the bar is certainly a major draw. Formerly built, owned, and operated by a local artist, the Hondo Lodge was designed in Western style with a Swiss overlay. This place rolls with fun and gemütlichkeit. Some say it looks as though John Wayne just checked out. The condos are across the lane from the main lodge in their own quiet—but convenient—building. Spacious and private, this is a great place for the social skier—you don't have to drive home when the bars close up.

5 INNSBRUCK LODGE & CONDOS
Taos Ski Valley, NM 87571, 800-243-5253, 1BR $137, 2BR $238
Amenities: Gym, game room, hot tub

One of the original developments at Taos Ski Valley, this Tyrolian-style lodge is owned and operated by Theresa Voller. Half of the property is a lodge with hotel rooms and a smashing berghof restaurant where you'll find hearty Austrian and American meals. The other half are the condos. Older and a little faded, the advantage here is the authentic atmosphere. You can also have meals included for a little more, where you'll dine at common tables. If you're lucky, the hostess will tell tales of the early days at TSV.

6 **THE KANDAHAR**
P.O. Box 72, Taos Ski Valley, NM 87525, 800-756-2226
1BR $85–250, 2BR $110–330
Amenities: Recreation center with exercise room, sauna, hot tub

The Kandahar was one of the first condo projects built in Taos Ski Valley in the early 1970s and it's beginning to show its age. It's located away from the main village along the side of the hill. You can ski out. The condos are in a series of two-story buildings and the units are on top of each other. Each condo has a private adobe-style fireplace. Some have cathedral ceilings with oak beams, giving the unit a spacious, airy feeling. But the decor dates from the early '70s, when incomes bulged with money from the oil fields. Today, they seem a little dowdy. The Kandahar is good for families with children as it's easy to keep track of young skiers. A health center with an exercise room, a steam bath, and a hot tub is provided.

8 **LAKE FOREST**
Taos Ski Valley, NM 87525, Rental agent: 505-883-6161
Amenities: None

Brand new at Taos Ski Valley, these large two-bedroom condos have private jacuzzi tubs and steam showers—a mini-steam room which is a delight in winter. No on-site management, so call one of the reservation agencies. Lake Forest is private, pretty, and spacious.

 LOS PIÑONES
Box 5244, Taos Ski Valley, NM 87525, 505-758-7989, $200/night

Located 8 miles south of Taos where the table plain meets the soaring Santa de Christo Mountains, this casa sits amid a stand of piñion trees with excellent mountain views. Southwestern in style, there are Saltillo tile floors and ceilings. The large living-dining room has a fireplace at each end. Peppered with Santeros and North American art pieces, this home has three bedroom/baths and there's a private sauna and a jacuzzi tub.

7 **POWDERHORN**
Box 69, Taos Ski Valley, NM 87525
1BR $150–205, 2BR $220–250
Amenities: Complimentary breakfast, hot tub

This should have been named "powder hound" because this is the place where hot doggers want to be—right next to the majestic Al's Run. These brand new condos are in a building which borrows from the Swiss Alpine chalet for style. European style continues on the inside with blond Bavarian cabinetry and Austrian patterned floral fabrics. Light and cheerful, you'll enjoy the camaraderie around the hot tub in the evenings.

8+ QUAIL RIDGE INN
P.O. Box 707, State Road 150, Taos, NM 87571, 800-624-4448
Studio $92–120, 1BR $120–200
Amenities: Tennis club (6 courts and pro), pool, gym, sauna, hot tub

From the outside, Quail Ridge Inn looks like an adobe Pueblo. This impression vanishes, however, once you step inside the modern condos with polished wood and Southwestern Navajo and Hopi accent pieces. Each condo has a kiva fireplace and is decorated hotel style in pastel colors of the desert. Each has a small refrigerator and coffeemaker. The studio units have Murphy beds and the one-bedroom units have sofa beds in the sitting room. Pleasant with hotel style, it's the sports center which makes this a desired destination. Tennis is popular during the spring, summer, and fall, and racquetball is available all year round. There is a heated, covered swimming pool, a sauna and a hot tub. You'll need a car because this condo resort is four miles outside Taos. Skiing is available in the winter twenty miles away at Taos Ski Valley. The resort will arrange transportation for groups of skiers to the Ski area or to town.

7 RIO HONDO
Box 81, Taos Ski Valley, NM 87525, 505-776-2646
1BR $65–210, 2BR $80–250, 3BR $95–410
Amenities: Hot tub, sauna

This three-story modern wood structure contains some of the most spacious two-, three-, and four-bedroom condos to be found at Taos Ski Valley. Drawing more on the Western style, you'll find brick fireplaces and wood to be the highlights of interior decor. These could fit in nicely at Breckenridge and are clearly popular with the Texan crowd. The floor plan provides for two separate bed/bath set ups so these are good for two couples. The kids can camp out in the living room. The location is just a short walk from the ski lifts, yet it's not in the village. Surrounded by pines, you'll hear the babbling brook in summer.

6 SIERRA DEL SOL
Box 84, Taos Ski Valley, NM 87525, 800-523-3954
Studio $100–150, 1BR $150–200, 2BR $220–295
Amenities: Hot tubs, sauna

New and modern, these turn their backs on both the Santa Fe and the Swiss theme. Light and contemporary are the adjectives to describe the neutral decor of the Sierra del Sol condominiums. The living/dining area is separated from the kitchen by a breakfast bar. There's a round steel fireplace in the living room, while just outside there's a view of the creek and forest. Well maintained, these are private and comfortable condos.

7+   SONTERRA CONDOS
206 Siler St., Box 5244, Taos, NM 87571, 505-758-7989
1BR $44–115, $300/wk
Amenities: None

Looking for the best value in New Mexico? Here it is. There's no other place like this condo resort, just 4 blocks from the historic Taos Plaza. Surrounded by an adobe wall and latilla fence, these 10 condos have a wide front porch with frontier rockers and chili ristras hanging on the wall. Facing a quiet inner courtyard with a Mexican fountain, each cozy unit is individually furnished in warm Southwestern style; some with traditional kiva fireplaces. The bedroom opens onto a private patio. We were impressed with the Indian drum and tables, the mandilla shields on the wall, and the woven baskets in the kitchen. Quiet and understated, there's nothing slick here. Sonterra has a rustic charm and an unbeatable price for a couple looking for a little romance.

9+   ST. BERNARD CONDOMINIUMS
Taos Ski Valley, NM 87525, 505-776-8506, 2BR $275
Amenities: Hot tub

Convenient to the ski lifts and Hotel St. Bernard, the St. Bernard Condominiums are easily recognized by the fresco paintings of Francescan monks on the exterior walls. Inside, the European tradition continues with rough-hewn oak beams and Bavarian blond-wood furniture. Stone fireplaces are as tall as the two story cathedral ceilings. Some, however, have been Americanized by their owners who have added Chimayo rug wall hangings and accents of Indian pottery and weaving. Above all in TSV, these condos have style.

5   TAOS EAST
Box 657, Taos Ski Valley, NM 87525, 800-238-SNOW
1BR $105–140

For those who want to be alone, this collection of modern townhouse-style condos are along the banks of the Rio Hondo, on the side of the mountain, surrounded by the cedar and pine forest. Western in style, these have brick fireplaces and neutral, comfortable furniture that can fit in anywhere. If you're tired of the North American or the Swiss fantasy, try these for honest home style. Four miles away from the ski area, this location is good in winter but it's at its best in summer when the hills abound with wildflowers, and the stream becomes a magnet for anglers and rafters.

5 TAOS MOUNTAIN LODGE
Box 698, Taos Ski Valley, NM 87525, 505-776-2229
Loft suite $112–140
Amenities: Hot tub

Located on the road to the Ski Valley, this rustic lodge is surrounded by pine forest. The 12 loft suites here are small but comfortable and each has a kitchenette with a microwave and refrigerator. The downstairs bedroom is private but the loft overlooks the living room—kids will love it for a hideout. Interior decor is Southwestern in style but don't expect the artistic delicacy found in other local accommodations. Rustic and private, there's a special commonality that evolves between the guests here. We think it's due to the isolation.

7 TWINING CONDOMINIUMS
Box 696, Taos Ski Valley, NM 87525, 800-828-2472
Studio $55–95, 1BR $95–165, 2BR $120–210
Amenities: Hot tub

As one Texan said, "It's like home, only with snow." Lapsing back to the original name for the mountain at Taos Ski Valley, the Twining Condos are popular with "old hands" who've been coming here for years. These units are unpretentious on the outside but large and well-decorated on the inside. Each unit has two bedrooms plus a loft including the fold-out couch. These units can accommodate up to eight guests. We saw a rejection of the Santa Fe look in favor of the luxury of a contemporary River Oaks or North Dallas look. Located on the quiet side of the village, the No. 5 chair lift is just right outside your door.

6 VILLACITO CONDOMINIUMS
Box 49, Arroyo Seco, New Mexico 87514, 505-776-8778, $95–260
Amenities: Hot tub

This is 7 miles from Taos and 12 miles from Taos Ski Valley. Located on the Taos Ski Valley Road, near the Quail Ridge Inn, this tiny cluster of 4 condos has style. It's more like staying in a private guesthouse with as much or as little personal attention as you could desire. Although on the Taos Ski Valley Road, these are not skier-oriented. These are more for those who've come to paint, explore the trails amid the sagebrush and cañyon, or perhaps just like mountains. This location is for those who hear a different drum—you are alone in the middle of the high desert.

RENTAL RESOURCES
Taos Vacation Rentals, 800-788-7267
Christopher Webster Real Estate, 505-758-9229

3. RED RIVER AND ANGEL FIRE

Just thirty minutes north of Taos, you'll find Red River. Angel Fire is located just thirty minutes east of Taos. Each has its own character and appeal, although they pale by comparison with Santa Fe and Taos.

Red River is one of the most colorful cowboy towns you'll find in the U.S. Main Street. Shaded by towering pines, it has planked sidewalks and saloons which could double as a stage set for "Gunsmoke." The skier chair lifts rise from the center of town so this is the hub of the action. This is an old-fashioned family ski area—a place where everyone is going to feel at home. The condos and cabins nearby are casual and emphasize the anglo cowboy charm—such a change from the Pueblo culture of Taos and Santa Fe.

Angel Fire is altogether different. A super-modern real estate development, there's a California sophistication here. For more on the background of Angel Fire, read John Martin's *The Milagro Beanfield Wars,* which although fiction, borrowed from tales of the development in the 1960s. The resort offers challenging skiing and uncrowded slopes. The redwood condos at the base of the lifts are all conveniently located for skiers. With 375 acres of ski terrain and 22 runs ranging from simple to expert, all categories of skiers will enjoy this resort. In the summer, it's even better because of the cool mountain breezes, occasional showers, and pine-scented air. Angel Fire has its own aircraft landing strip for those with private planes. For those who enjoy uncrowded destinations, Angel Fire fills the bill.

7   AUSLANDER CONDOMINIUMS
Box 789, Red River, NM 87558, 505-754-2311
1BR $100, 2BR $150
Amenities: Indoor heated pool, hot tub, and sauna

Closest to the lifts, these one-, two-, and three-bedroom condos are in a three-story building located in the heart of Red River. Efficient with a hotel style, you'll find this a popular place in the evening when skiers gather around the indoor heated pool, hot tub, and sauna.

6   CARIBEL CONDOMINIUMS
Box 590, Red River, NM 87558, 505-754-2313
1BR $50–110, 2BR $75–160
Amenities: Pond

Conveniently located just a block from the main chair lift, this two-story condominium complex is on "backstreet" Red River. Most of the units have views over the meadow to the mountains in the distance. Each has a spacious living room with fireplace and a full kitchen. Although not really personalized, this is a pleasant place to stay in both winter and summer.

6   EDELWEISS CONDOMINIUMS
     Box 730, Red River, NM 87558, 505-754-2942
     1BR $80–120, 2BR $95–140
     Amenities: Pool, sauna

These spacious two-bedroom units are popular with groups and young skiers. Conveniently located in the heart of town, each unit is well designed for easy living with a fireplace and full kitchen.

8   LIFTS WEST
     Box 318, Red River, NM 87558, 505-754-2778
     Studio $39–79, 1BR $59–99, 2BR $79–119
     Amenities: None

Clearly the best and most popular choice in Red River—something is always going on here. This modern three-story condominium structure houses a number of studio, one-, and two-bedroom units. Decorated in "old Western" style, there's a touch of fantasy to the place. There's a restaurant on site and the hot tubs and bar are lively places after skiing in the evening.

6   STARFIRE LODGE
     Drawer B, State Highway 434, Angel Fire, NM 87710
     Amenities: Pool, restaurant

The Starfire Lodge overlooks Angel Fire and the ski slopes commanding the finest location in Angel Fire. It is the center of after-ski activity. It is operated as a hotel with guest privileges at the Country Club. A swimming pool and nearby restaurant are available. The units are studios and kitchen facilities are limited.

5   TELEMARK TOWNHOUSES
     Box 907, Red River, NM 87558, 505-754-2534
     Townhouse $65–75
     Amenities: Hot tub

Now this is a special set up. These spacious townhouses, built with Tyrolian touches for a little romance, are part of a larger property that includes a bed and breakfast. You can have the best of both worlds—privacy plus someone to take care of you when you don't want to cook. With the accent on hospitality, this one is choice in Red River.

RENTAL RESOURCES

Angel Fire Property Management, 800-633-7463
Forestwood Management, 800-545-2167
Four Seasons Property Management, 800-888-6062
Resort Properties, 800-338-2589
Sun Valle Rentals, 800-321-2361

4. RUIDOSO AND THE SOUTH

Driving from El Paso across the desert floor, near the White Sands desert, you suddenly see a mountain range. Drive up the mountain for ten minutes and you're in an Alpine forest. The change in climate is dramatic and unexpected as the mountains, lakes, and forest are so different from the desert down below.

Ruidoso is a town carved out of the surrounding Mescalero Apache Indian reservation. It is a Western town that began in the 1890s as a trading post, and stands out in sharp contrast to Santa Fe and Taos up north. Unlike culturally rich northern New Mexico, there really are not any sights to see. Rather, this is an outdoors destination, and a place to relax except for the high season in June and July when the American Fraternity Horse Races take place. In winter, there's skiing at Sierra Blanca, a mountain formerly called Ski Apache until a few years ago.

Most visitors drive to Ruidoso from Texas, Oklahoma, and other parts of New Mexico. Those who travel transcontinental will find the El Paso airport to be most convenient.

WHERE TO STAY

6   **CARRIZO LODGE**
       Carrizo Canyon Rd., Drawer A, Ruidoso, NM 88345, 800-222-1224
       1BR $55–85
       Amenities: Pool, sauna, hot tub, restaurant

Close to Ski Apache, this place has one of the most popular bars for après ski fun that you'll find in the area. The one-bedroom condos have kitchens and fireplaces in the living room. This is a family-oriented spot.

5   **CHAMPION'S RUN**
       P.O. Box 601, E. Highway 70, Ruidoso Downs, NM 88346,
       505-378-8080; 2BR $75–140
       Amenities: Pool located next door to Ruidoso Downs

Champion's Run is the new name for Triple Crown, which recently changed management. About three miles outside of town, this large condo complex is next door to Ruidoso Downs Racetrack and just above a workout paddock. You can enjoy watching champion racehorses as they exercise. The complex was originally developed by former Texas Governor John Connolly and, as you would expect, is a first class development. The furniture has a traditional, Virginia horse-country feeling that is quite a surprise in Ruidoso.

6 CROWN POINT

Crown Drive, Highway 70, P.O. Box 3299, Ruidoso, NM 88345, 505-258-5200; 2BR $75–140
Amenities: Hot tub, tennis, indoor pool, racquetball

Crown Point, High Sierra, and Tierra del Sol are three new condo developments in the Camelot Mountain area just south of town. Perched on the mountain, they offer spectacular views. The setting will remind you of a German castle. The indoor pool has a removable roof for summer; a sports center with a sauna and a racquetball court is provided. This may be the area's best value.

5 DAN DEE CABINS

310 Main Rd., Box 844, Ruidoso, NM 88345, 505-257-2165
Cabins $55–95
Amenities: None

These modern wooden structures are along the Ruidoso River. At their prime in summer, they are also popular with skiers in winter. Don't expect anything rustic here, for you'll find the emphasis is on comfort and service.

7 INNSBROOK VILLAGE

Hwy 68 North, Alto, NM 88312, 800-284-0294
Amenities: Pool

Located between town and Ski Apache, these modern condominiums offer spacious one-, two-, three-, and four-bedroom accommodations at a reasonable price. Some are duplexes. Comfortably-decorated, they are a superior choice in the area.

7 SPUR LANDING

P.O. Box 457, Cloudcroft, NM 88317, 505-682-2700
Amenities: Golf, pool, tennis

These brand new townhouses line the golf course and are located in the old resort town of Cloudcroft. The architecture is uninspired, but the condos have plenty of sunlight. They are fully furnished in earth tone colors. Each unit has a private fireplace and a microwave in the kitchen. Far and away, this resort is the most luxurious choice in Cloudcroft.

6 WEST WINDS CONDOS

208 Eagle Dr., Box 1458, Ruidoso, NM 88345, 505-257-4031
Amenities: Pool, hot tub

This popular motel added a cluster of luxury condos several years ago. You'll find these one-, two-, and three-bedroom condos each have a fireplace, comfortable "skierized" furniture and full kitchen. With all the activity at the motel, the indoor-heated pool and the hot tub are popular places to find the young and the restless in the evenings.

4 WHISPERING PINES CABINS

Box 326, Ruidoso, NM 88345, 505-257-4311
Amenities: None

Whispering Pines is a Ruidoso tradition. These cute cabins are located in the scenic Upper Canyon area. You'll find that these are not the standard one-room cabin. These have been designed to have one, two, and three bedrooms. There are stone fireplaces in the living rooms—a great place to spend a cool mountain night.

RENTAL RESOURCES

A-1 Resort Reservations, 800-545-9013
Century 21, 800-657-8980
Coldwell Banker SDC Property Management, 800-626-9213
Condotel Rentals, 800-545-9017
Four Seasons Property Management, 800-822-7654

NORTH CAROLINA

North Carolina has been called "variety vacationland" because of its diverse geography and range of recreational and cultural activities it offers. From skiing and golfing in the mountains to fishing or sightseeing on the Outer Banks, there's something for everyone here. With all of this diversity, we have divided North Carolina into five distinct vacation areas:

1. **Northern Mountain Resorts** — Covering the high point of the Appalachians just south of the Virginia state line, this section reviews the South's largest and most popular ski resorts. Included are Sugar Mountain and Beech Mountain as well as the smaller ski resort communities of Blowing Rock and Boone. These peaks are the highest in the Appalachian chain and Grandfather Mountain is just under 6,000 feet. Although natural snowfall can sometimes be a question mark at Christmas time, these ski resorts have extensive snowmaking equipment.

2. **Western Appalachian Highlands** — In the southwestern part of the state, just over the line from South Carolina and Georgia, these resort areas are at their prime in the summer with Floridians. Fishing, sailing, golf, and tennis are the most popular activities and social life has been flavored by the Appalachian heritage. The mild climate has made this one of the most popular areas for retirees in the U.S.

3. **Pinehurst** — In the mid-central sandhills, this golfing community has acquired a legendary fame. The mild climate and moderate summers appeal to Yankees as well as southerners looking for a break from the summertime heat.

4. **The Outer Banks** — Lying just off the eastern coast, these barrier islands have attracted a coterie of vacationers from Virginia and the metro Washington D.C. area. Seldom more than two miles wide, this area has been famous for powerful storms and shipwrecks. The main occupation during the 17th and 18th centuries was piracy and even today you'll notice the distinct Elizabethan English in the local dialect.

5. **Southern Beaches** — Surprisingly the shores, just a little farther south have a milder climate. The Brunswick County area, flush against the border with South Carolina's Myrtle Beach, has been transformed into a haven for golfers. You can comfortably play for ten months a year.

North Carolina is a state in which the resorts have been developed with an appreciation for the changing seasons and variety created by nature. One hallmark of this region is that resorts are well adapted to the land and climate, as opposed to more commercial resort centers like Las Vegas or Orlando where climate and topography are inconsequential considerations.

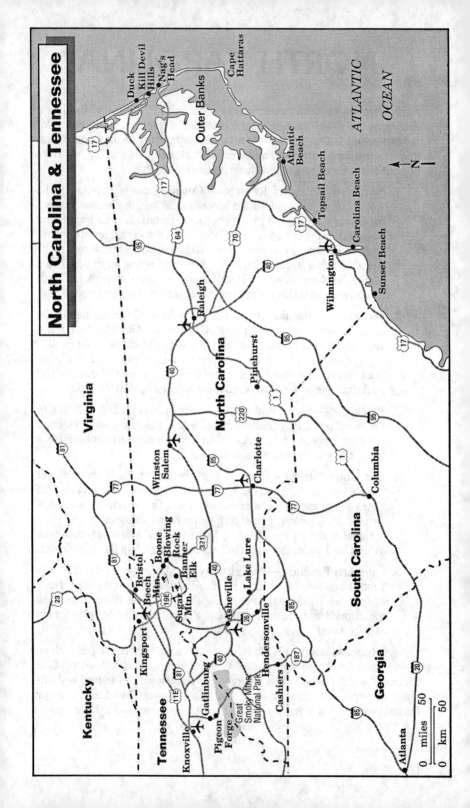

One important point about vacation rentals in North Carolina is the law. The law requires that condo and vacation home rentals be handled by a real estate agent. This has retarded the development of on-site property rental agents conducting a hotel-style operation. Instead of hospitality, the focus has been upon handling money and handing out keys. Therefore, unless the condos were an outgrowth of an existing hotel operation (as in the case of Chetola or Pinehurst) don't expect much by way of service at North Carolina resorts. This shows up in small, but important ways, with linens for example. **CAVEAT: Many of the resorts in North Carolina do not include sheets/linens or housekeeping services.** The custom in this area, especially in the beach resorts, is to **rent linens** from the management company or bring your own. Another feature of North Carolina is an absolute ban on accommodations for pets. Even if the condo manager could make arrangements for your dog, cat, or bird, the law prohibits it. So it's best to leave your pets at home, in the care of a vet or a trusted friend.

North Carolina is a state in which the resorts have been developed with a concern for the changing seasons and the variety created by nature. One hallmark of this region is that resorts are well adapted to the land and climate, unlike the more commercial resort centers like Las Vegas or Orlando where climate and topography are inconsequential considerations.

1. NORTHERN MOUNTAIN RESORTS

We all are seeking greener pastures and southerners often romanticize snow, skiing, and winter storms. The mountain resorts of Sugar and Beech were designed to fulfill those expectations. Built in the late '70s when the New South was rapidly rising in Atlanta, these communities borrowed upon the Alpine architectural design. Don't be surprised to see the green leaves of a live oak tree sheltering Heidi's proverbial mountain chalet.

Both Beech and Sugar Mountain are extensive master resort developments with hundreds of acres of woods, slopes, and golf fairways. You'll find small condo developments mixed in with communities of individual vacation homes. Almost none have a front desk, so don't bother writing or calling the resort directly. Accordingly, in each of these areas, large professional rental agencies have evolved to serve your needs. In between these master resort developments, there are several other condo developments ranging from the exquisite developments at Hound Ears or Club Yonahlossee to some of the budget properties like the Smoketree Lodge. Hawksnest is a ski mountain/golf resort "in between." Not nearly as extensive as the infrastructure at Sugar or Beech, skiing at Hawksnest is more like playing in the snow. Hound Ears also has its own private ski hill but don't expect much.

Blowing Rock has been a summer destination for Carolinians and the southern gentry for over 80 years. The cute town hides some of the grand old estates. Numerous cabin, condo, and vacation homes are available for rent in the vicinity of Blowing Rock. Only ten miles from skiing at Sugar or Beech, these properties double as prime vacation rentals in the winter season. Hound Ears, Linville Ridge, and Club Yonahlossee are their own private worlds and if you stay at any of these resorts, you're in for a special treat.

WHERE TO STAY

ACCOMMODATIONS CENTER OF BEECH
500 Beech Mountain Parkway
Banner Elk, NC 28604, 704-387-4246, 800-258-6198

Offering over 90 different condos, chalets, and private homes, this agency has the largest inventory of vacation rentals in the area. Most of the condos described in this chapter have some units available through the Accommodations Center. What need to be emphasized are the vacation home rentals. Since few of the condo complexes offer on-site amenities and guests at all Beech properties have access to the pool, this is one area where vacation homes compete favorably with the condos. Alan Holcomb, who runs the Accommodations Center, was the original real estate salesman when Beech Mountain was first developed, and today he is known as the sage of the mountain. If you have time, stop in and chat with Alan—you'll learn the whole history of the area. Professional and reliable, if anything goes wrong, you know you can count on these people.

5   ADAM'S APPLE RESORT
Route 1, Highway 105, Box 298, Banner Elk, NC 28604,
704-963-4950; 1BR $80, 2BR $100, 3BR $120
Amenities: Tennis

Adam's Apple Resort is located less than a mile from the Hawk's Nest Ski Resort. Adam's Apple is a sharp, modern establishment four miles from Banner Elk and 15 minutes from Beech Mountain, with easy access to nearby golf and ski resorts. The condos have been notched into the side of a hill and are interconnected to the main lodge by a series of planked walkways. The condos have absolutely beautiful views of the valley and Grandfather Mountain (the highest peak in the range). The modern decor features light woods, track lighting, fireplaces, and throw rugs. Years of use are starting to show and you'll find that some condos are rented by students working in the area. You can buy one of these condos for $18,000.

BEECH MOUNTAIN RESORT
Route 2, Box 56 M, Banner Elk, NC 28604
Amenities: Beech Mountain club with racquetball, tennis, pool, hot tub, saunas, skiing, golf

Beech Mountain competes with nearby Sugar Mountain for the honor of being the South's finest ski resort. Although the resort is queen of Carolina skiing, you shouldn't expect the challenge of Vermont or the dry snow of the Rockies. Less than 20 years old, the slopes around "The Beech" have been heavily "condominiumized." Rentals are available through local realtors such as the Accommodations Center described above. There is no one common theme to the condos at Beech. Some were developed in clusters as small as six units, others as large as 24. Most of them are semiresidential or vacation rentals since Beech is within driving distance of Charlotte and Winston-Salem. The decor is not standardized. Some condos have a "furniture package" with sturdy "skierized" furniture and water resistant plain materials. Others have been furnished in an "early attic" style. A few were the developer's models and have designer decor. The condos cascade down the backside of Beech Mountain Ski Resort and are actually five miles from the town of Banner Elk. You'll find twisted mountain roads and a couple of convenience stores. Social life revolves around the Sports Center at the top of the mountain with a pool, racquetball, tennis courts, hot tub, saunas, and video game room.

In this review, we have grouped the properties within the Beech Mountain development. Almost none have a front desk for mail or telephone requests. Prices should be in the range of $80 to $120 per night with discounts for longer stays. Dollar for dollar, we think you'll find the individual homes offer the best value, if your group is large enough to make use of all the bedrooms. There are other condos in the area or just over the property line that are as convenient to Beech Mountain skiing, *but they do not have access to the Beech Mountain Club.* Therefore, they are reviewed separately within this Northern Mountains section.

Grouse Ridge (7) Some of the largest and most stylish condos within the Beech Mountain community are part of this cluster of 12 units. Situated on the ridge, these two-story, four-bedroom beauties offer dramatic mountain views—the only rooms without a view would be the kitchen and the baths. The condo we saw was decorated in a sophisticated Appalachian country style with gingham touches and quilts on the bed—nothing overdone, just very comfortable. Great for groups of skiers, even better for extended families in summer when guest memberships for the golf club can be arranged.

Snow Plow (6) Another small complex of condominiums, these enjoy an excellent location on a ridge just below Fred's Mercantile. Here you are conveniently located near the crest of the mountain where you'll find a bevy of good restaurants and a small health club. This is one of the few Beech Mountain locations within walking distance of a number of destinations. These have nice touches like a flagstone entryway, a wood-burning fireplace, and a sweeping valley view from the master bedroom in the loft upstairs. Great for families, there's a separate bathroom on each level and the arrangement makes it easy to be away from the kids, yet keep an eye out.

Powder Ridge (7) These are some of the newer townhouse units within Beech Mountain. This small pocket project lacks the views afforded many of its neighbors, but inside these three-bedroom units, you'll be pleasantly surprised. Modern and classic, these owners have invested in a more sophisticated style, which seems more reminiscent of South Florida than the Carolina mountains. Check to find out which one is available. Reasonably priced, they make a pleasant part-time residence in winter or summer.

Tanglewood (8) These two-story townhouses are exceptional within the Beech Mountain preserve for a couple of reasons. The first is the architecture. Taking full advantage of the mountain views, each has a distinctive glass-bubble dome that breaks the slope of the two-story roofline. Inside, underneath, you'll find a private jacuzzi located just off the living room. We saw one surrounded by plants, which created the effect of a steamy jungle setting, yet the view included skiers on the slopes. These three-bedroom units on two different levels are great for groups or extended families.

Snow Tree Villa (6) Another collection of cute three-bedroom, 2 1/2 bath, townhouse condos. The configuration is good for groups of skiers as well as families.

Holiday Beech Villas (5) These units are considered the economy choice by Beech Mountain locals, but we found them to be much nicer than what you'd expect to find in the "student digs" category. The studios, at 400-square feet and with a room divider, are larger than some of the one-bedroom units we've seen. With a fold-out couch, this is adequate for a small family on a budget or a couple wanting a little extra space and privacy. The two-bedroom units, again, are extra large. Built 17 years ago, in a time of great expectations, the space is large but the construction is on the flimsy side. This is one where the developer ran out of funds and the central "clubhouse" building was in fact sold as a private home. Interior decor is dated with thick burnt orange carpet and inexpensive furniture.

Top of the Vineyard — This private home exemplifies some of the superior vacation homes available for rent within the Beech Mountain preserve. Step inside and you'll be impressed by the simplicity of design framing the mountain valley view. It suggests a Frank Lloyd Wright effect. The kitchen has a little extra wine bar upstairs, and down below, there's a large game room, a laundry room, and another two bedrooms/two baths.

Mariah North (7) There are two distinct phases of building at Mariah North: the detached chalets, which could be called inverted U-frame houses, and the condos, which are a series of triplex buildings. Here we found an elegant surprise—an interior with crystal chandeliers, baroque gilded mirrors, and a china cabinet displaying exemplary pieces. This truly does offer the "private guest house" feeling and you'll be charmed by the toys and surprises your nonresident host has left for you to play with.

Cedar Village — This little co-op project is a surprising find because it has its own recreation center featuring an indoor pool and hot tub and game tables. For families with small children, this has to be the choice at Beech Mountain. Inside, the units are a little on the small side and decor is a little down at the heels. But in 1993, the resort will undergo a comprehensive redecoration program. If it lives up to the interior decorators display of swatches and samples, it will be much better than when it was new. Expect to find an American Heritage style with lots of Carolina blue and salmon colors, offset by a classic flame stitch. Cedar Village is definitely an up-and-coming choice.

5   CAMERON'S COUNTRY CABINS
Rt. 1, Box 644, Blowing Rock, NC 28605, 704-295-4836
Cabins $115–130
Amenities: None

Featuring log cabins in a wooded area just 5 miles outside the town of Blowing Rock, this is a different vacation experience. Sylvan and serene, the views from the ridge extend for 75 miles of majestic rolling mountains. The resort occupies 25 acres and you can have your own wildlife experience right here. Each cabin has its own name and personality but every one has a stone fireplace and is decorated with country antiques, iron beds, stuffed animals, and a small kitchenette with a microwave oven. The Old Homestead cabin is the most romantic with a carved cedar bed and a two-person jacuzzi for romantic evenings.

8+   CHETOLA RESORT
P.O. Box 205, N. Main St., Blowing Rock, NC 28605, 800-243-8652
1BR $120, 2BR $165
Amenities: Health club, indoor pool, fishing, tennis, racquetball

Chetola Resort, one of the most renowned resorts in the North Carolina mountains, has had an established reputation for over 40 years. It is composed of a 75-acre planned development surrounded by Cone National Park. The centerpiece of the resort's beautiful setting is the stone and wood Chetola Lodge, built in turn-of-the-century architecture and overlooking a pond. Claire's restaurant is an upbeat dining experience located in the main lodge building. The condos are located on the hill behind the resort. Off to the left, there are the older timeshare units, in three-story wooden buildings surrounded by towering firs. Recently redecorated, you'll find they feature rose colors, designer fabrics, and a whirlpool in the master bath. Well maintained, they are a comfortable choice. Farther up the hill and built in essentially the same style, you'll find the condos. In our opinion, these are for a more sophisticated group of travellers. The interior decor belongs in the pages of *Southern Living* magazine. It's a surprise to find handsome oak millwork and English floral pattern fabrics around the window treatments. These spacious units are tailor made for those used to hanging around the country club. Although they don't have the jacuzzi whirlpools (as in the timeshares), these offer a higher level of luxury—probably because they are newer.

3   CHRISTIE VILLAGE
        100 Hornbeam Rd., Banner Elk, NC 28604, 704-387-2100
        Amenities: Beech Mountain Club

Located at Beech Mountain, this property gives you an idea of what budget lodgings are like. What used to be called a timeshare is now promoting itself as a condo rental property. Architecturally, these three-story units nestled in the pines have possibilities, but one sniff inside and you'll conclude that this property is stale. If nothing else is available, try this, but otherwise your money will go a lot farther at one of the other condo rental properties.

5   EVERGREEN
        Valle Crucis, NC. For reservations c/o Box 95, Sugar Grove,
        NC 28697, 704-963-7774; Cabins $125–175, $550–750/wk
        Amenities: None

Down a twisted mountain lane, just ten minutes from Boone, you'll find Evergreen featuring old-fashion Appalachian log cabins. Built the old way with hand-hewn logs and stack-stone fireplaces, each cabin is unique and with its own personality. Each cabin is well decorated with antiques, local crafts, and collectibles. All the modern appliances are available here. There are even the typical rockers on the front porch. Several have private hot tubs.

3   FLEETWOOD FALLS
        Box 128, Fleetwood, NC 28626, 919-877-1110
        Amenities: Lakes

Fleetwood Falls is a quiet place hidden in the Blue Ridge Mountains. Here, recreation doesn't move in the fast lane; its pace leaves one renewed. This private gated community of vacation homes is for those who want to get away from contemporary life and to escape into a rustic lifestyle. There are two lakes within the resort for swimming, fishing, and ice skating in winter. Several excellent golf courses are available in nearby Blowing Rock. Each of these vacation homes is custom-designed and decorated in a different style. A-frames, Bavarian chalets, and contemporary homes co-exist on lots of one to seven acres.

4   FOUR SEASONS AT BEECH
        Route 2, Box 56-F, Banner Elk, NC 28604
        Amenities: Pool, racquetball, sauna

Located about six miles outside of Banner Elk at the top of Beech Mountain, this resort has a Tudor-style inn atmosphere. The lobby area is dominated by a stone fireplace. The condos are actually suites in the lodge buildings with limited mini-kitchens. The interior floor plans and decor are disappointing. The units are decorated for heavy use with scotch-guarded fabrics and clunky wooden furniture. There are no on-site amenities, but you have guest privileges at the Sports Center, which is within walking distance for the hearty. There you'll find a pool, sauna, and racquetball.

HAWKSNEST SKI AND GOLF RESORT
Banner Elk, NC 28604

Located just over the ridge from Sugar Mountain and across the street from Grandfather, Hawksnest is a small ski resort with a rolling golf course. There are only three lifts and the grooming of the slopes/course doesn't compare with the quality of its neighbors. For a budget vacationer however, there are definite advantages. There are four condo developments here and prices should run from $400 per week for a one-bedroom, and $600 a week for a two-bedroom.

Hanging Rock Villas (7) A longtime favorite at Hawksnest, these uninspired buildings will surprise you with their interiors. Some have been recently redecorated in a sharp Virginia Heritage style, while others have functional furniture with "skierized" tweed material on the sofa and chairs.

Top of Seven (5) Undergoing extensive renovation during 1992, these one- and two-bedroom units are located midway up the mountain. A budget choice (you can buy one for $25,000), they are spacious with a stone fireplace and full kitchen. Time will tell about the redecoration.

Fifth Fairway Villas (5) Near the ski center, these are great in summer when you have an expansive view of the golf course and Grandfather Mountain.

Snow Cloud (3) These rounded, ten-sided structures enjoy great views, but the furnishings have deteriorated so much that we hesitate to recommend this one.

6   HIGHLANDS AT SUGAR
P.O. Box 892, Banner Elk, NC 28604
Amenities: Health club, hot tub, pool, game room

Highlands at Sugar is a condo village for skiers in the Carolina mountains. Its setting is beautiful: birch and evergreen trees on top of the mountain are complemented by the quality design. Some of the condos are two-story townhouses with rhododendron and mountain laurel landscaping. Others are spacious apartments in four-story buildings. The condos were recently redecorated and have contemporary furniture, such as blond bentwood chairs, fireplaces, modern electronic equipment, silk flowers, and (townhouse only) whirlpools in the master bathrooms. The mountaintop setting is beautiful especially in spring, summer, and fall. In the winter, the resort offers frequent shuttle bus service to the chair lifts at Sugar Mountain.

10 HOUND EARS CLUB
Box 188, Blowing Rock, NC 28605, 704-963-4331
2BR $800–1200/wk
Amenities: Golf, private ski hill, tennis

There are few places left in the world like the Hound Ears Club. This 700-acre resort is the quintessential country club community. Much has been preserved as woodlands but there is a championship golf course and a small ski area for the guests' use. Because demand for rentals so far outstrips the available rental inventory of 300 vacation homes and 80 condominiums, guests may only rent at Hound Ears for two years in a row. At the end of the third year, the cycle begins anew. Or you can snap up one of these properties when they come available for sale on the market. Not necessarily expensive, this is exclusive. Each of the homes are in architectural harmony as all modifications come under the Architectural Review Board. The homes range in size from 1200 square feet to over 9000 square feet. Interior decor ranges from "grandmother's heirlooms" to "starkly high tech." Plan on finding something that looks like a sitting room at your local country club. The condos are spacious but not ostentatious. We saw one that was showing its age, in a refined way, just like an English country home. Private and exclusive, you'll be happy if you already know some of the other club members or owners.

 THE JENKINS
321 Bypass & Sunset, Box 1003, Blowing Rock, NC 28605
704-295-9886, 800-438-7803

One of the largest condo/vacation home rental agencies in the state, this family-owned business offers extensive vacation rental properties. Specializing in chalets, cabins, and mountain homes, first-time vacationers to this area would do well to consult The Jenkins. Their inventory of properties includes The Cones, Royal Oak, Glen Burney, Pinnacle Woods, and The Village at Green Park, along the fairway at Blowing Rock.

8 KNOLL CONDOS AT ELK RIVER CLUB
P.O. Box 1555, Banner Elk, NC 28604
Amenities: Golf, tennis, pool, restaurant

Elk River is a private club community with the Knoll condos available for short-term rentals. These condos are 1,600 square feet in size with sweeping views of the forest and mountains. They are only a short walk from the clubhouse and tennis complex. The golf course was designed by Jack Nicklaus,

The living rooms of the condos have nine-foot-high ceilings and have been designed so that "pictures" of the view have been captured through the windows. Similarly, the bedrooms have sun decks and lots of glass windows. A stone fireplace and hearth set the tone for the living room.

9 LINVILLE RIDGE
Box 704, Linville, NC 28646, 704-898-5151
2BR $150–275, 3BR $220–385
Amenities: Golf, clubhouse with pool, health club spa, restaurant, tennis

One of the most talked about new resorts in the Carolinas, Linville Ridge benefits from a prime location in an area where the demand for "upscale" accommodations is growing rapidly. Unlike many of its neighbors, Linville Ridge is not rustic. Upon arrival, you'll notice the inspired modern architecture, which uses only natural materials like stone, oak, and glass in the spirit of Northern California. The condos, townhouses, and vacation homes continue this architectural theme with dramatic two-story living rooms, stone fireplaces, and open-beamed ceilings with angular pitches to allow for the best view. And the price ranges from $169,000 to $1.4 million, demonstrating that this was designed to be Yuppie Heaven. Just by way of comparison, at Hound Ears, you'll find the parking lot full of Cadillacs while at Linville Ridge, the preferred auto is obviously a Lexus or a BMW. Each condo and home has been professionally decorated and there's a strong preference for Drexel Heritage or alternatively, California Classic. All the right extras are here from the carved wooden decoy ducks to a pair of VTPs. No one is forced to watch the same video. As they say, Linville Ridge is above it all.

6+ THE PINNACLE INN
Box 1136 Banner Elk, NC 28604, 704-387-4276, 800-438-2097,
1BR $55–120, $300/wk; 2BR $65–95, $400/wk
Amenities: Sports center, pool, tennis

Boasting that it is the highest resort east of the Rockies, a claim contested by Maine's Sugar Mountain and Vermont's Killington, Pinnacle is a sprawling complex of three-story buildings just above Beech's "village," (the town hall, a convenience store, and a collection of real estate agencies). One note: these condos are not within the Beech Mountain master development and if you plan to play golf, you need to be sure there's a sponsor for a guest membership.

Overall, these units are neutral in tone and appearance. They are designed to appeal to the largest number of travellers and lack distinction or fantasy. Here you'll find few surprises. Each has been furnished in beige or tan tweed and the fireplace is the focal point. Unlike most accommodations at Beech, The Pinnacle has its own sports center with an indoor pool, steam, sauna, and exercise rooms. In the summer, there are two tennis courts and four outdoor hot tubs.

3 SKI COUNTRY CONDOMINIUM
Box 157, Banner Elk, NC 28604, 704-898-9877, 800-441-0465
1BR$70–95, 2BR $100–125
Amenities: Pool, tennis

Unique in the area, these are the only condos in the town of Banner Elk—and for that reason, they seem a little lost. Banner Elk is a practical town serving the nearby resort areas, and therefore, these would-be resort condos have actually become popular for year-round rentals by the local workers. The condos available for vacation seem a little bit worn from years of heavy use. There are several two-story buildings and a few A-frame homes. These are the larger three-bedroom models which have two bedrooms upstairs. Management is youthful and energetic, but the maintenance task here is formidable. In our opinion, this is a place to sleep and a good possibility for students on spring break.

4 SMOKETREE LODGE
Box 3407, Boone, NC 28607, 704-963-6505, 800-228-2968
1BR $77–300, 3BR $55–300
Amenities: None

Although technically the mailing address is Boone, this property is midway between Hawksnest and Sugar. Nestled at the foot of Grand Mountain, this pine, lodge-style building was built into the side of the hill and the units were carved into timeshare suites several years ago. No longer in active sales, today this resort has a casual mellow flavor. It is one of the few resorts in the area with its own health club including indoor pool, saunas, hot tub and exercise room. Each unit is more aptly described as a suite and the dimensions are on the small side. Everything is in order here and, dollar for dollar, the value is substantial.

SUGAR MOUNTAIN
Sugar Mountain, Banner Elk, NC 28604

The second largest ski resort in North Carolina, Sugar offers 18 runs, seven lifts, and the steepest vertical drop in the south—1200 feet. The success of this resort area is partially due to the well-developed vacation infrastructure of nearby Blowing Rock and Boone, but a lot has to do with the new wealth of Charlotte and the "reluctant millionaires" of nearby Winston-salem who were forced to sell their RJ Reynolds stock in the largest stock market sweepstakes of the century. In any case, Sugar has grown slowly but surely over the past 12 years, so there now are 15 condo developments and hundreds of vacation homes within the 400 acres surrounding the ski runs.

Sugar Ski and Country Club is described separately. As for the rest, they are typical of condo developments in the 80s with wood construction and inspired angular architecture that tries to capture the best views. Each development has its own character.

Skyleaf Villas & Condos (8) Located along the ski slope, you can ski out in the morning and take the lift home at night. The villas are perhaps the most luxuriously built units at Sugar, with each being part of a duplex. You'll find stone fireplaces, extra high ceilings, and sophisticated furniture in the Carolina-Virginia tradition. Antique reproductions and oriental carpets are in vogue. The condos have fantastic views and gas log fireplaces. This development attracts the up and coming young executives as well as the older statesmen of the community.

Briarcliff (6) These two-story townhouse condos are handsome from the outside, well located, and are surrounded by verdant landscaping. This is like a home in the woods and—surprise—it is one of the most reasonably-priced developments within Sugar. You can buy one of these one-bedroom models for a mere $30,000, although larger models are also available. Comfortably furnished, the accent is on function rather than style. Because of the proximity to the sports center in summer and the ski lodge in winter, this is also one of Sugar's high-demand vacation rentals.

The Glen (8) These condos are even better for families because they are within walking distance of the pool, golf, tennis, and skiing. More luxurious than many, the three- and four-bedroom condos are in duplex buildings surrounded by birch and pine. The stone foyer is a nice introduction and the kitchens are designed for family entertaining with JennAir grills for barbecuing in winter. Beautifully furnished, these have solid construction and will please the most discriminating traveller.

Hemlock Nob (5) These condos are among the oldest at Sugar and the ones we saw were definitely showing their age. Perhaps it's the barnlike exterior, but these just don't have style—although they are adequate and comfortable. If you stay here, negotiate a good rate.

Snowlake (5) These condos each have four bedrooms and four baths and although intended to be superior, these too have seen better days. Most popular with groups of young skiers because of the bedroom arrangements, they also have the prime position between the sports center, the ski lodge and the tennis center. These are right on the golf course and have great views in summer.

Bee Branch (7) We find these condos hard to categorize. We saw one that was exceptionally well decorated in the spirit of Appalachia (although few residents ever had it this good), and one that needed repair work, not just house cleaning. Conveniently located for skiers and golfers, check before you check in.

The Crest (8) Perhaps the most exclusive condos within Sugar, these units have private jacuzzi whirlpools and their hillside location provides great golf course views. Among the newest condos at Sugar, they are luxuriously decorated by someone turned loose at the nearby Hickory furniture mart.

Mossy Creek (9) Considered by locals to be the most luxurious because they are individual homes built on stilts in the forest. These have the distinction of having a private clubhouse with their own pool. These Logangate-style homes offer private whirlpools and, again, the decor offers the fruits of a buying spree at the nearby furniture mart.

Sugartop (also known as **The Citadel**) **(7+)** You can't miss these twin massive 12-story concrete towers atop Sugar Mountain. They are a landmark visible for miles around. This "visible" landmark caused environmentalists to enact the Ridge Law before they were completed. Essentially, this is a one-of-a-kind property because developers will never again be allowed to build on the ridge of the mountains in North Carolina and thereby destroy the view of the Appalachians. These units would fit in nicely in Florida or Chicago with their functional standardized design. Each has two bedrooms as well as a large living room with a spacious fireplace in the middle. With your back to the fire, you'll enjoy great views. Although these units are not as accessible to the slopes as at nearby Sugar Ski and Country Club, you can ski down in the morning and take the lift back in the evening. But it's quite a hike from the top of the lift to the entrance of Sugartop. One saving grace, this complex was designed for the handicapped and in summer this complex is perfect for those with disabilities who wish to enjoy the brisk mountain climate.

7   SUGAR SKI AND COUNTRY CLUB
Route 1, Box 169B, Banner Elk, NC 28604
704-898-9784, 800-634-1320,
1BR $112/daily $600/wk, 2BR$165/daily, $825/wk
Amenities: Clubhouse, pool

Atop the ski hill at Sugar, this is a great choice in the winter. In the morning you simply ski down the hill; in the evening take the ski lift back up. These condos are in 11 four-story shingle buildings on the crest of the hill. Advantageous for families with small children, this is one of the few resorts at Sugar that has its own activities center including an indoor heated pool, hot tub, sauna, and tennis courts. Another perk will appeal to the traveller who wants to get a little work done while on vacation: there's a business center with fax and a copy machine. The units are a little on the small side but highly efficient in the use of space. They are cute with vivid floral fabrics and lots of navy blue and white. In the one bedroom, there's a sleeping alcove where the Murphy bed folds up against the wall in the morning. It's a little like staying on a boat. Singles and executives favor this one because here, after a hard day of sports, you can truly unwind in the pool.

5 SWISS MOUNTAIN VILLAGE

Route 2, Box 86, Flat Top Rd., Blowing Rock NC 28605
704-295-3373
Suite $50–65, 1BR $55–75, 2BR $70–90, 3BR $85–100
Amenities: Clubhouse, pool

For those looking for a rustic retreat and a good family value, this little resort just outside of Blowing Rock is a surprising find. Built of stone and wood, these cabins are weathered on the outside, lovingly decorated with country charm on the inside. You'll find rockers on the front porch and quilts in the bedroom. Gas lamps are for decoration as are the ceramic pitchers and wash basins. As for modern amenities, there's a full kitchen complete with a washer/dryer. One bedroom will have a queen bed while another will have bunkbeds for kids. The best feature is the landscaped pond where the ducks swim and play all day.

TYNECASTLE

Hwys 105 and 184, Banner Elk, NC 28604 (no mail receptacle)

This is a master real estate development of permanent as well as second-home residences. Only a few are available for vacation rentals and those are for 30-day minimums. But what an experience this place is! It looks more like Wales or Sardinia than North Carolina because each of these homes is built of stone and half-timbered beams. Each is architecturally unique including one with a five-story tower. The romance of these homes cannot be overstated and although rentals are rare, they will provide a unique experience.

5 WILLOW VALLEY RESORT

Hwy. 105 S., P.O. Box 1782, Boone, NC 28607
Amenities: Golf, tennis, pool

Willow Valley Resort was formerly called Frontier Village, and some of the rustic cabins are still referred to as Frontier Village. The log cabins include stone fireplaces and country-style furniture and fabrics. Studio suites, available in the main lodge building, are decorated with contemporary furniture and are more attractive than the cabins. These don't, however, have the fantasy quality that the cabins have. Surrounded by mountains, Willow Valley is a complete resort on a plain. A private nine hole golf course, tennis courts, and an outdoor swimming pool are offered.

9 YONAHLOSSEE RESORT CLUB

Shull's Mountain Rd., Box 1397, Boone, NC 28607, 704-963-6400
1BR $125, 2BR $135–175, 3BR $155–195
Amenities: Clubhouse with tennis, pool, and restaurant.
Stables for horseback riding.

Until the early '80s, this was a girl's summer camp called The Trail of the Bear. But what a difference careful development can make. Today, it is one of North Carolina's finest summer resorts and an enviable place to stay for those who plan to ski Beech or Sugar Mountains. This private 140-acre complex is located in one of the rockiest sections of the Appalachians. Focusing on tennis, it has a premier program for intermediates who want to exponentially improve their game in a week's time. You'll find clay courts as well as indoor courts and a clubhouse where—you guessed it—the main topic of conversation is tennis. But it's the foliage surrounding the club, condos, and vacation homes that makes this special. Thick with rhododendron and hemlock trees, privacy is assured. The townhouse condos are pleasant and attractively furnished. You can tell that this is close to the Drexel Heritage furniture factory because these units each seem to be a showcase of their own. One of the bedrooms is a loft so these condos are best for families. The private homes have a number of bathrooms to match the number of bedrooms so they are great for two or three couples travelling together.

RENTAL RESOURCES
Barrett Realty, 704-898-5758
Beachwood Realty, 704-387-4251
Bears/Sugar Area Lodging, 704-898-4546,
   Extensive numbers of condos and homes for rent
Beech Mountain Chalet Rentals, 800-368-7404
Beech Mountain Realty and Rentals, 704-387-4293
Beech Mountain Rentals/Buchanan Real Estate, 704-387-4261,
   800-438-2095
Dereka's Sugar Mountain Accommodations, 704-898-9475
Elk Horn Company, 704-898-5333
ERA Resort Real Estate, 704-898-9746, Many condos at Sugar Mountain
High Country Realty, 704-963-6521, Hawksnest
Ridgeview Chalet Rentals, 305-758-4887, Beech Mountain
Slopeside Rentals, 800-692-2061, Beech Mountain
Wildwood Rentals, 704-963-6564, Hawksnest

2. WESTERN APPALACHIAN HIGHLANDS

Mountain music and clogging dancers, rolling golf fairways and clear rushing streams for fishing, legends from the past and morning mists, modern ski resorts and lakes for sailing: these are the images of the North Carolina Mountains. In the mountains, it's the scenery, not the climate that leaves you breathless. Beginning at Great Smokey National Park, it is possible to drive nearly 200 miles along one of the nation's most scenic parkways, the Blue Ridge. Don't expect to drive fast, because the twisting mountain roads mentioned in the fabled country songs are just as twisted and dangerous as the legends.

There are several centers in the Western Highlands: the towns of Asheville, Hendersonville, and Maggie Valley as well as the village of Cashiers. Asheville is a surprise, enjoying a mild year-round climate. In winter, it is protected by the mountains, which create a thermal belt, and is the cause for frequent dense fogs (hence the name "Smokey Mountains"), while in spring and fall it is vibrant with seasonal colors. Summer is short, green, and cool. Hendersonville has more of the same, only 25 miles away. Maggie Valley is perhaps the most touristy of the rural areas with a number of fine resort, golf club and retirement communities, and a village of shops and restaurants. Cashiers is beautiful. Situated at 3500 feet, it is surrounded by mountains and lakes. Winter can be a bit nippy but the six months of spring compensates. The surrounding forests are popular with hikers and rafters. The area's golf resorts are stunning to the eye and sapphire valley could have been a model for the Emerald City. Such a surprise to find this brisk, beautiful area so relatively undeveloped. Let's keep our secret!

For years, the business interests in this part of the Blue Ridge have been promoting the Western Highlands as an ideal place for retirement due to the mild climate and low cost of living. About 15 years ago, success arrived as the region was named the fastest growing retirement area in the U.S. That trend has been continuing and a large number of developments have been created in the past 15 years, which are both retirement and vacation home communities.

Transportation to the Western Appalachian Highlands is relatively easy as the airport at Asheville handles frequent commuter flights from Nashville in the west and Charlotte, Atlanta, and Raleigh in the east. Be forewarned: fog often causes flights to divert from Asheville to Greensboro or to Charlotte.

WHERE TO STAY

 APPLE REALTY
Box 396, Haywood Rd, Dillsboro, NC 28725, 704-586-3450

Dillsboro is a rural area and lacks a center, but like parts of Northern California or Wisconsin, there are a large number of vacations homes for rent here. Private and picturesque, these mountain retreats, for the most part, have been decorated in the Appalachian spirit with handmade quilts, antiques, brass beds, planked floors, and other fine touches. Located midway between Cashiers and Maggie Valley, golfers can choose from several topnotch courses while those who admire nature will find themselves surrounded by National Forest. Apple Valley Realty offers over 100 of these vacation homes, located "nowhere in particular," but convenient to the sports and area attractions.

7+ COTTAGE INN
Box 818, Cashiers, NC 28717, 704-743-3033
Amenities: Pool, tennis, restaurant

For more than a half century, southern families have been vacationing at this resort. This is a collection of 13 different and distinctive cottages offering one and two bedrooms. Each has a kitchen and fireplace. Furnishings range from rustic simplicity to the contemporary decor of the newer A-frames. Sorry, there are no phones here. This is a retreat from the modern world where only the moon provides a glow at night. The grounds are heavily wooded and feature split rail fences, flowering shrubs, and a walkway. But this is not the roughing-it kind of place. There's a heated outdoor pool, a tennis court, and a picnic area complete with dutch ovens. For a different view of the world, try a week here.

7 FAIRFIELD MOUNTAINS at LAKE LURE
201 Boulevard of the Mountains, Lake Lure, NC 28746,
704-625-9111; 1BR $95–120, 2BR $120–165
Amenities: Lake, golf, tennis, horseback riding, restaurants,
indoor/outdoor pools

Ever since parts of the movie "Dirty Dancing" were filmed on some of the 1,000 acres of Fairfield Mountains, the resort has never been the same. While the movie was being filmed, the resort instituted weekly Dirty Dancing parties for rocking into the wee hours of the morning. The resort's 133 condos feature vaulted ceilings, stone fireplaces, and a whirlpool in the master bath. They are professionally decorated with plaid fabrics and earth tone colors. The Apple Valley Villas have studio units and are the best rentals for short-term stays. Hospitality sports and activity programs are spotlighted here. There's something for everyone, from families with small children to senior citizens. Several social directors work hard in order to acquaint you with the full array of vacation activities. The golf course and country club occupy about a quarter of the land at this property. Much has been left to forests with hiking and horseback-riding trails. Trail rides are a specialty. The country club restaurant provides a quiet, enjoyable ambiance for dinner or lively, late afternoon sports conversation around the 19th hole. There are indoor/outdoor swimming pools as well as the lake where you can sail, water ski, or canoe. Fishermen can enjoy streams and the lake.

8+ FAIRFIELD SAPPHIRE VALLEY
4000 Hwy. 64 W., Sapphire, NC 28774, 704-743-3441
1BR $135, 2BR $165, 3BR $205
Amenities: Golf, tennis, marina, clubhouse with pool and
restaurant, horseback riding, mini-golf.

Fairfield Sapphire Valley may not be the Wild West, but it certainly has a western flavor. For example, a weekly "pack trip" takes place on a mule train. The destination is a base camp in the Great Smokies National Park. Tents are set up and dinner is cooked over a campfire. The meal consists of steak fries and trout that, hopefully, you caught yourself. Apart from the western experience, Fairfield is a golfer's paradise that provides challenging and rolling courses, plus a country club lounge for bragging about the great shots of the day. The club's swimming pool is popular during the day. It is also possible to join one of the nearby organized white water rafting expeditions on the Chattanooga River. This body of water is a designated "National Wild and Scenic River" and considered to be one of the most beautiful passages in the world (comparable to Colorado or Washington state). Cookouts take place at the end of the day. There are also organized bass and trout-fishing expeditions on Fairfield Lake. Blue Grass music and clogging performances take place in the evenings. Clogging is unique to the western mountains and involves a lot of stomping and square dancing maneuvers. In winter, there's a small private ski area where rental equipment is available, as are ski lessons. The townhouse condos, located in a landscaped hillside environment have living rooms with vaulted cathedral ceilings and a loft bedroom. The interior design is stylish with a variety of color combinations. The wing chairs and traditional furniture are befitting a country club resort. The Sunburst program for children, at $18 a day with lunch, is one of the best values you'll find anywhere. It's like a day camp for children with different activities planned each day."

5 **FONTANA VILLAGE RESORT**
Highway 28, Box 68, Fontana Dam, NC 28733, 800-849-2258
1BR $72, 2BR $90–$135, 3BR $180
Amenities: Lake, marina, fishing, boating, horseback riding, pool waterslide, restaurant, craft & art center, children's playground, mini-golf, tennis.

This resort has great potential but on our visit we were appalled by management's indifference to guests. A beautiful facility, this property is situated in a valley of the Blue Ridge, and the lake has a 31-mile shoreline. A great place for waterskiing and fishing as there are numerous private coves. For children, the swimming pool has dual waterslides. But, the accommodations reflect neglect. There are three styles of cottages and the pricing reflects the age of the units. Decor is drab and functional. Too bad, because with a little lift, this could be a great place. Certainly the price is right for all of the amenities that are available.

8+ **HIGH HAMPTON**
N.C. Hwy. 107 S., Cashiers, NC 28717, 800-334-2551
Amenities: Golf, pools, tennis, horseback riding, restaurant, gardens, children's playground, fishing, fitness trail, sailing.

The southern Appalachian heritage survives in the refined atmosphere of High Hampton. The resort is the former estate of Civil War General Wade Hampton, and imbues the proud self-reliant culture which has largely disappeared. It grows its own vegetables for dining room meals. The rustic central lodge has rough-hewn timbered walls and hoop-stitched rugs. The two- and three-bedroom vacation homes are along and near the golf course. These homes have spacious rooms with cathedral ceilings, fireplaces, large porches, and fully equipped kitchens. You can be on your own or you can have the option of taking the meal plan. In the summer, there are organized activities for children. The high point of the year comes at Thanksgiving when the resort celebrates a monumental four-day party; it's a time when many returning guests renew their friendships. All of the furniture at the resort is handcrafted. The condominiums are located away from the main lodge, and although new, they give off an all-natural "timeless" feeling. Stone fireplaces, wide plank wood floors, exposed beams and bentwood chairs are characteristics of the condos. The bathrooms are functional and as you can imagine, don't include whirlpools. This is the kind of place where you would want to curl up with a good book by the fire. The main charm of the resort is its forest and 2,000 acres of landscaped gardens. The resort features an 18-hole golf course, two pools, eight tennis courts and horseback-riding stable. You have the option of enjoying the simple life in the privacy of your condominium or joining the activities at the main lodge. The resort is closed during the winter.

6   HIGHLAND LAKE
P.O. Box 1026, Flat Rock, NC 28731
Amenities: Pool, tennis, canoes, fishing

Located between Hendersonville and Tryon in the Carolina hunt country, this resort offers a different slice of life. Promoting itself as the perfect place for a family reunion, you will feel like the guest of an extended family. Stay on the manor set on 180 acres. There are an abundance of country activities on site, the sort of fun adventures you haven't had since summer camp. Yet, you don't have to be a teenager to participate. Many wholesome adventures await you here with horseback trails and riding, streams with overhanging ropes in the trees where you can swing Tarzan style. Drop by the organic garden to pick, sniff, and nibble on berries or extraordinary tomatoes. This is where memorable salads and grilled veggies originate. For more sophisticated fun, there's a golf course, the Flat Rock Playhouse, and the Carl Sandburg home just across the street.

6   MAGGIE VALLEY RESORT
340 Country Club Road, Maggie Valley, NC 28751, 704-926-1616
1BR $70–120, 2BR $80–145
Amenities: Golf, tennis, clubhouse with pool and restaurant, conference center

Scenically beautiful, this country club resort community lacks the panache of many of its neighbors. If you are into golf, and can negotiate a great deal, then this can be a good value. But hospitality and the cleanliness one expects to find in a golf country club community, is sadly lacking here. Maybe it was a busy day, but it was alarming to see the pool area with all the leftover dirty towels early in the morning. The gardens are extensive, but need to be tended. Half a loaf is sometimes more discouraging than none at all. The golf course is the draw card and has been the site of the North Carolina Open Golf Tournament four times. The front nine is on the valley floor while the back nine rolls through the hills. The condo villas are large, but interior decor was selected for durability rather than aesthetic appeal. The restaurant has a great view and seems to be a convivial place after a day of golf. Maggie Valley receives mixed reviews.

6   MILL HOUSE LODGE
Box 309, Flat Rock, NC 28731, 704-693-6097
Amenities: Historic mill and grounds, restaurant, pond with beach, pool, tennis

Located just 3 miles south of Hendersonville, this is a country inn-cum-cottages. Known for 130 years as the Old Mill, the building was completely remodeled to create a charming inn surrounded by a cool oasis for swimming, canoeing, and fishing. The cottages have one, two, or three bedrooms and either a kitchen or kitchenette. All have fireplaces and the misty evening is fragrant with smoke, laurel and boxwood. For serious dining, the main lodge provides some of the best cuisine to be found in the area.

5   PEPPERTREE VACATION CLUB / GREAT SMOKIES HILTON
One Hilton Dr., Asheville, NC 28805
Amenities: Golf, restaurant, pool

This resort is a popular conference center that is situated on over 300 acres of rolling fairways, just minutes from downtown Asheville. The Hilton Hotel dominates the entrance to the property. Keep right on going, you'll want to stay at the condos in back. They are rounded ten-sided spacious structures. Unlike the hotel part, the condos are on the golf course facing away from the forest. The decor is contemporary, and these are the preferred units for executives attending conferences at the hotel. Alternatively, this is a good resort for golfers and families. Take advantage of room service or dine at the Hilton.

5   RICHMOND HILL INN VILLAS
87 Richmond Hill Drive, Asheville, NC 28806, 800-545-9238
Amenities: Restaurant

This is a local landmark as well as an inn-cum-cottages. Originally, the Queen Anne-style mansion was the home of a U.S. senator and ambassador.

After a million dollar renovation, the mansion is now on the Register of Historic Places. You can stay in the inn or the croquet cottages that surround the croquet court behind the inn. Here you can enjoy the mountain view from a rocking chair on the front porch of your cottage. Inside, you'll find a fireplace in the living room, fresh modern fabrics on contemporary furniture, and a four-poster bed in the bedroom.

7   WAYNESVILLE COUNTRY CLUB
Box 390, Waynesville, NC 28786, 800-627-6250
Amenities: 27 holes of golf, tennis, pool, restaurant,
conference center

Located in Maggie Valley Waynesville Country Club is in the heart of the Great Smokies and the Blue Ridge Mountains, just off Interstate 40. Originally developed in the 1920s by prominent Southern families looking to escape the hot summer sun, this development was carved out of a crested hillside where rushing streams and mountain forests provide a fragrant ambiance. The golf course was carefully crafted. It seems to be a series of green ribbons running through the mountains. In addition to the active pursuits of golf and tennis, this resort offers old-fashioned, unhurried hospitality. The country villas provide comfortable lodging in a very private setting directly on the golf course. Decorated in a crisp country style, without the usual number of knickknacks, these villas are a pleasant respite. The Senator and Governor Cottages are older and not as complete, yet the charm more than compensates. You'll find stone fireplaces and leather wing back chairs where you can relax at the end of a lengthy day. The villas are complete and you can cook to your heart's delight, but don't miss out on candlelight dinners in the tap room.

RENTAL RESOURCES
Appalachian Properties, 704-627-9859
Bit o' Country Rentals, 704-586-3450, Dillsboro
Brookstone Rentals, 704-743-5022, Sapphire Valley
Century 21 High Country, 704-926-0891, Maggie Valley
Cherokee Hills, 704-837-5853
Maggie Valley Accredited Reservations, 704-926-3786
Main Street Realty, 704-452-2227, Waynesville
Mountain Village Vacations, 704-743-2377, Cashiers
Old Mill Cottages, 704-524-5226, Franklin
Peppertree Resort Villas, 704-926-3811
Realty World Heritage, 704-926-0871, Maggie Valley
Town & Mountain Realty, 704-926-9101, Maggie Valley
Wolf Laurel Realty, 704-689-9777, Mars Hill

3. PINEHURST

This legendary "capital of golf" began in 1895 when a Boston millionaire acquired 5,800 acres of "pine barrens" to build a resort where guests could enjoy the mild climate and recuperative "southern airs." Shortly after the resort was opened, a local dairyman complained of a guest who was "striking a little white ball about" and hitting the dairyman's cattle. Suddenly, golf was conceived as an additional attraction for the resort's guests. A Scotsman was hired to design a golf course, and thus began not only a new career, but a golfing legend.

The Pinehurst Hotel and Country Club has five courses that begin and end at the main clubhouse. In addition, two other modern courses are nearby. The hotel/inn is exceptional for the number of courses it provides and the unique Scottish design of these courses. For over 75 years the hotel was called the Carolina Inn. However, the name has been changed within the past decade to reflect the name of the master resort community. Many people still refer to it as The Inn, so we refer to it as The Inn to avoid confusion.

In addition to The Inn property, the small village of Pinehurst has grown up over the years to become one of the most exclusive resort villages in the U.S. Today, the turn of the century village with homes from the '20s and '30s has been preserved as a historic district.

Eleven other golf courses and master golf resort communities are within 15 minutes of The Inn. They are not as celebrated, but most have a distinct style. The Pinehurst/Southern Pines area has been rated as one of the nation's most desirable retirement areas. North Carolina has surpassed Florida as the destination for active retirees to pursue healthy sports and activities. Therefore, most of the homes and condos in this land of golf courses are semiresidential.

Although golf is the reason to come, there are over 100 tennis courts in the area and horseback riding/polo are popular sports with a more limited following.

Air travellers will want to use the airport at Raleigh/Durham. This is a major international airport only 45 minutes from Pinehurst.

WHERE TO STAY

5 **FOXFIRE RESORT AND COUNTRY CLUB**
Hoffman Rd., P.O. Box 711, Pinehurst, NC, 919-295-5555
1BR $500/wk, 2BR $825/wk
Amenities: Golf, lake, pool, tennis, restaurant

Located just 15 minutes from Pinehurst, Foxfire offers a relaxed rustic environment for a golf holiday. The two-story condo buildings with flats and townhouses overlook a fairway on the 36-hole golf course, sheltered by groves of pine forest. All of the condos are within walking distance of the clubhouse. The resort offers more intimacy than some of its neighbors and is a popular choice for families (especially if one or two members are golf nuts). The social life centers around the clubhouse, its Golfer's Grill, the 19th hole and the 25 meter swimming pool (popular with children, but also given over to adult lap swimming for an hour a day). The condos are well-furnished with contemporary furniture. Unlike Pinehurst, which allows owners to personalize the decor, these condos are more standardized, so there are no surprises. All of them have fireplaces and screened porches. The porch allows one family member to escape from the company of other loved ones.

PINEHURST HOTEL AND COUNTRY CLUB
P.O. Box 4000, Pinehurst, NC 28374, 800-334-9560
1BR $425–635/wk, 2BR $850–1275/wk, 3BR $1275–1910/wk
Amenities: Golf, tennis, pools, hot tubs

Beginning with The Inn as its heart, accommodations in this community radiate out along the fairways with The Inn as the hub.

Dogwood Townhouses (7) Just off Dundee Road, Dogwood Townhouses may be the most private and spacious in the area. In a community where most of the condos are upper and lower-level apartments in a two-story building, these are the ones where you won't have a neighbor overhead or underfoot. Decorated in a contemporary style, these are within a three-minute walk of the village. This is best for adults as there is no pool or outside play area for children nearby.

Prince Manor (8) The best decorated condos in Pinehurst, the "A List," are in Prince Manor or Lakeview. The Prince Manor condos are located in Pinehurst Village, a stone's throw from The Inn. The setting is beautifully manicured. The condos are in a two-story building with contemporary furniture and modern peach and sea-foam colors. The screened porches make an extra room nine months of the year. It is convenient for dining and tee times.

Lakeview Condos (8+) The Lakeview Condos are another story. In a remote, private setting on the shores of Lake Pinehurst, these may be the most romantic because of the lake view. Since they are new, they may have the best decor in the area. Lakeview provides privacy in addition to the three pool/recreation centers for fun. The condos are only a five-minute walk down to the lake's beach club, restaurant, and marina.

St. Andrews Condominiums (8) St. Andrews Condominiums, located at the intersection of Lost Tree Road and Lake Forest, offer attractive, well-decorated condos across from another swimming center. It's an easy walk to the tennis center too.

Erin Hills Condos (6) The condos are adequate and some of the decor needs to be improved upon.

The Brae Burn Treehouses (5–6) The Brae Burn Treehouses are "mushroom-shaped" affairs where you walk up a flight of stairs to find your condo in the trees. Many of these are currently being redecorated, so expect to see improvements in the near future.

WOODLAKE COUNTRY CLUB
Lake Surf Blvd., Vass, NC 28394, 919-245-4031
Amenities: Golf, tennis, pool, lake

Woodlake, located only 20 minutes from Pinehurst, has one of the area's most challenging 18-hole golf courses. It surrounds Lake Surf (which is two miles long and one mile wide) and offers enchanting lake-hill vistas. Lake Surf takes its name from the original developer, who planned wave-making equipment for would-be surfers in North Carolina. Instead, it became a semi-residential master golf course development. Sailing, boating, and fishing are popular activities. Two groups of condominiums are available:

Cove Villas (7) These one and a-half-story villas overlook a scenic cove filled with mallows and Carolina cattails. The living rooms and loft bedrooms are spacious. Each condo includes a fireplace and a private patio overlooking the sound; they are comfortable for extended stays.

The Shore Villas (7) These villas are situated on the first fairway overlooking the lake. They feature spacious living rooms, balcony lofts, and cozy fireplaces. The clubhouse and its 19th-hole lounge for golf is the center of activity.

RENTAL RESOURCES
Highland Hills, 919-692-4434
Pinehurst Properties, 800-334-9553
The Pines, 919-281-3165
Whispering Pines Country Club, 919-949-3777

4. THE OUTER BANKS

These resorts are within easy reach of cities such as Raleigh, Fayetteville, Wilmington and Norfolk, Virginia. New Bern, at one time a colonial capital, is a charming southern city. Tryon Palace, home of the colonial governor during British rule, has been restored to its former grandeur in a manner similar to Williamsburg. It is not on the ocean and, in fact, is 30 minutes from the beach. The resorts here take advantage of their location on Pamlico Sound. The nearby town of Oriental is a sailor's paradise.

Steeped in history and legend, the Outer Banks was only recently discovered as a vacation destination. The Outer Banks run for 110 miles from the Virginia border south, until they break off into bits of islands like Ocracoke. The land is primarily sand, and the dunes shift a little each year.

One, Jockey Ridge, is over 15 stories high and is used as a jumping-off point for hang gliders.

Times have changed in Nag's Head since the natives hung lanterns around horses' heads to give the appearance to sailors that ships lay dead ahead. The area was the graveyard of the Atlantic, and plundering shipwrecks was a respected occupation. Today, the area is a major destination for travelers from Virginia or the metro Washington, D.C. area. Pamlico Sound is a major barrier between the Outer Banks and the population centers of North Carolina. Consequently, the Outer Banks area is more isolated than other coastal areas of North Carolina.

If you come, be advised that the population was sparse until the 1970s. You won't find a traditional southern or Carolina population. Instead, a different cultural heritage was created by pragmatists who follow, a code of rugged individualism. The local citizens developed these character traits in order to protect themselves from adversities of nature, such as high tides or dealing with land that was scarcely arable. Coastal Carolina is a quiet, comfortable place for family vacationers. There are over 200 condominium developments in this area and 1600 vacation homes available for rent. We have given you a representative overview—good, bad, and indifferent. Most accommodations in this area are very low key. Barrier Island is different with all of its activity and that's because it's a timeshare with on-site management. For the most part, vacationers come to the Outer Banks because of their friends, other family members, and to have a few weeks away in a "home-away-from-home" environment. There aren't a lot of sights to see, but there are unlimited sporting activities, most of which are associated with the sea.

Located only a couple of hours south of Norfolk airport, the preferred access to this vacation destination is through Virginia. Do not fly to Raleigh. It is a much longer trip due to Pamlico Sound and you'll have to take a ferry. Once there, you'll never forget the endless stretch of sand or the gentle culture with its strong Elizabethan heritage.

WHERE TO STAY

8 BARRIER ISLAND STATION
S.R. 1200, Duck, NC 27949, 800-395-2525
Amenities: Beach, tennis, indoor and outdoor pool, spa, restaurant

Pull out all the bells and whistles. Barrier Island Station, located in Duck, has every "extra" you could want. It caters predominantly to Yuppies from Washington, D.C., and is the only Outer Banks resort with "flash." Two pools, a health spa, an oceanfront snack bar, and restaurant are available. The resort development covers 26 acres, including the houses. The three-story condo buildings are unusual, characterized by outdoor wooden stairwells, steeply gabled roofs, and three-sided bay windows. A natural wooden plank wall surrounds a fireplace that has a huge plate glass window on both sides. Indirect track lighting accents the stylish California contemporary decor with glass-top tables, Chinese lamps, and decorator accessories. A whirlpool is located in the master bath.

Special features include a large outdoor pool, tennis courts, and children's playground. In addition, you can enjoy the huge greenhouse that encloses the indoor pool, hot tub, steamroom, and sauna. Wooden walkways pass through sea oats and barrier dunes to the beach, where an intriguing gazebo awaits. There is nothing else like this on the Carolina coast.

5 DUNES SOUTH
Mile Post 18, Nag's Head, NC 27959, 919-261-7230
Amenities: Beach, pool

If you can look beyond the superficial, these duplex units are large and have ocean views. The furniture is boxy and clunky.

6 OCEAN VILLAS I AND II
Mile Post 16 1/4, Nag's Head, NC 27959, 919-441-4090
Amenities: Beach, pool, hot tub

Ocean Villas is composed of two sections: Ocean Villas I, a series of small beach bungalows running between the ocean and the highway and Ocean Villas II, (two sizable three-story buildings with well-decorated apartments, private patios, and ocean views). The pool area overlooks the beach and ocean and a whirlpool is located in the gazebo. The condos in Ocean Villas II are cheerfully decorated with contemporary decor.

7 THE QUAY
Mile Post 14 1/2, Route 158, Nag's Head, NC 27959
Amenities: Beach, pool, tennis

Luxury oceanfront townhouses. The Quay has over 1,500-square feet of living area plus spacious decks and a carport on the ground floor. Each condo has been tastefully decorated with casual, contemporary furniture. The fireplace is the centerpiece of each living room.

7 SEA RANCH II
P.O. Box 325, Kill Devil Hills, NC 27948, 919-441-4445
Amenities: Beach, indoor pool, restaurant, tennis

Sea Ranch II is one of the largest condo/hotel complexes in the area. The two-bedroom suites are better decorated than most of the resorts in this area. The furniture is traditional and the fabrics are red and black. This resort is one of the most professionally managed properties on the Outer Banks. Service is the key: the employees cater to all of your expectations. The indoor pool in the greenhouse is a pleasure. The full-service health club will help you develop a cardiovascular training program during your vacation. A posh New York-style restaurant features an ocean view and at night, a bar becomes a nightclub.

8+ SEA SCAPE
P.O. Box 276, Kitty Hawk, NC 27949
Amenities: Golf, indoor and outdoor pools, tennis, snack bar

Sea Scape is one of our favorite resorts on the Outer Banks. It is located on a golf course and greens fees are included in the cost of a condo rental. The condo flats are located in cedar-shingled two-story buildings with a New England weathered look. Half of the buildings are clustered around the pool and recreation complex. The interiors are just a little on the small side, and the decor dates from nine years ago when the condos were built. You'll find plank wood walls, laminated wood furniture, natural cotton and wool fabric, and an overhead ceiling fan to catch the brush of summer breezes. Extra touches include a whirlpool in the master bath and steam bath/shower in the second bathroom. Each condo has two televisions and a VTP. The recreation center provides two pools and a hot tub. Two tennis courts and a "putt-putt" putting green complete the picture. It is located only a block from the beach.

THE VILLAGE AT NAG'S HEAD
Milepost 15, Route 158 By-Pass, Nag's Head, NC 27959,
800-548-9688

Most of the condos on the Outer Banks are beach oriented, but this is the major exception. The Village at Nag's Head is a master golf course development with 12 separate condo developments. Most are on the golf course; a few are on the beach. There are two clubhouses: Nag's Head Golf Links Clubhouse, and the Village Beach and Tennis Club. The golf course has been designed around the dunes in the "true Scottish tradition." This is the sort of first-class development that the Outer Banks has needed for many years. We have reviewed a few of the condo developments within this master resort.

Heron Cove (8) A modern four-story concrete structure, Heron Cove is on the beach just across the street from the golf course. These new condos are crisp, efficiently designed and handsomely decorated. For those who want to be in a solid mid-rise building and also be part of the Village, this is your choice next door to the Village Beach and Tennis Club.

Marsh Links (8) A golfer's delight, Marsh Links has individual two-story villas grouped in a cluster along the golf course that are contemporary in design. The living room has sliding glass windows in the gable. Guest privileges at the Village Beach Club are included.

The Ridges (8) A golfer's choice. Located on the 11th fairway of The Links Golf Club, it's only a short walk over to the clubhouse. They have spacious loft units and living rooms with cathedral ceilings and superior furniture. Not on the beach, the owners have tended to dress these up more. Each unit is a separate detached villa with a large screened porch and deck overlooking the golf course and the sound in the distance. Guest privileges at The Village Beach and Tennis Club are included.

Sea Pointe (8) Located right on the beach, but slightly recessed behind an area of dunes and sea oats, these duplex townhouses offer lots of space for a family on vacation. At first glance they resemble New England cottages with the dormer windows and gabled roofs. Inside, you'll find a spacious living room (with a fireplace and wet bar), a full kitchen and a whirlpool in the master bath.

7   THE VILLAS OF ROANOKE SOUND
Milepost 11, Route 158, Nag's Head, NC 27959
Amenities: Pool, clubhouse

Located on Roanoke Sound, just behind Jockey Ridge National Sanddune, these offer comfortable accommodations. The beach is a five-minute walk away. Inside, you'll find superior contemporary decor, not the usual "island-style" rattan furniture prevalent here at the beach. These villas have their own clubhouse with a large swimming pool.

RENTAL RESOURCES
Bodie Island Beach Club, 919-441-2558
Cape Hatteras Beach Club, 919-995-4115
Cove Realty, 800-635-7007
Dolphin Real Estate, 919-986-2241, Hatteras
Duck's Real Estate, 919-261-4614
Eighteen South, 919-261-4646
Golden Strand, 919-261-7808
Hatteras Cabanas, 919-986-2562
King's Grant Realty, 919-441-5981, 800-548-2033 Nag's Head
Kitty Dunes Rentals, 800-334-DUNE
Kitty Hawk Rentals, 919-441-7166
Nag's Head Realty, 919-441-2134, 800-222-1531
Ocean Pines, 919-261-4181
Outer Banks Beach Club, 919-441-6321
Outer Banks Ltd., 919-441-5000
Outer Banks Resort Rentals, 919-441-2134, Nag's Head
Re/Max Island Realty, 919-453-8700
Resort Realty, 919-261-8383, 800-458-3830, Kitty Hawk
Seaside Realty, 800-395-2525
Sea Scape Beach & Gulf Villas, 919-261-3881

Southern Shores Realty, 919-261-2111, 800-334-1000
Sun Coast Company, 919-261-4171, 800-933-4800
Sun Realty, 800-334-4745, Kill Devil Hills
Twiddy & Co., 919-261-3521, Duck
Village Realty, 919-480-2224, 800-548-9688, Nag's Head
The Villages at Ocean Hill, 919-453-8866
The Young People, 919-334-6436, 800-334-6436
Windjammer, 919-441-4811
Wright Property Management, 919-261-2186

5. SOUTHERN BEACHES

This is a large area of the coast stretching from Moorehead City south to South Carolina's border and Myrtle Beach. Moorhead City is a quiet fishing port but the beaches from Ocean Isle to Atlantic Beach have dozens of new condos and pleasant, spacious beach cottages available for rent. Prices here are the lowest for any region along the Atlantic Seaboard and a two-bedroom vacation home—not just a condo—really will rent for $550 a week.

Heading farther south, the beach areas around Wilmington, Topsail, and Wrightsville Beach, have boomed in popularity with the opening of the new highway connecting Wilmington to the rest of the interstate system. This sleepy port has been growing at a pace unprecedented since before the Civil War. You'll find Topsail to be slightly more upscale while Wrightsville, because it's only 30 minutes from the city of Wilmington, has become more residential and less vacation oriented.

The real boom towns are Sunset Beach and Ocean Isle just over the state line from South Carolina's Myrtle Beach. This area of Brunswick County has seen the development of a dozen new golf courses, with vacation homes and condos, and 40 new condo developments. You'll find that these communities have a quiet "boomtown" atmosphere. They should, after all, this is one of the healthiest real estate markets in the U.S., and if you are thinking of buying a beach home along the Atlantic Coast, this may be the best buying opportunity of 1993.

With so many properties, we have not focused on all the resorts in the area. Instead, we have provided you with extensive lists of rental agents. Once you have picked an area, ask the rental agents to send you their catalogues. They are huge.

Air transportation to the area is best through either Wilmington or Myrtle Beach. USAir has numerous flights to Myrtle Beach and a host of bargain-priced airfares.

8+ BALD HEAD ISLAND
Ferry Dock — Indian Plantation Marina, 704 E. Moore St.,
Southport, NC 28461, 800-234-1666; Homes $220–550
Amenities: Pools, restaurant, grocery store, golf, tennis

Bald Head Island is a special place isolated from the mainland by the sea and salt marshes. It's located at the southern tip of North Carolina's barrier islands along the Atlantic Coast. Development has only taken place in the past few years, at a time when we became conscious of the importance and natural beauty of the wetlands. Accessible only by boat, Bald Head Island is a step back in time. Once on the island, transportation is either by bicycle or electric cart. Cars are not allowed on Bald Head Island. The golf course has been designed around a forest and marsh. You'll find a swimming pool, clubhouse, restaurant, and grocery store. The two and one-half-story wooden condos have gabled roofs, loft bedrooms, and cathedral ceilings. The brand new decor is casual, contemporary, and the locations provide for nice views. Remember, they're not making more islands, and this one has been carefully developed for travellers in the next century.

BEACH CONNECTION
c/o Margaret Rudd Realty
1023 N. Howe St., Southport, NC 28461, 919-278-6523

Serving Long Beach, Yaupon, and the Oak Island-Southport area, this rental agency has a "lock" on the inventory. Years of customer satisfaction and service to the owners has paid off. Offering over 200 vacations homes plus a large number of the condos at Oak Island Beach Villas, you'll find these to be value priced for a vacation at the beach. A one-bedroom condo generally rents for $300 to $475 a week, a two-bedroom will go as low as $265 to a high of $475 for a week in the summer, and a three-bedroom goes for $335 to $550 for a week. Vacation homes are priced between $225 and $1400 for a week. Prices in the $650 range are a ballpark median for summertime.

BRICK LANDING PLANTATION
Route 2, Box 210, Ocean Isle Beach, NC 28459, 800-438-3006
1BR $120–220, 2BR $139–250
Amenities: Golf, tennis, pools, restaurant

Built on the site of a landing used for the unloading of bricks in the 17th Century, Brick Landing is surrounded by water. A 20-foot bluff overlooks the intracoastal waterway, creeks, and inlets. Three separate condo developments at "The Brick" include Southern Oak Villas, Mariners Wacche, and Windsong Plantation.

Southern Oaks Villas (8) Southern Oaks Villas are three-story condominium townhouses overlooking a fairway. They are brand new and beautifully furnished with stylish and contemporary decor. You'll discover blond woods and rich, navy blue Williamsburg-style floral patterned fabrics. All of the villas feature a fireplace and whirlpool. The golf club is the social center, providing pools and 19th-hole lounge. Tennis is also available, but "The Brick" was voted by *Golf Digest* as one of the Top 50 courses in the U.S. As you can imagine, the resort is predominantly populated by golfers.

Mariner's Wacche Condos (6) These condos are situated in three-story buildings on a bluff overlooking the golf courses and the intracoastal waterway. The views of the Atlantic Ocean are spectacular. Each unit includes a screened porch balcony that doubles as an extra room during the winter months. A private pool is available, and a whirlpool is located in the master bath.

Fair Winds Townhomes (7) Fair Winds Townhomes are generally semi-residential. They are spacious units, but they're not as popular as the other condo clusters. Brick Landing guests have use of a beach house located on the Ocean Isle beach.

5   CAROLINA SHORES RESORT
Route 7, Box 342, Calabash, NC 28459, 919-579-7001
Amenities: Pool, tennis, hot tub

The condos at Carolina Shores Resort are an economy choice. Located across from the entrance to the Marsh Harbor Golf Course, they overlook the Carolina Shores Golf Club. The modular condominiums are three-stories high with smallish units, screened porches, basic furnishings, and full kitchen.

7   FAIRFIELD HARBOUR
750 Broad Creek Rd., New Bern, NC 28560, 919-638-8011
Amenities: Golf, marina, restaurant, tennis, pools

This resort differs from other North Carolina coastal resorts in that it is not on the ocean; it is on the sound. The surf of the ocean is a good hour away. Fairfield did well in choosing this site because of its location on Pamlico Sound. This is an area favored by yachtsmen. The Labor Day Michelob Cup Sailing Regatta from Oriental to New Bern is the premier sailing event in North Carolina with over 150 yachts racing. The harbor and marina at this resort are picturesque in summer. The resort has its own private yacht which is available for day charters. In addition to sailing, all sorts of water sports (such as fishing, water-skiing, and diving) are available. Another feature of this resort is the 18-hole golf course. With both the marine and golfing activity, this resort offers an exceptional combination of community and recreational activities. The condos are among the most stylish in this part of North Carolina. This is a national destination resort attracting vacationers from all over the U.S. The condos are wooden structures located near the marina; residential retirement homes are located on the golf course. Inside the condos, generally, you'll find casual, contemporary interiors with soft aqua or green colors. A wing back chair in the living room distinguishes the decor, reminding you that you are in colonial North Carolina. Activities at the resort center around the three swimming pools, 11 tennis courts, two golf courses, two marinas, horseback riding, boating, fishing, miniature golf, and the children's playground. The country club offers some of the finest dining in the area.

One exceptional activity available to all guests with imagination is the "Who-dun-it" murder mysteries offered weekly. One particular week's adventure involved solving a "murder" based on clues, one of which was spelled out at the Bingo party.

6+ THE PLANTATION AT OYSTER BAY
(The Colony Condominiums)
900 Shoreline Dr., Sunset Beach, NC 28459, 800-222-1524
1BR $79–129, 2BR $99–159
Amenities: Golf, tennis, pool

The Plantation at Oyster Bay is located in Sunset Beach just over the state line from Myrtle Beach S.C. It is actually part of the Sea Trail master golf development. The Oyster Bay course has a much-photographed," island" putting green on the 5th hole. The main part of Sea Trail Plantation is located about a quarter of a mile north. The only condos developed so far are located at The Colony at Oyster Bay. These three-story condos overlook the first and second fairways at Oyster Bay. The top units have lofts, while others feature open air balconies and bay window screened porches. These condos are exceptionally well decorated for this area. A kitchen, living room, and breakfast bar are included for some units. A designer look similar to what you may have seen in *House Beautiful* has been created in some. A nearby golf clubhouse (with a pool and restaurant) and the Plantation Tennis Center (providing two courts) provide recreational activities.

PLEASURE ISLAND
Highway 421, Carolina Beach, NC 28428

Pleasure Island is the name given to this strip of Carolina Beach which contains numerous condos, second homes, and motels. Offering a wide sandy beach, it attracts vacationers from the Carolinas. Some of the condos available are:

Ocean Dunes (6) At the far end of the beach by Ft. Fisher, this has a great location for those who love nature and tranquility. New two-story townhouse condos, each one faces the beach. All have pleasant interior decor plus a clubhouse, tennis court, indoor pool, and outdoor pool.

Pelican Watch (5) The largest structure on Pleasure Island, it is 12-stories high. Condos are either two or three bedrooms with casual decor and an indoor and outdoor pool.

Sea Colony (4) This three-story building is on the beach and has its own pool.

Sands IV and Sands V (4) Some of the most popular beachfront condos on Pleasure Island, the Sands have spacious units that are good for families.

7   **ST. REGIS RESORT**
        Box 4000, North Topsail Shores, Snead's Ferry, NC 28460,
        919-328-0778, 800-682-4882; 1BR $39–119
        Amenities: Beach, pool, exercise room, restaurant, conference center

St. Regis is located on the beach at North Topsail and is convenient to the historic port of Wilmington. It has been carefully developed with a concern for the area's ecology. The condos, located in a seven-story concrete building, are new and tastefully decorated with a rich ambiance that has been created by the use of pearl grey and dusky rose-colored fabrics and dark wood furniture. St. Regis prides itself on its conference center designed for executive gatherings and seminars. The resort is geared towards the executives who make use of the center, but families will enjoy the resort's amenities. A weight room with exercise equipment, an outdoor pool, hot tub, saunas, and steam bath are provided. A gazebo is located at the beach.

5   **SANDS VILLA RESORT**
        Ft. Macon Rd., P.O. Box 1140 A.D., Atlantic Beach, NC 28512,
        919-247-2636
        Amenities: Beach, indoor and outdoor pools, tennis

Sands Villa Resort is a six-story concrete condo building located on the beach. The beach is wide, white, and ideal for walking. The 90 condos in this three-story wooden-shingle structure are spacious and newly decorated. The furniture is more luxurious than you would expect to find in Atlantic Beach condos. They are decorated in soft pinks and blues with plenty of mirrors and silk flowers. A private whirlpool is included in the master bath. Each condo overlooks the lawn and pool. This resort is easily the best choice in Atlantic Beach.

6+   **SEA TRAIL PLANTATION**
        301 Clubhouse Rd., Sunset Beach, NC 28459, 919-579-8949
        1BR $68, 2BR $122, 3BR $162
        Amenities: Golf, tennis, pool, exercise room, restaurant

Sea Trail Plantation offers 54 holes of challenging golf. It is one of the premier golf resorts of the Carolina Coast and features courses created by three designers. Sea Trail covers over 1,500 acres of low country wetlands which have been transformed into a full resort atmosphere. It is surrounded by hardwood forests, pines, lagoons and a manmade lake. The master resort technically includes another 500 acres down the street at The Plantation at Oyster Bay, but since it is a quarter-mile away and has its own identifiable character, Oyster Bay has its own separate review. The Club Villa town-houses are located on the first and eighth fairways. Low Country cottages elevated on stilts, can be rented as large three-bedroom condos or locked off into separate units. Each cottage has two screened porches and the kitchen is separated from the living room by a breakfast bar. When the cottages are "locked off," the one-bedroom unit has only a small kitchenette. The Clubhouse features a pool, an exercise room, tennis courts, restaurant and, of course, a 19th hole for reliving the day's golf stories.

 ### SUN-SURF REALTY
3103 Emerald Drive, Emerald Isle, NC 28594, 800-553-SURF

One of the largest real estate agencies on the North Carolina Coast, this rental agency handles over 200 vacation homes in this area plus another 150 condominiums. The vacation homes rent for prices ranging from $600 to $1700 per week and are generally simple beach cottages. Many are on stilts because of high surf in the winter. Those with ambulatory problems should check first for accessibility. Condominiums are less expensive, generally renting for $350 to $650 per week depending upon the size.

 ### WILLIAMSON REALTY
119 Causeway Rd, Ocean Isle Beach, NC 28469, 919-579-2373

This real estate company has over 250 condo and villa properties available for rental in the Ocean Isle area. Rentals are on a weekly basis and a one-bedroom condo will go for $375 to $525 a week, a two-bedroom for $575 to $975, and a three-bedroom for $725 to $1100. Houses begin around $600 and quickly go up (in high season) to a maximum of $3,275 per week. As you know, prices can be negotiable, so check with other rental agencies in the area.

1   WINDS OF OCEAN ISLE
310 E. First St., Ocean Isle Beach, NC 28459, 919-579-6275
Amenities: Beach, pool, hot tub

Advertising itself as "a unique beach resort" with a pair of beat-up sneakers as the resort's trademark can be a risky promotion. Some would find humor, but actually the symbolism is literal. The resort is dirty and needs an extensive overhaul. The beachside location, the landscaping, and the cathedral ceilings of the upper-floor loft units cannot redeem the overriding decay here. Decor includes oversized Mexican flowers and dated rattan empress chairs. It may have been groovy in the '70s, but time has passed this one by. So should you.

RENTAL RESOURCES

Alan Holden Realty, 919-842-6061, Holden Beach
A Place at the Beach III, 919-247-2636
Bald Head Island, 800-443-6305
The Beach Connection, 919-278-6523
Belvedere Plantation, 919-270-2761
BLF Associates Property Management, 919-458-4844, Carolina Beach
Bogue Banks Country Club, 919-726-1034
Bowser Calabash Properties, 919-579-7001
Bryant Real Estate, 800-322-3764, Wrightsville Beach
Carolina Beach Realty, 919,-458-8211, Carolina Beach
Carolina Golf & Beach Resorts, 919-579-7181, 800-843-6044, Ocean Isle
Century 21 Action, 800-255-2233, Topsail Beach
Coastal Concepts, 919-328-1750, 800-726-8642, Surf City
Cooke Realty, 919-579-3535, Ocean Isle
Emerald Isle Realty, 919-354-3315
Hobbs Realty, 919-842-2002, Holden Beach
Intracostal Realty, 919-256-3780, 800-346-2463, Wrightsville Beach
Kennedy Company, 919-328-0335, Snead's Ferry in Topsail
Margaret Rudd, 919-457-5258, Southeast coast
Pebble Beach Resort, 919-270-2761
Peppertree Atlantic Beach, 800-334-8427, Atlantic Beach
Point Emerald, 800-682-3423
Rains Realty & Rentals, 800-445-2055, Atlantic Beach
Realty World-Surf City, 919-328-5011, Topsail Island
Sand Dollar Realty, 919-579-7038, Ocean Isle
The Sands, 800-682-4985
Shell Island Resort, 919-256-5050, Wrightsville Beach
Sloane Realty, 919-579-6217, Ocean Isle
Spectrum Real Estate, 800-682-3423, Emerald Isle
Sunset Vacations, 919-579-9000, 800-331-6428
Surf Condos, 919-256-2275, Topsail Beach
Topsail Dunes, 919-328-0639
Topsail Realty, 919-328-2301
Tucker Brothers, 919-458-8211, Carolina Beach
United Beach Vacations, 919-458-9073, Carolina Beach
The Whaler, 919-247-4169
Winds Oceanfront Resort, 919-579-6275, Ocean Isle

OREGON

Oregon offers a surprisingly diverse range of vacation experiences. The area around Mt. Hood/Columbia River Gorge is one of the few spots in the world where you can ski in the morning and windsurf in the afternoon. Contrary to popular myth, the rain falls only on the western portion of the state. The Cascade Mountains break the storms and the eastern portion of the state is semi-arid. Bend, located on the eastern slope of the Cascades, enjoys bright sunny weather yet the area is lush because of water runoff from the Cascades. Throughout the state, temperatures rarely drop below 25 degrees nor do they rise above 80 degrees. We have split Oregon according to the two major regions of resort destinations. The first part concerns the resort communities along the Pacific Coast from Seaside to Newport. The second involves the mountain resort communities around Bend/Mt. Batchelor and Mt. Hood.

1. OREGON'S COAST

Oregon enjoys miles of broad beaches that are perfect for beachcombing and hunting for driftwood. Forested capes rise hundreds of feet above the Pacific Ocean surf. Wave-sculpted offshore rocks invite sightseeing and photography. Tidal pools expose many species of small delicate creatures. Busy bay fronts serve as ports for picturesque fleets of fishing boats and yachts. These are the images of the Oregon Coast.

Moving from north to south with a coastal drive beginning at Seaside, you'll find a beachfront promenade dating from the '30s. Seaside is a popular resort destination for families from Portland and the Willamette Valley because of the golf, beachfront horseback riding, and amusement centers.

Cannon Beach enjoys an artistic, easy going environment. This small, quaint village has three stores selling kites, and on any day you'll see kites soaring above the dunes. The town is filled with European-style boutiques and craft shops, yet only a few feet away, the wide sandy beach seems endless and the Pacific mysterious. Haystack Rock is a 232-foot monolith jutting out from the ocean. Tillamook County is famous for its cheese, rugged coastline with cliffs and vistas, and again, for the wide beach at Rockaway. This is a limited growth area that offers a respite from the fast-paced 20th Century.

Lincoln City and Gleneden Beach offer a 23-mile strip of over 50 ocean-front condo developments and motels. Growing increasingly popular with the semiretired because of the high quality of life and relatively low cost, Lincoln City now offers three golf courses and an abundance of not-so-strenuous activities such as crabbing on the beach.

Newport is a nautical community like its sister city, Newport, Rhode Island. This is a picturesque community that surrounds Yaquina Bay where you'll see the fishing fleet bobbing in the harbor. There are several

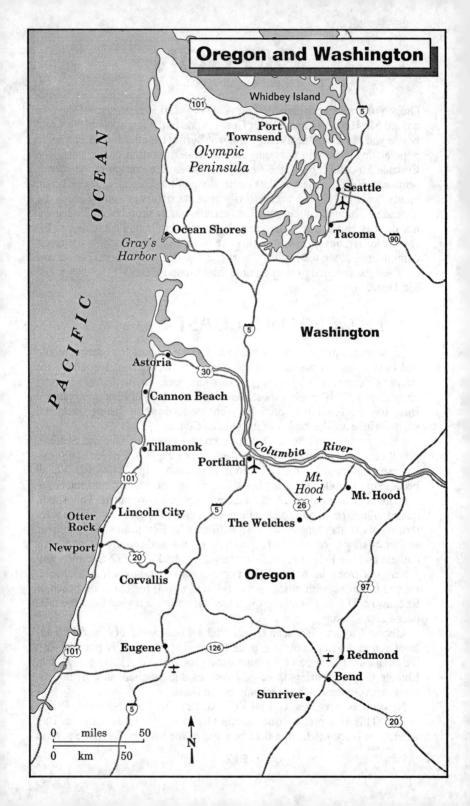

new attractions here, such as the aquarium (like Undersea Gardens), the Mark Hatfield Marine Science Center, and an exhibition of American Indian artifacts.

Air transportation is through Portland. Then it's a drive through the spectacular Cascade Mountains to the beach resort of your choice. There are several alternate routes through the mountains and, although the distances look short, driving can be slow. Check with the Oregon visitors bureau before setting out on trips through the mountains over to the shore.

WHERE TO STAY

6+ EMBARCADERO
1000 S.E. Bay Blvd., Newport, OR 97365, 503-265-8521
Amenities: Indoor pool, hot tub, sauna

Embarcadero is pretty to look at. It is located at the end of the harbor and takes advantage of its nautical setting. The Embarcadero buildings hug the shoreline and encircle the marina on Yaquina Bay, so each unit has a harbor or ocean view. Inside the condos, you'll be impressed by the high ceilings and the abundance of glass, which provides for great views. Every condo is well decorated with quality, contemporary furniture, an individual fireplace, and a private sundeck overlooking the harbor. The Embarcadero has a popular restaurant and cocktail lounge. A recreation center with an indoor swimming pool, hot tub and sauna is available. The children's playground, the special fish cleaning station and the crab cooker are special touches. Embarcadero provides a nice choice.

6 GEARHART BY THE SEA
10th & Marion, Gearhart, OR 97138, 503-738-8331
Amenities: Beach, golf, tennis, indoor pool, hot tub, restaurant

Gearhart by the Sea is the largest condo complex in Seaside. It offers an ideal setting for beach lovers and golfers. The 350 condos are located in the two-story wings or the luxurious six-story high-rise. The condos vary in size and floor plan, but each has a spacious living room with a private fireplace, a kitchen and one or two bedrooms. Interior decor varies from "early attic" to professionally designed. Generally, you can expect to find contemporary furnishings with soft pinks and blues, as well as many amenities to give each condo personalized appeal. The units in the new Gearhart House high-rise building are superior to those in the older wooden structures, called Pacific View and Pacific Palisades. There is a heated indoor swimming pool and hot tub. The beach is right outside your door and a golf pro shop is part of the resort.

8 THE INN AT OTTER CREST

P.O. Box 50, Otter Rock, OR 97369, 503-765-2111
Amenities: Beach, tennis, pool, restaurant

Otter Crest is a jewel on the Oregon coast. It is on a compact peninsula about 400 feet below the Pacific Coast highway. Take a meandering trail down to the inn where you'll find a unique, relaxed atmosphere. The inn itself, is a cluster of three-story buildings on several levels, notched into the rocky peninsula. At night, you can lie in bed and listen to the surf pounding below. The condos are attractive, comfortably furnished in colors of the forest and have a well-placed fireplace so you can lie by the fire and watch those glorious Pacific sunsets. There's a putting green perched on a most picturesque cliff where you'll feel as though you are on top of the world. Also, there is an outdoor heated swimming pool next to the path that leads to Otter Crest's private beach. When you stay here, you won't want to go back up the hill to civilization.

7 THE INN AT SPANISH HEAD

4009 S. Highway 101, Lincoln City, OR 93767, 503-996-2161
Amenities: Beach, pool, restaurant

A fabulous oceanside resort, the Inn doesn't look like much from the highway—just a couple of Spanish tiled two-story buildings. Once inside, however, you'll be impressed by the size and scope of this resort. It is built along the side of a cliff and cascades 10 stories down to the beach. The 146 condos are constructed of modern solid concrete. Each has an ocean view, so everyone can enjoy the surf. In the Pacific Northwest it seems unusual to find Spanish-style architecture, but the theme is carried through (including the condo interiors, which have that heavy Spanish carved wood furniture). A few units are hotel rooms, but the majority are one or two-bedroom condos with full kitchens. La Plaza restaurant and cocktail lounge are popular for dinner and dancing.

9 RIVER PLACE ALEXIS HOTEL

1510 S.W. Harbor Way, Portland, OR 97201, 503-228-3233
Amenities: Pool, restaurant

This resort is a real surprise. Located in downtown Portland on a narrow strip of land running along the Willamette, it is composed of a pink fantasy village of three- and four-story condos. This is Yuppie Heaven. Most of River Place Alexis is a hotel with defined hotel rooms or suites, but for a truly elegant stay, the residential condos offer every luxury you could want. They are unique and sophisticated. The lobby has elegant floral arrangements and light classical music in the background. The condos are designer decorated with pastel pinks and yellows and possess an abundance of accessories. Six of the units have private wood burning fireplaces and some have a private whirlpool. This is a choice for couples seeking a romantic stay in one of North America's most liveable cities or for families who want the space.

7   SURFVIEW
1400 S. Hemlock, Cannon Beach, OR 97110, 503-436-1566
Amenities: Indoor pool, hot tub, restaurant

If you want to be close to Portland and enjoy a week at the beach in a cute town where the main occupation seems to be flying kites, then Surfview is for you. This is a select choice because of setting, design, and atmosphere—nothing fancy or elaborate, just solid comfort and value. Surfview occupies an enviable spot on a dune overlooking both the widest white beach in Oregon and mysterious Haystack Rock jutting up from the ocean, just offshore. This cluster of three-story buildings was designed so most units have balconies and ocean views. Each condo has a comfortable living room and wood-burning fireplace. Some units have a private whirlpool large enough for two. An indoor swimming pool, hot tub, cocktail lounge, and Cade's restaurant are all on-site. Surfview is about four blocks south of the main part of Cannon Beach, so you have easy access to the town without having to endure the traffic congestion caused by weekenders from Portland.

2. OREGON'S MOUNTAINS

This area provides one of the best travel surprises in the U.S. No matter what you read, you won't be prepared for the constant assault on your senses by the area's natural beauty. And then you'll ask, why didn't someone tell me about this before! The Cascade Mountains form a series of peaks in this area dotted with over 100 lakes and 235 miles of streams. You'll be impressed by the dense fragrant forest. And when the sun shines, you'll be dazzled by the light. The mountain chain is broken by the deep chasm of the Columbia River, separating Washington from Oregon. At one spot, the river becomes so wide that it is actually broader than most lakes. This is called the Columbia River Gorge. Because of the mountain wind currents and their effect on the water, this is one of the most popular centers for windsurfing in North America.

Mt. Hood and the Columbia River Gorge are geologic wonders within 30 miles of each other. The portion of the river gorge between Multnomah Falls and the Dalles has been designated by the U.S. Congress as a national scenic area. This 24-mile scenic route passes waterfall-draped, forested cliffs. The Dalles was founded in 1840 and marked the western terminus of the Oregon Trail. Once a shipping center, the harbor is now filled with windsurfers who cruise the gorge toward Hood River.

Travelers by air have two choices. Bend has a regional airport with commuter flights from Seattle, Portland, and San Francisco. Or it may be easier to fly to Portland, rent a car, and drive three hours past scenic Mt. Hood and the dusty plains of central Oregon.

WHERE TO STAY

10 BLACK BUTTE RANCH
P.O. Box 8000, Black Butte Ranch, OR 97759, 800-452-7455
Amenities: Golf, tennis, pools, horseback riding

There is no other resort quite like Black Butte. To begin with, it's a self-contained resort community of more than 900 condos and vacation homes just outside Bend, Oregon. The climate is perfect if you like cool, dry weather, and Bend has more than 250 days of sunshine a year. Black Butte Ranch is situated in a meadowlands area with forest trails on the property. The lodge has been designed to make the most of the magnificent view of Mt. Batchelor. The condos are generally two-story townhouses that have been constructed in groups of 12 or 16 units at various spots on the property. The elite from Portland and the Willamette Valley come to play at this resort, so accordingly, many of the condos have an impressive decor. Some are "Northwoods" in style, others are "High Tech." The Big Meadow restaurant in the main lodge, is strikingly handsome and has one of the best views of the Cascade Mountains to be found anywhere. In addition to the requisite horseback riding stables, the ranch has two 18-hole golf courses, 18 tennis courts, four heated swimming pools, and rental canoes. Don't miss the "Posse Dinner Ride"—it's an unforgettable cookout.

7   DESCHUTES RIVER RANCH
20210 Swalley Rd., Bend, OR 97701, 503-382-7240
Amenities: Pool, skiing, horseback riding

Deschutes River Ranch is located on a bluff overlooking the Deschutes River. The condos are large three-bedroom individual houses offering rural privacy in the Bend area. The interior decor is a tasteful Pacific Northwest style with lots of space. Staying here will give you a taste of central Oregon ranch life because this is an actual working ranch (110 acres set aside for growing crops). Guests can take part in ranch activities and chores if they so desire. There are many trails for horseback riding and hiking. Deschutes River Ranch is fun for all, but especially for a family vacation because of the abundance of special activities for children.

7   THE INN AT THE MOUNTAIN
68010 E. Fairway Ave., Welches, OR 97067, 503-622-3101
Amenities: Golf, tennis, pools, horseback riding, restaurant

The Inn at the Mountain was formerly known for years as Rippling River, and today many still refer to it as Rippling River. It is located in the mountains about 23 miles south of the Columbia River and close to Mt. Hood ski areas. It is an exceptional resort. Built on pine-covered slopes, the spacious condos have been designed to have a rustic look with beamed ceilings and large stone fireplaces. Lots of glass brings views of the forest and the mountainside. This is what you would hope to find for a vacation home in Oregon. It covers over 60 acres. You can fish in the streams for steelhead trout in summer and cross-country ski in the winter. A shuttle bus travels to the nearby ski lifts of Mt. Hood. This is the one of the few areas where you can ski all year long. There are stables and organized trail rides, two restaurants in the main building, gym, exercise room, and sauna. The heated indoor and outdoor pools are used year-round.

8+ INN OF THE SEVENTH MOUNTAIN
P.O. Box 11207, Bend, OR 97709, 503-382-8711
Amenities: Pools, horseback riding, game room, tennis, restaurant

This resort is located on a bluff above the Deschutes River and has a spectacular setting in Cascades Mountain country. It is one of the most popular resorts in Central Oregon. The resort is great for families and couples seeking a luxury get away. The condos (over 300 are available) are located in four-story wooden buildings scattered throughout the property. There are two swimming pools, including one with a 64-foot waterslide. There are also saunas, hot tubs, tennis courts, and a recreation building with a game room. Many of the condos are studios with Murphy beds that pop down at night. Each condo has a private fireplace, which is cozy on winter nights after a hard day of skiing at Mt. Batchelor (16 miles away). Recreation counselors are available to help arrange your participation in white-water raft trips, mountain-bike trail rides, and horseback rides. For fisherman, the resort has a private stocked lake. It is also possible to fish in the Deschutes River. There's even a mini-golf course and several 18-hole courses nearby. In any event, you won't be bored (no matter what your age) because this resort has something to please everyone.

7 MT. BATCHELOR VILLAGE
19717 Mt. Batchelor Dr., Bend, OR 97702, 503-389-5900
Amenities: Pool, hot tub, sauna

This resort is a good choice for skiers because these condos are the closest to Mt. Batchelor. These 96 condos are in cedar-sided buildings. They are comfortably furnished with lots of tweeds and dark colors (as you would expect for lodgings in a forest). Each condo has a wood-burning fireplace. A swimming pool, a hot tub, and a sauna are also provided. Although the resort is convenient to the ski lifts, this choice on Mt. Batchelor is a little lonely, since most of the action is down in Bend.

9   SUNRIVER LODGE & RESORT
P.O. Box 3609, Sunriver, OR 97707, 303-593-1221, 800-547-3922
Amenities: Golf, tennis, pools, marina, gym, horseback riding,
restaurant

Twenty years ago, Sunriver Lodge started the community of Sunriver. It is located in Oregon's high desert and enjoys a mild, dry climate. While it's especially inviting in summer, the winters are also enjoyable, especially for people from soggy Willamette Valley or Portland. In the winter, the resort reaches its peak of popularity because of the skiing facilities at Mt. Batchelor. Sunriver Lodge Resort spreads over 5,500 acres of alpine meadowlands along the banks of the Deschutes River. The condos are well-designed, quality-built, and individually decorated, generally in the style of "elegant simplicity." You'll also find that a lot of Pacific Northwest paraphernalia has been used to accessorize the condos. As for amenities, the list goes on forever: two restaurants; 28 tennis courts; two 18-hole golf courses; two heated swimming pools including one that is Olympic size; a marina with canoes and white-water raft launchings; a gym with exercise room, saunas, and lap pool; and a horseback riding stable. Best of all, is the Kids Klub which offers supervised activities for young children, including field trips. A great resort for families, this resort has it all.

RENTAL RESOURCES
Butte Properties, 503-549-9526
Coldwell Banker First Resort, 503-593-1234
Deschutes River Ranch, 503-382-7240
Mountain Country Properties, 503-593-8652
Prudential Deschutes Realty, 503-593-2451, 800-423-5443, Sunriver
Ridgepine, 503-593-1211
Summit Realty, 503-593-2431
Sunray, 800-531-1130, Sunriver
Sunset Realty, 503-593-5018
Village Properties, 503-593-1653

PENNSYLVANIA

The Keystone State straddles the Appalachian mountains. The section of the mountains which passes through eastern Pennsylvania is called the Poconos, a name given by the Indians meaning "stream between the mountains." The resorts in the Poconos pride themselves on their rustic mountain settings, although the Indian heritage exists in name only.

Pennsylvania's Pocono Mountains extend from the Delaware Water Gap to the Appalachian Mountains. Just an hour east of Newark and the bedroom communities of New Jersey, the Poconos offer a variety of recreational activities within close proximity to the New York Metropolitan area. Golf and skiing are the two most noteworthy activities.

Thousands of vacationers come to the Poconos each summer for boating, fishing, hiking, horseback riding and golf. In addition, Delaware Water Gap National Park features thousands of wilderness acres and sylvan lake settings. In the winter, several ski areas succeed simply because they have the highest elevation within an hour or so of metropolitan New York. Prodigious efforts have been made to improve the quality of the resorts with snow-making equipment but let's face it, four lifts and a vertical drop of only 240 feet will not provide the challenge of Vermont's slopes. The ski resorts provide sports programs in the summer.

The Poconos are mainly famous for their "couples" resorts. Heart-shaped or champagne-glass bathtubs are common. This book features a "couples" resort, but don't get the wrong idea—it successfully combines private hedonistic pursuits within a healthy family atmosphere. Several Poconos resorts extend over vast acreages. Often the condos are hidden in the forest or are located along lakes overlooking the fairways. You'll find they grew from resort hotels which catered to the same clientele year after year. Condo development on the resort property was a natural—so is the clubbiness. Tamiment, for example, relies heavily upon vacationers from northern New Jersey who have now made summertime friends. But Tamiment also has a national appeal to people who don't know the Poconos and who are surprised to find Las Vegas-style entertainment in a nightclub setting each evening.

Generally, the condos are attractive and, as previously mentioned, sometimes include hedonistic bathtubs. The condos are comfortable and a few of them were designed with bedrooms on different sides of the living room (with the understanding that even the closest families want a little privacy from the in-laws).

Our selections feature some outstanding resorts as well as descriptions that are representative of what you can expect to find in condos within the "rating" category.

WHERE TO STAY

6+ **CAESAR'S BROOKDALE**
Brookdale Rd., Scotrun, PA 18355, 717-226-2101
Amenities: Lake beach, indoor pool, exercise room, tennis, restaurant

Caesar's Brookdale provides a touch of decadence in a traditional family resort. The condos feature one-of-a-kind champagne-glass whirlpool baths for two. A few of them also feature private heart-shaped swimming pools. Others have a private sauna or a private shower/steam bath for two. Aside from describing the private baths and saunas, the condos are luxuriously decorated with red velvet, sunken living rooms, small kitchens, and lots of mirrors. It allows adults to live according to their fantasies. This resort is a very popular family resort. Camp counselors lead supervised activities programs for juniors. Best of all, parimutuel betting takes place at the swimming pool on the winner of a pool circuit swim. And who are the contestants? Three to five year olds in inflated seahorses who paddle Ben-Hur style circuits along the circumference of the pool. This is one of the most amusing poolside activities we've seen to date.

FERNWOOD
Bushkill, PA 18324, 717-588-6661
Studio $77–99, 1BR $107–172, 2BR $175–242
Amenities: Golf, tennis, indoor and outdoor pool, skiing

Fernwood is one of the most bustling timeshare resorts in the Poconos. It is a master development encompassing a private golf course, and a private ski slope. It also offers tennis and horseback riding stables. Fernwood has been developed over 20 years and each phase is progressively more spectacular.

Dream Suites (7) The Dream Suites are condos which offer private pear-shaped whirlpools and private saunas. The bedroom walls and ceilings are mirrored. The decor is in California contemporary style and the blond wood is covered with peach and seafoam green fabrics. Decorator accessories and silk flowers round out the picture.

Treetops Villas (6) Treetops Villas are clusters of townhouses located along the golf course. Features include skylights, split-level designs, and private whirlpools. The interior decor consists of pearl gray fabrics and delicate patterned prints. Treetops has been designed for families or golfers who enjoy the outdoor environment along the fairway. It's a long walk to the main part of Fernwood, which features a restaurant, game rooms, and an exercise center.

SHAWNEE RESORT
Shawnee-on-Delaware, PA 18356, 717-421-1500
Amenities: Golf, tennis, skiing horseback riding, pools, Fred
Waring Theater/Playhouse, health club, restaurants

Shawnee is one of the largest resorts in the Northeast. This 600-acre resort is located on the Delaware River, just north of the Delaware Water Gap. For years, Shawnee was the home of Fred Waring and his Pennsylvanians. But in the late 1970s the property was purchased with the intent to create a carefully planned real estate development. The Inn, a four-story, red-roofed building constructed in 1905, is the center of Shawnee. A main dining room and a cocktail lounge are featured. In the summer, you can sit on the veranda and watch croquet or simply enjoy the view of the river. Eleven separate condo developments exist at Shawnee. Some of the condos are brand new and others are up to ten years old. The quality of the condos varies considerably with age.

Shawnee Village Villas (8) These villas have various locations throughout the Shawnee Resort. They are either high atop a ridge overlooking the Shawnee Inn, in the center of the activity area, or on a hilltop overlooking the Shawnee Golf course. A few of them are Pennsylvania-style brick and clapboard cottages with screened porches. They have been furnished with Early American furniture, thick carpets, and pine paneling. The units on the hillside are newer two and one-half story units. The furnishings are similar, but they have a cabin-in-the-woods feeling. Every condo has a private fireplace.

Valley View Townhouses (7) Valley View Townhouses are two story condos that can be locked off into separate studios and one-bedroom apartments. Or the whole townhouse can be rented. They are well designed for an extended family visit. The Early American style furniture is practical.

Northslope Townhouses (8) Northslope Townhouses are definitely superior in design and furnishings. They have gabled roofs and architectural flourishes such as half-circle Federalist windows. Fireplaces and two person whirlpools are provided.

Northslope Chateaus (8) Northslope Chateaus are separate cottages with furnishings similar to the townhouses. All of them have three bedrooms.

Shawnee is a great place for young children. The "Shawnee Place" Play and Water Park (designed by the creators of Sesame Place) will keep them entertained. A 3,000-foot daring lift ride, two waterslides, pony rides, and a discovery trail are featured. Fifteen available activities include a ball crawl with 40,000 plastic balls and cargo ropes. Older children and the young at heart will enjoy the Shawnee Adventures that feature bicycle and backpack expeditions on the nearby Appalachian Trial.

6 SNOW RIDGE VILLAGE
Big Two Resorts, Jack Frost Mountain, Box 704, Blakeslee, PA 18610
717-443-8428
Amenities: Pool, hot tub

Snow Ridge Village is located on Jack Frost Mountain. It consists of one- and two-story townhouse-style condos that feature a split-level design and sleeping lofts. Each condo has a stone fireplace, neutral colors, "skierized" furniture, a full kitchen, and a dining area. A few of them have private hot tubs. You'll discover comfortable family living here. There are no activity programs, but a recreation center provides an outdoor pool and an indoor hot tub. This is an especially comfortable choice for skiers and golfers. You'll enjoy privacy and the convenience of staying at Snow Ridge.

7   TAMIMENT
Lake Estates, Tamiment, PA 18371, 717-588-6652
1BR $115, 2BR $175, 3BR $205
Amenities: Golf, pools, tennis, racquetball, exercise room, lake, sailboats, restaurant, Las Vegas showroom

Tamiment is where people from metropolitan New York/New Jersey come to play. The resort's social life is similar to a club. Couples and families return year after year to play with friends from the neighborhood or to rekindle special summertime friendships. This lavish 2,200-acre resort, with all of the celebrities and comedians who perform in the showroom during the summer, has a touch of Las Vegas. Tamiment was developed by Wayne Newton. This fact may explain the connection with big name entertainers.

The condos are located in two-story wooden buildings with four condos per building. They are surrounded by a dense forest in a section that is separate from the main hotel/restaurant area. They are spacious, private, and luxurious. In contrast to the forest environment, you will find sophisticated interior decor that features chrome, glass, and white fabrics. Private fireplaces and fully equipped kitchens are provided. The individual outdoor patios are great for family barbecues and entertaining.

RENTAL RESOURCES
C. R. Baxter Rentals, 717-646-1000
Camelback, 717-629-3661
Chateau, 717-629-5900
Coldwell Banker Marshall Assoc., 717-222-9222
Nomi Village, 717-595-2432
Sawcreek Resort Survices, 717-588-6614
Ski Side Village, 717-629-2939
Snow Ridge Village, 717-443-8428
Split Rock Resort, 717-722-9111
Tanglewood, 717-226-3000
Village at Sciota, 717-992-5659

RHODE ISLAND

Rhode Island may be small, but Newport's resort community is a prime destination. It is connected to the mainland by a scenic bridge that crosses Rhode Island Sound. Newport, located less than 45 minutes from Providence and Interstate 95, is within an hour and a half of Boston. The map of Rhode Island can be found on page 368. The climate is brisk even in summer when the yachts dot the harbor, so be sure to bring sweaters and jackets. Newport winters have a quiet charm. The cold north wind blows over the water, making visitors appreciate the warmth of a fire or the conviviality of Newport's restaurants and pubs.

All of the condo resorts in Newport are within a few blocks of each other along Thames Street with the exception of Oceancliff, which is out along "millionaire's row" just off of Bellevue Avenue. The resorts along Thames Street are all tucked away down alleyways behind antique storefronts or century-old stone walls. All of these resorts have been created within the past eight years and all are thoroughly modern, even spiffy, on the inside—just like the polished brass rail on a yacht.

Air transportation is either through Providence or Boston.

WHERE TO STAY

7   INN ON LONG WHARF
142 Long Wharf, Newport, RI 02840, 401-847-7800,
800-225-3522; 1BR $130–180
Amenities: None

The Inn on Long Wharf is different from the other condo resorts in the Newport area. It is removed from the historic preservation of Thames Street and sits alone on the Wharf. The resort is composed of a modern five-story building that is only a short walk to Old Newport and Thames Street. The main advantage of the Inn is that it is surrounded by the sights and smells of the ocean. Although the individual accommodations are condo suites, they have been designed to look and function like a hotel. The hospitality is gracious. The Inn on Long Wharf is the sister property to the Inn on the Harbor. This location provides a strong nautical feeling, perhaps because the views feature boats in the harbor. The condos are small but very attractive (like a ship's cabin). Each condo has a private whirlpool. No full kitchens are available, but a refrigerator and coffee maker are provided.

8   INN ON THE HARBOR
359 Thames St., Newport, RI 02840, 401-849-6789, 800-225-3522
1BR $110–175
Amenities: Exercise room, hot tub, saunas, restaurant

Seemingly operated as a hotel, this condo resort is right in the heart of historic Newport. Every inch of space on the property has been put to good use. The restaurant/bar is a popular gathering place in Newport. This complex is built of brick with plenty of glass and wood and blends in with the historic part of town. The more desirable rooms overlook the harbor. The units are like suites. They are attractively decorated with nautical themes and stylish contemporary furniture. A popular brass and mahogany hole-in-the-wall bar is located downstairs. No kitchens are available, but a refrigerator and coffee maker are provided.

8+ NEWPORT BAY CLUB & HOTEL
America's Cup Ave. & Thames St., Newport, RI 02840,
401-849-8600; 1BR $150–250, 2BR $175–275
Amenities: Restaurant, shops

This resort is located within the Perry Mill warehouse in a recently renovated building. The 100-year-old building was completely made over. Brick walls, oak floors, oriental rugs, leather wing chairs, and brass lanterns grace the lobby. The condos, located above the ground level shops are one-bedroom suites and two-bedroom townhouses with different floor plans. The nautical furnishings are complemented by exposed wooden beams, brass lamps, lantern lamps, and seamen's wood carvings. The small kitchens are efficient. A restaurant is located near the lobby, and the ground floor contains the Perry Mill Market (which is full of boutiques). The rooms have views of the harbor and historic Newport. The location is advantageous because the resort is within walking distance of the harbor, wharfs, and historic Thames Street. This landmark resort is expensive.

8+ NEWPORT ON SHORE
405 Thames St., Newport, RI 02840-6600, 800-225-3522
1BR $150–250, 2BR $170–280
Amenities: Pools, hot tub

This renovated, unassuming brick building in the heart of Thames Street probably has the largest and most elegant units in the historic Newport area. Once inside the door, you'll notice a change of pace from the bustle of Thames Street. The beautiful condos have elegant interior decor with wood trim, cool pink fabrics, and silk flowers. A private whirlpool is located in the master bath. No kitchens are provided, only refrigerators and coffee makers. Considering the space and quality in this community, rentals here are a good value. Since Newport Onshore is the sister resort of the Wellington, guests have full use of the Wellington's Health and Tennis Club only six blocks away.

7+ OCEANCLIFF

Okdust Street, Ocean Dr., Newport, RI 02840, 401-846-6667
1BR $150–225
Amenities: Pool, hot tub, tennis, dining room

Oceancliff, one of Newport's legendary "summer homes" dating from 1893, is a unique resort. It is Gothic in style and built of red granite. The roof is made of Irish ironstone, which couldn't be reproduced today. Barbara Hutton, the Woolworth heiress, leased Oceancliff during the 1940s. The home was renovated in 1983 and carved into suites. Later, the two-story garden condo apartments were added on the ridge and designed so each unit had a view of the bay. The central lobby and restaurant/bar are located in the main building. The restaurant is one of the area's most exceptional. Gourmet specialties such as peppered duck or clams benedetto are prepared each evening. You can stay in the main house; the tower suites are the most fun. No full kitchens are provided. Grand stairwells and small turret-style windows add to the Gothic romance. Conversely, the garden villas are condo flats in a two-story building. They are modern with perhaps more comfort, but the style isn't the same.

8+ THE WELLINGTON

543 Thames at Wellington, Newport, RI 02840, 401-849-1770
1BR $150–175, 2BR $200–275
Amenities: Marina, pools, health club, tennis

Although The Wellington's address is Thames Street, the resort is a block from the street in a wide open space. Therefore, each unit has a full view of the harbor. The Wellington, which offers 54 units, is one of the largest resorts in the area. It also has a rare commodity here: an activities program for children and a full-service health club/tennis complex for adults. The individual condo interiors are beautiful, graced with lots of brass and nautical accessories. The wooden floors are varnished and covered with area rugs. A private whirlpool is located in the master bath. The location gives easy access to Old Newport's walking district. The Wellington is the area's best choice for families.

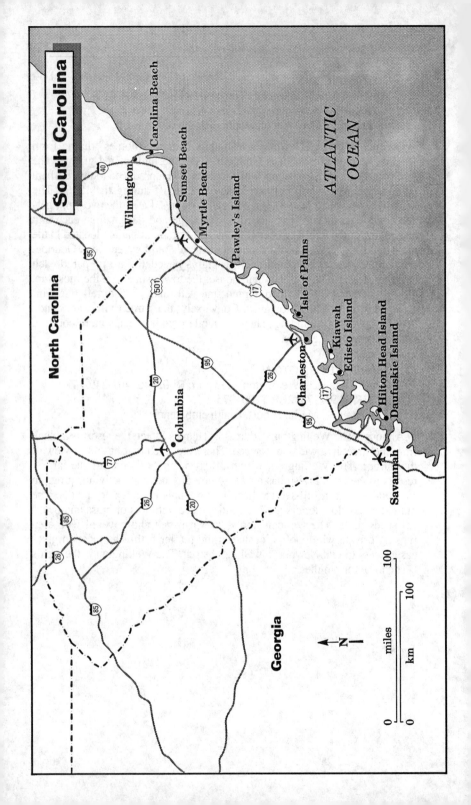

SOUTH CAROLINA

South Carolina will surprise you; it has a lot to offer. Some of the nation's best family beach resorts are in South Carolina. And if you are looking for a wild and riotous vacation, Myrtle Beach hosts the world's biggest beach party. Thousands of college students and teenagers come to Myrtle Beach to celebrate the rites of spring. For contrast, visit the very exclusive and private offshore island communities such as Kiawah and Hilton Head Island. Developers actually heightened the natural beauty of the settings by creating some of the most imaginatively landscaped golf courses to be found anywhere.

The state enjoys a mild climate year-round and the coastal regions sprout a few palms as well as extensive forests of palmettos and southern pines. The weather is perfect for golf, tennis, and biking all through the year. Snowbirds flock to South Carolina from November through March when nonbeach activities like golf and tennis can be enjoyed during a mild winter climate. Surprisingly, another surge of visitors arrives in the summer when families from the inland cities come to enjoy the cool breezes of the coastal communities.

South Carolina has two topographies: the lower foothills of the Appalachian Mountain chain roll into the fertile Piedmont; and the Low Country, the coastal area which officially begins south of Charleston. The Low Country features a ten-mile-wide band of marshlands between the ocean and the Piedmont. The land breaks up into a series of islands, several of which have been developed into some of the nation's top golf and tennis resorts such as Hilton Head Island, Edisto Island, Kiawah, Seabrook, and Isle of Palms.

This chapter is divided into three sections:

1. Hilton Head on the southern end of the coast;
2. Myrtle Beach at the northern end of the coast; and
3. Charleston's Islands, including the private developments on Kiawah, Seabrook, Isle of Palms, and Edisto.

1. HILTON HEAD

If Hilton Head island were viewed as a foot, then Sea Pines Plantation would be the toe. Sea Pines was the original "plantation" development and is home to the famous Harbortown Golf Course. Begun in the 1950s by the legendary Charles Frazier (who believed that development should be done with an eye for preserving the environment), Sea Pines set the standard and tone for future resort development. Hilton Head is the beneficiary of Mr. Frazier's vision. Forest Beach is a buffer zone of "off-plantation" land with shops, restaurants, motels, and lots of condos. Many of Hilton Head's "off-plantation" condos are on the shore in this Forest Beach section of Hilton Head.

The twin plantations of Shipyard and Wexford are located at the island's arch. Shipyard has been developed primarily with condos along the golf course and there are a few private homes here. Shipyard is a marvel of landscape architecture, with rolling fairways that follow the natural contours of the underlying sand dunes. You'll find a myriad of lagoons and an occasional napping alligator. Hilton Head is a subtropical island, but for some reason the island's alligators are unusually somnolent and rarely attack. Wexford, across the parkway from Shipyard, is an area of exclusive homes and condos. There are very few owners at Wexford who rent their homes or villas on a short-term basis, so Wexford is not covered herein.

Palmetto Dunes and Shelter Cove are the next areas of the island located a little higher up on the arch. Palmetto Dunes is a plantation; Shelter Cove is not. Shelter Cove is merely a Mediterranean-style condo village with boats and a marina. Palmetto Dunes is an exclusive area of homes and condos that offer the three "designer" courses by George Fazio, Robert Trent Jones, and Arthur Hills, as well as the sensational Rod Laver Tennis Center.

The Folly Beach area is another buffer zone of "off-plantation" homes and condos. At the heel of the island is Port Royal, primarily a community of villas for part-time residents or retirees who rarely rent their vacation homes. Hilton Head Plantation, above Port Royal at the island's ankle, is similar to Port Royal.

You'll find that most condo properties on Hilton Head Island are quiet and semiresidential. This is a timeless, noncommercial destination where everything fits within the organic environment. Accordingly, most condo resorts do not have front desks; you'll probably need to go through one of the rental agents if you want to rent a condo or vacation home. With over 50 rental resources, you'll find that most have a sense of competition and the rental rates we have provided are the rack-rate quotes. You should be able to negotiate a lower price, especially if you plan to stay more than a week. The one exception, however, is Heritage Golf Week when the prices double.

There are several options for transportation to Hilton Head. Many drive from their homes. One tip: avoid the town Bluffton with its notorious speed trap set at 25 M.P.H. This trap is located just five miles from the bridge to the island. You can bypass Bluffton by staying on Highway 170 and avoiding the Route 46 turnoff. Air travelers prefer Savannah, only an hour away. Charleston is less than two hours and the drive through the low country is quite pretty. There are frequent shuttle buses to Hilton Head from both Savannah and Charleston.

WHERE TO STAY

9 **THE BARRINGTON**
Ocean Ln., Palmetto Dunes, Hilton Head Island, SC 29928
800-845-6130, 1BR $175, 2BR $225, 3BR $270
Amenities: Beach, pool, hot tub, children's playground

On the beach and within Palmetto Dunes Plantation, it offers the best of both worlds. These new condos are in a six-story structure overlooking the beach on one side and a small lagoon on the other. You can walk to the Palmetto Dunes Golf Club or the Rod Laver Tennis Center. Guests at the Barrington enjoy all guest privileges at all the Palmetto Dunes recreational facilities. They have snappy interior decors and most condos have VTPs and microwaves. This is equally as good for families as for couples or groups coming to Hilton Head for a week of golf.

7 **THE BEACH VILLAS**
South Forest Beach Dr., Hilton Head Island, SC 29928
1BR $140, 2BR $180, 3BR $220
Amenities: Beach, pool

Oceanfront in the Forest Beach area, these are among our favorites for off-plantation condos. Here you won't pay extra for access to the golf course. The condos in these two-story townhouses are in a lovely landscaped environment. Each condo has a private patio or balcony. There's a small pool, but you'll probably prefer the beach.

5 **BREAKERS**
South Forest Beach Dr. Hilton Head Island, SC 29928
1BR $80, 2BR $100, 3BR $115
Amenities: Heated pool

Located on the beach in the Forest Beach section of the island, the condos in this wooden three-story building provide casual accommodations. The units are a little on the small side, so this is a choice for couples or a small family. Decorated for practicality and many feature bunk beds in the entryway to the living room as well as a separate master bedroom.

7 **BRIGANTINE QUARTERS**
Shipyard, Hilton Head Island, SC 29928, 803-785-6446
800-845-6446, 1BR $145, 2BR $185
Amenities: Pool, tennis, golf

Brigantine Quarters is one of the most famous resorts on Hilton Head Island. It soared to notoriety in 1986, when it was hailed as the harbinger of "quarter ownership," the phrase for four families sharing ownership of one condo. Brigantine is a quiet resort; there is no real activity center or hospitality program, although cocktail parties sometimes occur in the evenings by the swimming pool. The condos, duplexes on the fairway, and lagoons of the Shipyard Plantation Golf Club are some of the most spacious and well-designed lodgings on Hilton Head Island. The townhouses are luxuriously decorated and designed to allow lots of interior sunlight. Skylights and bright designer fabrics give these condos a "youthful" feeling. Each unit has a VTP, stereo system, and a private whirlpool in the master bath. The beach is a short drive or bike ride away.

8   CAPTAINS WALK
Ocean Ln., Palmetto Dunes, Hilton Head Island, SC 29928
1BR $175, 2BR $220, 3BR $275
Amenities: Beach, pool

Occupying one of the prime oceanfront locations in Palmetto Dunes, Captain's Walk offers a well-rounded choice for a Hilton Head vacation. The beach is outside your door and tennis and golf are only a short walk away. The loft units on the top floor feature living rooms with cathedral ceilings. Captains walk is tastefully decorated.

6   HARBOURSIDE I AND II
Shelter Cove, Hilton Head Island, SC 29928, 800-845-6130
1BR $110, 2BR $120, 3BR $155
Amenities: Marina, tennis, pool

High-rise condos located in the Shelter Cove marina area, these two eight-story buildings have orange roofs and architectural flourishes that suggest the Mediterranean. Each condo has a balcony and a view of the inlet. Social life centers around the pool here.

8   HARBOURSIDE III
Shelter Cove, Hilton Head Island, SC 29928, 800-845-6130
1BR $140, 2BR $180, 3BR $220
Amenities: Marina, pool, hot tub, tennis

Don't confuse Harbourside III with Harbourside I and II. It is actually next door, and provides a more luxurious interior decor. Newer than its neighbors, these condos have the word "Yuppie" almost written on all the designer fabrics. The condos are located in five-story buildings with harbor views and are part of the Mediterranean "village" at the Shelter Cove yacht marina. These units overlook the inlet and are popular with families. Harbourside III is noteworthy because ownership rentals include complimentary greens fees and tennis across the street at Palmetto Dunes Plantation. This is a major amenity at Hilton Head and amounts to a $200 value or more each day. The Palmetto Dunes golf course and Rod Laver Tennis Club are only a three-minute drive away.

6 **HILTON HEAD ISLAND BEACH & TENNIS CLUB**
40 Folly Field Rd., Hilton Head, SC 29928, 803-842-4402
Studio $65, 1BR $120
Amenities: Pools, tennis, snack bar, recreational area

Located "off-plantation" in the Folly Beach area, this may be your best bet for reasonably priced accommodations on Hilton Head. This resort is a huge condo village with 18 separate three- and four-story buildings in an area recessed from the beach by about 30 yards. There is a lot of activity around the ten tennis courts, pro shop, super-pool (an Olympic size eight lane lap pool) and shallow children's pool. Next to the pool is a beach cafe and gazebo. The one- and two-bedroom condos are adequate. Built 20 years ago when island building codes were more relaxed, the walls are a little thin and sometimes you can hear your neighbors. A few of the condos have beachfront views, but most of them overlook the canals, tennis courts, or landscaped grounds. Wood paneling makes the condo interiors seem dark and old in style. They are equipped with full kitchens and the sturdy furniture can withstand abuse. The advantage of staying at this resort is the price.

4 **ISLAND CLUB**
85 Folly Field Rd., Hilton Head Island, SC 29928
803-785-5221, 800-528-9336
Amenities: Beach, hot tub, pool, tennis, playground

The Island Club is an "off-plantation" property in the Forest Beach area. Built in 1977, the resort offers over 100 condos in six five-story buildings. They are arranged in such a way that half of the condos have ocean views. But it is time to redecorate. An active three-tiered pool area is surrounded by children and young adults. The resort features a complete health spa with saunas and hot tubs. A large children's playground is popular, and supervised activity programs are offered for children in the summer.

7 **KINGSTON COVE**
Shipyard, Hilton Head Island, SC 29925
1BR $140, 2BR $180, 3BR $220
Amenities: Pool, complimentary golf, greens fees

Located in a private section of Shipyard Plantation, Kingston Cove brings out the best of South Carolina's beauty. The condos are located in an area of live oaks with Spanish moss and quiet lagoons for fishing or just relaxing. They are in a great location because you have the best of the natural environment, yet you are within the Shipyard Plantation. The villas are actually spacious three-bedroom homes. Each villa is beautifully decorated with designer furniture and lots of fabric everywhere. VTPs and private whirlpools are included. Best of all, guests receive complimentary golf and tennis privileges, which amounts to a benefit of $200 a day on Hilton Head.

9   MARRIOTT'S HERITAGE
Harbortown, Sea Pines, Hilton Head Island, SC 29938
803-785-2040, 800-527-3490
Amenities: Clubhouse with lounge and game room, pool,
    golf, tennis

Marriott's Heritage has a prime position at Harbortown village within Sea Pines Plantation. The resort is located on a tiny piece of land across from the Harbortown Golf Clubhouse, an exclusive setting. The structure is a five-story concrete building that looks like a Marriott Hotel on the outside. Inside, you know you have entered another world. Mahogany paneling, brass lamps, and oriental carpets are characteristic of the interiors that look like something you would see in *Architectural Digest* magazine. The theme is elegance. Guests at this property also have membership rights in the exclusive Harbortown Golf Club next door. This is an extra benefit worth as much as $200 per day on Hilton Head. Bring dressy clothing. Men should expect to wear a jacket in the Clubhouse.

9   MARRIOTT'S MONARCH
Seas Pines, Box 6959, Hilton Head Island, SC 29938
803-671-5034, 800-527-3490
Amenities: Beach, pool, hot tub. Tennis nearby

Located on six acres within Sea Pines Plantation, Marriott's Monarch is one of South Carolina's leading resorts. It consists of four six-story concrete buildings arranged so every condo has an ocean view. The beach is wide, white, and sandy at this part of the island. The property is separated from the beach by sand dunes and sea grass. A wooden walkway will take you from the beach to the sand dunes and Monarch's wooden beach gazebo. A pool is slightly sheltered by the property and the Sea Marsh Golf Course is across the street. The condos are luxuriously decorated with designer fabrics, art objects, VTPs, and more.

What makes this property outstanding is the landscaping. There is a lagoon with little ponds and gazebos for enjoying the moss-laden live oaks and crepe myrtles. Swans float over the water and Japanese koi fish bob to the surface for bread crumbs. There is no other park area on Hilton Head to compare with this. This resort is perfect for vacationers of all ages.

8   OCEAN PALMS
35 S. Port Royal Dr., Port Royal, Hilton Head Island, SC 29928
Amenities: Pool, health club, golf, tennis

Elegantly decorated condos next to the Westin Hotel & Conference Center, this is as close to "glitz" as you'll find in South Carolina.

6 OCEAN WALK
South Forest Beach Dr., Hilton Head Island, SC 29928
Amenities: Pool, tennis, hot tub, sauna

These are superior condos in the Forest Beach section of Hilton Head. They are built around an atrium courtyard and the units are spacious. Expect island style interior decor. Ocean Walk is quiet, casual, comfortable.

ℭ PALMETTO DUNES PLANTATION
(Many condos described are within this development.)
P.O. Box 5606, Hilton Head, SC 29938, 803-785-1181
800-826-1649, 1BR $105–195, 2BR $140–210, 3BR $175–305
Amenities: Golf, tennis, pools, activities program,
dock with restaurant

Palmetto Dunes Plantation contains over 1,800 acres of golf course and forest along the "sole" of the Hilton Head Island "foot." Both the Intercontinental and Hyatt Hotels are located on the beach of Palmetto Dunes. This "plantation" has a different feel to it; it is slightly more go-go with a younger urban clientele. The Rod Laver Tennis Center offers 25 courts and one of the finest instructional programs in the United States. A week at Palmetto Dunes will do wonders for your game. The same is also true for golf. There are three designer courses that will provide play for an amateur and challenge for the best. The three-mile beach is one of the widest walking beaches on the entire Atlantic Seaboard.

The condos within Palmetto Dunes range from economy to luxurious. Unlike Shipyard, a variety of architectural styles are offered. Some structures are five-story condo apartment buildings and a few are townhouses. Eleven restaurants within the Palmetto Dunes community range from high-style formal to Low Country shrimp boils.

In summertime, a supervised activities program is available for children. It focuses on beach activities for younger children and golf and tennis instruction for preteens. Or, you can just enjoy one of the 18 pools scattered throughout the plantation. Each separate cluster of condos comes with its own pool. Fish Creek Landing is a boat dock with a restaurant. It rents canoes, paddle boats, rowboats, and fishing equipment.

8+ PORT O'CALL
Shipyard, Hilton Head Island, SC 29928; 1BR $170, 2BR $215
Amenities: Pool, ocean, beach, tennis, complimentary greens fees

Port O'Call, one block from the Atlantic Ocean, is made up of one-, two-, and three-bedroom villas. In addition, a three-story structure features condo townhouses. On-site amenities include a complete pool complex (steam, sauna, spa, barbecue grills) and a Shipyard Racquet Club. The advantage is its ideal location. This is one of the few properties within Shipyard where you can slip out the back gate, walk down a short lane, and be on the beach.

Greens fees and tennis fees at Shipyard Golf Club and Racquet Club are included in the price of a vacation rental. The villas and apartments are luxuriously decorated; you'll find designer fabrics and VTPs. The pool is the resort's social center.

 ### SEA PINES PLANTATION
(Many condos described are within this development.)
Sea Pines Reservations, P.O. Box 7000, Hilton Head Island,
SC 29938, 803-785-3333, 800-645-6131
1BR $80–120, 2BR $100–210, 3BR $120–250
Amenities: Beach, golf, tennis, pools, marina restaurants,
snack bars, shops

In the history of American resorts, Sea Pines stands out as the prototype of a master golf resort community with condos and vacation homes. The condo resort trend flourished here in 1957. This was also one of the first resorts to employ landscape architecture. The "mold" of tract development around a golf course typical in Florida was broken. The success of Sea Pines broke the tradition of the grand resort hotel and opened an entirely new dimension in resort development. Charles Frazier's concept of a "plantation" has now been incorporated in many of the new, ecologically sensitive resorts in the U.S. such as Amelia Island, Sawgrass, and Boca West.

Sea Pines Plantation is a master-resort community where 22 separate condo villages now accommodate over 7,000 guests per day. Yet, Sea Pines retains the sense of woods and wilderness. Tidal marshes and a 605-acre forest preserve have been set aside within the plantation as a wildlife sanctuary with a couple of nature trails. Five miles of beach have been protected with only single family homes and one condo resort that is hidden behind the natural coastal landscape and barrier sand dunes. This is one of the few beaches on the East Coast that is actually growing. More sand is deposited by the ocean each year. There are over 40 miles of bike trails within Sea Pines as well as ponds and a 15-acre fishing lake.

Sea Pines has three championship golf courses that wind through 5,000 acres of pine, palmetto, and live oak. The MCI Heritage Classic takes place on Harbortown Course each spring and rental rates double (if you can find space). Sea Pines Racquet Club has 29 courts and is home of the Family Circle Tennis Classic, another major sporting event on the island. The Stan Smith Tennis Academy offers clinics as well as private instruction.

Harbortown is the almost too cute New England-style sailor's village by the Lighthouse. This is where you'll find restaurants and shops.

There are no large hotels in Sea Pines. All accommodations are in low-rise, three-to-five-story condo buildings or townhouses hidden by the trees. The term used on Hilton Head is villa, but a villa here does not mean a separate house or some lavish structure. A villa on Hilton Head is a condominium. All are spacious, and most are of wood construction. All have full kitchens. Some overlook Harbortown village and others are in the South Beach area. Most have top quality or even luxurious designer decor.

6-9 SHIPYARD PLANTATION
Hilton Head Island, SC 29928, 803-785-4256
1BR $105–170, 2BR $150–215, 3BR $180–255
Amenities: Beach, pools, golf, tennis, conference center

After the success of Sea Pines, the developer turned to Shipyard Plantation to duplicate the master-planned community. Shipyard is near the center-sole of the "foot" island and enjoys two golf courses and miles of unspoiled beach. Shipyard includes one hotel on the beach and a condo property. The rest of the beach is lined with sand dunes and Low Country beachfront homes. Shipyard is like Sea Pines, only a little newer and little less stylish.

The condos here are mainly contemporary townhouses, and you'll find several almost identical groupings such as **Tennismaster, Sailmaster** and **Harbormaster.** These are wooden two-story townhouses with their own private walled patio. **The Evian** townhouses and flats at the center of the Plantation are the best. Enter through wrought iron gates and drive down a cobblestone lane through a forest of live oaks and magnolias. There's a clubhouse just for Evian with saunas, hot tub, and large pool. The Evian condos are marked by a French style and some even have huge gourmet kitchens, separate breakfast rooms, screened porches, and private patios. The Cottages are Low-Country style homes with sloping roofs and dormer windows. The condos in **The Cottages** surrounding a conference center, were designed to be rented to executives and doctors for corporate retreats and seminars. The furniture is sharp, but there is a slight touch of the commercial around this condo resort.

Each condo group offers guest membership privileges at Shipyard Golf and Tennis Clubs. Shipyard Beach Club, with a gazebo and changing rooms, is available during beach time since most of the condos line the golf fairways and are not on the beach.

6 SHOREWOOD
South Forest Beach Dr., Hilton Head Island, SC 29928
Amenities: Beach, pool

A modern five-story building on the beach, Shorewood is in the Forest Beach section. Each condo has a view of the beach across the pool. The perspective from the pool enhances the view. In an area popular with families, Shorewood has a slightly more dignified ambiance. Popular with golfers as well as beach lovers, it is well maintained and has comfortable interior decor.

8+ VILLAMARE
1 Ocean Ln., Palmetto Dunes, Hilton Head Island, SC 29928
803-686-3391, 800-635-3896
1BR $95–185, 2BR $125–245, 3BR $155–275
Amenities: Beach, pool, health club. Golf and tennis nearby

Located within Palmetto Dunes Plantation, Villamare is a rare beachfront condo property on Hilton Head Island. You can actually walk to the golf club or tennis center and the ocean is right outside your door. Viewed from the beach, you can't miss Villamare; it's the cluster of soft pink four-story buildings with bright green balcony rails. Surrounded by landscaping that includes palmettos, a free-form pool, and lawn and lagoon, the condos have been designed so each has an ocean view or garden views. Inside, the unusual angular design makes these two-bedroom condos seem large. There's a full kitchen and dining area, as well as the living room. The master bath is as large as a bedroom at some other condominiums, and you'll find a Roman-style whirlpool bath large enough for two. These condos are professionally decorated. You'll notice top-of-the-line contemporary furnishings with lots of glass-top tables, accessories, and designer fabrics covering the furniture as well as curtains and window treatments.

RENTAL RESOURCES
Bayside Realty, 803-785-5522
Beach Rental Company, 803-785-9499
Coastline Rentals, 803-842-5866
E.S.P. 803-671-4700, 800-368-5975
Dunes Marketing Group, 803-842-1111
Haig Point Realty, 803-686-4244
Hilton Head Accommodations, 803-785-3464
Hilton Head Island Reservations, 803-785-5271
Hilton Head Island Villas Rentals, 803-686-3066
Hilton Head Ocean Front Rentals, 803-785-8161
Hilton Head Plantation, 803-681-3307
Hilton Head Realty, 803-785-3311
Lancaster Lynhaven, 803-785-3817
Melrose Plantation, 803-785-8528
Palmetto Bay Marina Villas, 803-842-5555
Paradise Vacation Rentals, 803-842-2424
Port Royal, 803-681-7500
R.H. Rentals, 803-842-6212
Rose Hill Plantation, 803-842-2828
SandDollar Management, 803-785-7300
Sea Side Villas, 803-785-7061

Shoreline Rental Company, 803-842-3006
Trident Villas Rentals, 803-785-3447
Vacation Villa Rentals, 803-686-6226
Villa Rental Company, 803-785-6446

2. MYRTLE BEACH

Myrtle Beach has been called the "Seaside Golf Capital" of the world. With a 32-mile long expanse of beach and over 65 topnotch golf courses, it's no wonder. From its humble origins as a regional beach resort, Myrtle Beach is now rocketing to fame as an internationally acclaimed vacation destination. The weather is mild, and even though it's just 150 miles north of Hilton Head, the climates are different. Myrtle Beach is at the edge of the coastal plain, close to the Piedmont. Hilton Head is in the marshy "Low Country."

Myrtle Beach has several distinct sections. The area now stretches from North Myrtle Beach along the border with North Carolina down to Pawley's Island and Litchfield, which just ten years ago were sleepy little beach communities. The truth is that Myrtle Beach now spills over across the North Carolina state line, which is where a dozen of the new super golf "plantation" resorts are located. These are described in our North Carolina chapter.

North Myrtle Beach is home to Vanna White, who personifies the clean, wholesome, fun-filled life style of the area. This is a resort for family vacations. Activities have been designed so families can do things together from mini-golf to 18-hole golf on the 65 courses; from ping pong to tennis on over 125 courts; from amusement park snack bars to 25 of the nation's top-rated 250 restaurants. Springtime sees college students celebrating the rites of spring for a couple of weeks. Otherwise, Myrtle Beach is fairly sedate. Fall, winter, and early spring, Myrtle Beach is filled with semiretired snowbirds who come for two weeks of golf or tennis when the beach crowds have gone and the kids are in school.

Starting from the south, the Grand Strand can be divided into several distinct areas. Pawley's Island has a 350-year-old history where Gullah, a dialect mixture of African banter and Elizabethan English, is spoken. Famous for hammocks, today there is the super-deluxe Pawley's Plantation with the golf course designed by Jack Nicklaus. Pawley's is an area bound to change.

Murrell's Inlet is home to restaurant row and you can watch the shrimp and fish being unloaded from the boats while sitting on the veranda. Litchfield enjoys some prestigious golf course communities and is popular with retirees. Garden City is an offshore sandbar with unpretentious beach houses, and a strip of high-rise condos that were badly damaged by Hurricane Hugo. The condos of Garden City are not rated this year while the rebuilding takes place. Some condos may not reopen.

The southern half of Myrtle Beach, from the city limits up to the amusement park at the center, has a strip of unending high-rise condos just as massive as Ft. Lauderdale. Very few are residential. In the summer, this area can be packed with beach lovers, souvenir hunters in the shops, and in the distance, you can hear the screams from the roller coaster.

With over 350 condominium developments, including those all-suite resort hotels that look like condominiums, resort property rentals are big business in this area. Myrtle Beach is blessed with some of the largest and most organized vacation rental companies in the business, including Chicora Realty and Condotels. Chicora offers condos at over 120 developments as well as several hundred vacation homes. Condotels is a property management company that is now expanding beyond Myrtle Beach to Florida and California. On a national level, these are two of the strongest players so, as you can imagine condo rentals in Myrtle Beach are very competitive as well as professional. This should work to your benefit as you negotiate the cost of a week's vacation accommodations.

There are 252 condo rental agencies in the Myrtle Beach area. There may be more, but we have counted advertisements from 252.

Transportation to Myrtle Beach gets easier every year. U.S. Air has frequent service from many destinations in the Northeast and Midwest. Delta offers connections through Atlanta and Cincinnati, while American offers commuter flights from Raleigh. If you do fly, we urge you to rent a car because Myrtle Beach—The Grand Strand—stretches for 32 miles.

WHERE TO STAY

7   **BEACH COLONY**
5308 N. Ocean Blvd., Box 276, Myrtle Beach, SC 29577
803-449-4010, 800-222-2141, Studio $45–79
1BR $45–91, 2BR $77–104, $3BR 85–129
Amenities: Beach, pools, guest privileges at Myrtle Beach
Tennis & Swim Club

Beach Colony is unquestionably one of Myrtle Beach's best high-rise condo towers. Its 21-story tower is just north of the zoning line separating the prestigious Ocean Forest residential area of private homes from the condo towers. All of the condos face north or south, so everyone enjoys a sweeping view of the beach and ocean. The southern exposure condos have an unobstructed view for miles over the residential neighborhood of private homes. The condos are spacious and well designed for families or groups of golfers. The new interior decor includes natural ash woods or white painted woods and designer fabrics (in shades of aqua blue, celadon green, or frosted pink). The condos are equipped with microwaves and other kitchen appliances. Several units also have televisions and VTPs. Leisure and activity resources include an indoor and outdoor pool, hot tub, exercise/weight room, sauna, and free guest membership at the Myrtle Beach Tennis & Swim Club. The club offers the use of twelve tennis courts and an Olympic-sized pool.

6+ BLUEWATER RESORT

2001 S. Ocean Blvd., Box 3000, Myrtle Beach, SC 29578
803-626-8345,800-845-6994, 1BR $18–76, 2BR $24–82
Amenities: Beach, pools, weight/exercise room, game room, restaurants

Bluewater Resort, built as a 16-story condominium tower, offers a few units that are privately owned, but the majority were sold to one owner who operates Bluewater like a hotel. The decor makes this resort distinctive. Each unit has carved blond wood or Bavarian-style furniture. Expect to see rich decor with emerald green or ruby red carpet and fabrics. It's a bit heavy for a beach environment, but is certainly distinctive. You'll find Bergére chairs with carved wooden backs, and ball and claw feet on both tables and chairs. It is just a bit European. Bluewater has grown by taking over the low-rise four-story wooden condos on the second "back row" that are a block from the beach. Called "the villas," the condos have an informal family atmosphere with casual contemporary decor and views out over the palmettos and gardens toward the beach. All of the condos in the tower and the villas have full kitchens.

The resort is operated as a condo/hotel and offers lots of activities and benefits, such as room service. There's an outdoor "river ride," a donut-shaped pool with a swift current. You make circuits of the pool in inner tubes. There are seven other pools (including a large indoor pool) and five super-sized hot tubs. Bluewater is a favorite for families.

7+ CARAVELLE RESORT HOTEL & VILLAS

6900 N. Ocean Blvd., Myrtle Beach, SC 29572, 803-449-3331
800-845-0893, Studio $52, 1BR $65, 2BR $79
Amenities: Beach, pools, tennis

The Caravelle, located in a pocket of development just north of the Ocean Forest residential area, offers a lot of services and amenities. It is one of the largest resorts in Myrtle Beach, yet you don't feel caught in the usual hustle and bustle. Caravelle has managed to grow while maintaining its original low-key ambiance. There are eight buildings here including a hotel and four condo towers. St. Clements Tower condominiums are the newest condos. They offer two-room suites and a wide balcony, which is almost an extra room. The interiors consist of stylish and contemporary furniture and designer fabrics. Celadon green and rose are the prevailing colors. The units are small and almost "too efficiently" designed to feel like a relaxed vacation home. The Carolina Dunes Villas, in an eight-story concrete structure, are more spacious and better furnished. They have stylish furniture, grass cloth wallpaper, designer patterned fabrics, and lots of accessories. Caravelle Towers offers studios and Sea Mark Tower is only a block from the beach. For low-key vacation-home living, the Caravelle has three separate three-story condo buildings. They don't have the stylish furniture and fabrics, but they have more space and a relaxed atmosphere.

Operated as a condo/hotel, Caravelle offers lots of amenities and services, including activities programs for children during the summer. One of the best attractions at Caravelle is the "river ride," a pool with a swift current where adults and children can float in inner tubes in a circuit around the pool. There are eight other pools at Caravelle as well as a full sports center with an exercise room, saunas, and video game room.

5   CORAL BEACH

1105 S. Ocean Blvd., Box 2037, Myrtle Beach, SC 29578
803-448-8421, 800-843-2684, Suites $38–110
Amenities: Beach, pools, hot tubs, exercise room

This brand new twelve-story high rise near the center of the Myrtle Beach strip and amusement parks was badly damaged by Hurricane Hugo. The condos were some of the most luxurious in this part of Myrtle Beach, and the reconstruction of the early 1990s resulted in an even better Coral Beach. The condos are located in a solid concrete structure designed so each condo has a balcony and view north or south of the beach and ocean. Coral Beach is a large and active condo resort built with the needs of the family vacation in mind. A unique outdoor pool with waterfalls lit by colored lights and indoor pool are available. A hot tub bubbles in the grotto. Coral Beach has separate children's pools for playing and adult pools for swimming or sun-bathing. A "river ride," donut-shaped pool has a strong current and is fun for inner tubing. A full exercise/weight room is perfect for health nuts. This is a good choice for families on a budget.

7   FOREST DUNES

5511 N. Ocean Blvd., Myrtle Beach, SC 29577, 803-449-0864
800-845-7787, Studio $22–95, 1BR $38–95,
2BR $60–160, 3BR $55–170
Amenities: Beach, pools, sauna, exercise room

Forest Dunes, an 18-story tower located on the beach, is close to the zoning line that separates the prestigious Ocean Forest residential sections from the high-rise condo area at Myrtle Beach. All of the condos facing south have an almost unobstructed view of the beach and ocean. To the north, the view is also impressive, but there are only a couple of other resort towers in this pocket of high-rise development. The property is appropriate for people who want to be on the beach and near the activities, yet separated from the hubbub of central Myrtle Beach. It is popular with golfers, beach lovers, and families. The condos on the top three floors have three bedrooms and a private terrace. The living rooms and master bedrooms are spacious. The two- and three-bedrooms have two twin beds. Both the master bedroom and second bedroom have private baths and dressing rooms. They are a good choice for two couples. The condo interiors are decorated in a casual contemporary style with lots of pink and blue-gray colors. There's a dining area and countertop breakfast bar. Glass-top tables and silk flower arrangements add to the sense of height and openness. The one-bedrooms have similar decor, but lack the spaciousness of the oversized living rooms in the three-bedroom units. For fun, try the sauna, exercise in the exercise room, or ride an inner tube around the "river ride" pool.

4 GOLF COLONY RESORT
1 Colony Dr., Surfside Beach, SC 29587
Amenities: Golf, pool

Overlooking the fairways at Deertrack Golf Course, these condominiums offer some of the most spacious accommodations in the Myrtle Beach area. Some of the condos are in three-story buildings surrounding a pool, others are individual townhouses surrounded by Carolina pines. Some of the condos are decorated in an island style with rattan furniture, glass-top tables, and tropical fabrics. Spiral staircases lead to the second floor loft bedroom. This is a quiet resort for golfers, yet there is also a strong appeal for families. There are no organized activities or sports programs, but juniors can take advantage of the Deertrack golf and tennis programs and lots of children congregate by the pool in summer.

8 KINGSTON PLANTATION
9770 Kings Rd., Myrtle Beach, SC 29577, 803-449-0006
800-421-5432, Studio $65–110, 1BR $79–140
2BR $99–185, 3BR $110–205
Amenities: Beach, sports complex with racquetball,
aerobics classes, saunas, pools, restaurant

From the moment you pass the security gate, you'll be impressed by the landscape of this forested "island" in the heart of Myrtle Beach. Unique in Myrtle Beach, this is a 145-acre, master-resort development with two major areas of tree shaded townhouse condos surrounding a 20-acre lagoon where you'll see swans gliding over the water. Across the foot bridge are two massive high-rise condominium towers. This arrangement makes Kingston Plantation unique.

Starting with the twin condo towers (one pink, one blue), these solid structures have been designed and placed perpendicular to the beach so that all units have a beach and ocean view. Spacious, airy units with lots of light, each has been individually decorated. Expect superior decor. We saw one decorated with 18th-century Charleston reproduction furniture, another in a more modern style with a butcher block table and simple, almost

Scandinavian wood chairs. We saw a third decorated with heavy dark Victorian furniture blended with light, zesty fabrics. Whirlpool tubs large enough for two are provided. The best feature is the long balcony running the length of each unit. This is, indeed, a great place for outdoor gatherings or just watching the sunset.

There are several clusters of townhouse developments. Prices are highest near the ocean and drop as you head toward the interior of the plantation. This decrease in price is surprising because the sylvan setting is so tranquil and well landscaped that we preferred the condos away from the beach. Quite a change of pace to find this "forest" in the heart of Myrtle Beach. **Richmond Park** townhouses are slightly newer and have more "bells and whistles" with skylights, dormer windows, and cathedral ceilings. The decor is almost universally done by professional interior designers. You'll find a variety of styles, including "fluffy pink fantasy," high tech and lavender beige decor in these condos. The gourmet kitchens have the sinks, faucets, and appliances you may have seen pictured in *Architectural Digest,* but no one else really has these accouterments at home. The townhouses in West Hyde Park are just as snappy.

There is a beach club and restaurant with a swimming pool just for condo resort guests. Best of all is the sports center, which is one of the finest in the area. It has nine tennis courts and a stadium court for professional matches. A tennis pro offers private lessons as well as clinics for juniors and adults.

4   **MYRTLE BEACH RESORT**
Kings Highway, P.O. Box 15423, Surfside Beach, SC 29587
803-828-8000, 800-845-0359
Studio $40–70, 1BR $50–83, 2BR $70–85
Amenities: Beach, pools, exercise room, game room, tennis

Spread over 24 acres in an area just north of Surfside Beach and just south of Myrtle Beach, this resort offers a wide variety of vacation accommodations. There are condo apartments in several different five-story buildings scattered throughout the property that range from beachfront to secluded-in-the-forest settings. The **Bristol** condos surround an atrium and indoor swimming pool. The 21-story **Renaissance Tower** with an ocean view to the north and south was badly damaged by Hugo. The ground floor lobby has been repaired and actually improved during 1991. The condo interiors are a little disappointing. For example, they are decorated with basic hotel-style furniture. The **Five Seasons** condos surround six tennis courts. Although most people want to reside on the ocean, the Five Seasons provides the newest condos.

8 OCEAN CREEK RESORT & CONFERENCE CENTER

10600 N. Kings Hwy, Box 1557, Myrtle Beach, SC 29577
803-272-3511,803-272-7724, 800-845-0353
Studio $55, 1BR $67, 2BR $88, 3BR $99
Amenities: Beach, pools, tennis, conference center, restaurant

Right in the middle of the string of high-rise condos and motels along Myrtle Beach, you'll find the Ocean Creek Club and its 57 acres of protected woodlands. It is different from the other resorts at Myrtle Beach. The master development provides several condominium styles including the townhouse **Tennis Villas,** the three-story lodge apartments and the high-rise towers overlooking the beach. The Tennis Villas are two-story townhouses or quardriplexes with two condos, both on ground level and upstairs. Each condo is moderately priced and has a private entry and screened porch. The interior decor is comfortable and stylish featuring solid colors and light woods. The Tennis Villas are, as you would expect, located next to the seven tennis courts and pro shop. **The Lodge** units offer a good value. Each cluster of 42 condos is grouped around a swimming pool. The Lodge condos, each with easy access to the Conference Center and restaurant, were designed for vacationers as well as conference attendees. Many offer the casual decor and neutral furniture typical in hotels. Each of the 15-story oceanfront towers has luxurious condos with tile floors, wet bar in the living room, and deluxe kitchens. The best features are the wide balcony extending the length of the bedroom and living room that gives each unit an "extra" outdoor living room. The beach club is the social center of Ocean Creek. It offers a snack bar, pool, and children's playground.

3 OCEAN FOREST

5601 N. Ocean Blvd., Myrtle Beach, SC 29577
800-845-0347, 1BR $35–80
Amenities: Pool, guest card to nearby health club.
Across from the beach

Ocean Forest is a popular cluster of three-story condos north of the Ocean Forest residential neighborhood. The condos have low ceilings and wood paneling. The dark walnut stain creates a small, dark feeling which could be appreciated on hot summer days. A large hot tub and small pool area are available. A guest privilege card allows you to use the health club at the Sand Dunes.

5 THE PALACE

1605 S. Ocean Blvd., Myrtle Beach, SC 29577, 803-448-4300
800-334-1397, Studio $50–90, 1BR $70–120, 2BR $90–160
Amenities: Beach, pools, exercise/weight room, game room, restaurant

The Palace, a 23-story tower that has been converted into a condo hotel, is a classic suite resort. Many guests return year after year. The lobby was damaged by Hurricane Hugo and in early 1990 was totally redecorated with more classic furniture. The management is friendly and the social environment makes it possible to get to know your neighbors. The resort's drawback is the small size of the condos. The units are furnished similarly, but with style. You'll find standardized, upgraded hotel furniture with patterned fabrics and lots of burnt orange, aqua, and peach colors. There are full kitchens and tiny pillbox balconies barely large enough for two chairs. An indoor lap pool connects with a free-form outdoor pool.

5 THE PALMS
2500 N. Ocean Blvd., Box 3937, Myrtle Beach, SC 29578
803-626-9747, 800-528-0451, 1BR $51–109
2BR $79–158, 3BR $79–184
Amenities: Beach, pool, exercise/weight room, card room

The Palms consists of twin 18-story towers near the central part of Myrtle Beach. It is brand new and very stylish. The lobby is beautifully decorated with Chinese paintings, vases, an oriental inlaid ivory desk, and fabulous sprays of silk flowers. The condos were luxuriously decorated by a professional. They are characterized by blond wood furniture, rattan chairs with art deco palm-shaped backs, and many extravagant silk flower arrangements. They call it "barefoot elegance" but we don't know what's barefoot about it. The dimensions of the condos are smaller than average, but mirrors add a feeling of space. The condos are either flats or two levels connected by a spiral staircase.

PAWLEY'S PLANTATION GOLF & COUNTRY CLUB
P.O. Box 2070, Pawley's Island, SC 29585, 800-367-9959
2BR $110–150, 3BR $145–195
Amenities: Golf, clubhouse, tennis, restaurant

Pawley's Plantation is a brand new development designed by Jack Nicklaus. It was destined to become one of the nation's premier golf communities. It is located at the southern end of the Myrtle Beach strip, about 30 minutes from the center. A journey from Charleston takes about an hour. A security gate separates this master community from the surrounding environment. The Plantation covers 582 acres of forest and rolling green fairways. Centuries-old live oaks that are draped with Spanish moss have been preserved here. There's a lavish clubhouse that brings out the best of Charleston. It has a "great room" with a fireplace and conveys the feeling of an English Country home.

Pawley's Glen (8+) These villas are representative of the variety of condos available for rent. Situated along the 9th fairway, the two-story Low

Country buildings have peaked roofs and were designed to look like manor houses set in the woods. They are spacious and well designed. The wet bar in the living room is perfect for entertaining, and the screened porch is ideal for private time. The decor is professional with plenty of fabric around the window treatments. There are almost too many pillows. The Charleston reproduction furniture includes four-poster beds. This is quite a break from traditional lodgings in the Myrtle Beach area. The resort is fairly new and hasn't created any activities programs yet.

5 **THE PLANTATION**
1250 U.S. Hwy. 17 North, Surfside Beach, SC 29575, 803-238-5556
800-845-5039, Studio $35–70, 1BR $50–100, 2BR $65–125
Amenities: Golf, pool, racquetball, exercise room, tennis

The Plantation, located inside the Deercreek development on the Deertrack Golf Course, offers accommodations in three-story buildings. The resort is in a serene environment, but families abound. A large sports center features an indoor pool, small outdoor pool, racquetball, tennis courts, sauna, and hot tub. The golf course and tennis center provide professional clinics for juniors and adults. The ground floor condos are one-bedroom units. The second-story units are two level townhouses. The townhouses are more inviting because of their vaulted ceilings and upstairs sleeping lofts. They are elegantly furnished by interior decorators who used boldly designed fabrics, art deco chairs with fluted backs, and top quality china and linens. You'll be so spoiled here you won't want to leave.

6-7 **SANDS OCEAN CLUB/SANDS BEACH CLUB**
1000 Shore Dr., Myrtle Beach, SC 29577, 803-449-1531
800-845-6701, Studio $32–65, 1BR $50–95
2BR $70–120, $95–145
Amenities: Beach, indoor/outdoor pool, tennis, health club, marina, restaurant

The Sands Ocean and Beach Club are two of the largest resorts in the area. They are mammoth twin 16-story towers that look more like Miami or Ft. Lauderdale than Myrtle Beach. There are two restaurants, a large cocktail lounge, night club, and private yacht marina. The Sands Beach Club occupies a strip of land with a large beach park and marshland area for walks. Unlike the other developments on the beach "strip," this has the feeling of a private community with a large coastal sand dunes area for the enjoyment of Sands Beach Club guests. The compact condos are among the most beautifully decorated in Myrtle Beach. They feature blond wood furniture, soft green and prink colors, lots of silk flowers, and designer accessories. Next door at the Sands Beach Club, you'll find a similar twin tower plus groups of low-rise, three-story wooded "beach house" condos. In short, the Sands resorts offer accommodations to suit all tastes. The Sands specializes in golf packages, and arrangements have been made for discounted greens fees for Sands' guests. This group also developed the prestigious new Jack Nicklaus golf course down at Pawley's Plantation so there are even better golf rates at this sister resort. The Sands Resort offers a special activity program for children. The social director takes children on special one-day outings each day with either a picnic lunch or a visit to McDonald's just off the property.

6   **SCHOONER II**
       2108 N. Ocean Blvd., Myrtle Beach, SC 29577, 803-448-6229
       1BR $45–112, 2BR $60–140
       Amenities: Beach, pool, hot tub, weight room, racquetball

You'll feel like an honored guest at Schooner II. The resort, located in central Myrtle Beach, tries hard to deliver personalized and attentive service to all guests. It offers attractive, but rather small condo apartments. The living room and bedroom walls have mirror panels, which create an optical illusion of space and expand the ocean view. The pale pastels and pearl gray colors create a calm ambiance. The full-service exercise room is the best feature; a glass wall allows you to watch the beach as you get into shape. A racquetball court and hot tub are also available. For tennis, you'll need a guest membership at the Myrtle Beach Racquet Club. The resort provides overall good service and value.

5   **THE YACHTSMAN**
       1400 N. Ocean Blvd., Myrtle Beach, SC 29577, 800-868-8886
       Studio $45–120, 1BR $55–135, 2BR $60–155
       Amenities: Pools, health club, fishing pier, restaurant

You will find this large resort complex right in the heart of Myrtle Beach. With a park in front and the boardwalk nearby, this is a good choice for vacationers without a car. There are several condo sizes available. The Clipper unit has two bedrooms and professionally designed interiors with mirrors, silk flowers, and a whirlpool in the master bath. The condos are well decorated and carefully maintained. Each unit has an ocean view. An indoor pool and two outdoor pools are provided, and, of course, there's always the ocean. The resort has a neighboring hotel tower with services, including bellmen for assistance and room service. There is a full activity program, including organized volleyball games, aerobics, and organized cocktail or beach parties.

RENTAL RESOURCES
Able Property Management, 803-238-5197
Arcadian Management, 803-449-1596
Barefoot Vacations, 803-448-8358, 800-845-0837
Booe Realty, 803-449-4477, 800-845-0647

Chaz Condo Rentals, 800-423-8813
Chicara Beach Holiday, 803-272-7070, 800-845-0833
Coastal Rentals, 803-449-7447
Condo World, 803-249-6422
Condominium Rental Service, 803-272-3662
Condos Unlimited, 803-272-7293
Condotels, 803-249-2700, 800-845-0631
Defender Resorts, 803-449-1354
Dunes Realty, 803-651-2116
Elliott Realty, 803-249-1406
Garden City Realty, 803-651-2116
Grand Strand Realty, 803-249-1404
Independence Vacations, 803-448-2269
Leonard Call Taylor & Associates, 803-626-7676
Noble Company, 803-449-6625
Resort Rental Service, 803-249-5448
Sea Breeze Realty, 803-238-5139, 800-446-4010
Surfside Realty, 803-238-3435

3. CHARLESTON'S ISLANDS

South of Charleston exist two of the finest resort islands found in the U.S:
Kiawah and Seabrook. Kiawah shot to fame in 1974 after the Emir of
Kuwait purchased the entire island and announced plans for creating the
finest resort community in the world. The best golf course designers, landscape architects, and construction engineers were hired in an era when
money was no object. This has blessed Kiawah with an exceptionally good
infrastructure of roads, villages, and golf courses. Speed limits are 15 M.P.H.
on the island and are strictly enforced. After all, humans share the island
with one of the largest communities of breeding Loggerhead turtles remaining on the East Coast. This statement described the attitude on Kiawah.

Seabrook, the other fine resort, is much more contemporary and less of an
environmentalist's dream than Kiawah. Beautifully developed with care for
the natural surroundings, Seabrook is a vacation resort for families and
golfers, as well as a conference center for business people. Seabrook prides
itself on hosting high-level executive conferences and medical seminars.
The condos are clustered primarily in a village, so attendees can walk to the
conference center and evening banquets.

Just north of Charleston is the Isle of Palms, an offshore island, which has
been one of Charleston's "summer homes" for more than 150 years. Even
before the Civil War, southern planters would escape the summer heat in
favor of the cooling and healthy breezes on this island. In the 1970s, the

undeveloped half of the island was transformed into a Hilton Head-style master plantation and christened as Wild Dunes.

Not as famous as the two islands to the south, Wild Dunes has landscaped architecture and a golf course design rivaling, and even surpassing, its celebrated neighbors to the south. The beauty of Wild Dunes is known in some circles, but it just hasn't been as prestigious—therefore, the prices are lower. Wild Dunes delivers one of the best values for a vacationer in South Carolina, but—shhh!—don't tell anyone or the price might go up.

Finally, there is Edisto Island, as a tag along. Located just south of Kiawah and Seabrook, Edisto's main economy is still "shrimping." Every afternoon you can watch boats come in, laden down with shrimp for shipment all over the U.S. Edisto may look close, but the access road makes the trip to Charleston a long hour through marshes and forests. Edisto has also been partially transformed into a master plantation named Ocean Ridge. Formerly the vacation retreat of the DuPont family, Ocean Ridge has a beautiful southern environment, with lanes shaded by live oaks and magnolias. A golf course that follows the rolling contours of this sandy barrier island, Ocean Ridge has a chain of lagoons and ponds, with even a fishing hole and lots of crickets in the background. Each of these islands is a special place and will deliver an exceptional vacation experience to you.

On Kiawah Island, like so many other destinations in the Carolinas, most of the condo and vacation home rentals are through the off-site rental agencies. Most are located next door to each other in a building at the small Bohicket Marina, just before you cross over to noncommercial Kiawah Island. Seabrook, Wild Dunes, and Edisto Island are not in this category. Seabrook and Wild Dunes are operated as conference centers for a very elite clientele. Therefore, most of the rentals are through the front-desk operations at those resorts. Edisto Island is a master real estate development controlled by fairfield Communities, so again no real off-site group of rental agents has arisen to give Fairfield competition.

WHERE TO STAY

6 **FAIRFIELD OCEAN RIDGE**
P.O. Box 27, King Cotton Rd., Edisto Island, SC 29438
803-869-2561, 800-622-6569, Studio $75
1BR $85–100, 2BR $100–125, 3BR $125
Amenities: Golf, tennis, marina, pools, beach, restaurant

Edisto Island is 45 miles south of Charleston. Take Highway 17 to Highway 174 for a 22-mile drive through the Low Country. (It's a quiet little island with some generations-old wooden beach homes, and the main industry is shrimping.) Fairfield developed over 300 acres into a self-contained resort community that has the same climate as Hilton Head, but without the creeping urbanization. The island represents a new trend towards carefully planned South Carolina beachfront property, which has been done with an eye to preserving the environment. The broad, sandy beach is good for shelling or ocean fishing and the golf course is excellent. Throughout the property are clusters of townhouse condos, shaded by cypress and moss-laden live oak trees. Carry me back to the Old South. Each townhouse has been decorated with southern charm and just a touch of flashy Yankee money. Contemporary furniture, light woods, designer fabrics, and VTPs are included in the units. The condos provide an attractive, luxury environment for a Carolina beach or golf vacation. Edisto offers the charm of the Old South, but nightlife is limited. The Ocean Ridge Country Club, a social center for the island, offers good food, light music, a sports bar, and conviviality.

KIAWAH ISLAND
P.O. Box 12357, Charleston, SC 29412, 803-768-2121
800-654-2924, 1BR $100–125, 2BR $140–170, 3BR $155–275

Kiawah Island has won so many awards for preserving the natural environment, protecting wildlife, and imaginative development, it's almost redundant to describe Kiawah as a beautifully deigned resort community. Kiawah just might be the best resort when viewed from the perspective of ecologically sensitive development.

Kiawah consists of 10,000 acres of semitropical marshes, forests of oak and palmetto, and ten miles of wide Atlantic beach. The condos, homes, and inn are clustered in two areas of development. The island encompasses two golf courses, one haunted antebellum mansion, and natural wildlife. The two villages are about equal in size, although West Village is more active. The speed limit is 15 M.P.H. so biking, hiking, and jeeping are the best way to explore the island. It is the home for one of the remaining colonies of Loggerhead turtles (over 3,000 baby turtles are hatched each summer).

Kiawah's golf courses, designed by Jack Nicklaus and Gary Player, deserve mention. Dramatic in design and challenging for play, Kiawah's Ocean course was the site of the 1991 Ryder Cup golf tournament. Tennis is another reason to come to Kiawah since the tennis clinics and programs have been ranked as one of the top 50 in the U.S. Both West and East Village have 16 tennis courts, but the real heart of the operation is in West Village. Bohicket Marina is across the bridge for boating enthusiasts.

Fairway Oaks (7) Fairway Oaks offers condo units in two-story build-ings along the 16th and 17th fairways of the Marsh Point Golf Course. Their location allows easy access to all of Kiawah's amenities including the West Beach Tennis Center, Straw Market shops, the Inn, pools, and beach. The condos have slate entry foyers, fully equipped kitchens, and sun decks.

Mariner's Watch Villas (9) These cedar-shingled villas are reminiscent of turn-of-the-century seaside cottages. They overlook a lagoon but have ocean views. Spacious with vaulted ceilings and a fireplace in the living room, you'll find beautiful furnishings and soft yellow and peach colors.

Shipwatch Villas (8) These oceanfront condo suites, located on the best area of Kiawah, are adjacent to the Inn, Straw Market shopping, and tennis in West Beach Village. This four-story building features penthouses. All of the villas are tastefully decorated and feature balconies with direct views of the ocean. Only kitchenettes are provided. This is a perfect location for those who want to be near the center of activity.

Tennis Club Villas (7) Located adjacent to East Beach Tennis Club and Town Center, the Tennis Club Villas are close to the beach, sports, dining and shopping. The architecture is interesting. Details such as colorful awnings, latticework, bay and dormer windows, and exposed rafters set these condos apart. The second floor villas have unique screened porches.

Turtle Point Villas (8) Ideally located along the scenic 17th and 18th fairways of Turtle Point, the soft Low Country architecture of these condos creates the perfect retreat for island living. Some are flats and others are townhouses that include screened porches, sun decks, skylights, and fire-places. The three-bedroom units include a second-level master bedroom with a balcony and great views of Turtle Point finishing holes.

Windswept Villas (8) Tucked away in the dunes and overlooking the ocean, Windswept Villas offer the best of both worlds. They provide the solitude of a quiet oceanfront retreat and activity of Kiawah's East Beach Village. These luxurious condos feature enormous cathedral ceilings, private balconies, fireplaces, wet bars, and full kitchens.

8   SEABROOK ISLAND RESORT
P.O. Box 32099, Charleston, SC 29417, 803-922-2401
800-845-2475, 1BR $65–195, 2BR $100–240, 3BR $140–295
Amenities: Beach, beach club, pools, golf, tennis, health club, conference center, children's programs

Seabrook Island has its own distinct flavor. Located only 23 miles south of historic Charleston, the entire 2,500-acre island was developed by one person. Seabrook is popular with families and golfers, but prides itself on having one of the finest conference centers in the South. Catering facilities are available for seminars as well. A social director operates an exciting activity program for children in the summer and it emphasizes skills as well as play: nature hikes, art classes, and puppet shows are featured. On some nights teens can attend the "Rock by the Sea" dances. Most of the 350 con-dos are clustered around the village, but some stand alone and overlook the marsh or golf course. Most are designed in Low Country style with peaked or sloping, shingled roofs. Some are flats and others lofts under the peaked roofs. All of them are modern and beautifully maintained. Seminar attendees stay in the condos that are conveniently clustered around the conference center and village. The Beach Club Villas are clustered near the water, the Golf Villas along the fairways, Spinnaker units next to the tennis courts, and Tarpon Pond cottages face lagoons and moors.

9 WILD DUNES

P.O. Box 1410, Charleston, SC 29402, 803-886-6000
800-845-8880, 1BR $88, 2BR $110, 3BR $142
Amenities: Beach, golf, pools, tennis, marina, restaurants

Wild Dunes is a sleeping giant of a resort, located just across the Cooper Bridge from downtown Charleston. Although its only 20 minutes away from Charleston, this resort is a world apart. It's a master-resort community designed to enhance the natural landscape. The golf course follows the natural lines of the dunes and water hazards created by lagoons and canals. The 15th green on the Links Course is one of the most photographed in the U.S. because the green is surrounded by water hazards.

Located on the Isle of Palms, half of the island has been sealed off for the master plantation of Wild Dunes. Once inside the security gate, you'll notice that you are in another timeless world. This is how the Carolina barrier islands looked before development by man. You'll see snowy egrets glide over the marsh to roost on a palmetto. The two courses at Wild Dunes, the Links and the Harbor courses, follow the natural contour of the dunes with sunken "forests" and natural below-sea-level depressions. Wild Dunes is also a tennis center with 19 courts and two stadium courts that are used when Wild Dunes hosts championship tournaments.

During the summer, Wild Dunes offers some of the best children's programs found anywhere. There's the Dune Bugs' Club, which is like a summer camp with supervised activities that include crafts and swimming races. The Wild Adventures Club is for children eight to twelve with more skilled games and sports, craft-making experiences, and the "afternoon mystery tour" to historic forts, battleships, crabbing adventures. Golf and tennis clinics are held for children beginning at age six and there's an optional tennis camp where the children are immersed in tennis for five hours a day. They can then socialize with their tennis buddies during the "down-time." In the evenings, there are treasure hunts, kids' pizza parties, wacky water sports, teen dances, and children's movies.

The condos in Wild Dunes are called villas even though they are flats in four- to eight-story concrete buildings or townhouses. Several different locations appeal to the special interests of vacationers including the beachfront, or overlooking the tennis courts or marina. There are several choices of condos on Wild Dunes. The most popular are listed.

Wild Dunes Ocean Club — These seven-story concrete buildings are the exception to what you will find at Wild Dunes. They are popular with families who want to be near the main resort center. Each condo has a view of the dunes. Contemporary in design, most have been professionally decorated. They have carpet and tile floored kitchens, lots of wood cabinets, and wood trim over the large whirlpool in the master bath. Some are Low Country casual; others have the sophistication of Washington, D.C., or Miami. All are luxurious.

Seascape — The units are popular with families although they are much less luxurious. Located on the beach, the Seagrape units are next door to the Beach Pavilion Center.

The Beach Club Villas — The Beach Club Villas are actually two-story townhouses with screened porches. Some are right on the beach.

RENTAL RESOURCES
Beachwalker Rentals, 803-768-1777, 800-334-6308, Kiawah
Benchmark Rentals, 803-768-9000, 800-992-9666, Kiawah
Edisto Sales, 803-869-2527, 800-443-5398, Edisto
Island Realty, 803-886-8144, 800-476-0400, Wild Dunes
Kiawah Island Villa Rentals, 800-845-3911
Pam Harrington Rentals, 803-768-0273, 800-845-6966, Kiawah
R.H. Rentals, 803-842-6212, Kiawah

TENNESSEE

Mountain forests with little patches of fog. Grannies in bonnets and aprons making baskets or canning fresh fruit. An old stone mill on the stream where the waterwheel still creaks along. Country music jamborees, wildflowers and patches of lavender mountain rhododendron. Welcome to the mountains of Tennessee.

A Tennessee vacation is for those who want to go back in time to the days when life was less complex—free of auto pollution and demands for increased production on the job; back to times when "Have a Nice Day" had some meaning, and before "party" became a verb. If you value your heritage and you are looking for healthy outdoor fun, Tennessee is the place for you.

The region to visit is the mountainous area called the Smokey Mountains. When you see them, you'll know why they were so named. No matter what the season, you'll encounter little patches of blue fog. Pretty to look at, when you're in one of those thick fogs, everything kind of stops. Gatlinburg is the capital of this region. It is at the entrance to the Great Smokies National Park. Built on a steep grade descending to a river valley, Gatlinburg had little room to grow. Today, the popular attractions line the strip of highway known as Pigeon Forge. Only 80 miles east of Knoxville and its airport, this mountainous region is 80 years away from today. A detailed map of this area is on page 482.

Another area, less developed, is about 60 miles west of Knoxville and 100 miles east of Nashville. This Cumberland Gap region is becoming a playground for weekenders from Indiana as well as growing cities like Nashville. Beautiful resort areas have been cultivated around golf courses, lakes, and forest. This area is in step with the "New Nashville." It lacks the culture/sightseeing of the Gatlinburg area, but it offers sporting opportunities instead.

Summer is the most popular vacation time because of the area attractions that appeal to children and teens on vacation. Spring is a lengthy season with blooming trees and shrubs as well as crisp weather. The fall, when the leaves turn color, is when the locals say the area is at its best. The Great Smokies National Park and Ober-Gatlinburg are great places to sit back and realize just how good life is.

Most of the condos and villas in the Smokey Mountains are handled by real estate agents. While there is a smattering of condo resorts, as listed below, most of the resort property accommodations in this region are individual cabins or, in many cases, A-frame chalets. For this reason, the most important tool at your disposal is the Rental Resources section at the back of this chapter listing the rental agencies where you can find condo/villa accommodations.

WHERE TO STAY

 ALAN'S MOUNTAIN RENTALS
Box 77, Gatlinburg, TN 37738, 615-436-2512, 800-843-0457

This reservations service handles rentals for over 70 vacation homes in the vicinity of Great Smokey Mountain National Park. Many of these are cute country cabins, while others are modern A-frames. The following is a description of some of the possibilities:

Uncle Jim's Cabin — This is rustic, but modern. If you like the Ole Time atmosphere with all the modern appliances, this three-bedroom cabin is a possibility, at $70–80 a night.

Vanessa's Villa — A plush modern chalet, Vanessa's is situated on an acre of forested mountainside, with a view of the mountains off in the distance. This three-bedroom home rents for $95 a night.

Alan's Cabin — More romantic than most, the large living room is dominated by the stone fireplace. This is a cedar log cabin where you'll find Appalachian quilts, a hook rug, and antique bed frames. The best feature is the private hot tub (for 5) and the private sauna. It is available at $115 a night.

8   **BROOKSIDE RESORT**
East Parkway, Route 4, U.S. 321 North, Gatlinburg, TN 37738,
800-251-9597; Studio $45–95, 1BR $60–110, 2BR $69–125
Amenities: Pools, Brookside shopping village across the street

One of the largest vacation villages in the area, this combines condo convenience with a hotel-style operation that offers an array of services. Located at the North Gateway to the Great Smokey Mountains National Park, this has a sylvan setting surrounded by dense forest. The units vary from simple studios to two-bedroom condominiums where there is a jacuzzi whirlpool and a private steambath. Family oriented, you'll find lots of children around each of the three pools. There's also a large children's playground.

7   **CONDO VILLAS OF GATLINBURG**
201 Parkway Gatlinburg, TN 37738, 800-325-9992 (TN)
800-223-6264 (US); 2BR $55–110, 3BR $79–155
Amenities: None

This is a colony of vacation homes built into the hillside about three miles outside of town. Some are rounded "cedar villas" with either one or two bedrooms plus a personal jacuzzi spa. There are also the log villas, built in the traditional boxy style yet, more spacious. The upper floor condos have two bedrooms plus a loft for the kids, and downstairs the living room has a cathedral ceiling. Most have private jacuzzi whirlpools.

7   **CUMBERLAND GARDENS**
Box 95, Highway 70, Crab Orchard, TN 37723, 615-484-5285
800-443-3017; 1BR $65–90, 2BR $75–105, 3BR $85–115
Amenities: Golf, tennis, lake, pool, hot tub

The mountaintop location, perched high above the Cumberland plain, is one of this resort's best features. The resort caters to golfers, fishermen, and tennis enthusiasts and there is a ski slope on site. Briarwood Country Club is the social center nearby. Each condo has a brick fireplace as the focal point and, being fairly new, they are decorated in contemporary style.

7+   **DEER RIDGE RESORT**
Route 3, Box 849, Gatlinburg, TN 37738, 615-436-2325
Amenities: Golf course, pool, clubhouse, tennis

Located 11 miles from town, this resort is a world unto itself. There are 84 condos along the fairways of the golf course, situated to make the most of the mountain view. Interior decor has neutral furniture, just like an all-suite hotel. There's a golfer's green sandwich shop and restaurant for socializing. This is Gatlinburg's only country club resort.

7   **FAIRFIELD GLADE**
P.O. Box 1500, Fairfield Glade, TN 38555, 800-262-6702 (TN)
800-251-6778 (US); 1BR $59–105, 2BR $77–131, 3BR $95–145
Amenities: Golf, pools, marina, tennis, horseback riding

This is a self-contained resort community, which is a destination in and of itself. The development is on 12,000 acres near the Catoosa Wildlife Management Preserve. There are four 18-hole PGA golf courses as well as Druid Hills Country Club. The restaurant at Druid Hills is one of the better choices in this part of Tennessee and there is an evening dinner theater at the Cumberland County Playhouse within Fairfield's Country Club. There are lakes for boating, sailing, and fishing as well as trout streams. For tennis fans there is a John Newcombe tennis center and pro shop where you can undertake a week's intensive training. Children will enjoy the indoor swimming pool, the playground or perhaps, the more sedate outdoor pool at the country club. The best time to visit is in the spring when the dogwoods bloom for six weeks, or in the fall when the leaves turn color. Summer remains the most popular season.

1   **FOX RUN RESORT**
Dollywood Ln., Pigeon Forge, TN 37863, 615-453-9800; 1BR $35
Amenities: Clubhouse with recreation room, pool

This timeshare resort is remote, located on a mountain top about five miles out of Gatlinburg/Pigeon Forge. This is for people looking for bargain lodgings. There is a pool and some of the condos have a private whirlpool. Each condo has a private terrace that offers beautiful views of the Tennessee Mountains.

5   GATLINBURG TOWN SQUARE
259 Airport Rd., Gatlinburg, TN 37738, 615-436-2039,
800-424-1943; 2BR $75–150
Amenities: Indoor and outdoor pools, exercise/weight room

Located just about a mile from downtown Gatlinburg, this timeshare resort has the advantage of being close to but not in the main part of town. Vacationers familiar with Gatlinburg know that the town can have major traffic jams in spite of the strong pull to the surrounding beautiful mountain area. This resort is also less than a mile from the entrance to Great Smokies National Park. It is one of the largest condo developments in the Gatlinburg area. Each condo is spacious, has a private whirlpool, and the units are newly redecorated with light pink and blue colors. It offers some of the most attractive condos in this part of Tennessee. There is an indoor pool and an outdoor pool as well as an exercise room. Management is quietly efficient.

7   HIGH ALPINE CONDOMINIUMS
Route 2 Box 786, Upper Alpine Way, Gatlinburg, TN 37738
615-436-6643, 800-666-6643; 2BR $79–99, 3BR $109–119
Amenities: Outdoor pool in summer

These new condominiums are in a serene location, on a hilltop just before you get to Ober Gatlinburg. Convenient for skiers, those who come to enjoy the natural beauty of the Smokies will be impressed with the way these condos fit into the landscape. Inside, each has a stone fireplace and the interior decor ranges from practical "skierized" furniture to romanticized "country charm" or "ski the Alps." This is a pleasant choice that is reasonably priced.

7   THE HIGHLANDS
Rt 4, Box 369, Campbell-Lead, Gatlinburg, TN 37738-9502
615-436-3547, 800-233-3947; 1BR $89 2BR $104, 3BR $119
Amenities: Outdoor pool, hot tub, saunas, tennis

Located just off the road up to the ski mountain, these condos have an enviable forested location. Each has a stone fireplace and a private jacuzzi whirlpool large enough for two. Interior decor is modern and cheerful. Maybe you'll find one with a rocker, but overall this is a sophisticated choice. The upper units have a loft bedroom and a cathedral ceiling in the main living room. Each has a stone fireplace.

5 **HONEYMOON HIDEAWAYS CHALETS**
1 Honeymoon Hill, Gatlinburg, TN 37738, 615-436-7837,
800-331-3782; Chalets $95
Amenities: None

These chalets are for special people. On the outside, the cute honeymoon cottages look as though they come from a Hansel and Gretel story book, But those kids never had mirrors over the heart-shaped waterbed or heart-shaped jacuzzi tubs for two. If you have great bodies, maybe you'll enjoy all the mirrors.

 JOHNSON'S CHALETS
c/o Johnson's Inn, Baskins Creek Rd., Box 392, Gatlinburg,
TN 37738, 615-436-4881; 1BR $61–77, 2BR $78–110, 3BR $90–122
Amenities: Inn's facilities

This is a collection of eleven local homes that have nothing in common except management by the folks at the Johnson Inn. Spread up and down the length of the parkway, each of these homes has been individually designed, built, and decorated. We saw one with contemporary decor and another that had gingham and antique reproduction furniture. If you stay at one of these homes you can use the amenities at the Inn, including the pool, sauna, and tennis court.

 LeCONTE CHALET RENTALS
611 Oak St., Suite 9, Gatlinburg, TN 37738, 615-436-3126

This rental agency offers 45 mountain homes, a few of which have location on the edge of a town. All have fireplaces and a few have jacuzzi tubs for two. We saw the ultra-modern **Timberhaus,** which has a spare boxy style, more like what you'd expect to find in California. Then there's **Smokey Heights,** a restoration of the first cabins built on the Pigeon River. This is truly a fisherman's paradise and it is available at only $65 a night.

5+ **MARINER'S POINT AT THUNDER HOLLOW**
Route 9, Sparta Hwy., Crossville, TN 38555
Amenities: Golf, tennis, marina, horseback riding

Thunder Hollow is a major development near Cumberland Mountains State Park. Most of the community is for early retirement or second home vacationers. Mariner's Point is a condo development within this community on Lake Holiday, which offers short-term vacation rentals. There are two two-story condo buildings and each unit has a private balcony. Recently decorated, the condos are attractive and contemporary in design. There is a wide range of activities within the Thunder Hollow development including golf, tennis, swimming pools, a lake for boating or sailing, and horseback trails.

MOUNTAIN LAUREL CHALETS
Rt 2, Box 648, Ski Mountain Rd., Gatlinburg, TN 37738
615-436-5277

One of the largest vacation home rental agencies in Gatlinburg, you'll find they have a large selection of vacation homes priced from $65 a night. The advantage here is the personalized service and the follow through to ensure that your expectations are fulfilled.

4 **MOUNTAIN MEADOWS RESORT**
850 Rolling Hills, Pigeon Forge, TN 37863, 615-428-2897
2BR $75–125
Amenities: Pool

Large, spacious townhouses, Mountain Meadows is tucked away behind the commercial strip of Pigeon Forge. You'll find a swimming pool, but no hospitality program other than the on-site manager. This is a place to stay if you are planning on enjoying the Park, Gatlinburg, Dollywood, etc. The condos are beautifully decorated, spacious, and larger than many homes.

4 **OAKMOUNT**
555 Middle Creek Rd., Pigeon Forge, TN 37863, 615-453-3240
1BR $55–70, 2BR $75–90
Amenities: Indoor/outdoor pool, hot tub, weight room

This resort complex is up the hill and away from the commercial center of Pigeon Forge. It enjoys a quiet hillside setting with views of the Great Smokey Mountains. Each condo is luxuriously decorated by a professional designer and has a private stone fireplace. Best feature: whirlpool in the master bathtub. There is an indoor/outdoor heated pool, sauna, an exercise room for adults, and a full playground for children. The only drawback is the very active timeshare sales program.

5 **OLDE GATLINBURG PLACE CONDOMINIUMS**
211 Baskins Creek Rd., Gatlinburg, TN 37738, 615-436-3117,
800-367-2325
Amenities: Outdoor pool, hot tub

This in-town, eight-story condominium is convenient for those who don't have a car. You are only two blocks from the shops and near the entrance to Great Smokey National Park with its hiking trails. The units are small and very efficient. Best for a couple or a family with small children. Decorated in neutral blues and tans, this is efficient but lacking the flavor of the area. Each unit has a fireplace.

2 PEPPERTREE LAUREL POINT
Ski Mountain Rd., Gatlinburg, TN 37738, 615-436-3765
Amenities: Indoor/outdoor pool

This property is about two miles out from downtown Gatlinburg. It enjoys a cool, wooded location on the mountain looking out over the valley. This resort is for families. You will see children at play in the pool area. The condos are decorated with contemporary furniture that could be spruced up, however. Management will help you become acquainted with the area.

4 PINECREST TOWNHOUSES
300 Plaza Way, Pigeon Forge, TN 37863, 615-453-6500
2BR $75–122
Amenities: None

Tucked away behind Dollywood, this is a community of spacious two-bedroom condos with large, well-built units with mountain stone fireplaces. Tastefully decorated, they give you lots of room for an extended stay in this area. Located on a hill above Dollywood, you can hear the music softly coming through the trees at night.

ℭ SKI MOUNTAIN CHALETS & CONDOS
Box 770, Gatlinburg, TN 37738, 615-436-7846

This reservations service handles over 50 mountains chalets and condos at competitive prices of $65 to $150 per day, depending upon the size, quality, and location of the vacation home. One plus: they could find accommodations over Christmas when everyone else was full.

3 SKI VIEW MOUNTAIN RESORT
Ski View Dr., Gatlinburg, TN 37738
Amenities: Clubhouse with indoor pool

Way up Ski View Drive, these condos have beautiful views of the forest. Not all the condos are on one piece of land, some are down the hill from others. There is a small indoor pool and a sundeck where there are evening cocktail parties. This is a quiet resort for families who plan a week exploring the Park, Dollywood, etc. You plan your own fun here.

STANFILL'S MOUNTAIN RENTALS
Box 830, Gatlinburg, TN 37738, 615-436-9274

Stanfill's may have the largest selection of mountain homes available for vacation rentals. Some are cute with gingerbread façades or log cabin-style.

Inside you'll find many Appalachian heritage items including quilts, hooked rugs, etc. Our favorite is the **Executive Berghaus** with two hot tubs (one inside, one out on the deck), a striking living room, and a drop-dead mountain view. Prices begin at $135 a night for this jewel, but there are also a number of bungalows where the rental rates at $70 a night.

7   THE SUMMIT
Ski View Drive, Box 1247, Gatlinburg, TN 37738,
800-843-3456 (TN), 800-843-3455 (US)
Amenities: Indoor pool, hot tub

The Summit is good in the summer, even better in the winter because of its proximity to Gatlinburg's Ski Mountain. This modern four-story condo complex, occupies a prime hilltop location overlooking the smokies. Modern and clean, we were disappointed with the condos interior decor. The ones we saw seemed to be just a little bit spare in comparison with some of the other properties. The two-bedroom condos are on two levels with a spiral staircase. They are far superior to the boxy one-bedroom models.

7   TREETOPS
Roaring Fork Rd., Box 1009, Gatlinburg, TN 37738, 615-436-6559
1BR $75–100, 2BR $125–150
Amenities: Tennis, indoor/outdoor pool, exercise/weight room

This has an excellent location about two miles outside of downtown Gatlinburg and less than a mile from the entrance to Great Smokey Mountain National Park. The project has been carefully developed and with a little fantasy also. It's the streamside setting, landscaping, and all the pines that make this resort outstanding. There is a swimming pool and in summer there are two social directors to make sure children as well as adults have a wonderful vacation. Each condo is spacious, well decorated, and has a stone fireplace and a whirlpool in the master bath. Interior decor features furnishings typical of a mountain home. There is an Early American feeling accentuated by the ruffles and quilts.

ℂ   VOLUNTEER REALTY
Route 2, Box 875, Gatlinburg TN 37738, 615-436-2866, 800-346-2217

Volunteer Realty handles a wide range of mountain homes, some well-decorated, at prices beginning at $90 a night or $500 per week.

RENTAL RESOURCES
Acuff Mountain Home Rentals, 615-938-3760
Acorn Vacations, 615-436-8898
Alan's Mountain Rentals, 800-843-0487
Barbara's Chalet Rentals, 615-436-7400

Bogles Vacation Villas, 615-436-4222, 800-231-3701
Chalet Rentals of the Smokies, 615-436-3063, 800-334-3080
Edelweiss Condominiums, 615-436-7846
Fairview Chalets, 615-693-4544
Gatlinburg Chalet Rentals, 615-436-3199, 800-225-3834
Holly Ridge Condominiums, 615-453-3717
Le Conte Chalet Rentals, 615-436-3126
Leisure Condo & Chalet Rentals, 615-436-4222, 800-231-3701
Mountain Laurel Chalets, 615-436-5277
Schweigert Enterprises, 800-242-4853
Ski Mountain Chalets & Condos, 615-436-7846
Stanfill's Mountain Rentals, 615-436-9274
Village Stream Condo, 615-436-6614
Volunteer Realty, 800-346-2217
Windy Oaks Condos, 615-436-6971

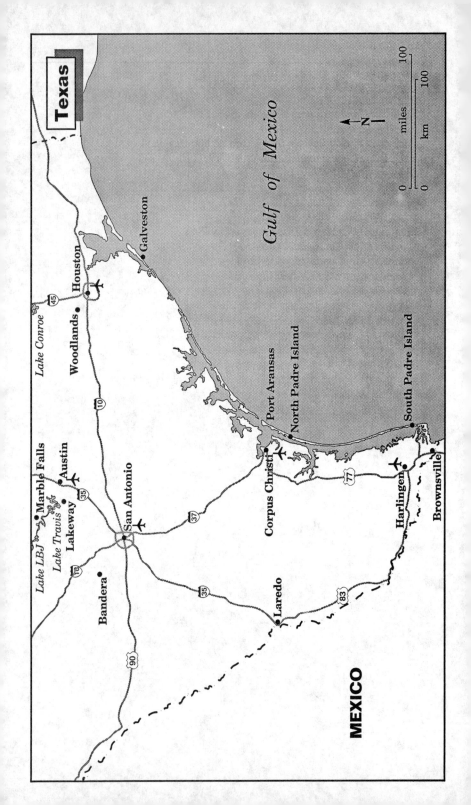

TEXAS

The resorts in Texas all center around a healthy, outdoor life. Recreation of some sort, whether it's trail riding or beach life, is promoted and readily available. These vacation areas offer good vacation opportunities for families with growing children. The climate along the coast is warm in winter and can be hot in the summer except for the cool breezes. Padre Island, and in particular South Padre Island, offers the best warm weather vacation climate in the U.S. dollar for dollar. Conceived and built to be a summer beach resort, Padre Island now attracts thousands of snowbirds each winter—especially from areas in the Midwest. South Padre Island is less than an hour away from the Mexican border. An international flavor provides Padre with a cultural as well as climatic advantage. If an inexpensive trip to Mexico is not what you want, consider the Brownsville area. One of the most romantic resorts in the U.S. is located just minutes away from the border.

Galveston Island is just enough farther north so that its climate is easily ten to fifteen degrees cooler than Padre in summer. For this reason, Galveston is best in spring, summer, and fall.

Heading inland the Texas Hill Country near Austin offers the cowboy experience as well as spectacular tennis, golf, and boating facilities. This is where the topography changes from rolling farmlands to the dry plains of the southwest. During the spring, west Texas turns into fields of bluebonnets inspiring trail rides.

Lake Conroe and the Woodlands are less than 25 minutes from Houston's Intercontinental Airport. This is an area popular with business executives for group meetings and conferences. Several exceptional golf courses are located here and 60-mile-long Lake Conroe offers boating opportunities. The best time to visit is in the spring when the dogwoods are in bloom.

Renting resort property in Texas is one of the best vacation values in the United States. Not only are the resort areas overbuilt for the local market, and relatively undiscovered by the national market, but also there's an intensive competition between the off-site rental agencies and the on-site rental firms. You'll find that about half the condos have on-site rental firms, and half do not. With those that don't, expect to find four or five off-site rental agencies offering the same condos at a wide array of prices.

Padre Island has a reputation for spring breakers. With lots of music, dancing, and poolside parties, there are many attractions besides warm water and the beach. In fact, Padre's reputation as a spring vacation destination is eclipsing Ft. Lauderdale. Nevertheless, not all of these condominiums share our enthusiasm for youthful enjoyment, so many have policies that discriminate against "spring breakers." When this policy is disclosed, we have so noted. There's no sense going to a condo resort where you'll be constantly reminded of the need for peace and quiet.

We have divided Texas into the following geographic regions:

1. South Padre Island
2. Brownsville
3. North Padre Island/Port Aransas
4. Galveston Island
5. The Hill Country
6. Lake Conroe/The Woodlands

1. SOUTH PADRE ISLAND

Padre Island is the place to be if you enjoy the beach. Most of the island has been dedicated to the Padre Island National Seashore Park under the protection of the U.S. Forest Service. Padre offers over 200 condo resorts to choose from, either at the northern end around Port Aransas or at South Padre. You'll find prices, in general, to be quite reasonable and some are just downright low.

The National Seashore Park is an area of sand dunes and sea grass. It's wide and open. You can venture into the Park from either end of the Island, and you will feel far removed from civilization. **Do not attempt to drive from one end of the Island to the other;** the park service will not allow through traffic and there is no paved road. Pirates buried their treasures here, and Spanish ships were lost off the coast. The U.S. Park Service has banned the use of metal detectors in this area, eliminating the threat of possible disturbance by treasure hunters.

South Padre Island is over 160 miles away. You must drive south from Corpus Christi/Port Aransas on the north end and you must recross to Corpus Christi on the mainland before returning back to the southern tip of the island. South Padre has been developed with numerous hotels and high-rise condominiums. This area was a hot bed of development during the late '70s when both Texans and Mexicans were flush with money. Today, the atmosphere is much more tranquil and there are some genuine real estate bargains here. South Padre has a distinct Mexican flavor, perhaps because Mexico is just across the water.

The Rio Grande Valley communities of Brownsville and Harlingen have become the home to Winter Texans because of the year-round golfing, fishing, and social life. Brownsville is a genuine border town that looks more like Mexico than the U.S. with bilingual signs, high Mexican-style street curbs, palm trees, and stores filled with shoppers from Mexico. Matamoros, Mexico is just an hour away and it offers nortes americanos shopping opportunities in the colorful markets.

Air transportation to this area is quite easy with frequent flights to Harlingen Airport 45 minutes away. Limo or shuttle bus service over to the resorts is easy to arrange. Brownsville has its own airport but with only a fraction of the flights that are available through Harlingen.

WHERE TO STAY

6 **AQUARIUS CONDOMINIUMS**
2000 Gulf Blvd., Box 2640, So. Padre Island, TX 78597
512-761-1325; 2BR $77–119
Amenities: Beach, pool, game room, tennis

This is a surprisingly well-priced value. The condos in this seven-story structure are right on the beach and rentals are priced low when compared to its neighbors. These two-bedroom units are functional in design and make the most of the space. However, each is a corner unit with a wraparound balcony that actually becomes a second living room. Island-style interior decor with lots of rattan furniture and uninspired durable fabrics prevail. Only one bath per unit. Although budget priced, this appeals to quiet vacationers and "spring breakers" are not welcome. It is functional but provides solid value.

6-7 **BAHI'A MAR RESORT**
6300 Padre Blvd., Box 2280, So. Padre Island, TX 78597
512-761-1343, 800-531-7404
Studio $110–170, 1BR $145–220, 2BR $175–230
Amenities: Beach, pool, tennis, disco

Located on the northern end of the commercial resort development on Padre Island, Bahi'a Mar is in two parts: a twelve-story hotel tower, and unusually designed three-story condos clustered around the garden. This was one of the first resorts built on South Padre Island, so it has more land than most resorts. An attractive stream flows through a landscaped garden creating a "tropical lagoon" effect. Over by the hotel tower there's a clover-shaped pool where you'll always find lots of activity. The condos are spacious; some with lofts. All have a few "bubble" porthole windows that give the condos at Bahi'a Mar a unique design. All have full kitchens and private patios. Some have interior decorator furnishings, others are very casual. Some are downright dreary. Ask about which one you will get before you rent. There's a dining room in the hotel tower and at night the place jumps with a disco. But you'll probably want to be out by the pool, playing tennis or on Padre's famous beach. If you're looking for that low-rise, townhouse style, then this is one of the best picks on the island.

5 **THE BEACH HOUSE I, II, III**
Gulf Blvd. at Bahama St., So. Padre Island, TX 78597
1BR $80–114, 2BR $135–220
Amenities: Beach, pools, tennis, hot tub

A series of pleasant five-story buildings on the beach at Padre. This is a friendly resort that concentrates on family vacations. Children, teenagers,

and adults quickly form friendships around the pool or over on the beach.
The units are spacious but casually furnished. Each has a small patio overlooking the beach.

7   **THE BREAKERS**
        708 Padre Blvd., So. Padre Island, TX 78597
        1BR $92, 2BR $125–155
        Amenities: Pools, tennis, racquetball, exercise/weight room

The Breakers is one of the most popular choices on Padre Island for vacation rentals because of all the activities. These units are just in front of the
high-rise Franke Plaza Tower and the beach can get very crowded here.
You'll be sure to make friends or find a volleyball game, however. The units
are on the small side but there's efficient use of space. You'll probably want
to be outside on the balcony overlooking the beach and Gulf. Interior decor
is superior and even stylish in some units. Some of these condos have recently been redecorated with cool southwestern colors and motifs. It is a superior
and quiet spot.

9   **BRIDGEPOINT**
        333 Padre Blvd., Box 3590, So. Padre Island, TX 78597
        512-761-7969, 800-221-1402
        1BR $100–250, 2BR $130–285, 3BR $175–400
        Amenities: Beach, pool, tennis, exercise/weight room

An island landmark, this 28-story tower is the tallest building on the
island and the first one to be noticed when you cross the bridge from the
mainland. Bridgepoint is the latest word on elegance in south Texas. The
lobby is beautiful with marble floors, sculpted area rugs, and intimate sitting
areas, brass, glass, and lots of flowers everywhere. Keep right on going. The
condos are smashing—spacious and decorated in luscious colors with striking contemporary furniture and a breathtaking view of the island and Gulf.
Large with gourmet kitchens, each unit has a separate maid's quarters
(which many owners have chosen to use as a den). If you're a cliff-dweller
looking for the best, this is your best choice.

3   **CASA DEL SOL**
        Gulf Blvd. at Amberjack, So. Padre Island, TX 78597
        1BR $55–75, 2BR $85–129
        Amenities: Pool, hot tub

This small three-story condo building is a budget choice offering two-
bedroom units in a mid-island location. Not on the beach, it's close to a cul-
de-sac offering beach access. The units are spacious and attractive with both
a living room and a dining area. It has a small pool and it's a quiet place
to stay.

4 CASTAWAYS
3700 Gulf Blvd., So. Padre Island, TX 78597
Amenities: Beach, pool

A quiet, economical place that offers attractive rates for daily, weekly, and monthly rentals. Popular with winter Texans, the Castaways offers spacious two-bedroom condos on the beach.

5 CONTINENTAL
4908 Gulf Blvd., Box 2113, So. Padre Island, TX 78597
512-761-1306, 1BR $60–119, 2BR $115–159
Amenities: Beach, pool

Enjoying a prime beachfront location, the Continental is a white stucco, three-story building. The lower units can be noisy because the walls are thin. It's a pleasant place where many families show up on weekends.

7 EDGEWATER
2216 Gulf Blvd., So. Padre Island, TX 78597
1BR $69–129, 2BR $129–195
Amenities: Beach, hot tub, pool, tennis

One of the more popular resorts on South Padre Island, the Edgewater offers solid spacious condos overlooking the beach. Good value, the units are nicely decorated with contemporary furniture that feature soft colors and seashore accents. There's a pool and hot tub but they are never crowded. For those who want peace and quiet or privacy in a condominium, the Edgewater fits your style. There is no on-site management.

8 EMBASSY
2600 Gulf Blvd., So. Padre Island, TX 78597
1BR $100, 2BR $180
Amenities: Pool, hot tub, beach, tennis

This solid beachfront condominium benefits from excellent management. Quietly efficient, everything is in good working order. Spacious units with balconies overlook the beach in this six-story building. It is quiet with few children in sight.

7 FLORENCE I AND II
Gulf Blvd. at Morningside, So. Padre Island, TX 78597
Studio $50–75, 1BR $75–129, 2BR $100–209
Amenities: Beach, pool, hot tub

Located near the northern end of the South Padre Island development, this seven-story condominium provides an attractive environment for a vacation at the beach. Each condo has a private patio with a view of the beach and the

Gulf. An intimate pool and hot tub are located directly on the beach. Casual contemporary decor, this is a good spot for families who want a week at the beach. There is no on-site management.

8 FRANKE PLAZA
706 Padre Blvd., So. Padre Island, TX 78597
2BR $105–155, 3BR $129–219
Amenities: Beach, indoor and outdoor pools, exercise/weight room, racquetball, game room

An 18-story tower where the condos begin on the 6th floor. This is truly a luxurious condominium building where each of the two- or three-bedroom condos has a sweeping view of the Gulf and the beach. The units have an efficient design that allows a view of the water from both the living room and the master bath. There are lots of extra touches in each unit, such as the floors and a wet bar in the living room. It's the amenities that make Franke Plaza outstanding: a full service gym with exercise/weight room and two racquetball courts. Not only are there two outdoor pools, but Franke Plaza has the largest indoor pool on the island. It is a great choice for couples, families, or winter Texans; "Spring breakers" need not apply. Call Franke Realty at 512-761-2606.

2 GALLEON BAY
4901 Laguna Blvd., Box 2687, So. Padre Island, TX 78597
512-761-7808, 1BR $75–95, 2BR $110–125
Amenities: Pool, boat dock

Located on the bay side of the island, Galleon Bay is not beachfront property. This eleven-story, high-rise tower features unusual architecture with open breezeways on each floor. If you're staying on the upper floors, get everything weighted down so it won't be swept away by the wind when you open the door. This building needs improvement in exterior maintenance and several of the condos we saw had worn furniture. With a little sprucing up, these spacious condos could offer a pleasant vacation environment.

4 GULFPOINT
100 Padre Blvd., So. Padre Island, TX 78597
1BR $49–99, 2BR $69–119
Amenities: Pool

Located on the southern tip of the island next to Isla Blanca Park, these condos, in a three-story building surrounding a garden and pool, provide a quiet, off-the-beach address. Attractive on the outside, the interior decor is fading. Long term rentals for a month or two are offered at an advantageous price.

6 **GULFVIEW I AND II**
250 Padre Blvd., Box 3290, So. Padre Island, TX 78597
512-761-5910 (G. I), 512-761-6416 (G. II)
1BR $69, 2BR $99–129
Amenities: Pool, tennis, boat dock, hot tub

Located right as you come across the bridge from the mainland, these condos are choice for those who don't have a car. Within easy walking distance of the beach, shops, and restaurants, this is a village of two-story shingle buildings designed to evoke the image of a fishing village. Cute on the outside, they are attractively furnished on the inside with new rattan or contemporary decor.

6 **ISLA DEL SOL**
Gulf Blvd., So. Padre Island, TX 78597
1BR $65–108, 2BR $125–192
Amenities: Beach, pool, landscaped park

These condos are in a four-story building on a prime section of the beach at Padre Island. This is one of the few resorts where you really don't need a car. There are so many things to do within walking distance. Best feature: large lawn area that other nearby resorts don't have. This is a good place for active, young children. The spacious interiors are well maintained. Some could use new furniture; others were recently redecorated in a contemporary late 1980s style. The units are solid and are in a good location.

4 **INVERNESS AT SOUTH PADRE**
5600 Gulf Blvd., So. Padre Island, TX 78597, 512-761-7919
1BR $100, 2BR $125
Amenities: Beach, pool

A popular place that is always full, it is located on the northern section of the beach. It is an eleven-story tower with spacious units and a good location. This property suffers from almost too much popularity. There are waits for the elevator and a daily need to tidy up the common areas. The outdoor pool is on the third floor and is a lively place for families or seniors to gather.

5 **LA INTERNACIONAL**
5008 Gulf Blvd., Box 2113, So. Padre Island, TX 78597
512-761-1306, Studio $42, 1BR $64
Amenities: Beach, pool

This is an average condo resort that was designed in a semicircle so that each unit is slightly wedge-shaped. We don't know why or how they do it, but this place is always full. There's nothing exceptional about the location or the units, but management has created a friendly environment where guests make friends and want to return year after year. All the units are one-bedroom models that accommodate a maximum of four guests. Winter Texans just love La Internacional.

3 LA PLAYA
2308 Gulf Blvd., Box 2122, So. Padre Island, TX 78597
512-761-1066, 1BR $260–400/wk, 2BR $315–600/wk
Amenities: Beach, pool

This is a small, wood-shingle resort on the beach. There is no on-site management and this may explain the run-down appearance of these condos. They offer weekly rentals only.

6+ MARISOL
1700 Gulf Blvd., Box 2310, So. Padre Island, TX 78597
512-761-1193
Amenities: Beach, pool

A cute, small condo building on the beach, it is constructed of brick, which is unusual for Padre Island. The architect blessed Marisol with flourishes and a hint of the English Tudor style. Pleasant, cheerful units where space has been carefully planned for maximum use. The condos are a little on the small side but nicely furnished. Attentive management makes sure this stays in tiptop shape and that each guest receives a warm reception. It is an intimate spot.

6-8 OCEAN VISTA TOWERS
Gulf Blvd at Whiting, So. Padre Island, TX 78597; 2BR $109–179
Amenities: Beach, pool, tennis, hot tub

Ocean Vista consists of two massive eight-story towers that overlook the beach. Currently being renovated, this resort has all the key ingredients to become a prime vacation destination. The rating reflects what we saw and what it might become.

8 PADRE GRANDE
2100 Gulf Blvd., Box 2489, So. Padre Island, TX 78597
512-761-7290, 1BR $95–125, 2BR $155–195
Amenities: Pool, hot tub

This is one of the most attractive resort condo developments on Padre Island. The impressive lobby lives up to its name with the two-story high ceiling and massive bronze doors, tile floors, mirrors, and a full-service reception area. Step outside and discover the pool and large hot tub. Upstairs, the same elegance is carried through. Floor coverings are carpeted with some tile work at the entrance and around the dining room. Decorated with lots of mirrors to bring in the view, in daylight you'll find the units are dazzling. This is a quiet resort where you're more apt to find energetic grandparents than young families with kiddies.

4 PADRE OASIS
111 E. Morningside, Box 2868, So. Padre Island, TX 78597
512-761-4689, 1BR $69–129, 2BR $79–159
Amenities: Pool, hot tub

Located mid-island, it's an easy walk from this three-story condo building over to the beach. A quiet, low-key place to stay, this doesn't have the transient resort atmosphere. Many of the condos here are residential or semi-residential because they are used by their owners on weekends.

5 PADRE SOUTH
1500 Gulf Blvd., Box 2338, So. Padre Island, TX 78597
512-761-4951, 1BR $80–100, 2BR $100–125
Amenities: Beach, pool, snack bar

Near the center of the commercial area, Padre South was one of the first condos built on South Padre. Located on the beach, there is a cute gazebo, large pool, and a good little cafeteria for snacks. The pier is nearby for fishing. The beach is at a gentle slope here and the calm water is just right for getting your feet wet or swimming. There is an activities program, and in summer a social director plans programs for small children. Although a nice resort it is now showing years of use.

2 PADRE VISTA
1323 Palo Blanco Dr., Laguna Vista, TX 78578
Amenities: Pool

These condos are not on Padre Island, but rather on the flats between Harlingen and the island. Near the lagoon, these townhouses attract short-term visitors. Each week trips are arranged to Matamoros, Mexico, and because it is popular with fisherman, fishing charters are frequently arranged for the guests. However, the location is far from the mainstream resort community.

4-3 PARK LANE
Morningside at Padre Blvd., Box 2257, So. Padre Island, TX 78557
1BR $39–69, 2BR $49–99
Amenities: Pool

This three-story wooden structure has a mid-island location. It is inexpensive and you can't miss this one because of its bright blue color. The beach is only a short walk away.

9   PARKSHORE
7000 Gulf Blvd., So. Padre Island, TX 78557
2BR $105–179, 3BR $129–219
Amenities: Beach, pool hot tub, tennis

One of the more exclusive resorts, this enjoys a quiet north beach location. Separated from the remainder of the condo/hotel strip by geography, entry to this resort is carefully controlled by a security gate and guard. You'll find large spacious units in this eight-story building, each with sweeping view of the Gulf of Mexico. Those on the north end have a special unobstructed view of the sand dunes of Padre Island National Seashore Park. It has consistently superior interior decor. Some have Mexican furniture, others have contemporary furniture in pinks and seafoam colors. No spring breakers.

5   PUESTA DEL SOL
Laguna Blvd. at Acapulco, So. Padre island, TX 78557
1BR $65–69
Amenities: Pool

Although a budget choice, this offers spacious units, attractive landscaping, and attentive on-site management. The only drawback is that it's located on the bay side of the island, not on the beach. The beach is a six-minute walk away, across the island. This is a quiet two-story building offering an inexpensive choice on Padre Island.

8+   RADISSON BEACH CLUB (See also Royale Beach Club)
500 Padre Blvd., So. Padre Island, TX 78597
Studio $75, 1BR $129, 2BR $219
Amenities: Pools, restaurants, tennis

There are four buildings with 270 condos at this property. One building is managed by the Radisson hotel group. The other three buildings are individually owned condos. The hub of activity on the island, you'll always have plenty to do. Generally you'll find large units with handsome contemporary decor. Most are superior to what is commonly found on the island, although there are some in need of redecoration. We saw one cheerfully decorated in rose pinks and seafoam green colors, that was every bit as inviting as a movie set. There was a large-screen television and a tape player for the times you want to stay inside. Overall, this is one of the best choices for a first-time visitor to South Padre because of all the entertainment, services, and activity.

8   REGENCY
Gulf Blvd. at Palm, So. Padre Island, TX 78597
2BR $69–104, 3BR $129–185
Amenities: Beach, pools, tennis

The Regency enjoys a convenient location just north of the main area of shops around the Sunchase Mall. As the name implies, this is a top-quality, six-story condo building with two- and three-bedroom units on the beach. It has solid construction, a small pool, and a lawn separating the building from the beach. Many of the units have been professionally decorated by interior decorators. There's a second courtyard pool that becomes a clubby place for cocktails in the evenings. The Regency is very nice.

8+   ROYALE BEACH CLUB
410 Padre Blvd., Box 2809, So. Padre Island, TX 78597
800-292-0204, 1BR $85–190
Amenities: Pools, restaurants, tennis

This is a timeshare development within one of the four towers at the massive Radisson Beach Club condo complex. Guests can use all the facilities of the Radisson resort including the pools, restaurants, tennis courts, etc. Here you have condo convenience combined with hotel activity. The Royale Beach Club goes a step beyond the hospitality offered at neighboring condo towers by featuring organized day trips to Mexico. Social directors are on hand to schedule a variety of on-site activities for adults and children. Our favorite: the afternoon crab races with parimutuel betting. It's lots of fun and a great mixer. The views of the island and ocean are spectacular here.

5   SAND CASTLE
200 W. Kingfish, Box 2220, So. Padre Island, TX 78597
800-221-5218, 1BR $35–64
Amenities: Beach, pool

Located on the Laguna Madre, the Sand Castle is two blocks away from the ocean. Simple and decorated in motel style furniture, this is one resort that welcomes—and provides special packages for guests at Easter week.

7   SEABREEZE BEACH RESORT
5400 Gulf Blvd., Box 3169, So. Padre Island, TX 78597
800-541-9901
Amenities: Beach, pools, hot tub

Do not confuse this with Seabreeze I, which is next door. This is a special place because of personalized attention from management. Seabreeze Beach Resort has two modern six-story, concrete buildings on the beach. These units are solid, functional, and comfortable. You'll find lots of rattan, island-style furniture but some units have been dressed up by interior decorators. There are large kitchens with all of the modern appliances. For those who don't want to be in a high-rise tower but who are looking for a superior vacation spot, this may be your choice.

6   **SEABREEZE I**
          4300 Gulf Blvd., Box 3559, So. Padre Island, TX 78597
          512-761-7734
          Amenities: Beach, pool, hot tub

A small six-story, 28-unit concrete condo building right on the beach. It is intimate, and owners and guests quickly get to know each other. These condos are well-maintained under the watchful eye of the manager. The units are on the small side, but have efficient, functional design.

6   **SUMMIT**
          900 Padre Blvd., So. Padre Island, TX 78597
          1BR $88–104, 2BR $129–219
          Amenities: Beach, pools, hot tub, tennis

Simple and unpretentious, this is one of our favorite choices for value. Located on a good section of beach, it's far enough away from the main cluster of activity so it can be classified as more residential. Each unit faces the beach and the living room enjoys great views. Furniture ranges from comfortable to island style, although some are a little aged; a few units have new decor. This is a friendly, quiet place to stay and is priced lower than many lesser properties.

7   **SUNCHASE I, II, III**
          1016 Padre Blvd., Box 2638, So. Padre Island, TX 78597
          512-761-1660
          Amenities: Beach, pool, health club racquetball

This is one of the largest complexes on the island and is completely separate from Sunchase IV located next door. These three towers have intriguing architecture. The towers on either end are designed in the shape of a stepped triangle and the central tower is rounded. Altogether the complex, viewed from the air, appears to be a large bird about to take flight. The key advantage here is full-time, front-desk service to attend to your needs. There are lots of people, and lots of activities. For the first time visitor this is a good choice because of the central location (the Sunchase shopping mall has some of the best shops on the island) and because of the services for visitors. Upstairs the condo units vary in quality. You can expect to find lots of rattan, island-style furniture accented by treasures from the markets in Mexico.

9   **SUNCHASE IV**
          1000 Padre Blvd., Box 2820, Padre Island, TX 78597, 512-761-5521
          1BR $94–129, 2BR $129–179, 3BR $159–219
          Amenities: Beach, pool, restaurant, health club

Sunchase IV is one of the island's best. Centrally located, it's convenient to the bridge and other activities. This is a luxury choice and you'll feel it the minute you step into the gleaming marble lobby chilled by air conditioning. You'll be as impressed by the grandeur of open empty space as by the charm of one of the concierges at the front desk who is eager to serve. Upstairs, it's even better. Each unit is a corner unit that captures multiple views and lots of sunlight. We saw two and each had over $50,000 worth of interior decor. The place gleams with marble floors, modern chrome and glass furniture, and bright emerald green fabrics outlined by beach ebony. Only three colors: white, green, and black. This is what you would expect in Houston's River Oaks, not down on the beach. The second one also looked like an interior decorators showroom with rose-colored fabrics and lots of ceramic vases and flowers as accents. Furnishings were more traditional, but the high-back upholstered chairs made the atmosphere distinctive.

6   SUNTIDE II
Gulf Blvd. at Saturn St. So. Padre Island, TX 78597
1BR $75–125, 2BR $99–175
Amenities: Beach, pool, hot tub, tennis

Located right on the beach, in the middle of the island activity, Suntide offers fairly new condos in a six-story building. The living room opens out onto your balcony with views of the Gulf. This is the best feature. Interior decor runs to neutral colors and tweed fabrics. The free-form pool is attractive in design but can be crowded.

7   SUNTIDE III
3000 Gulf Blvd., Box 2397, So. Padre Island, TX 78597
512-761-1307
Amenities: Beach, pool, tennis, hot tub, saunas

Modern, sleek, and on the beach, this tower offers spacious condos and a host of services for vacationers. Upstairs, the condos are spacious and decor is superior with contemporary or island-style, rattan furniture. The living room has a wall of glass and there's an additional space of a little breakfast nook. This is a good setup for a week or a month at the beach. This is one of the few resorts with both an indoor and outdoor pool.

4   TIKI
6608 Padre Blvd., Box 2398, So. Padre Island, TX 78597
512-761-2694, 1BR $59–77, 2BR $62–99
Amenities: Beach, heated pools, sauna

Located up on the north end of the South Padre community, near the entrance to the national seashore park, the Tiki enjoys a quiet location. Polynesian architecture rules the day and the resort was designed with style.

But that was twenty years ago. Unfortunately, the interior decor is dark and dreary. The romance of this unique resort has been lost, in our opinion. It's a pleasant place to stay, but with a little effort on the part of the owners, it could be so much better.

RENTAL RESOURCES

Condo Rentals of South Padre, 800-537-2373
Conrow Realty, 800-327-1608
Franke Realty, 512-761-2606
Furcron Realtors, 512-761-6961
Gulf Rentals Plus, 800-346-4046
Gulf View Realty, 512-761-2608, Port Isabel side, across the bay
Island Services, 512-761-7901
Padre Island Rentals, 800-292-7520
Padre Rentals, 512-761-5100
SandDollar Realty, 800-531-4541, 512-761-7857,
    Largest selection of condo rentals on South Padre
So. Padre Island Rentals, 512-761-1709
Staley Properties, 512-761-6426
Sunchase Realty & Management, 512-761-7711
Sunny Isles, 512-762-4689
Tropical Condominium Service, 800-221-5218

2. BROWNSVILLE

One of the most historically important towns in Texas, Brownsville sits on the Rio Grande just a stone's throw from the markets of Mexico. Unlike any other community in the U.S., this border town is "foreign." The Anglo and Mexican cultures have truly combined in this international city.

A chief reason to visit Brownsville is Rancho Viejo, one of the most romantic resorts we've visited. This paradise for golfers is also popular as a conference center for small executive meetings. The climate is dry and warm all year. In summer, on hot days, the beaches of Padre Island are only a few minutes away.

WHERE TO STAY

7 **FT. BROWN CONDOSHARES**
    Elizabeth St., Box 2255, Brownsville, TX 78520, 800-582-3333
    1BR $80–110
    Amenities: Pool, health club, tennis, children's playground

Just across from Mexico, along the shores of the Rio Grande, you'll find the 17-acre Ft. Brown Hotel. Surrounded by a Spanish resaca (lagoon), a waterfall, and lush greenery, this has in many respects been the social center of Brownsville for years. Twelve years ago part of the acreage was set aside as a condo village of two-story, adobe-style townhouses. Many have been purchased by Mexican nationals who will come over to Brownsville for a few days of fun, restaurants, golf, and shopping. Interior decor includes contemporary blond wood furniture and pastel pink, blue, or green fabrics. There's a little variation and none have been personalized by the owners. This is a unique resort within walking distance of the markets of Mexico Brownsville has its own character and attitudes, having been a part of the U.S. for less than 140 years. This is Mexico in the U.S.

9+   RANCHO VIEJO
Hwy 77 North 83, P.O. Box 3918, Brownsville, TX 78520
512-350-4000, Studio $95, 2BR villa $170, 3BR villa $245
Amenities: Golf, tennis, pool

Rancho Viejo is what you would hope to find in Texas. This 1400-acre resort captures the flavor of both Old Texas and Old Mexico. Located on a tributary stream of the Rio Grande, this property just 20 minutes north of the border, continues to use the Spanish names. The map is on antique paper and immediately brings to mind an old pirate's map. Ranch Viejo is a 400-year-old working ranch that still retains some of the citrus groves. Today, the ranch has been enhanced by championship golf courses with condos, bungalows, and villas lining the fairways. These two-, three-, and four-bedroom units are either duplexes or townhouses. Interior decor is superior with designer touches and themes. We saw one in all beige with bright teal and rose pillows and accents. Another had a collection of satin-stuffed pillows "snakes" suggesting the primitive Santa Fe style. Many have been decorated with no expense spared. All this is for you to enjoy as a rental condo or villa. There are two 18-hole golf courses, El Angel and El Diablo, that were former sites for a PGA tour qualifying school. The school is gone but the facilities and instructors are there for you with golf clinics for all levels. For tennis players there are eight courts. Rancho Viejo has huge, landscaped pools with a cascading waterfall and a swim-up bar. Beach lovers—it's only 30 minutes over to South Padre Island. A major attraction is the Casa Grande Supper Club and getting there is half the fun. You can take a cruise aboard the Delta Dawn down the three-mile resaca (tributary stream) to the clubhouse. You'll be served cocktails on board and serenaded by a mariachi band. The Supper Club is actually the ranch's original hacienda where roving Mexican troubadours contribute to the ambiance. Staying here is unique for it provides a marvelous blend of Old Mexico and Texas.

3. NORTH PADRE ISLAND / PORT ARANSAS

Starting at the north end of the island, Port Aransas encompasses a small fishing port and is the postal address for fifteen miles of beachfront condos that stretch down to the entrance of the National Seashore Park. The area has been blessed with an average annual temperature of 71 degrees. The cultural flavor here is decidedly Anglo-Mexico. You can reach Port Aransas by causeway from neighboring Corpus Christi or take a 20-minute ferry ride across the Bay separating North Padre Island from the city. Just south of Port Aransas, the stretch of beach is known as Mustang Island. You'll find a few resorts with high-rise towers and super free-form pools. Most condos here are low-rise apartments or townhouses where families or couples can enjoy a few days of fishing or walking the beach.

Air transportation is easy with frequent nonstop flights to Corpus Christi from most Texas cities and direct flights to much of the Midwest and desert southwest.

WHERE TO STAY

4   **ARANSAS HARBOR**
230 S. Cut-Off Rd., Box 1760, Port Aransas, TX 78373
512-749-4122, 1BR $49–69, 2BR $79–99
Amenities: Pool, tennis

Occupying a unique location in the town of Port Aransas, these are the first condos you'll come to after crossing the Corpus Christi Ship Channel via ferry. Spread over twelve acres, there are ten, two-story brick buildings that provide a "non high-rise" atmosphere. At first glance this looks like a residential condo project because it is not near the beach. This is a quiet place to stay and is convenient for fisherman or boating enthusiasts. You'll find these units offer solid construction, spacious floor plans, and neutral furniture. Friendly, vivacious management will help you get acquainted with the area. But for the location, this would earn higher marks.

5   **ARANSAS PRINCESS**
720 Beach Access Rd., Box 309, Port Aransas, TX 78373
512-749-5118, 2BR $130–195
Amenities: Pools, beach, tennis

This is a nine-story, high-rise condo with 112 gorgeous units located on the beach at Mustang Island. It is just three miles south of the town of Port Aransas. Beautifully designed, these units provide tasteful charm. But due to problems in the real estate market and developer financing, most of these spacious condos sit empty—lonely damsels waiting for their charms to be discovered. Because of the ghost-town atmosphere, this is for the adventurous only.

2   BAY TREE
900 N. Station, Drawer A, Port Aransas, TX 78373, 512-749-5859
Amenities: Fishing pier, boat dock, pool, tennis

Located on the Corpus Christi Ship Channel, the condos in these two-story buildings have good views of the bay and the harbor. Baytree offers some of the most inexpensive studios to be found on the island. But the design and construction remind us more of a converted motel than a designed condo. Management is friendly and it is convenient for fishermen.

5   BEACHHEAD RESORT
1319 11th St., Box 1577, Port Aransas, TX 78373, 512-749-6261
Amenities: beach, tennis, game room

Located along the strip of beachfront condos just south of town, Beachhead offers a modest vacation retreat at a very reasonable price. These condos have relatively more privacy than many of the other developments in this area because they are in a series of two-story quadriplexes. Wood construction creates that casual "beach house" environment where a little sand on the floor is acceptable. Each condo is situated so there is a view of the beach and the Gulf of Mexico. One real plus: a very attractive lobby and management that arranges weekly shopping or sightseeing trips to Mexico. This is one of the most popular spots in the area for "Winter Texans" in January and February.

6+   CASADEL
Highway 361, Box 1149, Port Aransas, TX 78373, 512-749-6942
Studio $65, 1BR $125, 2BR $160
Amenities: Beach, pool, tennis, game room

Unlike most other condos in the area that were constructed 200 yards away from the beach, Casadel is right on the beach. Sit on your balcony at this six-story building and listen to the surf gently lap the shore. The units are new and functionally designed to make the best use of the space. The result: good value and economical price. It is popular with families who have small children. Summertime brings planned activities and programs for children.

6   CHANNEL VIEW
631 Channelview Dr., Box 776, Port Aransas, TX 78373
512-749-6649, 1BR $52–125, 2BR $67–200, 3BR $90–230
Amenities: Heated pool, boat dock

Located at the very northern tip of the island at the edge of town, these condos enjoy the convenience of a "marina" location along with the privacy that comes from having a view of the limitless water and horizon. Spaciously designed for complete privacy, you'll find extra-large living rooms. Some have brick fireplaces. Some of the units have superior interior decor. We saw one done in "old fashioned country style" with quilts on the beds and lots of ruffles and needlepoint pillows. Convenient for the family that wants to go in several directions on vacation: the beach, boating, fishing, or strolling through town. On-site management treats each guest like a member of the family.

9 CLINE'S LANDING
1000 Station St., Box 1628, Port Aransas, TX 78373
512-749-5274, 2BR $125–140, 3BR 175–200
Amenities: Heated pool, hot tub, tennis, children's playground

This is one of the top choices along this part of the Texas Riviera. This six-story luxurious condo building dominates the skyline of Port Aransas. Overlooking the Corpus Christi Ship Channel, each condo has been designed with a wall of glass offering a sweeping view of the bay. The architect took great pains to ensure the privacy of each unit, so each balcony is at an angle and can't be seen by its neighbor. The units are spacious and well designed. Interior decor is superior and some owners have used rich colors and quality fabrics to enhance the vacation home environment. Each unit has wood cabinets in the kitchen, a travertine marble breakfast bar, and track lighting. It is deluxe. The Sunset Lounge is a private spot atop the building, and afford the best views of the town and Aransas Pass.

7 CORAL CAY
1423 11th St., Box 448, Port Aransas, TX 78373, 512-749-5111
Studio $59–75, 2BR $69–89, 3BR $79–99
Amenities: Pools, tennis

Nestled on the beach with its coral tiled roofs, Coral Cay has three two-story buildings containing 84 units. This resort features seaside charm with creature comforts at a moderate price. Lovely landscaping has been thoughtfully placed to compliment the native grasses and wild flowers of the sand dunes. Friendly, on-site management will help you make the most of your vacation at the beach. Inside, the condos have "much loved" ambiance. Several units have been personalized by their owners so you can expect to find toys or games tucked away in a closet. Comfortable furniture.

8 THE DUNES

1000 Lantana, Box 1238, Port Aransas, TX 78373, 512-749-5155
1BR $70–120, 2BR $90–155, 3BR $130–215
Amenities: Beach, heated pool, tennis, exercise room,
card room, fishing pier

The Dunes is one of the most popular choices in the area year-round. It is full of laughing families in the summer, and it is a choice spot for retirees in winter. Why? There are so many social activities that friendships are quickly formed and a cheerful, club-like atmosphere evolves. This is not expensive and certainly not luxurious, but this is a resort with character. The location is on the beach within easy walking distance to town. From each of the balconies of this nine-story building you'll have a sweeping view of the Gulf of Mexico. The condos are functionally designed to make the best use of space. Generally, decor includes rattan furniture that creates a "tropical-island" feeling. Best feature: the pool and party patio. Screened from the wind and ringed with tropical flora, the pool and spa area is quite inviting.

6+ EL CORTES VILLAS

Highway 361, Box 1266, Port Aransas, TX 78373
512-749-6206, 1BR $45–65, 2BR $65–85
Amenities: Pools, tennis, beach

Located three miles south of town along the endless Padre Island beach, this is a cluster of nine, two-story quadriplexes with distinctive "plantation house"-style roofs. Set back 500 yards from the beach, this is a community that attracts those who want to be close but not necessarily on the beach. For golfers, the Padre Isles Country Club is nearby. Each unit is two stories and has two bedrooms. There's a main living room on the ground floor, but also a second sitting room upstairs. There's lots of space.

3 EXECUTIVE KEYS

700 Beach Access Rd., Box 1087, Port Aransas, TX 78373
512-749-6272, Rates $38–110
Amenities: Beach, pool, recreation/card room

Driving by you can't help but notice these bright blue condos. This is a casual, friendly place at the beach with extra large units. Most are two- or three-bedroom models and some are two-story townhouses. Interior decor is casual and in some cases, dates from the 1970s. Overall, this is a friendly place for people who want a vacation at the beach. Executive Keys has its corps of loyalists who want to return to this resort year after year.

4   GULF SHORES
Park Rd. 53, Box 1298, Port Aransas, Texas 78373, 512-749-6257
2BR $60
Amenities: Beach, pool, tennis, game room

Located six miles south of Port Aransas and seven miles north of the causeway to Corpus Christi, this resort occupies a prime beachfront location. The sands of Padre Island stretch endlessly in either direction. Each condo has a private balcony recessed from its neighbors, overlooking the beach and the Gulf. Contemporary furnishings in some units; island-style, rattan furniture in others. A few have relics that can best be described as "early attic." This is a quiet choice that is modestly priced.

5   GULFSTREAM
14810 Windward Dr., Corpus Christi, TX 78418
512-949-8061, 2BR $80–100
Amenities: Beach, heated pool

The Gulfstream enjoys an unspoiled location on Padre Island beach even though it is technically within the Corpus Christi city limits. Here, a seawall protects the property from occasional storms coming from the Gulf of Mexico. This is a six-story, U-shaped apartment-style structure where each condo has a view of the Gulf. Interior decor features rattan furniture and dark, patterned fabrics. There is a heated outdoor swimming pool that is more popular than the beach in spring and fall. These are straight forward, no-nonsense lodgings that are well maintained.

6   ISLAND DUNES
715 Beach Access Rd., Box 1784, Port Aransas, TX 78373
512-749-4923, 1BR $60–80. 2BR $70–90, 3BR $85–110
Amenities: Pool

Located at the end of 11th street where the wide expanse of Padre Island begins, Island Dunes is a cluster of two-story duplexes. This complex was very well planned and built with solid construction. There's lots of space, privacy, a courtyard, and a free-form pool. Interior decor is stylish and contemporary. The units are either two- or three-bedrooms. The only drawback here is the RV park wedged between Island Dunes and the beach; boxy RV's tend to spoil the view.

5   ISLAND RETREAT
P. O. Box 637, Port Aransas, TX 78373, 512-749-6222
Studio $44, 1BR $46, 2BR $48, 3BR $54
Amenities: Beach, pool, tennis

These are condos on the beach at the northern end of Padre Island. This is a family resort where children and adults can let their hair down. It is very casual. Some units are motel-style rooms, others are two- and three-bedroom apartments. The first thing you notice about the condo interiors is the wood paneling. This makes the interiors a little bit darker than those that you would find elsewhere. You'll find cowhide upholstered furniture and couches covered with lots of tweed fabrics. This creates almost a "Texas-ranch" atmosphere, yet right out the window you'll see the ocean. There's a swimming pool surrounded by a chain link fence as protection against wandering toddlers. There are two lighted tennis courts and a host of activities in nearby Port Aransas. You'll find relaxed living by the beach. Long-term rentals are available and encouraged.

6   LA MIRAGE

Highway 361, Box 506, Port Aransas, TX 98373, 512-749-6030
Amenities: Pool, beach, tennis

Located midway between Port Aransas and the causeway to Corpus Christi, La Mirage is a huge 120-unit condo project in the middle of nowhere, with endless beach in either direction. The ground floor is actually a parking garage and the first floor of condos is actually the second floor. New management is working hard to bring this to life. The units are attractive, but the few visitors gives this an erie feeling. Press hard to get good rental rates for these attractive, spacious condos.

9   MAYAN PRINCESS

Park Rd. 53, Box 281, Port Aransas, TX 78379
512-749-5183, 1BR $75–140, 2BR $115–170
Amenities: Pools, hot tub, tennis, beach

One of the most beautiful resorts on Padre Island. The Mayan Princess is located nine miles south of Port Aransas and four miles north of the causeway to Corpus Christi. Surrounded by sand dunes, the beach stretches endlessly in either direction. The Mayan Princess is noteworthy for its distinctive architecture; it looks like it belongs in Cancun. Architecturally this complex includes white angular structures with a painted Mayan motif bordering the roof line. Open the massive Mexican-style front door and step inside to the cool, dark, luxury of a Mexican establishment. Service at the front desk is courteous, helpful, and professional. Now step outside to the garden and immediately you'll feel like you are in Cancun with the free-form pool, swim-up bar, and palapa restaurant. Inside, each condo is stunning because of the garden views. A Mexican-style stone/concrete wall dominates the living room. There are superior modern furnishings, many with the touch of an interior designer. Expect contemporary colors of peach, teal, and aqua. Stylish, prices are more reasonable than you would expect.

6   MUSTANG ISLAND BEACH CLUB AND RESORT
Highway 361, Box 166, Port Aransas, TX 78373
512-749-5446, 1BR $70, 2BR $90
Amenities: Pool, hot tub

This resort sits back from the beach. It is an attractive set of four condo buildings surrounding a pool and hot tub. A little bridge crosses the pool area and gives the project romance. The units are newly decorated in soft apricot and green colors. The resort is very quiet. There is a small clubhouse, but basically this is for people who value their privacy.

2   MUSTANG ISLE APARTMENTS
2025 11th St., Box 37, Port Aransas, TX 78373, 512-749-6011
1BR $33, 2BR $55
Amenities: Fish cleaning facilities

Located on the beach just south of the town of Port Aransas, these condos are tired and uninspired.

6   MUSTANG TOWERS
Highway 361, P.O. Box 1870, Port Aransas, TX 78373
512-749-6212, 2BR $75–200, $95–225
Amenities: Pool, hot tub, tennis

A nine-story, high-rise on the Padre Island beach it stands alone with no neighbors. Located midway between Port Aransas and the Corpus Christi causeway, the location is great for beach/nature lovers. There are lots of visitors here and the elevator is always in use. During the summer, there are organized shopping tours to Mexico and trips to San Antonio as well as planned activities for children.

4   THE PELICAN
1107 S. 11th St., P.O.Box 1690, Port Aransas, TX 78373
512-749-6226, 2BR $46, 3BR $52
Amenities: Pool, basketball backboard, children's playground

The Pelican consists of a cluster of two- and three-story buildings with distinctive French mansard roofs. Inside, the condos are disappointing because they are smaller than average and having tiny kitchens. The decor is neutral. If you plan to do lots of fishing you'll find other soul mates here.

8   PORT ROYAL
Highway 361, P.O. Box 336, Port Aransas, TX 78373
512-749-5011, 1BR $79–140, 2BR $99–180
Amenities: Pool, waterslide, tennis, restaurant

One of the best choices on North Padre Island, Port Royal is a fairly new four-story complex that is beach front, but slightly recessed to preserve an area of sea oats. The handsome condos are well decorated, with light, upbeat colors and rattan furniture. They are designed so each condo has a spacious living room and a view of the beach or harbor. There are private fireplaces and a whirlpool in the master bath. Some condos have private steam rooms! There's lots of activity here around the supersize lagoon pool—the largest in this part of Padre Island. There are cascading waterfalls, swim-up bars, and even a waterslide. There is an attractive restaurant overlooking the lagoon pool. The fresh seafood restaurants of Port Aransas are within walking distance. This is a well-run operation that has a top-flight resort environment.

7   SANDCASTLE
800 Sandcastle Dr., Box 1688, Port Aransas, TX 78373
512-749-6201, Studio $69, $1BR $99–109, 2BR $155
Amenities: Pool, tennis courts

Located on the edge of town, yet having a prime beachfront location, this is one of the most popular resorts on Padre Island. Designed and built in a U-shape, each of the 108 condos in this five-story building has its own sweeping view of the Gulf. The centerpiece is the garden and landscaped pool area. Somewhat recessed from the beach, there's a bridge and footpath over to the water. Excellent management makes this spot popular year round. There are organized tours to San Antonio, there is shopping in Mexico, and trips out west to the dude ranch country of Kerrville. The condos are spacious and well-designed so the living room enjoys the magnificent view. Thanks to a breakfast bar, that same view is also available from the kitchen, while the cook continues to enjoy everyone else's company. This is a friendly place.

8   SANDPIPER
Highway 361, Box 1268, Port Aransas, TX 78373, 512-749-6251
1BR $70–110, 2BR $90–120, 3BR $130–170
Amenities: Beach, pool, hot tub, tennis

Like the Sea Gull, this is one of the best built and most attractive condo towers on Padre Island. Somewhat newer, you'll find spacious, well-designed units with superior contemporary decor. Most have style as well as space. A beautiful landscaped garden and swimming pool area is available.

8   SEA GULL
Highway 361, Box 1207, Port Aransas, TX 78373, 512-749-4191
1BR $70–110, 2BR $90–150, 3BR $130–210
Amenities: Beach, pool, tennis

Located eight miles south of Port Aransas and five miles north of the Corpus Christi causeway, the Sea Gull is the twin property to the Sandpiper. A massive, ten-story building with two arms forming a V. Every condo overlooks a beautifully landscaped garden and the free-form pool—absolutely dynamite. This is what a condo resort should be. Just for whimsy, there's a little footbridge over the pool. The condos are spacious and solidly built. The living room is long and follows the glass wall overlooking the Gulf. The kitchen and bedrooms are in the rear. Social activities center around the pool and beach. Count on seeing small groups congregate by the pool each evening for cocktails while the sun sets. This provides great value.

RENTAL RESOURCES
Coldwell Banker, 800-366-6693
M.G. Management, 512-749-4871
Padre Island Realtors, 512-949-7036
Port Aransas Realty, 512-749-4000

4. GALVESTON ISLAND

Although only an hour from downtown Houston by Interstate highway, Galveston has a character all its own. Its history predates Houston, and it was a major part of the early settlement of Texas. Reputedly, the Pirate Jean Lafitte made his headquarters here when not busy raiding the Spanish Main or ships from Cartagena. Every now and then a Spanish coin or some other evidence of the pirates crops up, and the fortune hunters flock to the beaches.

Galveston has been hit by hurricanes several times during its history. Seawall Boulevard was begun in 1900 primarily to protect from flooding, so all the resorts are across the street from the beach. You'll see children at play in the sand, people walking the Seawall and occasional volleyball games. The warm surf from the Gulf of Mexico is gentle. In spring and early summer, the city is at its peak, when thousands of oleanders produce pink and white blossoms. The climate is semitropical. Palm trees flourish here. Expect temperatures in the 60s during spring and fall, with 80s during the summer.

Although there are many condos in Galveston, and these are without a doubt the newest accommodations, Galveston has a rich inventory of 19th-Century cottages available for vacation rentals. Some are sharp, some are owned by investors, some are cute, and some are funky. Before committing to a Galveston vacation, call some of the vacation realty firms and at least check out the opportunities.

Transportation to Galveston is easy because it's only an hour from Houston's Hobby Airport on the south side of town. Houston Intercontinental (on the north side of town) is at least one and one half hours from Galveston, depending upon city traffic.

WHERE TO STAY

8   **THE SAN LUIS**
5220 Seawall Blvd., Galveston, TX 77551
409-740-0219, 800-445-0090
Amenities: Pool, tennis, health club

Probably the largest high rise structure on Galveston Island, the units here are large apartments, and each has a sweeping ocean view. Galveston is a "laid-back" beach area, but this resort is the quality trendsetter. These have got to be among the most elegantly decorated condos on Galveston Island. The best feature is the million dollar tropical heated pool, that includes a rock cascade. The San Luis is across the street from the beach like all Galveston resorts.

6   **SEASIDE POINT**
7820 Seawall, Galveston Island, TX 77551, 409-730-3030
1BR $75–210, 2BR $95–265
Amenities: Pool, tennis, hot tub

Brand new condos in two, three-story buildings across the street from the beach. These casual, contemporary condos have decor designed for beach-front living—a sofa covered with water-resistant fabric and a table with canvas deck chairs. Well managed and maintained, there is a crisp style here. The swimming pool is popular six months of the year and volleyball games are common on weekends.

7   **THE VICTORIAN**
6300 Seawall Blvd., Galveston, TX 77551, 409-740-3555
800-231-6363, 1BR $79–129, 2BR $95–155
Amenities: Beach, heated pool, hot tub

This is a great choice on Galveston Island because this delivers good value for a modest price. Although designed to look Victorian in style, this is a fairly new condo resort. Each unit in this three-story building has a private balcony and all offer views of the ocean across the street or of the resort's large swimming pool. This is a great resort for families as well as for a couple who wants to get away to the quiet of the beach. Choose one- or two-bedrooms, each with a queen-size bed. Every suite provides additional sleeping accommodations with a sleeper, a sofa, and two bunk beds. Most of these condos are stylishly decorated with pinks and greens and lots of white.

RENTAL RESOURCES

Breakers Condos, 409-740-0588
By the Sea Condos, 409-740-0905
Casa del Mar Condos, 409-740-2431
Century 21 Bay Reef, 490-737-2300, 800-527-7333
Gallion Condos, 409-744-2244
Galvestonian Condos, 409-765-6161
Grover & Associates, 409-737-2663
Islander East Condominiums, 409-765-9301
Mitchell / Pirate's Beach, 409-737-2771
Sand n' Sea, 409-737-2771
Wolverton & Associates, 409-737-1430

5. THE HILL COUNTRY

The Hill Country begins around Austin and continues west for about 100 miles of rolling countryside. The area encompasses tidy German farming communities and a series of manmade lakes with hundreds of little coves and angular peninsulas. During the '70s and '80s some superlative golf, tennis, and boating resorts were created in this area—each one a separate master resort development unto itself. This is LBJ Ranch country and you might want to visit the Ranch and the Presidential Library. Perhaps not as informative but more exciting are the Texas "dude ranches" in this area. Offering a unique opportunity for children to experience the Wild West (as well as for those who never gave up that adventurous spirit), these ranches provide a unique and unforgettable family vacation. Although the quality and facilities are among the best on a national level, these resort areas have not yet attracted scores of vacationers from the other parts of the U.S. Too bad. That just leaves so much more of the open range for you to explore.

The centerpiece is 60-mile-long Lake Travis. You'll find the Horseshoe Bay and Lago Vista developments on the north shore. On the south shore you'll find Lakeway. Although separated by a narrow body of water, it takes a good hour to drive from one to the other. Located at the western edge of the fertile farming country, this is where the climate begins to turn dry. You won't find the desolate "scrub country" of west Texas, but rainfall is limited. January is the only really cold month and August is the time when the lake waters are most attractive.

Vacationers here can always dash into San Antonio for sightseeing or urban sophistication. San Antonio is a major tourist attraction with its history, Riverwalk, and new Sea World theme park. Nearly a century ago Mark Twain said that San Antonio was one of four cities in the U.S. with individual character. This is still true today. The languid Mexican heritage has mellowed the energy of Anglos and Germans in Texas to create a sparkling new culture.

Thirty miles northwest of San Antonio is Bandera, a town whose main business is "dude ranching." This is where horse lovers can come to play and families can learn to appreciate the Old West together on trail rides.

Air transportation to the Hill Country is easy with direct air service from most major cities to either San Antonio or Austin. Austin may be slightly more convenient but you'll surely want an excuse to visit San Antonio.

The Hill Country's climate and beauty attracted Texas' earliest settlers. This is where they chose to live. Come visit and you'll see why.

WHERE TO STAY

7   BANDERA HOMESTEAD RANCH
       P.O. Box 1434, Bandera, TX 78003, 512-796-3051
       1BR $85, 2BR $95, 3BR $105
       Amenities: Trail riding, pools, tennis

Bandera is the cowboy capital of the world and the dude ranch center of Texas. There's nothing else like it anywhere. For those seeking an active vacation or urban families who want to experience, not just look at, western life, this is it. Bandera Homestead condominiums are located on the 1800-acre River Ranch, five miles out of town. The rustic log cabin condos are nestled on a scenic bluff overlooking the Medina River. Although you may be hankering for the "rough and ready" adventure, don't overlook the fact that these condos have a private whirlpool in the master bath. Built townhouse style, you'll have privacy, or you can go down to the pool and socialize. Poolside barbecues are regular events here. For those who want adventures other than riding, this resort offers tennis and hiking trails (watch the rattlesnakes!) Great value and fun.

7   LAKEWAY INN / WORLD OF TENNIS RESORT
       101 Lakeway Dr., Austin, TX 78734, 512-261-6600
       1BR $140–160, 2BR $220–240, 3BR $330–360, 4BR $440–480
       Amenities: Golf, tennis, pool

Lakeway is actually two resorts. It encompasses 5,500 acres of rolling Texas hill country 20 miles northwest of Austin on a peninsula jutting into Lake Travis. Primarily, guests at Lakeway resort focus on golf, in particular, two 18 hole courses including one designed by Jack Nicklaus. Then, one of the nation's best tennis clinics, World of Tennis, is located within the master Lakeway development. However, World of Tennis focuses on—guess what—tennis, with 36 courts including a spectator arena around the stadium courts. The best feature here is the professional instruction you'll receive. It is geared to all levels of players. There's a great program for juniors with weekly competitions. The swimming pool at World of Tennis is shaped like a tennis racquet. The condos at World of Tennis were built to blend into the environment with natural wood and stone townhouses. These have full kitchens and fireplaces. Lakeway offers suites in the main lodge and the nearby villas. The suites have kitchenettes and no fireplaces. The villas do have kitchenettes and fireplaces. There are restaurants and there's lots of socializing around the tennis club. The best rentals, including many vacation homes, are through Austin Hills (512-263-5606).

2   RAYBURN COUNTRY RESORT AND COUNTRY CLUB
P.O. Box 36, Sam Rayburn, TX 75951, 409-698-2444
1BR $55–125, 2BR $65–150, 3BR $180
Amenities: Golf, tennis, pool

Located midway between Houston and Dallas, this resort is "under-visited" so the facilities are wide open for use. It's difficult to rate this one because it's a well-planned resort offering just about everything: lake, golf course, and country club lifestyle. But the grounds have been attacked by weeds and the furnishings, at the club and inside the condos, are worn out. If you want to play golf and not worry about the tee time, this may be for you. The condo interiors were fancifully decorated a dozen years ago to create a luxury environment, but frankly they seem out of place at this resort, which is now "down-at-the-heels." In addition to the 18-hole golf course, there are four lighted tennis courts, a 25-meter swimming pool, and a sports center with volleyball, basketball, miniature golf, and shuffleboard facilities. Think twice about where you're going and why you are planning a vacation. These wide open spaces might be for you.

5   TANGLEWOOD
P.O. Box 265, Pottsboro, TX 756076, 800-833-6569
1BR $110–150, 2BR $150–225
Amenities: Golf, tennis, lake with marina, pool

Nestled in the rolling, wooded hills overlooking Lake Texoma, the Tanglewood condominium tower is quite a surprise poking up toward the sky. While the upper floors have views of the lake, the lower floors have surprising views of the trees. You feel like you are living in the forest. Nearby Lake Texoma offers great boating opportunities and there is an 18 hole golf course. Down below, there are lighted tennis courts and four cascading swimming pools. For entertainment or private parties, this resort has its own 55-foot party yacht. Given this setting, the condo interiors are a disappointment. The Furniture is without style and some is a little worn. Tanglewood caters to those from the Dallas/Ft. Worth Metroplex who seek a nearby place in the woods for some family fun or a weekend retreat.

5 **VISTA GRANDE**
     1918 American Dr., Box 4826, Lago Vista, TX 78645
     512-267-1161, 1BR $90–120, 2BR $120–150
     Amenities: Privileges at Lago Vista Country Club, marina

Located 30 miles north of Austin within the spectacular Lago Vista resort community, this resort specializes in comfortable vacation homes for golfers and boaters. A green oasis bordered by blue waters it is surrounded by the dusty, boulder strewn hills. Upon arrival a bellman will take you by golf cart to your condo villa. Most are single-story structures with new, light pastel blue and apricot decor. The condos are villas made of stone and spread over the acreage to give each villa a real sense of privacy—nothing bold to break the peaceful harmony. There are great views from the back porch out over the lake. This is an idyllic setting for a week's vacation. Guests receive guest membership privileges for the length of their stay at the Lago Vista Country Club. These rolling courses have wooded grottos and waterfalls for you to play around. Boaters will also enjoy waterskiing, available at the marina, or pontoon boat rentals for floating and fishing in this 60-mile lake.

8 **WOODCREEK RESORT**
     One Woodcreek Dr., Wimberly, TX 78676
     Amenities: Pools, golf, tennis, marina

Located on Cypress Creek three miles north of town, Woodcreek Resort exemplifies everything that is best about the Texas Hill Country. This really is the heart of Texas with rolling hills, woodlands, creeks, and just a touch of the Old West. There are two separate areas of development within Woodcreek. You'll find detached, western-style cottages and contemporary townhouse condos—all have kitchenettes and are decorated in Texas style. You're likely to find antique reproductions and country quilts. All have either a patio or a porch deck. Some have fireplaces. Others are located on the golf course and reflect a country club environment. In addition to the golf, there's a sports center where you'll find 14 tennis courts, a teaching tennis pro, and three racquetball courts. There's also a complete health center with weight room, pool, saunas, and hot tubs. Over on the river, there's a small marina with canoes and paddleboats.

RENTAL RESOURCES
Austin Hills Resort Rentals, 512-263-5606

6. LAKE CONROE /
THE WOODLANDS

Lake Conroe, a 21,000-acre lake in a wooded area about 25 miles north of downtown Houston, has a long shoreline with numerous coves. Because of good highways, the trip from Houston's Intercontinental Airport is only half an hour. The area lures visitors with unlimited water activities on the calm lake, a long, nine-month season, numerous golf courses and tennis centers, and forested hills. Limited development has taken place here, but some of it is outstanding. Each one of the resorts reviewed below is a separate, self-contained community. You have the privacy of your condo and the convenience of a kitchen. For sports, social life, and dining the attractions are within the resort you choose.

WHERE TO STAY

7   **APRIL SOUND**
          P.O. Box 253, Conroe, TX 77301, 409-588-1101
          1BR $70, 2BR $125, 3BR $150
          Amenities: Marina, golf, tennis, racquetball, pools

Located 50 miles north of Houston and only 30 miles north of Intercontinental Airport, you'll be amazed by the difference once you drive inside the gates of April Sound Resort. The lanes are shaded by live oaks and you'll see gardens everywhere. April Sound strives to create the enchanted forest environment on the shores of Lake Conroe. Primarily a golf resort with three nine hole courses, the centerpiece is the country club at the marina. This is where tennis and golf players gather after the game or children splash in the pool. Separately, there are two other "adult-only" pools for lap swimming or quiet sunbathing. You'll find lots of condominiums in different styles within April Sound. Try to get one with a view out over the lake. Most are contemporary townhomes with spacious, full kitchens, and with comfortable furniture. Nothing special—just a pleasant environment for family getaways or gatherings of small groups.

7   **DEL LAGO**
          600 Del Lago Blvd., Montgomery, TX 77356, 409-582-6100
          800-833-8389, Villas $155–180
          Amenities: Golf, conference center, health spa, tennis, pool,
          restaurants, marina

You can't miss Del Lago when you visit Lake Conroe. It's the only 20-story, high-rise tower for miles around. Lake Conroe is located 25 miles from Houston in a serene setting of hills, woodlands and the Sam Houston National Forest. With a mild climate and close to a major city like Houston, Del Lago provides the perfect location for executive conferences as well as for family vacations. There's an 18-hole golf course, 13 tennis courts, a marina with power and sailboat rentals, and a health spa/fitness center. The tower is composed of suites with kitchenettes, but the best choice is to be in some of the townhouse condos lining the fairways. Spacious, with full kitchens, it's the backyard patios with vistas of the golf course or lake which offer the most charm.

5   THE LANDING AT SEVEN COVES
700 Kingston Cove, Willis, TX 77378, 713-223-3980
1BR $70, 2BR $99
Amenities: Pool, tennis, boat ramp, restaurant

On the north shore of Lake Conroe, Seven Coves is a development of two- and three-story condominiums for persons who enjoy boating. The Landing at Seven Coves is the heart of the development with a fabulous new Yacht Club. There are racquetball and tennis courts, a health club, and aerobics classes. Sail and power boat rentals are available. This is a great place for water-skiing. The condos are newly decorated in soft pastel colors, with modern appliances. There's even an authentic riverboat, not just a houseboat built on a barge, which is part of the resort, and several times a week brunch and dinner parties are offered on scheduled cruises.

8   WALDEN ON LAKE CONROE
14001 Walden Rd., Montgomery, TX 77356, 409-582-6441
1BR $101, 2BR $150
Amenities: Golf, marina, pools, tennis, exercise room

This is a beautiful golf course resort set amid the forests of Sam Houston National Park in southeast Texas. The designer took a 1200-acre peninsula jutting into Lake Conroe and turned it into an enchanted world of rolling fairways, spits of land, and water hazards. Located throughout the rolling resort acreage, the condos are in three-story wooden buildings along the fairways or in the forest. The top units are most desirable with cathedral ceilings, skylights, and lofts. Decorated with contemporary furniture, some could be spruced up. Each has a full kitchen and you can go to the 10th Hole Grill or the formal Commodore dining room in the Yacht Club. Walden is popular for group outings and executive retreats since it is only 45 minutes from Houston's Intercontinental Airport. Although there is a pool for each condo cluster, families with children will probably want to be near the pool center at the Yacht Club.

9   THE WOODLANDS INN
2301 N. Millbend Dr., The Woodlands, TX 77380
713-367-1100, 1BR $95–160, 2BR $120–235
Amenities: Golf, tennis, pools, restaurant

This is Houston's very own local resort. Although it's close to the city and Houston's Intercontinental Airport, the Woodlands is a surprising nature preserve on 23,000 acres. It sits where the San Jacinto River loses its way in the woodlands and creates several creeks. If the Woodlands were located elsewhere, it would be viewed as a destination resort because every sort of service and vacation activity is available here. However, as it is close to Houston, its popularity stems primarily from its ability to attract conferences and executive retreats. There are two championship golf courses here and 24 tennis courts. Partially a residential community and partially a resort, the Woodlands offers condo accommodations in two-story lodges, each with 16 condo suites. All of this is connected by walkways and covered passageways with the main part of the resort.

RENTAL RESOURCES
Lake Conroe Properties, 409-588-1108
Resort Rentals of Walden, 409-582-6595, 800-444-6495

UTAH

In the 19th Century the Mormons, following the lead of Brigham Young, found the green Salt Lake valley in the foothills of the Wasatch Mountains. Not in the mainstream of American life, Salt Lake City and surrounding communities developed and flourished on their own. Only recently have vacationers discovered the allure of the beautiful Wasatch mountains. Incredible as it may seem, within 30 minutes of the Salt Lake City airport, this is another world removed from the Mormon community. Park City is the resort town that first became popular with Californians. Today it is home to the U.S. Ski Team and hosts thousands of visitors annually. Once up in the mountains, you'll feel worlds apart from the commercial center of Salt Lake.

There are two main resort areas in Utah—the Park City/Deer Valley ski complex, which including Deer Valley has over 250 separate condominium developments, and the Little Cottonwoods Canyon complex with the formidable ski areas of Alta and Snowbird. Cottonwoods Canyon is steep and narrow limiting potential development to only a handful of select locations. There are other ski areas that are in canyons also easily accessible from Salt Lake City such as Brighton, Solitude, and Sundance, but these don't have a similar selection of condo accommodations.

1. PARK CITY / DEER VALLEY

Park City sits on the edge of a broad plain and was thoroughly "condominiumized" in the craze of the late '70s. The resort developments are in an area seven miles long and three miles wide stretching from Parkwest to Deer Valley. Park City's condominiums are in several distinct pocket neighborhoods. Deer Valley is the most exclusive ski resort in the U.S. With a limited number of lift tickets for sale each day, Deer Valley caters to Hollywood celebrities as well as families used to the fast-paced worlds of Beverly Hills, Scarsdale, or Highland Park. At the ultra-modern Deer Valley, attendants will hand you a tissue to clean your sunglasses as you stand in line for the chair lift. Up on the mountain, cafeteria food is gourmet or "spa lite." The condominiums in Deer Valley are spread over the hillside in small clusters with many quality resorts having only one or two dozen condominium units. Starting prices for purchase of these condos begin with an entry level of $300,000 and rapidly rise to over a million dollars. Although within sight of Park City and seemingly a part of the Park City complex, Deer Valley is a distinct neighborhood. These condos are operated differently from the other condominiums in the area. Generally, there is no on-site management but the rental office and maintenance personnel are within two miles down in the Deer Valley business center. Therefore, because there are no on-site offices, very few of the condo properties that we have described have telephone numbers. You must rent the properties from a rental agency, if you don't happen to know an owner. Most of the condos in Deer Valley have ski-in, ski-out access to the mountain, so you need not be concerned with shuttle buses in Deer Valley. Generally, you won't find a common swimming pool/hot tub complex for socializing at each resort. Instead the individual condos at Deer Valley often have their own private hot tubs, large enough for four or six. You'll find some in special glass enclosed greenhouses just off the living room where you can soak up the waters and the mountain view. This is the prevailing style in Deer Valley.

Park City began as a miner's town over 100 years ago and the Main Street area has been declared a national historic district. Lined with Victorian storefronts, saloons, and restaurants, today's Main Street area (including the small side streets) was built with a "neo-Victorian" facade. A few establishments have carried the theme inside with brass beds, globe lamps, and perhaps a private hot tub just off the living room. Short on space yet with lots of charm, this is an interesting spot to choose for a vacation.

The main, modern part of Park City radiates away from the Resort Center where the gondola and chair lifts are located. These condo developments generally will have 100 or more units that are modern, decorated in contemporary style, and each has a recreation center with a pool, hot tub, or sauna which is the hub of social activity. It provides a friendly and wholesome sporting environment. Lots of skiers in their 20s or 30s from cities like Phoenix, Atlanta, and St. Louis vacation here.

On the western edge of town lies Prospector Square, a sprawl of condos dating from the early '80s, and Park Meadows, another mass of condos around the golf course. Prospector Square has its own village of shops and restaurants within easy walking distance of all these condos. Two miles farther west is the Parkwest area at the base of the ski mountain. At 5 P.M. when the ski lifts close, Parkwest vacationers go home to dinner by their fireplace while a few venture into town on the shuttle bus. Powderwood and Jeremy Ranch claim a Park City location, but actually they sit down on the Interstate Highway four and five miles from the ski areas and town.

Convenient air transportation is one of the keys to the success of this area. Salt Lake is a hub for Delta Airlines and they offer nonstop flights to over 70 cities in the U.S. and Canada. Then it's only 35 miles by highway, around the Wasatch, to the Park City ski area. A new airline, Morris Air, has recently emerged offering budget fares to California, Seattle, Portland, Phoenix and Denver. For those who live in those cities, airfares can be as low as one-third of what the other airlines charge. United, Continental, Northwest, and American also fly to Salt Lake City several times daily.

WHERE TO STAY

9   ASPENWOOD
        Deer Valley, UT 84060 (no mail)
        Amenities: None

These condos are imposing. Located in the Snow Lake area, they are just on the other side of the Deer Valley ski lift parking lot although you'd never know it because of the forested landscaping. These two and one-half story structures are mostly duplexes and they face out over Snow Park and the Snow Park Lodge. Each condo has a private hot tub, a stone fireplace, and a private indoor garage. They are deluxe. Every little need has been attended to in planning the interior decor. You'll find these condos sumptuously furnished with deep carpets, comfortable chairs and love seats, and a real dining room that does justice to the concept of a special room for dining. The living rooms have vaulted ceilings and the open wooden beams create a clubby atmosphere. These are beautiful condos, however, there is no on-site management nor is there a central gathering area like a swimming pool. It is definitely for those who value privacy.

7   **BLUE CHURCH LODGE**
P.O. Box 1720, Park City, UT 84060, 800-626-5467
Studio $85–125, 1BR $95–170, 2BR $115–230, 3BR 155–260
Amenities: Hot tub

The Blue Church Lodge offers a real change of pace. This small condo resort is like a country inn, filled with antiques and located in the heart of Park City's historic district. It is really for couples or sensible families because exquisite decor could also be easily damaged. You are close to the restaurants and shops on Main Street, but you'll need to take the shuttle bus to get to the Ski areas. There is an indoor hot tub for soaking at the end of an active day.

8+   **COURCHEVEL**
Deer Valley Drive East, Park City, UT 84060
Amenities: None

This condo development is the one closest to the Deer Valley ski lifts. It over looks the parking lot for the ski area. The condos are beautifully decorated with a French accent that creates a warm, luxury environment. After all, you are in Deer Valley. Each condo features a private fireplace, sun deck, and a whirlpool. This may seem expensive but it's one of the best bargains if you want to stay in the Deer Valley area.

9+   **DAYSTAR**
Queen Esther Dr., Park City, UT 84060 (no mail)
Amenities: None

Absolutely deluxe townhouses in the Deer Valley area, about a half mile from the chair lift. No hospitality programs, but who needs them with this splendid privacy. Each condo has a private greenhouse off living room with a private sunken hot tub that is large enough for two to four good friends.

This is luxury. The condos are designer decorated with soft peach colors, track lighting, and nice decorator accents. After soaking in the hot tub and looking out over the valley, you can dry off by the fire in your private fireplace. These are an elegant choice and great for families because you have everything you need for a holiday.

5   EDELWEISS HAUS
1482 Empire Ave., Park City, UT 84060, 800-438-3855
1BR $95–180, 2BR $130–255
Amenities: Indoor pool, hot tub, sauna

This is located across the street from the Resort Center and the Park City ski lifts. Edelweiss Haus has a good location, pleasant environment, and, best of all, an outdoor heated swimming pool, hot tub, and sauna area for after skiing. The condos have that traditional "skierized" look and are decorated in earth tones, beige, and brown. A few have been personalized with whimsical accents. The resort has on-site management to help you find your way around or choose the best restaurants. There are bargain weekly rentals.

6   EMPIRE COALITION
Empire Ave., Park City, UT 84060
Amenities: Pool, hot tub

This has about as convenient a location as you could want in Park City. It is right on Park Avenue at the turn to the entrance to the Resort Center and the Park City ski lifts. You can walk to the ski lifts from here. Each unit is sizable and nice with a private fireplace and "skierized" furniture in neutral beige and tweed fabrics. You can walk to the grocery store and ski shops right across the street.

7   PARK MEADOWS RACQUET CLUB CONDOS
Little Kate Rd., Park City, UT 84060
Amenities: Golf, tennis, racquetball, pool, health club

Located midway between Park City and Parkwest, this area is in itself becoming a destination. Why? Because of the Racquet Club, racquetball and indoor tennis courts, the golf course, and all the socializing these sports attract. The Racquet Club condos are boxy two-story townhouses arranged in a courtyard fashion. Downstairs, you'll find a kitchen and living area with a private fireplace. Upstairs, are two bedrooms and a loft bedroom. Don't plan on using the loft as a third bedroom for adults. It's cramped in space. Furnishings here are of the "skierized" variety with lots of tweeds and neutral colors. Management is encouraging redecoration, so you may be pleasantly surprised.

8   PARK MEADOWS RACQUET CLUB VILLAS
Little Kate Rd., Park City, UT 84060
2BR $145–205, 3BR $260–330
Amenities: Golf, health club w/racquetball, heated pool, tennis

Located on the Jack Nicklaus designed golf course, these patio homes are among the best choices in the Park City area. The Racquet Club condos are about two miles away from the Park City ski lift or 3 miles from the Parkwest lifts. Why are these a good choice? They all have space, privacy, and a view. The units are large and furnished with handsome contemporary furniture. The Racquet Club offers a full health club with racquetball courts, indoor/outdoor tennis, a year-round heated swimming pool, and hot tub and sauna. Sneakers private club restaurant is here and is available to all in-house guests. Although removed from the main part of town, this resort is self-contained with full-service hospitality to make your stay a great vacation.

9+   PINE INN
Deer Valley, Park City, UT 84060
Amenities: None

You couldn't have a better location in Deer Valley for skiers. This is the only condo complex next to the Wasatch chair lift. The buildings are a sight to behold. They look like log cabins at first. Inside, the tone is anything but rustic. You'll find these to be richly decorated with the best furniture, fabrics, and wallpaper. Indirect lighting and good use of the wooden beams creates a warm, Alpine atmosphere. This is really living in style. Each condo has a private outdoor hot tub—relax in the bubbling waters and then roll in the snow! Everything has been provided here—VTPs in some units; microwaves in all units. Each condo has a private underground heated garage. There is no on-site management or swimming pool. You are about a two-minute walk away from the shops and restaurants of Deer Valley Resort Center.

8   PINNACLE
Pinnacle Drive, Deer Valley, Park City, UT 84060
3BR $600, 4BR $700
Amenities: None

Located at the entrance to Deer Valley, Pinnacle is just across from the Lake (summer) or Snow Park (winter). You'll have great views from these yellow two- and three-story townhouses that line the hillside. You could walk over to Deer Valley Plaza, but in winter this could be an endurance test. These condos are new and like everything in Deer Valley, expensively furnished. You'll be impressed by the split-level living areas and the stairway in four sections that truly deserves the word "designed." However, there is no on-site management or a swimming pool. Here the advantage is simply the condos themselves. With the vaulted ceilings and breathtaking views, we believe you'll find these a good choice. There are some "10" rated properties that aren't as nice as these condos, but without central amenities or on-site management, we can't go any higher with our rating.

5   **POWDERWOOD RESORT**
6975 N. 2200 W., Park City, UT 84060, 801-649-2032
1BR $85–155, 2BR $105–205
Amenities: Health club, pool, hot tub, shuttle bus

This resort is not in Park City—it's 6 miles away. The advantage here is accessibility to all of the Park City ski areas as well as convenience to Salt Lake Park City is 10 minutes away; the city lights are only 20 minutes away in Salt Lake. These condos are new, spacious, and well maintained. There's great hospitality here and you'll always find something to do. The Powderwood shuttle bus runs every 20 minutes in to town, so the shops and restaurants are always close at hand. Each condo has a private gas log fireplace, sliding glass doors, and spacious units. Decor is contemporary and cheerful. Every morning a Continental breakfast is served in the main lodge and there's a wine and cheese party. There is a full health club here with an exercise gym, steamroom, and an outdoor hot tub in a gazebo. This full service resort can be a great choice as long as you understand that it's **not** in Park City.

5-7 **PROSPECTOR SQUARE**
2200 Sidewinder Dr., Box 1698, Park City, UT 84060, 801-649-7100
Studio $75–145, 1BR $120–240, 2BR $175–290
Amenities: Health club, pool, sauna, indoor tennis, racquetball, aerobics classes

Prospector Square is a resort within a resort. This complex of nine buildings, not all of which are adjacent, lies about a mile from the ski lifts in what has been called the Prospector Square section of town. It is the only property that has a complete health club for your enjoyment. By the way, this is where members of the U.S. Olympic Ski Team work out, so don't feel overwhelmed by your competition in the weight room. Prospector Square was started in the late '70s during a period of rapid growth and ramshackle construction. That changed during the '80s and the newer buildings are much better built. Some of the units are worn out on the inside; others are decorated with a country French style. You will socialize more here because you'll keep seeing the same people at the Health Club or the restaurants surrounding Prospector Square. This is a budget to value choice, depending upon which building your stay in.

7   RED PINE CHALETS/RED PINE TOWNHOMES
2500 Chalet Dr., Park City, UT 84060
1BR $65–95, 2BR + Loft $85–140
Amenities: Pool, hot tub, sauna, tennis

Although a special place, these condos are not located in Park City. They are 3 miles away at Parkwest. Parkwest is a great mountain, often over-looked by most first-time visitors to Utah. But the secret is starting to get out and recently Parkwest has zoomed in popularity. Red Pine is a self contained village with over 300 chalets and townhomes. There are 2 heated swimming pools, a sauna, a hot tub large enough for 24, and 8 tennis courts. In response to the distance from town, there's a convenience store and there are shuttle buses but this is one resort where you need a car. The chalets are pleasant and decorated with lots of wood and forest green colors. Each has a private fireplace and an unobstructed mountain view. The townhouses are two stories and very spacious. They have a better floor plan than the chalets but many don't have that mountain view. This is indeed a surprising find—our secret.

7+   RESORT CENTER LODGE
Resort Center, Park City, UT 84060, 800-824-5331
Studio $105–170, 1BR $130–235, 2BR $200–325
Amenities: Pools, ice skating, skiing, sauna, hot tub

The Resort Center is where you'll come to buy lift tickets, have your skis repaired, browse the shops, and enjoy after-ski activity. These four-story brick structures house condos upstairs. Space is a premium here and these are some of the most ingeniously efficient studios. The one bedrooms are in a word, cramped. But if you want to be in the center of it all, this is the place. During the celebrity ski tournaments, many attend from Hollywood or are ski circuit celebrities. Interior decor is modern with an emphasis on soft greens and maroon, while the newer ones have sky blue and pink interiors. Kitchen facilities are adequate, but tight if you plan to cook a feast. The Resort Center has its own health club with swimming pool, saunas, and hot tub. Down below, there's an ice skating rink and some condos have views of the evening skating activity.

8   SHADOW RIDGE RESORT HOTEL
50 Shadow Ridge St., Park City, UT 84060, 800-451-3031
Studio $70–245, 1BR $95–285, 2BR $120–385
Amenities: Restaurant, pool, hot tub

This four-story condo resort is right at the parking lot for the Resort Center ski lifts. At first glance, this looks like a hotel because of all the activity in the lobby. The lobby is elegant with brass chandeliers and French bergére chairs. Go upstairs and you'll find a similar level of quality decorat-

ed with wooden armoire, brick fireplaces, and quality dining room furniture
that looks like it belongs in Williamsburg. You'll find brass beds and
whirlpool tubs. There's an elegant restaurant (however, in the spirit of Utah,
casual attire is acceptable) and a very active swimming pool area where
you'll find a hot tub and sauna. Shadow Ridge is a long-standing favorite
with those who know Park City. It's been said that to get reservations at
Christmas, you must be "born" with reservations rights.

7   SILVER CLIFF VILLAGE
        1485 Empire Ave., Park City, UT 84060, 800-331-8652,
        2BR $220–300
        Amenities: Pools, sauna, hot tub, skiing

Located right next to the Park City lift, this is a great choice for skiers.
Skiing is convenient and at night you can take the shuttle bus to the Main
Street area with its shops and restaurants. The three buildings at Silver Cliff
have been designed to have a "lodgelike" environment. The condos are well
designed so that four will feel comfortable in a one-bedroom apartment and
a two-bedroom can easily accommodate six. Each has a private fireplace, an
individual washer/dryer, and a whirlpool in the master bathroom.

7   SILVER KING CONDOMINIUMS
        P.O. Box 2818, Park City, Utah 84060, 801-649-5500
        2BR $240–320, 3BR $280–400
        Amenities: Pools, sauna, hot tub, skiing

Silver King is a four-story, apartment-block structure across from the
Resort Center and the main chair lifts which go up Park City Mountain. Step
inside the lobby and you'll feel as through you are in a first class hotel where
there's always a roaring fire in the lobby. These condos seem like hotel
suites with mini-kitchens featuring a small refrigerator and a microwave
oven. Furnishings are new, featuring blond woods, pastel fabrics, and contemporary styles. Some of the condos have a private hot tub just off their living room where you can sit and look out your window at all the activity on
the mountain. There's a community hot tub and a swimming pool, which is
popular after skiing. We recommend this for those who want modern convenience as well as easy access to the ski slopes and town. With children, you
may want a less sophisticated atmosphere.

5   SNOW CREST
        Empire Ave., Park City, UT 84060
        Amenities: Pool

Located right at the turn to the Resort Center and the Park City ski lift,
you can walk to the ski lifts only two blocks away. This is a popular budget
choice with nice units that are simply furnished. They've seen lots of use

and some condos look a little tired. There is a swimming pool. Snow Crest is a great choice for young skiers. There's always lots of action around the pool. It is also good for golfers in the summer because the Park City Golf Course is across the street.

7   SNOWFLOWER CONDOMINIUMS
400 Silver King Dr., Park City, UT 84060, 801-649-6400
1BR $225, 2BR $275
Amenities: Skiing, pools, hot tub

For years this has been one of the most popular choices in Park City because it's located at the base of the mountain, right behind the golf course. You can ski home at the end of the day. The best feature is that, although Snowflower is located right in the center of things, it enjoys a wooded location and most units have a mountain view. Most of the condos are furnished in yellows and neutral colors, although a few have some individuality. Each condo has a private fireplace and a whirlpool tub in the master bathroom. The loft units are great for families. There is an outdoor heated pool that buzzes with children and teenagers in the late afternoon.

9   STAG LODGE
Royal St. E, Deer Valley, Park City, UT 84060, 800-453-3833
3BR $1000, 4BR $1250
Amenities: Restaurant

Located high in the mountains, near Guardsman's Pass and Silver Lake Lodge, the Stag Lodge is unique because of the furnishings. Architecturally handsome, it looks like a movie set. The furnishings are smashing—this is where Ralph Lauren would want to be. The interior decor is a combination of rough wood and stone with floral prints and bronze art pieces. Some of these spacious condos offer over 3,000 sq. ft. of living space. There's a large outdoor hot tub and you'll love the view of Park City. Stag Lodge has ski-in/ski-out accessibility. Although it wants to be a summer resort (and should be because of its location) we found it to be very quiet. Philippe's restaurant is one of Park City/Deer Valley's best and most exclusive. Presidents of Fortune 500 corporations would feel comfortable here.

10   STEIN ERIKSEN LODGE
7400 Flat Lake Rd., Park City, UT 84060, 801-649-3700,
800-453-1302; Suite $800
Amenities: Pool, spa, restaurant, exercise room

One of the most elegant ski lodges in the world, everything here is perfect. When you check in, you'll be impressed by the service. The concierge can answer any questions and help you with any matter. The lobby is beautiful with a massive stone fireplace and Norwegian/Austrian carved furniture.

The floral arrangements on display are unforgettable. There are two gourmet restaurants, the Birkebeiner and Glitretind. Upstairs, the furnishings are elegant—again you'll find carved blond-wood Bavarian furniture and pretty floral fabrics that you would expect to find in Scandinavia. It is almost over-furnished. There's an outdoor swimming pool as well as a full service spa with exercise room, hot tub, saunas, and a massage room.

6   TREASURE MOUNTAIN CONDOS
     255 Main St., Park City, UT 84060, 800-344-2460
     Studio $75–120, 1BR $95–160, 2BR $135–210
     Amenities: Heated pool (summer), hot tub, game room

For those who want to be in the center of it all this is one of the few possibilities. It is right on historic Main Street. These condos raised a hue and cry when they were built 15 years ago because the rest of Main Street is Victorian while Treasure Mountain is decidedly contemporary. Today, you'll find that Treasure Mountain has quietly faded into obscurity. The units are modern, cheerful, and with a stone wall surrounding the fireplace which adds a decided touch of glamour. The primary advantage is that in the evenings you can walk to the restaurants, shops, and nightspots along historic Main Street. Another advantage is the Great Room off the lobby with its billiards table.

5   THREE KINGS
     Three Kings Rd., Park City, UT 84060, 800-245-6417
     Amenities: Pool, saunas

Located in the central part of Park City (not the old Main Street area) just off Park Avenue, this resort has been a popular choice with families for over a decade. The condos are each basically a large studio. Two studios combine to form a one bedroom, which includes a kitchen half and a bedroom half. How about interior decor? Look elsewhere. These are decorated with functional, "skierized" furniture to withstand heavy use. Here, the price is right. Ample space, good location, cooking facilities, and all of this for less than the price of a motel room makes this a reasonable choice.

6   THE YARROW
     P.O. Box 1840, Park City, UT 84060, 801-649-7000
     Studio $69–89, 1BR $65–159
     Amenities: Pool, hot tubs, pub, restaurant

Formerly the Holiday Inn, this resort is the gateway to Park City. Turn left to go to Park City's "new" town and Prospector Square; turn right to go to the ski area and historic Main Street. Totally redecorated and in some cases rebuilt, these condos offer plush accommodations and hotel style services in a prime location. The kitchens are actually kitchenettes and the condos are a little bit small. But the stunning interior design and VTPs/stereos compensate for the lack of space. There's an outdoor heated swimming pool, sauna, and spa area. In the summer, you can golf at the Park City golf course directly across the street.

RENTAL RESOURCES

ABC Reservations Central, 800-523-0666
Acclaimed Lodging, 800-552-9696
Advance Reservations, 800-453-4565
Affordable Luxury Lodging, 800-321-4754
All Seasons Condominiums, 800-331-8652
Blooming Enterprises, 800-635-4719
Budget Lodging, 800-522-7669
Charnonix Groupe, 801-649-2618
Condominium Rentals, 800-221-0933
Deer Valley Central Reservations, 800-424-3337
Deer Valley Connection, 800-458-8612
Deer Valley Lodging, 800-453-3833
Identity Properties, 800-245-6417
Owners Resorts & Exchange, 800-748-4666
Park City Reservations, 800-453-5789
Park City Resort Lodging, 800-545-7669
Park City Travel Lodging, 800-421-9741
PMA Lodging, 800-645-4PMA
R & R Property Management, 800-348-6759
Resort Property Management, 800-243-2932
Silverton Lodging, 800-666-9022
Ski Reservation HQ, 800-522-7669
Snow Country Lodging, 800-421-9741
Tri-Mountain Ski Properties, 800-678-2498
Vacation Enterprises, 800-477-5590

2. ALTA / SNOWBIRD

The Alta/Snowbird ski complex at the end of Little Cottonwoods Canyon offers some of the most spectacular skiing to be found anywhere. The location, only 30 minutes from downtown Salt Lake City, is both a blessing and a misfortune. Because it is so close, this area is considered to be part of metropolitan Salt Lake and has little separate resort identity of its own. Part of this is due to the geology of the area—steep slopes at a 45° angle, and only a narrow canyon road for access. These conditions have made resort development very difficult and only a few properties have been (or could be) built along the slopes of Snowbird or Alta.

Snowbird is the ultra-modern resort with the tram that rises 5,000 feet in just a few minutes. With over 500 inches of snowfall each year at mid-mountain, Snowbird technically would be open all year long. In fact, some years it closes on Memorial Day weekend. The accommodations around Snowbird fit within the village style. They, too, are ultra-modern and you'll find a range of accommodations from luxury studios up to super deluxe three bedroom condominiums.

Alta was one of the first ski areas to be developed in North America and consequently has quiet, old-fashioned comfort. The few condos in the Alta area show their age and you should expect to pay less than in neighboring Snowbird.

The two ski areas sit side by side and at the base it's hard to tell where one ends and the other begins. Those who stay here have the option of skiing two different mountains and won't need a car. In fact a car is a hindrance here since there's a shortage of parking, and shuttle buses to the Salt Lake airport are plentiful and cost only $12 per person.

WHERE TO STAY

6   **BLACK JACK CONDOMINIUMS LODGE**
         Alta, UT 84092, 801-742-3200; Studio $70, 1BR $115
         Amenities: Hot tub, restaurant, bar

These condos are isolated, but great for hearty athletic types who want to stay at and ski Alta/Snowbird. Here you are deep in the mountains midway between Alta and Snowbird. There's a four-wheel drive vehicle to take you over to the chair lift each morning. Strong skiers can ski home at the end of the day. The living rooms have private fireplaces and great mountain views. There's absolutely no nightlife nearby although Black Jack has a lounge with a friendly fireplace area.

7   **HELLGATE CONDOMINIUMS**
         Box 8008, Alta, UT 84092, 801-742-2020
         Studio $105–130, 1BR $170–210, 2BR $220–280, 3BR $280–350
         Amenities: Hot tub

Conveniently located just above the Alta parking lot, these condos attract serious skiers. Not fancy, you'll find these units decorated in a Western style with full kitchens and wood-burning fireplaces for those cold, high altitude evenings. Hellgate provides a convenient shuttle service over to the ski area.

8   **IRON BLOSAM LODGE**
         Snowbird, UT 84092, 801-742-2222
         Studio $79–149, Studio loft $89–270
         Amenities: Heated pool, Saunas, hot tub, tennis

This all-studio condo complex is unusual in design and fits right in with Snowbird's high tech image. There are two styles of studios. The studio loft model is two stories and has beds for ten. The master sleeping area is an upstairs separated by a brightly painted and functional steel-rail loft, while downstairs there are a number of couches and banquettes which convert into beds. Each has a fireplace, full kitchen, and great views of the mountains. The smaller studios are only on one floor and lack the fun of the two-story affairs.

9+ THE LODGE AT SNOWBIRD
Box 9000, Snowbird, UT 84092, 800-453-3000
Studio $89–145, 1BR $168–270, 1BR + Loft $247–395
Amenities: Heated pool, saunas, hot tub, restaurant, exercise room, tennis, shops

Crisply modern, this condo hotel is the heart of the buildings which call themselves Snowbird Village. Efficient and luxurious, there's a modern European style—like the new German or French ski resorts. Unlike most other condos, this is operated as a hotel with all of the attendant services such as bellmen, valet parking, and room service. It is a popular spot with a convenient location.

8 POWDER RIDGE CONDOMINIUMS
Box 920025, Snowbird, UT 84092, 801-943-1842
3BR $270–400, 4BR $300–475
Amenities: Sauna, outdoor hot tub

These traditional condos at Snowbird are huge. Each has a private hot tub and a private garage—a rarity for any resort condo complex. Located on the hillside at Alta, the management company for check-in and mail is next door at Snowbird. It's great for families or groups of skiers because each bedroom has its own bath.

9 SUGARPLUM
P.O. Box 5, Snowbird, UT 84092, 801-943-1872
2BR $190–310, 3BR $274–425
Amenities: Sauna, outdoor hot tub

These luxury condominiums at Snowbird make the best use of the limited land at Snowbird. A high-tech-style, four-story condominium, you'll find high ceilings and sweeping mountain views. The hallways and recreation area seem a little spartan at first because of the bare concrete walls and splashes of bright, bright color. The design of the units captures the best view of the mountains and each has a large hearth fireplace and a private jacuzzi hot tub. Angular and spare, these units make an impact upon the eye. Most of the condo owners have also elected to furnish their units in the same dramatic style. Condos at Sugarplum are generally luxurious and seem to have a European flair. We don't know where the furnishings came from but you've only seen styles like this in New York, Zurich, or Tokyo. The townhouses next door are huge and frequently rented by the Hollywood set. You'll remember your vacation at this one.

8 VIEW CONDOMINIUMS
Alta, UT 84092, 801-277-7172
1BR $225, 2BR $275–320, 3BR $355–420
Amenities: Hot tub

Appropriately named, these condos have excellent views. Two walls of the living room are solid glass so the spectacular scenic view is the main reason to choose this property. The ski-in/ski-out location also has a special advantage. Sharply decorated, the one we saw was all white, which created a mountain aerie feeling when viewing the snow covered slopes. All units have private hot tubs.

RENTAL RESOURCES
Alta Reservations Service, 801-942-0414
Canyon Services, 800-562-2888
Snowbird Reservations, 800-453-3000
Utah Ski Retreats, 801-742-2000

VERMONT

Vermont offers something for everyone, from exceptional ski instruction for children and budding athletes, to "leaf peeping" on a sunny fall afternoon. One of the nation's most popular playgrounds, Vermont offers some of the best condo resorts to be found. There are over 600 condo developments and thousands of private vacation homes. Many are truly second homes with pictures on the end tables or zebra-striped sheets. You won't find those within these pages. We have focused upon the primary ski resorts and their offspring condominiums. Today, with the decline in the number of skiers, many of these ski resorts are developing a new reputation as Alpine villages in order to attract summertime visitors. Several new golf courses have been opened during recent years and the number of summer visitors has grown at an impressive rate. Most of these ski resorts/Alpine resorts are just off Vermont's Route 100, which runs north to south along the state's central spine. For more detail, the map of Vermont can be found on page 448.

The location may be New England, but some of these resorts have nothing to do with austerity — not when there's a hot tub and a private sauna in individual units! Also, there are condo resorts that specialize in family vacations. Some, such as Smugglers' Notch and Sugarbush, have exceptional ski programs for children, and the accommodations won't break your budget.

Although skiing is a dominant theme in Vermont, you'll find that some vacation condos have sprung up on the grounds of successful inns. These are great for people who want to play golf in the summer, view the maples in the fall, and cross-country ski in the winter. Expect these resorts to offer a convivial atmosphere in order to compete with the resorts on the slopes.

As with states like Florida and Colorado, we have organized the material according to the major destinations:

1. Jay Peak
2. Killington/Pico
3. Mt. Snow
4. Okemo/Hawk
5. Smugglers' Notch
6. Stowe
7. Stratton
8. Sugarbush

The land is beautiful, but the weather is harsh. Skiing in January with the cold wet snow on icy slopes can be an endurance test. Bring warm clothing. In the summer, the temperatures are cool; a great relief from the city heat. When a breeze comes up in the mountains, you'll want a sweater or jacket.

Transportation to the Vermont ski areas is usually by car from the major metropolitan areas of the northeast. For travelers from New York or Southern New England driving up the interstate, at Brattleboro just cross over to Route 100 and follow the trail of cars north. For those who plan to fly, there are several airports to choose from. Those planning to visit the resorts of southern Vermont will want to consider Hartford/Springfield airport. It's a straight shot by interstate highway to Brattleboro and then by Route 100 to your destination. For those who plan to vacation in central or northern Vermont, Burlington airport is your best bet with nonstop service from Boston, Pittsburgh, Newark, and Chicago. Rutland also offers a number of flights from New York, Washington, and Pittsburgh. Those planning to visit Jay's Peak or flying from Canadian cities might want to consider Montreal, just an hour from the border.

1. JAY PEAK

Located about as far north as you can go and still be in Vermont, this attracts hard core advocates. One of the quietest resort areas in Vermont, Jay attracts families or vacationers who bring their own fun with them.

Jay Peak is one of the highest mountains in the state and there is an average annual snowfall of 300 inches. However, because it is so far from the metropolitan areas of New York and Hartford, ski lines are almost nonexistent during the week.

There are three groupings of condos here, all of which were developed by the Hotel Jay as almost annexes. Therefore, condo guests are invited to use the hotel pool after skiing and encouraged to use the dining room. The central reservations number for these condos is 800-451-4449. One of the best features at Jay is the well-developed children's program that includes skiing in the day and a special children's table in the dining room each evening. This is great for those evenings when you choose to stay by the fire at home and send the kids out.

WHERE TO STAY

6 **MOUNTAINSIDE CONDOS**
Route 242, Jay, VT 05859, 1BR $99, 2BR $139, 3BR $189
Amenities: Sauna, hot tub, pool, tennis, restaurant.

These condos are townhouses on the far side of the parking lot and close enough so you can walk to the ski lifts. Most of the decor includes unpretentious furniture with tweeds and neutral colors. Mountainside Condos are nothing special but they are quite private and comfortable.

7 **SLOPESIDE CONDOS**
Route 242, Jay, VT 05859, 2BR $139, 3BR $189
Amenities: Sauna, hot tub, pool, tennis, restaurant.

These condos are the best. Located just slightly up above the Hotel Jay, you can ski-in/ski-out. You'll be treated to solid comfort, lots of space, and sturdy furniture.

5 STONEY PATH CONDOS
Route 242, Jay, VT 05859, 1BR $99, 2BR $139
Amenities: Sauna, hot tub, pool, tennis, restaurant.

These condos are the most economical and they are about a half mile from the ski lift and the Hotel Jay. They are simple, functional, and good for families.

RENTAL RESOURCES
Snowbowl Townhouses, 802-334-7341
Guest Houses & Chalets, 802-988-2611

2. KILLINGTON / PICO

Killington is a destination that just keeps on getting bigger and better each year. The only drawback is that Killington lacks one of those quaint New England villages, and the condos are primarily along Killington Road (Route 4) between Route 100 and the parking lot for the ski lifts. The central point is the main parking lot for the ski area. Directions are usually given in terms of how far the resort is from this point. New development is springing up on the far western edge of the ski area around the Northeast Passage gondola. With a super health club, a lively bar, and some of the area's best units, there are hopes that this will someday become a village. But that's probably ten years from now and in the meantime, located three miles from the parking lot and even farther from the string of developments along Killington Road, this new area seems a little too quiet.

Killington offers six mountains for skiing with an average annual snowfall of 250 inches. This amount is supplemented by the most extensive snow-making equipment in the East. With over 300 trails, this is closest to European-style skiing. It has one of the longest interconnecting ski circuits that you will find in New England. Killington tries hard to be the best. Each year old lifts are replaced and new trails are opened on the mountain. Only Colorado's Breckenridge and Canada's Whistler can compete with this intense effort for improvement.

Recently, the Killington SKI Corporation acquired nearby Pico mountain, six miles away. Although it doesn't interconnect with the six Killington ski mountains, it sets a new boundary for the Killington ski area that now encompasses all of the development between the two ski centers. With frequent shuttle bus service provided by the SKI Corporation, supplemented by service from the condo resorts, skiers will have an even wider selection of ski runs and terrain.

The resort accommodations are primarily in four areas along Route 4 or Killington Road. Killington Village is **not** a village, rather it's a cluster of eight condo developments managed by the SKI Corporation. It is spread over 600 acres and focuses on a central health club/conference center. The western edge of development has luxury townhouses such as **Sunrise**. Five miles away there are condos around the base of Pico Mountain and extending along Route 100 to Rutland. Each area offers a broad range of accommodations, although the more inexpensive lodgings are those farthest away from the ski area.

WHERE TO STAY

9 **COLONY CLUB TOWNHOUSES**
        School House Rd., Killington, VT 05751, 802-773-4202
        3BR $250, 4BR $400
        Amenities: None

Located just off the Killington Road on the side of the hill, these enjoy some of the best views of the mountain and the valley. These new townhouses are on three levels and there's lots of space. The living room, on the second floor, has a brick fireplace and a cathedral ceiling. Interior decor is new and exciting with a vivid Scandinavian touch. The one we saw had a blond wood dining table and the high back wooden chairs had been painted red in the Swedish style. Fabrics combine reds and blacks on a beige field in interesting geometric designs. Almost all have video tape players, washer/dryer units, and some have whirlpools. These are among the area's best accommodations.

7 **EDGEMONT**
        Roaring Brook East Rd., Killington. VT 05751, 802-773-4202
        1BR $80–150, 2BR $100–180, 3BR $140–280
        Amenities: None

These condos were once part of Killington Village. Originally designed by Killington 17 years ago to be an integral part of the village at the bottom of Edgemont run, the individual condo owners decided to take rental matters into their own hands and they divorced themselves form Killington Village Management. In order to attract guests, these aging units were rehabbed from top to bottom, inside and out. What appears to be a cluster of New England barns actually turns out to be a cheerful skiers' vacation village. The centerpiece of these units is the fireplace. Decor is new and contemporary in style. Lots of personal mementos or "house presents" accessorize and personalize the interiors. Guests here have the option of using the Killington Village Health Club and Pool, just up the road, for a modest fee of $5 per day. This is a good value because these are not only better, but also less expensive than the neighboring condos.

7 FOX HOLLOW CONDOMINIUMS
Route 4, Rutland, VT 05701, 802-422-3244
2BR $145–290, 3BR $220–320
Amenities: Pico sports center across Route 4

Located six miles from Killington, these condos are across the street from Pico. These spacious units are a real sleeper. Often overlooked, they are large, stylish, and well equipped. Each of the two and three-bedroom units has a full kitchen, fireplace, washer/dryer, and a whirlpool. Some have private steam rooms. The buildings were designed with gables to create a broken roof line and lots of intriguing designs for the interiors of the upstairs units. Some condos have cathedral ceilings that make them even more attractive. Yet because they are at less posh Pico, the price is considerably discounted from what you would pay at Killington.

8 GLAZEBROOK
Killington Rd., P.O. Box 21, Killington. VT 05751, 802-422-4425
2BR $140–180, 3BR $185–290
Amenities: Private saunas and whirlpools

These new townhouses are as close to the main ski lifts at Killington as you can be without staying in the Village. Situated on 21 wooded acres, hidden from Killington Road, each of the 44 two-story units has either a two-bedroom or a three-bedroom floor plan as well as a private sauna and a whirlpool. Interior decor varies greatly. We saw one that was barely furnished with hotel supplies furniture. Another was cute with Austrian curtains and frills everywhere—a Hansel & Gretel home in the woods. Each has a full kitchen, fireplace, washer/dryer, and a videotape player. Built by Red Glaze who owns the Peak Performance Ski Shop nearby, ski rentals are at discount rates for Glazebrook guests. Well designed and well located it provides good value and is worth every penny.

5 HOGGE PENNY INN CONDOS
U.S. 4 West, P.O. Box 914, Rutland, VT 05702, 802-773-3200
1BR $127, 2BR $150, 3BR $210
Amenities: Restaurant, bar

Half a motel, half a condominium resort, the Hogge Penny is 12 miles away from Killington in the town of Rutland, Vermont. This does have an exuberant resort atmosphere in both winter and summer in the evenings. The bar and restaurant are popular stopovers for athletes after a day of hard skiing. Surprisingly, the condo units are away from the main hotel, in an intimate condo village setting. These two-story buildings have gabled roofs, lots of sunlight, and contemporary decor dating from 1985 when the condos were built. Many have been accessorized by owners with mementos, art, and videotape players. The restaurant is a real temptation not to use the kitchen in your condo.

4   KILLINGTON GATEWAY CONDOMINIUMS
U.S. 4 West, Mendon, VT 85701, 802-773-2301
1BR $100–200, 2BR $135–215, 3BR $160–280
Amenities: None

These condos are located midway between Rutland and Killington. The Killington Gateway condos are 9 miles from the ski lifts. They are not close enough to the ski area to be resort condos, yet they are not in the city where guests could enjoy the restaurants. If you have a car and plan to ski Okemo and Pico as well as Killington, then this is a good choice. The 34 condos in this wood building are spacious although uninspired. Each condo has a fireplace and full kitchen. Furnished in the collegiate maple look with inexpensive, Early American-style furniture, this is an economy choice. Young skiers will appreciate that rental rates average $22 to $30 a night per person when four or more share a condo.

4   KILLINGTON RESORT APARTMENTS
Killington Rd., RR 1, Box 2333, Killington. VT 05751, 802-422-3417
1BR $110, 2BR $160
Amenities: None

These ten apartments have seen better days. Located on the main access road, they are close to the ski lifts and you can walk to restaurants nearby. But the style is an old fashion neo-Austrian chalet and the wood has been repainted many times over the past 17 years. Although friendly, fully equipped, and convenient—think twice before choosing this one.

KILLINGTON VILLAGE
R.R. 1, Box 2460, Killington, VT 05751, 802-422-3312
Amenities: Pool, hot tub, racquetball, conference center.

Killington encompasses an area of six mountains spread over 720 acres. However, no real village has developed. Instead, lodgings, condos, and restaurants line the access road on Route 4 leading from Rutland, Vermont. The SKI Corporation controls the condo developments in this area known collectively as Killington Village. It has eight separate condo projects in different locations and each is suited for different budgets. The site for each of the condo developments listed below is a bit different and you'll find a wide range of quality within these accommodations. There's a central lodge and conference center with a swimming pool, hot tubs, and a racquetball court. Guests at any of the condos may use these central facilities.

Fall Line Condos (8) 1BR $160–200, 2BR $255–300, 3BR $320–400. Located in a peaceful wooded setting near the end of a ski trail, these new condos have some of the most beautiful interiors to be found in the Killington area. To begin with, the architect made the most of the location and provided windows to bring in the mountain views. These are some of the most expensive condos in the area. The local interior decorators were almost in competition to see who could provide the most beautiful living environment. Inside the condos, you'll find designer fabrics combined with quality contemporary or English traditional furniture. Each condo has a private whirlpool big enough for two, a VTP, and a microwave oven.

Highridge (9) 802-422-9611. This is Killington Village's most prestigious address. The views of the surrounding Green Mountains are spectacular. The architect made the best use of the site with panoramic views and lots of glass. These contemporary condos have split-level floors and "confident" environments created by interior designers. The condos are decorated with top-of-the-line furnishings (nothing ostentatious) and all the latest electronics equipment such as stereos, VTPs, and microwaves. These condos have their own private saunas or hot tubs in each unit. We found the interiors to be "better than home." You can use the Killington Resort facilities or Highridge also has its own private sports center with a pool.

Pinnacle (6) 1BR $135–160, 2BR $190–250, 3BR $270–355. These condos are located within walking distance of the shops and restaurants of the Killington Village registration/convention center. Many feature cathedral ceilings in the living room and great views of the mountains. You'll find functional, "skierized" furniture with lots of wood, tweed fabrics, and brown/beige colors. Some of the condos (not all) have VTPs, microwave ovens, and stereos. Pinnacle provides a sturdy, solid and unpretentious atmosphere.

Trail Creek Condos (7) 1BR $160–200, 2BR $275–300, 3BR $320–400. Located just off the Snowshed ski trail, these condos have ski-in/ski-out convenience. Fairly new, these condos are contemporary and upbeat. Best of all, the three-bedroom units have private hot tubs and saunas. Up at the Killington Village recreation center by the registration/convention center, there's a sports complex that features an indoor swimming pool. These condos offer a central location in Killington, yet you'll take a shuttle bus over to the ski lift in the morning. This is a good place for both couples and families.

Whiffletree (5) 1BR $120–149, 2BR $150–190, 3BR $188–234. Killington's oldest condos, these cozy one and two-bedroom condos are located on the golf course and overlook the mountains. You'll need to take the shuttle bus to get to the ski lift or the village. The living/dining area is one large room with a breakfast bar. Furnishings are often "early attic" with tweed sofas and lots of wood. In our opinion, some of the interiors look tired. In Killington Village, this is a budget choice.

5+   MOUNTAIN GREEN
Route 1, Box 2841, Killington, VT 05751, 802-422-3000
Studio $70–120, $1BR $100–165, 2BR $120–195
Amenities: Heated pool, health club with lap pool, racquetball

A brand new four-story condo complex, Mountain Green is located just at the entrance to Killington (not part of the Killington Village Master Resort Development described above). You'll need to take the shuttle bus to get over to the restaurants, shops, and ski lifts. The studio apartments are basically one large room with the refrigerator and stove over on one side. The small studios have fireplaces; the detachable hotel-room bedroom units don't. These are basic condos and uninspired, but the health club is a distinct advantage.

5   NORTHBROOK CONDOMINIUMS
Telefon Trail, P.O. Box 236, Killington. VT 05751, 802-422-3610
1BR $75–150, 2BR $85–170, 3BR $95–225
Amenities: None

Located two miles from the ski lifts, these condos are tucked away in a vale just down the hill from the main highway. Well situated and enjoying peaceful mountain views, the Northbrook offers "spacious economy". For example, a three-bedroom condo plus loft (which can accommodate up to 12—two families with children) rents for as little as $200 a day during ski season. The unit interiors, however, are starting to show years of wear and tear. Furniture is also a bit dated with dark wood cabinets and gold or avocado appliances. For those who aren't concerned about the ambiance these offer a good value.

6   NORTHSIDE
Route 4, Rutland, VT 05702, 802-422-3244, 1BR $170, 2BR $230
Amenities: Pico sports center within walking distance

These new condos are four miles from Killington in a serenely wooded area. Located across the street from Pico ski area, it's a healthy walk over to the ski area. Recently built, these have gabled roofs, multiple levels, skylights, and dramatic archways. Some have loft balconies that overlook the living room. Interior decor is contemporary in style with blond woods, Bentwood chairs, and colorful woven fabrics that suggest faraway places. Northside is very pleasant, and after skiing the Pico sports center and the après-ski bar are fun places to be.

6+ PICO RESORT HOTEL
Sherburne Pass, Route 4, Rutland, VT 05701, 802-747-3000
1BR $150
Amenities: Restaurant, sports center with indoor pool,
exercise/weight room, aerobics classes, sauna/hot tub area

Pico is a small resort located close to Killington yet favored by families or
day-trippers. Pico offers challenging skiing but lacks the glamour and social
life of Killington. The condos in the Pico Resort Hotel are perfect for skiers.
They are located right in the lodge at the base of the ski lift. The condos are
either spacious studios or, with interconnecting hotel rooms, they become
one-bedroom apartments. Nicely decorated, you'll find these provide a comfortable environment for families on vacation. Although there is a restaurant
here, you'll find an abundance of private parties in the condos where new
friends get together to discuss the day's adventures around the fireplace.
You'll also find very good value here.

5 SKYE PEAK
RR 1 Box 3153, Killington. VT 05751, 802-422-3984
1BR $99, 2BR $150
Amenities: Restaurant

This is about as close to the Killington ski lifts as you can be without
being in the Killington Village condos. These efficient one- and two-bedroom units are above Hooligan's Restaurant and the ski shop. Bare bones,
but fully equipped, the "personal residence" touch is missing. Sky Peak provides good value because it is close to the lifts and is modestly priced.

8+ SPRUCE GLEN
Roaring Brook East Rd., Killington. VT 05751, 802-422-3244
2BR $150–300
Amenities: Private sauna

Located on Killington's Great Eastern Trail, these townhouses are huge.
Older and eclectically decorated, they have character. The interiors are a little dark but recent additions such as mirrors and track lighting have spruced
things up. Each has a private sauna as well as a video tape player, full
kitchen, and a washer/dryer. Rental rates are low considering the size and
the space.

9 SUNRISE
Roaring Brook East Rd., Killington. VT 05751
1BR $130–195, 2BR $180–295, 3BR $260–375, 4BR $350–510
Amenities: Pool, health club, tennis, pond

Sunrise is absolutely elegant but very remote. These 85 new units are close to the Northeast Passage Gondola and the triple chair, so you have quick and easy access to the skiing. But you are four miles from the main ski lifts and the beginning of Killington Road with all the restaurants and resort services. Some units are single level, others are townhouses. All are contemporary and stylishly decorated. We saw one with Oriental throw rugs in the living room and brass beds with down quilts. The larger deluxe units have their own private saunas, hot tubs, or both. There's also a sports center for the exclusive use of Sunrise guests with a pool, tennis courts, and exercise room. This has the best ski-in/ski-out access in all of Killington, but it can be very lonely here.

9 TELEMARK VILLAGE
Route 100 North, Killington. VT 05751, 802-432-3244, 2BR $320
Amenities: Cross-country skiing

Located near the intersection of Routes 100 and 4, these two-story townhouses are next to the Mountain Meadows cross-country ski center. You can cross-country ski for miles from right outside your door. These condos are luxurious. Surrounded by a forest of birch and pine, the setting is quite peaceful. Inside, the condos are larger proportioned than average and the master bedroom is a suite with its own private sauna and whirlpool bath. Even the downhill racers will enjoy the confident charm of these units. They are built for the more relaxed cross-country types.

3 WINTERGREEN
Route 100 North, Killington. VT 05751, 800-238-3007, 1BR $120
Amenities: Sauna, hot tub

You have to wonder why these were ever built. Located ten miles north of the main ski lifts at Killington, these condos are in the middle of nowhere. Dating from the late 1970s, the architecture is a cross between ultra-modern and neo-Austrian chalet. Inside the units have well-ripened furniture and quaint Vermont wood-burning stoves for heat. These may have been ideal for the Age of Aquarius, but aren't we beyond that now?

ℂ WISE VACATION RENTALS
Killington Rd., P.O. Box 231, Killington. VT 05751, 802-773-4202

There are more than 200 private vacation homes in the Killington area, locally referred to as the chalets. Some are simple and very private, tucked away in a grove of birch and maples. Others are truly outstanding and for a splurge vacation you'll long remember, consider one of these:

Tropical Vermont — Imagine a Florida home with an indoor flagstone patio and a private pool surrounded by tropical plants, flooded with sunlight! Quite a surprise in rustic Vermont. This five-bedroom home is perfect for the executive who plans to entertain, or two families planning a vacation. The recreation room has a ping-pong table and of course there are videotape players. Want to revive the spirit of a ski chalet? There's an outdoor hot tub steams in winter. This home is available from $275 per night in low season.

The Overlook — A modern contemporary home with lots of glass walls, it is located right on the mountain overlooking the ski trails. There's an outdoor hot tub on the patio deck.

Mill Stream — This is the quintessential Vermont home. It is surrounded by maples overlooking a lively brook. There's a stone fireplace in the living room where you'll find a mix of Early American and comfortable contemporary furniture.

Of course, in most of these vacation homes you can expect a videotape player in the living room, extra space for entertaining, and many have a private spa, sauna, or a jetted whirlpool tub in the bath.

10 THE WOODS AT KILLINGTON
R.R. 1, P.O. Box 2210, Killington, VT 05751, 802-422-3100
1BR $135–260, 2BR $200–420, 3BR $240–560
Amenities: Sports center, health club/spa, pool, restaurant, conference center

We don't know what could be done to improve this "La Costa of Vermont." The Woods is a super-deluxe spa resort located about five miles from Killington Village. Surrounded by a forest, you'll find the name is appropriate for this group of condos. Yet inside each condo, you'll find an environment reflecting the sophisticated 1990s. Each condo interior was professionally decorated with lots of wallpaper and top quality furniture. The townhouses are luxurious; the cluster homes are even better, as most have a private sauna and a whirlpool for two. For entertainment, you'll find all the latest electronics such as VTPs, stereos, and microwaves. At the Woods, you can choose to enjoy group activities or you can enjoy the privacy afforded by a Vermont forest.

RENTAL RESOURCES
Killington Mountain Rental, 802-773-4717
Killington Rentals, 802-422-3244
Killington Reservations, 802-422-3306
Martin Associates, 802-462-2407
Wise Vacation Rentals, 802-773-4202

3. MT. SNOW

Mt. Snow has modern lifts and snow-making systems, allowing for more skiers than any other ski area in the east except Killington. Its close proximity to New York and Hartford also accounts for some of its popularity, but you'll find skiers here from everywhere. This ski resort has been developed by SKI Corporation, which also operates the Killington ski area. The 3,600-foot-high mountain has three faces and has been expanded over the years. Today, there are 50 separate ski lifts, all of which are needed on a crowded winter weekend. At the base of the lift, a small skier's village has been developed around the lodge. There you'll find four restaurants and a sports center with a heated pool and racquetball. Ice skating is available and is especially popular in the evenings. In summer when the snow melts, a golf course emerges and the Country Club opens. There are condos within this development but you'll find more to choose from in the nearby countryside around Haystack Mountain, or in the quaint New England villages of Wilmington or West Dover.

WHERE TO STAY

6   **BEAR CREEK CONDOS**
         Route 30, Box 100, Rawsonville, VT 05155, 802-297-1700
         2BR $200, 3BR $250
         Amenities: Tennis, sauna, pools, shuttle. Golf nearby

Although skiers may choose these, the Bear Creek Condos are more suited for those who want to enjoy the Vermont countryside for the change of seasons or golf. Located on Route 30 about 15 miles from either Stratton or Mt. Snow, skiers in winter have their choice of driving to either ski resort. There is a main building for reception with a restaurant and cocktail lounge. The atmosphere is casual "North Woods" with plenty of wood and moose-heads. The beer flows at night, so don't expect Bob Newhart's country inn. The two and one-half-story townhouses are spread over seven acres. You'll find solid comfort and privacy here.

         MT. SNOW RESORT
         Route 100, West Dover, VT 05356, 802-464-3333
         1BR $90–180, 2BR $110–260
         Amenities: Sports center w/pool and racquetball, sauna, exercise
         room, ice skating, golf, tennis, restaurants

These condos are part of the whole Mt. Snow ski area development. Although each complex is separate and distinct, guests staying here have special privileges at the Mt. Snow Health Club and the golf course.

Seasons Condos (8) The most expensive in Mt. Snow village, these condos are located on a winding mountain road between the two major ski lifts. Many have superior interior decor. You'll like the brick hearth fireplaces and the small outdoor patios overlooking the forest or ski trails. Convenient for skiing, this is a good choice for families.

Snow Mountain Village (7) These condos are located at Mt. Snow Village but they are too remote to be called "slopeside." If you stay here, you must drive or take the shuttle bus to the ski lifts. Each condo has a fireplace with a gas log. The advantage here is that each bedroom can become a separate suite because each has individual bathrooms. Therefore, this is a good choice for two couples sharing a condo.

Snow Tree Condominiums (5-6) Located in Mt. Snow Village, you can walk to the ski lifts. Some are trail side, so you can ski straight back to your condo in the evening. These are average condos with large living rooms, fireplaces, kitchens, and one or two bedrooms upstairs depending on the size of the condo you have selected. Surrounded by trees, there is a sense of privacy here. These are good for young families because the Mt. Snow day care center (the Pumpkin Patch) is directly across the street. Snow tree is a comfortable choice.

6 SPYGLASS HILL CONDOS
Mann Rd., Wilmington, VT 05363, 802-464-5321
Amenities: None

Haystack Mountain Ski Resort is located at the center of an ambitious new real estate development in Southern Vermont. Although Haystack has been a destination for day trippers, now the resort offers a new area for lodging. Spyglass Hill Condos was the first part of this development. One advantage here is the closeness to Mt. Snow. You have a choice of ski areas. These two and one-half-story condos actually seem like fully detached houses. Spacious and modern, we found wide variation in the quality of furnishings. One had a Scandinavian look while another showed lots of use by teenagers. Spyglass Hill is almost next to the Haystack Country Club with its 18-hole golf course. It's perfect for golfers in the summer, but there is no swimming pool or activities center. Try to negotiate a good rental rate here. These condos seem a little lonely.

9 TIMBER CREEK
P.O. Box 191, West Dover, VT 05356, 802-464-2323
2BR $160–320, 3BR $200–400
Amenities: Sports Center, indoor pool, exercise room, whirlpool, racquetball, saunas, tennis, horseback riding

What a surprise in Southern Vermont! These new two and one-half-story condos line a ridge overlooking the creek and Mt. Snow. The design is California style with lots of wood, architectural angles, and skylights. Each condo is over 2,000 square feet. Best of all, many of the condos have a sauna or private hot tub large enough for four people. Some condos have both, with the hot tub upstairs off the master bedroom and the sauna down below. These are the sort of condos you'd expect to find in Southern

California, not Vermont. The condos at Timber Creek are designed for millionaires. For space, comfort, and quality, these are the best in the area.

RENTAL RESOURCES
Palmiter Rentals, 802-464-1200
Snow Mountain Village, 802-464-2407

4. OKEMO / HAWK

This is the one area that is not just off of Route 100. Okemo used to be just a friendly, family resort in southeastern Vermont. It attracted local day trippers and maybe a few visitors from western Massachusetts, but it wasn't in the league with Killington or Stowe.

Eight years ago, management changed and a new master plan was created. The plan called for the development of numerous condominiums. Several have come on stream and Winterplace is the best of the new wave.

Nearby, the Hawk Inn has lovely condos and one of Vermont's best restaurants. Not catering to any of the downhill ski resorts, this is where the accommodations have become the "destination," not some gnarly ski area.

WHERE TO STAY

9+ **HAWK INN**
Route 100, P.O. Box 64, Plymouth, VT 05056, 802-672-3811
2BR $155–180, 3BR $170–210, 4BR $190–255
Amenities: Indoor pool, exercise room, ice skating pond, tennis

The Hawk Inn is located eight miles from Killington in the west and eight miles from Okemo in the east. Not an Alpine ski area, the Hawk Inn offers a cross-country Nordic ski route. You will also find a full-service, glass-enclosed spa/gym, horse drawn sleigh rides, afternoon bonfires around the skating pond, and some of Vermont's best dining at the Hawk's River Tavern. The clientele is somewhat different from what you'd find at Killington; here the guests seem more content to contemplate and enjoy the quality of nature rather than count to see who can make the most downhill ski runs. Many guests don't even bother to leave this resort for the lure of Killington or Okemo. At Hawk Inn, the condos are spacious and individually designed by interior decorators. The centerpiece of each unit is the impressive stone fireplace. This is a resort for people who know Vermont. You'll find Yankee austerity combined with warm hospitality to create a comfortable social atmosphere here.

8 **WINTERPLACE CONDOMINIUMS**
Okemo Rd., RFD #1, Ludlow, VT 05149, 802-228-5571
2BR $130–260, 3BR $170–350
Amenities: Pool

Okemo use to be just a friendly, family resort that was popular with day trippers from nearby Vermont and New Hampshire. In days gone by, skiers from the big cities rushed past Okemo to other Vermont resorts. That is now changing. Three new condominium developments have recently sprouted at Okemo. Their design, convenience to the ski slopes, and the relatively "unhurried" Vermont lifestyle have started to make Okemo a destination resort that draws visitors for more than just a weekend. Winterplace condos are the best of the three developments. Located at the summit of the mountain's lower quad chair lifts, you are removed from civilization. Ski down the hill in the morning to take the lifts up to the mountaintop. You'll find these spacious two- and three-bedroom condos have private fireplaces and new, stylish interior decor. Okemo's best advantage: family-oriented children's ski programs.

RENTAL RESOURCES
Hawk North, 800-832-8007

5. SMUGGLERS' NOTCH

Smugglers' Notch is emerging as one of Vermont's best resorts because of good planning and careful development. The condos and hotels fan out from the central pedestrian village. There are no cars, but you can walk anywhere. However, taking the road to Smugglers' Notch from Stowe is not as easy. One of Vermont's most tortuous mountain roads is here. It is often reduced to a single lane of traffic because of the giant boulders ("the notch") lining the road at one point. In short, just because Smugglers' Notch looks close to Mt. Mansfield and Stowe, don't plan on traveling frequently between the two resorts.

Smugglers' Notch has some of Vermont's best snow because of the mountain's elevations. In summer, Smugglers' Notch becomes a tennis resort and a center for families who want to enjoy the Vermont countryside. Increasingly, Smugglers' Notch is gaining importance as a conference center, probably because of the good design of the pedestrian village.

There are many condos to choose from in the village. All have been developed and are managed by the same corporation. The telephone number for all rentals at Smugglers' is 802-644-8851. Rental rates vary according to size: Studio $99–199, 1BR $159–279, 2BR $195–390, 3BR $249–440. The distinctions lie with the age of the condos (although none are more than 15 years old) and their proximity to the center of the village and the sports center.

WHERE TO STAY

8   HAKONE
Route 108, Smugglers Notch, VT 05464
Amenities: Health club w/indoor tennis. Aqua Center w/heated pool nearby

The most interesting condos in this three-story building are those on the first floor. They open on to a private Japanese garden area and a whirlpool bath. You are right across from the ski lifts and only two minutes away from the Aqua Center.

7   NORDLAND
Route 108, Smugglers Notch, VT 05464
Amenities: Health club w/indoor tennis. Aqua Center w/heated pool nearby

Nordland offers new one-bedroom condos at Smugglers' Notch. The condos are in a two-story building, each with a private balcony and fireplace. Well designed for families, some have an extra loft bedroom upstairs. You'll find pleasant interior decor. Nordland condos are next to the ski lifts, two minutes from the Aqua Center where you'll find the indoor swimming pool, hot tub, and sauna. Nordland also has its own Scandinavian spa and hot tub just for the few families staying at Nordland.

7   VILLMARKSAUNA
Route 108, Smugglers Notch, VT 05464
Amenities: Health club w/indoor tennis. Aqua Center w/heated pool nearby

Some say these are the best condos at Smugglers' Notch because of their location and solid comfort. The ski lift up to Mid Station is right out your door. You don't need a car here because Smugglers' is a walking village and, although small, it is complete with restaurants and shops. These condos have a living room with a bedroom on either side, and is perfect for two couples sharing a condo. The units are furnished with practical skierized furniture and have a complete kitchen. Villmarksauna is definitely a good value.

6. STOWE

Although Killington may have outgrown Stowe in the size of the ski terrain and Sugarbush offers both sophisticated restaurants and New England charm, Stowe continuous to be Vermont's most famous ski resort. The town of Stowe is quaint, with the typical New England church steeple and classical Georgian architecture along Main Street. But the condos, for the most part are outside of Stowe along Mountain Road, and are part of a five-mile strip of lodgings and restaurants between the village of Stowe and Mt. Mansfield, the ski area.

There's a wide range of condos from the luxurious **Topnotch** to the simple. Some are unusual such as **Stoneybrook,** which is part of a working farm. Many condo resorts are planned or themed, such as the **Trapp Family Lodge** built by the famous "Sound of Music" family. Some have grown as extensions of older, popular hotels, such as the condos around the **Golden Eagle.**

One reason for selecting Stowe has to be the après ski activity, which is the most varied in Vermont. You'll find great athletic facilities as well as intimate Austrian stubes, just perfect for wine and cheese. Some of Vermont's best restaurants are located here such as Villa Tragara, Isle de France, and the Green Mountain Inn.

Air transportation to Stowe is through nearby Burlington, the air center of Vermont. With nonstop flights throughout the northeast and service from Washington, Chicago, and Florida, you're bound to find convenient flights.

WHERE TO STAY

8 **COVERED BRIDGE**
Stowe, VT 05676
Amenities: Pool, tennis, cross-country ski trail access

Cross a charming covered bridge, drive up a winding mountain road and you'll discover these luxurious condos tucked away in a wooded setting punctuated by boulders, ponds, and streams. Built in 1985, these are some of the most stylish units in the area with imaginative architecture and designer decor. Each two-story building houses two, three-bedroom condos. Sloping roofs and skylights provide views at just the right angle. Inside you'll find modern kitchens, blond woodwork, Bentwood chairs, and a brick hearth around the fireplace. The one we saw had Laura Ashley fabrics in the bedrooms and a whirlpool in the master bath. Quiet and removed from the mainstream of Mountain Road, these have a country charm.

4 **FOUR SEASONS TOWNHOUSES**
Stowe, VT 05676
Amenities: Outdoor pool

A cluster of townhouses in a quiet setting, Four Seasons is spacious and comfortable. However, there's not a sense of vacation here, because of the residential apartment environment.

5   **GOLDEN EAGLE**
P.O. Box 1090 B, Mountain Rd., Stowe, VT 05672, 802-253-4811
1BR $95–160
Amenities: Health Club with indoor pool, outdoor pool, tennis, trout
pond, game rooms, restaurant.

This is the story of the resort that grew and grew and grew. The Golden
Eagle is exceptional because it is located within walking distance of the town
of Stowe. Most other lodgings or condos stretch along Mountain Road
between the town of Stowe and Mt. Mansfield. Originally a well-run motel,
the Golden Eagle developed some condominium units on nearby land. Here,
the condos are actually about a half mile from the main part of the inn which
houses the dining room and sports complex. The condos are in New England-
style, two-story buildings, and each has a full kitchen and a brick hearth fireplace. You'll find Early American furniture and attractive patterned fabrics
just like home. You don't need a car here because the shuttle bus will take
you four miles up to the Mt. Mansfield ski area, and the shops and restaurants
of Main Street are within walking distance. The emphasis is on hospitality
and service and explains the reason for the Golden Eagle's popularity.

7   **HILLCREST**
West Hill Rd., Stowe, VT 05672
Amenities: Outdoor pool, pond

Perched on a knoll, these two and one-half-story buildings offer a great
view of Mt. Mansfield. These condos are relatively new and accordingly
have contemporary decor. Some have been dressed up. We saw one with a
rock wall in the living room, dotted with plants that were potted into the
wall. Another was designed for entertaining with a full wet bar in the living
room. The location is a little remote, but those who are familiar with the
noise from Mountain Road will appreciate this location.

8   **HORIZONS TOWNHOUSES**
Stowe, VT 05672
Amenities: Pool, hot tub, tennis, paddle tennis, trout pond

These superior units have the privacy of a country estate and the convenience of townhouse living. These five townhouses occupy eight acres of
land on a knoll, strategically angled to capture the best mountain views.
Built in 1984, one building has two units and the other has three. Incredibly
there's a pool, hot tub, tennis court, paddle tennis court, and a trout pond for
the exclusive use of persons staying at Horizons. The one we saw had a private hot tub out on the deck. There are impressive townhouses.

3   INN AT THE MOUNTAIN CONDOMINIUMS
Mountain Rd., Stowe, VT 05672
Amenities: Pool, tennis, ski access

The Inn in many respects is the hub of activity around Mt. Mansfield in the wintertime. The condos in this three-story, motel-style building may be small and ugly, but you can't beat 'em for convenience. Nominally, they are considered one-bedroom units because the bedroom is partitioned off from the living room. It would take a shoe horn to get two adults and two teenagers into one of these units. Good for young skiers or beginning families, anyone else should consider the alternatives here such, as the Lodge, the Mountain Club, or the Townhouses.

6   LODGE CONDOMINIUMS AT MT. MANSFIELD
Mountain Rd., Stowe, VT 05672
Amenities: Pool, tennis, ski access

Built only a few years ago, these are some of the newest units among the collection of condos at Mt. Mansfield ski area. Strap on your skis and head straight down to the Toll House lift in the morning. Ski home in the afternoon. These condos are in three four-story buildings and each unit is long and deep so there is limited window space. There are several models: either a one-bedroom, a single-story, two-bedroom, or a two-story, two-bedroom. Although the location is wonderful, the design and interior decor are totally uninspired, neutral, and faceless. Gratefully, there might be a television or some books to break the monotony. Although a good location and popular with first timers, it is not a true "vacation home."

4   MT. MANSFIELD TOWNHOUSES
Mountain Rd., Stowe, VT 05672, 802-253-7311
1BR $247, 2BR $330, 3BR $385
Amenities: Sports center next door

Part of the family of condos at the Mt. Mansfield ski area, these are down from the highway, along a hillside. You are right next to the sports center, which is the place to be at night in the wintertime. Built a dozen years ago of wood and concrete, it's hard to imagine how such a great ski area could harbor such unattractive properties. Construction is concrete for the first floor and painted wood for the second. Inside, they're even worse. Split level, you can expect aging appliances, a sunken living room with a small fireplace, and "skierized" furniture. This stuff has been scotchguarded so often that smokers should be hesitant to light a match. There are several floor plans for one, two, three, or four-bedroom units. Message to owners and management: please redecorate, this is good real estate.

7+   MOUNTAIN CLUB
Mountain Rd., Stowe, VT 05672
Amenities: None

These are the newest and by far the best units among the condos at the Mt. Mansfield ski area. Located on the shore of a pond in summer, this site is just above the entrance to the Toll House lift. Completed in 1988, these individual buildings have style with gabled roofs and painted pine exteriors. Inside, there's a contemporary decor using the colors of the forest: brown, tan, and green. All have videotape players and there's a whirlpool in the master bath. Although a good location with attractive units, it is way overpriced.

3   MOUNTAIN VIEW CONDOMINIUMS
Mountain Rd., Stowe, VT 05672
Amenities: None

Funky is the word to describe the atmosphere around these condos. Some are vacation homes and others are occupied by long-term renters who work in the ski area. Here, you'll get a chance to meet and mix with the locals. These two-bedroom units have a large living room, but unlike so many Stowe area condos, no fireplace. Conveniently located on Mountain Road, just off Route 100, you can walk to the commercial area of Stowe and the Mt. Mansfield shuttle bus stops nearby in winter. These condos provide a budget choice that is best for the college crowd.

7   MOUNTAINSIDE
Mountain Rd., Stowe, VT 05672, 802-253-8610
Amenities: Pool, hot tub, sauna

This is located on Mountain Road midway between the village of Stowe on Route 100 and the ski area of Mt. Mansfield. These 16 two-bedroom condos occupy 17 acres of land. The setting is serene, and distinguishes these from most of the mountain road properties. Spacious and well furnished, they are often overlooked when locals speak of Stowe area accommodations. What a mistake! With their own pool, hot tub, and sauna, it's like staying on a private estate. Mountainside is quiet and understated.

7   NOTCHBROOK CONDOS
Stowe, VT 05672
Amenities: Pool, sauna, clubhouse

Quiet and serene, this community of 74 condos has its own distinct atmosphere. Tucked in the woods, well away from the commotion of Mountain Road, this complex has its own pool, sauna, and clubhouse. There are two basic sizes: the ground floor studios where the bedroom has been separated from the living room and there is a Pullman kitchen; and the two-bedroom units. In the two bedroom, you'll find a split-level design with a bedroom on the entry level, then a kitchen/dining area up a half flight of stairs. The same is true for the living room and the second bedroom. This configuration makes these particularly well suited for two couples traveling together.

7 SEVEN SPRINGS
Taber Hill Rd., Stowe, VT 05672
Amenities: None

Built in 1985, these contemporary condos enjoy a peaceful wooded setting on the far side of Route 100 from the ski areas. Don't think of staying here unless you have a car. It's about seven miles to the ski area. New and modern, this is also private. There are only eight condos on this hillside location. Pretty on the inside, we saw one decorated in beige and sky blue colors. There's a tiled fireplace hearth and a dining area with a table for eight. Bentwood chairs and one sofa made the unit seem extra light. The second one we saw had more comfortable furniture with three sofas arranged in a "U" shape and lots of coral pink throw pillows. The pink theme was continued in the bedrooms with thick fluffy quilts for those cold winter evenings. Some units have extra upstairs lofts.

9 STONYBROOK
P.O. Box 669, Stowe, VT 05672, 802-253-9701
2BR $875–1400/wk, 3BR $1200–1700/wk
Amenities: Fishing ponds, game room, indoor and outdoor pools, tennis, five hole "pitch & putt", cross-country skiing

Stonybrook is exceptional. Before Stowe became a winter resort, farming was the main industry. This former farm, just off Mountain Road, midway between the village of Stowe and the ski area, has been partially developed into a condominium resort. Half of the property is still operated as a family farm in the summertime. This unusual combination gives Stonybrook condos great views in winter and a wholesome charm in summer. On approach you can tell that this resort is outstanding, for there are New England stone walls and lots of flowers. The two-story townhouse condos are in a row and slightly staggered so you never look out on your neighbor's patio. Each has a spacious floor plan and, almost unique for Stowe, a private glassed-in hot tub large enough for four. Expect the interior decor to have country charm with light colors and blond woods. The armoire in the living room hides a television. Upstairs the bedrooms have thick goose down quilts. Everything at Stonybrook is very well done, however, it is expensive.

3 STOWE CONDOMINIUMS
Route 100 North, Stowe, VT 05672
Studio $105–200, 1BR $150–300, 2BR $250–400
Amenities: None

These condominiums are vacation area homes in name only. Although many were purchased for vacation rentals, what we saw had all the charm of a local apartment complex.

8+ STOWEFLAKE LODGE
Mountain Rd., Stowe, VT 05672, 802-253-7355
Amenities: Health club, tennis, indoor pool, outdoor pools, putting green, restaurant

These are among the most popular condos in Stowe because of residential privacy, yet there is easy access to the bustling hotel. Just off Mountain Road overlooking a meadow, the back side of the property opens up to cross-country ski trails. These units are rented either as studios or as two-bedrooms. Actually each is a three bedroom townhouse, but the master suite was designed as a lock off. Inside, you'll find a spacious living room with a brick hearth fireplace, a kitchen, a bedroom, and an upstairs loft bedroom. There's also a master suite: a bedroom that can be locked off to a studio with its own kitchenette. Most are decorated with California contemporary furnishings on the inside. This lodge is substantial and exudes a contemporary charm.

8 TEN ACRES LODGE
Lace Hill Rd., R.R. #3, Box 3220, Stowe, VT 05672, 802-253-7638
Cottages $225–275
Amenities: Pool, tennis, hot tub, cross-country skiing

Ten Acres Lodge began as a farm, was converted to an inn with fireplace suites, and now is developing small cottage "condos" on the grounds for skiers and vacationers who want more space and privacy. These cottages are perfect for a family or two couples. They are complete with everything you would hope to find in a vacation home. The furniture can best be described as "Old New England" with wing chairs, loomed rugs, and perhaps an antique wooden chair or table. Although the kitchens are complete, you may want to enjoy the Lodge's dining room.

10 TOPNOTCH AT STOWE
Mountain Rd., P.O. Box 1458, Stowe, VT 05672, 802-253-9705
Amenities: Spa with pool, gym, restaurant, outdoor pool at main lodge, tennis, horseback riding. Golf nearby

Topnotch is an accurate name for this resort. You'll be dazzled at first sight. Next to the lobby there is a beautiful sunken reading room with brick floors, oriental rugs, brass lamps, and windows for walls that look out on exquisite landscaping. There is an attractive landscaped pool area at the hotel and the condos have their own health club with an indoor spa which, again, has walls of glass and a pool with cascading waters. How about the condos?

They are all brand new, spacious three-bedroom units that are luxuriously decorated. All the small touches have been remembered, such as whirlpool tubs, VTPs and extra space for all of your sports paraphernalia, including skis and golf clubs. Although the condos have full kitchens, you may sometimes want to dine in the restaurant (rated as one of Stowe's best). Golf is available to guests at the nearby Stowe Country Club. Truly topnotch.

8+ **TRAPP FAMILY LODGE**
Lace Hill Rd., Stowe, VT 05672, 802-253-8511
1BR $150–280, 2BR $200–400
Amenities: Golf, cross-country skiing, pools, theater, restaurants, sports center with indoor pool, tennis

Remember "The Sound of Music" about the Austrian Baron Von Trapp, his wife, and the singing children who fled the Nazis for the U.S.? Well, the children grew up and the Trapp Family Lodge has been developed into a major condominium resort that has style, and lots of it. First, they have reproduced an Austrian-style environment in the hills of Vermont. You'll notice the carved wood and the cheerful Tyrolian architecture as you drive up. Fresh flowers abound and a truly European atmosphere exists with painted motifs on the moldings in the main reception areas. For those not counting calories, there are German/Austrian specialties in the dining room and an Austrian tea house with all the cakes and pies. They have included a style that reflects a noble family and their celebrated career as singers as well as the Broadway musical and the movie. The video "The Sound of Music" is available to play on your individual VTP and the local theater troupe often performs the musical. Johannes Von Trapp is a major figure in the village of Stowe, especially at festival time, and you're likely to meet him at the Lodge. There are actual condos that really look like little Austrian chalets, with two bedrooms, two baths, and a full kitchen. Each has European-style, Austrian decor with patterned fabrics and blond wood carefully balanced by American convenience—a winning combination. In ski season, you can take the shuttle bus to Mt. Mansfield and the resort has its own cross-country track. There are two heated outdoor swimming pools that have a smashing view of Vermont's Green Mountains and there is an indoor pool and sports center. The resort offers guided nature walks in the hills during the summertime.

7 **VILLAGE GREEN**
Cape Cod Rd., Stowe, VT 05672, 802-253-9705
Amenities: Indoor and outdoor pool, tennis, game room. Golf nearby

These modern two-bedroom townhouse condominiums are located just off Mountain Road in a meadowlands area overlooking the greens of the Stowe Country Club. Each building is actually a duplex that houses two units. Interior decor is "pragmatic" with tile floors in the entry hall and kitchen, and neutral colored carpet in the living/dining area. There's an Ethan Allen table and six Bentwood chairs in the dining area and indestructible off-white tweed furniture in the living room. Color comes from the throw pillow accents. The master bath has a whirlpool.

9   WEEKS HILL MEADOWS
Weeks Hill Rd., Stowe, VT 05672
Amenities: None

Among Stowe's most elegant vacation homes, Weeks Hill Meadows is located on the hillside above Bloody Brook. It enjoys views of Stowe Country Club as well as the surrounding mountains. Built as single story-plus-loft units, the roofs seem to dominate the outside architecture. Originally called Strawberry Hill, the name was changed a couple of years ago. Inside, you'll be impressed by the stone hearth fireplace and the solarium window nooks with windows overhead. We saw one that looked "Puritan" with a deacon's bench and lots of Bentwood chairs. Another was more contemporary with a pair of neutral colored love seats and a wall of mementos from travels around the world. Track lighting highlights the reading areas as well as the decorative accents. Upstairs the loft can house both a study and a bedroom. These loft units provide lots of space in a quiet location.

RENTAL RESOURCES
1836 Cabins, 802-253-7351
All Seasons Rentals, 800-54-STOWE
Evans Realty, 800-639-6084
Rentals at Stowe, 800-848-9120
Simoneau Realty, 802-253-4623
Stowe Area Association, 800-24-STOWE
Stowe Country Rentals, 802-253-8132

7. STRATTON

Located at the base of a 4,000 foot mountain, this resort is a weekend destination for many New Yorkers fleeing the city. Less than four hours by car from New York, Stratton is the first major resort that travelers come to on the highway leading from the megapolis. We use the word major because although Mt. Snow is farther south, it hasn't developed the special charm that one hopes to find in a major ski resort. Stratton has it. Carefully developed over the past 15 years, there are now over a dozen condo complexes to choose from in this 400-acre setting. In keeping with the modern trend to create year-round "Alpine" resorts (as opposed to seasonal ski resorts) an 18-hole golf course was added several years ago, and the tennis center offers twelve courts.

There is a village plaza with six restaurants at the base of the gondola and the ski lifts. A few sporting goods stores are located here, but for shopping you'll want to go into the nearby towns of West Dover or Manchester. The condos are arranged along the side of the ski runs and cascading down from the mountain plaza to the tennis club below. All were built by the same developer, so the quality and ratings reflect the newness of the units and the efforts to create a pleasing interior environment.

WHERE TO STAY

5 **BROMLEY VILLAGE CONDOS**
Route 11, Peru, VT 05152, 802-824-5458
1BR $90, 2BR $110, 3BR $130
Amenities: Pool. Golf nearby

Looking for a resort with great ski facilities and a neighboring golf course in summer? Someplace where you and your family will be recognized and remembered? Then consider Bromley. Overshadowed by its popular neighbor, Stratton Mountain, located five miles away, Bromley ski resort is one of Vermont's favorite family resorts. Its reputation has been known for its popularity with day trippers or those looking for an economical lift ticket. After all, Bromley provides good skiing without all the hype. These condos are for Bromley devotees who don't need the social life of the large resorts. Because of the relative isolation however, social relationships will easily be formed with others staying in the condo townhouses. These condos are two stories high with all the comforts of home and standard "skierized" furniture with tweeds and lots of brown and fawn colors.

STRATTON MOUNTAIN RESORT
Stratton Mountain Rd., Stratton Mountain, VT 05155, 802-297-2200
Amenities: Sports center with indoor pool, weight room, exercise classes, tennis restaurants, golf

This resort village has been developed over the past 12 years at the base of a 4,000-foot mountain. Formerly, lodging was in the nearby towns of Manchester and West Dover, but all that has changed for the better with the emergence of this new village. Stratton offers the most challenging skiing within its radius from New York City. This super resort covers 400 acres and includes a golf course and country club as well as the ski resort. The tennis center has 12 courts and is home to the Volvo Classic in the summer time. Whether you arrive in winter, summer, or fall, the resort center will be bustling with activity. The central check-in office, the inn, and six restaurants are located at the base of the ski lifts. The condos are new and are scattered throughout the property. There are distinctions based upon location and the units are priced according to size: 1BR $70–135, 2BR $90–180, 3BR $150–210. Of the 12 condo groupings available, these are our choices:

Crown Point (7) These attractive condos are fairly new and located far enough from the main village so that you'll need to take the shuttle bus to go skiing. They have handsome contemporary interior decor with cheerful pastel fabrics and a private fireplace for capturing the evening's glow. In addition to all of the sports facilities available to all Stratton Mountain Resort guests, Crown Point guests have a private platform tennis court and an outdoor pool for summertime use. The tennis club is directly across the street. This is a good choice for tennis buffs and those seeking quality lodgings with the peace of a forested setting.

Mountain Ridge (8+) Located at the end of the village mall, these Stratton condos have all the advantages: short walk to the ski slopes; privacy of a forest setting; and immediate access to the village restaurant and shops. These two-story wooden condo buildings stand out because they are painted a bright "poison-green" color. These units are brand new and each has three bedrooms, a flagstone fireplace, and the most elegant interior decor in Stratton Village. Everything you could want has been provided, including VTPs and microwave ovens. The Sports Center is only a short walk away. Mountain Ridge is one of Stratton's best.

Ober Tal (5-6) These condos were the first built in Stratton Village. The oldest, they enjoy the advantage of being within walking distance of the village and the ski lifts. However, at first sight these condos look worn. Inside, you'll find aged furniture and decor styles dating from the early '70s. The Sports Center is almost across the street so the location is convenient after skiing. Ober Tal is a good choice for a young couple or those looking for price bargains in Stratton Village.

Styles Brook (8) Styles Brook consists of tri-level cluster townhouses located across the street from the sports center. It is a great location for tennis in the summer or après-ski activity. A shuttle bus makes trips to the ski slopes. These condos are desirable for families since they are large and have a loft bedroom. Surrounded by woods, this is a peaceful setting. In the summertime, you may want to sit by the outdoor pool and read. Inside, the floor plans provide an impressive 1,500 to 2,500 square feet of living space. Interior decor seems to be basic American contemporary or perhaps a touch of Danish modern design. Styles Brook is great for families or large, informal groups.

Vantage Point (7) Located approximately one mile below the village, the shuttle bus is necessary for traveling to the ski lifts. These condos have architectural flourishes such as angles and gables that offer surprising views of the surrounding forest. The privacy and spaciousness provided by these condos results in a great mountain retreat for a family or two couples. Each condo includes a fireplace, and the light from the southern exposure windows creates a warm, toasty feeling. Furniture here is average, however. A small outdoor swimming pool is available during the summer. For after ski activities, you'll want to be up in the main part of the village.

8. SUGARBUSH

This is one of the most beautiful and well-designed resort areas in New England. Quality seems to be the order of the day here. There are two towns serving this area: Warren and Waitsfield. Both have retained their New England architecture, although the character has been softened over the years by hordes of skiers. There are also two ski mountains: Sugarbush and Sugarbush South (formerly called Mt. Ellen). The main ski area is Sugarbush, which has a village plaza and a cluster of some of the best restaurants found in Vermont. You'll find that some condos are part of this village cluster, others are on the opposite side of the ski run for ski-in/ski-out access.

Some of the better condos are hidden in the woods just off the three-mile long access road between either town and Sugarbush Mountain. This triangle of land offers some of the most spacious condos to be found in Vermont. Architects have blessed these projects with walls of glass to capture the sunlight and the forest view.

Both Warren and Waitsfield are right on Route 100 and all transportation is by car. Both the regional airports of Burlington and Rutland are each about 90 minutes away.

WHERE TO STAY

8 **THE BATTLEGROUND**
Route 17, Mad River, Warren, VT 05674, 802-496-2288
2BR $170–240, 3BR $210–270
Amenities: Small pool, cross-country skiing, tennis

There is no battle here. Everyone likes this one because of its distinctive setting and ambiance. It is located in Mad River, about four miles from Sugarbush Village. Mad River has its own complex of ski lifts, but lacks its neighbor's vertical drop. It is popular with families from New England who are proud of their straightforward Yankee heritage. Although considered part of the Sugarbush resort center, guests at Mad River are more likely to be found on the cross-country Nordic trails that begin at the Battleground. These condos are solid and spacious with small private patios and comfortable furnishings. The flagstone hearth in front of the fireplace makes you feel like you are at home. You'll like the small pool in the woods, but for exercise or conviviality, go to the sports center in Sugarbush. The Battleground (what an odd name for such a resort) is the very picture of contentment on a Saturday evening in the summertime with patio barbecues and tinkling wind chimes.

6   **THE BRIDGES**
Sugarbush Access Rd., Warren, VT 05674, 802-583-2922
1BR $102–180, 2BR $130–240, 3BR $200–360
Amenities: Sports center with pool, racquetball

Less than a half mile away from the village, these condos have a unique construction. Built in a modern Swiss style, you'll find a pair of two and one-half-story buildings connected by a glassed-in bridge on the second floor. The second-story units have an extra loft which means cathedral ceilings and great views of the pine forest and the mountains. Some have aged (and this shows) with gold or avocado colored appliances and carpets that are now dingy. Others have been recently redecorated with crisp blue and white fabrics, bentwood chairs, and Ethan Allen furniture. This is definitely for the sports-minded. There is a complete recreation center here with a 25-meter indoor pool, hot tub and racquetball court. It is very popular with groups of skiers or two couples sharing a condo.

8   **CASTLEROCK**
Sugarbush Village, Warren, VT 05674
3BR $280–320, 4BR $295–345
Amenities: None

Like a cluster of aging New England barns, these wood-sided condos are just above the Village on the north side of the Lower Village run. Some truly have ski-in/ski-out access. For others, it's a short two-minute walk. Inside, you'll be surprised to find these are among the warmest, most well-designed units for families or two couples possible. The price tags for these units are often three times that of the neighboring condos, yet the rental rates are all the same. These are far superior with deluxe, stylish interiors and contemporary wood furniture that has been accented with designer fabrics. Some have themes that create the European-chalet environment or the rustic North Woods look. Each has three bedrooms and a cozy living room area. There are no gimmicks at Castlerock just solid comfort.

CLUB SUGARBUSH (See Sugarbush Country Townhomes)

6   **FIDDLEHEAD**
German Flats Rd., Sugarbush North, Fayston, VT 05673
Amenities: Pool, hot tub, sauna, tennis

Tucked away in the forest, these stylish condos are by the Sugarbush North ski area, but you'll have to take a shuttle over to the lifts. These units are functional in design, but decorated with superior blond wood furniture. The one we saw was a "doll house" complete with a bookshelf lined with miniatures. Fiddlehead is cute and very private, but you could get lonely here.

6 GLADES
Sugarbush Village, Warren, VT 05674, 1BR $102–180,
2BR $151–271
Amenities: None

Located at the edge of the village, these small one and two-bedroom condos are great for the first time skier or families with young children. Ski school is only a few steps away. More private than Mountainside, these units are surrounded by trees instead of buildings. The Glades units are also newer with "skierized" furniture, neutral decor, and tiny fireplaces. Reasonably priced, these are a good value.

5 MOUNTAINSIDE
Sugarbush Village, Warren, VT 05674
1BR $113–180, 2BR $144–256
Amenities: None

Mountainside probably has one of the most convenient locations in the Village because one side faces the village square and the other side is on Lower Village Run. There is true ski-in/ski-out accessibility. Because it is located in the pedestrian village, you can walk everywhere. The condos in this five-story building are modern and handsomely furnished. A kitchen/breakfast bar is part of the larger living area. Each condo has a private fireplace and is comfortable for a family on vacation. The romantic French bistro Chez Henri and the Chinese Dragon are next door.

6 PARADISE
Sugarbush Village, Warren, VT 05674
1BR $102–180, 2BR $151–271
Amenities: None

Located on the edge of Sugarbush village and a short walk over to the ski slopes, these are some of the most well-decorated condos in the area. Paradise condos are in a three and four-story building next door to the Sports Center. Some living rooms have cathedral ceilings and lots of glass flood the units with sunlight during the day. All have a brick hearth fireplace, which provides a cozy atmosphere in the evenings. Expect to see tasteful interior decor ranging from "high tech" to "sweet Scandinavian." These are great for two couples sharing a condo because the floor plan allows for two separate bedroom suites and the location is so convenient.

7 SNOW CREEK
Sugarbush Village, Warren, VT 05674, 2BR $239–281
Amenities: Pool in summer

These are among the most popular condos in the area because they have the best access for skiers. Located on the south side of the Lower Village run, they are right at the Spring Fling triple chair. The Sugarbush ski area parking lot is farther down hill, and skiers have to take another lift before they can access Spring Fling. This means that you and your neighbors have the privilege of a head start on the area's best skiing. These units are small and functional two bedrooms. If two couples share them, they'd better be good friends. Otherwise, these are perfect for families. Decor is uninspired: contemporary furniture with skierized interiors. The "Scotch Guard" on the fabrics is a little bit thick. Snow Creek has its own outdoor pool which, unfortunately, is open only in summer.

6 **SNOWSIDE**
German Flats Rd., Sugarbush North, Fayston, VT 05673
2BR $178–208
Amenities: Pool, tennis

What was formerly the Mt. Ellen ski area has been renamed Sugarbush South. This is a smaller ski area, midway between main Sugarbush and the Mad River area. It is great for beginners, although the best instruction is over at the main part of Sugarbush. This area is quiet and is a great place for the second-time skier to get in lots of practice. These units are tucked away, out of sight from the ski area. Each is a functional two-bedroom model and the decor is contemporary; early 1980s with diagonal pine paneling, greys and peach colors, and blond wood furniture. Each has a private fireplace and overlooks Snowside's private outdoor pool. Although good in winter, these are at their best in summer when the hills are alive with birds.

9 **SOUTH VILLAGE**
Sugarbush Village, Warren, VT 05674
2BR $183–234, 3BR $295–343
Amenities: Pool, hot tub, sauna, clubhouse

This is a community of private homes on the south side of the Lower Village run. The location is next to the Spring Fling chair lift—some homes are close to the lift, other guests have to walk across the South Village parking lot. These two-, three- and four-bedroom homes are some of the best at Sugarbush because of space and privacy. The living room has a three-story ceiling and you'll find a glass enclosed corner where the sunlight through the trees creates a "cathedral of the forest" effect. The upstairs bedrooms have ceiling fans to capture the summer breezes.

9 **SOUTHFACE**
Sugarbush Access Rd., Warren VT 05674, 802-583-3000
2BR $262–312
Amenities: Sauna, hot tub

These are large duplex condos located about one mile from Sugarbush Village on the access road next to the Sugarbush Inn. You'll recognize them by the their distinctive architecture; there's a three-story, glassed-in atrium which exudes a special sense of openness and brings the surrounding forest indoors. Some have kept this an open space, others have installed a private hot tub, large enough for six. These duplexes are so large that they could become permanent, full-time homes. The buildings are well-spaced in a park-like environment surrounded by towering fir trees. This creates the feeling of a private residential neighborhood. The ground-to-roof windows provide lots of sunlight (and heat from solar energy). You'll enjoy the views of Sugarbush Mountain and its ski trails. Some condos here have a private hot tub or sauna just off the ground level bedroom. These are a good choice for groups of skiers or two to three couples sharing a condo because each bedroom suite has a private bath. For all the space and good design, the interior decors are a little lacking. Some are beautifully decorated; others have the basic Danish modern look. All social life is located at the Inn or the Sports Center. This is a quiet retreat for those who want space and privacy, away from the hustle of Sugarbush Village.

2   SUGAR LODGE
Sugarbush Village, Warren, VT 05674
Amenities: None

Formerly called the Hotel Sugarbush, this has had a name change, we suspect, to conceal its true identity. Great location, these hotel room condos are popular and now show years of high usage. This is a great location right on the village plaza, but this can be noisy with late night singers and early morning skiers. Maybe the time was right for a name change. Now a face lift is in order.

9   SUGARBUSH COUNTRY TOWNHOMES
Sugarbush Access Rd., P.O. Box 307, Warren, VT 05674,
802-583-2400
Amenities: Conference center

Formerly the Sugarbush Inn Townhouses, and then the "Club Sugarbush," this year these are known as the Sugarbush Country Townhomes. Across the street from the Inn, this is a community of extra-large luxury one, two or three-bedroom townhouses. Each has a large glass solarium for passive heat and all the glass makes these units sparkly. Well decorated, each is more personalized than most of the condo properties at Sugarbush. We saw one that was simple, bright and Scandinavian in effect. Another was reminiscent of Florida with house plants and vivid yellow furniture in the solarium. Another had the American heritage look, more in keeping with the colonial Sugarbush Inn across the street, with Williamsburg furniture, oriental throw rugs, and shining brass accessories.

There is a conference center here and guests at the Sugarbush Country Townhomes can avail themselves of room service from the Inn.

7   SUMMIT
Sugarbush Village, Warren, VT 05674, 3BR $215–360
Amenities: None

Located at the top of Sugarbush Village, these two-story condos are only ten years old. This means they are newer than most of the units in the village and their location is farthest away from the center. You might not want to walk to the village on a cold, icy evening. These three-bedroom units have privacy, however, because only one wall is attached to the neighboring unit. Contemporary decor is generally the rule here, with light woods and modern, "skierized" furniture. You'll be delighted with the view, but if you're a first-time skier you might want to stay down in the village as early morning access to the Lower Village run is a little rocky. Summit is spacious and solid.

3   UNIHAB
Sugarbush Village, Warren, VT 05674, 1BR $94–114, 2BR $150–190
Amenities: None

Dating from 1964 when technology was going to revolutionize the construction industry, these townhouses are actually modular construction boxes stacked on top of each other. They have two styles, a two-bedroom, and a four-bedroom unit. What was ultra-modern then can be dreary today. Others have recently changed hands and have been dressed up. The location is excellent and part of this complex borders the Lower Village run for ski-in/ski-out access. Best feature: the views of the village below and the wide sweep across the valley.

RENTAL RESOURCES
Castlerock Management, 802-583-2374
Graves Realty, 802-496-7500
Jennings Real Estate, 802-496-2591
Mill Brook Real Estate, 802-496-6679
Sugarbush Real Estate, 802-583-3000
Sugarbush Reservations, 800-53-SUGAR
Sugarbush Valley Real Estate, 802-496-3507
Sundown Country Homes, 802-496-2124
Trudy Wolf Real Estate, 802-496-2124

VIRGINIA

Virginia is for lovers. Whether you love your spouse or your children or the nation's heritage, you'll have your passions aroused by a vacation in Virginia.

The Tidewater area is where the English first settled in 1606. Traditions ran strong and the colonial heritage has been retained as part of daily life. In the 1930s John D. Rockefeller commenced an archeological and historic preservation project at the town of Williamsburg. Over 50 years ago the former colonial capital was purchased by the Rockefeller Foundation and transformed into a living museum. With the College of William and Mary at one end of town and the Colonial House of Burgesses at the other, the town has been restored to the condition of its mid-1700s elegance. The revival of numerous arts and crafts as well as a whole tradition in furniture, has been encouraged through economic subsidies. Today you'll see appropriately dressed cobblers, pharmacists, and haberdashers tending to their trades and offering their handmade products for sale. This is a living museum with romantic gardens and taverns. You can sit playing colonial games under the grape arbor while sipping a colonial "sangaree."

Virginia Beach, just 45 minutes south of Williamsburg, represents another side to the Tidewater. This is modern, progressive Virginia where NASA scientists have chosen to make their homes at "the Beach." Virginia Beach once was an exclusive resort community in the '20s. With the growth of the military complex at neighboring Norfolk, it has become a familiar resort community crowded with families on vacation in the summer. Today "the Beach" has matured with recognition that this natural resource is to be preserved. Development has now turned upscale and you'll find some choice high-rise condos on the beach where you can hear the surf at night.

The mountains are a world apart from tidewater Virginia. While the Tidewater revels in its colonial heritage and its progressive modern cities, the mountain folk cling to the "frontier" culture of the 19th Century when the area was settled. As part of Appalachia, this has a cultural heritage all its own. With luck, you'll attend a gathering of clogging dancers or perhaps buy a handmade quilt. Skyline Drive National Park just might be the most beautiful part of the Appalachian Mountains. Beginning at Front Royal, famous for its mountain berry jams, the drive passes along the crest of the Blue Ridge. It is one of the most romantic sections of the countryside you'll ever find. Follow along one of the many nature trails to see rare native plants and wildflowers. Mornings and evenings are especially romantic along Skyline Drive as you can see little wisps of fog in the hollows down below.

WHERE TO STAY

8+ FAIRFIELD WILLIAMSBURG
Route 60 West, Williamsburg, VA 23187, 804-220-1776
1BR $120, 2BR $200
Amenities: Pool, tennis, hot tub, restaurant

Fairfield Williamsburg is located on the grounds of the Colonial Williamsburg-style Holiday Inn Resort. The condos are a separate development that draw upon the Inn's core facilities. The condos are in an 18th Century brick and wood village of colonial "homes." Each home contains four condos. They are luxuriously decorated in a Federalist style. Antique reproduction furniture such as wing chairs and bold Williamsburg prints are characteristic. Each condo has a small kitchen and most have a fireplace. The Holiday Inn provides an indoor pool, hot tub, sauna, and an elaborate Colonial style bar/restaurant.

This is the choice for people who want to visit Williamsburg and live in a Colonial-style condo without giving up the convenience or privacy in a home away from home.

7 FOUR SAILS
33rd and Oceanfront, Virginia Beach, VA 23457, 804-491-8100
Amenities: Pool, weight room, restaurant

Four Sails' condos are spiffy suites in a 12-story building. The resort is located on the beach and every condo has an ocean view. The floor plan is efficient. The condos are rather small, although they include small patios. They are decorated in light contemporary woods and fabrics with several shades of blue. Everything is in perfect working order. The maintenance is meticulous, and a lot of truly helpful hospitality makes this resort a good value choice. The greenhouse enclosed pool is on the fifth floor; a popular place for families. But, of course, you can always enjoy the beach and the gentle surf. For sports enthusiasts, an indoor exercise room is available with saunas next door.

9 KINGSMILL RESORT
1010 Kingsmill Rd., Williamsburg, VA 23185, 804-253-1703
1BR $150, 2BR $240, 3BR $350
Amenities: Golf, tennis, pools, health club, restaurants

Developed by the Anheuser Busch Corporation nearly 20 years ago at a time when Busch Gardens in Williamsburg was also being conceived, this master golf resort just gets better and better. The resort is located on the shores of the James River just ten minutes from colonial Williamsburg and Busch Gardens. Two 18 hole golf courses include a design by Arnold Palmer. Kingsmill Resort provides several clusters of condominiums. The best condos are located on the peninsula's headland. The two story buildings contain condo flats elegantly decorated in a neocolonial style. Wing back chairs, Colonial print fabrics, brass accessories, and wooden duck decoys complete the picture. The other group of condos are flats in two story townhouse-style buildings located away from the central inn building along the fairway. The condos are also well decorated with traditional furniture and Williamsburg style fabrics. Everything is immaculate and in perfect working order.

The central inn offers two restaurants and a cocktail lounge, but the golf clubhouse is a livelier area. Kingsmill provides an outdoor pool, a health fitness center, intensive golf programs and tennis instruction (during selected times of the year). The resort is worth the expense. You will be so busy with sports and on-site recreational opportunities that you won't have time to see Colonial Williamsburg or Busch Gardens.

6 MASSANUTTEN

Route 644, Harrisonville, VA 22801, 703-289-9441
1BR $150, 2BR $225
Amenities: Golf, tennis, health club, indoor/outdoor pool

Massanutten occupies over 5,000 acres of Virginia's Blue Ridge Mountain and offers a variety of activities suited to the four seasons such as golf, hiking, riding in the mountains, skiing, and fishing. A wide variety of condo accommodations in different settings are available. Essentially, the two choices are either a quiet wooded setting or a spot in Massanutten Village. The interior decor varies according to the age of the condos. Some of them were developed fifteen years ago and have older furniture styles such as "ruffled country" with burnt orange colors. Others are newer and emphasize beige or aqua colors. All of the condos (except the studios) include full kitchens, private patios or balconies, and whirlpools surrounded by mirrors. The deluxe units have private saunas.

An 18-hole golf course and a fabulous sports complex, Le Club, are on-site. The sport complex provides racquetball, tennis, and swimming facilities.

4 POWHATTAN PLANTATION

3601 Ironbound Rd., Williamsburg, VA 23187, 804-220-1220
Amenities: Pool, weight room, racquetball, tennis

Powhattan Plantation features townhouse condominiums in the middle of nowhere, approximately 15 minutes from colonial Williamsburg or Busch Gardens. The entrance is grand; it leads to the 1735 Manor house. The Manor is beautiful. It features Williamsburg-style furniture, oriental carpets and gleaming brass accents. The townhouse condominiums are furnished in a colonial or Georgian style. They are characterized by cathedral ceilings, loft bedrooms, Chippendale wing chairs, four poster pine beds, and colonial fabrics. The interiors were planned well, but are worn.

The best feature is the sun deck that has a bubbling pine-sided hot tub. A sports center includes indoor/outdoor pools, racquetball courts, a weight room and a video game room.

Powhattan Plantation is an ambitious project, but the service and maintenance have fallen flat.

8-9+ WINTERGREEN
Route 664, Wintergreen, VA 22958, 804-325-2200, 800-325-2200
1BR $165, 2BR $230, 3BR $295, 4BR $355
Amenities: Golf, tennis, lake, pools, restaurant, health club

Wintergreen spreads over 11,000 acres of the Blue Ridge Mountains in western Virginia. It is one of the premier mountain resorts of the mid-Atlantic region. Just 150 miles from Washington D.C. and 40 miles from Charlottesville, Wintergreen attracts large numbers of weekenders and a growing number of executive conferences. It is a four-season resort with special activities for different times of the year i.e., skiing in winter, golf, and tennis in the summer.

There are over 3,000 vacation condos here in different parts of the resort. With the exception of the studios, all have full kitchens and fireplaces. Some are slopeside, hidden in the trees, others are townhomes close to the main lodge. The sophisticated contemporary decor often includes marble-top or glass-top tables, neutral colored but designer quality fabrics, and many brass or wood accessories. The championship 18 hole golf course hosts many small tournaments including some corporate challenges. The Tennis Center at Devil's Knob was rated among the Top 50 in the U.S. by *Tennis* magazine. Lake Monocan offers sailing and canoeing opportunities and there's an Olympic size pool and clubhouse. In summer, organized sports instruction programs and an extensive arts and crafts program are offered for children.

Wintergreen is great for families and couples. Remember, this is what they thought of when the state adopted the "Virginia is for Lovers" theme.

RENTAL RESOURCES
Atkinson Realty, 804-428-4441, Virginia Beach
Beach Quarters, 804-422-3186, Virginia Beach
Bryce Resort, 703-856-2111, Mountains
Chincoteague Island Vacation Cottages, 804-336-3720
Colony, 804-425-8689, Virginia Beach
Marjac Condominiums, 804-425-0100, Virginia Beach
Massanutten Property Owners, 703-289-9466, condos and homes by the week
Seibert Realty, 804-426-6200
VA Beach Resort, 804-481-9000

WASHINGTON

The Pacific Northwest is a bank where nature has deposited some of her greatest natural resources. The geography of the state is dominated by the majestic Cascade mountain peaks and the ocean, which has created harbors and beaches. The resort properties in Washington fall into three categories:

1. Mountain/sea resorts along the rugged Olympic Peninsula
2. Beach resorts around Gray's Harbor
3. Mountain/lake resorts along the Cascades or Lake Chelan

More detail on the state's geography can be found on the maps on pages 518 and 678.

The story of Washington begins with the Cascade mountain range. To the west of the snowy crest of the Cascades, lies an area of dense forests and rich agriculture. To the east, Washington state is a land of rolling wheat fields and dry sagebrush country. The Olympic Peninsula, on the northwest tip of the state, is one of the wettest areas in the world with annual rainfall between 150 and 200 inches. This has created dim, mysterious forests shrouded by fog and legend. The eastern shore of the Olympic Peninsula is a little dryer than the Pacific side as the rain falls mainly between the ocean and the crest of Mt. Olympus. Here you'll find both a unique seafaring world with its own history (barely one hundred years old) and ancient Indian legends with village names like Snohomish, Puyallop, and Stillaquamish. The culture has been enriched by Scandinavian immigrants who created their own Norwegian-style towns like Poulsbro.

Visitors come to the Olympic Peninsula for the sailing, hiking in the forests, or just poking around this huge nature preserve. This is the "Amazon of North America" and attracts vacationers looking for adventure as well as outdoor sports. After all, it's in this part of Washington that you'll often hear "We don't tan, we rust."

The southwestern beaches around Gray's Harbor have a milder, dryer climate. The residents of Ft. Lauderdale, however, need not fear that beach lovers will forego their fair beaches for Washington State. Oh no. But there is a mild, warm summer season from June through September when, after a short morning fog, you can expect clear sunny weather day after day with only a light shower in the afternoon.

The inland mountain resorts offer the romance of "Twin Peaks." You are in an environment of rugged mountains, totem poles, misty shrouds, and spectacular mountain scenery on a sunny day.

The condo resorts on Puget Sound and around the Olympic Peninsula have a national popularity. You'll find guests from all over the U.S. who have come to see the unique Roche Harbor and Port Ludlow developments. But otherwise, this is mainly an area for visitors from the northwestern states or Canada. By all means, go now before the area is discovered.

Tourism in Washington has been growing at over 10 percent each year, making tourism one of the state's booming industries.

Transportation to the resorts in Washington is by car or boat. If you fly, Seattle is the only choice. Travelers to Roche Harbor need to know that a two hour ferry boat ride is involved, past the thimble islands of Puget Sound.

WHERE TO STAY

6 **CANTURBURY INN**
P.O. Box 310, Ocean Shores, WA 98569, 1BR $64–134,
206-289-3317; 2BR $120
Amenities: Beach, pool, recreation room, restaurant

Located at Ocean Shores beach near Gray's Harbor, you'll find this to be an attractive three-story condo resort, which looks like a large motel from the street. All condos have sliding glass doors that open on to your private patio or terrace. A perfect place to admire the beach, sand dunes, and the surf. At Canturbury, you are on the beach and the beach is everything in this community. The condos are decorated with durable furniture, appropriate for a beach resort. The larger units have gas log fireplaces. The Canturbury has a popular restaurant, a real recreation room with billiards and video games, an indoor swimming pool, and a hot tub.

5 **KALA POINT VILLAGE**
42 Prospect Avenue, Port Townsend, WA 98369, 206-385-6650;
1BR $100, 2BR $150
Amenities: Beach, pool, hot tub, tennis

A planned development of condos and vacation homes Kala Point is just south of Port Townsend right on Puget Sound. There are two defined sections: The Bluffs, which are vacation homes and partly residential; and timeshare condos, which are dressed up and well-decorated. The timeshare condos are operated on a condo/hotel basis with check-in facilities and housekeeping. These two bedroom townhouses are in a landscaped setting overlooking the sound. At Kala Point you are in a deep forest and right next to a beach. Although located in the rainy Olympics, geography has created a small sunbelt on this part of the peninsula. During any week, you can expect a few days of sunshine along with periods of clouds and rain. Kala Point has a clubhouse with an indoor/outdoor pool, sauna, hot tub, and tennis courts.

7 **OCEAN CREST RESORT**
Sunset Beach, Mochips, WA 98562, 206-276-4465
Studio $35–46, 1BR $74–85, 2BR $78–95
Amenities: Pool, hot tub, exercise room, restaurant

Ocean Crest has a sense of style that many of the other Ocean Shores resorts lack. Located about nine miles north of Ocean Shores, the Ocean Crest Resort is in a world of its own. It has handsome design and architecture, good landscaping. Inside these condos, you have great sunlight and most have ocean views. Each condo has a private wood-burning fireplace for those chilly evenings along the Washington Coast. There's an attractive restaurant and a piano bar lounge where you can join impromptu sing-a-longs. The recreation center has a large heated indoor pool, hot tub, sauna, and fully equipped exercise room. This is a good choice for a family vacation, but be advised you are 15 minutes away from the restaurants and activity of Ocean Shores.

8 POINT BROWN RESORT
P.O. Box 877, Ocean Shores, WA 98569, 208-289-4421
1BR $90, 2BR $120, 3BR $145
Amenities: Beach, privileges at the Ocean Shores Club. Golf nearby

Point Brown bills itself as "Washington's finest oceanfront resort." This may be true. Most of Washington's resorts are on Puget Sound, in the San Juan Islands, or in the mountains. Only recently with the growth of Ocean Shores as a planned development community, have vacationers begun to appreciate the beauty of Washington's shore-line. Point Brown has 179 condos located on a spit of land at the entrance to Gray's Harbor. The four developments that make up Point Brown have been named after the streets in the game Monopoly: Park Place, Pacific Avenue, Atlantic Avenue, and St. James. Of the four, Atlantic Avenue, is the best decorated, The townhouse condos feature ocean views and sunken living rooms. There are lots of pastel colors and decorator accessories here and they are definitely the most beautiful condos in the Ocean Shores area. Each condo has a gas log fireplace, electronic entertainment center including VTP, and a whirlpool in the master bedroom. No swimming pool on site, but guests have membership privileges at the Ocean Shores Club with three swimming pools, saunas, and tennis courts. The other condos are townhouses and flats: spacious and with sweeping harbor views, but lacking in high style interior decor. Nearby is the Ocean Shores golf course, but the real reasons to come are the miles of ocean dunes, fishing, surfing, and boating opportunities.

5 THE POLYNESIAN
291 Ocean Shores Blvd., Ocean Shores, WA 98569, 206-289-3361
1BR $49–109
Amenities: Beach, indoor pool, recreation room

Designed with flamboyant architecture to resemble a Polynesian "long house," this Pacific Northwest establishment was built of stone and timber. The Polynesian offers a lodge-type setting with 70 condo apartments facing the dunes and beach at Ocean Shores. All are nicely decorated units with an

ocean view and a private wood-burning fireplace. The rattan Island-style furniture is about the only thing Polynesian about this resort. A good indoor
heated lap pool and a recreation area for children and teens are provided.
The Polynesian is a good choice for those families who want a week on the
Washington beaches of its good location and friendly, social atmosphere.

8+ THE RESORT AT PORT LUDLOW
Paradise Bay Rd., Port Ludlow, WA 98365, 206-437-2222
1BR $135
Amenities: Golf, marina, pool, tennis

One of the top choices in Washington State by a wide margin. The Resort
at Port Ludlow is located in a storybook setting surrounded by ocean, mountains, firs and cedars, and the rocks of Puget Sound. The golf course and the
marina are the twin hearts of this 460-acre resort complex so it has appeal for
those who enjoy the country club lifestyle as well as for those who enjoy
yachting. The harbor has both sail and powerboat rentals available. Whidby
Island is just across the sound where the mountain peaks are often shrouded
with mists. Formerly, the land was home to a lumber mill and some of the
buildings have been retained as destinations for hikers. The beach club is
located on a spit of land jutting into the harbor. This is where you'll find a
large heated outdoor swimming pool as well as a smaller indoor pool. Port
Ludlow also offers seven tennis courts and bike rentals. Both are very popular on this semiprivate peninsula. There's a supervised activities program for
children in the summer. With the glorious setting and all the activities, the
condo interiors are a little disappointing. Casual, comfortable furniture, but
as bland as a suburban hotel. They do provide private wood-burning fireplaces, however. All things considered, this is a top choice.

9 ROCHE HARBOR RESORT
P.O. Box 4001, Roche Harbor, WA 98250, 206-378-2155, 1BR
$75–180
Amenities: Tennis, fishing, scuba diving, pool, restaurant

Island living! There's something about the two-hour ferry ride from the
mainland over to Friday Harbor on San Juan Island that severs your ties to
reality. Ravens caw in the early morning mist. According to the local Indian
legends, this is the "Land of the Raven." Roche Harbor is tucked away in the
San Juan islands, accessible only by ferry from Anacortes. Surrounded by
woods and nine miles from the port of Friday Harbor, Roche Harbor Resort
has a curious history dating from 1866 when it was created as a company
town producing lime for the concrete industry. Lime production ended in
1957 and the company town, including the small hotel, was sold to a developer. The town has been transformed into one of the nation's most unusual
resorts with accommodations surrounding the ice plant, the worker's cottages, and the customs house. The owner's mansion is now the main dining

room. The 1880s vintage Hotel de Haro is a three-story wooden structure which originally housed visiting executives and dignitaries, including Teddy Roosevelt. The location has a magnificent view of the natural harbor where picturesque yachts frequently moor in the summer. The resort is on the National Register of Historic Places.

The modern condos are actually set back away from the harbor where you can enjoy the pristine forest tranquility. Each has a private patio as well as a full kitchen and a fireplace. You'll find a wood trimmed "clubby" interior decor with earth tones and Pacific Northwest accessories for accents. The Lagoon Shores condos are more contemporary with designer fabrics and VTPs and are not as "woodsy." This is a great resort for those who like tennis, sailing, fishing, or, for the very brave, year-round scuba diving in the rich waters of the Japanese current.

8+   SUN MOUNTAIN LODGE
P.O. Box 1000, Winthrop, WA, 509-996-2211
1BR $120, Cabins $135
Amenities: Lake, pools, tennis, horseback riding, restaurant. Golf nearby

If you liked "Twin Peaks" you'll love Sun Mountain. Set amid some of the most gorgeous scenery in the Cascades, this Lodge was forged from stone and wood. Having all the modern conveniences, the condos in these two-story buildings also have the flavor of a wilderness home. Decor is contemporary accented by Pacific Northwest touches and Indian weavings. The small cabins by the lake are a good choice for a family adventure. This resort is an escapist environment with hiking trails (for those who want to be alone) and a pool center with a huge rock hot tub. The bar is where everyone gravitates at night. Quite an interesting group of visitors find their way here.

5   SURFCREST
P.O. Box 445, Copalis Beach, WA 98539, 206-289-2157; 1BR $75
Amenities: Beach, pool

Located five miles north of Ocean Shores, this is in the quiet community of Copalis Beach. Surrounded by 100 acres of spruce woods on one side and the ocean on the other, Surfcrest sits all alone in a village of 54 two-story condos arranged in a V-shape with a community recreational area in the center. Friendly management will give you a good introduction. This is a social resort where most guests make friends quickly; children play with their friends and adults find others with similar interests. The condos are modestly furnished as you would expect to find at a beach house. The indoor pool is a popular place and the upstairs "adults only" lounge is a place for parents to escape from their children. A pleasant spot for a quiet family vacation.

RENTAL RESOURCES
Beach Haven Resort, 206-376-2288
Blue Fjord Cabins, 206-468-2749
Canturbury Inn, 206-289-3317
Century 21 Ocean Shores, 800-562-6670
Cherie L. Lindholm Real Estate, 206-376-2202
Dockside Property Company, 206-378-5060
Iron Springs Resort, 206-276-4230
Kala Point Realty, 206-385-2367
The Nautilus, 206-289-2722
Northwest Vacation Homes, 206-321-5005
Ocean Crest Resort, 206-276-4465
Ocean Shores Reservations, 206-289-2430
San Juan Properties, 206-378-2101
Smugglers Villa Resort Condos, 206-376-2297
Surfcrest Resort, 206-289-2157
Windjammer Condominiums, 206-289-3388

WISCONSIN

Wisconsin constantly appeals to the visitor to slow down, turn off the highway, and follow those rambling roads back into the countryside. Ground by glaciers so that today the land is flat, Wisconsin has an extensive road network and a series of bicycle routes. There are bike trails to take you from one side of the state to the other, all in the crisp, exhilarating country air.

The state has several distinct vacation areas and we have divided this chapter into two parts: Door County, and the Lake and Ski Resorts. Door County is the tiny thumb of the state that juts into Lake Michigan above Green Bay. Situated on the Great Lakes, this area is more like Maine than the Midwest. There's a rocky shore with a lighthouse, two-foot waves, gulls, and the clean fresh smell of an ocean breeze. Meanwhile, the inland Lake and Ski Resorts are shallow and warm enough for swimming in summer. This is the land of the great North Woods—before Timberland and Land's End began selling the clothing to fit the lifestyle. The Lake and Ski Resorts section reviews five resort areas: Minocqua, Rhinelander, the Wisconsin Dells, and Lake Geneva.

Wisconsin is a destination for all seasons and, as long as you approach it with the attitude that you want to slow down, the resort areas will fulfill your expectations.

1. DOOR COUNTY

Door County attracts artists and those who yearn for Cape Cod. The peninsula is a 70-mile long finger of land that juts into Lake Michigan. Door's low-key resorts, shining summer weather, and cherry and apple orchards offer an escape from 20th Century America. The name "Door County" comes from the French explorers who labeled it "Porte des Mortes" (Door of the Dead) because of the treacherous waves and currents that shipwrecked sailors. Scuba divers come in the summer to search and hunt for the remains of over 200 charted shipwrecks. In addition to the geographic location on Lake Michigan, another distinguishing feature of this area is the number of restaurants, shops, and tourist attractions. Even the sedentary can find a lot to do in Door County and "antiquing" is a major sport here. Not as aerobic as some activities, it does require physical endurance to browse and inspect the thousands of items for sale in the shops and Saturday flea markets. The sights include the Bjorklunden Chapel, a Norwegian stavkirke, the Cana Island Lighthouse, and the Ridges Sanctuary, which is the largest natural flower preserve in the U.S.

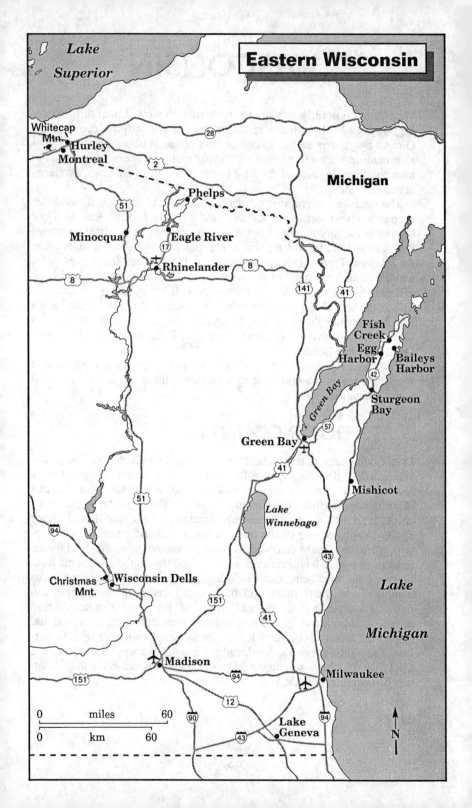

WHERE TO STAY

6   BAILEYS HARBOR YACHT CLUB
Ridges Road, Baileys Harbor, WI 54202; 2BR $550/wk
Amenities: Pool, tennis. Yacht Club next door.

While most Door County establishments are on the Green Bay side of the peninsula, only a few are to be found on the quieter Lake Michigan side. Baileys Harbor offers a cute collection of little cabins and condos next door to the marina. Fairly new, the condos are in the boxy Bauhaus style with pitched roofs and cedar-shingled siding. Inside decor is generally very simple with nautical touches. The kitchens are small but open, giving these units an extra sense of spaciousness.

8+   BAY SHORE INN
4205 Bay Shore Dr., Sturgeon Bay, WI 54235, 414-743-4551
1BR $75–140, 2BR $85–165
Amenities: Indoor and outdoor pools, tennis, beach, game room, restaurant

The Bay Shore Inn has been located on the shores of Green Bay for many years, but it was completely rebuilt in 1990. Spacious and light with lots of windows, the units are beautifully decorated in gray with rose and blue and have a view of the water. Each unit has a whirlpool and the one we saw had a dressing room in the master bath. Although the kitchens are stylish and brand new, you may want to try some of the homemade pastries or the traditional Door County fish boil at the Garden Sea Restaurant. Pleasant and helpful management is there to assist you.

6   BEOWULF LODGE
Box 3775, Fish Creek, WI 54212, 414-868-2046, 800-433-7592
1BR $82–94
Amenities: Indoor pool, tennis, conference center

This all-suite hotel looks like a condo resort, but all the amenities and services put it into the hotel category. What you will find are spacious accommodations that have been nicely decorated. Each has a kitchen. There's a recreation center with the heated pool, sauna, and restaurant. Beowulf Lodge provides condo space in a hotel style.

☏   DOOR COUNTY REALTY
4027 Main St. Box 303, Fish Creek, WI 54212, 414-868-2111

Many of the best accommodations in Door County are private homes available for weekly, monthly, or seasonal rentals. Some of the owners are a little particular about renting out their homes, which may have been in the family for generations. Door County Realty handles over 70 vacation home or resort condo rental properties and has proved to be a good source for both short and longer term visitors. A quiet efficiency here ensures that every one of the properties is well scrubbed and in perfect shape for your visit.

For an exceptional find that reflects the traditions of Door County, contact this agency to find your summer home rental.

7   FISH CREEK CONDOS
Fish Creek, WI 54212, 414-868-2111
2BR $495–650/wk, 3BR $850/wk
Amenities: Pool, tennis

Located near Peninsula State Park in a picturesque birch woods setting, Fish Creek Condos are also within walking distance of downtown Fish Creek. The two-bedroom models are all on one level while the three-bedroom models are of a townhouse design. You'll find a spacious living room with a fieldstone fireplace and a cozy kitchen. Interior decor tends to be contemporary in beige with blue or rose. Dashes of country classic fabrics in the Laura Ashley style accent the decor. Fish Creek Condos offer a good location and great value, and they are a solid choice.

5   FOX HILLS RESORT
Mishicot, WI 54228, 800-950-7615
Studio $69–135, 1BR $99–179, 2BR $139–219
Amenities: Golf, tennis, indoor and outdoor pools, health club, horseback riding

Laying claim to be "at the doorstep to Door County," this resort can more accurately be described as on the road to Door County. Near Manitowoc, With 45 holes of golf, this is a major development that has potential as a weekend destination. The courses have a resemblance to Scotland or Florida with their berms and rolling terrain, but our concern was with hospitality. The timeshare sales program seemed to dominate the resort experience. The units are modern in two-story buildings with pleasant contemporary decor. The private whirlpool tub is an inviting amenity. There's an outdoor pool and it also has one of the few indoor pools in northern Wisconsin. Don't be outfoxed by the sales program.

7   FOX POINT CONDOMINIUMS
Egg Harbor, WI 54209; $650/wk
Amenities: Tennis

Located on a bluff overlooking the waters of Green Bay just south of Egg Harbor, these attractive units enjoy a beautiful forested setting. In fact, the 13-acre forest preserve surrounding the buildings and buffering this development from the encroachment of civilization, may be its best feature. The condos blend into the environment. Inside, the units are modern and furnished in a contemporary style. Expect to find lots of beige carpeting and rose fabrics. Occasional accents by owners will remind you of Door County's quaint country charm. Each unit has a view of the Bay. Bear in mind that there is no pool, but honestly how important is pool swimming when you're on the shores of this lovely bay?

7 **HARBOR GUEST HOUSE**
Box 108, Fish Creek, WI 54212, 414-868-2284
1BR $57–127, 2BR $132–177
Amenities: Pool, tennis

There are six suites in this romantic Tudor-style lodge on the lake, and a cluster of private condominiums hidden behind in the woods. It's the design here that adds a touch of romance: stone walls, stone fireplaces, patios on the beach, and views of Green Bay. The decor consists of "collegiate maple" but is clean and comfortable. Each has a full kitchen. The pool is actually over at Hidden Harbor Condominiums.

7 **HIDDEN HARBOR CONDOMINIUMS**
Box 303, Fish Creek, WI 54212; 414-868-3245
2BR $850/wk, 3BR $950/wk
Amenities: Pool, tennis, paddle tennis, boat docks

These condos enjoy a lovely wooded setting in a grove of fragrant cedar trees within walking distance to downtown Fish Creek. You can sit on your screened porch and enjoy nature. Located on the bay side of the peninsula, some of the units have private boat slips. These two- and three-bedroom units in two-story buildings are good for a family or friends vacationing together. There's a large living room with a fieldstone fireplace. Interior decor relies upon Door County's rural heritage and traditions with quilts, Scandinavian wreaths, and some even have rocking chairs.

5 **THE INN AT LITTLE SISTER HILL**
2715 Little Sister Hill Rd., Sister Bay, WI 54234, 414-854-2328
1BR $84, 2BR $92–130
Amenities: Heated outdoor pool

These two-story modern townhouses enjoy an attractive setting. In a land of cozy cabins, these are a welcome change. Interior decor includes inexpensive contemporary furniture. The big surprise is the absence of fireplaces.

6-7 **THE LANDING**
7741 Egg Harbor Rd., Box 16, Egg Harbor, WI 54209, 414-868-3282
1BR $69, 2BR $85–125
Amenities: Pool, tennis, playground

Hidden in the woods on a small ridge just above the town of Egg Harbor, this is a cute "condo in the country." The air is fragrant and hiking trails are accessible from here. Sadly, the interiors are a drab disappointment. They are furnished much like the reception area at your doctor's office. They have smallish rooms and the second bedroom is actually a loft.

8 LANDMARK
7643 Hillside Rd., Box 260, Egg Harbor, WI 54209, 414-868-3205
1BR $47–95, 2BR $59–114, 3BR $110–155
Amenities: Tennis, pools, exercise room, game room, restaurant, conference center

Located on a bluff overlooking Green Bay and the Alpine Golf Course, this condo/hotel offers a high level of hospitality. Taking pride in its conference center, the Landmark attracts many small meeting groups and seminar attendees. There's an attractive indoor free-form swimming pool as well as an outdoor pool. Some of the units are suites with only a sitting room; others are larger with a full kitchen as well as separate bedrooms. It is contemporary with hotel-style furniture in light woods and fabrics in moss or forest green colors. With beautiful views of the forest and the water, this is equally suitable for a romantic getaway as for a family vacation.

8+ THE RUSHES
3014 Rushes Rd., P. O. Box 630, Sturgeon Bay, WI 54235,
414-839-2730
Amenities: Lake, indoor pool, cross country ski trails

The Rushes provides stylish accommodations in Door County. Occupying 160 acres on the sandy shores of Kangaroo Lake, these contemporary two-story condos evoke a California style. Interiors are spacious and comfortably furnished with forest green carpets, wood and glass-top tables, and a stone fireplace with bench. The living rooms have cathedral ceilings and are designed to capture the best views of the lawn and lake. Popular with families who want to go "nowhere" for some fun and relaxation will enjoy this spot.

9 SISTER BAY RESORT & YACHT CLUB
P. O. Box 496, Sister Bay, WI 54234, 414-854-2993
1BR $79–149, 2BR $89–169
Amenities: Boat slips, tennis, fishing pier, "toobies"

One of Wisconsin's best resorts, it is an imposing three-story lodge structure on the south shore of Door County's Sister Bay. Sister Bay offers several floor plans as options for your vacation. There are the "honeymoonette" one-bedroom suites with their own private hot tubs (not a whirlpool bath, but a real hot tub); and two-bedroom units designed for privacy and lots of space on a family vacation. A special feature is the fireplace in the master bedroom. This resort radiates a special air of confidence and contentment with the world. Everything is well ordered, nothing is rushed, and management is available to take care of small, special favors— or to respect your privacy if that's what you're after. Not too fancy, not too plain, this one's just right.

7 SISTER BLUFF ESTATES

Highway 42, Sister Bay, WI 54234; 3BR $650/wk, 4BR $975/wk
Amenities: Pool, tennis, children's playground

One of Door County's largest collections of condos, Sister Bluff has a lot to offer. These townhouses, which have two bedrooms and a loft are a good choice for families. This is one of the few developments that also has four-bedroom models. Each unit has a fieldstone fireplace in the living room and the interior decor tends to be superior to many other area accommodations. Many owners have accented their condos with mementos from Door County's nautical past or the Scandinavian heritage. With a pool, 8 tennis courts, and a children's playground, this choice means less driving for mom and dad.

7+ WAGON TRAIL

1041 Highway ZZ, Ellison Bay, WI 54210, 414-854-2385
2BR $70–155
Amenities: Indoor pool, sauna, restaurant

One of Door County's most popular destinations, Wagon Trail provides a range of accommodations that includes suites and private homes in the woods. Located near the end of the Door County Peninsula, this has an advantageous setting on "the quiet side" of the peninsula overlooking Lake Michigan. Just across the bay, Newport State Park has a rugged shoreline reminiscent of Maine. Wagon Trail occupies 200 wooded acres along this shoreline. Starting with a core lodge, Grandma's Bakery attracts many Door County visitors with its famous pecan rolls and Scandinavian treats. It's cute with a gift shop to boot. The suites in this Scandinavian country inn have low ceilings and oak beams. The living rooms, recently updated, are attractive and comfortable, but the kitchens are relics from back in grandma's days. The vacation homes are something else again. Each has been individually designed and decorated. You'll find a rustic looking log cabin that has a modern interior and all the electronic entertainment equipment you could want. Several are in the style of Cape Cod cottages while some are just simple Wisconsin cottages. Interior decor is highly personalized which is part of the charm of staying in vacation homes. This is where you want to be— snuggled by the fire with a box of Grandma's pastry.

8   WINDING BROOK
Ephraim, WI 54211; 3BR $900/wk
Amenities: Beach

Ephraim is one of those quiet communities where time stands still. Stop in the filling station for gas and enjoy a soda. Winding Brook is a good compliment to the community standards. These attractive condos are across the street from the private beach and each has a lovely view of Eagle Harbor and the waters of Green Bay. There are only seven units in this development, so it's very much like having your own vacation home. The one we saw was beautifully decorated with a fieldstone fireplace and three bedrooms. Spacious and well planned, these units also feature a large utility room for sporting equipment and for keeping the mud out of the house. The beach can be seen by all, but enjoyed only by the residents of Winding Brook.

2. LAKE AND SKI RESORTS

Just as Door County resembles Maine, so do the inland Lake and Ski Resorts resemble New Hampshire or the north woods of Canada. In the fall, you'll be amazed by the colors of the foliage contrasted against the clear blue of the sky and lakes. The advantage to "leaf peeping" in Wisconsin is that you'll find a tenth as many people as in New England. Winter is brutal but the Scandinavian settlers brought their traditions, sports, and food to this land, which can have 200 inches of snowfall a year. The five major ski resorts in Wisconsin may lack the vertical drop of Vermont, but the compensation lies in the gemütlichkeit of the after-ski activities. Spring is a myth, but summer can last a solid four months. Indian summer lasts a solid six weeks thanks to the moderating influences of the Great Lakes and the warmth captured in the small inland lakes.

In this section, there are five target resort areas. The first is the Hurley Whitecap mountain area. It is located just at the intersection of Lake Superior and the Michigan Upper Peninsula border. Due to the proximity of four ski mountains, this area is at its peak in winter. Rental rates are lower in summer, however, when nearby resorts charge full high-season prices. In summer, this area is beautiful and it's a sleeper because of low summertime prices.

Another area is Minocqua. It is southeast, in the center of the Chain O' Lakes. Here, the focus is on rustic cabins and the cute North Woods town, which looks as though it could double as a set for "Northern Exposure." Eagle River, a third resort area, is just 35 miles farther east, and it shares the same ambiance and attitudes.

Dropping down to the center of the state, about an hour north of Madison, you'll find the Wisconsin Dells and Christmas Mountain. Popular with massive numbers of Chicagoans fleeing the summertime heat, the Wisconsin

Dells are almost too close to the major metropolitan areas to retain the indigenous charm during the summer months. Finally, there is Lake Geneva, just an hour north of Chicago's suburbs. This classic vacation-home community where the Wrigleys, the Swifts, and the Armours had their summertime estates, has seen its caché fade.

Each of these communities has scores of vacation homes and cabins available for rent. The availability of condos is a debatable issue. Where you find ski mountains you'll find condos. A few lake resorts added condos in the '80s, but this is more a land of persons seeking untamed nature, rather than carefully cultivated resorts.

The Wisconsin Dells in the central part of the state offers a popular area for vacations. Over the centuries, the Wisconsin River has carved a spectacular seven-mile gorge through the rock. Today, you'll hear the laughter of children on "duck-boats," amphibious car-boats that carry sightseers through the region. You'll see bizarre stone formations in the sheer cliffs.

The Lake Geneva area, in the southeast, is an easy hour from metropolitan Chicago. You'll see some spectacular summer homes and glittering resorts with top quality restaurants to attract visitors from the sophisticated cities.

Air transportation to these Wisconsin resorts is primarily by commuter service from the hubs of Chicago, Detroit and Minneapolis. The Rhinelander airport serves the Land O' Lakes region and the Wisconsin Dells are only an hour or so away from the airport at Madison. The Lake Geneva resorts are an easy hour from Milwaukee's airport or a long hour from Chicago's O'Hare.

WHERE TO STAY

7+ **THE ABBEY**
Highway 67, Fontana, WI 53125, 414-275-6811; 2BR $235
Amenities: Marina, pool, spa, tennis, restaurants

Located just an hour from metropolitan Chicago, The Abbey is a major center of attention. The main hotel lodge offers a full range of scheduled activities as well as recreational opportunities. Most of the Abbey property consists of hotel rooms in a series of buildings tucked away in a forested setting. The condos are located away from the main lodge and enjoy a peaceful section of the lake front. These units undeniably have a touch of hotel management and lack the warm personal atmosphere of a condo. Although it has attractive decor, there is nothing classic that would befit this grand resort. The conference center attracts group gatherings. Regardless of where you stay in the area, you'll surely drop by this landmark resort at least once.

1   **BEACONS OF MINOCQUA**
         8250 Northern Rd., Minocqua, WI 54548, 715-356-5515
         2BR $150, 3BR $185
         Amenities: Lake, pool, dock, putting green

This timeshare complex is home to a dozen attractive units in a two-story wooden structure on the shores of Lake Minocqua. Each unit has a personal jacuzzi whirlpool. But indifferent management leaves us cold. What's worse is "the hole," an abandoned construction site on the grounds that remains a hazard.

8   **CHRISTMAS MOUNTAIN**
         County Highway H, Wisconsin Dells, WI 53965, 608-253-1000
         Cabin $89–159, 2BR $115–300
         Amenities: Golf, skiing, horseback riding, pool, tennis, restaurant

Located four miles away from the motels and adventures of the Dells, Christmas Mountain offers a Wisconsin "Country Club" vacation. This master development includes several condo clusters around the 18-hole golf course—each designed to satisfy several different groups of guests. Christmas Mountain provides a choice of cabins, golf villas, and separate houses. Billed as budget lodgings, you'll be pleasantly surprised by the log **Cabins.** They have hardwood floors with old-fashioned hook rugs, and cute interior decor including country ruffles around the bed. These have style and a touch of whimsy. The **Pines** golf villas are two-story contemporary California-style redwood buildings. These have spacious living rooms and kitchens; upstairs a whirlpool bath surrounded by mirrors and large enough for two. The newest are the **Oaks**—same floor plan and private whirlpool. The Oaks are separate detached houses surrounding their own swimming pool/hot tub area.

6+   **DEER RUN**
         Box 356, St. Germain, WI 54558, 715-479-6884
         2BR $350–450, 3BR $440–610/wk
         Amenities: Lake

Located on the shores of Big St. Germain Lake, this is a fishing club that has evolved into a condo resort. Only 30 minutes north of Rhinelander, this is the site of the Musky Inn Supper Club, an ongoing operation since 1904. The duplex and individual cottages are clustered together but there are 63 acres of private backwoods for your recreational enjoyment. Although rustic in appearance, it's the social ambiance here which makes this like summer camp for grown-ups. Although your kitchen may be great for fixing macaroni for the kids, grown-ups will appreciate the conviviality of the Musky Inn.

EAGLE BLUFF CONDO RENTALS
100 Silver St., Hurley, WI 54534, 800-336-0973

This reservations service handles over 180 condo and vacation home properties in Northern Wisconsin. Whether you plan to ski Indianhead in winter, or long for the pristine beauty of Lake Gogabic, you'll be able to find your choice of accommodations here.

5 ED GABE'S LOST LAKE RESORT CONDOMINIUMS
Box 24, St. Germain, WI 54558, 715-542-3079
1BR $385-450/wk, 2BR $525-650/wk, 3BR $800/wk
Amenities: Pool, tennis, recreation center

This collection of cabins and townhouse condos along the lake has had an enduring reputation among repeat visitors and in the local community. Simple, clean, and friendly with no pretensions, this offers great value.

7 HAVEN NORTH CONDOMINIUMS
Hurley, WI 54534, 715-561-5626
1BR $52-100, 2BR $78-152, 3BR $97-175
Amenities: Lake, tennis

Located in the heart of the Big Snow country, these attractive condominiums are convenient for skiers planning to visit Indianhead, Big Powderhorn, Black Jack, or Porcupine ski mountains. This is a cluster of two-story quadruplexes on the lakeshore. Each was decorated a dozen years ago, and the style is a little aged, but good care hides the age. Expect simple "skierized" furnishings accented by the owner's personal taste for country antiques or nautical knickknacks. This is a popular, family-oriented resort and there is a cadre of vacationers who return to the spot year after year.

6 MINOCQUA SHORES
Box 313, Minocqua, WI 54548, 715-356-5101
3BR $110-200, 4BR $145-225
Amenities: Lake, dock, boat rentals

Located on a private island in Lake Minocqua, about a mile from town, this has been a traditional favorite with vacations. The condos are huge, three- and four-bedroom units. Interior decor is a little on the stale side with "collegiate maple" furniture and lots of Scotch-guarded fabrics.

8 THE POINTE RESORT
Highway 51 South, P.O.Box 880, Minocqua, WI 54548,
715-356-7799; 1BR $84-146, 2BR $15-190
Amenities: Tennis, indoor pool, restaurant

Located in the Land O' Lakes region of northern Wisconsin, Minocqua is a place where all the world is at peace, or at least "gone fishing." These luxurious lakeside condominiums are in a contemporary wooden structure which blends in with the environment. Every window is "placed" in order to frame a view. The superior decor is, in fact, among the best in Wisconsin. These are lots of decorator touches and designer fabrics. Each unit has a fireplace, and many have lofts and cathedral ceilings in the living rooms. Part of this resort is a hotel where you'll find an indoor pool, restaurant, recreation facilities, and a conference center.

7   WHITECAP MOUNTAIN
Montréal, WI 54550, 800-933-SNOW; 1BR $90–145, 2BR $102–150
Amenities: Ski lodge, restaurant

Located just south of Lake Superior and Michigan's Upper Peninsula, this is Wisconsin's largest ski resort. True, there is a hotel lodge, but most of the accommodations are in small (ten-unit) condominium buildings each separately named and clustered together in a skiers' village. Some of the specific condo buildings include **Mountain Meadows, Woodland, Valkomen,** and **St. Moritz.** Most units have private hot tubs large enough for four and all have fireplaces in the living room. Interior decor is casual/contemporary, but we were impressed by the effort to recreate a Swiss village with little touches such as Swiss cowbells, European andirons in the fireplace and, of course, poster art of European skiing. What's best is that the price goes down in the summer, when this area reaches full bloom. The lodge restaurant is open year-round and here's a north woods experience with a touch of gemütlichkeit.

RENTAL RESOURCES... WISCONSIN
Big Snow Country Rentals, 414-739-2825, Montreal
Coldwell Banker/Door County, 414-868-2373
Door County Realty, 414-868-3245, 800-962-4161
Glister Co., 414-351-2377, Door County
Mallard Cove Vacation Homes, 800-876-9751, Lake Gogebic
Montreal Haus Rentals, 414-733-5766, Montreal
Whitecap Lodging, 715-561-2776, Hurley

WYOMING

It used to be that Wyoming was overlooked by travel agents as a vacation destination because it had little to offer besides Yellowstone National Park, sheep ranches, and those wide open spaces. In the 1950s, Laurence Rockefeller—with amazing foresight and tenacity, realized the incredible beauty of the jagged Grand Teton mountain range and caused the United States Congress to create a second national park just south of Yellowstone. Today the Grand Teton Mountains National Park may be one of the world's most photographed. Just south of these two major parks lies Jackson, a cowboy town that has gained popularity as a center for mountain expeditions, horseback riding, tennis, golf, river rafting, and skiing. Jackson includes this entire area, originally named Jackson's Hole after Davey Jackson, the fur trapper, who worked this valley or "hole."

Besides the two national parks there are thousands of acres of forest lands with unlimited opportunities to experience the outdoors. Miles of trails offer easy walks and invigorating mountain hikes. Mountain biking has zoomed in popularity and bikers can explore the wilderness on trails too steep or narrow for a horse. If you're in shape you can climb the 13,770-foot Grand Teton.

Above all though, the stunning 50-mile-long valley of Jackson Hole is the gateway to one of the wonders of the world, Yellowstone National Park. Encompassing 2.2 million acres of unspoiled land, Yellowstone includes pine forests and rolling meadows, high mountains, and deep canyons. Old Faithful Geyser is the best known example of Yellowstone's geologic rarities. Others are boiling hot pools, bubbling mud pots, and sulphur-smelling geyser basins, which you can explore via miles of boardwalks and trails. You can also see 1,000-foot canyons, thundering waterfalls, and massive walls of the yellow stone for which the park is named.

In winter, the story is even better. Home to three major ski resorts, Jackson Hole has the reputation of providing some of the finest and most challenging powder skiing to be found anywhere. The main Jackson Hole ski resort (Teton Village) is 12 miles northwest of town and is surrounded by a "new town" with over 20 different condominium developments and lodges. This area is actually two mountains that connect at the same base. Après Vous Mountain offers a wide terrain of beginner and intermediate slopes; Rendezvous Mountain at 10,450 feet offers some of North America's best Black Diamond skiing. Snow King Resort, the second ski area, is actually in the town of Jackson. Mainly for beginners and intermediates, it offers a fun day in the snow. Finally, Grand Targhee, an hour away on the other side of the mountains, is a special place with over 500 inches of snow per year. It is favored by those who thrill at powder skiing. Although blessed with the challenging reputation, Grand Targhee is more intermediate than Rendezvous Mountain. The town of Jackson is still a frontier village with log cabin exteriors, western-covered plank boardwalks, a country store selling sun bonnets as well as neon-framed shades, and "Antlers Park," the town square with archways made of elk antlers. An unusual convergence of different cultural trends, you will find nothing else like Jackson today. Over the past few years with the growth of Jackson Hole's popularity, designers such as Ralph Lauren and Benetton have opened boutiques here. Quite a surprise in a community of 9,000, cut off from the major highways by the mountains.

When planning a vacation, there are several neighborhoods to choose from. There's the actual town of Jackson with its shops and restaurants. There's Teton Village, the skiers village of condominiums, which becomes a horseback riding center in summer. There's the Jackson Hole Racquet Club/Teton Pines area five miles south of Teton Village but ten miles north of the town of Jackson. The Racquet Club/Teton Pines area has over 32 tennis courts (many of which offer instruction and clinics) and a championship 18-hole golf course designed by Arnold Palmer. Up by the airport, ten miles away from town in a different direction, there's Teton Shadows at the Jackson Hole Golf Course, designed by Robert Trent Jones, Jr. Fourth, in this litany of vacation home neighborhoods in the orbit of Jackson town, comes Spring Creek Resort. Set on a bluff overlooking the valley, these condos have the best view of the Grand Teton Mountains that you could imagine. Southwestern in tone, this is a special place to observe the area's natural beauty. Finally, there's Grand Targhee, fully an hour away on the other side of the mountain accessible only by driving 50 miles, 30 of them in Idaho. For more detail, a map of this area has been provided on page 426. This is an exceptional resort community, and it becomes more affordable each year. Once you vacation in Wyoming, you'll place it high on your list of spots to return to.

One factor contributing to Wyoming's current attraction has been its limited population and the lack of transportation from major eastern cities or California. Jackson Hole, more than most other resort destinations, is a "fly in" community. Surrounded by steep mountain passes on three sides, the driver's best approach is from the north, i.e., Montana, a state with a similarly low population density. That is beginning to change with the introduction of non-stop air service from Chicago, Denver, and Dallas. Travelers from the west will probably fly to Jackson via connections in Salt Lake City.

WHERE TO STAY

8   **THE ASPENS (See Jackson Hole Racquet Club)**
Moose-Wilson Rd., Jackson Hole, WY 83001 (no mail)
800-443-8616, 1BR $75–110, 2BR $110–150, Homes $300–450
Amenities: Jackson Hole Racquet Club, pool, tennis

This is a new phase of expansion at the Jackson Hole Racquet Club, which is next door to The Aspens. These vacation homes and condos are superior with contemporary decor accented by Indian fabrics. Many have additional art pieces to create a fanciful environment.

6 **COLTER BAY VILLAGE**
Grand Teton National Park, P.O. Box 240, Moran, WY 83013
Amenities: Lake, restaurant

Set in a wooded area along the shores of Jackson Lake, this resort is one of three to have operating permits within the Grand Teton National Park that was created by Laurence Rockefeller. This is a village of log cabins and, for those wishing to be close to nature, tent cabins. These 209 snug cabins do not have kitchen facilities, but there are ice chests and outdoor barbecue grills. For those less adventurous, there's the unpretentious Chuckwagon restaurant overlooking the lake.

6 **COWBOY VILLAGE RESORT**
120 S. Flat Creek Dr., Box 1747, Jackson Hole, WY 83001
800-962-4988, cabins $66–84
Amenities: Hot tubs

Appropriately named, you'll like this community of log cabins close to the center of Jackson Hole town. Your children will love the queen-sized bunk beds, complete with a ladder. These 82 log cabins are very simple and natural with a small cooking area to one side. The larger two-room cabins have a full kitchen with a stove. This is a fun place to stay where impromptu volleyball games take place in the summer and young skiers will regale stories of the day's adventures around the hot tub at night. It's not quite a dude ranch but it is certainly blessed with the frontier spirit.

8+ **GRAND TARGHEE**
P.O. Box SKI, Alta, WY 83422, 800-433-8146, 1BR $67–103
Amenities: Restaurant, indoor pool, exercise/weight room, kat skiing

This is an exceptional resort for skiers. On the map it looks like it is part of the Jackson Hole or Teton Mountains ski complex; in reality, it's not. When you stay at Grand Targhee, you stay at Grand Targhee. Access to Jackson Hole for those without a car is by daily shuttle bus—at least a one hour trip. You may be well advised to fly in to Idaho Falls. Do not underestimate this steep mountain pass rising 6,000 feet in less than 12 miles. It's an unforgettable trip and your ears will pop.

Once there, Grand Targhee is well worth the trip. With exceptional skiing, this is an escape from the 1990s. There's no other ski resort in the U.S. like Grand Targhee because of the spectacular mountain setting and the view of the jagged Teton Mountain peaks. You'll feel as though you are on top of the world. One special treat is the daily "cat-skiing" in winter. Just like the famous helicopter ski trips, Grand Targhee has a fleet of caterpillars to take you up to the top of the mountain peaks (virgin terrain) where you can ski down in the light powder snow. It's a unique experience and one that draws skiers from around the world to Grand Targhee. Up here, you will find a strong spirit of camaraderie born of the isolation. Sit by the fireplace in the lobby/reception area or soak in the hot tub as you make new friends. In the spring of 1990, the main restaurant burned. A new building has arisen in its place, which is much better than the old with more space for restaurants and socializing than in the old days.

Some of the condos are small, functional suites. Others are large corner units decorated with "Cheyenne Indian" flair featuring kiva-adobe fireplaces and woven rugs. The flavor here is unique with understated uncomplicated cowboy hospitality. You will notice the pale sunlight on the sawtooth mountain peaks in the evenings. Guaranteed good snow and for the adventurous, this resort offers cat-skiing away from lift lines and groomed trails. This is as close to being Shangri-la as any place we've seen.

6   THE INN AT JACKSON HOLE
P.O. Box 328, Jackson Hole, WY 83001, 800-842-7666 ; 1BR $150
Amenities: Pool, hot tub

The Inn has the only condominiums in Teton Village with hotel-style services. Most of the property offers motel rooms with only a couple of select condos in back, on the mountain. It has a very central location.

4   JACKSON HOLE LODGE
Box 1805-VC, Jackson Hole, WY 83001, 307-733-2992
1BR $60–$90
Amenities: Indoor pool, children's pool, hot tubs, sauna

Three blocks from the center of town, these timeshare suites are especially well suited for active families with the indoor pool, children's pool, two hot tubs, and a sauna. There's lots of activity all the time. Interior decor can best be described as collegiate.

7+   JACKSON HOLE RACQUET CLUB
3535 N. Moose-Wilson Rd., Star Route 36A, Jackson Hole, WY 83001
800-443-8616, 1BR $75–110, 2BR $100–130, 3BR $130–190
Amenities: Tennis, pool, hot tub, restaurant

Seems like only yesterday that this resort was trying to tell the world about its charms. Today, it is getting hard to find availability. Located eight miles north of the town of Jackson and just four miles away from the ski area of Teton Village, this resort has easy access to the best of both worlds. Crisp air, views of the mountains, and an unmatched setting for a conference. Stiegler's is a wonderful Austrian restaurant that gets even better in summer with patio dining overlooking the pool. This resort is home to John Gardner's Tennis Clinics and offers eight courts. Next door is the championship 18-hole Teton Pines Golf Club designed by Arnold Palmer. The Racquet Club is a master development with several areas for homes, lots, and condominiums. The first group of condos are called The Aspens, 18 two-story wooden ranch buildings each housing four units. Spacious and unpretentious, they are comfortable with casual furniture and an interior decorator's touch.

The second area of condo development is the **Balsam Lodge**. Again, these two-story modern wood buildings have been designed to fit right in to the landscape. Each building has four condos, however the furnishings are new and more stylish. Well planned and executed, the Racquet Club condos have been designed with lots of land and trees surrounding each building so that you have a sense of living in the forest rather than in a cluster of condos. The Racquet Club is at its best in the summer when visitors plan golf, horse-back, and mountaineering activities. However, this resort is equally popular in winter with its full-service health club attracting visitors after a day of skiing. Everything here is well done with an emphasis on convenience rather than stylishness. It is a great choice—if you can get a reservation.

6   JENNY LAKE LODGE
Grand Teton National Park, P.O. Box 240, Moran, WY 83013
Amenities: Lake, horseback riding, dining room

This resort is socially prestigious but because it is so rustic, we can only rate it a "6." When Laurence Rockefeller lobbied for Grand Teton National Park to be created, he caused the U.S. Forest Service to grant rights to oper-ate a couple of lodges in the park. Jenny Lake Lodge is a cluster of 30 rustic, yet deluxe, cabins nestled around a central building. These cabins have elec-tric blankets and fireplace *but no kitchen facilities are available.* Instead all meals—and they are gourmet quality—are served in the main building's dining room. It is a special, social place on the shores of Jenny Lake within the expanse of the park.

6   SNOW KING RESORT/PITCHFORK CONDOS
Box SKI, Jackson Hole, WY 83001, 800-522-KING
1BR $100–130, 2BR $135–175
Amenities: Pool, hot tub, tennis, restaurant

Snow King ski area, located in the town of Jackson, offers an easy entry for those who want to learn to ski, although there are runs and facilities for all levels of skiers. At the base of the ski hill, Snow King Resort offers a hotel and the **Pitchfork** condominium complex which is built around a con-vivial lodge. These one-bedroom condos are furnished hotel style and each has kitchen facilities. Not very imaginative but very convenient for those who want to be near the shops, restaurants, and cowboy bars of Jackson Hole. It's a good choice for groups of singles or families with young chil-dren and it is convenient.

8+ SPRING CREEK RESORT
P.O. Box 3154, Jackson Hole, WY 83001, 800-443-6139
1BR $250, 2BR $350
Amenities: Pool, hot tub, tennis, restaurant

This thousand-acre estate has a unique setting atop a butte, 700 feet above the Jackson Hole valley floor. No other accommodations in the Jackson Hole area have such breathtaking views of the Grand Teton Mountains. The developer has made the best use of this setting by situating each cluster of two-story condo buildings so that each unit has a view of the mountains. The condos are spacious and solidly constructed. Inside, the vaulted ceilings and stone fireplaces are complimented by lodgepole furniture and Indian-design fabrics. Occasional art pieces compete with the views from the window for your attention. Although rustically elegant, our only hesitation is that on our last inspection, management seemed to have slipped and some of the freshness was gone. For fun, the Granary restaurant with its three-story-high ceiling and glass terrace offers the most spectacular view of the Tetons that you'll find in Jackson Hole. Although it's a 15 minute drive from the town of Jackson Hole and 25 minutes from the ski slopes, this is a choice destination for romantics because of the view.

8-9 TETON PINES
3450 N. Clubhouse Drive, Jackson Hole, WY 83001
800-238-2223, $210–430
Amenities: Golf, tennis, health spa with pool, restaurant

Certainly this is one of Jackson's most stylish addresses. About eight miles outside of the town of Jackson and three miles from the ski lifts at Teton Village, you will find Teton Pines. This is a luxurious resort with its own Arnold Palmer golf course, John Gardner tennis courts, and Jack Dennis Fly Fishing School. These are new condominiums where interior designers were unleashed from the normal constraints of a budget. Sunlight streams through the windows on to pastel colors and blond ash furniture. The only drawback is that the condo units have no kitchens. The 191 homes come fully equipped. Stylized western or Indian art works complete the picture. At the clubhouse, there is a 19th hole and an excellent dining room. In winter, the golf course becomes a cross-country ski trail.

6 TETON SHADOWS
245 W. Pearl Ave., Jackson Hole, WY 83001 (no mail), 1BR $65–95
Amenities: Golf, clubhouse, hot tub

The development is five miles north of town in a direction different from Teton Village/Jackson Hole Racquet Club or Spring Creek Resort. Separated by the mountains from the main Jackson Hole ski area, it's a 25-minute drive over to the tram at Teton Village for skiers. Teton Shadows is located on the Jackson Hole Golf Club, an 18-hole championship course which was home to the U.S. Open in 1992. These two-story condos are spacious and have great views of the fairway and the mountains in the distance. Interior decor is contemporary and comfortable. Some owners have dressed up their units with Indian fabrics or western furniture. Others have allowed the furniture to age. All in all, this was designed for golfers who want a week in the area, although the space and location make them perfect for those who want to explore Yellowstone and The Grand Teton National Park. A country club ambiance prevails.

TETON VILLAGE
Teton Village Rd., Jackson, WY 83001 (no mail)
Amenities: Pools, restaurants, ski lifts

This condominium village at the base of the skiers' mountain almost defies description. There are fourteen separate condominium developments offering virtually the same experience, but they are in buildings with several different styles. Strangely, none of these separate developments have their own front desk or office for check-in, so the owners have made arrangements with the four rental companies which have offices in Teton Village. You will check-in with the management company with whom you booked your reservation and from there you will be sent to your designated vacation home. The village is so compact that nothing is further than a four to five-minute walk. Some of the individual condominium complexes within Teton Village are:

Eagle's Rest (7) Spacious two- and three-bedroom condos, some have private saunas on the ground floor. This is the only condo development in Teton Village with a heated outdoor pool.

Four Seasons (7) Spacious two and three-bedroom condos with massive stone fireplaces, these units have great views of the mountains and their location is convenient to the core of Teton Village and the tram.

La Chonmine (7) The convenient location just across from the core of Teton Village and the studio and one-bedroom units make this popular with singles and young people.

Nez Perce (8) These luxury two- and three-bedroom condos are in a three-story Austrian chalet structure set away from the tram and the center of the Village. Each has a large living room with a stone fireplace. Beautifully furnished, some have lodgepole furniture and southwest Indian accents.

Rendez Vous (8) These spacious condos in a three-story wooden ranch-style building are spacious and designed for a comfortable family holiday. Each has a stone fireplace; some have vaulted ceiling living rooms and loft bedrooms. Located next door to the Sundance Tennis and Swim Club, this is Teton Village's best location for families with children.

Sleeping Indian (7) These are some of the oldest and most reasonably priced condos to be found in Teton Village. This three-story building has studios as well as one and two-bedroom units. It is convenient to the Sundance sports center.

Snowridge (7) Some of the most luxurious condos in Wyoming. Many have interior decor by professional designers.

Teewinot (9) Tucked in between Rendez Vous and Wind River, you'll find the quiet Teewinot condos. This three-story Austrian chalet-style building has some condos with vaulted ceilings. Close to the Sundance Tennis and Swim Club, these two- and three-bedroom condos are perfect for families or groups of active skiers. As a footnote, these are the only condos in Wyoming with heated garages.

Tensleep and Gros Ventre (6) These two buildings contain some of the smaller one- and two-bedroom condos to be found at Teton Village. Only three minutes from the tram, the location is convenient.

Timber Ridge (8) These four-bedroom townhouses are larger than most homes. Each has its own private sauna on the ground floor level, a two-story living room, and an extra loft on the third floor, which children with sleeping bags will surely want to be a "fifth" bedroom. It provides great views of the wide open spaces of the valley.

Tram Towers (9+) The condos closest to the ski lifts, these brand new townhouses are the only ski-in/ski-out condos at Teton Village. It truly exemplifies Wyoming's new standard for luxury.

Wind River (7) The lap of luxury, these deluxe three-story townhouse condos are the farthest away from the tram and the village center, and insure the most privacy. Breathtaking two-story living rooms capture incredible mountain views. The centerpiece is a dramatic stone fireplace and a whirlpool spa downstairs on the ground floor. The location makes it possible to ski-in directly to your condo after a day on the slopes.

RENTAL RESOURCES
Accommodations of Jackson Hole, 800-422-2927
BBC Property Management, 800-325-8605
Ely & Assoc., 800-735-8310
Fraine/Sheppard Condo Rentals, 408-249-6843
Jackson Hole Lodge, 307-733-2992
Jackson Hole Management, 307-739-3000
Jackson Hole Property Management, 800-443-8613
Mountain Property Management, 800-992-9948
Real Estate of Jackson Hole, 800-443-6130
Teton Village Property Management, 800-443-6840
Village Center, 800-733-0914

CANADA

Clearly one of the best vacation areas in North America, this vast landscape stretching from the Bay of Gaspé to Vancouver Island in the west has some of the most exciting and scenic resort areas that we've ever visited. The ski resorts are far more international then their U.S. cousins. Québec appeals to Europeans and over 35% of the skiers in Banff or Whistler are from Japan. The food is fabulous, benefitting from 30 years of massive European immigration and more recently from the Orient. Customs are slightly different; life moves a little more slowly and with due deliberation. And the mountains—you'll never forget the gentle hills and forests of French Québec, or the fantastic heights of Alberta's Rockies that dramatically jut up from the prairie lands.

What's most surprising is that U.S. visitors have overlooked Canada's traditional winter ski resorts in the summertime. With championship golf, lakes for sailing and windsurfing, mountains for hiking and biking, and endless forests and streams for observing or stalking wildlife—why do so many forget about Canada as a summertime destination? You'll find the skier villages of condos to be quiet yet offering the same restaurants and nightlife at lower, summertime prices.

For many, a quick trip to Canada is like a mini-vacation to Europe. You'll notice women wearing different fashions in an effort to be à la mode of Europe. Canadians are more clothes conscious than their U.S. cousins. And the men have a firm but gentle helpfulness in the tradition of England. For years Canada's "open-door" policy has attracted millions of European immigrants. Québec remains a land of opportunity for the young and restless of France and Italy. Vancouver, a city which many call the California of Canada because of climate, culture, and the film industry, has attracted enormous wealth from the Orient, especially Hong Kong, because that city-state faces an uncertain economic future after 1995. On some days there are as many as 12 non-stop flights to Vancouver from Hong Kong and Tokyo. But it's not the starving Chinese who are coming; it is the wealthy entrepreneurial class that has transferred its capital to Canada.

What has this meant for Western Canada? There's a tremendous boom in real estate prices, new building, new businesses, and—best of all—new resort development. Vancouver's real estate market could only absorb so much new money, so the investors headed east. Whistler has been transformed from a quiet town with good skiing to a pulsating resort center with three new championship golf courses. Then came the resort areas of Banff and Lake Louise, where limited development has resulted in rising prices. Beyond investing in the gleaming cities of Toronto and Montréal, the resort areas of the Laurentians have nearly doubled the number of luxury condo properties in the past six years. Turning away from the simpler and picturesque Canadian frontier style, today's new developments are modern, functional, and loaded with resort amenities.

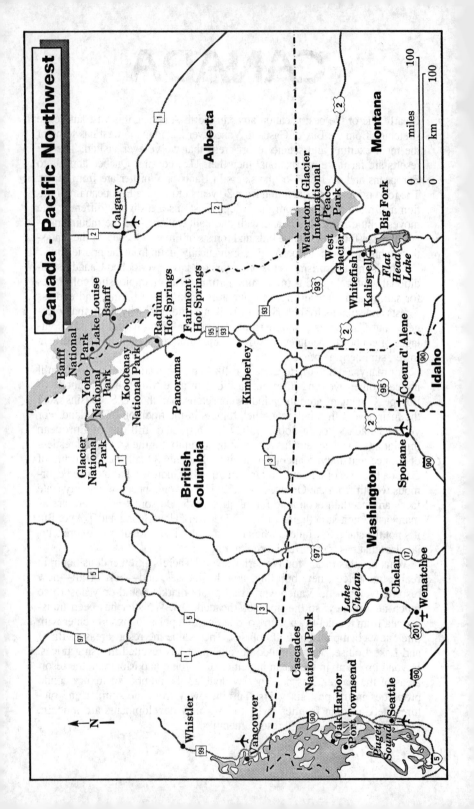

But best of all, you'll find Canada's resorts to be generally less expensive than resorts in the U.S. Even the resort areas of Banff and Lake Louise, fabled as destinations for wealthy heli-skiers and celebrity fishing expeditions, have accommodations priced below their U.S. counterparts.

We have focused only on those resort areas where you'll find a wide range of resort properties, and which have easy transportation from the U.S. as well as Canada. Therefore, the resorts we cover are all within easy reach of Vancouver, Calgary, or Montréal airports.

CHOOSING YOUR DESTINATION

Canada's resort areas each have their own distinct personality. The condo communities in Canada are all in the environs of a ski resort area. This means that in summer, they are prime destinations for those who enjoy the cool mountain breezes. Prices will vary and you should be aware that there is less price-flexibility in Canada than in the U.S. We've found less of a willingness to cut the price in order to fill up the units. You should also be aware that each Province has a GST (government services tax) which will run from 8 to 18% depending upon the locale. For non-Canadians, **YOU MAY HAVE THE TAX REFUNDED.** That's right—simply collect your receipts from lodging, meals, rental cars, and goods purchased and submit them to the appropriate Provincial government. You'll get a check for the refund in approximately three months.

In this section we cover the following provinces:

ALBERTA — Home of the cowboy culture, here all of the resorts are within two hours driving time of Calgary's International Airport. The rolling Canadian prairie stops suddenly as the spectacular Rockies rise at Calgary's western edge. All of the resorts are within Banff National Park. Beginning with the town of Banff on the southern end, resort development follows the narrow valley of the Bow River for 50 kilometers north to Lake Louise. Banff was built by the Canadian Pacific Railroad as a reason to travel out west. Today, you'll find an abundance of modern condo-style accommodations radiating out from its core.

BRITISH COLUMBIA — British Columbia has two major areas of condo resort development—Whistler Village and the Valley of a Thousand Peaks. Vancouver offers the nearest airport (two hours away). U.S. visitors seeking economical or nonstop flights could try Seattle. Seattle is just two hours further south of Vancouver by a fast, four-lane Interstate highway. Surprisingly, Whistler is very European in style with its architecture and lively restaurants.

The Valley of a Thousand Peaks has a collection of mega-resorts, each of which has its own private ski mountain. Adequate for good skiers, these ski mountains don't offer the challenge or nearly as many ski runs as in the Whistler and Blackcomb complex.

QUÉBEC — This is another world and soon may be a separate country. Québec was tamed by the French nearly 400 years ago and in spite of immigration from many nations (including an English speaking minority that comprises 35 percent of the population), it remains fiercely French today. Visitors to Québec from the U.S. compare it to a mini-trip to Europe. Not only are the languages and foods different, but so are the condo resorts. The dimensions of the individual units are generally smaller, as in France. You will find less emphasis on material comfort and more on the social environment. One resort even features European-style group skiing, a departure from the individualist approach at U.S. ski areas such as Vermont or Colorado.

RENTING RESORT PROPERTY & CANADIAN DOLLARS

Most of the condo resorts in Canada have been built with on-site management offices. Because of Canadian investment laws, many developments **REQUIRE** that rentals be through the resort's front office. Where this happens, you won't find the same play in prices as at resorts where you can negotiate between the on-site and the off-site rental agents. In general, Whistler is an area where there is price competition but you won't find negotiable prices in Alberta at all and only in rare instances in Québec. Nevertheless, the price will decline depending upon how long you plan to stay. For example, the price may be $125 each for the first two nights, but if you stay for three nights or more, the price drops to $75 per night.

The prices we've quoted are in Canadian dollars. Generally, you can discount the prices we've quoted by 22% to get the equivalent price in U.S. dollars. DO NOT CONFUSE CANADIAN DOLLARS WITH U.S. DOLLARS. The U.S. dollar has a significantly higher exchange rate. Although Canadian prices may seem higher at first blush, the price may be lower than in the U.S. because most of our readers will be paying in U.S. dollars.

When planning a trip to Canada, it is wise to consider buying travellers checks in Canadian dollars. In Canada, each time you go to a bank to convert U.S. dollars to Canadian dollars, there is a transaction charge which may range from $2 to 1% of the transaction's value. You'll save money if you convert beforehand in the U.S. In addition, travellers checks are safer when it comes to loss or theft.

CANADIAN ADDRESSES AND TELEPHONE NUMBERS

In the U.S. section of this book, we have given addresses with states and zip codes. Canadian addresses require the street address, the town, the province, and the six-digit postal code. When addressing a letter, be sure to add "Canada" at the end. For example, if you were writing to Gray Rocks, the address would read:

Gray Rocks
Route 327 Nord, P.O. Box 1000
Mt. Tremblant, Québec JOT 2H0
CANADA

Telephone numbers use the same area code plus seven digits as in the U.S. There is no need to go through the international access/country code system when calling Canada.

ALBERTA

For years we've been recommending that savvy consumers consider the vacation condo rental rates afforded by Alberta's resort areas of Banff and Lake Louise. These are some of the most beautiful and carefully developed resorts in the world. Yet, for some reason, travel to Western Canada has never even approached its potential. Banff National Park offers an incredible Rocky Mountain experience because the mountains are so dense. Nowhere else do the mountains loom so massively and so near. It's quite a shock to wake up and see the silhouette of a mountain peak just outside your window at dawn.

The province of Alberta is considered to be Canada's "wild west." In addition, Calgary and Edmonton are the capitals of business and government; and the 1988 Olympics brought international recognition to the area. Calgary is the city that travellers pass through to reach the destinations we've described in this book. An oil metropolis, it has a gleaming downtown with 80-story skyscrapers that rise in sharp contrast to the flat prairielands and the endless shopping malls radiating away from the city.

We've concentrated on Banff and Lake Louise in the National Park, just an hour away to the west. The hot springs, for which Banff originally became famous, were discovered by railroad workers in 1883. Their value was immediately recognized. Two years later the territorial government created Canada's first national park at Banff. Here the mountains soar to 12,000 feet as the result of the earth's faulting, and the valleys are boulder-strewn as the result of glacial action. The national park extends throughout both the provinces of Alberta and of British Columbia.

On the Alberta side there are the villages of Banff and Lake Louise, separated by a distance of approximately 35 miles. This wilderness area is the valley of the Bow river which flows on to Calgary about an hour away. Banff is a sprawling town of 6,000 radiating away from the central main street, Banff Avenue. This avenue is the axis from which local distances are measured. Unlike Whistler, with its core walking village, the themes to development at Banff reflect either a desire for a convenient in-town location, or a desire to be out on the edge of the hiking trails. A few resorts have remote, end-of-the-road locations that give them unique appeal.

What we find so surprising is that although this is little more than an hour from the major international airport at Calgary, this area hasn't been discovered. What makes it even more attractive is that airfares to Calgary, dollar for dollar, are some of the lowest in the world. Although many North Americans overlook Banff as a destination, the Japanese love it. It's only 10 hours from Tokyo and today it's estimated that 35% of the resort's visitors are from Japan.

What do these new arrivals like best? It's definitely the incredible spaciousness and luxury of a condo. Although the area is targeted for skiing and sightseeing, many Japanese visitors become enamored of their condo accommodations and have been known to spend days luxuriating in a jacuzzi or trying to use all of the appliances in what we hear are truly deluxe kitchens. You'll see groups of young Japanese visitors in the winter with their slick ski clothing. Local ski instructors report that the oriental skier is more inclined to "ski extreme" and take advantage of every opportunity. Visit the shops and restaurants and listen to the conversations around you. You'll find that many of the local workers are French-speaking Québecois who are trying to sell an item to Japanese tourists where both sides are using fractured English.

Lake Louise claims to be a village, but we wish you more success than we had in finding it. What we saw was another impressive 19th-Century Canadian Pacific chateau, two hotels, and a small shopping center. Skiers will enjoy quick access to the slopes at Mt. Lake Louise, but restaurants are almost non-existent and nightlife consists of a disco in the chateau. Yet, Lake Louise has the most beautiful scenery and the lack of development makes the mountains seem even more majestic.

In winter, skiing is the main reason to visit. There are three ski mountains here—Sunshine, Mount Norquay, and the mountain at Lake Louise 35 miles down the road. Just for the sake of comparison, the Lake Louise area with 11 square miles of ski terrain is the largest in Canada: larger than Whistler and Blackcomb combined.

To the uninitiated visitor, the diversity is overwhelming. You can ski for a week and never do the same run twice. Offering a full range of runs (the resort is 25% novice, 45% intermediate and 30% expert), you'll never tire of the dramatic views of the geometric peaks across the valley. Experts will thrill to the backbowls.

Just outside the village of Banff, Sunshine Village is another massive area that continues to win awards from *Ski* and *Snowcountry* magazines year after year for its dedication to service. The ski school features the best Canadian and European instructors and there's a special concentration on the kids ski programs. Get an early start on your day and marvel at the pinks and purples of dawn on top of the world.

Mt. Norquay is just on the other side of Banff and, while not as large as the other two, offers some unique ski programs. For good skiers, there's the Club 35,000, which is a cut above the usual Black Diamond Skiing. You can ski 35,000 vertical feet (27 runs) in one day on the Norquay chutes and qualify for a gold pin. For the skiers who thinks they've done it all, go for the super gold pin—50,000 vertical feet in one day (38 runs) and no lift lines. You can do it if you have stamina.

Finally, a note about accommodations in this chapter. All of the accommodations, except the all-suite hotel (Prince Royal Inn) in Calgary, are "condo style." They look like condos but development in the national park has been tightly controlled so that the Canadians who need to live and work in the area can afford housing. The Park District will issue developers 99-year leases under certain conditions. The condominiums must have a "need to reside" permit. Therefore there can be no second home ownership nor resort condos within the national park. The condo complexes we describe below are truly condo hotels where the owner/manager owns all the units and rents them in a hotel operation. Therefore, interior decor is standardized and the "condo price negotiation" game can't be played because one person owns all the units.

Air transportation to the area is through the Calgary International Airport. This is one of the hubs for Canadian Pacific Airlines. Between Canadian Pacific and Air Canada, there are dozens of flights each day to Canadian destinations. As for U.S. travellers, connections must be made through Denver, Salt Lake, Seattle, Spokane, San Francisco, or Chicago. Of the U.S. carriers, Delta and United have the most flights and these offer convenient connections, through their own hubs, to cities throughout the U.S. America West and American offer flights to their hubs in Phoenix and Dallas. Japan Airlines comes in twice a day and British Air, KLM, and Lufthansa fly in from Europe several times a week.

WHERE TO STAY

6   BAKER CREEK CHALETS
Box 66, Lake Louise, Alberta TOL 1EO, 403-522-3761
Cabins $70–90
Amenities: Restaurant, horseshoes, cross-country skiing

Located just six miles east of Lake Louise on the Bow Valley Parkway, this self-contained village of 26 log cabins is favored by those who appreciate cross-country skiing. Surrounded by wildflowers, these country cabins have a European flair. Surprisingly well-decorated, each has a fireplace and cozy quilts for those cold winter nights. The Baker Creek bistro is an exceptional spot in the north woods complete with characters straight from *Northern Exposure*. Summer is the most popular season when fishing and hiking are popular activities.

220 BEAVER STREET
220 Beaver Street, Banff, Alberta TOL 0C0

This collection of downtown Banff homes, dating from the railroad and logging era of the 1920s, has been remodeled into homey guest quarters.

8+   BANFF ROCKY MOUNTAIN RESORT
Banff Ave, Box 100, Banff, Alberta TOL 0C0, 403-762-5531,
800-66RELAX; Studio $95, 1BR $110–165, 2BR $150–205
Amenities: Indoor pool, outdoor hot tub, health club, racquetball, restaurant

This is the only resort that can sell property inside Banff National Park. This timeshare is spiffy and modern. The studio, one- and two-bedroom units are all on the small side, but very well decorated by Banff standards. Each has a kitchen, fireplace, and accents of Native American art. The loft units are far better in our opinion because of the extra sense of space. One of the liveliest resorts in the area, this is popular with families.

9   BUFFALO MOUNTAIN LODGE
Tunnel Mountain Road, Box 1326, Banff, Alberta T0L 0C0,
403-762-2400, 800-661-3518
Studios $85–135, 1BR $125–170, 2BR $135–190
Amenities: Indoor pool, hot tubs, racquetball, squash courts

Located about a mile out of town, next to Tunnel Mountain Park, where you'll feel as though you are on top of the world, yet you're surrounded by awesome peaks, this is one of the most distinctive resorts in the area. We say this cognizant that the complex involves a number of two-story buildings in a parklike setting. What we like is the decor—furnishings made from bent branches made usable with pillows. Lodgepole chairs and a canopied bed with a huge eiderdown duvet. This has a touch of fancy. The two-story townhouse units are more expensive but definitely superior. Over at the main lodge there's a New York-style coffeehouse complete with a reading rack and crackling fireplace. This has an end of the line ambiance, spiritually akin to *Northern Exposure.*

6   CASTLE MOUNTAIN VILLAGE
Highway 93A South, Box 1655, Banff, Alberta T0L 0C0,
403-762-3868
Amenities: Indoor pool, hot tub

Searching for the wilderness adventure? There's nothing around this cute little colony of cabins for 15 miles or so. Self-contained, the guests can have as much privacy or camaraderie as they desire. These cabins have beds while the deluxe versions have two sleeping nooks that can be separated by curtains. Although the potential exists for this to be a truly romantic spot, management opted for the functional, so you'll find decor completely uninspired. For a sense of community, folks gather at the little convenience store on-site for a cup of coffee.

7+ DOUGLAS FIR RESORT
Tunnel Mountain Road, Box 1228, Banff, Alberta T0L 0C0,
403-762-5591, 800-661-9267
1BR $102–114, 2BR & Chalets $132–148
Amenities: Waterslides, pool, hot tub, gym, racquetball courts

One of our favorites in the area, you'll find this a friendly place with delightful management and a very popular pool area. What's the attraction? An indoor waterslide two stories high with chutes that spiral into the pool. Clearly the best choice in the area for families with young children. If you can't stay here, come and use the pool anyway for minimal charge. Most of the condos are in two-story buildings. Decor is functional with indoor-outdoor carpeting and collegiate maple furniture. The loft units are better because of the space, but the little cabins are best.

6   HIDDEN RIDGE CHALETS
Tunnel Mountain Rd., Box 519, Lake Louise, Alberta T0L OCO, 403-762-3544, 800-661-1372; 1BR $95–135, Chalets $ $90–150

This condo village offers a collection of units in quad buildings dating from the mid '30s, as well as individual chalets. The best feature here is the view. You are alone on a ridge with the most dramatic views of the Rockies imaginable. The A-frame chalets are best for groups of travellers, because there are three sleeping areas. For socializing, there's a large outdoor hot tub.

5   LAKE LOUISE INN
Village Rd., Box 209, Lake Louise, Alberta T0L IEO, 403-522-3791, 800-661-9237; Studio $50–70
Amenities: Indoor pool, sauna, hot tub

Located two miles away from Mt. Lake Louise, this is an economy choice. The five buildings here offer a wide choice in accommodations from suites with kitchens to economy hotel rooms.

6   THE POST HOTEL
Box 69, Lake Louise, Alberta T0L IEO, 403-522-3989, 800-661-1586
Amenities: Pub, indoor pool, hot tub

A combination of homey comfort and youthful good cheer is the combination here. Built in the style of an alpine chalet (without the Tyrolian flourishes and chintz), this hotel offers studios with kitchens. Many gourmets choose these units to economize.

7   PRINCE ROYAL INN
618 5th Ave. SW, Calgary, Alberta T2P 0M7, 403-263-0520
1BR $79
Amenities: Pool, restaurant, gym

Although Alberta is a great destination for those seeking the space and privacy of a condo, Calgary seems to be the capital of 200 motels. This is the only all-suite property in town and, for those with families and who didn't drive to Canada, you'll probably need to know about this hotel either right after or just before your flight. Located in the heart of downtown, this has residential style. You'll have a living room and kitchen. Convenient to Calgary's river parks, plan some extra time to enjoy the city.

5 RUNDLE MANOR

348 Marten St., Box 1077, Banff, Alberta T0L OCO, 403-762-5544
1BR $62, 2BR $77
Amenities: Pool privileges at Inns of Banff

Located in the heart of Banff, just one building off of Banff Avenue, this resort offers large condos in what appears from the outside to be just a motel. It's not. Instead, this is like a small apartment complex and the units will surprise you with their spaciousness. The one-bedroom model is adequately furnished but you'll do much better by upgrading to the two-bedroom unit. It's huge and all the hallways could almost be used as extra rooms. The furniture is dreary. This is a real home away from home. It is one of the best choices for those who don't have a car, because the slopes are nearby.

7 TUNNEL MOUNTAIN CHALETS

Tunnel Mountain Road, Box 1137, Banff, Alberta T0L OCO,
403-762-4515, 800-661-1859; 1BR $93–143, 2BR $118–168

This is a friendly place as a result of personalized attention from the resident managers/owners. It's almost as though you are welcomed into their home, yet the condos are large and completely private. Interior decor features wood paneling and lots of tan and brown fabrics. This makes the units seem dark but you'll be brightened by the glowing stone fireplace in the evenings. The two-story "chalets" are far superior to the one-bedroom condos because of the second-story loft. Tunnel Mountain is rustic in design and decor; English in attitude and hospitality.

BRITISH COLUMBIA

Canada's westernmost province offers some of the most spectacular scenery found in North America. The ragged coastline along Puget Sound gives way to some of the most rugged mountains found anywhere. This has resulted in conditions favoring two major resort areas: Whistler, and the Valley of a Thousand Peaks.

Whistler is a polished jewel of a ski resort with a walking village rivaling Vail, Colorado. With all the French restaurants, Japanese sushi bars, and European-style discos, this is an exciting spot. Over in the Valley, life is more tranquil. Each of the resorts caters to those seeking enjoyment of the great outdoors as much as an escape from urbanization. Highly civilized, you'll be impressed by the Canadian style.

With this in mind, we have divided B.C. into two sections: Whistler, and the Valley of a Thousand Peaks.

1. WHISTLER

The Whistler recreation area, with a planned pedestrian village at its core, has been skillfully developed over the past 20 years. What began as a ski resort is now recognized as one of Canada's leading summer resorts for people who want to see the majestic Rockies, the towering Douglas firs, and the clear Alpine lakes. The village has an Alpine look with winding streets, gabled roofs, and buildings four to five stories high.

Radiating out from the village, with a population of 3,000, you'll find Whistler's newer neighborhoods. The Blackcomb Benchlands is a twin village which has been evolving since 1988. With a luxurious 12-story "chateau" as the village centerpiece, Blackcomb is more upscale than Whistler Village. The condos in the Blackcomb area are larger and much more luxurious yet very few know about Blackcomb. For this reason condo rental rates (and real estate prices) are on a parity with accommodations in Whistler. The net result for consumers is that you get much more for your money in Blackcomb than in Whistler Village.

Just to the north of Whistler Village is the new "North Village" where sewer pipes are currently being laid. This will more than double the size of Whistler Village and this new, upscale development is destined to become the new "core of Whistler" within ten years.

Across the highway and up the mountain is the Alta Lake area and the Blueberry Hill development. Alta Lake is one of the most picturesque lakes to be found anywhere with majestic snow-capped mountains and clear blue water. The homes and condos of the Blueberry Hill area have been built within the past three years so they are "new" and much more spacious than the earlier generation condos in Whistler Village.

Down the valley, four kilometers toward Vancouver, there's the Whistler Creek area. This area was built 15 years ago as an alternate base of the mountain to accommodate the hordes of day trippers from Vancouver and Seattle. This area is now changing. The old gondola has been replaced and a new high-speed chair lift has been added. The new lift more than doubles the capacity of the chair lifts to take skiers up the mountain. Over 4,000 people an hour can now be accommodated and that up from just 700 a few years ago. With easy access, Whistler Creek has now become an area of new shops and restaurants competing with its sister villages of Whistler or Blackcomb Benchlands. Many new condos of varying levels of quality have been built here during the past four years. One special place, just up the road from Whistler Creek, is the Highland Vale area with its restaurants and disco.

North of the Whistler area, around Lost Lake, a new Robert Trent Jones golf course has been built. This backs up to Alta Lake and promises to be the next area of Whistler's booming expansion.

Much of this boom has been fueled by the massive infusion of Asian capital into British Columbia during the past five years. With as many as 12 flights a day from Hong Kong to Vancouver and the anticipated "closing door" of Hong Kong's 1997 annexation into China, billions of dollars are flowing into Whistler from Hong Kong. Today, there are over 60 condo developments to choose from. Within three years, there will probably be 40 more. What began as a ski resort is now recognized as one of Canada's leading summer resorts for people who want to see the majestic Rockies, the towering Douglas fir, and clear Alpine lakes.

Located just 4 hours north of Seattle (or one and one-half hours from Vancouver), getting there is half the fun. You'll pass majestic mountains, sparkling fjords, scenic vistas, and endure a tortured journey through desolate, almost lunar mountains. You'll never forget the drive through "sea-to-sky country." Or, alternatively, take the train from Vancouver through the towering snow-capped mountains. The afternoon trip back to Vancouver provides one of Canada's most uproarious après-ski parties in North America.

The charm of Whistler lies in the foreign romance. You know you are not in the U.S. by all the exciting ethnic (Japanese, Italian, French, Bavarian, and Chinese) restaurants and European clothes. The language is the same, but there's a certain touch to the way things are done that makes Whistler decidedly foreign.

In the summer, Whistler offers crystalline lakes, Alpine meadows bursting with flowers, forest trails, and views of the glacier-capped mountains. Enjoy golfing or go boating on the lakes. Biking, tennis, and summer skiing are popular, too. In the winter, Whistler receives over 450 inches of heavy Pacific snow. It's not the dry powder snow that you'll find in Colorado or Montana. Whistler is one of the few ski areas that remains open almost all year. Glacier skiing takes place during summer mornings. In either season, you'll enjoy the rich variety of restaurants for all tastes and pocketbooks. Whistler's après-ski night life compares favorably with resorts all over North America, with cafes, discos and ice-skating parties. As one pundit said "It's

Vail at half the price." Dollar for dollar, this is one of the best vacation values in North America.

Generally, the condos in the Village are a little smaller than what you would find in the U.S. Studios really are designed to sleep two; however they can accommodate four good friends with two in a bed and two on twin sofas. Surprisingly, in all of Whistler Village there is only one indoor pool and only a handful of resorts offer the private whirlpools and saunas that are so popular at luxury U.S. ski condos. Kitchens are also European style and are much more compact. Many studios only have a refrigerator, hot plate, and microwave. The new condos in Blackcomb, the Alta Lake area, and Whistler Creek are generally much larger with better quality construction and furnishing. These newer properties are less inclined to be operated as hotel condominiums. More private and often better furnished, many of these do NOT have on-site management, so you'll have to contact one of the condo rental agencies to make a reservation.

If you drive to Whistler, parking garages are available under the town. If you stay for a week in the village, chances are good that you'll never need your car. If you fly into Vancouver, avoid the wheel-gripping drive and take the train.

WHERE TO STAY

7 **BLACKCOMB**
Whistler Village, Box 400, Whistler, BC V0N 1B0, 604-932-4155
Studio $65–100, 1BR $130
Amenities: Indoor pool, sauna, hot tub

Blackcomb is located on the main square in the heart of the village. It only takes three minutes to walk to the gondola. The resort is a three-story building with a lodgelike atmosphere. Since many tour packages use this as their choice in Whistler, the lobby is always humming with porters and tour organizers. The Blackcomb units are small and you'll feel like you're in a cabin cruiser when you sleep in them. The studio with a loft is definitely far superior; the queen size and two twin beds provide plenty of sleeping space.

9+ **BLUEBERRY HILL**
St. Anton Way, Whistler, BC V0N 1B0
1BR $165–210, 2BR $195–265
Amenities: Pool or hot tub

Located near the shores of Alta Lake, with some of the most breathtaking views of the majestic Canadian mountains, Blueberry Hill Estates was designed to be a top-of-the-line area for homes with a few condos. These deluxe condos sit behind the 18-hole Arnold Palmer golf course and are just one kilometer from Whistler Village. Although popular with skiers in winter, these are an exceptional find for summertime visitors. Each two or three-bedroom condo has a full kitchen, fireplace, whirlpool, and a double shower.

3   **CARLTON LODGE**
         Mountain Square, Box 519, Whistler, BC V0N 1B0, 604-932-2972
         Studio $85, 1BR $99
         Amenities: None

Carlton Lodge, a five-story structure at the Whistler Express ski gondola, is one of the largest condo lodges. Skiers don't ever need to go outside to take the lift up the mountain. There is no lobby. These are some of the oldest condos in Whistler Village. You can tell because they are quite a bit larger than what's being built today. The living rooms are spacious. Full kitchens are provided. The indifferent decor and poor hospitality spoil the picture. The contemporary furniture is mixed with bean bag chairs and too-soft, almost formless sofas. Carlton Lodge has a 1970s style. It is an economy choice.

5   **THE CLOCK TOWER**
         4341 Village Lane, Box 172, Whistler, BC V0N 1B0, 604-932-4724
         Studio $60–90, 1BR $80–120
         Amenities: Sauna

The Clock Tower is located in the heart of the village approximately one minute from the ski lifts. The resort is composed of a four-story lodge with European ski village architecture. The units are small and the hallways are narrow.

5   **FIREPLACE INN**
         4520 Village Stroll, Box 310, Whistler, BC V0N 1B0, 604-932-3200
         Studios $60
         Amenities: Hot tub, skiing

The Fireplace Inn and The Clock Tower share the same lobby, but they have different front desks. The studios are small and the furniture is functional, but they have a great location and kitchenettes.

7   **FITZSIMMONS CONDOMINIUMS**
         7124 Nancy Greene Dr., Whistler, BC V0N 1B0, 604-932-3338
         1BR $65–80
         Amenities: Hot tub, disco

Located in the heart of Whistler Village, you can feel the pulse of activity right outside your window. These spacious and superior units have been beautifully decorated to enhance the rustic wood paneling and open-gable architecture. There's a hot tub on the roof for soaking under the stars and a disco, Club 10, two floors below in the basement. Some of the Fitzsimmons condos have been incorporated into the Whiski Jack timeshare; see the description under Whiski Jack.

8 FOXGLOVE
4573 Chateau Blvd., Box 519, Whistler, BC V0N 1B0, 604-932-2276
Amenities: None

The Blackcomb Benchlands has become a sea of condos within the past three years. You'll find a dozen new names with more on the drawing board. Foxglove is representative of many of these new developments, such as Wintergreen Villas or Snowberry. This is a cluster of three condos in a two-story, gabled building. On the mountain, it has ski-in/ski-out access for the more daring skiers. Others may prefer the shuttle bus or to walk. Each one of these brand new one-, two-, and three-bedroom condos has a fireplace, kitchen, VTP, microwave, washer/dryer, and a balcony/patio. Well designed for active families, they are and superior to most of the older condos in Whistler Village. Rentals are available only through the realtors.

8 FOREST TRAILS
4737 Spearhead Dr., Whistler, BC V0N 1B0
2BR $95–140, 3BR $140–210
Amenities: None

These condos enjoy a central location in the Blackcomb Benchlands and you are only steps away from the Wizard Express and all the activities of the Chateau Whistler shopping mall. Just completed in 1991, these two- and three-bedroom townhouse condos feature attractive gabled architecture and superior, interior decorator furnishings. Each has a full kitchen, fireplace, and a whirlpool. One unique feature: a private garage to store your car.

8 THE GABLES
4510 Blackcomb Way, Whistler, BC V0N 1B0
1BR $89–170, 2BR $105–199, 3BR $125–210
Amenities: None

Completed in 1988, The Gables enjoys one of the best locations in the Blackcomb Benchlands, directly across from the Wizard high-speed chair lift and just down from the shopping mall and the luxurious Chateau Whistler Hotel. These are new and very stylish with, as you would expect, lots of gables that create little nooks and crannies. The one-, two-, and three-bedroom condos all have new furniture packages and the units are light and charming. Each has a kitchen, washer/dryer, fireplace, and whirlpool tub. It is not like many of the older buildings with their efficient European floor plans. These are among the most luxurious condos, with the best location in all of Whistler.

9+   **GLACIER LODGE**
4573 Chateau Blvd., Box 726, Whistler, BC V0N 1B0, 604-932-2882
1BR $120, 2BR $200
Amenities: Restaurant

The Glacier Lodge is "the village" of Blackcomb. The Blackcomb Benchlands village is just emerging and there are several core buildings with ground floor shops and restaurants. The Glacier Lodge is one of those buildings. Very convenient and with just as much to recommend it as any condo over in the core village of Whistler. These stylish condos on the second and third floor were completed in 1988 and feature full kitchens, gas log fireplaces, and balconies. Operated as a full-service hotel, there is a 24-hour front desk. Right next to the Wizard Express lift, you couldn't have a much more central location.

6   **GONDOLA VILLAGE**
Highway 99, Box 519, Whistler, BC V0N 1B0, 604-932-4184
Studio $85, 1BR $99, 2BR $132
Amenities: Skiing

Located four kilometers from the main village of Whistler, the Gondola Village is in the Whistler Creek area. It's for those who love the great outdoors and want to wake up to a view of the majestic mountains instead of another hotel. The gondola lift is right here for your convenience. These condos are 12 years old and starting to show their age. Some have "early attic" decor; others have any discount store's best. Each has a fireplace and the ambiance for a family place to stay. It is very convenient building for skiers.

9   **GREYSTONE LODGE**
4905 Spearhead Pl., P.O.Box 1044, Whistler, BC V0N 1B0,
604-932-2888; 1BR $110, 2BR $185
Amenities: Outdoor pool, indoor hot tub

Located just above the Chateau Whistler, overlooking the base of Blackcomb and the Wizard Express chair lift, Greystone truly has ski-in/ski-out convenience for all levels of skiers. Completed in 1991, these are new, luxurious condos with decorator-designed interiors, kitchens, and gas log fireplaces. The second floor units have lofts with cute dormer windows. Children love it.

HIGHLAND VALE
Highway 99, Whistler, BC V0N 1B0, 800-663-8070
Rates: From $45 on up
Amenities: Hot tub, cafe

This cluster of four separate condo developments is located along Highway 99 within walking distance of the gondola lift at Whistler Creek. Five minutes by car or bus from the main village, there's a sense at Highland Vale that you're in your own little world. Friendships form quickly around the rustic bar in the main lodge building or the Rim Rock Cafe, which is one of the most popular night spots in the whole Whistler area. Accommodations range from rustic hotel rooms for singles to spacious condos for families in the Vale building.

Highpointe (7) This is the newest addition at the south end of Highland Vale. You're only a short 200 meters from the gondola lift. These studio loft units are well designed for a family of five or for a couple that wants superior accommodations with fireplace, full kitchen, and whirlpool tubs.

Vale (7) Located on the north side of the Highland Vale complex, these are the largest condos with separate bedrooms, living room, dining area, kitchen, and fireplaces. It is the choice for families. There's a hot tub and a laundry room.

Highland (7) Just like Vale except a little older.

The Lodge (6) Known for the crackling fires and the rustic charm of its friendly dining room, The Lodge serves as the center point for most activities at Highland Vale. The Rim Rock Cafe and the Oyster Bar are also housed in this building. Here the units are studios or studios with loft. They are rustic with wood paneling and country charm decor. Each has a small kitchenette.

9+ LE CHAMOIS

4557 Blackcomb Way, P.O. Box 1044, Whistler, BC V0N 1B0, 604-932-8700; 1BR $220–300, 2BR $230–450, 3BR $350–650
Amenities: Outdoor heated pool, hot tub, gym

Just opened in 1991, these luxury units have a *great* location, right at the base of Blackcomb's Wizard Express in an area developing as Blackcomb Village. Operated as a full-service, all-suite hotel with its own front desk, Le Chamois has appeal for small executive conferences or seminars for doctors. Le Chamois has more amenities than most other resorts at Whistler/ Blackcomb including an outdoor heated pool, hot tub, exercise room, and a small shopping arcade. Best feature: a concierge at the 24-hour front desk to help you get acquainted with the area. Inside, the condos have been furnished by an interior decorator with superior furniture and beautiful patterned, coordinated fabrics. There are almost too many silk flowers. Each unit has an efficient kitchenette for preparing breakfast or light meals.

9 THE MARQUISE

4809 Spearhead Dr., Whistler, BC V0N 1B0, 604-938-1484
1BR $185–340, 90 units
Amenities: Hot tub, heated outdoor pool

Brand new for 1991, these are among the most luxurious condos found at Whistler. Located in the Blackcomb Benchlands, they are on the hillside, only steps above the village. You have ski-in/ski-out access using the high-speed Wizard Express chair lift. Although very few places in the Whistler area have indoor pools, the Marquise has an outdoor heated pool and a unique clear-dome covered hot tub. These one-bedroom condos are luxuriously furnished with interior decorator accents but the real beauty comes from the panoramic views through the window. Each has a full kitchen and fireplace, the Marquise is top-of-the-line, by local standards.

8+ MOUNTAINSIDE LODGE

4417 Sundial, Whistler, BC V0N 1B0, 604-932-4511, 800-777-8135
Studio $70–103, 1BR $100–150
Amenities: Pool, hot tub. Golf and tennis nearby

Mountainside Lodge is located in the village and two of the ski lifts are right outside the back door. One of the first lodges built in Whistler, it enjoys a great location. It is an established resort with guests and owners who return year after year. Why? For the ambiance. Although the pool area in and of itself is nothing special, you will meet interesting people there. The resort's focal point: Umberto's restaurant, which has a cozy atmosphere and genuine Northern Italian cuisine. The condos are disappointing considering the romance of Umberto's. The units are boxy and were designed to accommodate as many people as possible in the smallest amount of space while leaving room for a whirlpool. The "skierized" furniture has tweeds and neutral colors. The loft units are definitely superior because of the bay windows and private saunas. With a bubbling fountain, courtyard flowers, and an outdoor swimming pool overlooking the mountain, it is one of the best choices around.

8 NANCY GREENE'S OLYMPIC LODGE

4150 Village Green, Box 280, Whistler, BC V0N 1B0, 604-932-4724
Studio $60–90, 1BR $80–120
Amenities: Pool, hot tub, steam room

Billed as "the friendliest resort in Whistler," Canada's most famous skier has her own lodge and condo resort in the heart of Whistler village. And it's got some of the most professional management/services in the village. The lodge offers restaurants and an active après-ski cocktail lounge. You can see Nancy's Olympic trophies on display. The condos were added in 1989 with expansion into the Crystal Lodge condos. The condos are completely remodeled and are very spacious. You'll find lofts, private fireplaces, Laura Ashley-style wallpaper and sophisticated country charm touches. With its central location, only three minutes from the ski lifts, everyone comes to Nancy's for the après-ski at some point during their vacation.

5 PLAZA SUITES
4202 Village Sq., Whistler, BC V0N 1B0; 2BR $110–199
Amenities: Sauna, village center

In the heart of Whistler Village, these units are ten years old yet they offer spacious two-bedroom units with kitchens, fireplaces, and two bathrooms for families or group that want space and to be located right in the heart of the action.

7 POWDER HORN
4821 Spearhead Dr., Whistler, BC V0N 1B0
1BR $85–122, 2BR $122–170, 3BR $171–215
Amenities: Hot tub

Nestled in the backwoods of the Blackcomb Benchlands, these large one-, two-, and three-bedroom condos have full kitchens, gas log fireplaces, a whirlpool tub, simple decor with "skierized" furniture in neutral colors, and lots of pine wood. It's a comfortable environment for a family. Powder Horn is one of the few condo developments that really has ski-in/ski-out access for all levels of skiers.

6 POWDERVIEW
Gondola Way, Whistler, BC V0N 1B0
Amenities: None

Located at the south end of the village, these units are still part of "the village" but not in the popular central core. If you want a convenient location, yet don't want to be in the thick of the crowds, these condos are for you. The Whistler mountain express is a 2-minute walk away and some units overlook the golf fairway in the summertime. Each of these one- and two-bedroom units has a full kitchen and a fireplace.

7 RAINBOW CONDOMINIUMS
4205 Village Sq., Whistler, BC V0N 1B0
Amenities: Sauna

Located in the core village of Whistler, these one and two-bedroom condos have a quiet charm that appeals to families. Each has a full kitchen, stone fireplace hearth, parquet floors and soft, neutral interior decor. They offer a great place to stay after a day of skiing or biking.

8   **ST. ANDREWS HOUSE**
4433 Sundial Place, Whistler, BC V0N 1B0
Amenities: None

Located right in the heart of Whistler Village, overlooking Sundial Square, these two units offer spacious accommodations and a remarkable location. There's a full kitchen, fireplace, two-bedrooms, and a whirlpool. The popular Val d'Isere restaurant is right down below and its outdoor cafe in the summer provides a unique view.

8   **SNOWRIDGE**
Spearhead Dr., Whistler, BC V0N 1B0
Amenities: None

Located on the side of Whistler Mountain's south base and overlooking the south end of Whistler Valley and the Tantalus Mountain range, Snowridge features some of the largest condos to be found on the edge of "the village." These are two-bedroom, two-bedroom loft, three-bedroom and three-bedroom loft condos built in 1989 when Whistler area developers began creating larger and more luxurious units. Each condo has a full kitchen, fireplace, and a genuine steam bath in one of the bathrooms. Snowridge is great for families, two couples or small groups.

8   **SNOWY CREEK**
Blackcomb Way, Whistler, BC V0N 1B0
Amenities: None

These townhouse condos straddle the small gap between the Blackcomb Benchlands and Whistler Village. It's a two-minute walk down to Whistler Village and the Blackcomb ski lift. Or its a two-minute schuss down to Blackcomb's Magic Chair or Wizard Express. They offer superior lodgings. These cluster buildings with stone facades and gabled roofs are some of the largest units to be found in the Whistler area. Completed in 1989, they are richly decorated (for Canada) and equipped with a full kitchen, two bathrooms, a fireplace, and some have their own private "hot tub room" as a special addition. It is a good choice for families, groups, or two couples.

7   **SUNDIAL CRESCENT**
Westbrook, 4340 Sundial Crescent, Whistler, BC V0N 1B0,
604-932-2321
Amenities: Rooftop hot tub

Sundial Crescent is a brand new resort. The condos have attractive, professionally designed interiors. Drawing upon the forest setting for inspiration, you'll find deep green carpets, beige fabrics, and lots of polished brass and glass. A few potted palms and plants further enhance the decor. The deluxe units have their own whirlpools. The kitchenettes are without dishwashers. The village location is close to the gondola for skiers.

7 **TANTALUS**
4200 Whistler Way Box 340, Whistler, BC V0N 1B0,
604-932-4146; $99–260
Amenities: Golf

Located just a two-minute walk from the south end of Whistler Village, these spacious two-bedroom condos are by themselves along the mountain, overlooking the golf course. A good skier can ski home but others may rely upon the shuttle bus. This is however, one of the most popular spots for golfers in the summer. In spite of the great location and views, the interiors are a little small. These units were built in the days when little attention was given to soundproofing.

7 **WESTBROOK**
4340 Sundial Crescent, P.O. Box 1043, Whistler, BC V0N 1B0,
604-932-6500; Studio, $65–99, 1BR $85–190, 2BR $110–240
Amenities: Hot tub

This eight-story building is just one building away from the Whistler Express gondola. Skiers would be hard pressed to find other accommodations at a more convenient location in Whistler village. The condos are operated as a hotel, which controls the furnishings and management. Functional in design with a kitchen that opens onto the dining table and living room, you'll feel more like you're in a hotel suite than a condo. Lots of service, you'll find a 24-hour front desk and an outdoor rooftop hot tub for relaxation after a hard day of skiing, golf, or biking in the mountains.

WHISKI JACK RESORTS
Box 344, Whistler, BC V0N 1B0, 604-932-6500
Studio $65–99, 1BR $85–190, 2BR $110–240
Amenities: Pools, saunas, hot tub, gym

There are five locations to choose from at Whiski Jack Resorts. Four of them are in the village and one is in Whistler Creek. These timeshare condos have the most dressed-up interior decor in the Whistler region. The newer condos have been designer decorated with high style, bright dramatic fabrics, lots of mirrors, and silk flowers. The older condos, such as the original Whiski Jack, have "skierized" interiors, boxy wood furniture and tweed fabrics. Some of the condos are two-story units with a spiral staircase. Whiski Jack provides VTPs and deluxe kitchens in every condo (which is rare in Whistler). In addition, all of the condos include private fireplaces and private whirlpools. A few of them even have private saunas.

Whistler View (7) Whistler View is located in the Village. It is convenient to the Whistler and Blackcomb chair lifts. Some of the two-bedroom condos have either private saunas or hot tubs.

Fitzsimmons (8) Fitzsimmons is located in the village. Every one- and two-bedroom condo has a private sauna. The rooftop hot tub is popular at night.

Village Gate House (7) The Village Gate House condos don't have saunas or rooftop hot tubs, but every condo includes a whirlpool large enough for two. The central village location is very convenient.

Snowbird (9) Snowbird is a short walk from the village in the Benchlands section, next to the Wizard lift. These are the only townhouse condos in the area and they are perhaps the most luxuriously decorated of any at Whistler. VTPs are included. Sorry, no private saunas or hot tubs are available.

Whiski Jack (8) The original Whiski Jack can be found in the Whistler Creek area. You'll spot the townhouses by their brightly colored roofs. The condos include private saunas. The mountain views are great—you just don't get this in the village.

5 **WHISTLER ON THE LAKE**
3262 Archibald, Whistler, BC V0N 1B0
Amenities: Lake. Golf nearby

If you want the best of both Whistler worlds—a peaceful setting and village excitement—Whistler on the Lake may be the choice for you. As Whistler's only waterfront property, this year-round facility is located on the south shore of Alta Lake, almost a chip shot from the Whistler Golf Club, and a five-minute drive from Whistler Village. You'll be surrounded by mountains, evergreen trees, and the clearest water you've ever seen. From the shore you can look right down to the lake bottom. After a hectic day of skiing or a night of socializing, you can retreat to tranquil wilderness beauty.

All Whistler on the Lake condos are one and two-bedroom units with full kitchens, fireplaces, and patio/balconies that serve up panoramic lakeside views of everything from baby ducks to small boats passing by. Inside, decor is cheerful and functional. "Hotel-style" furniture prevails but who cares with those large picture windows and gorgeous lake views? This is truly a find in the Whistler area.

6 **WHISTLER RESORT & CLUB**
2129 Lake Placid Rd., Box 279, Whistler, BC V0N 1B0,
604-932-5756; Studio $99–115, 1BR $180–220
Amenities: Lake, pool, hot tub, sauna, tennis

The Whistler Resort Club, located three kilometers from Whistler Village, houses condo suites on the shores of Lake Nita. The setting is beautiful, especially during the summer. Unlike most of the other condos in Whistler, this resort has a social ambiance that enables guests to get to know each other. The surroundings are rustic and the decor is casual. Each unit has a full kitchen and a fireplace. Victorian stuffed chairs and attractive bouquets of artificial flowers are special touches. Whistler tries to create the ambiance of an English resort. Skiers will appreciate easy access to the Whistler Creek gondola and the Olive chair lift.

5   **WHISTLER VILLAGE INNS (The Keg and The Powder)**
Sundial Crescent, P.O. Box 970, Whistler, BC V0N 1B0,
604-932-4004; Studio $65, 1BR $100
Amenities: Outdoor heated pool, hot tub, saunas, restaurant

Two of the oldest condo buildings at Whistler, they were built over 20 years ago when Whistler was just getting started. Nevertheless, they enjoy a prime location on Sundial Crescent, just a building away from the Whistler Express gondola lift. This is where the buses drop off skiers staying at other resorts. Operated as hotels with full-time, full-service front desks, you'll feel more like you're staying in a hotel than a condo. These are small, efficient studio units with cheap furniture and cramped floor plans. They do, however, have full kitchens. Ask for a "studio loft" as these are much more spacious. You'll be treated to simple, practical, full-service, and a great location. The Keg and Powder are identical lodges on two sides of the square. The Keg has a friendly lobby where you can always enjoy a complimentary pot of coffee or tea by the fireplace with friends.

7   **WILDWOOD LODGE**
4749 Spearhead Dr., Box 604, Whistler, BC V0N 1B0,
604-932-3252; 1BR $180, 2BR $250
Amenities: Outdoor pool, indoor hot tub

Wildwood Lodge is located about 3 kilometers from Whistler village by car, and about 1 1/2 kilometers by the foot path. A fireplace is included in every condo. A pastel decor, patterned fabrics, and vertical blinds are the standard. The loft units are the best choice because they have vaulted ceilings in the living room.

6   **WINDWHISTLE**
Whistler Way, Whistler, BC V0N 1B0
Amenities: None

This quiet group of condos in Whistler village offers one-bedroom units for good value. Efficiently designed with inexpensive furniture, these units do have full kitchens, fireplaces, and whirlpool tubs. They are convenient for two; tight for four.

10 **WOODRUN LODGE**
4910 Spearhead Dr., Whistler, BC V0N 1B0, 604-932-3317
1BR $180, 2BR $250
Amenities: Pool, hot tub, exercise room

Just opened in 1991, Woodrun Lodge was built by the developer of Blackcomb Resort to be a mountainside showpiece. It's beautiful. The Lodge is six stories high with lots of glass picture windows to capture the view, turrets and bay windows to provide architectural flourishes, and intriguing floor plans. The condos have stone hearth fireplaces and have been decorated by interior designers with color-coordinated fabrics and "pieces" such as a chest for a coffee table or wingback chairs. Woodrun Lodge is truly superior. Everyone has ski-in/ski-out access and you're only steps from the center of Blackcomb village shops and restaurants. It is an excellent resort.

RENTAL RESOURCES
Crown Resort Accommodations, 604-932-2215
Four Seasons Rentals, 604-932-3252
Nordic Accommodations, 604-681-0999
Northern Comfort, 604-932-5403
Powder Property Management, 604-681-0695
Sea to Sky, 604-932-2972, 604-932-4184
Whistler Chalets, 800-663-7711
Whistler Exclusive Properties, 604-932-5353

2. VALLEY OF A THOUSAND PEAKS

Southeastern British Columbia is favored with that increasingly rare combination of undiminished natural beauty and diverse recreational opportunities. Several mega-resorts, which offer summertime sports as well as skiing in the winter, have recently opened in the Valley of a Thousand Peaks. Several years ago a decision was made to create a golfing center in this part of the Rocky Mountains and the resorts here are a result of that thoughtful planning. There are eleven major courses, each one within 22 miles of the other running along Routes 93-95. Less than three hours east of Calgary and three hours north of Spokane, Washington, this is a spectacular setting for all outdoor pursuits from hunting to skiing, golfing and fishing.

Extending from Golden in the north to Elkwood in the south, the B.C. Rockies are the high skyline that cradles a playland of forests, meadows, lakes, rivers, and streams. Radium Hot Springs and Fairmont Hot Springs are international favorites with their natural mineral hot pools. Panorama offers a luxurious Alpine retreat while the condos clustered around Kimberley Ski and Mountain Resort have all been designed in a Bavarian style with quaint shutters and flower boxes full of geraniums in the summer.

Transportation to the area is the major inhibition for most visitors. The nearest major airport is Calgary for those going to the resort areas in the northern part of the valley, and Spokane is three to four hours away from resorts at the southern end of the valley. Either way, it's a long trip by plane and car (or by car) from the major population centers of North America. But for those who endure the trip, you'll be well rewarded with a glimpse of the Rockies that you'll treasure for years to come.

WHERE TO STAY

8 EMERALD LAKE LODGE
Hwy 1, Box 10, Field, BC V0A 1G0, 800-663-6336
Junior Suites$100–210
Amenities: Large hot tub, gym, sauna

This is an end-of-the-road/Shangri-la-style resort. Built as a hunting lodge in the 1920s, this was grandfathered before the provincial moratorium on new construction in the national park. This has a lakeside location and has been carefully developed to create an environment appealing to the senses. Built of stone, and lined with mooseheads, the main lodge is a reminder of by-gone days. Each junior suite has a sitting room and fireplace. No kitchens—and no nearby Safeway. Catch or shoot whatever you will, the chef will prepare it in a grand European hunters' style. The best feature is the personalized service and the camaraderie which develops among the marooned guests. If you really want to explore the wilderness, guides can be arranged on a daily basis. Emerald Lake provides a different experience.

9 FAIRMONT HOT SPRINGS RESORT VILLAS
Box 10, Fairmont Hot Springs, BC, V0B 1L0, 604-365-6341
1BR $80–155, 2BR $100–200
Amenities: Golf, skiing, hot springs, pool, tennis, health club

Fairmont Hot Springs Resort enjoys one of those spectacular settings, which you've always hoped to find in the Canadian Rockies. This 6,000 acre resort complex is in the shadow of the Fairmont Range where peaks soar to an altitude of 15,000 feet. Fairmont is three hours west of Calgary and five hours north of Spokane. The remote location has heretofore limited the number of visitors so the surrounding forest is almost pristine. Golden eagles, bald eagles, and osprey soar overhead. Deer, elk, mountain longhorn sheep, and mountain goats roam through the surrounding wilderness. The Columbia River meanders past the condos and in the fall the spawning salmon are so plentiful that they almost turn sections of the river red.

This resort is in two sections, mountain and river. The mountain side was the first to be developed with golf and forested hiking trails. There is a small ski hill but it pales by comparison to Whistler or Banff. The condos are townhouses with private fireplaces and patios. Across the road, the new river golf course has just been completed, and the condos are in a three-story building. Glamorously decorated, they are no comparison to the "skierized" decor of the mountain condos. The river condos are a melody of fabrics and furniture better than most of us have at home. The style is a cross between French Empire and British Sporting Club. There's nothing else like this in Canada, as each two-bedroom River condo has four televisions, connected for satellite reception, and two electronic entertainment centers, each with a VCR.

The resort has a couple of health clubs with a pool where the walls can be retracted in the summer. There's the championship 18-hole Riverside golf course, site of many regional tournaments, and the resort has its own ski hill. Unique to Fairmont is the crystal clear, odorless "hot springs" from which the resort draws its name. The only drawback is the omnipresence of the timeshare sales force.

This is a destination resort, which will certainly provide an unforgettable vacation experience.

KIMBERLEY SKI AND SUMMER RESORT
350 Ross St., Kimberley, BC V1A 2Z9
Amenities: Skiing, golf, tennis, pools, hot tubs

Kimberley nestles on the edge of the Purcell Mountains at the southern end of the Valley of a Thousand Peaks. This is one of Canada's most picturesque towns because it is entirely themed to be a Bavarian village. Local children play in dirndls and lederhosen. A mile above town Northstar Mountain offers skiing in winter and biking trails in summer. Not an international destination, this nevertheless has its own charms especially when combined as a stopover on a circle trip through the B.C. Rockies. You'll find condos and townhouses in a series of discrete two-story buildings lining the hillside. Some of the choices are:

Purcel Condos (6) Just minutes away from the slopes, these skier condos are simple, clean, and practical. 1BR $72–113, 2BR $110–161

Rocky Mountain Club (6) These units are the accommodations closest to the lift. Located next door to the Racquetball and Indoor Tennis Club, this is for those who want to be active after a day of skiing. 1BR $72–114, 2BR $110–162

Silver Birch Chalets (7) These two- and three-bedrooms are what passes for the luxury choice in the area. Spacious, they are not stylish. Each has a stove fireplace and your own private sauna. They are great for families and groups. 2BR $110–142, 3BR $127–201

Rentals in the Kimberly area are through Mountain Trench Enterprises, Box 339, Kimberly, BC VIA 2Y9, 604-427-5385.

For those planning two or three days in the area, or even a week, this is clearly your best bet.

9 PANORAMA RESORT

Panorama, BC V0A 1T0, 800-268-8880; 1BR $80–150, 2BR $90–180
Amenities: Skiing, horseback riding, tennis, pools, hot tubs, restaurants. Golf and lake nearby

Known as Canada's Alpine resort because of the invigorating climate, Panorama lives up to its name. The setting is spectacular beneath the snow-capped face of Mt. Nelson and along the banks of Toby Creek. This is "deluxe wilderness." Hard to reach, this one is worth the trip. Panorama is its own self-contained community and, for us, this qualifies as Shangri-la. Just in case you didn't feel overwhelmed by the altitude, your surroundings, and the tortured mountain drive—the main buildings are outlined at night by little tiny white Christmas lights. Maybe it's the altitude or the wine but the effect is emotional.

There are two separate condominium developments here: **Horse Thief** and **Toby Creek.** The floor plans are the same. The one-bedroom units are a little boxy; the two-bedroom models seem far superior, especially when you note they have a slightly higher price. Toby Creek condos enjoy a creekside location where you can hear the water and enjoy an unobstructed view. The Horse Thief condos are on the other side of the lodge. Because they are newer, the interior decor is slightly better. Expect to find a neutral, woodsy ambiance with lots of beige and butterscotch colors. Each has a fireplace and a full kitchen that is great for breakfast or a light lunch. After a day of the outdoors, you'll appreciate the Starbird dining room or the more intimate Strathcona pub with its inimitable Scottish style. Panorama Resort is unique.

7 RADIUM HOT SPRINGS RESORT

Box 310, Radium Hot Springs, BC V0A 1M0, 800-655-3585
1BR $130, 2BR $145, 3BR $160
Amenities: Hot springs, spa, pool, golf, horseback riding, tennis, skiing

Located at the western boundary of Kootenay National Park, Radium Hot Springs Resort commands a unique location, one well worth a scenic detour. The resort's Aquacourt is a crystal clear, odorless, therapeutic mineral spring, which has been transformed into a huge outdoor "hot tub." The near-by Olympic-sized swimming pool is a more temperate 80°. The resort is connected to the village by a walking trail and there are extensive linking trails heading up into the hills behind the resort. This is the gateway to the Height of the Rockies Wilderness Preserve which runs along Canada's Continental Divide with its hiking and biking trails. For those who prefer less rigorous activity, there's a championship 18-hole golf course, tennis courts, horseback riding, and a full gym.

The resort offers condominiums in a series of four-story buildings overlooking the golf course, and a clutch of single-family, free-standing villas. Interior decor varies from "efficient Canadian," a budget style that borrows the efficient use of space from European condos, to the more luxurious executive villas, which have superb decor and contemporary style. The one-bedroom condos have kitchenettes while the two- and three-bedroom condos and villas have full kitchens.

This is a unique spot where you'll want to be outside among nature's marvels. You'll appreciate the convenience of your own vacation home where you can set your own schedule of activities.

RENTAL RESOURCES
Kimberly Vacations, 604-427-3666
Mountain Trench Enterprises, 604-427-5385

QUÉBEC

La Belle Province is beautiful not only because of the villages and landscape of the Laurentians, but also because of the people and culture. Québec provides a bit of France in North America. Settled by the French who explored the rivers and forests in the 16th Century, Québec was ceded to the British under a European treaty. Although annexed to British Canada, Québec has continued its traditions and developed a unique culture.

The resorts of the Laurentians are where the Québecois go to play. And play they do—French style topped off with plenty of after-ski fun and enthusiastic windsurfing on the lakes. Golf, tennis, windsurfing, and skiing are popular sports, but this is one area where the activity will be memorable because of the cultural experience. We have divided Québec into two sections, each about an hour's drive away from Montréal:

1. The Laurentians
2. St. Lawrence Lakes

In French Canada you'll find an attitude that just doesn't exist in other parts of North America. There is a joyful, playful spirit in the way things are done. And you'll also find a very macho desire to test the limits of human endurance and skill. In the Laurentians, you'll find skiers never complain of the cold, and many of them attempt off-track skiing (through the trees) to a level unimagined on the groomed slopes of Colorado. Windsurfing on the lakes is also highly competitive, but afterwards the wine and cheese parties have a camaraderie you just wouldn't find in Boston or New York.

Condomania has recently boomed in Québec. Everywhere along the highway or in the resort villages there are signs advertising condos for sale. While this sort of development blossomed in the U.S. in the '70s and '80s, it is now just becoming very popular in Canada. As a result, all the accommodations described herein are new. Generally, you should expect to see style and flair at every resort, but the drawback is that units are notably smaller than U.S. versions. You'll find studio and one-bedroom condos the size of some hotel rooms. Furthermore, the kitchen appliances generally are miniature versions of what you would find in the U.S. Many studios only have a mini-fridge and a microwave.

1. THE LAURENTIANS AND MT. TREMBLANT

The Laurentians are the oldest mountains in North America. Peaks of granite have been worn into tumble-down valleys following the river beds. The Laurentians can be cold, windy, and icy in winter. In summer, they can present a fantasy fulfilled when the sun shines through the trees and sparkles on the lakes, but there are many overcast gray days too, when you need a

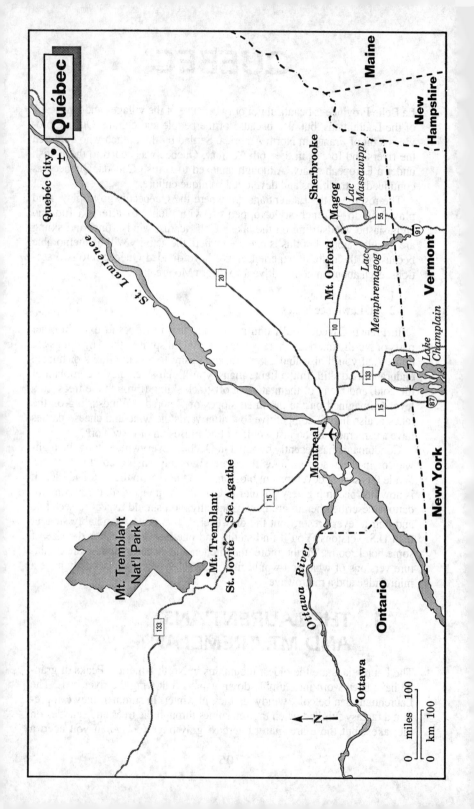

sweater to play golf or a warm jacket for sailing. Recently, plans to build a skiers' village at Mt. Tremblant were announced by the same group which had such success in developing Whistler. Within a short time Mt. Tremblant could emerge as the most glamorous ski resort in the East.

Located an hour north of Montréal and only minutes away from Montréal's international airport at Mirabel, there is a series of ski hills, which grow larger until you reach the highest, Mt. Tremblant. Our advice to you is to bypass the charms of St. Jovite and St. Agathe, and head straight to Mt. Tremblant. This is the resort area of distinction. You'll find several prestigious resorts along Lake Tremblant, about three miles outside of town. Lake Tremblant with the forests, steeply-rising shoreline, canoes, and sailboats is what you would hope to find in Canada. The town of Mt. Tremblant serves the resorts, but has not yet evolved into a tourist village with shops and restaurants. Consistent with the generally high quality of French cuisine in Québec, the Tremblant area offers a variety of outstanding restaurants. Don't give in to the pressure to take a hotel's meal plan and thereby commit yourself to just one restaurant. Don't stay home at night either. After all, you are in Canada, where the playful spirit of France reigns. Many nights you'll choose between your own kitchen or a hotel dining room.

WHERE TO STAY

8+ AUBERGE DU MT. TREMBLANT / TREMBLANT CLUB
Tremblant Club, Ave. Cuttle, Mt. Tremblant, Québec J0T 1Z0, 819-425-2731, 800-363-2413
Amenities: Lake, indoor and outdoor pools, tennis, health spa, ski school, horseback riding, restaurant

Formerly known as Cuttle's Tremblant Club, this resort has attracted the same clients year after year. You can't have better praise than to continuously thrive on repeat customers. Obviously they do something right. What is it? Maybe it's the proverbial "Moosehead Bar" overlooking Lake Tremblant. We think it's the casual, clubby atmosphere where families play together and the bar rings with ribald songs at one a.m. This is an "Anglo" outpost in French-speaking Québec. The Tyrolian-style chalet condos have ten units of various sizes. They are simply decorated in a north woods style. The studios have coffee makers; the larger ones have kitchenettes. All have individual fireplaces. Only four miles from the very French Gray Rocks, this is a world apart in style.

Auberge du Mt. Tremblant has it's own ski school and eight instructors. Video critiques are presented in the evenings for serious skiers. There's a health club with an indoor pool and gym, and an outdoor pool. Boats and canoes are available for guests to enjoy the lake. The location is beautiful. This is one of the top choices in Québec.

3   CONDOLETS
2154 Chemin de Montagne, Mt. Tremblant, Québec J0T 1Z0
Amenities: None

Condolets' condos may be tiny, but at least they're functional. They are located at the base of the mountain near the ski lifts. A metal "acorn" fireplace is provided for burning a log or two. A stove and refrigerator are also included, but there's no telephone and no television. Although the condos are designed for budget travelers, you would be better off joining a group in a larger unit because the space is so tight.

9   GRAY ROCKS
Route 327 Nord, P.O. Box 1000, Mt. Tremblant, Québec, JOT 2H0, 819-425-2771, 800-567-6767; 1BR $164–191, 2BR $240–360
Amenities: Sports complex, skiing, tennis, saunas, pool

If you enjoy the camaraderie of European-style group skiing, you'll love Gray Rocks. There is no other place like it in North America. A bit of European culture is combined with the convenience of North America. Although this resort offers condominium lodgings, you'll find that many people take the meal plan in order to enjoy a different party each evening at the Inn. The condos are about a mile away from the main part of Gray Rocks Inn on the shores of Lake Ouimet. They offer some of the most spacious townhouse condos and superior furnishings in Québec. Expect to find quality furniture, designer accessories, and cool modern colors. What's special about Gray Rocks? It's the private Gray Rocks ski mountain where groups are formed among skiers with similar abilities and you ski and play together for a week, just like they do in France or Austria. The after-ski life is even merrier with lots of private parties around the fireplaces in the evenings. You'll make new friends for a week and will want to rendezvous at Gray Rocks in the future. Summertime may be even better. You'll enjoy boating, tennis, swimming, hiking, and all that strong Canadian beer. Again, the group learning experience is encouraged with skill and humor. Although many condo travelers stay at home in the evening, we urge you to sample the nightlife around the inn. Unlike most condo resorts, rates at Gray Rocks are per person. A vacation here is well worth every penny.

5   HARVE DU VILLAGE
213 Rue de Couvent, Mt. Tremblant, Québec J0T 1Z0, 819-425-3763
Amenities: Tennis, pool, golf, ice skating, cross country skiing

Harve Du Village is located in the village of Mt. Tremblant, three minutes from the shore of Lake Mercier. To ski at Tremblant, you'll either have to take the shuttle from the village or drive by car. The unpretentious condos, located in a four-story wooden frame building, are simply furnished with European futuristic pillow chairs and wooden butcher block tables and chairs. Every condo is equipped with the basics. In addition, small luxuries such as televisions and private fireplaces are provided. The kitchenettes are fully equipped for cooking, but you may want to sample the French bistros in the village. This condo village is functional and clean.

7   MT. TREMBLANT LODGE
Lac Tremblant, Mt. Tremblant, Québec JOT 1Z0, 819-425-8711, 800-461-8711; 1BR $232
Amenities: Golf, pool, skiing

Located near the base of Mt. Tremblant, the lodge offers ski-in/ski-out accommodations. You won't need a car if you stay here. Everything that you need is available; you can ski and hike in the daytime and visit the piano bar or the disco in the evening. The lodge has a full-service restaurant, and even though the condos are equipped with full kitchens, you will be encouraged to take the meal plan. The condos are little bungalows on the grounds of the lodge. Every unit has a private fireplace. An outdoor swimming pool and tennis court are available in the summer. Although the condos are cute on the outside, we were disappointed with the homogenized hotel-style furnishings.

7   NANSEHAUS CONDOMINIUMS
Route 327 Nord, Box 388, Mt. Tremblant, Québec JOT 1Z0, 819-425-2771
Amenities: Lake, golf, skiing

Nansehaus Condominiums are located in a wooded area at the base of the mountain. A car is necessary for getting to the ski lift. The condos are designed to look like chalets, but they are actually townhouses with connecting walls. Since every entry is on a separate level, guests will feel as though they have a private chalet. These are some of the largest, most spacious, private condos in the area. Most Québecois condos are actually suites in two- or three-story buildings, but these are separate little structures. There is no on-site management or hospitality, but the activity around Auberge Mt. Tremblant is only a short walk away. The condo interiors are spacious, but the interior decor that we saw was a little disappointing. The units are furnished, not decorated. This resort is the best choice in the area for people seeking space and a home in the woods.

8   PINOTEAU VILLAGE
Pinoteau Village, Lac Tremblant, Québec JOT 1Z0, 819-425-3503
Amenities: Bar, restaurant, ice skating, pool, lake

Pinoteau Village, a landmark on Lake Tremblant, is one of the largest condo villages in the area. Mt. Tremblant ski lifts are only about one km away and it is possible to get there by bus. The condos are in five separate mini-subdivisions within the Pinoteau complex since they were built at different times. The condos closest to the lake are older, but have the best views. The condos at the rear of the property are slightly more spacious and have the best interior decor. Expect to find light wood contemporary furniture, two convertible sofa beds, full kitchen, private fireplace, and either a patio or balcony. The decor is a cheerful combination of light colored walls and carpet with mauve or burnt orange colored sofas. Many of them have a great view of Mt. Tremblant. A recreational center with an exercise room and two hot tubs is available. A restaurant is on-site and you can stay on the meal plan if you don't want to cook.

6   VILLA BELLEVUE
        Mt. Tremblant, Québec JOT 120, 819-425-2734
        Amenities: Lake, pool, hot tub, restaurant

Located on the shores of Lake Ouimet, this summer resort is a popular destination for winter sports activities as well. Primarily a hotel, this resort has a bevy of spacious condos. Built of wood and decorated in earth tone colors, there's little romance about these functional lodgings. Nevertheless, this is one of the few area resorts that won't try to force you into one of their hotel meal plans. Each has a kitchen. The advantage here is freedom, in addition to the space and convenience.

2. ST. LAWRENCE LAKES

The St. Lawrence Lowlands is the area between the Vermont border and the St. Lawrence River. East of Montréal, the area is more Anglo-American than French. Although French is the official language of Québec, nearly 35 percent of the population is native English speaking. This is where they live. The St. Lawrence Lowlands are like an extension of Vermont, but without the mountain peaks for skiing. Mt. Orford at 2,400 feet is the highest and offers skiing. Magog and North Hatley are towns between the lakes. The lakes are calm and shallow, perfect conditions for windsurfers. Since the area fills up with vacationers in August, we suggest you choose another month to visit.

This is a regional resort area that seldom attracts visitors from far away. You'll find a certain clubbiness because vacationers generally have been returning to this resort area year after year. Only recently have these communities opened up and, in response, urban dwellers have began to flock here in appreciation of the area's unspoiled natural beauty.

WHERE TO STAY

4   CLUB AZUR
        81 Desjardins, Magog, Québec J1X 3W9, 819-847-2131
        Amenities: Pool, clubhouse, game room, tennis

Formerly called Village Rousillon, Club Azur occupies a choice beach-front location on the lake just outside the town of Magog. These two and three-story townhouse condos are fully equipped. The floor plans are functional and the furnishings casual. The condos seem to be decorated with toys. What this resort specializes in is FUN—it's like a mini Club Med. There are plenty of wild and crazy activities for children and adults. In the winter, Club Azur organizes group skiing on Mt. Orford which is only five miles away. The clientele is bilingual, but generally you'll hear French spoken. The prices are good.

3   CONDOTELS ORFORD
385 Rue du Moulin, Magog, Québec J1X 4A1, 819-847-2514
Amenities: Pool

This village of new townhouse condos is popular with families because of the variety of activities in the area. Lake Memphremagog and ski lifts at Mt. Orford are only two miles away. The condos are simply and adequately furnished (beds, tables, and chairs). Don't expect decorator touches. There is an outdoor swimming pool. You have to make your own fun here.

5   L'INTERVAL
2764 Chemin du Parc, Orford, R.R. 2, Magog, Québec J1X 3W3,
819-843-8960, 800-363-2413
Amenities: Pool, hot tub

French to the core, these brand new townhouse condos are located on the slopes of Mt. Orford. They are popular because the Magog area offers golf, watersports, and skiing within an hour of Montréal and within 25 minutes of the Vermont border. The condos are attractively decorated with lots of peach, soft pink, and white plastic or wood furniture. It is quite visually attractive. There's an indoor swimming pool and hot tub area that is popular all year long. For some reason, this resort attracts a French-speaking crowd which gives L'Interval a truly international flavor.

6   O'BERGE DU VILLAGE MAGOG
261 Rue Merry Sud, Magog, Québec J1Z 3L2, 819-843-6566
Amenities: Hot tub, racquetball, clubhouse, game room

O'Berge Du Village Magog is a self-contained village of condos. The name comes from a play on words from the Anglicized French word "auberge." The lakeshore resort, located on the edge of town, is lively, friendly, and mainly English speaking. You'll find children playing outside in the playground. Each building has a sauna. The sports center has racquetball courts and a kidney-shaped hot tub. The condos are cozy and nicely decorated with polished "raw wood" furniture, tweeds, and splashes of bright color to liven things up. Barbecues frequently take place in the summer, and wine and cheese parties abound in the winter.

5   VILLAGE MT. ORFORD
Route 141, Magog, Québec J1X 3W3, 819-843-8960
Amenities: Pool, tennis

Village Mt. Orford is located on Mt. Orford, which has combined with Mt. Sutton, Gromont, Glen Mountain and Owl's Head to form the "Ski East" interconnected ski complex. Skiers can take the lift up the mountain, ski down to the main "town" part of the Mt. Orford ski center, then take the lift back up and ski home at the end of the day. The boxy wooden townhouses, grouped in clusters, are spacious and have good views, but they are cheaply furnished. This is a family resort that is popular all year round because it is only an hour away from Montréal. Tennis and an outdoor pool are the summer attractions. In addition, the main part of Mt. Orford provides a sports center and golf course.

Appendix—List of Timeshares

Some of the condo resorts in this guide have units operated under a timeshare plan. Timeshare simply means that the ownership rights to a condo have been subdivided among 52 owners, each having the right to use that condo for a week. The reason we list these timeshares is that many timeshare owners exchange their occupancy rights to visit other resorts rather than renting.

Acapulco Clipper
Arroyo Roble Resort
Attitash
Banff Rocky Mountain
  Resort
Berkshire Beach Club
Berkshire by the Sea
Breakers, The (Florida)
Brewster Green
Bryan's Spanish Cove
Caesar's Brookdale
Caloosa Cove Resort
Campanilla Compound
Cape Cod Holiday
  Estates
Caribbean Beach
Carlsbad Inn
Carriage House (Nevada)
Casa Ybel
Cathedral Ledge
Cedar Village Condos
Champion's Run
Charter Club of Marco
  Beach
Club Donatello
Club Tahoe
Cold Spring Resort
Commodore Beach Club
Cove at Yarmouth
Desert Isle
Disney Vacation Club
Dover House
Dunes South
Eagle's Nest Beach
  Resort
East Rim Condos
Eastern Slope Inn
Fairfield Bay
Fairfield Flagstaff
Fairfield Glade
Fairfield Harbour
Fairfield Mountains
Fairfield Ocean Ridge
Fairfield Plantation
Fairfield Sapphire Valley
Fairfield Williamsburg

Fairmont Hot Springs
  Resort
Fairmont Hot Springs
  Resort Villas
Falls, The
Fantasy World Club
  Villas
Fernwood
Fort Brown Condoshares
Four Seasons at Beech
Fox Hills Resort
Fox Run Resort
Frostfire
Galleon Bay
Gatlinburg Town Square
Gold Point
Golden Strand
Grand Flamingo Club
Greens, The (Colorado)
Habitat 2000
Harbor Club Villas
Harve du Village
Highlands at Sugar
Hillcrest Inn
Hotel de L'Eaux Vives
Hotel de La Monnaie
Inn at Goose Rocks
Inn at Silver Creek, The
Islander Beach Resort
Isle of Bali
Jockey Club
Jupiter Reef Club
Kala Point Village
Kimberling Inn Condos
Kingston Cove
L'Auberge Del Mar
La Boca Casa
Laguna Shores
Laguna Surf
Lake Arrowhead Chalets
Lakeview at Silver Creek
Lakeway Inn/World of
  Tennis Resort
Landing at Seven Coves,
  The

Landmark Holiday
  Resort
Landmark, The
Las Olas Beach Club
Las Olas Beach Club of
  Cocoa Beach
Leisure Club
Leisure Club at
  Horseshoe Bay
Leisure Club
  International
Lido Beach Club
Lifetime of Vacations
Lighthouse Cove
Lion's Gate Pines Lodge
Lodge at Lake Tahoe,
  The
Lodge on Whitney
  Mountain, The
Longboat Bay Club
Loon Mountain—
  Mountain Club
Los Abrigados
Lucayan Resort
Maggie Valley Country
  Club
Magic Tree
Mardi Gras Manor
Marine Terrace
Mariner's Boathouse
Mariner's Point at
  Thunder Hollow
Marriott's Desert Springs
  Villas
Marriott's Heritage
Marriott's Monarch
Marriott's Royal Palms
  of Orlando
Marriott's Sabal Palms
Marriott's Streamside
Massanutten
Maverick
Mayan Princess
Mittersill
Mountain Meadows
  Resort

Mountainside at Silver
   Creek
Mustang Island Beach
   Club and Resort
Newport On Shore
O'Berge du Village
   Magog
Oak n'Spruce Resort
Oakmount
Ocean Club on
   Smuggler's Beach
Ocean Forest
Ocean Landings
Ocean Palms
Ocean Villas I and II
Olympic Village Inn
Orange Lake Country
   Club
Our House at the Beach
Outrigger Beach Club
Pacific Grove Plaza
Padre South
Padre Vista
Palm Beach Resort
Park Plaza
Parkway International
   Adventure
Peppertree Laurel Point
Peppertree Vacation Club
Pinecrest Townhouses
Polynesian Isles
Ponds at Fox Hollow
Port Elsewhere
Port O'Call
Poste Montaigne
Powell Place
Powhattan Plantation
Rayburn Country Resort
Resort World of Orlando
Ridge Sierra, The
Ridge Tahoe, The
Roark Resort
Samoset Resort
San Clemente Cove
San Clemente Inn
San Francisco Suites
Sand Pebble Resort
Sands Beach Club
Sands Ocean Club
Sands of Indian Wells
Sandstone Creek Club
Sanibel Cottages

Sarasota Sands
Schooner II
Scottsdale Camelback
   Resort
Sea Mist
Sea Scape (N. Carolina)
Shadow Mountain
   Quarters
Shanty Creek/Schuss
   Mountain
Sheffield Inn
Shell Winner's Circle
   Beach Club
Ski View Mountain
   Resort
Snow Cloud at Seven
   Devils
South Seas Plantation
Southern California
   Beach Club
Steele Hill Resort
Streamside at Vail
Summit at Silvercreek
Summit at Winter Park,
   The
Sun Bay Beach
   Club/Lodge
Tahoe Edgelake Beach
   Club
Tahoe Seasons (Nevada)
Tanglewood
   (Pennsylvania)
Tennis Club, The
Tortuga Beach Club
Trapp Family Lodge
Treetops (Missouri)
Treetops (Tennessee)
Turtle Inn
Vail International
Ventura
Veranda Beach Club
Vistana Beach Club
Vistana Resort
Wave Crest
Whiski Jack Resorts
Whistler Resort Club
White Sands of Longboat
   Key
Winners Circle Resort
Yachtsman, The
Yarrow, The

INDEX OF PROPERTIES

C

M

N

O